THE ARAB-ISRAELI CONFLICT

Volume IV: The Difficult Search

for Peace (1975–1988)

PART TWO

The Arab-Israeli Conflict

Volume IV: The Difficult Search for Peace (1975–1988)

PART TWO

EDITED BY

JOHN NORTON MOORE

SPONSORED BY THE

American Society of
International Law

Princeton University Press
Princeton, New Jersey

Library of Congress Cataloging-in-Publication Data

(Revised for vol. 4)

The Arab-Israeli conflict.

Includes indexes.   Bibliography: v. 3, p.
Contents: v. 1. Readings.—v. 2. Readings.—[etc.]—v.
4. The difficult search for peace (1975–1988).
1. Jewish-Arab relations—1917–   —Addresses, essays, lectures.
2. Jewish-Arab relations—1917–   Sources. I. Moore, John Norton, 1937–
II. American Society of International Law.
DS119.7.A6718   1975   956'.04   72-39792

Vol. 4 Part Two ISBN 0-691-05678-1

This book has been composed in Linotron Baskerville

Princeton University Press books are printed on acid-free paper,
and meet the guidelines for permanence and durability of the
Committee on Production Guidelines for Book Longevity of the
Council on Library Resources

Printed in the United States of America by Princeton University Press,
Princeton, New Jersey

10 9 8 7 6 5 4 3 2 1

Volume Four

THE ARAB-ISRAELI CONFLICT:

THE DIFFICULT SEARCH FOR PEACE (1975–1988)

PART ONE

Introduction by John Norton Moore

Acknowledgments

Maps

PART TWO

Maps

Permissions

Selected Bibliography on the Arab-Israeli Conflict and
International Law: 1975–1988

Volume *Four*

THE ARAB-ISRAELI CONFLICT:

THE DIFFICULT SEARCH FOR PEACE (1975–1988)

PART TWO

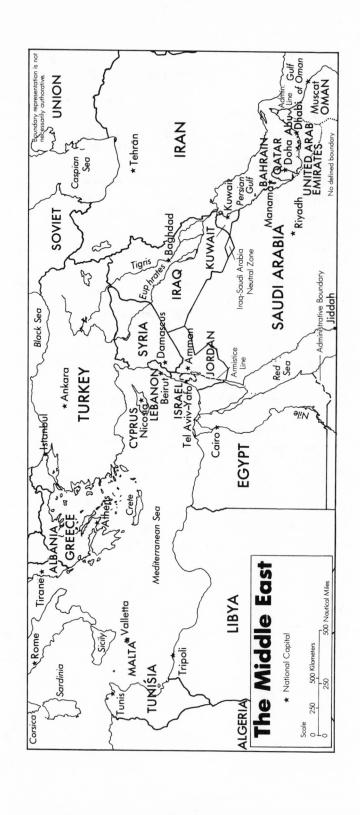

The Middle East

Scale

0   250   500 Kilometers

0   250   500 Nautical Miles

★ National Capital

Boundary representation is not necessarily authoritative.

SOVIET UNION

Caspian Sea

★ Tehrān

IRAN

Black Sea

★ Istanbul

Tigris

Euphrates

Baghdad

IRAQ

KUWAIT

★ Kuwait

Persian Gulf

BAHRAIN

Manamah★

QATAR

★ Doha

UNITED ARAB EMIRATES

Admin. Line

Gulf of Oman

Abu Dhabi★

★ Muscat

OMAN

No defined boundary

★ Ankara

TURKEY

SYRIA

Damascus★

LEBANON

Beirut★

CYPRUS

Nicosia★

ISRAEL

Tel Aviv-Yafo★

Amman★

JORDAN

Armistice Line

Iraq-Saudi Arabia Neutral Zone

SAUDI ARABIA

★ Riyadh

Red Sea

Administrative Boundary

Jiddah

Cairo★

EGYPT

Nile

GREECE

Athens★

ALBANIA

Tiranë★

★ Rome

Corsica

Sardinia

Sicily

MALTA

★ Valletta

Mediterranean Sea

Crete

TUNISIA

Tunis★

Tripoli

LIBYA

ALGERIA

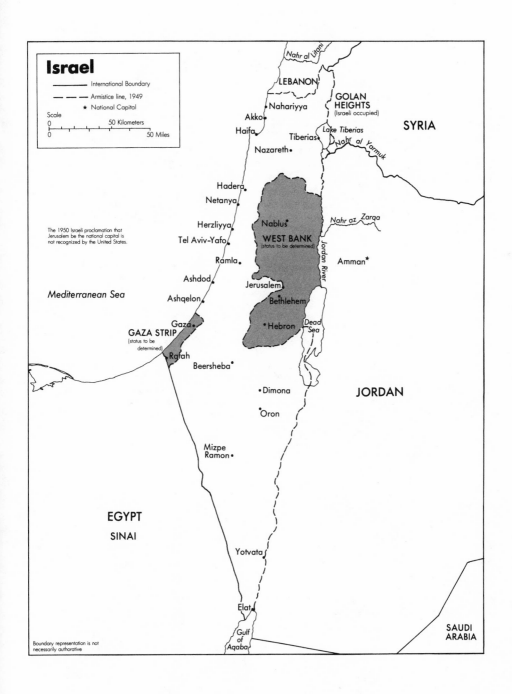

Israel

— International Boundary

- - - Armistice line, 1949

★ National Capital

Scale

0 ————— 50 Kilometers

0 ————— 50 Miles

The 1950 Israeli proclamation that
Jerusalem be the national capital is
not recognized by the United States.

Mediterranean Sea

Nahr al Litani

LEBANON

**GOLAN
HEIGHTS**
(Israeli occupied)

Nahariyya

Akko

Haifa

SYRIA

Lake Tiberias

Tiberias

Nahr al Yarmuk

Nazareth

Hadera

Netanya

Herzliyya

Nablus

WEST BANK
(status to be determined)

Nahr az Zarqa

Tel Aviv-Yafo

Ramla

Jordan River

Amman★

Ashdod

Jerusalem

Ashqelon

Bethlehem

Gaza

GAZA STRIP
(status to be
determined)

Hebron

*Dead
Sea*

Rafah

Beersheba

JORDAN

Dimona

Oron

Mizpe
Ramon

EGYPT

SINAI

Yotvata

Elat

*Gulf
of
Aqaba*

**SAUDI
ARABIA**

Boundary representation is not
necessarily authoritative

IV. THE WAR IN LEBANON:
JUNE 1982–AUGUST 1982

A. The Israeli Invasion of Lebanon

228. Security Council Resolution 508 Calling for a Cease-Fire in Lebanon, June 5, 1982*

* S.C. Res. 508, 37 U.N. SCOR (2374th mtg.) at 5, U.N. Doc. S/INF/38 (1982).

The Security Council,

Recalling its resolutions 425 (1978), 426 (1978) and its ensuing resolutions and, more particularly, resolution 501 (1982),

Taking note of the letters of the Permanent Representative of Lebanon dated 4 June 1982,[26]

Deeply concerned at the deterioration of the present situation in Lebanon and in the Lebanese-Israeli border area, and its consequences for peace and security in the region,

Gravely concerned at the violation of the territorial integrity, independence and sovereignty of Lebanon,

Reaffirming and supporting the statement made by the President and the members of the Security Council on 4 June 1982,[24] as well as the urgent appeal issued by the Secretary-General on 4 June 1982,

Taking note of the report of the Secretary-General,[27]

1. *Calls upon* all the parties to the conflict to cease immediately and simultaneously all military activities within Lebanon and across the Lebanese-Israeli border and not later than 0600 hours, local time, on Sunday, 6 June 1982;

2. *Requests* all Member States which are in a position to do so to bring their influence to bear upon those concerned so that the cessation of hostilities declared by Security Council resolution 490 (1981) can be respected;

3. *Requests* the Secretary-General to undertake all possible efforts to ensure the implementation of and compliance with the present resolution and to report to the Security Council as early as possible and not later than forty-eight hours after the adoption of the present resolution.

Adopted unanimously at the 2374th meeting.

[24] S/15163.

[26] *Official Records of the Security Council, Thirty-seventh Year, Supplement for April, May and June 1982,* documents S/15161 and S/15162.

[27] *Ibid., Thirty-seventh Year,* 2374th meeting.

229. Security Council Resolution 509 Calling for Israeli Withdrawal from Lebanon, June 6, 1982*

* S.C. Res. 509, 37 U.N. SCOR (2375th mtg.) at 6, U.N. Doc. S/INF/38 (1982).

The Security Council,

   Recalling its resolutions 425 (1978) and 508 (1982),

   Gravely concerned at the situation as described by the Secretary-General in his report to the Council,[28]

   Reaffirming the need for strict respect for the territorial integrity, sovereignty and political independence of Lebanon within its internationally recognized boundaries,

   1. *Demands* that Israel withdraw all its military forces forthwith and unconditionally to the internationally recognized boundaries of Lebanon;

   2. *Demands* that all parties observe strictly the terms of paragraph 1 of resolution 508 (1982) which called on them to cease immediately and simultaneously all military activities within Lebanon and across the Lebanese-Israeli border;

   3. *Calls* on all parties to communicate to the Secretary-General their acceptance of the present resolution within twenty-four hours;

   4. *Decides* to remain seized of the question.

Adopted unanimously at the 2375th meeting.

   [28] *Ibid.* [*Official Records of the Security Council, Thirty-seventh Year*], 2375th meeting.

230. European Community Statement on the Situation in Lebanon, June 9, 1982*

* 15 Bull. Eur. Comm. (No. 6) 79 (1982).

'The Member States of the European Community vigorously condemn the new Israeli invasion of Lebanon. Like the bombardments which preceded it and which caused intolerably high loss of human life, this action cannot be justified. It constitutes a flagrant violation of international law and of the most basic humanitarian principles. Furthermore it compromises the efforts to achieve a peaceful settlement of the problems of the Middle East and creates the imminent danger of a generalized conflict. The Ten reaffirm the importance they attach to the independence, sovereignty, territorial integrity and national unity of Lebanon, which are indispensable for peace in the region. The Ten strongly support the appeals made by the Secretary-General of the United Nations. They urgently call on all the parties concerned to act in accordance with Security Council Resolutions 508 and 509, and in particular on Israel to withdraw all its forces immediately and unconditionally from the Lebanon and to place the United Nations Interim Forces in Lebanon (UNIFIL) in a position to accomplish its mission without hindrance.

Should Israel continue to refuse compliance with the above resolutions the Ten will examine the possibilities for future action.

The objective of the Ten is to work for a Lebanon free from the cycle of violence which they have repeatedly condemned in the past. This cannot be dissociated from the establishment of a global, just and lasting peace in the region. They are ready to assist in bringing the parties concerned to accept measures intended to lower the level of tension, re-establish confidence and facilitate a negotiated solution.

The Ten will urgently examine within the institutions of the Community the use of the means at the disposal of the Community to give aid to the victims of these events.'

231. Security Council Resolution 511 Renewing the U.N.

Interim Force in Lebanon Mandate, June 18, 1982*

---

* S.C. Res. 511, 37 U.N. SCOR (2379th mtg.) at 6, U.N. Doc. S/INF/38 (1982).

The Security Council,

Recalling its resolutions 425 (1978), 426 (1978), 427 (1978), 434 (1978), 444 (1979), 450 (1979), 459 (1979), 467 (1980), 483 (1980), 488 (1981), 490 (1981), 498 (1981) and 501 (1982),

Reaffirming its resolutions 508 (1982) and 509 (1982),

Having studied the report of the Secretary-General on the United Nations Interim Force in Lebanon[31] and taking note of the conclusions and recommendations expressed therein,

Bearing in mind the need to avoid any developments which could further aggravate the situation and the need, pending an examination of the situation by the Security Council in all its aspects, to preserve in place the capacity of the United Nations to assist in the restoration of the peace,

1. *Decides,* as an interim measure, to extend the present mandate of the United Nations Interim Force in Lebanon for a period of two months, that is, until 19 August 1982;

2. *Authorizes* the Force during that period to carry out, in addition, the interim tasks referred to in paragraph 17 of the report of the Secretary-General on the Force;[32]

3. *Calls on* all concerned to extend full co-operation to the Force in the discharge of its tasks;

4. *Requests* the Secretary-General to keep the Security Council regularly informed of the implementation of resolutions 508 (1982) and 509 (1982) and the present resolution.

Adopted at the 2379th meeting by 13 votes to none, with 2 abstentions (Poland, Union of Soviet Socialist Republics).

---

[31] *Official Records of the Security Council, Thirty-seventh Year, Supplement for April, May and June 1982,* document S/15194 and Add.1 and 2.

[32] *Ibid.,* document S/15194/Add.2.

232. Security Council Resolution 512 Stressing the Need for Humanitarian Aid and Refraining from Violence Against Lebanon's Civilians, June 19, 1982*

* S.C. Res. 512, 37 U.N. SCOR (2380th mtg.) at 7, U.N. Doc. S/INF/38 (1982).

The Security Council,

Deeply concerned at the sufferings of the Lebanese and Palestinian civilian populations,

Referring to the humanitarian principles of the Geneva Conventions of 1949[33] and to the obligations arising from the regulations annexed to The Hague Convention of 1907,[34]

Reaffirming its resolutions 508 (1982) and 509 (1982),

1. *Calls upon* all the parties to the conflict to respect the rights of the civilian populations, to refrain from all acts of violence against those populations and to take all appropriate measures to alleviate the suffering caused by the conflict, in particular, by facilitating the dispatch and distribution of aid provided by United Nations agencies and by non-governmental organizations, in particular, the International Committee of the Red Cross;

2. *Appeals* to Member States to continue to provide the most extensive humanitarian aid possible;

3. *Stresses* the particular humanitarian responsibilities of the United Nations and its agencies, including the United Nations Relief and Works Agency for Palestine Refugees in the Near East, towards civilian populations and calls upon all the parties to the conflict not to hamper the exercise of those responsibilities and to assist in humanitarian efforts;

4. *Takes note* of the measures taken by the Secretary-General to co-ordinate the activities of the international agencies in this field and requests him to make every effort to ensure the implementation of and compliance with the present resolution and to report on these efforts to the Security Council as soon as possible.

Adopted unanimously at the 2380th meeting.

[33] United Nations, *Treaty Series*, vol. 75, Nos. 970-973.

[34] Carnegie Endowment for International Peace, *The Hague Conventions and Declarations of 1899 and 1907* (New York, Oxford University Press, 1915).

233. Text of Israeli Government Peace Proposal, June 27, 1982*

The Cabinet resolved that:

1. Israel will maintain the cease-fire in Lebanon. If the enemy violates the cease-fire, the I.D.F. will respond with full severity.

2. The Government of Israel recommends that the Lebanese Army enter west Beirut.

3. All of the 15 terrorist organizations of which the roof organization called the P.L.O. is comprised will hand over their weapons to the Lebanese Army. All members of the above-mentioned terrorist organizations, without any exceptions, will leave Beirut and Lebanon.

4. The departing column of the terrorists, under the protection of the International Red Cross, will move across the international Lebanese-Syrian border along the Beirut-Damascus road. The I.D.F. will insure that in the sector of that road which is under its control the column will have safe passage. If the terrorists prefer an alternative route, this will be made possible for them by the I.D.F.

5. With the liberation of west Beirut and the reunification of the Lebanese capital, the political negotiation between all the parties concerned will begin with a view to reaching an agreement which will guarantee the territorial integrity of Lebanon, the departure of all foreign forces from that country, its independence and the peace of its inhabitants. This agreement will insure security and peace of the Galilee and its inhabitants, of Israel and its citizens.

6. Israel will gladly accept the good offices of the United States to the negotiating parties, in order to reach this agreement.

234. General Assembly Resolution ES-7/5 on the Question of Palestine, June 26, 1982*

* G.A. Res. ES-7/5, ES-7 U.N. GAOR Supp. (No. 1) at 7, U.N. Doc. A/ES-7/14/Add. 1 (1982).

The General Assembly,

Having considered the question of Palestine at its resumed seventh emergency special session,

Having heard the statement of the Palestine Liberation Organization, the representative of the Palestinian people,[7]

Alarmed by the worsening situation in the Middle East resulting from Israel's acts of aggression against the sovereignty of Lebanon and the Palestinian people in Lebanon,

Recalling Security Council resolutions 508 (1982) of 5 June 1982, 509 (1982) of 6 June 1982 and 512 (1982) of 19 June 1982,

Taking note of the reports of the Secretary-General relevant to this situation, particularly his report of 7 June 1982,[8]

Taking note of the two positive replies to the Secretary-General by the Government of Lebanon[9] and the Palestine Liberation Organization,[10]

Noting with regret that the Security Council has, so far, failed to take effective and practical measures, in accordance with the Charter of the United Nations, to ensure implementation of its resolutions 508 (1982) and 509 (1982),

Referring to the humanitarian principles of the Geneva Convention relative to the Protection of Civilian Persons in Time of War, of 12 August 1949,[11] and to the obligations arising from the regulations annexed to the Hague Conventions of 1907,[12]

Deeply concerned at the sufferings of the Palestinian and Lebanese civilian populations,

Reaffirming once again its conviction that the question of Palestine is the core of the Arab-Israeli conflict and that no comprehensive, just and lasting peace in the region will be achieved without the full exercise by the Palestinian people of its inalienable national rights,

Reaffirming further that a just and comprehensive settlement of the situation in the Middle East cannot be achieved without the participation on an equal footing of all the parties to the conflict, including the Palestine Liberation Organization as the representative of the Palestinian people,

1. *Reaffirms* the fundamental principle of the inadmissibility of the acquisition of territory by force;

2. *Demands* that all Member States and other parties observe strict respect for Lebanon's sovereignty, territorial integrity, unity and political independence within its internationally recognized boundaries;

---

[7] A/ES-7/PV.22, p. 6.

[8] S/15178.

[9] *Ibid.*, para. 3.

[10] *Ibid.*, para. 4.

[11] United Nations, *Treaty Series*, vol. 75, No. 973, p. 287.

[12] Carnegie Endowment for International Peace, *The Hague Conventions and Declarations of 1899 and 1907* (New York, Oxford University Press, 1915).

3. *Decides* to support fully the provisions of Security Council resolutions 508 (1982) and 509 (1982) in which the Council, *inter alia*, demanded that:

(*a*) Israel withdraw all its military forces forthwith and unconditionally to the internationally recognized boundaries of Lebanon;

(*b*) All parties to the conflict cease immediately and simultaneously all military activities within Lebanon and across the Lebanese-Israeli border;

4. *Condemns* Israel for its non-compliance with resolutions 508 (1982) and 509 (1982);

5. *Demands* that Israel comply with all the above provisions no later than 0600 hours (Beirut time) on Sunday, 27 June 1982;

6. *Calls upon* the Security Council to authorize the Secretary-General to undertake necessary endeavours and practical steps to implement the provisions of resolutions 508 (1982, 509 (1982) and 512 (1982);

7. *Urges* the Security Council, in the event of continued failure by Israel to comply with the demands contained in resolutions 508 (1982) and 509 (1982), to meet in order to consider practical ways and means in accordance with the Charter of the United Nations;

8. *Calls upon* all States and international agencies and organizations to continue to provide the most extensive humanitarian aid possible to the victims of the Israeli invasion of Lebanon;

9. *Requests* the Secretary-General to delegate a high-level commission to investigate and assess the extent of loss of human life and material damage and to report, as soon as possible, on the result of this investigation to the General Assembly and the Security Council;

10. *Decides* to adjourn the seventh emergency special session temporarily and to authorize the President of the latest regular session of the General Assembly to resume its meetings upon request from Member States.

24th plenary meeting
26 June 1982

235. European Council Statement on the Middle East,

June 29, 1982*

---

* 15 Bull. Eur. Comm. (No. 6) 16 (1982).

1.5.4. '1. The Ten maintain their vigorous condemnation of the Israeli invasion of Lebanon. They are greatly concerned about the situation in that country and in particular in Beirut. They believe that the present cease-fire must at all costs be preserved.

This cease-fire should be accompanied on one hand by an immediate withdrawal of Israeli forces from their positions around the Lebanese capital as a first step towards their complete withdrawal, and on the other hand by a simultaneous withdrawal of the Palestinian forces in West Beirut in accordance with procedures to be agreed between the parties.

In order to facilitate this withdrawal the separation of forces would be controlled during this short transitional period by Lebanese forces and, by agreement with the Lebanese Government, by UN observers or forces.

2. The establishment of a final peace in the Lebanon requires the complete and prompt withdrawal of Israeli forces from that country as well as the departure of all foreign forces except those which may be authorized by a legitimate and broadly representative Government of Lebanon whose authority would be fully re-established over all its national territory. The Ten support all efforts for the achievement of these objectives.

3. For the present the Ten have decided to continue their activity to bring relief to the population in distress and, in this context, call on all parties to act in accordance with Security Council Resolutions 511 and 512 and to cooperate with the responsible international agencies as well as with UNIFIL. They are also ready in due course to assist in the reconstruction of the country.

4. Anxious to initiate, over and above the settlement of the Lebanese problem, the lasting restoration of peace and security in the region, the Ten wish to see negotiations based on the principles of security for all States and justice for all peoples. All the parties concerned should be associated with these and thus should accept one another's existence. Israel will not obtain the security to which it has a right by using force and creating *faits accomplis* but it can find this security by satisfying the legitimate aspirations of the Palestinian people, who should have the opportunity to exercise their right to self-determination with all that this implies.

They believe that for negotiations to be possible the Palestinian people must be able to commit themselves to them and thus to be represented at them. The position of the Ten remains that the PLO should be associated with the negotiations.

The Ten wish to see the Palestinian people in a position to pursue their demands by political means and wish that the achievement of these should take account of the need to recognize and respect the existence and security of all.'

236. European Council Statement on the Decision to Break Financial Ties with Israel, June 29, 1982*

* 15 Bull. Eur. Comm. (No. 6) 17 (1982).

On the Middle East, Mr Martens said that the Heads of State or Government had had a detailed discussion of the situation in Lebanon and the conflict in the Middle East and had agreed to confirm that the signature of the second Financial Protocol between the Community and Israel would be deferred, as would the next ministerial-level meeting of the EEC-Israel Co-operation Council. He stressed that the Member States were not selling any military equipment to Israel at present.

237. Humanitarian Assistance for the People of Lebanon Act, June 30, 1982*

---

* 22 U.S.C. Sec. 2292p (1982).

§2292p. Lebanon: emergency relief, rehabilitation, and reconstruction assistance

(a) Congressional policy and authorization

The Congress recognizes that prompt United States assistance is necessary to alleviate the human suffering and resettlement needs of the innocent victims of recent strife in Lebanon. Therefore, the President is authorized to furnish assistance, on such terms and conditions as he may determine, for the relief, rehabilitation, and reconstruction needs of such victims. Assistance provided under this section shall emphasize the provision of food, medicine, clothing, shelter, and water supply systems, and similiar efforts to ameliorate the suffering of the people in Lebanon.

(b) Authorization of appropriations

In addition to amounts otherwise available for such purpose, there is authorized to be appropriated to the President $50,000,000 to carry out this section. Amounts appropriated under this subsection are authorized to remain available until expended.

(c) Policies and general authority

Assistance under this section shall be furnished in accordance with the policies and general authorities contained in section 2292 of this title.

(Pub. L. 87-195, pt. I, §495J, as added Pub. L. 97-208, June 30, 1982, 96 Stat. 138.)

238. Security Council Resolution 513 Calling for Respect

of the Rights of All Non-Combatants in Lebanon,

July 4, 1982*

* S.C. Res. 513, 37 U.N. SCOR (2382nd mtg.) at 7, U.N. Doc. S/INF/38 (1982).

The Security Council,

Alarmed by the continued sufferings of the Lebanese and Palestinian civilian populations in southern Lebanon and in west Beirut,

Referring to the humanitarian principles of the Geneva Conventions of 1949[33] and to the obligations arising from the regulations annexed to The Hague Convention of 1907,[34]

Reaffirming its resolutions 508 (1982), 509 (1982) and 512 (1982),

1. *Calls* for respect for the rights of the civilian populations without any discrimination and repudiates all acts of violence against those populations;

2. *Calls further* for the restoration of the normal supply of vital facilities such as water, electricity, food and medical provisions, particularly in Beirut;

3. *Commends* the efforts of the Secretary-General and the action of international agencies to alleviate the sufferings of the civilian population and requests them to continue their efforts to ensure their success.

Adopted unanimously at the 2382nd meeting.

[33] United Nations, *Treaty Series*, vol. 75, Nos. 970-973.

[34] Carnegie Endowment for International Peace, *The Hague Conventions and Declarations of 1899 and 1907* (New York, Oxford University Press, 1915).

239. Security Council Resolution 515 Demanding That Israel Lift Its Blockade of Beirut, July 29, 1982*

* S.C. Res. 515, 37 U.N. SCOR (2385th mtg.) at 7, U.N. Doc. S/INF/38 (1982).

The Security Council,

Deeply concerned at the situation of the civilian population of Beirut,

Referring to the humanitarian principles of the Geneva Conventions of 1949[33] and to the obligations arising from the regulations annexed to The Hague Convention of 1907,[34]

Recalling its resolutions 512 (1982) and 513 (1982),

1. *Demands* that the Government of Israel lift immediately the blockade of the city of Beirut in order to permit the dispatch of supplies to meet the urgent needs of the civilian population and allow the distribution of aid provided by United Nations agencies and by non-governmental organizations, particularly the International Committee of the Red Cross;

2. *Requests* the Secretary-General to transmit the text of the present resolution to the Government of Israel and to keep the Security Council informed of its implementation.

Adopted at the 2385th meeting by 14 to none.[36]

[33] United Nations, *Treaty Series*, vol. 75, Nos. 970-973.

[34] Carnegie Endowment for International Peace, *The Hague Conventions and Declarations of 1899 and 1907* (New York, Oxford University Press, 1915).

[36] One member (United States of America) did not participate in the voting.

240. Communiqué of Arab Foreign Ministers Conference, Jeddah, July 29, 1982*

* 11–12 J. Palestine Stud. 314 (Summer/Fall 1982).

First: Urgent action to ensure maintenance of the cease-fire.

Second: The PLO announces its decision to move its armed forces from Beirut. The guarantees of this move and guarantees for the security of the camps are to be agreed upon between the Government and the PLO in Beirut.

Third: Act to lift the siege of the city of Beirut and its suburbs with the withdrawal of Israeli forces.

Fourth: The Lebanese Government is to undertake all measures leading to the insurance of the security and safety of the citizens of the city of Beirut and its suburbs, including the Palestinian camps.

Fifth: Participation of international forces in the operation guaranteeing the security and safety of Beirut and its suburbs.

Sixth: The Arab countries will undertake the necessary political action to help Lebanon to implement Security Council Resolutions 508 and 509 in their entirety.

241. Security Council Resolution 516 Calling for a Cease-Fire in Lebanon and Immediate Israeli Withdrawal, August 1, 1982*

* S.C. Res. 516, 37 U.N. SCOR (2386th mtg.) at 8, U.N. Doc. S/INF/38 (1982).

The Security Council,

Reaffirming its resolutions 508 (1982), 509 (1982), 511 (1982), 512 (1982) and 513 (1982),

Recalling its resolution 515 (1982),

Alarmed by the continuation and intensification of military activities in and around Beirut,

Taking note of the latest massive violations of the cease-fire in and around Beirut,

1. *Confirms* its previous resolutions and demands an immediate cease-fire, and a cessation of all military activities within Lebanon and across the Lebanese-Iraeli border;

2. *Authorizes* the Secretary-General to deploy immediately, on the request of the Government of Lebanon, United Nations observers to monitor the situation in and around Beirut;

3. *Requests* the Secretary-General to report back to the Security Council on compliance with the present resolution as soon as possible and not later than four hours from now.

Adopted unanimously at the 2386th meeting.

242. Security Council Resolution 517 Renewing the Call
for a Cease-Fire in Lebanon and Asking the Secretary-
General to Report on the Resolution's Implementation,
August 4, 1982*

* S.C. Res. 517, 37 U.N. SCOR (2389th mtg.) at 8, U.N. Doc. S/INF/38 (1982).

The Security Council,

Deeply shocked and alarmed by the deplorable consequences of the Israeli invasion of Beirut on 3 August 1982,

1. *Reconfirms* its resolutions 508 (1982), 509 (1982), 512 (1982), 513 (1982), 515 (1982) and 516 (1982);

2. *Confirms once again* its demand for an immediate cease-fire and withdrawal of Israeli forces from Lebanon;

3. *Censures* Israel for its failure to comply with the above resolutions;

4. *Calls* for the prompt return of Israeli troops which have moved forward subsequent to 1325 hours, eastern daylight time, on 1 August 1982;

5. *Takes note* of the decision of the Palestine Liberation Organization to move the Palestinian armed forces from Beirut;

6. *Expresses its appreciation* for the efforts and steps taken by the Secretary-General to implement the provisions of resolution 516 (1982) and authorizes him, as an immediate step, to increase the number of United Nations observers in and around Beirut;

7. *Requests* the Secretary-General to report to the Security Council on the implementation of the present resolution as soon as possible and not later than 1000 hours, eastern daylight time, on 5 August 1982;

8. *Decides* to meet at that time, if necessary, in order to consider the report of the Secretary-General and, in case of failure to comply by any of the parties to the conflict, to consider adopting effective ways and means in accordance with the provisions of the Charter of the United Nations.

Adopted at the 2389th meeting by 14 votes to none, with 1 abstention (United States of America).

243. Security Council Resolution 518 Calling for Israeli Cessation of Military Activities in Lebanon, Particularly in Beirut, August 12, 1982*

* S.C. Res. 518, 37 U.N. SCOR (2392nd mtg.) at 9, U.N. Doc. S/INF/38 (1982).

The Security Council,

Recalling its resolutions 508 (1982), 509 (1982), 511 (1982), 512 (1982), 513 (1982), 515 (1982), 516 (1982) and 517 (1982),

Expressing its most serious concern about continued military activities in Lebanon and, particularly, in and around Beirut,

1. *Demands* that Israel and all parties to the conflict observe strictly the terms of Security Council resolutions relevant to the immediate cessation of all military activities within Lebanon and, particularly, in and around Beirut;

2. *Demands* the immediate lifting of all restrictions on the city of Beirut in order to permit the free entry of supplies to meet the urgent needs of the civilian population in Beirut;

3. *Requests* the United Nations observers in, and in the vicinity of, Beirut to report on the situation;

4. *Demands* that Israel co-operate fully in the effort to secure the effective deployment of the United Nations observers, as requested by the Government of Lebanon, and in such a manner as to ensure their safety;

5. *Requests* the Secretary-General to report as soon as possible to the Security Council on the implementation of the present resolution;

6. *Decides* to meet, if necessary, in order to consider the situation upon receipt of the report of the Secretary-General.

Adopted unanimously at the 2392nd meeting.

244. Security Council Resolution 519 Renewing the U.N. Interim Force in Lebanon Mandate, August 17, 1982*

* S.C. Res. 519, 37 U.N. SCOR (2393rd mtg.) at 9, U.N. Doc. S/INF/38 (1982).

The Security Council,

Recalling its resolutions 425 (1978), 426 (1978), 427 (1978), 434 (1978), 444 (1979), 450 (1979), 459 (1979), 467 (1980), 483 (1980), 488 (1981), 490 (1981), 498 (1981), 501 (1982) and 511 (1982),

Reaffirming its resolutions 508 (1982) and 509 (1982), as well as subsequent resolutions on the situation in Lebanon,

Having studied with grave concern the report of the Secretary-General on the United Nations Interim Force in Lebanon[39] and noting its conclusions and recommendations and the wishes of the Government of Lebanon as set out therein,

Bearing in mind the need, pending an examination by the Security Council of the situation in all its aspects, to preserve in place the capacity of the United Nations to assist in the restoration of the peace and of the authority of the Government of Lebanon throughout Lebanon,

1. *Decides* to extend the present mandate of the United Nations Interim Force in Lebanon for a further interim period of two months, that is, until 19 October 1982;

2. *Authorizes* the Force during that period to continue to carry out, in addition, the interim tasks in the humanitarian and administrative fields assigned to it in paragraph 2 of resolution 511 (1982);

3. *Calls on* all concerned, taking into account paragraphs 5, 8, and 9 of the report of the Secretary-General on the Force, to extend full co-operation to it in the discharge of its tasks;

4. *Supports* the efforts of the Secretary-General, with a view to optimum use of observers of the United Nations Truce Supervision Organization, as envisaged by relevant resolutions of the Security Council;

5. *Decides* to consider the situation fully and in all its aspects before 19 October 1982.

Adopted at the 2393rd meeting by 13 votes to none, with 2 abstentions (Poland, Union of Soviet Socialist Republics).

---

[39] *Ibid.* [*Official Records of the Security Council, Thirty-seventh Year, Supplement for July, August and September 1982*], document S/15357.

B. The Initial Deployment of the Multinational Force

245. Exchange of Notes with Lebanon Over U.S. Participation in the Multinational Force, August 18 and 20, 1982*

* 82 U.S. Dep't State Bull. No. 2066, at 4 (September 1982).

Lebanese Note Requesting U.S. Contribution to MNF

Beirut
August the 18th, 1982

Ambassador Robert S. Dillon
U.S. Embassy, Beirut

Your Excellency,

I have the honor to refer to the many conversations between their Excellencies the President of the Republic of Lebanon, the Prime Minister and myself on the one hand, and with Ambassador Philip C. Habib, Special Emissary to the President of the United States of America, on the other hand, as well as to the resolution of the Council of Ministers passed today. I have the honor to refer to the schedule set up by the Government of Lebanon, after consultations with interested parties, in order to assure the withdrawal from Lebanese territory of the Palestinian leaders, offices and combatants related to any organization now in the Beirut area, in a manner which will:

(1) assure the safety of such departing persons;

(2) assure the safety of the persons in the area; and

(3) further the restoration of the sovereignty and authority of the Government of Lebanon over the Beirut area.

In this context, the Government of Lebanon is proposing to several nations that they contribute forces to serve as a temporary Multinational Force (MNF) in Beirut. The mandate of the MNF will be to provide appropriate assistance to the Lebanese Armed Forces (LAF) as they carry out the foregoing responsibilities, in accordance with the annexed schedule. The MNF may undertake other functions only by mutual agreement. It is understood that, in the event that the withdrawal of the Palestinian personnel referred to above does not take place in accord with the predetermined schedule, the mandate of the MNF will terminate immediately and all MNF personnel will leave Lebanon forthwith.

In the foregoing context, I have the honor to propose that the United States of America deploy a force of approximately 800 personnel to Beirut, subject to the following terms and conditions:

· The American military force shall carry out appropriate activities consistent with the mandate of the MNF.

· Command authority over the American force will be exercised exclusively by the United States Government through existing American military channels.

· The American force will operate in close coordination with the LAF. To assure effective coordination with the LAF, the American force will assign liaison officers to the LAF and the Government of Lebanon will assign liaison officers to the American force. The LAF liaison officers to the American force will, *inter alia*, perform liaison with the civilian population and manifest the authority of the Lebanese Governement in all appropriate situations.

• In carrying out its mission, the American force will not engage in combat. It may, however, exercise the right of self-defense.

• The American force will depart Lebanon not later than thirty days after its arrival, or sooner at the request of the President of Lebanon or at the direction of the United States Government, or according to the termination of the mandate provided for above.

• The Government of Lebanon and the LAF will take all measures necessary to ensure the protection of the American force's personnel, to include securing the assurances from all armed elements not now under the authority of the Lebanese Government that they will comply with the cease-fire and cessation of hostilities.

• The American force will enjoy both the degree of freedom of movement and the right to undertake those activities deemed necessary for the performance of its mission or for the support of its personnel. Accordingly, it shall enjoy all facilities necessary for the accomplishment of these purposes. Personnel in the American force shall enjoy the privileges and immunities accorded the administrative and technical staff of the American Embassy in Beirut, and shall be exempt from immigration and customs requirements, and restrictions on entering or departing Lebanon. Personnel, property and equipment of the American force introduced into Lebanon, shall be exempt from any form of tax, duty, charge or levy.

I have the further honor to propose, if the foregoing is acceptable to your Excellency's government, that your Excellency's reply to that effect, together with this note, shall constitute an agreement between our two governments, to enter into force on the date of your Excellency's reply.

Please accept, your Excellency, the assurances of my highest consideration.

FUAD BOUTROS
Deputy Prime Minister/
Minister of Foreign Affairs

U.S. Reply to Lebanese Note Requesting U.S. Contribution to MNF

August 20, 1982

I have the honor to refer to your Excellency's note of 18 August 1982 requesting the deployment of an American force to Beirut. I am pleased to inform you on behalf of my government that the United States is prepared to deploy temporarily a force of approximately 800 personnel as part of a Multinational Force (MNF) to provide appropriate assistance to the Lebanese Armed Forces (LAF) as they carry out their responsibilities concerning the withdrawal of Palestinian personnel in Beirut from Lebanese territory under safe and orderly conditions, in accordance with the schedule annexed to your Excellency's note. It is understood that the presence of such an American force will in this way facilitate the restoration of Lebanese Government sovereignty and authority over the Beirut area, an objective which is fully shared by my government.

I have the further honor to inform you that my government accepts the terms and conditions concerning the presence of the American force in the Beirut area as set forth in your note, and that your Excellency's note and this reply accordingly constitute an agreement between our two governments.

ROBERT S. DILLON
Ambassador of the
United States of America

246. Plan for the Departure from Lebanon of the PLO Leadership, Offices, and Combatants in Beirut, and Fact Sheets, August 20, 1982*

---

* 82 U.S. State Dep't Bull. No. 2066, at 2 (September 1982) (note omitted).

1. Basic Concept. All the PLO leadership, offices, and combatants in Beirut will leave Lebanon peacefully for prearranged destinations in other countries, in accord with the departure schedules and arrangements set out in this plan. The basic concept in this plan is consistent with the objective of the Government of Lebanon that all foreign military forces withdraw from Lebanon.

2. Cease-fire. A cease-fire in place will be scrupulously observed by all in Lebanon.

3. U.N. Observers. The U.N. Observer Group stationed in the Beirut area will continue its functioning in that area.

4. Safeguards. Military forces present in Lebanon—whether Lebanese, Israeli, Syrian, Palestinian, or any other—will in no way interfere with the safe, secure, and timely departure of the PLO leadership, offices, and combatants. Law-abiding Palestinian noncombatants left behind in Beirut, including the families of those who have departed, will be subject to Lebanese laws and regulations. The Governments of Lebanon and the United States will provide appropriate guarantees of safety in the following ways.

· The Lebanese Government will provide its guarantees on the basis of having secured assurances from armed groups with which it has been in touch.

· The United States will provide its guarantees on the basis of assurances received from the Government of Israel and from the leadership of certain Lebanese groups with which it has been in touch.

5. "Departure Day" is defined as the day on which advance elements of the multinational force (MNF) deploy in the Beirut area, in accordance with arrangements worked out in advance among all concerned, and on which the initial group or groups of PLO personnel commence departure from Beirut in accord with the planned schedule (see page 9).

6. The Multinational Force. A temporary multinational force, composed of units from France, Italy, and the United States, will have been formed— at the request of the Lebanese Government—to assist the Lebanese Armed Forces in carrying out their responsibilities in this operation. The Lebanese Armed Forces will assure the departure from Lebanon of the PLO leadership, offices, and combatants, from whatever organization in Beirut, in a manner which will:

(A) Assure the safety of such departing PLO personnel;

(B) Assure the safety of other persons in the Beirut area; and

(C) Further the restoration of the sovereignty and authority of the Government of Lebanon over the Beirut area.

7. Schedule of Departures and Other Arrangements. The attached schedule of departures is subject to revision as may be necessary because of logistical requirements and because of any necessary shift in the setting of Departure Day. Details concerning the schedule will be forwarded to the Israeli Defense Forces through the Liaison and Coordination Committee. Places of assembly for the departing personnel will be identified by agree-

ment between the Government of Lebanon and the PLO. The PLO will be in touch with governments receiving personnel to coordinate arrival and other arrangements there. If assistance is required the PLO should notify the Government of Lebanon.

8. MNF Mandate. In the event that the departure from Lebanon of the PLO personnel referred to above does not take place in accord with the agreed and predetermined schedule, the mandate of the MNF will terminate immediately and all MNF personnel will leave Lebanon forthwith.

9. Duration of MNF. It will be mutually agreed between the Lebanese Government and the governments contributing forces to the MNF that the forces of the MNF will depart Lebanon not later than 30 days after arrival, or sooner at the request of the Government of Lebanon or at the direction of the individual government concerned, or in accord with the termination of the mandate of the MNF provided for above.

10. The PLO leadership will be responsible for the organization and management of the assembly and the final departure of PLO personnel, from beginning to end, at which time the leaders also will all be gone. Departure arrangements will be coordinated so that departures from Beirut take place at a steady pace, day by day.

11. Lebanese Armed Forces Contribution. The Lebanese Army will contribute between seven and eight army battalions to the operation, consisting of between 2,500-3,500 men. In addition, the internal security force will contribute men and assistance as needed.

12. ICRC. The International Committee of the Red Cross (ICRC) will be able to assist the Government of Lebanon and Lebanese Armed Forces in various ways, including in the organization and management of the evacuation of wounded and ill Palestinian and Syrian personnel to appropriate destinations, and in assisting in the chartering and movement of commercial vessels for use in departure by sea to other countries. The Liaison and Coordination Committee will insure that there will be proper coordination with any ICRC activities in this respect.

13. Departure by Air. While present plans call for departure by sea and land, departures by air are not foreclosed.

14. Liaison and Coordination:

· The Lebanese Armed Forces will be the primary point of contact for liaison with the PLO as well as with other armed groups and will provide necessary information.

· The Lebanese Armed Forces and MNF will have formed prior to Departure Day a Liaison and Corodination Committee, composed of representatives of the MNF participating governments and the Lebanese Armed Forces. The committee will carry out close and effective liaison with, and provide continuous and detailed information to, the Israeli Defense Forces (IDF). On behalf of the committee, the Lebanese Armed Forces will continue to carry out close and effective liaison with the PLO and other armed groups in the Beirut area. For convenience, the Liaison and Coordination Committee will have two essential components:

(A) Supervisory liaison; and

(B) Military and technical liaison and coordination.

The Liaison and Coordination Committee will act collectively; however, it may designate one or more of its members for primary liaison contact who would of course act on behalf of all.

· Liaison arrangements and consultations will be conducted in such a way as to minimize misunderstandings and to forestall difficulties. Appropriate means of communications between the committee and other groups will be developed for this purpose.

· The Liaison and Coordination Commitee will continually monitor and keep all concerned currently informed regarding the implementation of the plan, including any revisions to the departure schedule as may be necessary because of logistical requirements.

15. Duration of Departure. The departure period shall be as short as possible and, in any event, no longer than 2 weeks.

16. Transit Through Lebanon. As part of any departure arrangement, all movements of convoys carrying PLO personnel must be conducted in daylight hours. When moving overland from Beirut to Syria, the convoys should cross the border into Syria with no stops en route. In those instances when convoys of departing PLO personnel pass through positions of the Israeli Defense Forces, whether in the Beirut area or elsewhere in Lebanon, the Israeli Defense Forces will clear the route for the temporary period in which the convoy is running. Similar steps will be taken by other armed groups located in the area of the route the convoy will take.

17. Arms Carried by PLO Personnel. On their departure, PLO personnel will be allowed to carry with them one individual side weapon (pistol, rifle, or submarine gun) and ammunition.

18. Heavy and Spare Weaponry and Munitions. The PLO will turn over to the Lebanese Armed Forces as gifts all remaining weaponry in their possession, including heavy, crew-served, and spare weaponry and equipment, along with all munitions left behind in the Beirut area. The Lebanese Armed Forces may seek the assistance of elements of the MNF in securing and disposing of the military equipment. The PLO will assist the Lebanese Armed Forces by providing, prior to their departure, full and detailed information as to the location of this military equipment.

19. Mines and Booby Traps. The PLO and the Arab Deterrent Force (ADF) will provide to the Lebanese Armed Forces and the MNF (through the Lebanese Armed Forces) full and detailed information on the location of mines and booby traps.

20. Movement of PLO Leadership. Arrangements will be made so that departing PLO personnel will be accompanied by a proportionate share of the military and political leadership throughout all stages of the departure operation.

21. Turnover of Prisoners and Remains. The PLO will, through the ICRC, turn over to the Israeli Defense Forces, all Israeli nationals whom they have taken in custody, and the remains, or full and detailed information about the location of the remains, of all Israeli soldiers who have fallen. The PLO will also turn over to the Lebanese Armed Forces all other prisoners whom they have taken in custody and the remains, or full and detailed information about the location of the remains, of all other soldiers who have fallen. All arrangements for such turnovers shall be worked out with the ICRC as required prior to Departure Day.

22. Syrian Military Forces. It is noted that arrangements have been made between the Governments of Lebanon and Syria for the deployment of all military personnel of the Arab Deterrent Force from Beirut during the departure period. These forces will be allowed to take their equipment with them, except for that—under mutual agreement between the two governments—which is turned over to the Lebanese Armed Forces. All elements of the Palestinian Liberation Army, whether or not they now or in the past have been attached to the Arab Deterrent Force, will withdraw from Lebanon.

FACT SHEETS ON THE DEPARTURE

Plan for the Departure of the PLO

A plan for the departure from Lebanon of the PLO leaders, offices, and combatants in Beirut has been accepted by the Governments of Lebanon, the troop-contributing countries, and Israel and by the PLO. That plan includes a schedule of departures which is also attached to the bilateral notes exchanged between the Government of Lebanon and the troop-contributing countries.

The PLO will go to various countries in the region including Jordan, Iraq, Tunisia, North Yemen, South Yemen, Syria, Sudan, and Algeria.

Departing PLO personnel will be accompanied by a proportionate share of the military and political leadership throughout all stages of the departure arrangements.

The PLO will turn over to the Lebanese Armed Forces their heavy and crew-served weapons, spare weaponry and equipment along with all munitions left behind in the Beirut area. They and the Arab Deterrent Force will also provide detailed information on the location of mines and booby traps to the Lebanese Armed Forces. On departure, PLO personnel may carry with them an individual side weapon and ammunition.

The Arab Deterrent Force (i.e., the Syrians) and those forces attached to the Arab Deterrent Force will also redeploy from Beirut during the period of the PLO departure. The Syrian military forces will take their equipment with them except for that which, by mutual agreement, is turned over to the Lebanese Armed Forces.

MNF Composition, Area of Operations, and Mission

Force Composition. The multinational force, which will be deployed to the Beirut area at the request of the Government of Lebanon, will be comprised of approximately 400 Italian, 800 French, and 800 U.S. military personnel. The U.S. portion of the MNF will be comprised of Marines of the 32d Marine Amphibious Unit presently serving with elements of the Sixth Fleet on duty in the eastern Mediterranean.

Area of Operations. The MNF will operate in and around the Beirut area. It will take up positions and operate from locations determined by mutual agreement between the various national contingents and the Lebanese Armed Forces through the mechanism of a Liaison and Coordination Committee.

Mission. The multinational force will assist the Lebanese Armed Forces in carrying out its responsibilities for insuring the safe and orderly departure from Lebanon of the PLO leaders, offices, and combatants in a manner which will insure the safety of other persons in the area, and which will further the restoration of the sovereignty and authority of the Government of Lebanon over the Beirut area.

Duration of the MNF Mandate. It has been mutually agreed between the Government of Lebanon and those governments contributing forces to the MNF that these forces will depart Lebanon not later than 30 days after arrival, or sooner at the request of the Government of Lebanon or at the direction of the individual government concerned. There is also provision for the immediate termination of the mandate of the MNF and for its withdrawal from Beirut in the event that the departure from Lebanon of PLO personnel does not take place in accord with the predetermined schedule.

Role and Mission of U.S. Forces in Beirut

U.S. forces will be deployed to Beirut as part of the multinational force based on an agreement between the U.S. Government and the Government of Lebanon.

The U.S. contingent of the multinational force will provide appropriate assistance to the Lebanese Armed Forces as they carry out their responsibilities concerning the withdrawal of PLO personnel in Beirut from Lebanese territory under safe and orderly conditions. The presence of U.S. forces also will facilitate the restoration of Lebanese Government sovereignty and authority over the Beirut area.

U.S. forces will enter Beirut after the evacuation is well underway (probably 5 or 6 days thereafter) in concert with the Italian MNF contingent and the remainder of the French force. Approximately 800 Marines from Sixth Fleet units will be deployed. Command authority for the Marines will be exercised by the National Command Authority (NCA) through normal American military channels (EUCOM). These forces will not engage in combat by [*sic*] may exercise the right of self-defense. They will have freedom of movement and the right to undertake actions necessary to perform their mission or to support their personnel. U.S. personnel will be armed with usual infantry weapons.

Close coordination will be maintained with the Lebanese Armed Forces. There will be an exchange of liaison officers among the elements of the MNF and the Lebanese Armed Forces. A Liaison and Coordination Committee composed of representatives from the U.S., French, Italian, and Lebanese armed forces will assist this process. The Government of Lebanon and the Lebanese Armed Forces are taking measures necessary to insure the protection of U.S. forces including having secured assurances from armed elements that they will comply with the cease-fire and cessation of hostilities.

The U.S. contingent will be in Beirut for no more than 30 days.

War Powers Resolution

The War Powers Resolution requires a report to Congress within 48 hours after the introduction of U.S. Armed Forces: (1) into foreign territory while equipped for combat; or (2) into hostilities or situations where imminent involvement in hostilities is clearly indicated by the circumstances.

There is no intention or expectation that U.S. forces will become involved in hostilities in Beirut. They will be in Lebanon at the formal request of the Government of Lebanon; we will have assurances regarding the safety and security of the multinational force. Although we cannot rule out isolated acts of violence, all appropriate precautions will be taken to assure the safety of U.S. military personnel during their brief assignment to Lebanon.

These matters will, in any event, be kept under constant review, and the President will report to Congress consistent with the reporting requirements of the War Powers Resolution.

Agreements and Assurances

U.S. forces will participate in the multinational force in Beirut pursuant to an agreement between the U.S. Government and the Government of Lebanon. That agreement is in the form of an exchange of notes signed by Ambassador Dillon on behalf of the U.S. Government and Deputy Prime Minister and Minister of Foreign Affairs Boutros on behalf of the Lebanese Government.

The agreement describes the missions of the Lebanese Armed Forces, the MNF, and the U.S. forces participating in the MNF. It contains provisions concerning command authority for U.S. forces, coordination with the Lebanese Armed Forces and immunities of U.S. personnel. Annexed to the agreement is the schedule for the PLO departure from Beirut.

In accordance with the agreement, the Government of Lebanon has secured assurances from all armed elements not now under the authority of the Lebanese Government that they will comply with the cease-fire and cessation of hostilities. The Government of Israel has provided appropriate assurances.

Role of the ICRC in Moving the PLO from West Beirut

The role envisaged for the International Committee of the Red Cross (ICRC) in moving the PLO from west Beirut is still being finalized on the basis of discussions in Geneva and Beirut.

In accordance with its charter, the ICRC will be expected to care for the sick and wounded combatants while in transit. Initially, the ICRC will arrange transport and provide medical care for the sick and wounded PLO personnel going to Greece.

Financing the Departure of the PLO From West Beirut

The cost of chartering transport of the PLO combatants to receiving countries will be funded through international organizations. The United States is prepared to provide initial funding from State Department funds.

Estimates regarding the cost of evacuating PLO forces from west Beirut currently range from $2 to $4 million. This figure could be increased, however, as the number of people to be transported and their ultimate destinations are finalized.

247. President Reagan's Letter to the U.N. Secretary-General on the Multinational Force, August 20, 1982*

* 82 U.S. State Dep't Bull. No. 2066, at 7 (September 1982).

Dear Mr. Secretary-General:

As you know, the Government of the Republic of Lebanon has requested the deployment of a multinational force in Beirut to assist the Lebanese armed forces as they carry out the orderly and safe departure of Palestinian personnel now in the Beirut area in a manner which will further the restoration of the sovereignty and authority of the Government of Lebanon over the Beirut area. The Lebanese Government has asked for the participation of United States military personnel in this force, together with military personnel from France and Italy.

I wish to inform you that the United States Government has agreed, in response to this request from the Lebanese Government, to deploy a force of about 800 personnel to Beirut for a period not exceeding 30 days. It is my firm intention and belief that these troops will not be involved in hostilities during the course of this operation.

The deployment of this United States force is consistent with the purposes and principles of the United Nations as set forth in Articles 1 and 2 of the Charter. It furthers the goals of Security Council resolutions 508 (1982) and 509 (1982) adopted in June at the beginning of the Lebanese conflict. The force will plan to work closely with the United Nations observer group stationed in the Beirut area.

This agreement will support the objective of helping to restore the territorial integrity, sovereignty and political independence of Lebanon. It is part of the continuing efforts of the United States Government to bring lasting peace to that troubled country, which has too long endured the trials of civil strife and armed conflict.

RONALD REAGAN

I have the honour to request that the present letter be circulated as an official document of the General Assembly, under item 34 of the provisional agenda, and of the Security Council.

KENNETH L. ADELMAN
Ambassador

248. President Reagan's Letter to the Congress on the

Multinational Force, August 24, 1982*

---

* 82 U.S. Dep't State Bull. No. 2066, at 7 (September 1982).

On August 18, 1982, the Government of Lebanon established a plan for the departure from Lebanon of the Palestine Liberation Organization leadership, offices, and combatants in Beirut. This plan has been accepted by the Government of Israel. The Palestine Liberation Organization has informed the Government of Lebanon that it also has accepted the plan. A key element of this plan is the need for a multinational force, including a United States component, to assist the Government of Lebanon in carrying out its responsibilities concerning the withdrawal of these personnel under safe and orderly conditions. This will facilitate the restoration of Lebanese Government sovereignty and authority over the Beirut area.

In response to the formal request of the Government of Lebanon, and in view of the requirement for such a force in order to secure the acceptance by concerned parties of the departure plan, I have authorized the Armed Forces of the United States to participate on a limited and temporary basis. In accordance with my desire that the Congress be fully informed on this matter, and consistent with the War Powers Resolution, I am hereby providing a report on the deployment and mission of these members of the United States Armed Forces.

On August 21, in accordance with the departure plan, approximately 350 French military personnel—the advance elements of the multinational force—were deployed in Beirut together with elements of the Lebanese Armed Forces, and the departure of Palestinian personnel began. To date, Palestinian personnel have departed Lebanon in accordance with the terms of the plan.

On August 25, approximately 800 Marines began to arrive in Beirut. These troops are equipped with weapons consistent with their non-combat mission, including usual infantry weapons.

Under our agreement with the Government of Lebanon, these U.S. military personnel will assist the Government of Lebanon in carrying out its responsibilities concerning the withdrawal of Palestinian personnel under safe and orderly conditions. The presence of our forces will in this way facilitate the restoration of Lebanese Government sovereignty and authority in the Beirut area. Our forces will operate in close coordination with the Lebanese Armed Forces, which will have 2,500–3,500 personnel assigned to this operation, as well as with a total of approximately 800 French and 400 Italian military personnel in the multinational force. Transportation of the personnel departing is being carried out by commercial air and sea transport, and by land. According to our agreement with the Government of Lebanon, the United States military personnel will be withdrawn from Lebanon within thirty days.

I want to emphasize that there is no intention or expectation that U.S. Armed Forces will become involved in hostilities. They are in Lebanon at the formal request of the Government of Lebanon. Our agreement with the Government of Lebanon expressly rules out any combat responsibilities for the U.S. forces. All armed elements in the area have given assurances that they will take no action to interfere with the implementation of the departure plan or the activities of the multinational force. (The departure has been underway for some days now, and thus far these assurances have been fulfilled.) Finally, the departure plan makes it clear that in the event of a breakdown in its implementation, the multinational force will be withdrawn. Although we cannot rule out isolated acts of violence, all appropriate precautions have thus been taken to assure the safety of U.S. military personnel during their brief assignment to Lebanon.

This deployment of the United States Armed Forces to Lebanon is being undertaken pursuant to the President's constitutional authority with respect to the conduct of foreign relations and as Commander-in-Chief of the United States Armed Forces.

This step will not, by itself, resolve the situation in Lebanon, let alone the problems which have plagued the region for more than thirty years. But I believe that it will improve the prospects for realizing our objectives in Lebanon:

- a permanent cessation of hostilities;
- establishment of a strong, representative central government;
- withdrawal of all foreign forces;
- restoration of control by the Lebanese Government throughout the country; and
- establishment of conditions under which Lebanon no longer can be used as a launching point for attacks against Israel.

I also believe that progress on the Lebanon problem will contribute to an atmosphere in the region necessary for progress towards the establishment of a comprehensive peace in the region under Camp David, based firmly on U.N. Security Council Resolutions 242 and 338.

Sincerely,

RONALD REAGAN

V. The Search for Peace and the Continuing Conflict in Lebanon: August 1982–December 1988

A. The Reagan Peace Initiative

249. President Reagan's Statement on U.S. Policy

for Peace in the Middle East,

September 1, 1982*

* 18 Weekly Comp. Pres. Doc. 1081 (September 6, 1982).

Today has been a day that should make us proud. It marked the end of the successful evacuation of PLO from Beirut, Lebanon. This peaceful step could never have been taken without the good offices of the United States and especially the truly heroic work of a great American diplomat, Ambassador Philip Habib.

Thanks to his efforts, I'm happy to announce that the U.S. Marine contingent helping to supervise the evacuation has accomplished its mission. Our young men should be out of Lebanon within 2 weeks. They, too, have served the cause of peace with distinction, and we can all be very proud of them.

But the situation in Lebanon is only part of the overall problem of conflict in the Middle East. So, over the past 2 weeks, while events in Beirut dominated the front page, America was engaged in a quiet, behind-the-scenes effort to lay the groundwork for a broader peace in the region. For once there were no premature leaks as U.S. diplomatic missions traveled to Mideast capitals, and I met here at home with a wide range of experts to map out an American peace initiative for the long-suffering peoples of the Middle East—Arab and Israeli alike.

It seemed to me that with the agreement in Lebanon we had an opportunity for a more far-reaching peace effort in the region, and I was determined to seize that moment. In the words of the scripture, the time had come to "follow after the things which make for peace." Tonight I want to report to you the steps we've taken and the prospects they can open up for a just and lasting peace in the Middle East.

America has long been committed to bringing peace to this troubled region. For more than a generation, successive United States administrations have endeavored to develop a fair and workable process that could lead to a true and lasting Arab-Israeli peace.

Our involvement in the search for Mideast peace is not a matter of preference; it's a moral imperative. The strategic importance of the region to the United States is well known, but our policy is motivated by more than strategic interests. We also have an irreversible commitment to the survival and territorial integrity of friendly states. Nor can we ignore the fact that the well-being of much of the world's economy is tied to stability in the strife-torn Middle East. Finally, our traditional humanitarian concerns dictated a continuing effort to peacefully resolve conflicts.

When our administration assumed office in January of 1981, I decided that the general framework for our Middle East policy should follow the broad guidelines laid down by my predecessors. There were two basic issues we had to address. First, there was the strategic threat to the region posed by the Soviet Union and its surrogates, best demonstrated by the brutal war in Afghanistan, and, second, the peace process between Israel and its Arab neighbors.

With regard to the Soviet threat, we have strengthened our efforts to develop with our friends and allies a joint policy to deter the Soviets and their surrogates from further expansion in the region and, if necessary, to defend against it.

With respect to the Arab-Israeli conflict, we've embraced the Camp David framework as the only way to proceed. We have also recognized, however, solving the Arab-Israeli conflict in and of itself cannot assure peace throughout a region as vast and troubled as the Middle East.

Our first objective under the Camp David process was to ensure the successful fulfillment of the Egyptian-Israeli peace treaty. This was achieved with the peaceful return of the Sinai to Egypt in April 1982. To accomplish this, we worked hard with our Egyptian and Israeli friends and, eventually, with other friendly countries to create the multinational force which now operates in the Sinai. Throughout this period of difficult and time-consuming negotiations, we never lost sight of the next step of Camp David—autonomy talks to pave the way for permitting the Palestinian people to exercise their legitimate rights. However, owing to the tragic assassination of President Sadat and other crises in the area, it was not until January 1982 that we were able to make a major effort to renew these talks.

Secretary of State Haig and Ambassador Fairbanks made three visits to Israel and Egypt early this year to pursue the autonomy talks. Considerable progress was made in developing the basic outline of an American approach which was to be presented to Egypt and Israel after April.

The successful completion of Israel's withdrawal from Sinai and the courage shown on this occasion by Prime Minister Begin and President Mubarak in living up to their agreements convinced me the time had come for a new American policy to try to bridge the remaining differences between Egypt and Israel on the autonomy process. So, in May, I called for specific measures and a timetable for consultations with the Governments of Egypt and Israel on the next steps in the peace process. However, before this effort could be launched, the conflict in Lebanon preempted our efforts.

The autonomy talks were basically put on hold while we sought to untangle the parties in Lebanon and still the guns of war. The Lebanon war, tragic as it was, has left us with a new opportunity for Middle East peace. We must seize it now and bring peace to this troubled area so vital to world stability while there is still time. It was with this strong conviction that over a month ago, before the present negotiations in Beirut had been completed, I directed Secretary of State Shultz to again review our policy and to consult a wide range of outstanding Americans on the best ways to strengthen changes for peace in the Middle East.

We have consulted with many of the officials who were historically involved in the process, with Members of Congress, and with individuals from the private sector. And I have held extensive consultations with my own advisers on the principles that I will outline to you tonight.

The evacuation of the PLO from Beirut is now complete, and we can now help the Lebanese to rebuild their war-torn country. We owe it to ourselves and to posterity to move quickly to build upon this achievement. A stable and revived Lebanon is essential to all our hopes for peace in the region. The people of Lebanon deserve the best efforts of the international community to turn the nightmares of the past several years into a new dawn of hope. But the opportunities for peace in the Middle East do not begin and end in Lebanon. As we help Lebanon rebuild, we must also move to resolve the root causes of conflict between Arabs and Israelis.

The war in Lebanon has demonstrated many things, but two consequences are key to the peace process. First, the military losses of the PLO have not diminished the yearning of the Palestinian people for a just solution of their claims; and, second, while Israel's military successes in Lebanon have demonstrated that its armed forces are second to none in the region, they alone cannot bring just and lasting peace to Israel and her neighbors.

The question now is how to reconcile Israel's legitimate security concerns with the legitimate rights of the Palestinians. And that answer can only come at the negotiating table. Each party must recognize that the outcome must be acceptable to all and that true peace will require compromises by all.

So, tonight I'm calling for a fresh start. This is the moment for all those directly concerned to get involved—or lend their support—to a workable basis for peace. The Camp David agreement remains the foundation of our policy. Its language provides all parties with the leeway they need for successful negotiations.

I call on Israel to make clear that the security for which she yearns can only be achieved through genuine peace, a peace requiring magnanimity, vision, and courage.

I call on the Palestinian people to recognize that their own political aspirations are inextricably bound to recognition of Israel's right to a secure future.

And I call on the Arab States to accept the reality of Israel—and the reality that peace and justice are to be gained only through hard, fair, direct negotiation.

In making these calls upon others, I recognize that the United States has a special responsibility. No other nation is in a position to deal with the key parties to the conflict on the basis of trust and reliability.

The time has come for a new realism on the part of all the peoples of the Middle East. The State of Israel is an accomplished fact; it deserves unchallenged legitimacy within the community of nations. But Israel's legitimacy has thus far been recognized by too few countries and has been denied by every Arab State except Egypt. Israel exists; it has a right to exist in peace behind secure and defensible borders; and it has a right to demand of its neighbors that they recognize those facts.

I have personally followed and supported Israel's heroic struggle for survival, ever since the founding of the State of Israel 34 years ago. In the pre-1967 borders Israel was barely 10 miles wide at its narrowest point. The bulk of Israel's population lived within artillery range of hostile Arab armies. I am not about to ask Israel to live that way again.

The war in Lebanon has demonstrated another reality in the region. The departure of the Palestinians from Beirut dramatizes more than ever the homelessness of the Palestinian people. Palestinians feel strongly that their cause is more than a question of refugees. I agree. The Camp David agreement recognized that fact when it spoke of the legitimate rights of the Palestinian people and their just requirements.

For peace to endure it must involve all those who have been most deeply affected by the conflict. Only through broader participation in the peace process, most immediately by Jordan and by the Palestinians, will Israel be able to rest confident in the knowledge that its security and integrity will be respected by its neighbors. Only through the process of negotiation can all the nations of the Middle East achieve a secure peace.

These, then, are our general goals. What are the specific new American positions, and why are we taking them? In the Camp David talks thus far, both Israel and Egypt have felt free to express openly their views as to what the outcome should be. Understandably their views have differed on many points. The United States has thus far sought to play the role of mediator. We have avoided public comment on the key issues. We have always recognized and continue to recognize that only the voluntary agreement of those parties most directly involved in the conflict can provide an enduring solution. But it's become evident to me that some clearer sense of America's position on the key issues is necessary to encourage wider support for the peace process.

First, as outlined in the Camp David accords, there must be a period of time during which the Palestinian inhabitants of the West Bank and Gaza will have full autonomy over their own affairs. Due consideration must be given to the principle of self-government by the inhabitants of the territories and to the legitimate security concerns of the parties involved. The purpose of the 5-year period of transition which would begin after free elections for a self-governing Palestinian authority is to prove to the Palestinians that they can run their own affairs and that such Palestinian autonomy poses no threat to Israel's security.

The United States will not support the use of any additional land for the purpose of settlements during the transitional period. Indeed, the immediate adoption of a settlement freeze by Israel, more than any other action, could create the confidence needed for wider participation in these talks. Further settlement activity is in no way necessary for the security of Israel and only diminishes the confidence of the Arabs that a final outcome can be freely and fairly negotiated.

I want to make the American position well understood. The purpose of this transitional period is the peaceful and orderly transfer of authority from Israel to the Palestinian inhabitants of the West Bank and Gaza. At the same time, such a transfer must not interfere with Israel's security requirements.

Beyond the transition period, as we look to the future of the West Bank and Gaza, it is clear to me that peace cannot be achieved by the formation of an independent Palestinian state in those territories, nor is it achievable on the basis of Israeli sovereignty or permanent control over the West Bank and Gaza. So, the United States will not support the establishment of an independent Palestinian state in the West Bank and Gaza, and we will not support annexation or permanent control by Israel.

There is, however, another way to peace. The final status of these lands must, of course, be reached through the give and take of negotiations. But it is the firm view of the United States that self-government by the Palestinians of the West Bank and Gaza in association with Jordan offers the best chance for a durable, just, and lasting peace. We base our approach squarely on the principle that the Arab-Israeli conflict should be resolved through negotiations involving an exchange of territory for peace.

This exchange is enshrined in United Nations Security Council Resolution 242, which is, in turn, incorporated in all its parts in the Camp David agreements. U.N. Resolution 242 remains wholly valid as the foundation stone of America's Middle East peace effort. It is the United States position that, in return for peace, the withdrawal provision of Resolution 242 applies to all fronts, including the West Bank and Gaza. When the border is negotiated between Jordan and Israel, our view on the extent to which Israel should be asked to give up territory will be heavily affected by the extent of true peace and normalization, and the security arrangements offered in return.

Finally, we remain convinced that Jerusalem must remain undivided, but its final status should be decided through negotiation.

In the course of the negotiations to come, the United States will support positions that seem to us fair and reasonable compromises and likely to promote a sound agreement. We will also put forward our own detailed proposals when we believe they can be helpful. And, make no mistake, the United States will oppose any proposal from any party and at any point in the negotiating process that threatens the security of Israel. America's commitment to the security of Israel is ironclad, and, I might add, so is mine.

During the past few days, our Ambassadors in Israel, Egypt, Jordan, and Saudi Arabia have presented to their host governments the proposals, in full detail, that I have outlined here today. Now I'm convinced that these proposals can bring justice, bring security, and bring durability to an Arab-Israeli peace. The United States will stand by these principles with total dedication. They are fully consistent with Israel's security requirements and the aspirations of the Palestinians.

We will work hard to broaden participation at the peace table as envisaged by the Camp David accords. And I fervently hope that the Palestinians and Jordan, with the support of their Arab colleagues, will accept this opportunity.

Tragic turmoil in the Middle East runs back to the dawn of history. In our modern day, conflict after conflict has taken its brutal toll there. In an age of nuclear challenge and economic interdependence, such conflicts are a threat to all the people of the world, not just the Middle East itself. It's time for us all—in the Middle East and around the world—to call a halt to conflict, hatred, and prejudice. It's time for us all to launch a common effort for reconstruction, peace, and progress.

It has often been said—and, regrettably, too often been true—that the story of the search for peace and justice in the Middle East is a tragedy of opportunities missed. In the aftermath of the settlement in Lebanon, we now face an opportunity for a broader peace. This time we must not let it slip from our grasp. We must look beyond the difficulties and obstacles of the present and move with a fairness and resolve toward a brighter future. We owe it to ourselves—and to posterity—to do no less. For if we miss this chance to make a fresh start, we may look back on this moment from some later vantage point and realize how much that failure cost us all.

These, then, are the principles upon which American policy toward the Arab-Israeli conflict will be based. I have made a personal commitment to see that they endure and, God willing, that they will come to be seen by all reasonable, compassionate people as fair, achievable, and in the interests of all who wish to see peace in the Middle East.

Tonight, on the eve of what can be a dawning of new hope for the people of the troubled Middle East—and for all the world's people who dream of a just and peaceful future—I ask you, my fellow Americans, for your support and your prayers in this great undertaking.

Thank you, and God bless you.

250. Text of "Talking Points" Sent to Prime Minister
Begin by President Reagan, September 9, 1982*

* *New York Times*, Sept. 9, 1982, at A10, col. 1. *See also* Quandt, "Appendix H: American Answers to Jordanian Questions, October 1978," in *Camp David: Peacemaking and Politics* 388–96 (1986).

Text of 'Talking Points' Sent to Begin by President

Special to The New York Times

WASHINGTON, Sept. 8 — Following is the text of what Administration officials called talking points accompanying a letter sent last week by President Reagan to Prime Minister Menachem Begin of Israel. The same points were presented to Arab governments as a prelude to Mr. Reagan's peace proposals.

GENERAL PRINCIPLES

A. We will maintain our committment to Camp David.

B. We will maintain our committment to the conditions we require for recognition of and negotiation with the P.L.O.

C. We can offer guarantees on the position we will adopt in negotiations. We will not be able, however, to guarantee in advance the results of these negotiations.

TRANSITIONAL MEASURES

A. Our position is that the objective of the transitional period is the peaceful and orderly transfer of authority from Israel to the Palestinian inhabitants.

B. We will support:

¶The decision of full autonomy as giving the Palestinian inhabitants real authority over themselves, the land and its resources, subject to fair safeguards on water.

¶Economic, commercial, social, and cultural ties between the West Bank, Gaza and Jordan.

¶Participation by the Palestinian inhabitants of East Jerusalem in the election of the West Bank-Gaza authority.

¶Real settlement freeze.

¶Progressive Palestinian responsibility for internal security based on capability and performance.

C. We will oppose:

¶Dismantlement of the existing settlements.

¶Provisions which represent a legitimate threat to Israel's security, reasonably defined.

¶Isolation of the West Bank and Gaza from Israel.

¶Measures which accord either the Palestinians or the Israelis generally recognized sovereign rights with the exception of external security, which must remain in Israel's hands during the transitional period.

FINAL STATUS ISSUES

A. U.N.S.C. Resolution 242

It is our position that Resolution 242 applies to the West Bank and Gaza and requires Israeli withdrawal in return for peace. Negotiations must determine the borders. The U.S. position in these negotiations on the extent of the withdrawal will be significantly influenced by the extent and nature of the peace and security arrangements offered in return.

B. Israeli Sovereignty

It is our belief that the Palestinian problem cannot be resolved [through] Israeli sovereignty or control over the West Bank and Gaza. Accordingly, we will not support such a solution.

C. Palestinian State

The preference we will pursue in the final status negotiation is association of the West Bank and Gaza with Jordan. We will not support the formation of a Palestinian state in those negotiations. There is no foundation of political support in Israel or the United States for such a solution. The outcome, however, must be determined by negotiations.

D. Self-Determination

In the Middle East context the term self-determination has been identified exclusively with the formation of a Palestinian state. We will not support this definition of self-determination. We believe that the Palestinians must take the leading role in determining their own future and fully support the provision in Camp David providing for the elected representatives of the inhabitants of the West Bank and Gaza to decide how they shall govern themselves consistent with the provision of their agreement in the final status negotiations.

E. Jerusalem

We will fully support the position that the status of Jerusalem must be determined through negotiations.

F. Settlements

The status of Israeli settlements must be determined in the course of the final status negotiations. We will not support their continuation as extraterritorial outposts.

ADDITIONAL TALKING POINTS

1. Approach to Hussein

The President has approached Hussein to determine the extent to which he may be interested in participating.

¶King Hussein has received the same U.S. positions as you.

¶Hussein considers our proposals serious and gives them serious attention.

¶Hussein understands that Camp David is the only base that we will accept for negotiations.

¶We are also discussing these proposals with the Saudis.

2. Public Commitment

Whatever the support from these or other Arab States, this is what the President has concluded must be done.

The President is convinced his positions are fair and balanced and fully protective of Israel's security. Beyond that they offer the practical opportunity of eventually achieving the peace treaties Israel must have with its neighbors.

He will be making a speech announcing these positions, probably within a week.

3. Next Procedural Steps

Should the response to the President's proposal be positive, the U.S. would take immediate steps to relaunch the autonomy negotiations with the broadest possible participation as envisaged under the Camp David agreements.

We also contemplate an early visit by Secretary Shultz in the area.

Should there not be a positive response, the President, as he has said in his letter to you, will nonetheless stand by his position with proper dedication.

251. Israeli Cabinet Communiqué on President Reagan's Peace Proposal, September 2, 1982*

* 12 J. Palestine Stud. 211 (Winter 1983).

The Cabinet met in special session today and adopted the following resolution:

The positions conveyed to the Prime Minister of Israel on behalf of the President of the United States consist of partial quotations from the Camp David Agreement or are nowhere mentioned in the agreement or contradict it entirely.

The following are the major positions of the Government of the United States:

1. Jerusalem

"Participation by the Palestinian inhabitants of East Jerusalem in the election for the West Bank-Gaza Authority."

No mention whatsoever is made in the Camp David agreement of such a voting right. The single meaning of such a vote is the repartition of Jerusalem into two authorities, the one—of the State of Israel, and the other—of the administrative council of the autonomy. Jerusalem is nowhere mentioned in the Camp David agreement. With respect to the capital of Israel letters were forwarded and attached to that agreement. In his letter to the President of the United States, Mr. Jimmy Carter, the Prime Minister of Israel, Mr. Menachem Begin, stated that "Jerusalem is one city, indivisible, the capital of the State of Israel." Thus shall it remain for all generations to come.

2. Security

"Progressive Palestinian responsibility for internal security based on capability and performance."

In the Camp David agreement it is stated:

"A withdrawal of Israeli armed forces will take place and there will be a redeployment of the remaining Israel forces into specified security locations.

"The agreement will also include arrangements for assuring internal and external security and public order."

It is, therefore, clear that in the Camp David agreement no distinction is made between internal security and external security. There can be no doubt that, were internal security not to be the responsibility of Israel, the terrorist organization called PLO—even after its defeat by the IDF in Lebanon—would act to perpetrate constant bloodshed, shedding the blood of Jews and Arabs alike. For the citizens of Israel this is a question of life and death.

3. 'A Real Settlement Freeze'

In the Camp David agreement no mention whatsoever is made of such a freeze. At Camp David the Prime Minister agreed that new settlements could not be established (though population would be added to existing ones) during the period of the negotiations for the signing of the peace treaty between Egypt and Israel (three months being explicitly stated). This commitment was carried out in full. That three-month period terminated on Dec. 17, 1978. Since then many settlements have been established in Judea, Samaria and the Gaza district without evicting a single person from his land, village or town. Such settlement is a Jewish inalienable right and an integral part of our national security. Therefore, there shall be no settlement freeze. We shall continue to establish them in accordance with our natural right. President Reagan announced at the time that the "settlements are not illegal." A double negative makes a positive, meaning that the settlements are legal. We shall act, therefore, in accordance with our natural right and the law, and we shall not deviate from the principle that these vital settlements will not lead to any eviction.

4. The Definition of Full Autonomy

"The definition of full autonomy as giving the Palestinian inhabitants real authority over themselves, the land and its resources, subject to fair safeguards on water."

Such a definition is nowhere mentioned in the Camp David agreement, which states:

"In order to provide full autonomy to the inhabitants (underlined, our emphasis), etc."

In the lengthy discussion at Camp David it was made absolutely clear that the autonomy applies not to the territory (underlined) but to the inhabitants (underlined).

5. Ties With Jordan

"Economic, commercial and cultural ties between the West Bank, Gaza and Jordan."

In all the clauses of the Camp David agreement there is no reference whatsoever to such ties.

6. Israeli Sovereignty

There is nothing in the Camp David agreement that precludes the application of Israeli sovereignty over Judea, Samaria and the Gaza district following the transitional period which begins with the establishment and inauguration of the self-governing authority (administrative council). This was also stated by an official spokesman of the Government of the United States.

7. *Palestinian State*

The Government of the United States commits itself not to support the establishment of a Palestinian State in Judea, Samaria and the Gaza district. Regrettably, the visible reality proves this to be an illusion. Were the American plan to be implemented, there would be nothing to prevent King Hussein from inviting his newfound friend, Yasir Arafat, to come to Nablus and hand the rule over to him. Thus would come into being a Palestinian state which would conclude a pact with Soviet Russia and arm itself with every kind of modern weaponry. If the PLO could do this in Lebanon, establishing a state-within-a-state, how much more so will the terrorists do so ruling over Judea, Samaria and the Gaza district. Then, a joint front would be established of that "Palestinian State" with Jordan and Iraq behind her, Saudi Arabia to the south and Syria to the north. All these countries, together with other Arab states, would, after a while, launch an onslaught against Israel to destroy her. It is inconceivable that Israel will ever agree to such an "arrangement" whose consequences are inevitable.

Since the positions of the Government of the United States seriously deviate from the Camp David agreement, contradict it and could create a serious danger to Israel, its security and its future, the Government of Israel has resolved that on the basis of these positions it will not enter into any negotiations with any party.

The Government of Israel is ready to renew the autonomy negotiations forthwith with the Governments of the United States and Egypt, signatories to the Camp David agreement, and with other states and elements invited at Camp David to participate in the negotiations, with a view to reaching agreement on the establishment of full autonomy for the Arab inhabitants of Judea, Samaria and the Gaza district, in total conformity with the Camp David accords.

252. Knesset Speech by Foreign Minister Yitzhak Shamir on President Reagan's Proposals, September 8, 1982*

* 21 Int'l Legal Materials 1158 (1982).

Mr. Speaker, Members of the Knesset,

When the first stage of Operation Peace for Galilee was completed, and the stronghold of the murder organizations in the Lebanese capital was eliminated, thereby opening up new possibilities for peace in our region, we were prepared to launch a peace offensive, to mobilize all the resources of goodwill in our own country and among our neighbors, in order to complete the process we began five years ago, the Camp David process.

We believed, and we still believe, that the uprooting of the terrorist plague has helped people understand that the path of violence will not lead to Israel's capitulation; there is but one way to solve the problems of the peoples and countries in the region and alleviate their distress, and that is direct negotiations for a comprehensive and honourable peace.

There was no need to rediscover this path or lay it down once again: the road is already paved. Israel, Egypt and the United States invested a great deal of thought and hard work, of mental and spiritual effort in bringing forth the peace treaty between Egypt and Israel and the Camp David Agreements. This past April—only a few months ago—Israel proved its total fidelity to the obligations it had assumed under these agreements. With profound misgivings and mental anguish, witnessed by the entire world, it completed the withdrawal from Sinai, pulling up, for the first time in its history, magnificent settlements built with the blood and sweat of its children.

We were ready to get on with completing with negotiations on autonomy for the Palestinian Arabs, in order to put into effect the remaining section of the Camp David accords and create the conditions for peaceful and honourable coexistence with the Arab residents of Judea, Samaria and Gaza. There is no doubt that, in these negotiations, it was first and foremost Egypt and the United States, partners in the negotiations from the very start, that were to have taken part. Only recently we held talks with representatives of the United States on the next stages in the peace process. We learned that they were busy studying the various issues of Camp David in order to formulate proposals and positions.

The Reagan Programme

Then, last Wednesday, 1 September 1982, the President of the United States delivered a speech to the American people in which he presented the US position on the various issues involved in a political arrangement for the areas of Judea, Samaria and the Gaza district. The main points in the American position were conveyed to the Prime Minister the day before by the US ambassador in Israel. The Cabinet met in special session on Thursday, 2 September 1982, and solemnly deliberated on the American proposals, as presented to the Prime Minister. It decided to reject the proposals, and to refrain from entering into any negotiations with any party whatsoever on the basis of these positions. This decision has now been placed before the Knesset.

The United States Government did not see fit to consult with us on this new programme, which concerns our borders, our security and our positions. This is something that is simply not done. It contradicts an explicit obligation which the US Government undertook on three separate occasions in the past. The Memorandum of Understanding of 20 December 1973, and President Ford's letter of 1 September 1975, which was reaffirmed in the Memorandum of Understanding of 26 March 1979, stated that the United States would confer with Israel fully, step by step, and would make every effort to coordinate its proposals with Israel. On the other hand, the American administration saw fit to confer with Arab countries that have repeatedly expressed their opposition to the Camp David Agreements. This is in itself a very serious matter; but the actual contents of the new American ideas are even more serious. We cannot accept them as a basis for the negotiation of peace agreements in the region.

The Camp David Accords

The Camp David Agreements were reached after difficult and penetrating debates. Every word in those agreements was the result of intense discussion. Any matter that was not included had been deliberately omitted. The United States participated in the talks, influenced the positions of the parties and mediated between them. The then-President of the United States signed the agreements as a witness.

Since that time, and during the entire negotiating process up to 1 September 1982, the United States abstained from taking any explicit public stand on the substantive issues under negotiation. The reason was obvious. Both partners to the agreement well knew that such a stand by the United States would impair the negotiations and the chances of reaching an agreement between the two parties.

The Camp David Agreements constituted a package, whose component parts were interrelated in a logical, political way, although there was no operational connection between them. Israel agreed to make far-reaching concessions in the Sinai in exchange for peace with Egypt, with the understanding that this would be the extent of its security and territorial risk, since, in the eastern sector, autonomy was agreed upon in Judea, Samaria and Gaza for a five-year transition period. During the negotiations, Egypt did indeed call for Arab sovereignty over the territories of Judea, Samaria and Gaza and a freeze on Jewish settlement. But its demand was not accepted, and Egypt agreed to autonomy for five years. This entire structure has now been undermined by the United States move, which ignores the interrelation between the various positions and concessions and revives demands and positions that were considered and rejected during the Camp David negotiating process. Thus the damage wrought by the American move lies not only in its contradiction of the explicit wording of the agreement, but even more in its attack on the whole conception and internal political structure of the Camp David accords. In reading the new US proposals, I can say that if at the time of Camp David the Americans had insisted on the positions they are now putting forth, we would not have signed the agreements.

Contradictions in the US Position

President Ronald Reagan, in his speech to the American people, declared that Israel has the right to exist behind secure and defensible borders, and the right to demand that its neighbours recognize this fact. He even pointed out that under the pre-1967 lines, Israel was less than ten miles wide at certain points, and that a large portion of its population lived within artillery range of hostile Arab armies. He announced that he had no intention of proposing that Israel return to those conditions. President Reagan also said that the peoples of the Middle East could achieve a secure peace only through the negotiating process. He declared that Jerusalem had to remain undivided, although its final status would have to be fixed by negotiations. Finally, he reiterated his earlier declarations concerning the absolute commitment of the United States to Israel's security.

These are important, positive statements, and we believe that they reflect a sincere, profound feeling of friendship toward Israel and of commitment to its future security. We must note with great regret, however, that the operative provisions that accompanied these declarations by the President contradict them; they constitute a danger to Israel's security, to the principle of a negotiated agreement, and to the chances for peace between Israel and its remaining Arab neighbours.

Erosion of the Camp David Agreements: Autonomy

The position paper we received from the US administration stated that full autonomy means that the inhabitants have "full authority" to govern themselves, the land and its water sources. In the Camp David Agreements the language used was the "granting of full autonomy to the inhabitants;" Israel made it clear in the negotiations that this referred to the inhabitants and not the territory.

The operational significance of this point was a subject of negotiations with Egypt. The United States has now taken a definite position of its own that deviates from the agreement and does great harm to the negotiating process. It turns upside down everything that was achieved in this regard by Israel's representatives through difficult, lengthy negotiations. It represents a change in the essence of the Camp David Agreements. We did not accept this position then, and we will not accept it today.

The United States also states that it will support economic, trade, social and cultural ties between Jordan and Judea, Samaria and the Gaza district.

The Camp David Agreements refer to the connection between autonomy, Jordan and Israel in careful, thoughtful language. The United States has deemed fit, in its new paper, to emphasize specifically the ties with Jordan and to ignore the ties that in any case already exist with Israel. In so doing, it invites pressure for severing ties with Israel in the future. Open borders and free movement are the fundamental principles which Israel has always advocated; until now, they were acceptable, as well, as far as we know, to the United States. How much more so is this the case when we are speaking of an area that is part and parcel of Eretz Israel (the Land of Israel), from which we will never be separated, not now and not ever.

Jerusalem was not mentioned in the body of the Camp David accords, since Israel did not agree to anything that would impair the status of Israel's united capital. Egypt does indeed differ with Israel's stand on this subject, and the positions of the parties may be found in letters that accompany the agreement. Now the United States has taken a stand completely contradictory to that of Israel. The participation of Jerusalem Arabs in the elections for the autonomy authority can have only one real result: the redivision of Jerusalem. To that we will never agree.

Jewish Settlements

The American call for a freeze on Jewish settlement in Judea, Samaria and Gaza during the transition period is negative and harmful. It is not by chance that there is no mention of this in the Camp David Agreements. No self-respecting Israeli Government could agree that the right of Jews to settle in all parts of Eretz Israel should be an issue for discussion or even for mention in any political document. The right of Jews to settle in the Land of Israel is fundamental and beyond question; it does not require anyone's approval. Even to raise the issue is an insult. Even worse, it will encourage Arab elements to believe that they can continue to strive to cut off segments of Eretz Israel and transfer them—"Judenrein"—to foreign ownership. It is impossible to understand how this position can be reconciled with the President's letter of 31 August to the Prime Minister; I quote: "This position does not contravene his deep recognition of the continued right of the Jews to live in peace in Judea, Samaria and Gaza." (Translated from Hebrew)

The subject of security was extensively discussed at Camp David. It is divided into two parts: the overall security of Israel from outside attack, and the security of its inhabitants from terror and sabotage attacks from among the Arab population of Judea, Samaria and Gaza. The key sentence in this matter in the Camp David framework states that all steps and measures will be taken to guarantee the security of Israel and its neighbours during the transition period and afterwards. In order to help achieve this security, a strong police force is to be established by the autonomy authority. This means that Israel would remain in charge of its security against both external attacks and terrorist acts during the transition period and beyond.

No Israeli representative to the negotiations conceived that the prevention of terror and the war against terror could possibly be turned over to a foreign element in Judea, Samaria and Gaza. The new American position seeks to give the Arab inhabitants responsibility for internal security, that is, beyond the defined area of police jurisdiction. The new definition differs significantly from that adopted at Camp David. It means turning over all responsibility for internal security to the autonomous authority. In practical terms, responsibility for fighting terror would not be under our jurisdiction. No sensible Israeli would support this position.

UN Security Council Resolution 242

In the preamble to each of the Camp David documents, and later, to the peace agreement between Israel and Egypt, Security Council Resolution 242 is prominently cited.

The participants at Camp David understood that the negotiations were designed, among other things, to fulfil the provisions of the resolution by means of peace treaties between Israel and its neighbours. In this manner, the parties gave the resolution a specific interpretation and agreed to implement it in practice. Now the US comes along and reopens the subject as though there were no Camp David, and as though there were no connections between 242 and the Camp David Agreements. Autonomy implements Resolution 242. But the new American interpretation does not stop there. It demands that Israel specifically withdraw from this area too.

When you put together all the American positions with all their facets— that is, the principle of withdrawal from Judea, Samaria and Gaza, the principle of territories in exchange for peace, the connection between the depth of the withdrawal and the degree of peace, the freezing of settlement, the opposition to Israeli sovereignty over the territories of Judea, Samaria and Gaza, and the granting of voting rights to East Jerusalem Arabs for the autonomy authority—what this package really means is Israel's return to the partition lines of 1967. When we add to this the rejection of Israeli sovereignty as a possible future option, and the equivocal language concerning the possibility of establishing a Palestinian state, the scenario that would result if these positions were realized is very clear and very grim.

The Camp David Agreements are being emptied of their content; everything that was proposed in Camp David by the Arab side and rejected by Israel reappears in the form of a 'presidential position' emanating from above, to subdue Israel and bend its will.

US-Israel Relations

The Government of Israel could not but reject these positions, even though they came to us from our friend, the president of our greatest friend and ally, the United States. Our relations with the United States are of a special character. Between our two nations there is a deep friendship, based on common values and identical interests. At the same time, differences between our two countries crop up occasionally, chiefly on the subject of our borders and how to defend our security. These differences of opinion are natural; they stem from changing conditions, and they express our independence and our separate needs. A true alliance can exist only between independent nations, each one knowing what is unique to it and what they have in common. Israel is a difficult ally, but a faithful and reliable one. We are certain that what we have in common with the United States is permanent and deep, while our disagreements are ephemeral. The permanent will overcome the ephemeral.

Conclusion

The Israeli people have seen changes and fluctuations, ups and downs in their relations with the US. They know and have known that on the fundamental life-and-death issues—such as security, Jerusalem, the 1967 borders, the danger of a Palestinian state—we have no choice but to stand by our position firmly, strongly and clearly—even against our great friend the United States. No different viewpoint, school of thought, or political party can justify taking any position that differs from the one which the Government of Israel has taken. The Israeli people will stand together and overcome.

253. Final Declaration of the Twelfth Summit Conference
of Arab Heads of State, Fez, Morocco,
September 6–9, 1982*

* Text provided by the Embassy of the Kingdom of Morocco, Washington, D.C., *reprinted in* 21 Int'l Legal Materials 1144 (1982).

Following is the full text of the final declaration adopted by the Twelfth Arab Summit of Fez, which convened September 6th through 9th.

The first part of the 12th Arab Summit was held in Fez on Muharram 27, 1402, which corresponds to November 25, 1981.

After it postponed its works, it resumed them from 17 to 20 Dou Al Kiada, 1402, corresponding to September 6th through 9th, 1982, under the Chairmanship of His Majesty King Hassan II of Morocco. All Arab countries have participated in the works of the Summit with the exception of Libya.

Given the dangerous and delicate circumstances the Arab nation is going through and the historical feeling of responsibility, their Majesties, their Highnesses and their Excellencies the Arab Kings, Presidents and Emirs of Arab states have examined important issues submitted to the Summit and have made the following decisions:

I. The Arab-Israeli Conflict

The Summit paid hommage to the resistance of the forces of the Palestinian revolution, of the Lebanese and Palestinian peoples, of the Arab Syrian Armed Forces and reaffirms its support to the Palestinian people in its struggle for the recovering of its inalienable national rights.

The Summit, convinced of the strength of the Arab nation for the achievement of its legitimate objectives and for putting an end to the aggression, on the basis of fundamental principles laid down by Arab Summits and out of Arab countries' concern to carry on the action by all means for the achievement of a just peace in the Middle East, taking into account the plan of His Excellency President Habib Bourguiba who considers the international legality as a basis for settling the Palestinian issue and the plan of His Majesty King Fahd Ibn Abdelaziz, related to peace in the Middle East, and in the light of discussions and remarks made by their Majesties, their Excellencies, and their Highnesses, the Kings, Presidents and Emirs, the Summit has agreed upon the following principles:

1) The withdrawal of Israel from all Arab territories occupied in 1967, including the Arab Al Qods (Jerusalem).

2) The dismantling of settlements established by Israel on the Arab territories after 1967.

3) The guarantee of freedom of worship and practice of religious rites for all religious in the holy shrines.

4) The reaffirmation of the Palestinian people's right to self-determination and the exercise of its imprescriptible and inalienable national rights under the leadership of the Palestine Liberation Organization (PLO), its sole and legitimate representative and the indemnification of all those who do not desire to return.

5) Placing the West Bank and Gaza Strip under the control of the United Nations for a transitory period not exceeding a few months.

6) The establishment of an independent Palestinian state with Al Qods as its capital.

7) The Security Council guarantees peace among all states of the region including the independent Palestinian state.

8) The Security Council guarantees the respect of these principles.

II. The Israeli Aggression Against Lebanon

1) The Summit strongly condemns the Israeli aggression against Lebanon and the Palestinian and Lebanese peoples, and draws the attention of the international public opinion to the seriousness and the consequences of this aggression on the stability and security of the region.

2) The Summit decides to support Lebanon in everything allowing the implementation of the Security Council resolutions and particularly resolutions 508 and 509 concerning the withdrawal of Israel from the Lebanese territory back to the internationally recognized frontiers.

3) The Summit reaffirms the solidarity of Arab countries with Lebanon in its trajedy and its readiness to grant all assistance that it would demand to solve its problems.

The Summit was informed of the Lebanese Government's decision to put an end to the mission of the Arab deterrent forces in Lebanon. To this effect, the Lebanese and Syrian Governments will start negotiations on measures to be taken in the light of the Israeli withdrawal from Lebanon.

III. Arab Stance on the Gulf War

The Summit has studied the situation in the Gulf and has noted with great affliction and regret the continuation of the Iraq-Iran war, despite repeated attempts to reach a cease-fire and despite offers of mediation and good offices on the part of international organizations, while lauding the positive initiative of Iraq to withdraw its forces back to international borders.

Taking into account the principle of solidarity and the unity of the Arab ranks and out of the Conference's concern to see an atmosphere of clarity, understanding and good neighborliness prevail between Arab countries and their neighbors, the Summit has decided to reaffirm its commitment to defend all Arab territories and to consider any aggression against an Arab country as being an aggression against all Arab countries, and to call upon the two involved parties to fully comply with the resolutions 479 of the year 1982 and 514 of the year 1982 of the Security Council and implement them.

The Summit asks all countries to abstain from taking any measure likely to encourage directly or indirectly the continuation of the war.

IV. The Horn of Africa

The Summit has taken note of what has been exposed by the Democratic Republic of Somalia regarding the incursion of Ethiopia in the Somalian territory and decided the following:

1) To support the Democratic Republic of Somalia to face the requirement of the safeguard of its sovereignty over its territories and to drive out the Ethiopian forces from the Somali territory.

2) The mutual respect by the two countries, Ethiopia and the Democratic Republic of Somalia of the sovereignty and independence of each state after the withdrawal of Ethiopia from the Somali territories.

3) Support of the Summit to the peaceful steps for solving, on this basis, the bilateral problems.

The Summit has decided to set up a committee entrusted with undertaking contacts with the permanent members of the United Nations Security Council fo [*sic*] follow up the Summit's resolutions on the Arab-Israeli conflict and to get informed on these countries' stance and to get informed concerning the position that the United States of America has made public during the past few days concerning the Arab-Israeli conflict. This committee will report regularly on the results of its contacts and endeavors with the Kings and Heads of State.

254. Secretary of State Shultz's Statement Before the Senate Foreign Relations Committee on the Reagan Peace Initiative, September 16, 1982*

---

* 82 U.S. Dep't State Bull. No. 2067, at 5 (October 1982).

I am very pleased to have this opportunity to discuss with you the Administration's recent policy steps in the Middle East. We have begun actions of a wide range and of immense importance. The positive bipartisan support for President Reagan's peace initiative has been evident to us and is deeply appreciated. That support is essential to the conduct of a vigorous and creative foreign policy and, accordingly, I deeply appreciate your willingness to meet with me on short notice.

A little over 2 months ago, I came before you as a nominee for Secretary of State. In those hearings, we were all clearly concerned about the problems presented by the Middle East and the Palestinian issues in particular. I emphasized then our efforts to secure a ceasefire in Lebanon, as the first step toward our goal of a united, sovereign Lebanon, freed from foreign forces. I also emphasized the importance of Israeli security and overall peace, while recognizing the legitimate rights of the Palestinians and their just requirements.

Since then, not just your attention but the world's attention was focused on the Middle East and particularly on our diplomatic efforts there to end the bloodshed and to bring a deeper and lasting peace to the area. With the successful evacuation of the Palestine Liberation Organization (PLO) from Beirut, we have turned to the next steps necessary for peace: the withdrawal of all foreign forces from Lebanon and the restoration of central authority in that country and, of prime importance, the reinvigoration of the Camp David peace process in an effort to resolve fairly the underlying Arab-Israeli dispute.

Lebanon, of course, has suffered grievously over the last several months, let alone the last several years. Phil Habib's [President's special emissary to the Middle East] and Morris Draper's [special negotiator for Lebanon] successful negotiation of the withdrawal of the PLO from Beirut established the first phase of our approach to the problem of Lebanon. The U.S. Marine contingent in the multinational force completed its withdrawal from Beirut at 2:00 this morning, well within the 30-day period the President specified in his notification to you. The French and Italian contingents will begin their withdrawal soon. The Government of Lebanon, meanwhile, is working carefully but surely to reestablish authority over all parts of Beirut, with the Lebanese Army and police increasingly assuming security responsibilities in the city.

The Next Step

A second phase in our Lebanon diplomacy is now before us. As all of you know, the President is sending Ambassador Draper to Lebanon to begin negotiations on withdrawal of foreign forces from that country. The President has made it clear that he personally intends to stay fully engaged in efforts to bring about a strong, free, united, and healthy Lebanon, sovereign throughout all its territories within internationally recognized borders.

The withdrawal of all foreign military forces from Lebanon must be accompanied by the creation of conditions in southern Lebanon to preserve Israeli security. In the immediate future, we will seek a further stabilization in the situation in Beirut. We must create an environment in Lebanon that will allow the newly elected Lebanese Government—free of outside pressure or imposed solutions—to carry on with its task of national reconciliation. The desparate need for economic reconstruction can be well served through such reconciliation and the withdrawal of foreign forces.

The United States is a staunch friend of the Lebanese people and will be a good partner in Lebanon's courageous effort to rebuild its economy and to strengthen its national institutions. We will exercise our responsibility and duty to give every opportunity to the Lebanese themselves to recreate a united but pluralistic society behind strong leadership from their newly elected president. We also look forward to cooperating with appropriate international institutions in the effort to ameliorate the destruction caused by the long and most unfortunate fighting.

These efforts to rebuild Lebanon and strengthen its institutions can only be helped by progress in the overall search for a Middle East peace. The problems of Lebanon are distinct and must be addressed whenever possible separately from our Middle East peace initiative, but both tasks must be carried on without delay. The President will, therefore, dispatch Ambassador Draper to Lebanon this weekend, while we also continue to work on the overall peace initiative.

U.S. Initiative

When I was before you in the confirmation hearings, I noted our commitment to solving the Palestinian problem within the Camp David framework. Right after your vote to report my nomination favorably to the full Senate, the President instructed me that he wished high priority be placed on addressing the underlying Arab-Israeli dispute, especially the Palestinian issues.

The President's statement last week began a fresh start on the Arab-Israeli dispute. The fundamental problems involved are of universal concern not just to the people of the region but to the United States and other countries as well. The events of the last month have demonstrated that we Americans have a special responsibility in the efforts to bring peace to the area. No one else has the credibility—and therefore the ability—to provide the crucial link to all sides.

The President's Middle East peace initiative is based on an intensive and detailed review of the problem. We have discussed the issues in detail with members of this committee and others in the Congress, with former government officials, and many other knowledgeable people. The paramount conclusions of that review are that (1) it is time to address, forcefully and directly, the underlying Palestinian issues, and (2) genuine success depends upon broadening participation in the negotiations to include, as envisaged in the Camp David accords, Egypt, Israel, Jordan, and the representatives of the Palestinian people.

In taking this initiative, the President established two conditions—we will remain fully committed to both the principles of the Camp David accords and to the security of Israel. The Camp David framework has one key element that all other peace plans lack: It has been successful. It produced the only treaty of peace between Israel and an Arab country and the completion of the disengagement and return of the Sinai. Moreover, the Camp David framework has the necessary room for negotiations to fulfill the legitimate rights of the Palestinian people and to reach peace treaties between Israel and its neighbors. As President Carter said a week ago, "There is absolutely nothing in the President's speech . . . nor in the information he sent to the Israelis which is contrary to either the letter or the spirit of Camp David. It is absolutely compatible with the Camp David agreement." Our initiative will give the provisions of Camp David their full meaning and a new dynamism.

This renewed dynamism for the Camp David negotiations will insure Israeli security, and we emphatically will require the product of the negotiations to do so. As the President's speech noted, this country, this Administration, and the President personally are committed to Israel's security. This same renewed dynamism also will provide appropriate regard to the "legitimate rights of the Palestinian people and their just requirements." Camp David itself calls for the residents of the West Bank and Gaza and other Palestinians as agreed to participate in negotiating the two primary means of achieving those rights—a 5-year transitional period of autonomous self-government and final status after the 5-year transitional period. By renewing the process, we seek to fulfill the hope of Camp David: Israel and its neighbors, Jordan, Egypt, and the Palestinians, engaged in fair, direct, and successful negotiations on how they will all live together.

The Camp David accords provide that these negotiated arrangements on final status must be "just, comprehensive, . . . durable," and "based on Security Council Resolutions 242 and 338 in all their parts." Security Council Resolution 242 sets forth the two key principles:

   (i) Withdrawal of Israeli armed forces from territories occupied. . . .

   (ii) Termination of all claims or states of belligerency and respect for and acknowledgement of the sovereignty, territorial integrity and political independence of every State in the area and their right to live in peace within secure and recognized boundaries free from threats or acts of force.

As it has often been summarized, peace for territory.

We believe these principles apply on all fronts, but our position on the extent of withdrawal will be significantly influenced by the extent and nature of the peace and security arrangements being offered in return. Israel, Jordan, Egypt, and the elected representatives of the inhabitants of the West

Bank and Gaza will negotiate the final boundaries, recognizing Palestinian legitimate rights, and securing what Resolution 338 calls a "just and durable peace." We will support positions in those negotiations which we believe are fair. Those positions include:

Israeli Sovereignty/Palestinian State. It is the President's belief that the Palestinian problem cannot be resolved through Israeli sovereignty or control over the West Bank and Gaza. Accordingly, we will not support such a solution. We will also not support the formation of a Palestinian state in those negotiations. There is no foundation of political support in Israel or in the United States for such a solution and peace cannot be achieved by that route. The preference we will pursue in the final status negotiations is some form of association of the West Bank and Gaza with Jordan.

Self-Determination. In the Middle East context, the term "self-determination" has been identified exclusively with the formation of a Palestinian state. We will not support this definition of self-determination. We do believe that the Palestinians must take a leading role in determining their own future and fully support the provision in the Camp David agreement providing for the elected representatives of the inhabitants of the West Bank and Gaza to decide how they shall govern themselves consistent with the provisions of their agreement in the final status negotiations.

Jerusalem. We will fully support the position that Jerusalem must be undivided and that its status must be determined through negotiations. We do not recognize unilateral acts with respect to final status issues.

Settlements. The status of Israeli settlements must be determined in the course of the final status negotiations. We will not support their continuation as extraterritorial outposts, but neither will we support efforts to deny Jews the opportunity to live in the West Bank and Gaza under the duly constituted governmental authority there, as Arabs live in Israel.

Negotiations on the final status of the area will not start until a self-governing authority for the territories is firmly in place. Negotiations about the transitional phase have been in progress for the last 3 years. In those negotiations we have consistently expressed our views to our negotiating partners, Israel and Egypt, as issues arose. Most recently, we informed our partners of how these separate expressions fit into our overall view of Palestinian self-government during a transitional period.

In our view, the objective of the transitional period is the peaceful and orderly transfer of authority from Israel to the Palestinian inhabitants, while insuring that all necessary measures are taken to assure Israeli security.

We have emphasized that this period is transitional, not final, and that, therefore, the provisions relating to it should not prejudice the final status. In light of those views, we have told our partners that we have supported and will continue to support:

· The definition of full autonomy giving the Palestinian inhabitants real authority over themselves, the land, and its resources subject to fair safeguards on water;

· The inclusion of economic, commercial, social, and cultural ties among the West Bank, Gaza, and Jordan;

· Participation by the Palestinian inhabitants of east Jerusalem in the election for the West Bank/Gaza authority; and

· Progressive Palestinian responsibility for internal security based on capability and performance.

Using those same standards, we have opposed and will continue to oppose:

· Dismantlement of existing settlements; and
· Provisions which represent a threat to Israel's security.

As the President noted in his speech, we are attempting to reinvigorate the autonomy negotiations. That effort would be assisted to a great extent by a freeze of the Israeli settlements in the occupied territories, which was requested during the Camp David negotiations. Our concern is not with their legality or illegality but with their effects on the peace process.

The President's initiative follows over 3 years of active negotiations, continuous discussions of the issues involved over the same period, and, most recently, two trips to the Middle East by the Secretary of State this year and additional trips by Ambassador Fairbanks [special negotiator for the Middle East peace process] and by others working on the negotiations. We have put these ideas in some detail to the Israelis and the key Arab states, including Jordan and Egypt. They are now examining the proposals. It would be surprising if they liked or disliked all of them. We have received reactions from some of our interlocutors. We are studying those reactions. We confidently expect to continue our discussions, with the Israelis, with the Arab countries, and with other friendly governments.

The President has now articulated a reasonable basis for a negotiated compromise among the parties. We emphasize that any agreement must be based on the free give-and-take of the negotiating process. We do not guarantee to any party the outcome of the negotiations on any issue. The President has now stated publicly some U.S. positions on key issues. We now call for the parties contemplated by the Camp David agreement to join us in seeking peace.

Time for Quiet Diplomacy

Mr. Chairman [Senator Charles H. Percy], I am very grateful for the words of support and encouragement that you and the members of this committee have given. Your emphasis in several interviews on the deep yearning for peace in the countries and peoples of this area; Senator Cranston's and Senator Boschwitz's support for the effort to broaden the process and involve the Jordanians and representatives of the Palestinians; and Senator Mathias' emphasis on the need for all to address this problem objectively are indications that the Congress and the Administration are together, focused on this essential task. As you put it, "There just isn't an alternative for finding a basis for lasting peace. . . . Think what could happen to this area in the Middle East if peace is found, and a basis for working together with its Arab neighbors is found by Israel and its Arab neighbors."

We now have the initial formal reactions from the Israeli Government and the Arab League summit. The Israeli Government, supported by a vote of the *Knesset*, has opposed the President's proposals. While not directly addressing the President's proposals, the Arab League summit has put forward its own proposals, key elements of which are at variance with our proposals. The President stands firmly behind his proposals. The reactions of the Israeli Government and of the Arab League are clear and graphic evidence that the position of both sides must be negotiated if we are to bring genuine peace and security to this troubled region.

The opening positions have been announced. Now is the time for quiet diplomacy to pursue the President's initiative and bring it to fruition.

In launching this initiative, the President determined that he would stay fully involved and fully committed to the principles he enunciated. We will be working hard over the next weeks in light of the new dynamic the initiative introduces to bring the peace process forward. I pledge to you that we will be exercising the creativity, the persistence, and the dogged determination to succeed which marked the successful effort in Beirut. I also emphasize to you that we recognize that our effort is to bring a lasting, effective, and just peace to this area. That goal can hardly be accomplished in a few short weeks. We ask you to stay with the President in his determination to sustain his effort and to look for the long-term, just solution. We believe, deeply and purposefully, that peace can come between Arabs and Jews. No greater purpose can be placed before us all than a just and lasting peace.

255. Report of PLO Central Council, November 25, 1982*

The PLO Central Council held a meeting on Thursday, November 25, 1982. The Council discussed at length the current Arab Palestinian issues and developments in the region.

1. The Council expressed pride in and appreciation of the position of our people inside the occupied territory, who affirmed their adherence to the PLO, their sole legitimate representative, for their adherence to their firm national demands—particularly their right to return, to self-determination and to the establishment of an independent state on their national soil—for their rejection of all the attempts at tampering with these rights and for their commitment to Palestinian representation solely through the PLO.

2. The Council expressed the view that the Reagan plan does not fulfill the inalienable rights of our people under the leadership of the PLO because the Reagan plan ignores the right of self-determination for our Palestinian people and the establishment of an independent Palestinian state under PLO leadership, without which no permanent and just solution can be reached for the Middle East problem and its central Palestinian issue.

3. Based on decisions by Palestine National Councils, Arab summits and the will of our Palestinian people in the occupied territory and in the diaspora, the Council affirms that the PLO is the sole legitimate representative of the Palestinian people inside and outside the occupied territory and that it is the sole spokesman for these people.

4. The Council members expressed great appreciation for the sacrifices and heroism of the Arab people of Egypt in defence of Palestine and the Arab nation, and reiterated that the Camp David agreements were the principal means by which Israel and the United States attempted to isolate Egypt from the Arab nation. The Council stressed the need for Egypt to return to the Arab ranks and for the Arabs to return to Egypt, away from Camp David.

5. The Council stressed the importance of Palestinian national unity. The members were unanimous that this unity is our strong bastion of struggle and is responsible for our epic of steadfastness in Lebanon. The Council stressed the importance of this unity so as to realize our people's inalienable national rights. The members also affirmed that the attempts of hostile forces to strike at national unity within the framework of the PLO would be doomed to failure.

It has been decided that intensive meetings will begin on the morning of November 26, in which the [PLO] Executive Committee Chairman and members will take part. These meetings will also be attended by the presidium of the Palestine National Council and the secretaries general of all the Resistance groups in order to draw up political, organizational and military plans to face the next stage and to fix a venue and date for the Palestine National Council's 16th session.

256. PLO Statement Outlining Its Position on Dialogue with Jordan and Rejecting the Reagan Peace Plan, Damascus, April 12, 1983*

* 12 J. Palestine Stud. 218 (Summer 1983).

In the light of the recent political developments and of the resolutions adopted by the Palestinian leadership at its meetings in Amman and Kuwait, we wish to make the following points clear:

1. The PLO's attitude has always been based on adherence to the resolutions of the Palestine National Council, especially those adopted at the recent session in Algiers, and on the resolutions of the Fez summit, which were unanimously accepted by the Arabs, who regard them as the basis for their political moves at the international level.

2. In its attitudes, the PLO has always stressed its refusal to regard the Reagan plan as a sound basis for a just and permanent solution to the Palestine issue and the Arab-Zionist conflict, inasmuch as neither in form nor in content does this plan comply with the inalienable national rights of the Palestinian people. It also calls on the Arabs to make fundamental concessions at the expense of those rights without providing minimum guarantees for the recovery of the occupied Arab and Palestinian territories, and for enabling our people to exercise their right to self-determination on their national soil.

The PLO has clearly and frankly stated its attitude to its brother Arabs, and in particular to its brothers in Jordan, during the discussions between us and them in recent months.

3. The Palestinian revolution, while insisting on the full and independent representation of the Palestinians by the PLO, affirms that it sees the Palestinian cause as the national cause of a people who have every right to liberation, independence and sovereignty on their national soil.

Excluding or minimizing this representation turns the Palestinian cause and the future of the occupied territory into a mere problem of frontiers and local regions, or leads to the fragmentation and invalidation of the rights of the Palestinian people.

In the light of the above, it has always been the Palestinian position to regard the issue of their rescue of Palestinian territory as a top priority and as the central objective of the Palestinian struggle.

4. Through the resolutions of the National Council, the PLO has stressed the importance of the special and distinctive relations with Jordan, in view of the vital interests that the two fraternal peoples have in common. The PLO has not seen future relations from a tactical viewpoint, or as being a mechanism to enable us to subscribe to the Reagan plan. On the contrary, it has seen the confederal relationship as a strategic goal regulating and reinforcing the links between the two peoples on a national basis after the establishment of the independent Palestinian state.

The PLO believes that the resolutions of the Fez summit have the mechanism for political moves through the UN Security Council, while the Reagan plan offers a picture similar to the Camp David plan, which was rejected by all the Arabs at the Baghdad summit conference as being a partial and separate solution, incompatible with Arab interests and comprehensive national rights.

5. The PLO has stressed that any political move on behalf of the cause of Palestine, as being an all-Arab cause, must be based on the resolutions of the Arab summits and within an Arab framework. Only this can guarantee the safety of such a move and that the best use is made of all Arab efforts and potentials. This Arab framework is capable of developing international attitudes to the advantage of our national rights.

6. During the talks of PLO delegations with Jordan which were held in Amman, it became clear that there was a common understanding on the lack of seriousness and credibility in the American stand. This has been and is being demonstrated particularly by current developments in Lebanon and by the criminal activities of Zionism in the occupied territories which the American administration is supporting and disregarding.

While affirming these facts, which have been recorded through documents exchanged with our brothers in Jordan, the PLO stresses the importance of continued dialogue and relations with Jordan in the interests of our common and all-Arab interests, for the confrontation of Zionist aggression in the occupied territories and the threat it constitutes to the security and sovereignty of fraternal Jordan and all the other Arab countries.

B. The Redeployment of the Multinational Force

and Efforts to Assure Lebanese Autonomy

257. U.S. Statements on Bashir Gemayel's Assassination, September 14 and 15, 1982*

---

* 82 U.S. Dep't State Bull. No. 2068, at 47 (November 1982) (notes omitted).

President's Statement, Sept. 14, 1982

The news of the cowardly assassination of Bashir Gemayel, President-elect of Lebanon, is a shock to the American people and to civilized men and women everywhere. This promising young leader had brought the light of hope to Lebanon. We condemn the perpetrators of this heinous crime against Lebanon and against the cause of peace in the Middle East. Our deepest sympathy goes to Mrs. Bashir Gemayel and their son, the entire Gemayel family, to President Elias Sarkis, to his government, and to the people of Lebanon. We join with them in mourning.

The tragedy will be all the greater if men of good will in Lebanon and in countries friendly to Lebanon permit disorder to continue in this war-torn country. This must not happen. The U.S. Government stands by Lebanon with its full support in this hour of need.

White House Statement, Sept. 15, 1982

This latest violent tragedy only reemphasizes the need for urgency in the search for peace in the Middle East. The United States intends to continue to press ahead vigorously with the President's initiative to broaden the participation at the peace talks.

We have been in frequent touch with senior officials of the Government of Lebanon and with other prominent Lebanese personalities. Our support for their efforts to maintain order should be clear. We have also contacted Israeli officials in Beirut, Washington, and in Israel. They told us that their military moves are limited and precautionary. We have urged they do nothing to increase tensions.

The central Government of Lebanon remains in place. We will be consulting with President Sarkis, Prime Minister Wazzan, and other Lebanese Government officials to explore ways we can support their efforts to maintain stability. We adhere to the goals we share with the Government of Lebanon of internal unity and withdrawal of all foreign forces.

While we deplore the shocking assassination of President-elect Gemayel, it is essential that we not lose sight of these important objectives which Lebanon has set for itself. The restoration of central government authority remains key to Lebanon's future. We will do everything we can to assist this process through this difficult period in the country's history.

Ambassador Draper has the full support of the President and will continue to work closely with the Government of Lebanon in pursuit of its objectives. Those objectives parallel our own support for:

· The withdrawal of all foreign military forces from Lebanon;

· The strengthening of the central government and the reestablishment of its authority throughout Lebanon;

· The creation of conditions which insure that Lebanon will never again be a launching pad for attacks against Israel; and

The promotion of national unity and reconciliation, along with strengthening of all national institutions, including the army.

Department Statement, Sept. 15, 1982

We deplore the shocking assassination of President-elect Bashir Gemayel. This latest violent tragedy only reemphasizes the need for urgency in the search for peace in the Middle East.

The central Government of Lebanon remains in place. We will be consulting with President Sarkis, Prime Minister Wazzan, and other Lebanese Government officials to explore ways we can support their efforts to maintain stability.

We have been in frequent touch with senior officials of the Government of Lebanon and with other prominent Lebanese personalities. Ambassador Draper [special negotiator for Lebanon] is in Lebanon today for meetings with Lebanese officials. Our support for their efforts to maintain order is clear. We have also contacted Israeli officials in Beirut, Washington, and in Israel. We have urged they do nothing to increase tensions and again call on all parties to exercise restraint.

President-elect Gemayel's death underscores the need that we not lose sight of the important objectives which Lebanon has set for itself. The restoration of central government authority remains key to Lebanon's future. We will do everything we can to assist this process through this difficult period in the country's history. Ambassador Draper has the full support of the President and will continue to work closely with the Government of Lebanon in pursuit of its objectives. Those objectives parallel our own support for:

· The withdrawal of all foreign military forces from Lebanon;
· The strengthening of the central government and the reestablishment of its authority throughout Lebanon;
· The creation of conditions which insure that Lebanon will never again be a launching pad for attacks against Israel; and
· The promotion of national unity and reconciliation, along with strengthening of all national institutions, including the army.

We will continue to pursue the goals we share with the Government of Lebanon of internal unity and withdrawal of all foreign forces. The United States intends, as well, to continue to press ahead vigorously with the President's initiative to broaden the participation at the Middle East peace talks.

258. European Parliament Resolution on the Assassination

of the President of the Lebanese Republic,

September 16, 1982*

* 25 O.J. Eur. Comm. (No. C 267) 43 (1982).

The European Parliament,

A. deeply moved by the cowardly assassination of the elected President of the Republic and other leading Lebanese Christians,

B. fearing that this tragic event will impede the progress on the current laudable attempts to find a peaceful solution to the problems of the Middle East,

C. hoping for the restoration of a strong Lebanese sovereign state and for reconciliation between all the elements which make up the nation and which have united to reconstruct the country together despite the bloody provocation of the partisans of civil war,

1. Condemns vigorously the odious attack which claimed the life of the elected President of the Lebanese Republic;

2. Stresses that the assassination of President Sadat and President Gemayel serves to help those forces which are attempting to prevent at any price a peaceful settlement between the Arabs and the Israelis and are endeavouring to make Lebanon a strategic base for efforts to destabilize the Middle East;

3. Takes the view that the Community must now more than ever continue to play a positive role in the attempts to achieve peace in the Middle East by adopting practical initiatives of a humanitarian, economic and political nature:

4. Instructs its President to forward this resolution to the Council, Commission and Foreign Ministers meeting in political cooperation.

259. Security Council Resolution 520 Condemning the
Israeli Incursion into Beirut and Calling for Immediate
Withdrawal from Lebanon, September 17, 1982*

---

* S.C. Res. 520, 37 U.N. SCOR (2395th mtg.) at 10, U.N. Doc. S/INF/38 (1982).

The Security Council,

Having considered the report of the Secretary-General of 15 September 1982,[40]

Condemning the murder of Bashir Gemayel, the constitutionally elected President-elect of Lebanon, and every effort to disrupt by violence the restoration of a strong, stable government in Lebanon,

Having listened to the statement by the Permanent Representative of Lebanon,[41]

Taking note of the determination of Lebanon to ensure the withdrawal of all non-Lebanese forces from Lebanon,

1. *Reaffirms* its resolutions 508 (1982), 509 (1982) and 516 (1982) in all their components;

2. *Condemns* the recent Israeli incursions into Beirut in violation of the cease-fire agreements and of Security Council resolutions;

3. *Demands* an immediate return to the positions occupied by Israel before 15 September 1982, as a first step towards the full implementation of Security Council resolutions;

4. *Calls again* for the strict respect of the sovereignty, territorial integrity, unity and political independence of Lebanon under the sole and exclusive authority of the Government of Lebanon through the Lebanese Army throughout Lebanon;

5. *Reaffirms* its resolutions 512 (1982) and 513 (1982), which call for respect for the rights of the civilian populations without any discrimination, and repudiates all acts of violence against those populations;

6. *Supports* the efforts of the Secretary-General to implement resolution 516 (1982), concerning the deployment of United Nations observers to monitor the situation in and around Beirut, and requests all the parties concerned to co-operate fully in the application of that resolution;

7. *Decides* to remain seized of the question and asks the Secretary-General to keep the Security Council informed of developments as soon as possible and not later than within twenty-four hours.

Adopted unanimously at the 2395th meeting.

[40] *Ibid.* [*Official Records of the Security Council, Thirty-seventh Year, Supplement for July, August and September 1982*], document S/15382/Add.1.

[41] *Ibid., Thirty-seventh Year,* 2394th meeting.

260. President Reagan's Statements on the Massacre of Palestinians in West Beirut, September 18 and 20, 1982*

* 82 U.S. Dep't State Bull. No. 2068, at 48 (November 1982) (notes omitted).

President's Statement, Sept. 18, 1982

I was horrified to learn this morning of the killing of Palestinians which has taken place in Beirut. All people of decency must share our outrage and revulsion over the murders, which included women and children. I express my deepest regrets and condolences to the families of the victims and the broader Palestinian community.

During the negotiations leading to the PLO withdrawal from Beirut, we were assured that Israeli forces would not enter west Beirut. We also understood that following withdrawal, Lebanese Army units would establish control over the city. They were thwarted in this effort by the Israeli occupation that took place, beginning on Wednesday. We strongly opposed Israel's move into west Beirut following the assassination of President-elect Gemayel both because we believed it wrong in principle and for fear that it would provoke further fighting. Israel, by yesterday in military control of Beirut, claimed that its moves would prevent the kind of tragedy which has now occurred.

We have today summoned the Israeli Ambassador to demand that the Israeli Government immediately withdraw its forces from west Beirut to the positions occupied on September 14. We also expect Israel, thereafter, to commence serious negotiations which will first lead to the earliest possible disengagement of Israeli forces from Beirut and, second, to an agreed framework for the early withdrawal of all foreign forces from Lebanon.

Despite and because of the additional bloody trauma which adds to Lebanon's agonies, we urge the Lebanese to unite quickly in support of their government and their constitutional processes and to work for the future they so richly deserve. We will be with them.

This terrible tragedy underscores the desperate need for a true peace in the Middle East, one which takes full account of the needs of the Palestinian people. The initiative I announced on Septebmer 1 will be pursued vigorously in order to achieve that goal.

President's Statement, Sept. 20, 1982

My fellow Americans, the scenes that the whole world witnessed this past weekend were among the most heartrending in the long nightmare of Lebanon's agony. Millons of us have seen pictures of the Palestinian victims of this tragedy. There is little that words can add. But there are actions we can and must take to bring that nightmare to an end.

It is not enough for us to view this as some remote event in which we ourselves are not involved. For our friends in Lebanon and Israel, for our friends in Europe and elsewhere in the Middle East, and for us Americans, this tragedy, horrible as it is, reminds us of the absolute imperative of bringing peace to that troubled country and region. By working for peace in the Middle East, we serve the cause of world peace, and the future of mankind.

For the criminals who did this deed, no punishment is enough to remove the blot of their crime. But for the rest of us, there are things that we can learn and things that we must do. The people of Lebanon must have learned that the cycle of massacre upon massacre must end. Children are not avenged by the murder of other children. Israel must have learned that there is no way it can impose its own solutions on hatreds as deep and bitter as those that produced this tragedy. If it seeks to do so, it will only sink more deeply into the quagmire that looms before it. Those outsiders who have fed the flames of civil war in Lebanon for so many years need to learn that the fire will consume them, too, if it is not put out. And we must all rededicate ourselves to the cause of peace. I reemphasize my call for early progress to solve the Palestinian issue and repeat the U.S. proposals which are now even more urgent.

For now is not the time for talk alone. Now is a time for action. To act together to restore peace to Beirut; to help a stable government emerge that can restore peace and independence to all of Lebanon; and to bring a just and lasting resolution to the conflict between Israel and its Arab neighbors, one that satisfies the legitimate rights of the Palestinians who are all too often its victims.

Our basic objectives in Lebanon have not changed, for they are the objectives of the government and the people of Lebanon themselves. First and foremost, we seek the restoration of a strong and stable central government in that country, brought into being by orderly constitutional processes. Lebanon elected a new president 2 short weeks ago only to see him murdered even before he could assume his office. This week a distressed Lebanon will again be electing a new president. May God grant him safety as well as the wisdom and courage to lead his country into a new and happier era.

The international community has an obligation to assist the Government of Lebanon in reasserting authority over all its territory. Foreign forces and armed factions have too long obstructed the legitimate role of the Lebanese Government's security forces. We must pave the way for withdrawal of foreign forces.

The place to begin this task is in Beirut. The Lebanese Government must be permitted to restore internal security in its capital. It cannot do this if foreign forces remain in or near Beirut. With this goal in mind, I have consulted with our French and Italian allies. We have agreed to form a new multinational force, similar to the one which served so well last month, with the mission of enabling the Lebanese Government to resume full sovereignty over its capital, the essential precondition for extending its control over the entire country.

The Lebanese Government, with the support of its people, requested this help. For this multinational force to succeed, it is essential that Israel withdraw from Beirut. With the expected cooperation of all parties, the multinational force will return to Beirut for a limited period of time. Its purpose is not to act as a police force but to make it possible for the lawful authorities of Lebanon to discharge those duties for themselves.

Secretary Shultz, on my behalf, has also reiterated our views to the Government of Israel through its Ambassador in Washington. Unless Israel moves quickly and courageously to withdraw, it will find itself ever more deeply involved in problems that are not its own and which it cannot solve.

The participation of American forces in Beirut will again be for a limited period. But I've concluded there is no alternative to their returning to Lebanon if that country is to have a chance to stand on its own feet.

Peace in Beirut is only a first step. Together with the people of Lebanon, we seek the removal of all foreign military forces from that country. The departure of all foreign forces at the request of the Lebanese authorities has been widely endorsed by Arab as well as other states. Israel and Syria have both indicated that they have no territorial ambitions in Lebanon and are prepared to withdraw. It is now urgent that specific arrangements for withdrawal of all foreign forces be agreed upon. This must happen very soon. The legitimate security concerns of neighboring states, including particularly the safety of Israel's northern population, must be provided for. But this is not a difficult task if the political will is there. The Lebanese people must be allowed to chart their own future. They must rely solely on Lebanese Armed Forces who are willing and able to bring security to their country. They must be allowed to do so, and the sooner the better.

Ambassador Draper, who has been in close consultation with the parties concerned in Lebanon, will remain in the area to work for the full implementation of our proposal. Ambassador Habib will join him and will represent me at the inauguration of the new President of Lebanon and will consult with the leaders in the area. He will return promptly to Washington to report to me.

Early in the summer our government met its responsibility to help resolve a severe crisis and to relieve the Lebanese people of the crushing burden. We succeeded. Recent events have produced new problems, and we must, again, assume our responsibility.

I am especially anxious to end the agony of Lebanon because it is both right and in our national interest. But I am also determined to press ahead on the broader effort to achieve peace between Israel and its Arab neighbors. The events in Beirut of last week have served only to reinforce my conviction that such a peace is desperately needed and that the initiative we undertook on September 1 is the right way to proceed. We will not be discouraged or deterred in our efforts to seek peace in Lebanon and a just and lasting peace throughout the Middle East.

All of us must learn the appropriate lessons from this tragedy and assume the responsibilities that it imposes upon us. We owe it to ourselves and to our children. The whole world will be a safer place when this region which has known so much trouble can begin to know peace instead. Both our purpose and our action are peaceful, and we are taking them in a spirit of international cooperation.

Tonight I ask for your prayers and your support as our country continues its vital role as a leader for world peace, the role that all of us as Americans can be proud of.

261. Security Council Resolution 521 Condemning the

West Beirut Massacre, September 19, 1982*

* S.C. Res. 521, 37 U.N. SCOR (2396th mtg.) at 10, U.N. Doc. S/INF/38 (1982).

The Security Council,

Appalled at the massacre of Palestinian civilians in Beirut,

Having heard the report of the Secretary-General[42] at its 2396th meeting,

Noting that the Government of Lebanon has agreed to the dispatch of United Nations observers to the sites of greatest human suffering and losses in and around that city,

1. *Condemns* the criminal massacre of Palestinian civilians in Beirut;

2. *Reaffirms* once again its resolutions 512 (1982) and 513 (1982), which call for respect for the rights of the civilian populations without any discrimination, and repudiates all acts of violence against those populations;

3. *Authorizes* the Secretary-General, as an immediate step, to increase the number of United Nations observers in and around Beirut from ten to fifty, and insists that there shall be no interference with the deployment of the observers and that they shall have full freedom of movement;

4. *Requests* the Secretary-General, in consultation with the Government of Lebanon, to ensure the rapid deployment of those observers in order that they may contribute in every way possible within their mandate to the effort to ensure full protection for the civilian populations;

5. *Requests* the Secretary-General, as a matter of urgency, to initiate appropriate consultations and, in particular, consultations with the Government of Lebanon on additional steps which the Security Council might take, including the possible deployment of United Nations forces, to assist the Government in ensuring full protection for the civilian populations in and around Beirut and requests him to report to the Council within forty-eight hours;

6. *Insists* that all concerned must permit United Nations observers and forces established by the Security Council in Lebanon to be deployed and to discharge their mandates and, in this connection, solemnly calls attention to the obligation of all Member States, under Article 25 of the Charter of the United Nations, to accept and carry out the decisions of the Council in accordance with the Charter;

7. *Requests* the Secretary-General to keep the Security Council informed on an urgent and continuing basis.

Adopted unanimously at the resumed 2396th meeting.

[42] *Ibid.* [*Official Records of the Security Council*], *Thirty-seventh Year, Supplement for July, August and September 1982*, document S/15400.

262. Statement by the EEC Foreign Ministers on the Middle East Situation, September 20, 1982*

*15 Bull. Eur. Comm. (No. 9) 53 (1982).

'The Ten express their profound shock and revulsion at the massacre of Palestinian civilians in Beirut. They strongly condemn this criminal act and call for the necessary measures to be taken to ensure the safety of the civilian population. They welcome UN Security Council Resolution 521 and are ready to support, up to the limit of their capabilities, appropriate additional steps, including the strengthening of the UN observers team in Beirut and the possible deployment of UN or multinational forces.

They strongly deplore the violation of the Habib plan and demand the immediate withdrawal of the Israeli forces from West Beirut. They are convinced that the interests of Lebanon and of the region require the earliest possible withdrawal of all foreign forces except those authorized by the government of Lebanon, whose authority should be fully re-established over all its national territory.

The Member States of the European Community remain greatly concerned about the situation in Lebanon as a whole. They strongly condemn the assassination of the President-elect of Lebanon. They appeal to all parties to show moderation and prevent further violence in that country.

The Ten reaffirm their solidarity with a friendly country whose population has suffered so cruelly and whose fragile stability is dangerously threatened. They are confident that the Lebanese people will be able to elect a new president in accordance with their constitution and to bring about national reconciliation. They renew their offer to assist in the relief and reconstruction of the country.

The tragic events in Lebanon have once again demonstrated that the Middle East can enjoy true peace and lasting stability only through a comprehensive settlement to be concluded with the participation of all parties, which means that the PLO will have to be associated with negotiations. Such a settlement should be based on the principles of security for all States in the region, including Israel's right to exist, justice for all peoples, including the right of self-determination for the Palestinians with all that this implies, and mutual recognition by all the parties involved.

The Ten note that the abovementioned principles are commanding increasing acceptance.

They therefore welcome the new American initiative contained in President Reagan's speech on 1 September 1982. In the view of the Ten it offers an important opportunity for peaceful progress on the Palestinian question and a step towards the reconciliation of the parties' conflicting aspirations.

The Ten appeal to all parties to seize the present opportunity to initiate a process of mutual *rapprochement* leading towards a comprehensive peace settlement.

In this connection they underline the importance of the statement adopted by Arab Heads of State of Government at Fez on 9 September, which they see as an expression of the unanimous will of the participants, including the PLO, to work for the achievement of a just peace in the Middle East encompassing all States in the area, including Israel.

They call now for a similar expression of a will to peace on the part of Israel.

They believe that discussions of the Franco-Egyptian draft resolution by the Security Council could play a useful part in establishing a common basis for a solution of the problems of the area.

The Ten continue to believe that a basic element for progress towards a negotiated comprehensive peace settlement in the region is the creation of a climate of confidence between the parties. Consequently, they consider that the Israeli decision to establish eight new settlements in the occupied territories is a serious obstacle to peace efforts as well as illegal under international law.

The Ten confirm that they will continue to be active in pursuing their efforts to promote a comprehensive, just and lasting peace settlement. In this context they will maintain and expand their contacts with all parties.'

263. Lebanon's Letter Informing the Security Council That It Desires the Reconstitution of the Multinational Force in Lebanon, September 20, 1982*

* 37 U.N. SCOR Supp. (July–Sept. 1982) at 82, U.N. Doc. S/15408/Annex II (1982).

Confirming our conversation of this morning, and in the context of the consultations you are conducting, I am writing to inform you that the Government of Lebanon has formally requested the reconstitution of the Multinational Force which was operating in Lebanon as of 21 August 1982.

You will recall that I had indicated before the Security Council, in the meeting held on Saturday 18 September [*2396th meeting*], that my Government was already discussing the possible return of the Multinational Force, the mandate of which we had hoped to see prolonged.

I am instructed to inform you that the Council of Ministers met this morning and decided to press its request for an early deployment with the Governments of the United States of America, France and Italy.

As soon as my Government receives the replies, which are expected very shortly, we will inform you of their contents.

My Government wishes to take this opportunity to reiterate, as in our letter of 20 August, Lebanon's commitment, in accordance with the Charter, to the Security Council resolutions relating to the situation in Lebanon, and more particularly, our continued readiness to give all necessary assistance to the United Nations Observer Group in fulfilling an extremely difficult mission for which we have the highest appreciation.

264. Exchange of Letters between the United States and Lebanon Concerning the Return of the Multinational Force, September 25, 1982*

* 82 U.S. Dep't State Bull. No. 2068, at 50 (November 1982).

Deputy Prime Minister Boutros' Letter

September 25, 1982

Your Excellency:

I have the honor to refer to the urgent discussions between representatives of our two Governments concerning the recent tragic events which have occurred in the Beirut area, and to consultations between my Government and the Secretary General of the United Nations pursuant to United Nations Security Council Resolution 521. On behalf of the Republic of Lebanon, I wish to inform your Excellency's Government of the determination of the Government of Lebanon to restore its sovereignty and authority over the Beirut area and thereby to assure the safety of persons in the area and bring an end to violence that has recurred. To this end, Israeli forces will withdraw from the Beirut area.

In its consultations with the Secretary General, the Government of Lebanon has noted that the urgency of the situation requires immediate action, and the Government of Lebanon, therefore, is, in conformity with the objectives in U.N. Security Council Resolution 521, proposing to several nations that they contribute forces to serve as a temporary Multinational Force (MNF) in the Beirut area. The mandate of the MNF will be to provide an interposition force at agreed locations and thereby provide the multinational presence requested by the Lebanese Government to assist it and the Lebanese Armed Forces (LAF) in the Beirut area. This presence will facilitate the restoration of Lebanese Government sovereignty and authority over the Beirut area, and thereby further efforts of my Government to assure the safety of persons in the area and bring to an end the violence which has tragically recurred. The MNF may undertake other functions only by mutual agreement.

In the foregoing context, I have the honor to propose that the United States of America deploy a force of approximately 1200 personnel to Beirut, subject to the following terms and conditions:

· The American military force shall carry out appropriate activities consistent with the mandate of the MNF.

· Command authority over the American force will be exercised exclusively by the United States Government through existing American military channels.

· The LAF and MNF will form a Liaison and Coordination Committee, composed of representatives of the MNF participating governments and chaired by the representatives of my Government. The Liaison and Coordination Committee will have two essential components: (A) Supervisory liaison; and (B) Military and technical liaison and coordination.

· The American force will operate in close coordination with the LAF. To assure effective coordination with the LAF, the American force will assign liaison officers to the LAF and the Government of Lebanon will assign liaison officers to the American force. The LAF liaison officers to the American force will, inter alia, perform liaison with the civilian population and with the U.N. observers and manifest the authority of the Lebanese Government in all appropriate situations. The American force will provide security for LAF personnel operating with the U.S. contingent.

· In carrying out its mission, the American force will not engage in combat. It may, however, exercise the right of self-defense.

· It is understood that the presence of the American force will be needed only for a limited period to meet the urgent requirements posed by the current situation. The MNF contributors and the Government of Lebanon will consult fully concerning the duration of the MNF presence. Arrangement for the departure of the MNF will be the subject of special consultations between the Government of Lebanon and the MNF participating governments. The American force will depart Lebanon upon any request of the Government of Lebanon or upon the decision of the President of the United States.

· The Government of Lebanon and the LAF will take all measures necessary to ensure the protection of the American force's personnel, to include securing assurances from all armed elements not now under the authority of the Lebanese Government that they will refrain from hostilities and not interfere with any activities of the MNF.

· The American force will enjoy both the degree of freedom of movement and the right to undertake those activities deemed necessary for the performance of its mission for the support of its personnel. Accordingly, it shall enjoy the privileges and immunities accorded the administrative and technical staff of the American Embassy in Beirut, and shall be exempt from immigration and customs requirements, and restrictions on entering or departing Lebanon. Personnel, property and equipment of the American force introduced into Lebanon shall be exempt from any form of tax, duty, charge or levy.

I have the further honor to propose, if the foregoing is acceptable to your Excellency's government, that your Excellency's reply to that effect, together with this note, shall constitute an agreement between our two Governments.

Please accept, Your Excellency, the assurances of my highest consideration.

[FOUAD BOUTROS]
DEPUTY PRIME MINISTER /
MINISTER OF FOREIGN AFFAIRS

Ambassador Dillon's Letter

September 25, 1982

Your Excellency:

I have the honor to refer to your Excellency's note of 25 September 1982 requesting the deployment of an American force to the Beirut area. I am pleased to inform you on behalf of my Government that the United States is prepared to deploy temporarily a force of approximately 1200 personnel as part of a Multinational Force (MNF) to establish an environment which will permit the Lebanese armed forces (LAF) to carry out their responsibilities in the Beirut area. It is understood that the presence of such an American force will facilitate the restoration of Lebanese Government sovereignty and authority over the Beirut area, an objective which is fully shared by my Government, and thereby further efforts of the Government of Lebanon to assure the safety of persons in the area and bring to an end the violence which has tragically recurred.

I have the further honor to inform you that my Government accepts the terms and conditions concerning the presence of the American force in the Beirut area as set forth in your note, and that Your Excellency's note and this reply accordingly constitute an agreement between our two Governments.

[ROBERT DILLON]
UNITED STATES AMBASSADOR

265. General Assembly Resolution ES-7/9 on the Question

of Palestine, September 24, 1982*

---

* G.A. Res. ES-7/9, ES-7 U.N. GAOR Supp. (No. 1) at 13, U.N. Doc. A/ES-7/14/Add.1 (1982).

The General Assembly,

Having considered the question of Palestine at its resumed seventh emergency special session,

Having heard the statement of the Palestine Liberation Organization, the representative of the Palestinian people,[19]

Recalling and reaffirming, in particular, its resolution 194 (III) of 11 December 1948,

Appalled at the massacre of Palestinian civilians in Beirut,

Recalling Security Council resolutions 508 (1982) of 5 June 1982, 509 (1982) of 6 June 1982, 513 (1982) of 4 July 1982, 520 (1982) of 17 September 1982 and 521 (1982) of 19 September 1982,

Taking note of the reports of the Secretary-General relevant to the situation, particularly his report of 18 September 1982,[20]

Noting with regret that the Security Council has so far not taken effective and practical measures, in accordance with the Charter of the United Nations, to ensure implementation of its resolutions 508 (1982) and 509 (1982),

Referring to the humanitarian principles of the Geneva Convention relative to the Protection of Civilian Persons in Time of War, of 12 August 1949,[21] and to the obligations arising from the regulations annexed to the Hague Conventions of 1907,[22]

Deeply concerned at the sufferings of the Palestinian and Lebanese civilian populations,

Noting the homelessness of the Palestinian people,

Reaffirming the imperative need to permit the Palestinian people to exercise their legitimate rights,

1. *Condemns* the criminal massacre of Palestinian and other civilians in Beirut on 17 September 1982;

2. *Urges* the Security Council to investigate, through the means available to it, the circumstances and extent of the massacre of Palestinian and other civilians in Beirut on 17 September 1982, and to make public the report on its findings as soon as possible;

3. *Decides* to support fully the provisions of Security Council resolutions 508 (1982) and 509 (1982), in which the Council, *inter alia*, demanded that:

(a) Israel withdraw all its military forces forthwith and unconditionally to the internationally recognized boundaries of Lebanon;

(b) All parties to the conflict cease immediately and simultaneously all military activities within Lebanon and across the Lebanese-Israeli border;

4. *Demands* that all Member States and other parties observe strict respect

---

[19] See A/ES-7/PV.32.
[20] S/15400.
[21] United Nations, *Treaty Series*, vol. 75, No. 973, p. 287.
[22] Carnegie Endowment for International Peace, *The Hague Conventions and Declarations of 1899 and 1907* (New York, Oxford University Press, 1915).

for the sovereignty, territorial integrity, unity and political independence of Lebanon within its internationally recognized boundaries;

5. *Reaffirms* the fundamental principle of the inadmissibility of the acquisition of territory by force;

6. *Resolves* that, in conformity with its resolution 194 (III) and subsequent relevent resolutions, the Palestinian refugees should be enabled to return to their homes and property from which they have been uprooted and displaced, and demands that Israel comply unconditionally and immediately with the present resolution;

7. *Urges* the Security Council, in the event of continued failure by Israel to comply with the demands contained in resolutions 508 (1982) and 509 (1982) and the present resolution, to meet in order to consider practical ways and means in accordance with the Charter of the United Nations;

8. *Calls upon* all States and international agencies and organizations to continue to provide the most extensive humanitarian aid possible to the victims of the Israeli invasion of Lebanon;

9. *Requests* the Secretary-General to prepare a photographic exhibit of the massacre of 17 September 1982 and to display it in the United Nations visitors' hall;

10. *Decides* to adjourn the seventh emerency special session temporarily and to authorize the President of the latest regular session of the General Assembly to resume its meetings upon request from Member States.

32nd plenary meeting
24 September 1982

266. President Reagan's Message to the Congress on the Return of the Multinational Force, September 29, 1982*

* 82 U.S. Dep't State Bull. No. 2069, at 42 (December 1982).

On September 20, 1982, the Government of Lebanon requested the Governments of France, Italy, and the United States to contribute forces to serve as a temporary Multinational Force, the presence of which will facilitate the restoration of Lebanese Government sovereignty and authority, and thereby further the efforts of the Government of Lebanon to assure the safety of persons in the area and bring to an end the violence which has tragically recurred.

In response to this request, I have authorized the Armed Forces of the United States to participate in this Multinational Force. In accordance with my desire that the Congress be fully informed on this matter, and consistent with the War Powers Resolution, I am hereby providing a report on the deployment and mission of these members of the United States armed forces.

On September 29, approximately 1200 Marines of a Marine Amphibious Unit began to arrive in Beirut. Their mission is to provide an interposition force at agreed locations and thereby provide the multinational presence requested by the Lebanese Government to assist it and the Lebanese Armed Forces. In carrying out this mission, the American force will not engage in combat. It may, however, exercise the right of self-defense and will be equipped accordingly. These forces will operate in close coordination with the Lebanese Armed Forces, as well as with comparably sized French and Italian military contingents in the Multinational Force. Although it is not possible at this time to predict the precise duration of the presence of U.S. forces in Beirut, our agreement with the Government of Lebanon makes clear that they will be needed only for a limited period to meet the urgent requirements posed by the current situation.

I want to emphasize that, as was the case of the deployment of U.S. forces to Lebanon in August as part of the earlier multinational force, there is no intention or expectation that U.S. Armed Forces will become involved in hostilities. They are in Lebanon at the formal request of the Government of Lebanon, and our agreement with the Government of Lebanon expressly rules out any combat responsibilities for the U.S. forces. All armed elements in the area have given assurances that they will refrain from hostilities and will not interfere with the activities of the Multinational Force. Although isolated acts of violence can never be ruled out, all appropriate precautions have been taken to ensure the safety of U.S. military personnel during their temporary deployment in Lebanon.

This deployment of the United States Armed Forces is being undertaken pursuant to the President's constitutional authority with respect to the conduct of foreign relations and as Commander-in-Chief of the United States Armed Forces.

I believe that this step will support the objective of helping to restore the territorial integrity, sovereignty, and political independence of Lebanon. It is part of the continuing efforts of the United States Government to bring lasting peace to the troubled country, which has too long endured the trials of civil strife and armed conflict.

    Sincerely,

RONALD REAGAN

267. European Parliament Resolution on the Situation in Lebanon, October 15, 1982*

* 25 O.J. Eur. Comm. (No. C 292) 111 (1982).

The European Parliament,

A. having regard to the atrocious slaughter of Palestinian civilians in the Sabra and Chatila camps in Beirut,

B. recalling that the massacres occurred at a time when Israeli troops had entered Beirut with the aim of guaranteeing public order in that part of the city,

C. having regard to the size of the demonstrations organized in Israel on 24 September in protest against the Begin government's policy in the Lebanon,

D. having regard to the near-unanimous election of Amin Gemayel as President of the Lebanese Republic following the assassination of his brother, Bashir,

E. having regard to the historic role incumbent on the European countries in helping find a solution to allow peace finally to return to this area,

F. approving the statement of the Foreign Ministers of the Community meeting in political cooperation on 20 September 1982,

1. Expresses its horror at the massacres in the Palestinian camps of Sabra and Chatila;

2. Sends the Palestinian people, which has so cruelly suffered, all its sympathy and expresses its solidarity in this time of trial;

3. Notes the establishing, albeit belated, of an official Israreli [*sic*] enquiry into the events in Sabra and Chatila and hopes that responsibility for them will be fully and clearly established;

4. Salutes the positive role being played by the troops of the peace-keeping force in Beirut in restoring the safety of the civilian population, in accordance with the resolution of the United Nations Security Council;

5. Calls for the immediate withdrawal from all Lebanese territory of all foreign forces which are present without the approval of the Lebanese Government;

6. Supports all recent efforts toward negotiations between all the parties concerned with a view to finding a comprehensive solution to the problem based on the political recognition of all the countries in the region, a homeland for the Palestinian people and the restoration of sovereignty and territorial integrity to the Lebanon,

7. Proposes that the Arab countries in OPEC, the USA and the EEC draw up a development programme for all States directly affected and ravaged by the Middle East conflict;

8. Instructs its President to forward this resolution to the Council, Commission and the Foreign Ministers meeting in political cooperation.

268. Security Council Resolution 523 Renewing the U.N. Interim Force in Lebanon Mandate and Authorizing Interim Humanitarian Acts, October 18, 1982*

* S.C. Res. 523, 37 U.N. SCOR (2400th mtg.) at 11, U.N. Doc. S/INF/38 (1982).

The Security Council,

Having heard the statement of the President of the Republic of Lebanon,[44]

Recalling its resolutions 425 (1978), 426 (1978) and 519 (1982),

Reaffirming its resolutions 508 (1982) and 509 (1982), as well as all subsequent resolutions on the situation in Lebanon,

Having studied the report of the Secretary-General[45] and taking note of its conclusions and recommendations,

Responding to the request of the Government of Lebanon,

1. *Decides* to extend the present mandate of the United Nations Interim Force in Lebanon for a further interim period of three months, that is, until 19 January 1983;

2. *Insists* that there shall be no interference under any pretext with the operations of the Force and that it shall have full freedom of movement in the discharge of its mandate;

3. *Authorizes* the Force during that period to carry out, with the consent of the Government of Lebanon, interim tasks in the humanitarian and administrative fields, as indicated in resolutions 511 (1982) and 519 (1982), and to assist the Government of Lebanon in ensuring the security of all the inhabitants of the area without any discrimination;

4. *Requests* the Secretary-General, within the three-month period, to consult with the Government of Lebanon and to report to the Security Council on ways and means of ensuring the full implementation of the mandate of the Force as defined in resolutions 425 (1978) and 426 (1978), and the relevant decisions of the Council;

5. *Requests* the Secretary-General to report to the Security Council on the progress of his consultations.

Adopted at the 2400th meeting by 13 voted to none, with 2 abstentions (Poland, Union of Soviet Socialist Republics).

[44] *Ibid.* [*Official Records of the Security Council*], *Thirty-seventh Year*, 2400th meeting.

[45] *Ibid., Thirty-seventh Year, Supplement for October, November and December 1982*, document S/15455 and Corr.1.

269. European Parliament Resolution on Reinforcing the

Multinational Force in Lebanon, December 16, 1982*

* 26 O.J. Eur. Comm. (No. C 13) 84 (1983).

The European Parliament,

A. conscious of the positive role the European Community and its Member States can play in establishing peace in Lebanon,
B. noting that the presence of the 'multinational force' currently made up of American, French and Italian troops is supported by all parties concerned and above all by the entire population of Lebanon;
C. recalling that the Lebanese Government, in response to the wishes of the Lebanese people, has asked for the multinational force to be doubled;

1. Requests Member States, as a gesture of European solidarity with the Lebanese people, to double the multinational force at present in Lebanon;

2. Suggests that, in addition to French and Italian troops, these reinforcements should preferably be supplied by other Community countries;

3. Instructs its President to forward this resolution to the Foreign Ministers meeting in political cooperation, to the Commission and to the American and Lebanese Governments.

270. Final Report of the Kahan Commission of Inquiry into the Events at the Refugee Camps in Beirut, 1983*

* Authorized Translation. For a different perspective, see "Israel in Lebanon: The Report of the International Commission to Inquire into Reported Violations of International Law by Israel During Its Invasion of Lebanon" (Macbride Report, 1983).

Introduction

At a meeting of the Cabinet on 28 September 1982, the Government of Israel resolved to establish a commission of inquiry in accordance with the Commissions of Inquiry Law of 1968. The Cabinet charged the commission as follows:

"The matter which will be subjected to inquiry is: all the facts and factors connected with the atrocity carried out by a unit of the Lebanese Forces against the civilian population in the Shatilla and Sabra camps."

In the wake of this resolution, the President of the Supreme Court, by virtue of the authority vested in him under Section 4 of the aforementioned law, appointed a commission of inquiry comprised as follows:

Yitzhak Kahan, President of the Supreme Court, commission chairman; Aharon Barak, Justice of the Supreme Court; Yona Efrat, Major General (Res.).

The commission held 60 sessions, hearing 58 witnesses. As per the commission's requests of the Cabinet Secretary, the Office of the Minister of Defense, the General Staff of the Israel Defense Forces (henceforth, the I.D.F.), the Ministry for Foreign Affairs, and other public and governmental institutions, the commission was provided with many documents, some of which were, in the course of the deliberations, submitted to the commission as exhibits. The commission decided, in accordance with Section 13(A) of the law, that there was a need to collect data necessary for its investigation. Appointed as staff investigators were: Ms. Dorit Beinish, Deputy State Attorney, and Ms. Edna Arbel, Senior Assistant to the District Attorney (Central District), who were seconded to the commission by the Attorney General; and Assistant Police Commander Alex Ish-Shalom, who was seconded to the commission by the Inspector General of the Israel Police. Judge David Bartov was appointed commission coordinator. The staff investigators collected, by virtue of the authority vested in them under Sections 13(C), 180 statements from 163 witnesses. Before the commission began its deliberations, it visited Beirut, but it was not allowed to enter the area of the events. The commission also viewed television footage filmed near the time of the events at the camps and their surroundings.

The commission published notices to the public in the press and other media, inviting all who wish to testify or submit a document or bring any information to the commission's attention to submit to the commission in writing details of the material he possessed or wished to bring to the commission's attention. There was not much response to these appeals. The commission made an effort to collect testimony also from people who live outside the juridical boundaries of the State of Israel; and all necessary steps were taken to bring witnesses from outside of Israel, when this was possible. The commission's requests in this matter were not always honored. For example, the "New York Times" correspondent Mr. Thomas Friedman, who published in the aforementioned newspaper a famous article on what transpired during the period under deliberation here, refused to appear before the commission, claiming that this was contrary to his paper's editorial policy. We did not receive a satisfactory answer as to why the paper's publisher prevented its reporter from appearing before the commission and thus helping it uncover all the important facts.

Some of the commission's hearings were held in open session, but most of the sessions were in camera. In this matter we acted in accordance with the instructions of Section 18(A) of the law, according to which a commission of inquiry is required to deliberate in open session but is entitled to deliberate in camera if it is convinced that "it is necessary to do so in the interest of protecting the security of the State. . .the foreign relations of the State. . ." and for other reasons stipulated in that section. It became clear to the commission that with regard to certain matters about which witnesses testified before it, open hearings would be liable to affect adversely the nation's security or foreign relations; and therefore it heard most of its testimony in camera. It should be noted that during sessions held in camera, witnesses also said things whose publication would not cause any harm; however, because of the difficulty in separating those things whose publication would be permissible from those whose publication would be forbidden, it was imperative in a substantial number of cases to hear the entire testimony in camera.

In accordance with Section 20(A) of the law, this report is being published together with an appendix that will be called Appendix A. In the event that we will need recourse in this report to testimony whose publication would not be damaging to the nation's security or foreign relations, we shall present it in a section of the report that will be published. On the other hand, in accordance with Section 20(A) of the law, a portion of this report, to be called Appendix B, will not be published, since, in our opinion, non-publication of this material is essential in the interest of protecting the nation's security or foreign relations.

As we have said, the commission's task, as stipulated by the Cabinet's resolution, is "to investigate all the facts and factors connected with the atrocity which was carried out by a unit of the Lebanese Forces against the civilian population of the Shatilla and Sabra camps." These acts were prepetrated between Thursday, 16 September 1982, and Saturday, 18 September 1982. The establishment of the facts and the conclusions in this report relate only to the facts and factors connected with the acts perpetrated in the aforementioned time frame, and the commission did not deliberate or investigate matters whose connection with the aforementioned acts is indirect or remote. The commission refrained, therefore, from drawing conclusions with regard to various issues connected with activities during the war that took place in Lebanon from 6 June 1982 onward or with regard to policy decisions taken by the Government before or during the war, unless these activities or decisions were directly related to the events that are the subject of this investigation. Descriptions of facts presented in this report that deviate from the framework of the commission's authority (as defined above) have been cited only as background material, in order to better understand and illustrate the chain of events.

In one area we have found it necessary to deviate somewhat from the stipulation of the Cabinet's resolution, which represents the commission's terms of reference. The resolution speaks of atrocities carried out by "a unit of the Lebanese Forces." The expression "Lebanese Forces" refers to an armed force known by the name "Phalangists" or "Keta'ib" (henceforth, Phalangists). It is our opinion that we would not be properly fulfilling our task if we did not look into the question of whether the atrocities spoken of in the Cabinet's resolution were indeed perpetrated by the Phalangists, and this question will indeed be treated in the course of this report.

The commission's deliberations can be divided into two stages. In the first stage, the commission heard witnesses who had been summoned by it, as well as witnesses who had expressed the desire to appear before it. The commission asked questions of these witnesses, and they were given the opportunity of bringing before the commission everything known to them of the matters that constitute the subject of the investigation. When this stage terminated, the commission issued a resolution in accordance with Section 15(A) of the aforementioned law, concerning the harm that might be caused certain people as a result of the investigation or its results; this was done in order to enable these people to study the material, to appear before the commission and to testify (for the text of the resolution, see section 1 of appendix A). In accordance with this resolution, the chairman of the commission sent notices to nine people; the notices detailed how each one of them might be harmed. The material in the commission's possession was placed at the disposal of those receiving the notices and of the attorneys appointed to represent them. During the second stage of the deliberations, we heard witnesses who had been summoned at the request of the lawyers, and thus some of the witnesses who had testified during the first stage were cross-examined.

Afterwards, written summations were submitted, and the opportunity to supplement these summations by presenting oral arguments was given. We should already note that involving the lawyers in the commission's deliberations did not in any way make the commission's work more difficult; it even helped us in fulfilling our task. The lawyers who appeared before us were able to clarify properly, though not at excessive length, the various points that were the subject of controversy; and thus they rendered valuable assistance to the commission's task, without in any way prejudicing their professional obligation to properly represent and defend their clients.

When we resolved to issue, in accordance with Section 15(A) of the law, notices about harm to the nine people, we were not oblivious to the fact that, during the course of the investigation, facts were uncovered that could be the prima facie basis for results that might cause harm to other persons as well. Our consideration in limiting the notices about possible harm to only nine persons was based on [the conception] that it is our duty, as a public judicial commission dealing with an extremely important issue — one which had raised a furor among the general public in Israel and other nations — to deliberate and reach findings and conclusions with regard to the major and important things connected with the aforementioned events, and to the question of the responsibility of those persons whose decisions and actions could have decisively influenced the course of events. We felt that with regard to the other people who were involved in one way or another in the events we are investigating, but whose role was secondary, it would be better that the clarification or investigation, if deemed necessary, be carried out in another manner, and not before this commission, viz., before the military authorities, in accordance with the relevant stipulations of the military legal code and other legislation. We chose this path so that the matters under investigation would not expand and become overly-complicated and so that we could complete our task in not too long a time.

In the course of the investigation, not a few contradictions came out regarding various facts about which we had heard testimony. In those cases where the contradictions referred to facts important for establishing findings and drawing subsequent conclusions, we shall decide between the variant versions in accordance with the usual criteria in judicial and quasi-judicial tribunals. Our procedures are not those of a criminal court; and therefore the criterion of criminal courts that stipulates that in order to convict someone his guilt must be proven beyond a reasonable doubt, does not apply in this case. Nevertheless, since we are aware that our findings and conclusions are liable to be of significant influence from a social and ethical standpoint, and to harm also in other ways persons involved in our deliberations, no finding of significant harm was established with regard to any one of those to whom notices were sent, unless convincing evidence on which to base such a finding was found, and we shall not be satisfied with evidence that leaves room for real doubt. We shall not pretend to find a solution to all the contradictions in testimony. In many instances, these contradictions relate to the content of conversations that took place between various people without the presence of witnesses, or when the witnesses' attention was not focused on the content of the conversation, and there are no exact notes on these conversations. In such cases, it is only natural that there exist several versions with regard to what was said, and the differences between them do not necessarily derive from a desire to conceal the truth but rather are sometimes the natural result of a failure of the human memory. We do not see the need to rule about those contradictions which surround unimportant details that do not influence the decision about points in controversy.

We shall conclude this part of the report by expressing appreciation and gratitude to all those who helped us in fulfilling our task. It is only fitting that we note that all the institutions and various functionaries in the Government, the I.D.F., and other authorities whose help we needed rendered us all the necessary assistance and placed at our disposal all the relevant material, without reservation. Our special thanks go to the coordinator of the commission, Judge David Bartov, who showed great capability in handling the administrative aspects of the commission's work and without whose enterprise and devoted and efficient work it is very doubtful whether we would have succeeded in properly carrying out our task. Our appreciation and gratitude go also to the staff investigators, Dorit Beinish, Edna Arbel and Alex Ish-Shalom, who, by virtue of their expertise, initiative and dedication, succeeded in placing at our disposal much material which served as the basis of the commission's deliberations and findings. Similarly, our thanks go to the entire staff of commission employees, whose loyalty and faithfulness enabled us to carry out and complete our task.

A Description of the Events

The Period Before the Events in Beirut

In 1975, civil war broke out in Lebanon. This war began with clashes in Sidon between the Christians and Palestinian terrorists and subsequently widened in a manner to encompass many divers [*sic*] armed forces — under the auspices of ethnic groups, political parties, and various organizations — that were active in Lebanon. In its early stages, this war was waged primarily between the Christian organizations on the one hand, and Palestinian terrorists, Lebanese leftist organizations, and Muslim and Druze organizations of various factions on the other. In the course of the civil war, Syrian army forces entered Lebanon and took part in the war, for a certain period of time on the side of the Christian forces, and subsequently on the side of the terrorists and the Lebanese leftist organizations. During the early years of the war, massacres on a large scale were perpetrated by the fighting forces against the civilian population. The Christian city of Damour was captured and destroyed by Palestinian terrorists in January 1976. The Christian residents fled the city, and the conquering forces carried out acts of slaughter that cost the lives of many Christians. In August 1976, the Christian forces captured the Tel Za'atar refugee camp in Beirut, where Palestinian terrorists had dug in, and thousands of Palestinian refugees were massacred. Each massacre brought in its wake acts of revenge of a similar nature. The number of victims of the civil war has been estimated at close to 100,000 killed, including a large number of civilians, among them women and children.

The Palestinians' armed forces organized and entrenched themselves in camps inhabited by refugees who had arrived in Lebanon in various waves, beginning in 1948. There are various estimates as to the number of Palestinian refugees who were living in Lebanon in 1982. According to the figures of U.N.R.W.A. (the United Nations Relief and Works Agency), the Palestinian refugees numbered approximately 270,000. On the other hand, the leaders of the Christian armed forces estimated the number of Palestinian refugees at approximately 500,000 or more. This estimate is most probably exaggerated, and the more realistic estimate is the one that puts the number of Palestinian refugees at approximately 300,000 — and in any case, not more than 400,000.

The main Christian armed force that took part in the civil war consisted mainly of Maronite Christians, though a small number of Shi'ites joined them. This force comprised several armed Christian organizations, the largest among them being the organizations under the leadership of the Chamoun family and of the Jemayel family. The head of the Jemayel family, Mr. Pierre Jemayel, founded the Phalangist organization; and the leader of this organization in recent years was Pierre's son, Bashir Jemayel. In the course of time, the Phalangist organization became the central element in the Christian forces; in 1982, the Phalangists ruled the Christian armed forces. Even though the "Lebanese Forces" formally comprised several Christian organizations, the dominant and primary force in this organization, at the time under our scrutiny, was the Phalangists, led by the Jemayel family.

When the war broke out in Lebanon in June 1982, the Phalangist force included a nucleus of approximately 2,000 full-time recruited soldiers. In addition, the Phalangists had a reserve armed force — that is, men who served part-time in their free hours or when they were called up for special service. When fully mobilized, the number of Phalangist soldiers reached 5,000. Similarly, the Phalangists had militias in the villages. There were no ranks in this military force, but it was organized along military lines, with Bashir Jemayel as the military and political leader who enjoyed unimpeachable authority. The Phalangists had a general staff comprised of several commanders. At the head of this general staff was a commander named Fadi Frem; at the head of the Phalangists' intelligence division was a commander by the name of Elie Hobeika.

The link between the Christian forces and the State of Israel was formed shortly after the start of the civil war. In the course of time, this link grew stronger, from both political and military standpoints. The Christian forces were promised that if their existence were to become endangered, Israel would come to their aid. Israel extended significant aid to the Christian armed forces, supplying arms, uniforms, etc., and also training and instruction. Over the course of time, a considerable number of meetings were held between leaders of the Phalangists and representatives of the Government of Israel and the I.D.F. In the course of these meetings, the ties between the leaders of the two sides grew stronger. The Institute for Intelligence and Special Assignments (henceforth, the Mossad) was made responsible for the link with the Phalangists; and representatives of the Mossad maintained — at various times, and in various ways — a rather close connection with the Phalangist leadership. In the course of these meetings, the Phalangist leaders brought up various plans for strengthening the Christian forces' position, as well as various ways of bringing about the end of the civil war in

Lebanon and restoring the independence of that nation, while [simultaneously] buttressing the status of the Phalangists and those allied with them in a regime that would be established in Lebanon. Israel's representatives expressed various reservations with regard to these plans and Israel's involvement in their realization.

A separate armed force is the military force in South Lebanon — the "Army of Free Lebanon" under the command of Major Haddad. This force comprises several hundred full-time soldiers. In addition, there is in South Lebanon a National Guard, which, under the command of local officers, does guard duty in the villages. Relations between the Phalangists and Haddad's men are not particularly close, for various reasons, and there were points of tension between these two forces. In 1982, soldiers of both Major Haddad and the Phalangists wore uniforms provided by Israel — and similar to those worn by the I.D.F. The Phalangists' uniforms bore an emblem consisting of the inscription "Keta'ib Lubnaniyeh" and the drawing of a cedar, embroidered over the shirt pocket. Major Haddad's soldiers had an emblem on the epaulet inscribed with the words "Army of Free Lebanon" in Arabic and the drawing of a cedar. During the war, Haddad's force advanced and reached the Awali River. Pursuant to I.D.F. orders, Haddad's army did not proceed north of the Awali River.

The subject of the Palestinian population in Lebanon, from among whom the terrorist organizations sprang up and in the midst of whom their military infrastructure was entrenched, came up more than once in meetings between Phalangist leaders and Israeli representatives. The position of the Phalangist leaders, as reflected in various pronouncements of these leaders, was, in general, that no unified and independent Lebanese state could be established without a solution being found to the problem of the Palestinian refugees, who according to the Phalangists' estimates, numbered half a million people. In the opinion of the Phalangists, that number of refugees, for the most part Muslims, endangered [both] the demographic balance between the Christians and Muslims in Lebanon and (from other standpoints as well) the stability of the State of Lebanon and the status of the Christians in that country. Therefore, the Phalangist leaders proposed removing a large portion of the Palestinian refugees from Lebanese soil, whether by methods of persuasion or other means of pressure. They did not conceal their opinion that it would be necessary to resort to acts of violence in order to cause the exodus of many Palestinian refugees from Lebanon.

As we have said, the Mossad was the organization that actually handled the relations between the Phalangists and Israel, and its representatives maintained close contacts with the Phalangist leadership. In addition, the Intelligence branch of the I.D.F. (henceforth Military Intelligence) participated, albeit in a more limited capacity, in the contacts with the Phalangists; and it, by virtue of its job was to issue a not insignificant number of evaluation papers on the Phalangists, their leaders, their aims, their fighting ability, etc. The division of labor between the Mossad and Military Intelligence with regard to the Phalangists, was spelled out in a document (exhibit 189). While this division of duties left room for misunderstandings and also duplication in various areas, there is no room for doubt that both the Mossad and Military Intelligence specifically dealt with drawing up evaluations on the Phalangists, and each one of them was obligated to bring these evaluations to the attention of all interested parties. Neither the head of the Mossad nor the director of Military Intelligence disagreed with this in his testimony before us.

From the documents submitted to us and the testimony we heard, it emerges that there were differences of opinion between the Mossad and Military Intelligence with regard to the relations with the Phalangists. The Mossad, to a not inconsiderable extent under the influence of constant and close contact with the Phalangist elite, felt positively about strengthening relations with that organization, though not ignoring its faults and weaknesses. This approach of the Mossad came out clearly in the testimony we heard from the person who was in charge of the Mossad's contacts with the Phalangists. The head of the Mossad, in his testimony before us on 27.12.82. said, inter alia (p. 1437), that "the Mossad tried, to the best of its ability, throughout this period, to present and approach the subject as objectively as possible; but since it was in charge of the contacts, I accept as an assumption that subjective, and not only objective, relations also emerged. I must accept that in contacts, when you talk to people, relationships are formed." In contrast, Military Intelligence was to emphasize in its evaluations the danger in the link with the Phalangists, primarily because of this organization's lack of reliability, its military weakness, and other reasons we need not specify here. A characteristic expression of the difference in approach between these two agencies, whose responsibility it was to provide evaluations on the Phalangists and the desirability of relations with them, can be found in the exchange of documents when one of the intelligence officers (henceforth intelligence officer A, whose full name appears in the list of names in section 1 of Appendix B) who served as a liaison officer on behalf of Military Intelligence in the Mossad's representation at Phalangist headquarters at the beginning of the war submitted an assessment (exhibit 171) on cooperation with the Phalangists. This Military Intelligence officer rendered a negative evaluation, from Israel's standpoint, of the Phalangists' policy during the war and their aims for the future. This criticism was vigorously rejected by the Mossad (exhibit 172).

The "Peace for the Galilee" war (henceforth the war) began on 6.6.82. On 12-14 June, I.D.F. forces took over the suburbs of Beirut and linked up with the Christian forces who controlled East Beirut. On 25 June the encirclement of West Beirut was completed and I.D.F. forces were in control of the Beirut-Damascus road. There followed a period of approximately one and a half months of negotiations on the evacuation of the terrorists and the Syrian forces from West Beirut, and during this time various targets in West Beirut were occasionally shelled and bombed by the I.D.F.'s Air Force and artillery. On 19.8.82 the negotiations on the evacuation of the terrorists and the Syrian forces from West Beirut were completed. On 23.8.82 Bashir Jemayel was elected president of Lebanon. His term of office was supposed to begin on 23 September 1982.

On 21-26 August, a multi-national force arrived in Beirut, and the evacuation of the terrorists and the Syrian forces began. The evacuation was completed on 1 September; however, according to information from various sources, the terrorists did not fulfill their obligation to evacuate all their forces from West Beirut and hand their weapons over to the Lebanese army but left in West Beirut, according to various estimates, approximately 2,000 fighters, as well as many arms caches, some of which were handed over by the terrorists to the Lebanese leftist militia "Mourabitoun." This militia numbered approximately 7,000 men in West Beirut, and it cooperated with the terrorists. After the evacuation was completed, the multi-national force left Lebanon (10-12 September 1982; cf. section 2 of Appendix A for dates of stages of the war).

At the beginning of the war, the Chief of Staff [Lt.-Gen. Rafael Eitan] told the Phalangists that they should refrain from all fighting. This order was issued because of the fear that if the Phalangists' force got into trouble while fighting, the I.D.F. would be forced to come to its aid, thereby disrupting the I.D.F.'s plan of action. Even after I.D.F. forces reached the Damour-Shouf line, the I.D.F.'s orders were that the Phalangists would not participate in fighting (testimony of the Chief of Staff, pp.195-6). After I.D.F. forces reached the area under Christian control, the Phalangist commanders suggested that a company of theirs of approximately 300 men set up a training base at a place called Beit Ad-Din, a site of historical importance in Lebanon. The Chief of Staff agreed to this, but made his agreement conditional on the Phalangist forces' exercising restraint and discipline, as the area was Druze. At first, this condition was honored; afterwards, there were outbursts of hostilities between the Phalangists and the Druze in Beit Ad-Din. The Druze committed some murders, and the Phalangists took revenge; a small I.D.F. force was stationed in the area in order to prevent such actions. In the early stages of the war there were also some acts of revenge and looting on the part of the Christians in Sidon; these were stopped by the I.D.F.

When I.D.F. forces were fighting in the suburbs of Beirut and along the Beirut-Damascus road, the Phalangists were asked to cooperate with the I.D.F.'s actions by identifying terrorists, a task at which the Phalangists' expertise was greater than that of the Israeli security forces. During these actions there were generally no acts of vengeance or violence against the Palestinian civilian population by the Phalangists who were operating with the I.D.F. Another action of the Phalangists' military force was the capture of the technical college in Reihan, a large building in Beirut not located in a built-up area. The Phalangists captured this place from the armed Shi'ite organization "Amal." One day after the place was taken, the Phalangists turned the building over to the I.D.F. and left the site (testimony of the Chief of Staff, pp.198-200).

The fighting actions of the Phalangists during that time were few, and in effect the fighting was all done by I.D.F. forces alone. This state of affairs aroused criticism and negative reactions from the Israeli public, and among I.D.F. soldiers as well. This dissatisfaction was expressed in various ways; and in the political echelon, as well as in the media, there was amazement that the Phalangists were not participating in the fighting, even though the war was their battle as well, and it was only right that they should be taking part in it. The feeling among the Israeli public was that the I.D.F. was "pulling the chestnuts out of the fire" for the Phalangists. As the number of I.D.F. casualties mounted, public pressure for the Phalangists to participate in real fighting increased. The plan formulated in mid-June 1982, when it was still uncertain whether the terrorists would agree to leave West Beirut, was that the Christian forces would fight to take control of West Beirut; the I.D.F. would not take part in that operation; and only in the event that it became necessary would the I.D.F. help out the Phalangists with long-range artillery fire. This plan was discussed in the Cabinet meeting of 15.6.82, where it was proposed by the Prime Minister, and his proposal was adopted by the Cabinet, namely, that I.D.F. forces would not enter West Beirut, and this job was to be done by other forces (meaning the Phalangists) with help they would be given by the I.D.F. (transcript of the Cabinet meeting of 15.6.82, exhibit 53). Even after this resolution, no real fighting was done by the Phalangists for the purpose of extending control over West Beirut; and, as we have said, eventually the terrorists were evacuated as the result of a political agreement, after the I.D.F. had shelled various targets in West Beirut.

In all the testimony we have heard, there has been unanimity regarding [the fact] that the battle ethics of the Phalangists, from the standpoint of their attitude to non-combatants, differ greatly from those of the I.D.F. It has already been noted above that in the course of the civil war in Lebanon, many massacres had been perpetrated by the various forces that had taken part in the fighting. When the war began in June 1982, the prevailing opinion among the Mossad agents who had maintained contacts with the Phalangist leadership was that the atrocities and massacres were a thing of the past, and that the Phalangist forces had reached a stage of political and organizational maturity that would ensure that such actions would not repeat themselves. This opinion was based both on personal impressions of the character of the Phalangist leadership, as well as on the recognition that the interest of the Phalangist elite to eventually rule an independent Lebanese nation, half or more of whose population is Muslim and would be interested in maintaining relations with the Arab world, requires moderation of actions against Palestinians and restraint as to modes of operation. At the same time, there were various facts that were not compatible with this outlook. During the meetings that the heads of the Mossad held with Bashir

Jemayel, they heard things from him that left no room for doubt that the intention of this Phalangist leader was to eliminate the Palestinian problem in Lebanon when he came to power — even if that meant resorting to aberrant methods against the Palestinians in Lebanon (testimony on pps. 16, 17, and 168 of the transcripts; exhibit 85 of 30 June 1982, clause 14 — section 2 of Appendix B). Similar remarks were heard from other Phalangist leaders. Furthermore, certain actions of the Phalangists during the war indicated that there had been no fundamental change in their attitude toward different segments of the Lebanese population, such as Druze and Palestinians, whom the Phalangists considered enemies. There were reports of Phalangist massacres of women and children in Druze villages, as well as the liquidation of Palestinians carried out by the intelligence unit of Elie Hobeika (testimony no. 105 of intelligence officer B before the staff investigators, part of which appears in section 3 of Appendix B; also, a document which mentions the Phalangist attitude toward terrorists they had taken prisoner — section 4 of Appendix B, exhibit 39). These reports reinforced the feeling among certain people — and especially among experienced intelligence officers — that in the event that the Phalangists had an opportunity to massacre Palestinians, they would take advantage of it.

The Assassination of Bashir Jemayel and The I.D.F.'s Entry into West Beirut

On Tuesday afternoon, 14.9.82, a large bomb exploded in a building in Ashrafiyeh, Beirut, where Bashir Jemayel was [meeting] with a group of commanders and other Phalangists. For the first few hours after the explosion, it was not clear what had happened to Bashir, and there were rumors that he had only been slightly wounded. Word of the attempt on his life reached the Prime Minister, the Defense Minister, the Chief of Staff, the director of Military Intelligence [Major General Yehoshua Saguy] and others in the early hours of the evening. During the evening, before it became clear what had befallen Bashir, the Defense Minister spoke with the Chief of Staff, the director of Military Intelligence, the head of the Mossad, and the head of the General Security Services about possible developments. He also spoke a number of times with the Prime Minister. Moreover, there were a number of conversations that evening between the Prime Minister and the Chief of Staff. Word of Bashir's death reached Israel about 11:00 P.M., and it was then that the decision was taken — in conversations between the Prime Minister and the Minister of Defense and between the Prime Minister and the Chief of Staff — that the I.D.F. would enter West Beirut. In one of the consultations between the Minister of Defense and the Chief of Staff, there was mention of including the Phalangists in the entry into West Beirut. The question of including the Phalangists was not mentioned at that stage in conversations with the Prime Minister.

One [*sic*] the decision was made to have the I.D.F. enter West Beirut, the appropriate operational orders were issued. Order Number 1 was issued at

12.20 A.M. on the night between 14.9.82 and 15.9.82 Orders Number 2 and 3 were issued on Wednesday, 15.9.82, and Order Number 4 was issued that same day at 2.00 P.M.; Order Number 5 was issued at 3.00 A.M. on 16.9.82; and Order number 6 was issued on the morning of 16.9.82. The first five orders said nothing about entering the refugee camps, and only in Order Number 6 were the following things stated (clause 2, document no. 6, exhibit 14):

"The refugee camps are not to be entered. Searching and mopping up the camps will be done by the Phalangists/Lebanese Army."

Clause 7 of the same order also states that the Lebanese Army "is entitled to enter any place in Beirut, according to its request."

Execution of the I.D.F.'s entry into West Beirut began during the early morning hours of 15.9.82.

On the night between 14.9.82 and 15.9.82, the Chief of Staff flew to Beirut with a number of people and met there with the G.O.C. Northern Command [Major General Amir Drori] and with the commander of the division (henceforth the division). Afterwards, the Chief of Staff, together with the people accompanying him, went to the Phalangists' headquarters, where, according to his testimony (p. 210), he ordered the Phalangist commanders to effect a general mobilization of all their forces, impose a general curfew on all the areas under their control, and be ready to take part in the fighting. The response of the Phalangist commanders who took part in that meeting was that they needed 24 hours to organize. The Chief of Staff requested that a Phalangist liaison officer come to the place where the division's forward command post was located (henceforth forward command post) under the command of Brigadier-General Amos Yaron. At that meeting, the Phalangist commanders were told by the Chief of Staff that the I.D.F. would not enter the refugee camps in West Beirut but that the fighting this entails would be undertaken by the Phalangists (Chief of Staff's testimony, p. 211). The Chief of Staff testified that the entry of the Phalangists into the refugee camps was agreed upon between the Minister of Defense and himself at 8.30 P.M. on the previous evening. The camps in question were Sabra and Shatilla. After the meeting in the Phalangists' camp, the Chief of Staff went to the forward command post.

The forward command post was located on the roof of a five-story building about 200 meters southwest of the Shatilla camp. The borders of the two camps were not defined exactly. The Sabra camp extended over an area of some 300 × 200 meters and Shatilla over an area of about 500 × 500 meters (testimony of the deputy assistant to the director of Military Intelligence, p. 29). The two camps were essentially residential neighborhoods containing, in the area entered by the Phalangists, as will be stated below, low permanent structures along narrow alleys and streets. From the roof of the forward command post it was possible to see the area of the camps generally but — as all the witnesses who visited the roof of the command post stated, and these were a good number of witnesses whose word we consider reliable — it was impossible to see what was happening within the alleys in the camp from the roof of the command post, not even with the aid of the 20 × 120 binoculars that were on the command post roof. Appended to this report are an aerial photograph and map of the area of the camps, as well as a general map of Beirut (sections 3, 4, and 5 of Appendix A).

It was not possible to obtain exact details on the civilian population in the refugee camps in Beirut. An estimate of the number of refugees in the four refugee camps in West Beirut (Burj el-Barajneh, Fakahani, Sabra, and Shatilla) is about 85,000 people. The war led to the flight of the population, but when the fighting subsided, a movement back to the camps began. According to an inexact estimate, in mid-September 1982 there were about 56,000 people in the Sabra camp (protocol, p. 29), but there is no assurance that this number reflects reality.

The Chief of Staff was in the forward command post from the early morning hours of Wednesday, 15.9.82. The I.D.F. began to enter West Beirut shortly after 6:00 A.M. During the first hours of the I.D.F. entry, there was no armed resistance to the I.D.F. forces, evidently because the armed forces that were in West Beirut were taken by surprise. Within a few hours, the I.D.F. forces encountered fire from armed forces that remained in a number of places in West Beirut, and combat operations began. The resistance caused delays in the I.D.F.'s taking over a number of points in the city and caused a change in the route of advance. In the course of this fighting three I.D.F, soldiers were killed and more than 100 were wounded. Heavy fire coming out of Shatilla was directed at one I.D.F, battalion (henceforth the battalion) advancing east of Shatilla. One of the battalion's soldiers was killed, 20 were injured, and the advance of the battalion in this direction was halted. Throughout Wednesday and to a lesser degree on Thursday and Friday (16-17.9.82), R.P.G. and light-weapons fire from the Sabra and Shatilla camps was directed at the forward command post and the battalion's forces nearby, and fire was returned by the I.D.F. forces.

On Wednesday, 15.9.82, the Minister of Defense arrived at the forward command post between 8:00 and 9:00 A.M. He met with the Chief of Staff there, and the latter reported on what had been agreed upon with the Phalangists, namely, a general mobilization, curfew, and the entry of the Phalangists into the camps. The Minister of Defense approved this agreement. From the roof of the command post, the Minister of Defense phoned the Prime Minister and informed him that there was no resistance in Beirut and that all the operations were going along well.

During the aforementioned meeting between the Minister of Defense and the Chief of Staff, present on the roof of the forward command post were the Defense Minister's aide, Mr. Avi Duda'i; the director of Military Intelligence, who came to this meeting together with the Minister of Defense; representative A of the Mossad (his full name appears in the list of names, section 1, Appendix B); Major-General Drori; Brigadier-General Yaron; Intelligence officer B; the head of the General Security Services; Deputy Chief of Staff Major-General Moshe Levi; and other I.D.F. officers who were accompanying the Minister of Defense. Duda'i recorded in his notebook what was said and agreed upon at that meeting. According to Dudai's testimony, he later copied these notes into another notebook, pages of which were presented before us (exhibit 103). These notes stated, inter alia, that the Phalangists were to be sent into the camps. The Minister of Defense spoke with the Prime Minister twice from the roof of the command post. According to the record of these conversations (exhibits 100 and 101), in one of them the wording of the I.D.F. Spokesman's announcement was agreed upon as follows:

"Following the murder of President-elect Bashir Jemayel, I.D.F. forces entered West Beirut tonight to prevent possible grave occurences [sic] and to ensure quiet.

"The entry of the I.D.F. forces was executed without resistance."

From the forward command post the Minister of Defense went to the Phalangist headquarters. A record was made of this meeting, which was attended by a number of Phalangist commanders as well as the Minister of Defense, the director of Military Intelligence, the head of the General Security Services and representatives of the Mossad (exhibit 79). At that meeting, the Minister of Defense stated, inter alia, that the I.D.F. would take over focal points and junctions in West Beirut, but that the Phalangist army would also have to enter West Beirut after the I.D.F. and that the Phalangist commanders should maintain contact with Major-General Drori, G.O.C. Northern Command, regarding the modes of operation. A record of this meeting was made by Intelligence officer B (exhibit 28). From there the Minister of Defense went to Bikfaya, to the Jemayel family home, to pay a condolence call.

From the meeting with the Jemayel family in Bikfaya, the Minister of Defense went to the airport, and on the way he met with Major-General Drori at a gas station. This meeting took place in the presence of a number of people, including the director of Military Intelligence, the head of the General Security Services, Mr. Duda'i, and the bureau chief of the director of Military Intelligence, Lieutenant-Colonel Hevroni. The situation of the forces was discussed at this meeting, and Major-General Drori reported on the course of events during the I.D.F.'s entry into West Beirut. From there the Minister of Defense went on to the airport and met there with the Chief of Staff and the Deputy Chief of Staff at about 2:00 P.M., after which the Minister of Defense returned to Israel.

That same day, 15.9.82, while the Minister of Defense was in Beirut, a meeting took place at 11:30 A.M. in the Prime Minister's Office between the Prime Minister and others from the American embassy in Israel. During that meeting (protocol of the meeting, exhibit 120), the Prime Minister informed Mr. Draper that I.D.F. forces had entered West Beirut beginning in the morning hours, that there were no real clashes, that the I.D.F. action was undertaken in order to prevent certain possible events, and that we were concerned that there might be bloodshed even during the night. The Prime Minister also said that the Phalangists were behaving properly; their commander had not been injured in the assassination and was in control of his forces; he is a good man and we trust him not to cause any clashes, but there is no assurance regarding other forces. He added that the primary immediate task was to preserve quiet, for as long as quiet is maintained it will be possible to talk; otherwise there might have been pogroms, and the calm was preserved for the time being (exhibit 120).

At 4:00 P.M. on Wednesday, 15.9.82, a briefing took place at the office of the Deputy Chief of Staff with the participation of the I.D.F. branch heads, including the assistant for research to the director of Military Intelligence. The meeting began with a review by the assistant for research to the director of Military Intelligence of possible political developments in Lebanon following the death of Bashir Jemayel. He stated, inter alia (page 4 of the transcript of the discussion, exhibit 130), that the IDF's entry into West Beirut was perceived as vital not only by the Christians but also by the Muslims, who regarded the I.D.F. as the only factor that could prevent bloodshed in the area and protect the Sunni Muslims from the Phalangists. The Intelligence officer also stated that according to what was known to Military Intelligence, the attack on Bashir was carried out by the Mourabitoun, though that was not certain. During the meeting, the head of Operations Department announced that the Phalangists "are encouraging entry into the camps" (p.7 of exhibit 130). The Deputy Chief of Staff reported his impressions of the meeting at Phalangist headquarters in Beirut that day and said that the intension was to send the Phalangists into the refugee camps and afterwards perhaps into the city as well. He added that this "might create an uproar," because the armed forces in West Beirut that were then quiet might stir up a commotion upon learning that Phalangists are coming in behind the I.D.F. (page 11, exhibit 130).

At 6:00 P.M. the Minister of Defense spoke with the Prime Minister from his home and reported (exhibit 99) that by evening the I.D.F. would be in all the places; that he had conveyed the Prime Minister's words to Pierre Jemayel; and that "everything is in order" and the decision made on the previous night to send the I.D.F. into Beirut had been most important and [indeed] should not have been delayed.

The Chief of Staff remained at the forward command post in Beirut and followed the development of the I.D.F. actions from there. On that day the Phalangist officers did not arrive at the forward command post to coordinate operations, but Major-General Drori met with them in the evening and told them generally that their entry into the camps would be from the direction of Shatilla. Major-General Drori, who was not at ease with the plan to send the Phalangists into the camps, made an effort to persuade the commanders of the Lebanese Army that their forces should enter the camps and that they should prevail upon the Prime Minister of Lebanon to agree to this move. The reply of the Lebanese Army at the time was negative.

In the early morning hours of Thursday, 16.9.82, the Chief of Staff left the forward command post and returned to Tel Aviv. That same morning, in the wake of political pressure, an order was issued by the Minister of Defense to halt the I.D.F.'s combat operations; but after a short time the Minister of Defense rescinded the order. At 10:00 A.M. the Minister of Defense held a consultation in his office with the Chief of Staff; the director of Military Intelligence, Brigadier-General Y. Saguy; Lieutenant-Colonel Zecharin, the Chief of Staff's bureau chief; and Mr. Duda'i (exhibit 27 is a record of what was said at that meeting). The meeting was opened by the Chief of Staff, who announced that "the whole city is in our hands, complete quiet prevails now, the camps are closed and surrounded; the Phalangists are to go in at 11:00-12:00. Yesterday we spoke to them. . . The situation now is that the entire city is in our hands, the camps are all closed." Later on in his statement, while pointing to a map, the Chief of Staff stated that the areas marked on the map were in the hands of the I.D.F. and that the Fakahani, Sabra, and Shatilla camps were surrounded. He also said that if the Phalangists came to a coordinating session and wanted to go in, it was agreed with them that they would go in and that the Lebanese Army could also enter the city wherever it chose. At this discussion, the Minister of Defense spoke of the heavy American pressure to have the I.D.F. leave West Beirut and of the political pressure from other sources. In the course of the meeting, the Chief of Staff repeated a number of times that at that moment everything was quiet in West Beirut. As for going into the camps, the Minister of Defense stated that he would send the Phalangists into the refugee camps (p.5, exhibit 27). At the time of the consultation, the Minister of Defense informed the Prime Minister by phone that "the fighting has ended. The refugee camps are surrounded. The firing has stopped. We have not suffered any more casualties. Everything is calm and quiet. Sitting opposite me is the Chief of Staff, who has just come from there. All the key points are in our hands. Everything's over. I am bringing the Chief of Staff to the Cabinet meeting. That's the situation as of now. . ." After this conversation, the Chief of Staff reported on the contacts during the night of 14.9.82 with the members of the Mourabitoun, in which the members of this militia said that they were unable to hide, that they were Lebanese, and that they would undoubtedly all be killed by the Phalangists, whether immediately or some time later. The Chief of Staff added that "there's such a dual kind of situation that they're confused. They're seething with a feeling of revenge, and there might have been rivers of blood there. We won't go into the refugee camps" (p.7, exhibit 27). As stated, participating in this consultation was the director of Military Intelligence, who in the course of the discussion stated a number of things that appear in the aforementioned record.

The commanders of the Phalangists arrived for their first coordinating session regarding the entry of their forces into the camps at about 11:00 A.M. on Thursday, 16.9.82, and met with Major-General Drori at the headquarters of one of the divisions. It was agreed at that meeting that they would enter the camps and coordinate this action with Brigadier-General Yaron, commander of the division. This coordination between Brigadier-General Yaron and the Phalangist commanders would take place on Thursday afternoon at the forward command post. It was likewise agreed at that meeting that a company of 150 fighters from the Phalangist force would enter the camps and that they would do so from south to north and from west to east. Brigadier-General Yaron spoke with the Phalangists about the places where the terrorists were located in the camps and also warned them not to harm the civilian population. He had mentioned that, he stated, because he knew that the Phalangists' norms of conduct are not like those of the I.D.F. and he had had arguments with the Phalangists over this issue in the past. Brigadier-General Yaron set up lookout posts on the roof of the forward command post and on a nearby roof even though he knew that it was impossible to see very much of what was going on in the camps from these lookouts. An order was also issued regarding an additional precautionary measure whose purpose was to ascertain the actions of the Phalangist forces during their operation in the camps (this measure is cited in section 5, Appendix B). It was also agreed that a Phalangist liaison officer with a communications set would be present at all times on the roof of the forward command post — in addition to the Mossad liaison officer at the Phalangist headquarters. The Phalangist unit that was supposed to enter the camps was an intelligence unit headed, as we have said, by Elie Hobeika. Hobeika did not go into the camps with his unit and was on the roof of the forward command post during the night (testimony of Brigadier-General Yaron, p.726). This unit was assigned the task of entering the camps at that time for two reasons, first — since the . . . Phalangists had difficulty recruiting another appropriate force till then; second — since the members of this unit were considered specially trained in discovering terrorists, who tried to hide among the civilian population.

On 16.9.82 a document was issued by the Defense Minister's office, signed by the personal aide to the Defense Minister, Mr. Avi Duda'i, which contained "The Defense Minister's Summary of 15 September 1982." This document is (exhibit 34) a summary of the things which Mr. Duda'i had recorded during his visit with the Defense Minister in Beirut on 15.9.82, as detailed above. In various paragraphs of the document there is mention of the Defense Minister's instructions regarding the entry into West Beirut. The instruction in paragraph F. is important to the matter at hand; it is stated there:

"F. Only one element, and that is The I.D.F., shall command the forces in the area. For the operation in the camps the Phalangists should be sent in."

The document is directed to the Chief of Staff, the Deputy Chief of Staff and the director of Military Intelligence. The document was received at the office of the director of Military Intelligence, according to the stamp appearing on the copy (exhibit 35), on 17.9.82.

In the testimonies we have heard, different interpretations were given to the instruction that only the I.D.F. command the forces in the area. According to one interpretation, and this is the interpretation given the document by the Chief of Staff (p.257), the meaning of the instruction is that in contacts with external elements, and especially with the Phalangists, only the I.D.F., and not another Israeli element, such as the Mossad, will command the forces in the area — but this does not mean that the Phalangist force will be under the command of the I.D.F. On the other hand, according to the interpretation given the document by the director of Military Intelligence (pp. 127, 1523), the meaning is that all forces operating in the area, including the Phalangists, will be under the authority of the I.D.F. and will act according to its instructions.

The entry of the Phalangists into the camps began at about 18:00 on Thursday, 16.9.82. At that time there were armed terrorist forces in the camps. We cannot establish the extent of these forces, but they possessed various types of arms, which they used — even before the entry of the Phalangists — against I.D.F. forces that had approached the area, as well as against the I.D.F. headquarters at the forward command post. It is possible to determine that this armed terrorist force had not been evacuated during the general evacuation, but had stayed in the camps for two purposes, which were — renewal of underground terrorist activity at a later period, and to protect the civilian population which had remained in the camps, keeping in mind that given the hostility prevailing between the various sects and organizations, a population without armed protection was in danger of massacre. It should be added here that during the negotiations for evacuation, a guarantee for the safety of the Muslims in West Beirut was given by the representative of the United States who conducted the negotiations, following assurances received from the government of Israel and from Lebanon.

Meanwhile, as we have said, the multi-national force left Lebanon, and all the previous plans regarding the control of West Beirut by the Lebanese government were disrupted due to the assassination of President-elect Bashir Jemayel.

The Events from the Entry of the Phalangists into the Sabra and Shatilla Camps until their Departure

On Thursday, 16.9.82, at approximately 18.00 hours, members of the Phalangists entered the Shatilla camp from the west and south. They entered in two groups, and once they had passed the battery surrounding the camps their movements within the camps were not visible from the roof of the forward command post or from the observation sites on other roofs. The Divisional Intelligence Officer tried to follow their movements using binoculars which he shifted from place to place, but was unable to see their movements or their actions. With the entry of the Phalangists into the camps, the firing which had been coming from the camps changed direction; the shooting which had previously been directed against the I.D.F.

now shifted in the direction of the Phalangists' liaison officer on the roof of the forward command post. G. (his full name appears in the list of names, Section 1, Appendix B) requested the I.D.F. to provide illumination for the force which was moving in, since its entry was taking place after dark. Initially, the illumination was provided by a mortar company, and subsequently also by aircraft; but because the illumination from the planes interfered with the evacuation of casualties of an I.D.F. unit, this source of illumination was halted; mortar illumination continued intermittently throughout the night.

At approximately 8:00 P.M., the Phalangists' liaison officer, G., said that the Phalangists who had entered the camps had sustained casualties, and the casualties were evacuated from the camps. Major General Drori was at the forward command post from approximately 7:30 P.M. and followed the fighting as it was visible from the roof of the forward command post. He left the site after 8:00 P.M.

Several Intelligence Branch personnel, headed by the Division Intelligence Officer, were in the building on whose roof the forward command post was situated. The Intelligence Officer, who wanted to obtain information on the Phalangists' activities, ordered that two actions be carried out to obtain that information (these actions are detailed in Section 5, Appendix B). No information was obtained in the wake of the first action. As a result of the second action the Intelligence Officer received a report according to which the Phalangists' liaison officer had heard via radio from one of the Phalangists inside the camps that he was holding 45 people. That person asked what he should do with the people, and the liaison officer's reply was "Do the will of God," or words to that effect. The Intelligence Officer received this report at approximately 20:00 hours from the person on the roof who heard the conversation. He did not convey the report to anyone else, because an officers' briefing was scheduled to take place at field headquarters shortly afterward.

At about the same time or slightly earlier, at approximately 7.00 P.M., Lieutenant Elul, who was then serving as Chef de Bureau of the Divisional Commander, overheard another conversation that took place over the Phalangists' transmitter. According to Lt. Elul's testimony, while he was on the roof of the forward command post, next to the Phalangists' communications set, he heard a Phalangist officer from the force that had entered the camps tell Elie Hobeika (in Arabic) that there were 50 women and children, and what should he do. Elie Hobeika's reply over the radio was; "This is the last time you're going to ask me a question like that, you know exactly what to do;" and then raucous laughter broke out among the Phalangist personnel on the roof. Lieutenant Elul understood that what was involved was the murder of the women and children. According to his testimony, Brigadier General Yaron, who was also on the forward command post roof then, asked him what he had overheard on the radio; and after Lieutenant Elul told him the content of the conversation, Brigadier General Yaron went over to Hobeika and spoke with him in English for about five minutes (for Lt. Elul's testimony, see pp. 1209-1210a). Lt. Elul did not hear the conversation between Brigadier General Yaron and Hobeika.

Brigadier General Yaron, who was on the roof of the forward command post, received from Lt. Elul a report of what he had heard. According to Brigadier General Yaron's testimony, the report conveyed to him by Lt. Elul stated that one of the Phalangists had asked the commander what to do with 45 people, and the reply had been to do with them what God orders you to do (testimony of Brigadier General Yaron, pp. 696 and 730). According to Brigadier General Yaron, he understood from what he had heard that the reference was to 45 dead terrorists. In his testimony, Brigadier General Yaron linked this report with what he had heard in the update briefing that evening — which will be discussed below — from the Divisional Intelligence Officer. From Brigadier General Yaron's remarks in his testimony it emerges that he regarded the two reports — from Lt. Elul and from the Intelligence Officer — as being one report from two different sources. We have no doubt that in this instance there were two different and separate reports. As noted, the report which the Intelligence Officer obtained originated in a conversation held over the radio with Elie Hobeika. Although both reports referred to a group of 45-50 persons, and it is not to be ruled out that the questions asked over the radios referred to the same group of persons, it is clear, both from the fact that the replies given were different in content — the reply of the liaison officer was to do with the group of people as God commands, while Hobeika's reply was different — that two different conversations took place regarding the fate of the people who had fallen into the Phalangists' hands. As noted, Brigadier General Yaron did not deny in his testimony that Lt. Elul had translated for him and told him what he had heard when the two of them were on the roof of the forward command post. We have no reason to think that Lt. Elul did not inform Brigadier General Yaron of everything he had heard. It is noteworthy that Lt. Elul testified before us after Brigadier General Yaron had testified and before the notices were sent in accordance with section 15(A) of the law; and his statement to the Staff Investigators (no. 87) was also given after Brigadier General Yaron's testimony. Brigadier General Yaron did not testify again after the notice in accordance with section 15(A) had been sent, nor was there any request on his part to question Lt. Elul. We assert that Lt. Elul informed Brigadier General Yaron of the content of the conversation which took place with Elie Hobeika as specified above.

An additional report relating to the actions of the Phalangists in the camps vis-a-vis the civilians there came from laison [sic] officer G. of the Phalangists. When he entered the dining room in the forward command post building at approximately 8:00 P.M., that liaison officer told various people that about 300 persons had been killed by the Phalangists, among them also civilians. He stated this in the presence of many I.D.F. officers who were there, including Brigadier General Yaron. We had different versions of the exact wording of this statement by Phalangist officer G., but from all the testimony we have heard it is clear that he said that as a result of the Phalangists' operations up to that time, 300 terrorists and civilians had been killed in the camps. Shortly thereafter, Phalangist officer G. returned to the dining room and amended his earlier report by reducing the number of casualties from 300 to 120.

At 20:40 hours that evening an update briefing was held in the forward command post building with the participation of various I.D.F. officers who were in the building at that time, headed by Brigadier General Yaron. The remarks made at that meeting were recorded by a Major from the History Section in the Operations Branch/Training Section. We were given the tape recording and a transcript thereof (Exhibit 155). At the meeting Brigadier General Yaron spoke of the I.D.F.'s progress and deployment, and about the Phalangists' entry into the camps and the combing operations they were carrying out. Following that briefing, the Divisional Intelligence Officer spoke. In the course of his intelligence survey regarding the terrorists and other armed forces in West Beirut, he said that following (pp. 4 and 5 of the transcript, Exhibit 155):

"The Phalangists went in today. I do not know what level of combat they are showing. It is difficult to see it because it is dark. . . The impression is that their fighting is not too serious. They have casualties, as you know — two wounded, one in the leg and one in the hand. The casualties were evacuated in one of their ambulances. And they, it turns out, are pondering what to do with the population they are finding inside. On the one hand, it seems, there are no terrorists there, in the camp; Sabra camp is empty. On the other hand, they have amassed women, children and apparently also old people, with whom they don't exactly know what to do (Amos, this refers back to our talk), and evidently they had some sort of decision in principle that they would concentrate them together, and lead them to some place outside the camps. On the other hand, I also heard from — (the Phalangists' liaison officer G.). . . that 'do what your heart tells you, because everything comes from God.' That is, I do not — "

At this point Brigadier General Yaron interrupted the Intelligence Officer and the following dialogue ensued between them:

Brigadier General Yaron: "Nothing, no, no. I went to see him up top and they have no problems at all."

Intelligence Officer: "People remaining in the field? Without their lives being in any danger?"

Brigadier General Yaron: "It will not, will not harm them."

Following this exchange, the Intelligence Officer went on to another subject. The Phalangists' actions against the people in the camps were not mentioned again in this update briefing.

In his testimony, Brigadier General Yaron explained his remark about his visit "with him up top and they have no problems at all" by saying that he had spoken several times that evening with the Phalangist officers on the roof of the forward command post after he had heard the first report about 45 people and also after the further report about 300 or 120 casualties; and even though he had been skeptical about the reliability of these reports and had not understood from them that children, women or civilians had been murdered in massacres perpetrated by the Phalangists, he had warned them several times not to harm civilians and had been assured that they would issue the appropriate orders to that effect (pp. 731-732).

Between approximately 22:00 hours and 23:00 hours the Divisional Intelligence Officer contacted Northern Command, spoke with the Deputy Intelligence Officer there, asked if Northern Command had received any sort of report, was told in reply that there was no report, and told the Deputy Intelligence Officer of Northern Command about the Phalangist officer's report concerning 300 terrorists and civilians who had been killed, and about the amendment to that report whereby the number of those killed was only 120. The divisional Intelligence Officer asked the Deputy Intelligence Officer of Northern Command to look into the matter more thoroughly. Intelligence Officer A. was in the room while that conversation took place, and when he heard about that report he phoned Intelligence Branch Research at the General Staff, spoke with two Intelligence Branch officers there and told them that Phalangist personnel had so far liquidated 300 terrorists and civilians (testimony of Intelligence Officer A., p. 576). He went on to add that he had a heavy feeling about the significance of this report, that he regarded it as an important and highly sensitive report which would interest the senior responsible levels, and that this was the kind of report that would prove of interest to the Director of Military Intelligence personally. In the wake of these remarks, the personnel in Intelligence Branch research of the General Staff Branch who had been given the report carried out certain telephone clarifications, and the report was conveyed to various persons. The manner in which the report was conveyed and the way it was handled are described in Section 6, Appendix B. Suffice it to note here that a telephone report about this information was conveyed to Lt. Col. Hevroni, Chef de Bureau of the director of Military Intelligence, on 17.9.82 at 5:30 A.M. The text of the report, which was distributed to various Intelligence units and, as noted, also reached the office of the director of Military Intelligence, appears in Appendix A of Exhibit 29. That document contained a marking, noting that its origin lay with the forward command post of Northern Command, that it was received on 16.9.82 at 23.20 hours, and that the content of the report was as follows:

"*Preliminary* information conveyed by the commander of the local Phalangist force in the Shatilla refugee camp states that so far his men have liquidated about 300 people. This number includes terrorists and civilians."

The action taken in the wake of this report in the office of the Director of Military Intelligence will be discussed in this report below.

On Thursday, 16.9.82, at 19.30 hours, the Cabinet convened for a session with the participation of — besides the Prime Minister and the Cabinet Ministers (except for 5 Ministers who were abroad) — a number of persons who are not Cabinet members, among them the Chief of Staff, the head of the Mossad and the director of Military Intelligence. The subject discussed at that meeting was the situation in Lebanon in the wake of the assassination of Bashir Jemayel. At the start of the session, the Prime Minister reported on the chain of events following the report about the attempt on Bashir's life. The Minister of Defence then gave a detailed survey. The Chief of Staff provided details about the I.D.F.'s operation in West Beirut and about his meetings with Phalangist personnel. He said, inter alia, that he had informed the Phalangist commanders that their men would have to take part in the operation and go in where they were told, that early that evening they would begin to fight and would enter the extremity of Sabra, that the I.D.F. would ensure that they did not fail in their operation but I.D.F. soldiers would not enter the camps and would not fight together with the Phalangists, rather the Phalangists would go in there "with their own methods" (p. 16 of the minutes of the meeting, Exhibit 122). In his remarks the Chief of Staff explained that the camps were surrounded "by us," that the Phalangists would begin to operate that night in the camps, that we could give them orders whereas it was impossible to give orders to the Lebanese army, and that the I.D.F. would be assisted by the Phalangists and perhaps also the Lebanese Army in collecting weapons. With respect to the consequences of Bashir's assassination, the Chief of Staff said that in the situation which had been created, two things could happen. One was that the entire power structure of the Phalangists would collapse, though as yet this had not occurred. Regarding the second possibility, the Chief of Staff said as follows (pp. 21-22 of Exhibit 122):

"A second thing that will happen — and it makes no difference whether we are there or not — is an eruption of revenge which, I do not know, I can imagine how it will begin, but I do not know how it will end. It will be between all of them, and neither the Americans nor anyone else will be of any help. We can cut it down, but today they already killed Druze there. What difference does it make who or what? They have already killed them, and one dead Druze is enough so that tomorrow four Christian children will be killed; they will find them slaughtered, just like what happened a month ago; and that is how it will begin, if we are not there — it will be an eruption the likes of which has never been seen; I can already see in their eyes what they are waiting for.

"Yesterday afternoon a group of Phalangist officers came, they were stunned, still stunned, and they still cannot conceive to themselves how their hope was destroyed in one blow, a hope for which they built and sacrificed so much; and now they have just one thing left to do, and that is revenge; and it will be terrible."

At this point the Chief of Staff was asked "if there is any chance of knowing who did it, and to direct them at whoever perpetrated the deed," and he continued:

"There is no such thing there. Among the Arabs revenge means that if someone kills someone from the tribe, then the whole tribe is guilty. A hundred years will go by, and there will still be someone killing someone else from the tribe from which someone had killed a hundred years earlier. . .

"I told Draper this today, and he said there is a Lebanese Army, and so on. I told him that it was enough that during Bashir's funeral, Amin Jemayel, the brother, said 'revenge'; that is already enough. This is a war that no one will be able to stop. It might not happen tomorrow, but it will happen.

"It is enough that he uttered the word 'revenge' and the whole establishment is already sharpening knives. . ."

Toward the end of his remarks, the Chief of Staff referred to a map and explained that with the exception of one section everything was in the hands of the I.D.F., the I.D.F. was not entering the refugee camps, "and the Phalangists are this evening beginning to enter the area between Sabra and Fakahani" (p. 25). At that meeting the Head of Mossad also gave a briefing on the situation after the assassination of Bashir, but made no reference to the Phalangists' entry into the camps. There was considerable discussion in that meeting about the danger of the United States at the I.D.F.'s entry into West Beirut, the general opinion being that the decision to go in was justified and correct. Toward the close of the meeting there was discussion regarding the wording of a resolution, and then Deputy Prime Minister D. Levy said that the problem was not the formulation of a resolution, but that the I.D.F.'s continued stay in Beirut was liable to generate an undesirable situation of massive pressure regarding its stay there. Minister Levy stated that he accepted the contention regarding the I.D.F.'s entry into Beirut, and he then continued (p. 91):

"We wanted to prevent chaos at a certain moment whose significance cannot be disregarded. When confusion exists which someone else could also have exploited, the situation can be explained in a convincing way. But that argument could be undercut and we could come out with no credibility when I hear that the Phalangists are already entering a certain neighborhood — and I know what the meaning of revenge is for them, what kind of slaughter. Then no one will believe we went in to create order there, and we will bear the blame. Therefore, I think that we are liable here to get into a situation in which we will be blamed, and our explanations will not stand up. . ."

No reaction was forthcoming from those present at the meeting to this part of Deputy Prime Minister D. Levy's remarks. Prior to the close of the session the Prime Minister put forward a draft resolution which, with certain changes, was accepted by all the Ministers. That resolution opens with the words:

"In the wake of the assassination of the President-elect Bashir Jemayel, the I.D.F. has seized positions in West Beirut in order to forestall the danger of violence, bloodshed and chaos, as some 2,000 terrorists, equipped with modern and heavy weapons, have remained in Beirut, in flagrant violation of the evacuation agreement. . ."

Here we must note that the Director of Military Intelligence was present at the outset of the meeting but left, after having received permission to do so from the Minister of Defense, no long after the start of the session, and certainly a considerable time before Minister D. Levy made the remarks quoted above.

Brigadier-General Yaron did not inform Major-General Drori of the reports which had reached him on Thursday evening regarding the actions of the Phalangists vis-à-vis non-combatants in the camps, and reports about aberrations did not reach Major-General Drori until Friday, 17.9.82, in the morning hours. On Friday morning Major-General Drori contacted Brigadier-General Yaron, received from him a report about various matters relating to the war, and heard from him that the Phalangists had sustained a number of casualties, but heard nothing about casualties among the civilian population in the camps (testimony of Major-General Drori, p. 404). That same morning Major General Drori spoke with the Chief of Staff and heard from him that the Chief of Staff might come to Beirut that day.

In the early hours of that morning a note lay on a table in the Northern Command situation room in Aley. The note read as follows:

"During the night the Phalangists entered the Sabra and Shatilla refugee camps. Even though it was agreed that they would not harm civilians, they 'butchered.' They did not operate in orderly fashion but dispersed. They had casualties, including two killed. They will organize to operate in a more orderly manner — we will see to it that they are moved into the area."

Lieutenant-Colonel Idel, of the History Section in Operations Branch/ Training Section, saw this note on the table and copied it into a notebook in which he recorded details about certain events, as required by his position. It has not been clarified who wrote the note or what the origin was of the information it contained, even though on this matter the staff investigators questioned many persons who held various positions where the note was found. The note itself was not found, and we know its content only because Lieutenant-Colonel Idel recorded it in his notebook.

The G.O.C. held a staff meeting at 8:00 A.M. in which nothing was said about the existence of reports regarding the Phalangists' actions in the camps.

Already during the night between Thursday and Friday, the report about excesses committed by the Phalangists in the camps circulated among I.D.F. officers who were at the forward command post. Two Phalangists were killed that night during their operation in the camps. When the report about their casualties reached the Phalangists' liaison officer, G., along with a complaint from one of the Phalangist commanders in the field that the I.D.F. was not supplying sufficient illumination, the liaison officer asked Lieutenant-Colonel Treiber, one of the Operations Branch officers at the forward command post, to increase the illuimation [sic] for the Phalangists.

Lieutenant-Colonel Treiber's response was that the Phalangists had killed 300 people and he was not willing to provide them with illumination (testimony of Lieutenant Elul, pp. 1212-1213). Lieutenant-Colonel Treiber subsequently ordered that limited illumination be provided for the Phalangists.

In the early hours of the morning, additional officers at the forward command post heard from the Phalangists' liaison officer, G., that acts of killing had been committed in the camps but had been halted (statements 22 and 167).

At approximately 9:00 A.M. on Friday, Brigadier General Yaron met with representatives of the Phalangists at the forward command post and discussed with them the entry of an additional force of Phalangists into the camps. Afterwards, according to the testimony of Major General Drori (p. 1600), he met with Brigadier General Yaron in the *Cite* of Beirut, where they discussed the activity of the I.D.F. troops and other matters related to the war; but Brigadier General Yaron said nothing to him at that meeting about excesses committed by the Phalangists, Brigadier General Yaron's testimony contains a different version of the talk between him and Major General Drori that morning. According to that testimony, Brigadier General Yaron received reports that morning about a woman who claimed that she had been struck in the face by Phalangists, [and] about a child who had been kidnapped and whose father had complained to the Divisional Operations Officer; and Brigadier General Yaron had seen liaison officer G. arguing with other Phalangists. From all this Brigadier General Yaron inferred that something was amiss, or as he put it, "something smelled fishy to me" (p. 700). He phoned Major General Drori and told him something did not look right to him, and as a result of this conversation, Major General Drori arrived at the forward command post at approximately 11.00 A.M. According to Major General Drori, he arrived at the forward command post without having heard any report that something was wrong in the camps, simply as part of a routine visit to various divisions. We see no need to decide between these two versions.

When Major General Drori arrived at the Divisional forward command post he spoke with Colonel Duvdevani and with Brigadier General Yaron. We also have differing versions regarding what Major General Drori heard on that occasion. In his statement (No. 2) Colonel Duvdevani related that he said he had a bad feeling about what was going on in the camps. According to his statement, this feeling was caused by the report of liaison officer G. about 100 dead and also because it was not known what the Phalangists were doing inside the camps. Colonel Duvdevani did not recall whether Major General Drori had asked him about the reasons for his bad feeling. Brigadier General Yaron testified (p. 701) that he had told Major General Drori everything he knew at that time, namely those matters detailed above which had caused his bad feeling. According to Major General Drori's testimony, he heard about three specific matters on that occasion. The first was the blow to the woman's head; the second — which was not directly related to the camps — was that in one neighbourhood, namely San Simon, Phalangists had beaten residents; and the third matter was that a feeling existed that the Phalangists were carrying out "an unclean mopping-up" — that is, their soldiers were not calling on the residents — as I.D.F. soldiers do — to come out before opening fire on a house which was to be "mopped up," but were "going into the house firing" (testimony of Major General Drori, pp. 408, 1593-1594). No evidence existed that, at that meeting or earlier, anyone had told Major General Drori about the reports of 45 people whose fate was sealed, or about the 300 killed; nor is there any clear evidence that he was told of a specific number of people who had been killed. After Major General Drori heard what he heard from Colonel Duvdevani and Brigadier General Yaron, he ordered Brigadier General Yaron to halt the operations of the Phalangists, meaning that the Phalangists should stop where they were in the camps and advance no further. Brigadier General Yaron testified that he suggested to Major General Drori to issue this order (p. 701). The order was conveyed to the Phalangist commanders. On that same occasion Major General Drori spoke with the Chief of Staff by phone about several matters relating to the situation in Beirut, told him that he thought the Phalangists had perhaps "gone too far" and that he had ordered their operation to be halted (p. 412). A similar version of this conversation appears in the Chief of Staff's testimony (pp. 232-233). The Chief of Staff testified that he had heard from Major General Drori that something was amiss in the Phalangists' actions. The Chief of Staff asked no questions, but told Major General Drori that he would come to Beirut that afternoon.

As mentioned above, the cable report (appendix exhibit 29) regarding 300 killed reached the office of the director of Military Intelligence on 17.9.82 at 5:30 A.M. The text of this cable was transmitted to the director of Military Intelligence at his home in a morning report at 6:15 A.M., as part of a routine update transmitted to the director of Military Intelligence every morning by telephone. From the content of the cable, the director of Military Intelligence understood that the source of the report is Operations and not Intelligence, and that its source is the Northern Command forward command post. According to the testimony of the director of Military Intelligence, the details of which we shall treat later, he did not know then that it had been decided to send the Phalangists into the camps and that they were operating there; therefore, when he heard the report, he asked what the Phalangists were doing — and he was told that they had been operating in the camps since the previous day (p. 120, 123). When the director of Military Intelligence arrived at his office at 8:00 A.M., he asked his bureau chief where the report had originated, and he was told that it was an "Operations" report. He ordered that it be immediately ascertained what was happening in the Sabra and Shatilla camps. The clarifications continued in different ways (described in section 6 of appendix B) during Friday morning, but no confirmation of the report was obtained; and the intelligence personnel who dealt with the clarifications treated it as a report which for them is unreliable, is unconfirmed, and therefore it would not be proper to circulate it according to the standard procedure, by which important and urgent intelligence reports are circulated. The content of the cable was circulated to a number of intelligence personnel (whose positions were noted on the cable form) and was conveyed to the Mossad and the General Security Services. Since the source of the report seemed to those Intelligence Branch personnel who dealt with the matter to be Operations, it was not accorded the standard treatment given reports from Intelligence sources, but rather the assumption was that Operations personnel were dealing with the report in their own way. The answers received by the director of Military Intelligence to his demand for clarification were that there were no further details. The director of Military Intelligence did not know that the report had been transmitted by Intelligence officer A. The report was transmitted verbally, incidentally, by the assistant to the bureau chief of the director of Military Intelligence to Lieutenant Colonel Gai of the Defense Ministry's situation room, when the latter arrived at about 7:30 A.M. at the office of the director of Military Intelligence. One of the disputed questions in this inquiry is whether Lieutenant Colonel Gai transmitted the report to Mr. Duda'i; we shall discuss this matter separately. Suffice it to say here that we have no evidence that the report was transmitted to the Defense Minister or came to his knowledge in another way.

At 7:30 A.M. on Friday there was a special morning briefing at the [office of] the assistant for research to the director of Military Intelligence. At the meeting, in which various intelligence personnel participated, the aforementioned report was discussed, and it was said that it can not be verified. The assistant for research to the directory of Military Intelligence gave an order to continue checking the report. He knew that the source of the report was Intelligence officer A. The assistant for research to the director of Military Intelligence also treated this report with skepticism, both because the number of killed seemed exaggerated to him and since there had been no additional confirmation of the report (pp. 1110-1113). The director of Military Intelligence took no action on his part regarding the aforementioned report, except for requesting the clarification, and did not speak about it with the Chief of Staff or the Minister of Defense, even though he met with them that morning.

As mentioned above, the reports of unusual things occurring in the camps circulated among the officers at the forward command post already during the night and in the morning hours of Friday, and they reached other I.D.F. officers and soldiers in the area. At approximately 8:00 A.M., the journalist Mr. Ze'ev Schiff received a report from the General Staff in Tel Aviv, from a man whose name he has refused to disclose, that there was a slaughter in the camps. The transmitter of the report used the Arabic expression *dab'h*. He was not told of the extent of the slaughter. He tried to check the report with Military Intelligence and Operations, and also with the Mossad, but received no confirmation, except the comment that "there's something." At 11:00 A.M. Mr. Schiff met with Minister Zipori at the minister's office and spoke with him about the report he had received. Minister Zipori tried to contact the director of Military Intelligence and the head of the General Security Services by phone, but did not reach them. At approximately 11:15 A.M., he called the Foreign Minister, Mr. Yitzhak Shamir, and spoke with him about the report he had received from Mr. Schiff. According to the testimony of Minister Zipori, he said in that telephone conversation with Mr. Shamir that he had received reports that the Phalangists "are carrying out a slaughter" and asked that Minister Shamir check the matter with the people who would be with him momentarily and whose planned visit was known to Minister Zipori (Minister Zipori's testimony, p. 1097). According to Mr. Schiff's statement to the staff investigators (no. 83), Minister Zipori said in that conversation that "they are killing in the camps" and proposed that "it is worth checking the matter through your channels."

We heard a different version of the content of the conversation from Minister Shamir. Minister Shamir knew of the entry of the Phalangists into the camps from what he had heard at the aforementioned cabinet meeting of 16.9.82. According to him, Minister Zipori told him in the aforementioned telephone conversation that he knows that Minister Shamir was to meet soon with representatives of the United States on the situation in West Beirut, and therefore he deems it appropriate to report what he had heard about what is occurring there. The situation in West Beirut is still not as quiet as it may seem from the media, and he had heard that three or four I.D.F. soldiers had been killed, and had also heard "about some rampage by the Phalangists" (p. 1232). Minister Shamir said in his testimony that as far as he could remember there was no mention in that conversation of the words massacre or slaughter. According to him, he was not asked by Minister Zipori to look into the matter, he did not think that he was talking about massacre, [rather] he got the impression from the conversation that its main aim was to inform him of the losses suffered by the I.D.F., and therefore he himself made no check and also did not instruct Foreign Ministry personnel to check the report, but asked someone in the Foreign Ministry whether new reports had arrived from Beirut and was satisfied with the answer that there is nothing new.

In addition, Minister Shamir thought, according to his testimony, that since a meeting would shortly be held at his office with Ambassador Draper, in which the Defense Minister, the director of Military Intelligence, the head of the General Security Services and their aides would be participating on the Israeli side, then he would hear from them about what is happening in West Beirut. This meeting was held at the Foreign Minister's office at 12:30, between Ambassador Draper and other representatives of the United States and a group of representatives of Israel, including the Minister of Defense, the director of Military Intelligence, and the head of the General Security Services (exhibit 124). The Foreign Minister did not tell any of those who came to the meeting about the report he had received from Minister Zipori regarding the actions of the Phalangists, and he explained this inaction of his by the fac [*sic*] that the matter did not bother him, since it was clear to him that everything going on is known to the persons sitting with him, and he did not hear from them any special report from Beirut (p. 1238). The meeting ended at 3:00 P.M., and then the Foreign Minister left for his home and took no additional action following the aforementioned conversation with Minister Zipori.

Let us return to what occurred on that Friday in West Beirut.

In the morning hours, Brigadier General Yaron met with Phalangist commanders for coordination, and agreed with them that a larger Phalangist force would organize at the airport, that this force would not be sent in to the camps until it receives approval from the Chief of Staff and after the Chief of Staff holds an additional meeting at Phalangist headquarters (pp. 705-706).

Already prior to the Chief of Staff's arrival, Major General Drori held a meeting with the commander of the Lebanese Army in which he again tried to persuade the commander, and through him the Prime Minister and Ambassador Draper, that the Lebanese Army enter the camps. Major General Drori told that commander, according to his testimony, the following (p. 1633):

"You know what the Lebanese are capable of doing to each other; when you go now to Wazzan (the Prime Minister of Lebanon) tell him again, and you see what is out here, and the time has come that maybe you'll do something, and you're going to Draper, to meet with Draper. . . get good advice from him this time, he should give it to you this time, he should agree that you enter the camps, it's important, the time has come for you to do it, and get good advice this time from Draper, or permission from him to enter or do it."

Major General Drori explained in his testimony that he had approached the commander so that the latter would speak with Ambassador Draper, since he had heard that Ambassador Draper had told the commander of the Lebanese Army a day earlier that the Americans would get the Israelis out of Beirut, that they should not talk to them and not negotiate with them. The answer which Major General Drori later received to his request from the commander of the Lebanese Army was negative.

On Friday, 17.9.82, already from the morning hours, a number of I.D.F. soldiers detected killing and violent actions against people from the refugee camps. We heard testimony from Lieutenant Grabowsky, a deputy commander of a tank company, who was in charge of a few tanks which stood on an earth embankment — a ramp — and on the adjacent road, some 200 meters from the first buildings of the camps. In the early morning hours he saw Phalangist soldiers taking men, women and children out of the area of the camps and leading them to the area of the stadium. Between 8.00 and 9.00 a.m. he saw two Phalangist soldiers hitting two young men. The soldiers led the men back into the camp, after a short time he heard a few shots and saw the two Phalangist soldiers coming out. At a later hour he went up the embankment with the tank and then saw that Phalangist soldiers had killed a group of five women and children. Lieutenant Grabowsky wanted to report the event by communications set to his superiors, but the tank crew told him that they had already heard a communications report to the battalion commander that civilians were being killed, [and] the batallion commander had replied, "We know, it's not to our liking, and don't interfere." Lieutenant Grabowsky saw another case in which a Phalangist killed a civilian. In the afternoon hours his soldiers spoke with a Phalangist who had arrived at the spot, and at the request of Grabowsky, who does not speak Arabic, one of the soldiers asked why they were killing civilians. The answer he received was that the pregnant women will give birth to terrorists and children will grow up to be terrorists. Grabowsky left the place at 16.00 hours. Late in the afternoon he related what he had seen to his commander in the tank battalion and to other officers. At their suggestion he related this to his brigade commander at 20.00 hours (Grabowsky testimony, pp. 380-388). In various statements made to the staff investigators, soldiers and officers from Lieutenant Grabowsky's unit and from other units stationed nearby related that they saw on Friday various acts of maltreatment by the Phalangist soldiers against men, women and children who were taken out of the camp, and heard complaints and stories regarding acts of killing carried out by the Phalangists. One of those questioned heard a communications report to the battalion commander about the Phalangists "running wild."

The battalion commander did not confirm in his statements (no. 21 and no. 175) and testimony that he had received reports on Friday from any of his battalion's soldiers about acts of killing or violent actions by the Phalangists against the residents of the camps. According to him, he indeed heard on Thursday night, when he was in the forward command post, about 300 killed, a number which was later reduced to 120 killed; but on Friday the only report he received was about the escape of a few dozen beaten or wounded persons northward and eastward, and this was in the afternoon. At a later date, after the massacre in the camps was publicized, the battalion commander made special efforts to obtain a monitoring report of the battalion's radio frequency and he submitted this report to us (exhibit 1240). In this document no record was found of a report of acts of killing or maltreatment by the Phalangists on Friday.

We did not send a notice as per Section 15 to this battalion commander, and this for the reasons explained in the Introduction. We have not arrived at any findings or conclusions on the contradictory versions regarding the report to the battalion commander, and it appears to us that this subject can and should be investigated within the framework of the I.D.F., as we have proposed in the Introduction. For the purposes of the matters we are discussing, we determine that indeed I.D.F. soldiers who were near the embankment which surrounded the camp saw certain acts of killing and an attempt was made to report this to commanders of higher ranks; but this report did not reach Brigadier General Yaron or Major General Drori.

The Chief of Staff reached the airport at Khalde near Beirut at 15.30 hours with a number of I.D.F. officers. At the airport he met with Major General Drori and travelled with him to a meeting at Phalangist headquarters. Major General Drori testified that he had told the Chief of Staff on the way what he knew regarding the Phalangists' actions. The Chief of Staff was satisfied with what he had heard and did not ask about additional matters (Drori testimony, pp. 415, 416). Brigadier General Yaron joined those travelling to the meeting with the Phalangist commanders. The Chief of Staff testified in his first appearance that he had heard from Major General Drori and from Brigadier General Yaron only those things which he had heard on the telephone, and does not remember that he asked them how the improper behavior of the Phalangists had expressed itself. In that testimony he explained that he had refrained from asking additional questions since the discussion had dealt mainly with the situation in the city, that he generally does not like to talk while travelling, and that he thought the matter would be clarified at Phalangist headquarters, where they were headed (testimony of the Chief of Staff, pp. 243, 234). In his additional testimony before us, when the Chief of Staff was asked for his response to Major General Drori's testimony that the latter had told the Chief of Staff about the three things which he knew about (see above), the Chief of Staff said that he is prepared to accept that these were the things said to him, but emphasized that the meaning of the things he had heard was not from his point of view that there had been acts of revenge and bloodshed by the Phalangists (p. 1663). In any case, according to his second testimony as well, the Chief of Staff was satisfied with hearing a short report from Major General Drori about the reasons for the halting of the Phalangists' actions, and did not pose questions regarding this.

At about 16:00 hours, the meeting between the Chief of Staff and the Phalangist staff was held. We have been presented with documents containing summaries from this meeting. In a summary made by Mossad representative A who was present at the meeting (exhibit 80 A) it was said that the Chief of Staff "expressed his positive impression received from the statement by the Phalangist forces and their behavior in the field" and concluded that they "continue action, mopping up the empty camps south of Fakhani until tomorrow at 5:00 A.M., at which time they must stop their action due to American pressure. There is a chance that the Lebanese Army will enter instead of them." Other matters in this summary do not relate to the matter of the two camps (a summary with identical contents appears in exhibit no. 37). We heard more precise details on the content of the meeting from witnesses who participated in it. The Chief of Staff testified that the Phalangists had reported that the operation had ended and that everything was alright, that the Americans are pressuring them to leave and they would leave by

5:00 A.M., and that they had carried out all the objectives. His reaction was "O.K., alright, you did the job."

According to the Chief of Staff, the discussion was very relaxed, there was a very good impression that the Phalangists had carried out the mission they had been assigned or which they had taken upon themselves, and there was no feeling that something irregular had occurred or was about to occur in the camps. During the meeting they requested a tractor from the I.D.F. in order to demolish illegal structures; the Chief of Staff saw this as a positive action, since he had long heard of illegal Palestinian neighborhoods, and therefore he approved their request for tractors (pp. 234-239). In his second testimony, the Chief of Staff added that the commander of the Phalangists had said that there was almost no civilian population in the camps, and had reported on their killed and wounded (p. 1666). He did not ask them questions and did not debrief them about what had happened in the camps. They wanted to send more forces into the camps, but he did not approve this; and there was no discussion at that meeting of relieving forces (pp.1667-1670). At the same meeting, the Chief of Staff approved the supply of certain arms to the Phalangists, but this has nothing to do with events in Beirut. Major General Drori testified during his first appearance that the commander of the Phalangist force, who was present at the meeting, gave details of where his forces were and reported heavy fighting — but did not make mention of any irregularities, and certainly not of a massacre. The Phalangist commanders spoke of American pressure [on them] to leave the camps. When Major General Drori was asked for additional details of that conversation he replied that he could not recall (pp. 415-420, 444-444). Brigadier General Yaron also testified that at that meeting the Phalangists commanders had said nothing about unusual actions in the camps, [that] the reason given for departure from the camps the next morning was American pressure, and that it seemed to him that the Chief of Staff even had had some good words to say, from a military standpoint, about their action. It was also agreed at that meeting that they would get tractors in order to raze illegal structures. At the end of the meeting it was clear to Brigadier General Yaron, as he testified, that the Phalangists could still enter the camps, bring in tractors, and do what they wanted — and that they would leave on Saturday morning (pp. 709-716).

In the matter of sending in additional Phalangist forces, Brigadier General Yaron testified that he did not think that limitations had been imposed on them with regard to bringing in an additional force, and he did not know whether they brought in an additional force after the meeting — but since they were supposed to leave at 5:00 A.M. on the following morning, there was no need for additional forces. On the same subject, Brigadier General Yaron also said that there was no restriction on the Phalangists' bringing in additional forces; it seemed to him that they had brought in a certain additional force — although the major force, at the airport, was not sent into the camps. He did not check whether they did or did not bring in additional forces, and from his point of view there was no inpediment [*sic*] to their bringing in additional forces until Saturday morning (pp. 715-747).

Also present at that same meeting were the Deputy Chief of Staff, Mossad representative A, the divisional intelligence officer (who took the minutes of the meeting) and other Israeli officers; and there is no need to go into details here of their testimony on this matter, since the things they said generally agree with what has already been detailed above. We would add only that in the matter of the tractors, the Mossad representative recommended to the Chief of Staff that tractors be given to the Phalangists; but at the conclusion of the meeting, an order was given to supply them with just one tractor and to remove I.D.F. markings from the tractor. The one tractor supplied later was not used and was returned immediately by the Phalangists, who had their own tractors which they used in the camps that same night and the following morning.

It is clear from all the testimony that no explicit question was posed to the Phalangist commanders concerning the rumors or reports which had arrived until then regarding treatment of the civilian population in the camps. The Phalangist commanders, for their part, didn't "volunteer" any reports of this type, and this matter was therefore not discussed at all at that meeting. The subject of the Phalangists' conduct toward those present in the camps did not come up at all that meeting, nor was there any criticism or warning on this matter.

During the evening, between 18.00-20.00 hours, Foreign Ministry personnel in Beirut and in Israel began receiving various reports from U.S. representatives that the Phalangists had been seen in the camps and that their presence was liable to lead to undesirable results — as well as complaints about actions by I.D.F. soldiers in the hospital building in Beirut. The Foreign Ministry personnel saw to the clarification of the complaints, and the charges against I.D.F. soldiers turned out to be unfounded.

After the Chief of Staff returned to Israel, he called the Defense Minister between 20.00-21.00 hours and spoke with him about his visit to Beirut. According to the Defense Minister's testimony, the Chief of Staff told him in that conversation that he had just returned from Beirut and that "in the course of the Phalangists' actions in the canps [*sic*], the Christians had harmed the civilian population more than was expected." According to the Defense Minister, the Chief of Staff used the expression that the Lebanese Forces had "gone too far," and that therefore their activity had been stopped in the afternoon, the entry of additional forces had been prevented, and an order had been given to the Phalangists to remove their forces from the camps by 5.00 A.M. the following morning. The Defense Minister added that the Chief of Staff also mentioned that civilians had been killed (testimony of the Defense Minister, pp. 293-294). According to the Defense Minister's statements, this was the first report that reached him of irregular activity by the Phalangists in the refugee camps. The Chief of Staff did not confirm that he had told the Defense Minister all the above.

According to him, he told the Defense Minister that the Phalangists had carried out their assignment, that they had stopped, and that they were under pressure from the Americans and would leave by 5.00 A.M. does not recall that he mentioned disorderly behavior by the Phalangists, but he is sure he did not speak of a massacre, killing or the like. When the Chief of Staff was asked whether the Defense Minister had asked him questions in that same conversation, his reply was that he didn't remember (p. 243). In his second round of testimony, the Chief of Staff said that it was possible and also reasonable that he had told the Defense Minister the content of what he had heard from Major General Drori, although he reiterated that he didn't recall every word that was said in that same conversation (pp. 1687-1688). At the conclusion of his second round of testimony, the Chief of Staff denied that there had been discussion, in the telephone conversation with the Defense Minister, of killing beyond what had been expected (p. 1692).

This conversation was not recorded by anyone, and the two interlocutors testified about it from memory. It is our opinion that the Defense Minister's version of that same conversation is more accurate than the Chief of Staff's version. It is our determination [*sic*] that the Chief of Staff did tell the Defense Minister about the Phalangists' conduct, and that from his words the Defense Minister could have understood, and did understand, that the Phalangists had carried out killings of civilians in the camps. Our opinion finds confirmation in that, according to all the material which has been brought before us in evidence, the Defense Minister had not received any report of killings in the camps until that same telephone conversation; but after that conversation, the Defense Minister knew that killings had been carried out in the camps — as is clear from a later conversation between him and Mr. Ron Ben-Yishai, which we will discuss further on.

On Friday at approximately 4:00 P.M., when the television military correspondent Mr. Ron Ben-Yishai was at the airport in Beirut, he heard from several I.D.F. officers about killings in the camps. These officers were not speaking from personal knowledge, but rather according to what they had heard from others. Likewise, he saw Phalangist forces comprising about 500-600 men deployed at the airport. The Phalangist officer with whom Mr. Ben-Yishai spoke at that time told him that the Phalangist forces were going to the camps to fight the terrorists, so as to remove the terrorists and the arms caches in the camps. Asked what explanation had been given to the soldiers, the officer replied that it had been explained to them that they must behave properly and that they would harm their image if they didn't behave in the war like soldiers in all respects. He heard members of the forces in the field shouting condemnations and making threatening motions toward Palestinians, but he attached no importance to this, since he had encountered this phenomenon many times during the war. Mr. Ben-Yishai went from the airport to Ba'abda; and there, at 8:30 P.M., he heard from various officers that they had heard about people being executed by the

Phalangists. At 23.30 hours, Mr. Ben-Yishai called up the Defense Minister and told him that a story was circulating that the Phalangists were doing unacceptable things in the camps. To the Defense Minister's questions, Mr. Ben-Yishai replied that he had heard this story from people he knew who had heard about civilians being killed by the Phalangists. The Defense Minister did not react to these words (statement 10 by Mr. Ben-Yishai, and testimony by the Defense Minister, p. 298). According to the Defense Minister, what he heard from Mr. Ron Ben-Yishai was nothing new to him, since he had already heard earlier about killings from the Chief of Staff; and he also knew that as a result of the report, entry by additional forces had been halted and an order had been given to the Phalangists to leave the camps (p. 298).

In concluding the description of the events of Thursday and Friday, it should be noted that no information on the reports which had arrived during those two days regarding the Phalangists' deeds, as these were detailed above, was given to the Prime Minister during those same two days. It should also be added that on Friday evening, there were several calls from U.S. representatives complaining about entry by Phalangist forces and about the consequences which might ensue, as well as about actions that had been taken in other parts of West Beirut. Foreign Ministry personnel handled these complaints, and a summary of them was also sent to the situation room at the Defense Ministry and was brought to the Defense Minister's attention at approximately 22.00 hours.

The Departure of the Phalangists and the Reports of the Massacre

The Phalangists did not leave by 5:00 A.M. on Saturday, 18.9.82. Between 6:30-7:00 A.M., a group of Phalangist soldiers entered the Gaza Hospital, which is located at the end of the Sabra camp and which is run by the Palestinian Red Crescent organization. These soldiers took a group of doctors and nurses, foreign nationals working in that same hospital, out of the hospital and led them under armed escort via Sabra St. We heard from three members of the group, Drs. Ang and Morris and the nurse Ellen Siegel, about what happened in that hospital from the time of Bashir's murder until Saturday morning. As this group passed along Sabra St., the witnesses saw several corpses on both sides of the street, and groups of people sitting on both sides of the street with armed soldiers guarding them. The members of the group also saw bulldozers moving along Sabra St. and entering the camp's alleyways. The group of doctors and nurses arrived, with those who, were leading them, at a plaza at the end of Sabra St.; they passed by the Kuwaiti Embassy building and were brought into a former U.N. building by their guards. There several members of the group were interrogated by the Phalangists, but the interrogation was halted, their passports restored to them, and they were taken to a building where there were I.D.F. soldiers — that is, the forward command post. After a while, the members of the group were taken by I.D.F. soldiers to another part of Beirut, where they were released; and several of them, at their request, returned to the hospital after receiving from one of the I.D.F. officers a document which was meant to grant them passage as far as the hospital. We will return again later to the testimony of three of the members of this group.

When Brigadier General Yaron realized that the Phalangists had not left the camps by 06:30 hours, he gave the Phalangist commander on the scene an order that they must vacate the camps without delay. This order was obeyed, and the last of the Phalangist forces left the camps at approximately 8:00 A.M. Afterwards there was an "announcement" — that is, it was declared over loudspeakers that people located in the area must come out and assemble in a certain place, and all those who came out were led to the stadium. There, refugees from the camps gathered, and the I.D.F. gave them food and water. In the meantime, reports circulated about the massacre in the camps, and many journalists and media personnel arrived in the area.

The Chief of Staff testified before us that on Saturday morning, the Prime Minister phoned him and told him that the Americans had called him and complained that the Phalangists had entered the Gaza Hospital and were killing patients, doctors, and staff workers there. The Chief of Staff's reply was that as far as he knew, there was no hospital called "Gaza" in the western part of the city, but he would look into the matter. At his order, an investigation was conducted in the Northern Command and also in the Operations Branch, and the reply he received was that there was indeed a hospital called "Gaza" but that no killings had been perpetrated, and he so informed the Prime Minister. According to the Chief of Staff's initial testimony, the Prime Minister called him on this matter at approximately 10:00 A.M. (p.243). In his second round of testimony, when the Chief of Staff was presented with the fact that the Prime Minister was in synagogue at 8:00 A.M. on that same Saturday, the first day of the Rosh Hashana holiday, the Chief of Staff said that the first telephone conversation with the Prime Minister had apparently taken place at an earlier hour of the morning. The Prime Minister stated in his testimony that he had gone to synagogue at 8:15-8:30 hours, returning at 13:15-13:30 hours; that he had had no conversation with the Chief of Staff before going to synagogue; that there had been no American call to him regarding the Gaza Hospital; and therefore, the conversations regarding the Gaza Hospital about which the Chief of Staff testified (pp. 771-772) had not taken place. The Defense Minister testified that the Chief of Staff apparently spoke with him by phone between 9:00-10:00 on Saturday morning and told him that the Prime Minister had called his attention to some occurrence at the Gaza Hospital; but the Defense Minister was not sure that such a conversation had indeed taken place, and said that he thinks that there was such a conversation (p. 300). We see no need, for the purpose of determining the facts in this investigation, to decide between the two contradictory versions regarding the conversations about Gaza hospital. We assume that the contradictions are not deliberate, but stem from faulty memory, which is understandable in view of the dramatic turn of events taking place in those days.

On Saturday, the Defense Minister received additional reports about the acts of slaughter. He heard from the Director-General of the Foreign Ministry, Mr. Kimche, that Ambassador Draper had called him to say that I.D.F. soldiers had entered banks on the Street of Banks and that Palestinians had been massacred. It emerged that the report about the entry into the banks was incorrect. Regarding the report about the massacre, the Defense Minister's reply to the Foreign Ministry Director-General, which was given at about 13:00 hours, was that the Phalangists' operation had been stopped, the entry of additional forces blocked, and all the forces in the camps had been expelled. At 15:00 hours, Major General Drori spoke with the Defense Minister and told him about the reports concerning the massacre, adding that the Phalangists had already left the camps and that the Red Cross and the press were inside (testimony of Maj. Gen. Drori, pp. 428-429). At about 17:00 hours, Major General Drori met with a representative of the Lebanese army and appealed to him to have the Lebanese army enter the camps. The representative of the Lebanese army replied that he had to get approval for such a move. Between 21:30 and 22:00 hours the reply was received that the Lebanese army would enter the camps. Its entry into the camps was effected on Sunday, 19.9.82.

After the Phalangists had left the camps, Red Cross personnel, many journalists and other persons entered them, and it then became apparent that in the camps, and particularly in Shatilla, civilians — including women and children — had been massacred. It was clear from the spectacle that presented itself that a considerable number of the killed had not been cut down in combat but had been murdered, and that no few acts of barbarism had also been perpetrated. These sights shocked those who witnessed them; the reports were circulated by the media and spread throughout the world. Although for the most part the reports said that the massacre had been executed by members of the Phalangists, accusations were immediately hurled at the I.D.F. and at the State of Israel, since, according to the reports published at that time, the Phalangists' entry into the camps had been carried out with the aid and consent of the I.D.F. On Saturday and the days following, the I.D.F. refrained as far as possible from entering the camps, for fear that should any I.D.F. soldiers be seen there, accusations would be forthcoming about their participation in the massacre. The burial of the dead was carried out under the supervision of the Red Cross, and the victims' families also engaged in their burial.

It is impossible to determine precisely the number of persons who were slaughtered. The numbers cited in this regard are to a large degree tendentious and are not based on an exact count by persons whose reliability can be counted on. The low estimate came from sources connected with the Government of Lebanon or with the Lebanese Forces. The letter (Exhibit 153) of the head of the Red Cross delegation to the Minister of Defense stated that Red Cross representatives had counted 328 bodies. This figure, however, does not include all the bodies, since it is known that a number of families buried bodies on their own initiative without reporting their actions to the Red Cross. The forces who engaged in the operation removed bodies in trucks when they left Shatilla, and it is possible that more bodies are lying under the ruins in the camps or in the graves that were dug by the assailants near the camps. The letter noted that the Red Cross also had a list of 359 persons who had disappeared in West Beirut between 18 August and 20 September, with most of the missing having disappeared from Sabra and Shatilla in mid-September. According to a document which reached us (Exhibit 151), the total number of victims whose bodies were found from 18.9.82 to 30.9.82 is 460. This figure includes the dead counted by the Lebanese Red Cross, the International Red Cross, the Lebanese Civil Defense, the medical corps of the Lebanese army, and by relatives of the victims. According to this count, the 460 victims included 109 Lebanese and 328 Palestinians, along with Iranians, Syrians and members of other nationalities. According to the itemization of the bodies in this list, the great majority of the dead were males; as for women and children, there were 8 Lebanese women and 12 Lebanese children, and 7 Palestinian women and 8 Palestinian children. Reports from Palestinian sources speak of a far greater number of persons killed, sometimes even of thousands. With respect to the number of victims, it appears that we can rely neither on the numbers appearing in the document from Lebanese sources, nor on the numbers originating in Palestinian sources. A further difficulty in determining the number of victims stems from the fact that it is difficult to distinguish between victims of combat operations and victims of acts of slaughter. We cannot rule out the possibility that various reports included also victims of combat operations from the period antedating the assassination of Bashir. Taking into account the fact that Red Cross personnel counted no more than 328 bodies, it would appear that the number of victims of the massacre was not as high as a thousand, and certainly not thousands. According to I.D.F. intelligence sources, the number of victims of the massacre is between 700 and 800 (testimony of the director of Military Intelligence, pp. 139-140). This may well be the number most closely corresponding with reality. It is impossible to determine precisely when the acts of slaughter were perpetrated; evidently they commenced shortly after the Phalangists entered the camps and went on intermittently until close to their departure.

According to the testimony we heard, no report of the slaughter in the camps was made to the Prime Minister on Saturday, with the possible exception of the events in the Gaza Hospital, regarding which we made no finding. The Prime Minister heard about the massacre on a B.B.C. radio broadcast towards evening on Saturday. He immediately contacted the Chief of Staff and the Defense Minister, who informed him that the actions had been halted and that the Phalangists had been removed from the camps (p.771).

When a public furor erupted in Israel and abroad in the wake of the reports about the massacre, and accusations were levelled that the I.D.F. and Haddad's men had taken part in the massacre, several communiques were issued by the I.D.F. and the Foreign Ministry which contained incorrect and imprecise statements about the events. These communiques asserted explicitly or implied that the Phalangists' entry into the camps had been carried out without the knowledge of — or coordination with — the I.D.F. The incorrect statements were subsequently amended, and it was stated publicly that the Phalangists' entry into the camps had been coordinated with the I.D.F. There is no doubt that the publication of incorrect and imprecise reports intensified the suspicions against Israel and caused it harm.

After the end of the Rosh Hashanah holy day, at 21.00 hours on Sunday, 19.9.82, a Cabinet meeting took place at the Prime Minister's residence with the participation of, in addition to the Cabinet members, the Chief of Staff, the head of the Mossad, the director of Military Intelligence, Major General Drori, and others. The subject discussed in that meeting was "the events in West Beirut — the murder of civilians in the Shatilla camp" (minutes of the meeting, Exhibit 121). At that meeting the Prime Minister, the Minister of Defense, the Chief of Staff and Major General Drori reported on the course of events. The Defense Minister stressed that the I.D.F. had not entered the camps, which were terrorist bastions, because it was our interest not to endanger even one soldier in the camps (p.5, minutes of the meeting). He added that on the day following the entry, "when we learned what had taken place there, the I.D.F. intervened immediately and removed those forces" (p.6). According to him (p.7) no one had imagined that the Phalangists would commit such acts. In his remarks, the Chief of Staff stressed, among other points, that in previous Cabinet meetings various Ministers had asked why the Phalangists were not fighting — after all, this was their war. He, too, noted that no one could have known in advance how the Phalangists would behave, and in his view even the Phalangists' commanders did not know what would happen, but had lost control of their men. The Chief of Staff added that "the moment we learned how they were behaving there, we exerted all the pressure we could, we removed them from there and we expelled them from the entire sector" (pp.9, 10). Major General Drori said that even before the Phalangists entered the camps, "we made them swear, not one oath but thousands, regarding their operation there. There was also their assurance that the kind of actions that were committed would not be committed. The moment it became clear to us what had happened, we halted the operation and demanded that they get out — and they got out." Major General Drori also told about the group of 15 persons, among them doctors, whom the I.D.F. had extricated from the hands of the Phalangists, thus preventing a major complication. He gave details of his appeal to the heads of the Lebanese army that they agree to enter the camps, and about the negative replies he had received (pp.18-22). Afterward the Chief of Staff spoke again, and according to the recorded minutes (p.25) he said as follows:

"On Friday, I met with them at around noon, at their command post. We did not yet know what had happened there. In the morning we knew that they had killed civilians, so we ordered them to get out and we did not allow others to enter. But they did not say they had killed civilians, and they did not say how many civilains [*sic*] they had killed; they did not say anything. . ."

In his second testimony the Chief of Staff explained that by his words, "in the morning we knew they had killed civilians," he was referring to reports that existed on Saturday morning and not to the reports that existed Friday morning, as might have perhaps been understood (p.1665). The remarks quoted above are not unequivocal; they are ambivalent. We accept the Chief of Staff's explanation that he was not referring to the reports in his possession of Friday, but to the reports that reached him on Saturday morning. This interpretation of the Chief of Staff's remarks is consistent with his other statements in this section of his remarks.

Several remarks were made in that meeting by the Prime Minister, who opened the session with a general survey in which he complained about accusations — in his view unfounded — which had been levelled against Israel. Various ministers took part in the discussion. In response to the remark of Minister Moda'i that the Prime Minister had spoken of "protecting life" as one of the goals of the entry into West Beirut, the Prime Minister stated (p.73, Exhibit 121):

"That was our pure and genuine intention. That night I also spoke of this with the Chief of Staff. I told him that we must seize positions precisely to protect the Muslims from the vengeance of the Phalangists. I could assume that after the assassination of Bashir, their beloved leader, they would take revenge on the Muslims."

To this, Minister Hammer commented that "if we suspected that they would commit murder, we should have thought before we let them enter." The Prime Minister's reply was, "In the meantime days have passed. What are you objecting to? At night I said that we must prevent this." When in the course of his testimony the Prime Minister's attention was drawn to these remarks of his — that on the night when the decision about the entry into West Beirut was taken, he had spoken with the Chief of Staff about the goal "to protect the Muslims from the vengeance of the Phalangists" — he confirmed having said this, although he had not known at that time that the Phalangists would enter the camps (p.764). In the Cabinet meeting of 19.9.82 the Chief of Staff did not react to these remarks by the Prime Minister, and did not deny them. In his second testimony the Chief of Staff said that in the conversation between him and the Prime Minister that night, the Prime Minister might have said "that there must be no rioting. . . they must not cross over or flee or not do things like. . .crossing from side to side"; but the Prime Minister had not gone into any greater detail (p.1690). Since that night conversation was not taken down and it is difficult to rely on the memory of the conversants regarding the accuracy of what was said, we cannot determine with certainty what the Prime Minister said at that time, except for the fact that he mentioned that one of the purposes of the entry was to prevent rioting. The meeting concluded with a resolution to issue a communique expressing deep regret and pain at the injuries to a civilian population done by a Lebanese unit which had entered a refugee camp "at a place distant from an I.D.F. position." The resolution added that "immediately after learning about what had happened in the Shatilla camp, the I.D.F. had put a stop to the murder of innocent civilians and had forced the Lebanese unit to leave the camp." It was stressed in the resolution that the accusations regarding I.D.F. responsibility for the human tragedy in the Shatilla camp were in the nature of "a blood libel against the Jewish state and its Government," were groundless, and "the Government rejects them with repugnance." The resolution also stated that had it not been for the intervention of the I.D.F., the number of losses would have been far greater, and that it had been found that the terrorists had violated the evacuation agreement by leaving 2,000 terrorists and vast stocks of weapons in West Beirut. The resolution concludes:

"No one will preach to us moral values or respect for human life, on whose basis we were educated and will continue to educate generations of fighters in Israel."

The furor that erupted in the wake of the massacre, and various accusations that were levelled, led those concerned to carry out debriefings and clarifications. A clarification of this kind was carried out on behalf of the General Staff (Exhibit 239) and in the office of the director of Military Intelligence (Exhibit 29 from October 1982). The summation of the Military Intelligence report states that "it emerges from a retrospective examination that the telephone report. . .had its source in a rumor/'gut feeling' that the (Intelligence Officer A) had happened to overhear, and that he himself was unable to verify that rumor in his on-site examinations, or in reaction to the briefings he had received. . ." The cable in question is Appendix A to Exhibit 29, which has already been quoted above; and from what has already been said above it is clear that is it was not based on a "gut feeling." This investigative report contains other inaccuracies, which we shall note when we come to discuss the responsibility of Mr. A. Duda'i. A more detailed clarification was carried out in a Senior Command Meeting (SCM) with the participation of the Chief of Staff. The minutes of that Meeting were submitted to us (Exhibit 241). At that meeting, the Chief of Staff said, inter alia, that whereas prior to the I.D.F.'s entry into Lebanon atrocities had been perpetrated throughout that country, after the I.D.F.'s entry "the Phalangists did not commit any excesses officially and did nothing that could have indicated any danger from them," and they looked to him to be a regular, disciplined army. In his remarks the Chief of Staff also stressed the pressure from various elements for the Phalangists to take part in the combat operations. Major General Drori related the course of events from his point of view, which in general lines is consistent with what he related in his testimony before us. He said, inter alia, that he had originally wanted the I.D.F. or the Lebanese army to enter the camps, and that he did not concur in the considerations which had led to the decision regarding the entry of the Phalangists. Major General Drori was asked by one of the participants why a tractor had been needed, and he replied that there was a plan of the Lebanese administration, including the Phalangists and the Lebanese army, to destroy all the illegal structures, including the many structures in the camps. Brigadier General Yaron also related the course of events. He said, inter alia, that when he had been informed by the command that approval had come to let the Christians into the refugee camp he had expressed no opposition or reservation, but had been quite pleased because it was clear to him that this camp contained many terrorists and the battalion had come under quite heavy fire from it. Brigadier General Yaron stressed that he warned the Phalangists not to harm civilians, women, children, old people or anyone raising his hands, but to clean out the terrorists from the camps, with the civilians to go to the area of the stadium. He said that until Saturday morning he did not know what was happening and when he saw the group of doctors and nurses, they had not told him about the acts of slaughter either. Following a quite lengthy debate, Brigadier General Yaron responded to the remarks of the participants by stating, inter alia (pp. 85 to 87, Exhibit 241):

"The mistake, as I see it, the mistake is everyone's. The entire system showed insensitivity. I am speaking now of the military system. I am not speaking about the political system. The whole system manifested insensitivity. . .

"On this point everyone showed insensitivity, pure and simple. Nothing else. So you start asking me, what exactly did you feel in your gut on Friday . . .I did badly, I admit it. I did badly. I cannot, how is it possible that a divisional commander — and I think this applies to the Division Commander and up — how is it possible that a Division Commander is in the field and does not know that 300, 400, 500 or a thousand, I don't know how many, are being murdered here? If he's like that, let him go. How can such a thing be"? But why didn't he know? Why was he oblivious? That's why he didn't know and that's why he didn't stop it. . .but I take myself to task. . .

I admit here, from this rostrum, we were all insensitive, that's all."

At the conclusion of his remarks, the Chief of Staff stressed that if the I.D.F. had provided the Phalangists with the tank and artillery support they had requested, far more people would have been killed (p. 121).

On 28.9.82 a Senior Comnand [sic] Meeting was held with the Defense Minister, who related the course of events from his point of view. His remarks at that meeting are consistent with what we heard in his testimony. Several senior I.D.F. officers expressed their views at that meeting (Exhibit 242).

The Responsibility for the Massacre

In this section of the report, we shall deal with the issue of the responsibility for the massacre from two standpoints: first from the standpoint of direct responsibility — i.e., who actually perpetrated the massacre — and then we shall examine the problem of indirect responsibility, to the extent that this applies to Israel or those who acted on its behalf.

The Direct Responsibility

According to the above description of events, all the evidence indicates that the massacre was perpetrated by the Phalangists between the time they entered the camps on Thursday, 16.9.82, at 18.00 hours, and their departure from the camps of Saturday, 18.9.82, at approximately 8:00 A.M. The victims were found in those areas where the Phalangists were in military control during the aforementioned time period. No other military force aside from the Phalangists was seen by any one of the witnesses in the area of the camps where the massacre was carried out, or at the time of the entrance into or exit from this area. The camps were surrounded on all sides: on three sides by I.D.F. forces, and on the forth side was a city line (that divided between East and West Beirut) that was under Phalangist control. Near the point of entry to the camps a Lebanese army force was encamped, and their men did not see any military force besides the Phalangist one enter the camps. It can be stated with certainty that no organized military force entered the camps at the aforementioned time besides the Phalangist forces.

As we have said, we heard testimony from two doctors and a nurse who worked in the Gaza hospital, which was run by and for Palestinians. There is no cause to suspect that any of these witnesses have any special sympathy fo [sic] Israel, and it is clear to us — both from their choosing that place of employment and from our impression of their appearance before us — that they sympathize with the Palestinians and desired to render service to Palestinians in need. From these witnesses' testimony as well it is clear that the armed military unit that took them out of the hospital on Saturday morning and brought them to the building that formerly belonged to the U.N. was a Phalangist unit. The witness Ms. Siegel did indeed tell of a visit to the hospital at 7:00 P.M. on Friday evening of two men dressed in civilian clothes who spoke to the staff in German, and she hinted at the possibility that perhaps they were Sephardic Jews; but this assumption has no basis in fact, and it can be explained by her tendentiousness. Ms. Siegel even said that these men looked like Arabs (pp. 499-500). It is clear that these men did not belong to an armed force that penetrated the camps at the time. The two doctors Ang and Morris did not see any other military force aside from the Phalangists, who presented themselves as soldiers of a Lebanese force. Dr. Ang also saw soldiers with a band with the letters M.P. in red on it. There is evidence that some of the Phalangist units who came to the camps wore tags with the letters M.P., and along the route the Phalangists travelled to the camps, road directions containing the letters M.P. were drawn. To be sure, Dr. Morris did not say specifically that the armed men who came to the hospital were Phalangists, but he described their uniforms, which bore Arabic inscriptions, and also heard them talking among themselves in Arabic and with someone from the hospital staff in French. Dr. Morris does not read Arabic, but Ms. Siegel, who does read Arabic, testified that the Arabic inscription was the one that signifies Phalangists. Therefore, the testimony of these three witnesses also indicates that the only military force seen in the area was a Phalangist one. A similar conclusion can be drawn from the statement of Norwegian journalist John Harbo (no. 62).

In the course of the events and also thereafter, rumors spread that personnel of Major Haddad were perpetrating a massacre or participating in a massacre. No basis was found for these rumors. The I.D.F. liaison officer with Major Haddad's forces testified that no unit of that force had crossed the Awali River that week. We have no reason to doubt that testimony. As we have already noted, the relations between the Phalangists and the forces of Major Haddad were poor, and friction existed between those two forces. For this reason, too, it is inconceivable that a force from Major Haddad's army took part in military operations of the Phalangists in the camps, nor was there any hint of such cooperation. Although three persons from southern Lebanon — two of them from the Civil Guard in southern Lebanon — were in West Beirut on Friday afternoon, and got caught in the exchanges of fire between an I.D.F. unit and Jumblatt's militia, with one of them being killed in those exchanges, this did not take place in the area of the camps; and the investigation that was carried out showed that the three of them had come to Beirut on a private visit. There is no indication in this event that Haddad's men were at the site where the massacre was perpetrated. We can therefore assert that no force under the command of Major Haddad took part in the Phalangists' operation in the camps, or took part in the massacre.

It cannot be ruled out that the rumors about the participation of Haddad's men in the massacre also had their origin in the fact that Major Haddad arrived at Beirut airport on Friday, 17.9.82. From the testimony of the I.D.F. liaison officer with Major Haddad's forces, and from Major Haddad's testimony, it is clear that this visit by Major Haddad to the suburbs of Beirut and the vicinity had no connection with the events that took place in the camps. Major Haddad arrived at Beirut airport in an air force helicopter at 8.30 A.M. on 17.9.82. The purpose of his visit was to pay a condolence call on the Jemayel family at Bikfaya. At the airport he was met by three vehicles with members of his escort party, who had arrived that morning from southern Lebanon. En route, they were joined by another jeep with three of Haddad's commanders, who also arrived to pay a condolence call. Major Haddad and his escorts paid their condolence visit at Bikfaya, and then for security reasons returned via a different route, arriving at the point where the road from Bikfaya meets the coastal road. From there, Major Haddad, along with about eight of his men, went to visit relatives of his in Jouniyeh. Following that visit to his relative, Major Haddad returned that same afternoon to his home in southern Lebanon, from where he phoned the aforementioned liaison officer that evening.

Hints were made about the participation of Haddad's men in the massacre on the basis of a southern Lebanese accent which several of the survivors mentioned, and they also said that a few of the participants in the massacre had Moslem names. This, too, does not constitute concrete evidence, since among the Phalangist forces there were also Shi'ites — albeit not many — and they were joined also by persons who had fled from southern Lebanon.

We cannot rule out the possibility — although no evidence to this effect was found either — that one of the men from Major Haddad's forces who was visiting in Beirut during the period infiltrated into the camps, particularly in the interim period between the departure of the Phalangists and the entry of the Lebanese army, committed illegal acts there; but if this did happen, no responsibility, either direct or indirect, is to be imputed to the commanders of Major Haddad's forces.

Here and there, hints, and even accusations, were thrown out to the effect that I.D.F. soldiers were in the camps at the time the massacre was perpetrated. We have no doubt that these notions are completely groundless and constitute a baseless libel. One witness, Mr. Franklin Pierce Lamb, of the United States, informed us of the fact that on 22.9.82 a civilian I.D. card and a military dogtag belonging to a soldier named Benny Haim Ben Yosef, born on 9.7.61, were found in the Sabra camp. Following that testimony, these details were investigated and it was found that a soldier bearing that name was in hospital after having undergone operations for wounds he sustained during the entry into West Beirut. A statement was taken from this soldier in Tel Hashomer Hospital. It emerged from his remarks that he is a soldier in the battalion, he arrived in Beirut on Wednesday, 15.9.82, his unit was moving not far from the Shatilla camp and was fired on; he was hit and the protective vest he was wearing began to burn. A medic cut the vest with scissors and threw it to the side of the road, as it contained grenades which were liable to explode. Personal documents belonging to the soldier were in the pocket of the vest. He was evacuated on a stretcher and taken by helicopter to Rambam Hospital. Already in the initial medical treatment his left arm was amputated; he was also wounded in the legs and in the upper left hip. It is clear that he was not in the camps at all. This testimony is confirmed by the statement of the medic Amir Hasharoni (statement 117). Evidently, someone who found the documents on the side of the road brought them to the camp, where they were discovered. The discovery of these documents belonging to an I.D.F. soldier in the camp does not indicate that any I.D.F. soldiers were in the camp while the massacre was being perpetrated.

Mr. Lamb also testified — not from personal knowledge but based on what he had heard from others — that cluster bombs were placed under bodies found in the camps, apparently as booby-traps. According to the witness, the I.D.F. used cluster bombs when the camps were shelled; these bombs explode easily and considerable caution is required in handling them, with only specially trained people having the technical knowledge to make use of these bombs as booby-traps. He raised the question whether the Phalangists, or the forces of Major Haddad — if any of them were in the camps — possessed the requisite technical skills to make use of these bombs as booby-traps. This question implies that the bombs were placed beneath the bodies by I.D.F. personnel. That implication is totally without foundation. As noted, Mr. Lamb had no personal knowledge regarding the use of such bombs as booby-traps, and it would be extremely far-fetched to view this section of Mr. Lamb's testimony as containing anything concrete pointing to direct involvement of anyone from the IDF in the massacre that was perpetrated in the camps.

Following the massacre, the Phalangist commanders denied, in various interviews in the media, that they had perpetrated the massacre. On Sunday, 19.9.82, the Chief of Staff and Major General Drori met with the Phalangist commanders. Notes of that meeting were taken by a representative of the Mossad who was present (Exhibit 199). The Chief of Staff told the Phalangist commanders that he had come from the camps, it was said that a massacre had taken place there, and that for the sake of their future they must admit to having perpetrated the acts and explain the matter, otherwise they would have no future in Lebanon. Their reaction was that if the Chief of Staff says they must do so, they would. The Chief of Staff formed the impression that they were bewildered, that it was possible that they did not know what had happened in the camps and had no control over their people there (testimony of the Chief of Staff, p. 251). Even after that meeting the Phalangist heads continued in their public appearances to deny any connection with the massacre. That denial is patently incorrect.

Contentions and accusations were advanced that even if I.D.F. personnel had not shed the blood of the massacred, the entry of the Phalangists into the camps had been carried out with the prior knowledge that a massacre would be perpetrated there and with the intention that this should indeed take place; and therefore all those who had enabled the entry of the Phalangists into the camps should be regarded as accomplices to the acts of slaughter and sharing in direct responsibility. These accusations too are unfounded. We have no doubt that no conspiracy or plot was entered into between anyone from the Israeli political echelon or from the military echelon in the I.D.F. and the Phalangists, with the aim of perpetrating atrocities in the camps. The decision to have the Phalangists enter the camps was taken with the aim of preventing further losses in the war in Lebanon; to accede to the pressure of public opinion in Israel, which was angry that the Phalangists, who were reaping the fruits of the war, were taking no part in it; and to take advantage of the Phalangists' professional service and their skills in identifying terrorists and in discovering arms caches. No intention existed on the part of any Israeli element to harm the non-combatant population in the camps. It is true that in the war in Lebanon, and particularly during the siege of West Beirut, the civilian population sustained losses, with old people, women and children among the casualties, but this was the result of belligerent actions which claim victims even among those who do not fight. Before they entered the camps and also afterward, the Phalangists requested I.D.F. support in the form of artillery fire and tanks, but this request was rejected by the Chief of Staff in order to prevent injuries to civilians. It is true that I.D.F. tank fire was directed at sources of fire within the camps, but this was in reaction to fire directed at the I.D.F. from inside the camps. We assert that in having the Phalangists enter the camps, no intention existed on the part of anyone who acted on behalf of Israel to harm the non-combatant population, and that the events that followed did not have the concurrence or assent of anyone from the political or civilian echelon who was active regarding the Phalangists' entry into the camps.

It was alleged that the atrocities being perpetrated in the camps were visible from the roof of the forward command post, that the fact that they were being committed was also discernible from the sounds emanating from the camps, and that the senior I.D.F. commanders who were on the roof of the forward command post for two days certainly saw or heard what was going on in the camps. We have already determined above that events in the camps, in the area where the Phalangists entered, were not visible from the roof of the forward command post. It has also been made clear that no sounds from which it could be inferred that a massacre was being perpetrated in the camps reached that place. It is true that certain reports did reach officers at the forward command post — and we shall discuss these in another section of this report — but from the roof of the forward command post they neither saw the actions of the Phalangists nor heard any sound indicating that a massacre was in progress.

Here we must add that when the group of doctors and nurses met I.D.F. officers on Saturday morning, at a time when it was already clear to them that they were out of danger, they made no complaint that a massacre had been perpetrated in the camps. When we asked the witnesses from the group why they had not informed the I.D.F. officers about the massacre, they replied that they had not known about it. The fact that the doctors and nurses who were in the Gaza Hospital — which is proximate to the site of the event and where persons wounded in combative action and frightened persons from the camps arrived — did not know about the massacre, but only about isolated instances of injury which they had seen for themselves, also shows that those who were nearby but not actually inside the camps did not form the impression, from what they saw and heard, that a massacre of hundreds of people was taking place. Nor did members of a unit of the Lebanese army who were stationed near the places of entry into the camps know anything about the massacre until after the Phalangists had departed.

Our conclusion is therefore that the direct responsibility for the perpetration of the acts of slaughter rests on the Phalangist forces. No evidence was brought before us that Phalangist personnel received explicit orders from their command to perpetrate acts of slaughter, but it is evident that the forces who entered the area were steeped in hatred for the Palestinians, in the wake of the atrocities and severe injuries done to the Christians during the civil war in Lebanon by the Palestinians and those who fought alongside them; and these feelings of hatred were compounded by a longing for revenge in the wake of the assassination of the Phalangists' admired leader Bashir and the killing of several dozen Phalangists two days before their entry into the camps. The execution of acts of slaughter was approved for the Phalangists on the site by the remarks of the two commanders to whom questions were addressed over the radios, as was related above.

The Indirect Responsibility

Before we discuss the essence of the problem of the indirect responsibility of Israel, or of those who operated at its behest, we perceive it to be necessary to deal with objections that have been voiced on various occasions, according to which if Israel's direct responsibility for the atrocities is negated — i.e., if it is determined that the blood of those killed was not shed by I.D.F. soldiers and I.D.F. forces, or that others operating at the behest of the state were not parties to the atrocities — then there is no place for further discussion of the problem of indirect responsibility. The argument is that no responsibility should be laid on Israel for deeds perpetrated outside of its borders by members of the Christian community against Palestinians in that same country, or against Muslims located within the area of the camps. A certain echo of this approach may be found in statements made in the cabinet meeting of 19.9.82, and in statements released to the public by various sources.

We cannot accept this position. If it indeed becomes clear that those who decided on the entry of the Phalangists into the camps should have foreseen — from the information at their disposal and from things which were common knowledge — that there was danger of a massacre, and no steps were taken which might have prevented this danger or at least greatly reduced the possibility that deeds of this type might be done, then those who made the decisions and those who implemented them are indirectly responsible for what ultimately occurred, even if they did not intend this to happen and merely disregarded the anticipated danger. A similar indirect responsibility also falls on those who knew of the decision; it was their duty, by virtue of their position and their office, to warn of the danger, and they did not fulfill this duty. It is also not possible to absolve of such indirect responsibility those persons who, when they received the first reports of what was happening in the camps, did not rush to prevent the continuation of the Phalangists' actions and did not do everything within their power to stop them.

It is not our function as a commission of inquiry to lay a precise legal foundation for such indirect responsibility. It may be that from a legal perspective, the issue of responsibility is not unequivocal, in view of the lack of clarity regarding the status of the State of Israel and its forces in Lebanese territory. If the territory of West Beirut may be viewed at the time of the events as occupied territory — and we do not determine that such indeed is the case from a legal perspective — then it is the duty of the occupier, according to the rules of usual and customary international law, to do all it can to ensure the public's well-being and security. Even if these legal norms are invalid regarding the situation in which the Israeli government and the forces operating at its instructions found themselves at the time of the events, still, as far as the obligations applying to every civilized nation and the ethical rules accepted by civilized peoples go, the problem of indirect responsibility cannot be disregarded. A basis for such responsibility may be found in the outlook of our ancestors, which was expressed in things that were said about the moral significance of the biblical portion concerning the "beheaded heifer" (in the Book of Deuteronomy, chapter 21). It is said in Deuteronomy (21:6-7) that the elders of the city who were near the slain victim who has been found (and it is not known who struck him down) "will wash their hands over the beheaded heifer in the valley and reply: our hands did not shed this blood and our eyes did not see." Rabbi Yehoshua ben Levi says of this verse (Talmud, Tractate Sota 38b):

"The necessity for the heifer whose neck is to be broken only arises on account of the niggardliness of spirit, as it is said, 'Our hands have not shed this blood.' But can it enter our minds that the elders of a Court of Justice are shedders of Blood! The meaning is, [the man found dead] did not come to us for help and we dismissed him, we did not see him and let him go — i.e., he did not come to us for help and we dismissed him without supplying him with food, we did not see him and let him go without escort." (Rashi explains that escort means a group that would accompany them; Sforno, a commentator from a later period, says in his commentary on Deuteronomy, "that there should not be spectators at the place, for if there were spectators there, they would protest and speak out.")

When we are dealing with the issue of indirect responsibility, it should also not be forgotten that the Jews in various lands of exile, and also in the Land of Israel when it was under foreign rule, suffered greatly from pogroms perpetrated by various hooligans; and the danger of disturbances against Jews in various lands, it seems evident, has not yet passed. The Jewish public's stand has always been that the responsibility for such deeds falls not only on those who rioted and committed the atrocities, but also on those who were responsible for safety and public order, who could have prevented the disturbances and did not fulfill their obligations in this respect. It is true that the regimes of various countries, among them even enlightened countries, have side-stepped such responsibility on more than one occasion and have not established inquiry commissions to investigate the issue of indirect responsibility, such as that about which we are speaking; but the development of ethical norms in the world public requires that the approach to this issue be universally shared, and that the responsibility be placed not just on the perpetrators, but also on those who could and should have prevented the commission of those deeds which must be condemned.

We would like to note here that we will not enter at all into the question of indirect responsibility of other elements besides the State of Israel. One might argue that such indirect responsibility falls, inter alia, on the Lebanese army, or on the Lebanese government to whose orders this army was subject, since despite Major General Drori's urgings in his talks with the heads of the Lebanese army, they did not grant Israel's requests to enter the camps before the Phalangists or instead of the Phalangists, until 19.9.82. It should also be noted that in meetings with U.S. representatives during the critical days, Israel's spokesmen repeatedly requested that the U.S. use its influence to get the Lebanese Army to fulfill the function of maintaining public peace and order in West Beirut, but it does not seem that these requests had any result. One might also make charges concerning the hasty evacuation of the multi-national force by the countries whose troops were in place until after the evacuation of the terrorists. We will also not discuss the question of when other elements besides Israeli elements first learned of the massacre, and whether they did all they could to stop it or at least to immediately bring the reports in their possession to Israeli and other elements. We do not view it as our function to discuss these issues, which perhaps should be clarified in another framework; we will only discuss the issue of Israel's indirect responsibility, knowing that if this responsibility is determined, it is not an exclusive responsibility laid on Israel alone.

Here it is appropriate to discuss the question whether blame may be attached regarding the atrocities done in the camps to those who decided on the entry into West Beirut and on including the Phalangists in actions linked to this entry.

As has already been said above, the decision to enter West Beirut was adopted in conversations held between the Prime Minister and the Defense Minister on the night between 14-15 September 1982. No claim nay [sic] be made that this decision was adopted by these two alone without convening a cabinet session. On that same night, an extraordinary emergency situation was created which justified immediate and concerted action to prevent a situation which appeared undesirable and even dangerous from Israel's perspective. There is great sense in the supposition that had I.D.F. troops not entered West Beirut, a situation of total chaos and battles between various combat forces would have developed, and the number of victims among the civilian population would have been far greater than it ultimately was. The Israeli military force was the only real force nearby which could take control over West Beirut so as to maintain the peace and prevent a resumption of hostile actions between various militias and communities. The Lebanese army could have performed a function in the refugee camps, but it did not then have the power to enforce order in all of West Beirut. Under these circumstances it could be assumed that were I.D.F. forces not to enter West Beirut, various atrocities would be perpetrated there in the absence of any real authority; and it may be that world public opinion might then have placed responsibility on Israel for having refrained from action.

Both the Prime Minister and the Defense Minister based the participation of the Phalangists in the entry into West Beirut on the Cabinet resolution adopted at the session of 15.6.82. We are unable to accept this reasoning. Although there was much talk in the meeting of 15.6.82 (Exhibit 53) about the plan that the I.D.F. would not enter West Beirut, and that the entry would be effected by the Phalangists with support from the I.D.F. — but the situation then was wholly different from the one that emerged subsequently. During the discussion of 15.6.82 the terrorists and Syrian forces had not yet been evacuated from West Beirut, and the entire military picture was different from the one that developed after the evacuation was executed and after Bashir's assassination. However, even if the Phalangists' participation was not based on a formal Cabinet resolution of 15.6.82, we found no cause to raise objections to that participation in the circumstances that were created after Bashir's assassination. We wish to stress that we are speaking now only of the Phalangists' participation in connection with the entry into West Beirut, and not about the role they were to play in the camps.

The demand made in Israel to have the Phalangists take part in the fighting was a general and understandable one; and political, and to some extent military, reasons existed for such participation. The general question of relations with the Phalangists and cooperation with them is a saliently political one, regarding which there may be legitimate differences of opinion and outlook. We do not find it justified to assert that the decision on this participation was unwarranted or that it should not have been made.

It is a different question whether the decision to have the Phalangists enter the camps was justified in the circumstances that were created. From the description of events cited above and from the testimony before us, it is clear that this decision was taken by the Minister of Defense with the concurrence of the Chief of Staff and that the Prime Minister did not know of it until the Cabinet session in the evening hours of 16.9.82. We shall leave to another section of this report — which will deal with the personal responsibility of all those to whom notices were sent under Section 15(A) of the law — the discussion of whether personal responsibility devolves upon the Defense Minister or the Chief of Staff for what happened afterward in the camps in the wake of the decision to have the Phalangists enter them. Here we shall discuss only the question of whether it was possible or necessary to foresee that the entry of the Phalangists into the camps, with them in control of the area where the Palestinian population was to be found, was liable to eventuate in a massacre, as in fact finally happened.

The heads of Government in Israel and the heads of the I.D.F. who testified before us were for the most part firm in their view that what happened in the camps was an unexpected occurrence, in the nature of a disaster which no one had imagined and which could not have been — or, at all events, need not have been — foreseen. It was stressed in the remarks made in testimony and in the arguments advanced before us, that this matter should not be discussed in terms of hindsight, but that we must be careful to judge without taking into account what actually happened. We concur that special caution is required so as not to fall into the hindsight trap, but that caution does not exempt us from the obligation to examine whether persons acting and thinking rationally were dutybound, when the decision was taken to have the Phalangists enter the camps, to foresee, according to the information that each of them possessed and according to public knowledge, that the entry of the Phalangists into the camps held out the danger of a massacre and that no little probability existed that it would in fact occur. At this stage of the discussion we shall not pause to examine the particular information possessed by the persons to whom notices were sent under Section 15(A) of the law, but shall make do with an examination of the knowledge possessed by everyone who had some expertise on the subject of Lebanon.

In our view, everyone who had anything to do with events in Lebanon should have felt apprehension about a massacre in the camps, if armed Phalangists forces were to be moved into them without the I.D.F. exercising concrete and effective supervision and scrutiny of them. All those concerned were well aware that combat morality among the various combatant groups in Lebanon differs from the norm in the I.D.F. that the combatants in Lebanon belittle the value of human life far beyond what is necessary and accepted in wars between civilized peoples, and that various atrocities against the non-combatant population had been widespread in Lebanon since 1975. It was well known that the Phalangists harbor deep enmity for the Palestinians, viewing them as the source of all the troubles that afflicted Lebanon during the years of the civil war. The fact that in certain operations carried out under close I.D.F. supervision the Phalangists did not deviate from disciplined behavior could not serve as an indication that their attitude toward the Palestinian population had changed, or that changes had been effected in their plans — which they made no effort to hide — for the Palestinians. To this backdrop of the Phalangists' attitude toward the Palestinians were added the profound shock in the wake of Bashir's death along with a group of Phalangists in the explosion at Ashrafiya, and the feeling of revenge that event must arouse, even without the identity of the assailant being known.

The written and oral summations presented to us stressed that most of the experts whose remarks were brought before the commission — both Military Intelligence personnel and Mossad personnel — had expressed the view that given the state of affairs existing when the decision was taken to have the Phalangists enter the camps, it could not be foreseen that the Phalangists would perpetrate a massacre, or at all events the probability of that occurring was low; and had they been asked for their opinion at the time they would have raised no objections to the decision. We are not prepared to attach any importance to these statements, and not necessarily due to the fact that this evaluation was refuted by reality. It is our impression that the remarks of the experts on this matter were influenced to a certain extent by the desire of each of them to justify his action or lack thereof, the experts having failed to raise any objection to the entry of the Phalangists into the camps when they learned of it. In contrast to the approach of these experts, there were cases in which other personnel, both from Military Intelligence, from other I.D.F. branches, and from outside the governmental framework, warned — as soon as they learned of the Phalangists' entry into the camps, and on earlier occasion when the Phalangists' role in the war was discussed — that the danger of a massacre was great and that the Phalangists would take advantage of every opportunity offered them to wreak vengeance on the Palestinians. Thus, for example, Intelligence Officer G. (whose name appears in Section 1 of Appendix B), a branch head of Military Intelligence/ Research, stated that the subject of possible injury by the Phalangists to the Palestinian population had come up many times in internal discussions (statement No. 176). Similarly, when Intelligence Officer A. learned on Thursday, in a briefing of Intelligence officers, that the Phalangists had entered the camps, he said, even before the report arrived about the 300 killed, that he was convinced that the entry would lead to a massacre of the rufugee camps' population. In a working meeting held at 7:00 P.M. between Major General Drori and the liaison officer with the Lebanese army at Northern Command [headquarters], the officer was told by Major General Drori that the Phalangists were about to enter the Sabra and Shatilla refugee camps; his reaction was that this was a good solution, but care should be taken that they not commit acts of murder (statement No. 4 and testinony [sic] of Major General Drori, pp. 402-403). In his statement, Captain Nahum Menahem relates that in a meeting he had with the Defense Minister on 12.9.82, he informed the Defense Minister of his opinion, which was based on considerable experience and on a study he had made of the tensions between the communities in Lebanon, that a "terrible" slaughter could ensue if Israel failed to assuage the inter-communal tensions in Lebanon (statement No. 161, p. 4). We shall mention here also articles in the press stating that excesses could be expected on the part of the Christian fighters (article in the journal *Bamahane* from 1.9.82, appended to the statement — No. 24 — of the article's author, the journal's military reporter Mr. Yinon Shenkar) and that the refugee camps in Beirut were liable to undergo events exceeding what had happened at El Tel Za'atar (article in a French paper in Beirut from 20.8.82 appended to the statement, No. 76, of the journalist Mr. Strauch). We do not know whether the content of these articles was made known to the decision-makers regarding the operation of the Phalangists in West Beirut, or to those who executed the decision. We mention them solely as yet another indication that even before Bashir's assassination the possibility of the Phalangists perpetrating a massacre in the camps was not esoteric lore which need not and could not have been foreseen.

We do not say that the decision to have the Phalangists enter the camps should under no circumstances have been made and was totally unwarranted. Serious considerations existed in favor of such a decision; and on this matter we shall repeat what has already been mentioned, that an understandable desire existed to prevent I.D.F. losses in hazardous combat in a built-up area, that it was justified to demand of the Phalangists to take part in combat which they regarded as a broad opening to assume power and for the restoration of Lebanese independence, and that the Phalangists were more expert than the I.D.F. in uncovering and identifying terrorists. These are weighty considerations; and had the decision-makers and executors been aware of the danger of harm to the civilian population on the part of the Phalangists but had nevertheless, having considered all the circumstances, decided to have the Phalangists enter the camps while taking all possible steps to prevent harm coming to the civilian population, it is possible that there would be no place to be critical of them, even if ultimately it had emerged that the decision had caused undesirable results and had caused damage. However, as it transpired no examination was made of all the considerations and their ramifications; hence the appropriate orders were not issued to the executors of the decisions and insufficient heed was taken to adopt the required measures. Herein lies the basis for imputing indirect responsibility to those persons who in our view did not fulfill the obligations placed on them.

To sum up this chapter, we assert that the atrocities in the refugee camps were perpetrated by members of the Phalangists, and that absolutely no direct responsibility devolves upon Israel or upon those who acted in its behalf. At the same time, it is clear from what we have said above that the decision on the entry of the Phalangists into the refugee camps was taken without consideration of the danger — which the makers and executors of the decision were obligated to foresee as probable — that the Phalangists would commit massacres and pogroms against the inhabitants of the camps, and without an examination of the means for preventing this danger. Similarly, it is clear from the course of events that when the reports began to arrive about the actions of the Phalangists in the camps, no proper heed was taken of these reports, the correct conclusions were not drawn from them, and no energetic and immediate actions were taken to restrain the Phalangists and put a stop to their actions. This both reflects and exhausts Israel's indirect responsibility for what occurred in the refugee camps. We shall discuss the responsibility of those who acted in Israel's behalf and in its name in the following chapter.

The Responsibility of the Political Echelon

Among those who received notices sent by the committee in accordance with Section 15(A) of the Commissions of Inquiry Law were the prime minister and two ministers, and in this matter no distinction was made between Cabinet ministers and officeholders and other officials. We took this course because, in our opinion, in principle, in the matter of personal responsibility, no distinction should be made between Cabinet members and others charged with personal responsibility for actions or oversights. We wish to note to the credit of the lawyers who appeared before us that none of them raised any argument to the effect that in the investigation being conducted before us, the status of Cabinet members differed from that of others. In our view, any claim that calls for a distinction of this sort is wholly untenable. We shall discuss this argument below, although it was raised not in the deliberations of the commission but outside them.

In the report of the "Commission of Inquiry — the Yom Kippur War" (henceforth the Agranat Commission), the subject of "personal responsibility of the government echelon" was discussed in Clause 30 of the partial report. It is appropriate to cite what was stated there, since we believe that it reflects the essence of the correct approach, from a legal and public standpoint, to the problem of the personal responsibility of the political echelon. The partial report of the Agranat Commission states (Section 30):

"In discussing the responsibility of ministers for an act or failure to act in which they actually or personally took part, we are obligated to stress that we consider ourselves free to draw conclusions, on the basis of our findings, that relate only to direct responsibility, and we do not see it as our task to express an opinion on what is implied by parliamentary responsibility.

"Indeed, in Israel, as in England — whence it came to us — the principle prevails that a member of the Cabinet is responsible to the elected assembly for all the administrative actions of the apparatus within his ministry, even if he was not initially aware of them and was not a party to them. However, while it is clear that this principle obligates him to report to the members of the elected assembly on such actions, including errors and failures; to reply to parliamentary questions; to defend them or to report on what has been done to correct errors — even the English experience shows that the traditions have not determined anything regarding the question of which cases of this kind require him to resign from his ministerial office; this varies, according to circumstances, from one case to the next. The main reason for this is that the question of the possible resignation of a Cabinet member in cases of this kind is essentially a political question *par excellence*, and therefore we believe that we should not deal with it. . ."

Later on in the partial report, the Agranat Commission deals (in Section 31) with the "direct personal responsibility of the Minister of Defense" and arrives at the conclusion that "according to the criterion of reasonable behavior demanded of one who holds the office of Minister of Defense, the minister was not obligated to order additional or different precautionary measures. . ."

The Agranat Commission also dealt (in Section 32 of its partial report) with the personal responsibility of the Prime Minister and arrived at the conclusion that she was not to be charged with any responsibility for her actions at the outbreak of the Yom Kippur War and afterwards.

From the above it is clear that the Agranat Commission did not in any way avoid dealing with the question of the personal responsibility of the Prime Minister and other ministers, and regarding responsibility of this kind it did not distinguish between ministers and other people whose actions were investigated by the commission. The Agranat Commission did not discuss the question of a minister's responsibility for the shortcomings and failures of the apparatus he heads and for which he should not be charged with any personal responsibility. It is not necessary to deal in this report with the question of a minister's responsibility for the failures of his apparatus which occurred without any personal blame on his part, and we shall not express an opinion on it.

The claim has been made, albeit not in the framework of the commission's deliberations, that the matter of a minister's judgment cannot serve as the subject of investigation of a commission of inquiry according to the Commissions of Inquiry Law, 1968, because a minister's judgments are political judgments; there are no set norms regarding judgments of this kind; and therefore one cannot subject such judgments to scrutiny. We reject this view. It is unfounded from both a legal and a public point of view. From a legal standpoint, it is a well known rule, and attested by many rulings of the Supreme Court (sitting in its capacity as the High Court of Justice), that any judgment of a public authority, including that of ministers, is subject to scrutiny and examination in court. Decisions made on the basis of unwarranted, irrelevant, arbitrary, unreasonable, or immaterial considerations have more than once been disqualified by the courts.

In examining the considerations that served as the basis for decisions, the court never distinguished between the obligations of a minister and those of any other public authority. The fact that there exists no hard and fast law stating that a public authority must reach its decision on the basis of correct and reasonable considerations after examining all matters brought before it in a proper manner, has not prevented the courts from imposing obligations of this sort on every public authority.

This has no bearing on the principle that the court does not substitute its own judgment for the judgment of the public authority and usually does not intervene in the policy that the authority sets for itself.

This is all the more reason for rejecting the above-mentioned view when the matter under discussion is the deliberations of a commission of inquiry that is obligated to consider not necessarily the legal aspects of the subject but also, and occasionally primarily, its public and moral aspects. The absence of any hard and fast law regarding various matters does not exempt a man whose actions are subject to the scrutiny of a commission of inquiry from accountability, from a public standpoint, for his deeds or failures that indicate inefficiency on his part, lack of proper attention to his work, or actions executed hastily, negligently, unwisely, or shortsightedly when —

considering the qualifications of the man who holds a certain office and the personal qualities demanded of him in fulfilling his duties — he should have acted perspicaciously. No commission of inquiry would fulfill its role properly if it did not exercise such scrutiny, in the framework of its competence, vis-a-vis any man whose actions and failures were under scrutiny, regardless of his position and public standing.

In conclusion, regarding personal responsibility, we will not draw a distinction between the political echelon and any other echelon.

Personal Responsibility

In accordance with a resolution adopted by the Commission on 24.11.82, notices were sent under Section 15(A) of the Commissions of Inquiry Law, 1968, to nine persons regarding the harm liable to be done to them by the inquiry and its results. We shall now consider the matter of each of those who received such a notice.

The Prime Minister, Mr. Menachem Begin

The notice sent to the Prime Minister, Mr. Menachem Begin, stated that he was liable to be harmed if the Commission were to determine "that the Prime Minister did not properly weigh the part to be played by the Lebanese Forces during and in the wake of the I.D.F.'s entry into West Beirut, and disregarded the danger of acts of revenge and bloodshed by these forces vis-a-vis the population in the refugee camps."

The Prime Minister's response to the notice stated that in the conversations between him and the Defense Minister in which the decision was taken to have I.D.F. units enter West Beirut, and in the conversations he had held with the Chief of Staff during the night between 14.9.82 and 15.9.82, nothing at all was said about a possible operation by the Lebanese Forces.

The Prime Minister testified that only in the Cabinet session of 16.9.82 did he hear about the agreement with the Phalangists that they would operate in the camps, and that until then, in all the conversations he had held with the Defense Minister and with the Chief of Staff, nothing had been said about the role of the Phalangists or their participation in the operations in West Beirut. He added that since this matter had not come up in the reports he received from the Defense Minister and the Chief of Staff, he had raised no questions about it. The Prime Minister's remarks in this regard are consistent with the testimony of the Defense Minister and the Chief of Staff, and with the existing documents concerning the content of the conversations with the Prime Minister. We have described above the two conversations between the Prime Minister and the Defense Minister from the roof of the forward command post on Wednesday, 15.9.82, in the morning hours. According to the testimony and the notes of those conversations, the matter of the Phalangists was not mentioned in them at all. In a further conversation between the Defense Minister and the Prime Minister, on Wednesday at 18.00 hours, nothing was said about the participation of the Phalangists in the entry into Beirut. Similarly, on Thursday, 16.9.82, when the Defense Minister spoke by phone with the Prime Minister during the discussion in the Defense Minister's office, the Defense Minister said nothing about the Phalangists. According to the content of the conversation (see Exhibit 27), his report to the Prime Minister was in an optimistic vein: that the fighting had ended, the I.D.F. held all the key points, and it was all over. The only mention of the camps in that conversation was that they were encircled.

We may certainly wonder that the participation of the Phalangists in the entry to West Beirut and their being given the task of "mopping up" the camps seemed so unimportant that the Defense Minister did not inform the Prime Minister of it and did not get his assent for the decision; however, that question does not bear on the responsibility of the Prime Minister. What is clear is that the Prime Minister was not a party to the decision to have the Phalangists move into the camps, and that he received no report about that decision until the Cabinet session on the evening of 16.9.82.

We do not believe that we ought to be critical of the Prime Minister because he did not on his own initiative take an interest in the details of the operation of the entry into West Beirut, and did not discover, through his own questions, that the Phalangists were taking part in that operation. The tasks of the Prime Minister are many and diverse, and he was entitled to rely on the optimistic and calming report of the Defense Minister that the entire operation was proceeding without any hitches and in the most satisfactory manner.

We have cited above passages from remarks made at the Cabinet session of 16.9.82, during which the Prime Minister learned that the Phalangists had that evening begun to operate in the camps. Neither in that meeting nor afterward did the Prime Minister raise any opposition or objection to the entry of the Phalangists into the camps. Nor did he react to the remarks of Deputy Prime Minister Levy which contained a warning of the danger to be expected from the Phalangists' entry into the camps. According to the Prime Minister's testimony, "no one conceived that atrocities would be committed...simply, none of us, no Minister, none of the other participants supposed such a thing..." (p. 767).The Prime Minister attached no importance to Minister Levy's remarks because the latter did not ask for a discussion or a vote on this subject. When Minister Levy made his remarks, the Prime Minister was busy formulating the concluding resolution of the meeting, and for this reason as well, he did not pay heed to Minister Levy's remarks.

We have already said above, when we discussed the question of indirect responsibility, that in our view, because of things that were well known to all, it should have been foreseen that the danger of a massacre existed if the Phalangists were to enter the camps without measures being taken to prevent them from committing acts such as these. We are unable to accept the Prime Minister's remarks that he was absolutely unaware of such a danger. According to what he himself said, he told the Chief of Staff on the night between 14 and 15 September 1982, in explaining the decision to have the I.D.F. occupy positions in West Beirut, that this was being done "in order to protect the Moslems from the vengeance of the Phalangists," and he could well suppose that after the assassination of Bashir, the Phalangists' beloved leader, they would take revenge on the terrorists. The Prime Minister was aware of the mutual massacres committed in Lebanon during the civil war, and of the Phalangists' feelings of hate for the Palestinians, whom the Phalangists held responsible for all the calamities that befell their land. The purpose of the I.D.F.'s entry into West Beirut — in order to prevent bloodshed — was also stressed by the Prime Minister in his meeting with Ambassador Draper on 15.9.82. We are prepared to believe the Prime Minister that, being preoccupied at the Cabinet session with formulating the resolution, he did not pay heed to the remarks of Minister Levy, which were uttered following lengthy reviews and discussions. However, in view of what has already been noted above regarding foresight and probability of acts of slaughter, we are unable to accept the position of the Prime Minister that no one imagined that what happened was liable to happen, or what follows from his remarks: that this possibility did not have to be foreseen when the decision was taken to have the Phalangists move into the camps.

As noted, the Prime Minister first heard about the Phalangists' entry into the camps about 36 hours after the decision to that effect was taken, and did not learn of the decision until the Cabinet session. When he heard about the Phalangists' entry into the camps, it had already taken place. According to the "rosy" reports the Prime Minister received from the Defense Minister and the Chief of Staff, the Prime Minister was entitled to assume at that time that all the operations in West Beirut had been performed in the best possible manner and had nearly been concluded. We believe that in these circumstances it was not incumbent upon the Prime Minister to object to the Phalangists' entry into the camps or to order their removal. On the other hand, we find no reason to exempt the Prime Minister from responsibility for not having evinced, during or after the Cabinet session, any interes [sic] in the Phalangists' actions in the camps. It has already been noted above that no report about the Phalangists' operations reached the Prime Minister, except perhaps for the complaint regarding the Gaza Hospital, until he heard the BBC broadcast towards evening on Saturday. For two days after the Prime Minister heard about the Phalangists' entry, he showed absolutely no interest in their actions in the camps. This indifference would have been justifiable if we were to accept the Prime Minister's position that it was impossible and unnecessary to foresee the possibility that the Phalangists would commit acts of revenge; but we have already explained above that according to what the Prime Minister knew, according to what he heard in the Thursday cabinet session, and according to what he said about the purpose of the move into Beirut, such a possibility was not unknown to him. It may be assumed that a manifestation of interest by him in this matter, after he had learned of the Phalangists' entry, would have increased the alertness of the Defense Minister and the Chief of Staff to the need to take appropriate measures to meet the expected danger. The Prime Minister's lack of involvement in the entire matter casts on him a certain degree of responsibility.

The Minister of Defense, Mr. Ariel Sharon

The notice sent to the Minister of Defense under Section 15(A) stated that the Minister of Defense might be harmed if the commission determined that he ignored or disregarded the danger of acts of revenge or bloodshed perpetrated by Lebanese forces against the population of the refugee camps in Beirut and did not order the adoption of the withdrawal of the Lebanese forces from the refugee camps as quickly as possible and the adoption of measures to protect the population in the camps when information reached him about the acts of killing or excesses that were perpetrated by the Lebanese forces.

In his testimony before us, and in statements he issued beforehand, the Minister of Defense also adopted the position that no one had imagined the Phalangists would carry out a massacre in the camps and that it was a tragedy that could not be foreseen. It was stressed by the Minister of Defense in his testimony, and argued in his behalf, that the director of Military Intelligence, who spent time with him and maintained contact with him on the days prior to the Phalangists' entry into the camps and at the time of their entry into the camps, did not indicate the danger of a massacre, and that no warning was received from the Mossad, which was responsible for the liaison with the Phalangists and also had special knowledge of the character of this force.

It is true that no clear warning was provided by military intelligence or the Mossad about what might happen if the Phalangist forces entered the camps, and we will relate to this matter when we discuss the responsibility of the director of Military Intelligence and the head of the Mossad. But in our view, even without such warning, it is impossible to justify the Minister of Defense's disregard of the danger of a massacre. We will not repeat here what we have already said above about the widespreaed knowledge regarding the Phalangists' combat ethics, their feelings of hatred toward the Palestinians, and their leaders' plans for the future of the Palestinians when said leaders would assume power. Besides this general knowledge, the Defense Minister also had special reports from his not inconsiderable [number of] meetings with the Phalangist heads before Bashir's assassination.

Giving the Phalangists the possibility of entering the refugee camps without taking measures for continuous and concrete supervision of their actions there could have created a grave danger for the civilian population in the camps even if they had been given such a possibility before Bashir's assassination; thus this danger was certainly to have been anticipated — and it was imperative to have foreseen it — after Bashir's assassination. The fact that it was not clear which organization had caused Bashir's death was of no importance at all, given the known frame of mind among the combatant camps in Lebanon. In the circumstances that prevailed after Bashir's assassination, no prophetic powers were required to know that concrete danger of acts of slaughter existed when the Phalangists were moved into the camps without the IDF's being with them in that operation and without the IDF being able to maintain effective and ongoing supervision of their actions there. The sense of such a danger should have been in the consciousness of every knowledgeable person who was close to this subject, and certainly in the consciousness of the Defense Minister, who took an active part in everything relating to the war. His involvement in the war was deep, and the connection with the Phalangists was under his constant care. If in fact the Defense Minister, when he decided that the Phalangists would enter the camps without the IDF taking part in the operation, did not think that that decision could bring about the very disaster that in fact occurred, the only possible explanation for this is that he disregarded any apprehensions about what was to be expected because the advantages — which we have already noted — to be gained from the Phalangists' entry into the camps distracted him from the proper consideration in this instance.

As a politician responsible for Israel's security affairs, and as a Minister who took an active part in directing the political and military moves in the war in Lebanon, it was the duty of the Defense Minister to take into account all the reasonable considerations for and against having the Phalangists enter the camps, and not to disregard entirely the serious consideraton mitigating against such an action, namely that the Phalangists were liable to commit atrocities and that it was necessary to forestall this possibility as a humanitarian obligation and also to prevent the political damage it would entail. From the Defense Minister himself we know that this consideration did not concern him in the least, and that this matter, with all its ramifications, was neither discussed nor examined in the meetings and discussions held by the Defense Minister. In our view, the Minister of Defense made a grave mistake when he ignored the danger of acts of revenge and bloodshed by the Phalangists against the population in the refugee camps.

We have already said above that we do not assert that the decision to have the Phalangists enter the camps should under no circumstances ever have been made. It appears to us that no complaints could be addressed to the Defense Minister in this matter if such a decision had been taken after all the relevant considerations had been examined; however, if the decision were taken with the awareness that the risk of harm to the inhabitants existed, the obligation existed to adopt measures which would ensure effective and ongoing supervision by the IDF over the actions of the Phalangists at the site, in such a manner as to prevent the danger or at least reduce it considerably. The Defense Minister issued no order regarding the adoption of such measures. We shall not dwell here on what steps might have been taken; this we shall consider below. Regarding the responsibility of the Minister of Defense, it is sufficient to assert that he issued no order to the IDF to adopt suitable measures. Similarly, in his meetings with the Phalangist commanders, the Defense Minister made no attempt to point out to them the gravity of the danger that their men would commit acts of slaughter. Although it is not certain that remarks to this effect by the Defense Minister would have prevented the acts of massacre, they might have had an effect on the Phalangist commanders who, out of concern for their political interests, would have imposed appropriate supervision over their people and seen to it that they did not exceed regular combat operations. It was related above that a few hours after the Phalangists entered the camps, soldiers at the site asked what do to do with the people who had fallen into their hands, and the replies they were given not only did not bar them from harming those people, but even urged them to do so. It is a highly reasonble [sic] assumption that had the commanders who gave that reply heard from the Defense Minister or from higher Phalangist commanders a clear and explicit order barring harm to civilians and spelling out the damage this was liable to cause the Phalangists, their reply to these questions would have been different.

Had it become clear to the Defense Minister that no real supervision could be exercised over the Phalangist force that entered the camps with the I.D.F.'s assent, his duty would have been to prevent their entry. The usefulness of the Phalangists' entry into the camps was wholly disproportionate to the damage their entry could cause if it were uncontrolled. A good many people who heard about the Phalangists' entry into the camps were aware of this even before the first reports arrived about the massacre. The Chief of Staff in effect also held the same opinion, as emerges from his reply to a question whether he would have issued orders for additional measures to be taken or would have sufficed with the steps that were in fact taken, had it been expected that the Phalangists would commit excesses. He replied as follows (p.1677):

"No, if I had expected that this was liable to happen, or if someone had warned me that this was liable to happen, they would not have entered the camps."

In reply to another question, whether he would have taken additional measures, the Chief of Staff said:

"They would not have entered the camps; I would not have allowed them to enter the camps."

Asked if he would not have allowed the Phalangists to enter the camps despite the aim of having them operate together with the I.D.F. and spare the I.D.F. losses, the Chief of Staff replied:

"Then maybe we should have acted differently, by closing the camps, by surrounding them, or bringing them to surrender in another week or in another few days, or shelling them with all our might from the air and with artillery. As for me, if I had anticipated that this is what would happen, or if such a warning had been given, they would not have entered the camps."

And the Chief of Staff added that if he had suspected or feared that what happened would happen, "they would not have entered the camps at all, they would not have come anywhere near the camps." We quote these remarks here in order to show that despite the usefulness of having the Phalangists enter the camps, that step should have been abandoned if a massacre could not have been prevented using the means in the I.D.F.'s hands.

We do not accept the contention that the Defense Minister did not need to fear that the Phalangists would commit acts of killing because in all outward aspects they looked like a disciplined and organized army. It could not be inferred from the Phalangists' orderly military organization that their attitude toward human life and to the non-combatant population had basically changed. It might perhaps be inferred from their military organization that the soldiers would heed the orders of their commanders and not break discipline; but at the very least, care should have been taken that the commanders were imbued with the awareness that no excesses were to be committed and that they give their men unequivocal orders to this effect. The routine warnings that I.D.F. commanders issued to the Phalangists, which were of the same kind as were routinely issued to I.D.F. troops, could not have a had any concrete effect.

We shall remark here that it is ostensibly puzzling that the Defense Minister did not in any way make the Prime Minister privy to the decision on having the Phalangists enter the camps.

It is our view that responsibility is to be imputed to the Minister of Defense for having disregarded the danger of acts of vengeance and bloodshed by the Phalangists against the population of the refugee camps, and having failed to take this danger into account when he decided to have the Phalangists enter the camps. In addition, responsibility is to be imputed to the Minister of Defense for not ordering appropriate measures for preventing or reducing the danger. [sic] of massacre as a condition for the Phalangists' entry into the camps. These blunders constitute the nonfulfillment of a duty with which the Defense Minister was charged.

We do not believe that responsibility is to be imputed to the Defense Minister for not ordering the removal of the Phalangists from the camps when the first reports reached him about the acts of killing being committed there. As was detailed above, such reports initially reached the Defense Minister on Friday evening; but at the same time, he had heard from the Chief of Staff that the Phalangists' operation had been halted, that they had been ordered to leave the camps, and that their departure would be effected by 5:00 A.M. Saturday. These preventive steps might well have seemed sufficient to the Defense Minister at that time, and it was not his duty to order additional steps to be taken, or to have the departure time moved up, a step which was of doubtful feasibility.

The Foreign Minister Mr. Yitzhak Shamir

The Foreign Minister, Mr. Yitzhak Shamir, was sent a notice under Section 15(A) that he might be harmed if the commission determined that after he heard from Minister Zipori on 17.9.82 of the report regarding the Phalangists' actions in the refugee camps, he did not take the appropriate steps to clarify whether this information was based in fact and did not bring the information to the knowledge of the Prime Minister or the Minister of Defense.

In the memorandum that the Foreign Minister submitted to us in response to the aforementioned notice, he explained that what he had heard from Minister Zipori about the "unruliness" of the Phalangists did not lead him to understand that it was a matter of a massacre; he thought, rather, that it was a matter of fighting against terrorists. Since he knew that many of them had remained in Beirut, together with their weapons, he could have had the impression from Minister Zipori's statement that perhaps the Phalangists' combat operations were carried out in a manner that differed from the way a battle was conducted by the I.D.F., but he did not understand that a massacre of civilians, women and children, was taking place. The Foreign Minister also explained his attitude to Minister Zipori's statement by stating that he knew that Minister Zipori had been long and consistently opposed to cooperation with the Phalangists, and he was also known in the Cabinet as a constant critic of the Minister of Defense, the Chief of Staff, and their actions. For these reasons the Foreign Minister restricted himself to asking a member of his ministry's staff whether there was any news from West Beirut and satisfied himself that there was no need for further investigation after the Minister of Defense and others responsible for security affairs came to his office and did not mention that anything extraordinary had occurred in Beirut.

It is not easy to decide between the conflicting versions of what Minister Zipori said to the Foreign Minister. We tend to the opinion that in the telephone conversation Minister Zipori spoke of a "slaughter" being perpetrated by the Phalangists, and it is possible that he also spoke of "unruliness." He had heard from the journalist Ze'ev Schiff of reports that a massacre was going on in the camps and had treated Schiff's information seriously; and it is difficult to find a reason why he would not have told the Foreign Minister what he had heard when the point of the telephone communication was to inform the Foreign Minister what he had learned from Schiff. Mr. Schiff, in a statement he has submitted, confirms Minister Zipori's version. Nevertheless, we are unable to rule out the possibility that the Foreign Minister did not catch or did not properly understand the significance of what he heard from Minister Zipori. The Foreign Minister likewise did not conceal that in relating to what Minister Zipori had told him, he was influenced by his knowledge that Minister Zipori was opposed to the policy of the Minister of Defense and the Chief of Staff regarding the war in Lebanon, and particularly to cooperation with the Phalangists.

The phenomenon that came to light in this case — namely, that the statement of one minister to another did not receive the attention it deserved because of faulty relations between members of the Cabinet — is regrettable and worrisome. The impression we got is that the Foreign Minister did not make any real attempt to check whether there was anything in what he had heard from Minister Zipori on the Phalangists' operations in the camps because he had an *a priori* skeptical attitude toward the statements of the minister who reported this information to him. It is difficult to find a justification for such disdain for information that came from a member of the Cabinet, especially under the circumstances in which the information was reported. As stated, the conversation between the two ministers was preceded by a Cabinet meeting on 16.9.82 at which Minister Levy had expressed a warning of the danger involved in sending the Phalangists into the camps. That Friday was the end of a week in which dramatic events had occurred, and the situation as a whole was permeated with tension and dangers. In this state of affairs, it might have been expected that the Foreign Minister, by virtue of his position, would display sensitivity and alertness to what he had heard from another minister — even if we were to accept unconditionally his statement that the point under discussion was only the "unruliness" of the Phalangists. The Foreign Minister should at least have called the Defense Minister's attention to the information he had received and not contented himself with asking someone in his office whether any new information had come in from Beirut and with the expectation that those people coming to his office would know what was going on and would tell him if anything out of the ordinary had happened. In our view, the Foreign Minister erred in not taking any measures after the conversation with Minister Zipori in regard to what he had heard from Zipori about the Phalangist actions in the camps.

The Chief of Staff, Lieutenant General Rafael Eitan

The notice sent to the Chief of Staff, Lieutenant General Rafael Eitan, according to Section 15(A), detailed a number of findings or conclusions that might be harmful to the Chief of Staff if the commission established them.

The first point in the notice has to do with the Chief of Staff disregarding the danger of acts of vengeance and bloodshed being perpetrated by the Phalangists against the population of the refugee camps and his failure to take the appropriate measures to prevent this danger. In this matter, the Chief of Staff took a position similar to that the Minister of Defense which was discussed above and which we have rejected. The Chief of Staff stated in his testimony before us that it had never occurred to him that the Phalangists would perpetrate acts of revenge and bloodshed in the camps. He justified this lack of foresight by citing the experience of the past, whereby massacres were perpetrated by the Christians only before the "Peace for Galilee" War and only in response to the perpetration of a massacre by the Muslims against the Christian population, and by citing the disciplined conduct of the Phalangists' while carrying out certain operations after the I.D.F.'s entry into Lebanon. The Chief of Staff also noted the development of the Phalangists from a militia into an organized and orderly military force, as well as the interest of the Phalangist leadership, and first and foremost of Bashir Jemayel, in behaving moderately toward the Muslim population so that the president-elect could be accepted by all the communities in Lebanon. Finally, the Chief of Staff also noted, in justifying his position, that none of the experts in the I.D.F. or in the Mossad had expressed any reservations about the planned operation in the camps.

We are not prepared to accept these explanations. In our view, none of these reasons had the power to cancel out the serious concern that in going into the refugee camps, the Phalangist forces would perpetrate indiscriminate acts of killing. We rejected arguments of this kind in the part of this report that deals with indirect responsibility, as well as in our discussion of the responsibility borne by the Minister of Defense, and the reasons we presented there likewise hold for the Chief of Staff's position. Here we will restrict ourselves to brief reasoning.

Past experience in no way justified the conclusion that the entry of the Phalangists into the camps posed no danger. The Chief of Staff was well aware that the Phalangists were full of feelings of hatred towards the Palestinians and that their feelings had not changed since the "Peace for Galilee" War. The isolated actions in which the Phalangists had participated during the war took place under conditions that were completely different from those which arose after the murder of Bashir Jemayel; and as one could see from the nature of [those] operations, in the past there had been no case in which an area populated by Palestinian refugees had been turned over to the exclusive control of the Phalangists. On a number of occasions, the Chief of Staff had harsh and clear-cut things to say about the manner of fighting between the factions and communities in Lebanon, and about the concept of vengeance rooted in them; and in this matter we need only refer to the detailed facts presented in this report. We have already said a number of times that the traumatic event of the murder of Bashir Jemayel and of a group of Phalangists was sufficient reason to whip up the Phalangists. It is difficult to understand how it was possible to justify ignoring the effect of this event on arousing a feeling of vengeance and hatred toward all those who were inimical to the Phalangists, and first and foremost the Palestinians. The consideration that the military organization of the Phalangists and their orderly and disciplined appearance attested to a change in their mode of fighting was specious, and we have already pointed this out.

The absence of a warning from experts cannot serve as an explanation for ignoring the danger of a massacre. The Chief of Staff should have known and foreseen — by virtue of common knowledge, as well as the special information at his disposal — that there was a possibility of harm to the population in the camps at the hands of the Phalangists. Even if the experts did not fulfill their obligation, this does not absolve the Chief of Staff of responsibility.

The decision to send the Phalangists into the camps was taken by the Minister of Defense and the Chief of Staff, and the Chief of Staff must be viewed as a partner to this decision and as bearing responsibility both for its adoption and for its implementation. The Chief of Staff did not express any opposition to or reservation about the decision to the Minister of Defense, and no one disputed that it was taken with his consent. There is no reason to doubt that had the Chief of Staff expressed opposition or reservation, this fact would have borne serious weight in the consideration of the decision; and had there been a difference of opinion between him and the Minister of Defense, he could easily have brought the matter before the Prime Minister for his decision. It emerges quite clearly from the Chief of Staff's testimony, as cited above, that his opposition to sending the Phalangists into the camps would have meant that they would not have been sent in, and other means (which he detailed in the statement cited above) would have been adopted for taking control of the camps.

If the Chief of Staff did not imagine at all that the entry of the Phalangists into the camps posed a danger to the civilian population, his thinking on this matter constitutes a disregard of important considerations that he should have taken into account. Moreover, considering the Chief of Staff's own statements quoted above, it is difficult to avoid the conclusion that the Chief of Staff ignored this danger out of an awareness that there were great advantages to sending the Phalangists into the camps, and perhaps also out of a hope that in the final analysis, the Phalangist excesses would not be on a large scale. This conclusion is likewise prompted by the Chief of Staff's behavior during later stages, once reports began to come in about the Phalangists' excesses in the camps.

It has been argued by the Chief of Staff, and in his behalf, that appropriate steps were taken to avoid the danger. A similar claim has been made by Major General Drori and Brigadier General Yaron. In our opinion, this claim is unfounded.

As stated, one of the precautions was a lookout posted on the roof of the forward command post and on another roof nearby. It may be that this lookout was of value in obtaining certain military information on combat operations, but it was worthless in terms of obtaining information on the Phalangists' operations within the camps. Another step was taken to obtain information on exchanges over the communications sets between the Phalangist forces in the field and their commanders. It is difficult to regard this step as an efficient way to discover what was going on in the camps, because it was based on the assumption that what was said over the communications network would provide an accurate picture not only of the combat operations but also of any atrocities, and this assumption was not sufficiently grounded. It is true that the first reports of the massacres came from this source of information, but that was merely fortuitous; and just as questions had been asked about the fate of 45 to 50 people, it could have happened that such questions would not have gone over the communications network. As stated, the fact of 300 dead was not discovered as a result of listening in on the communications set; and it is a fact that whatever was said over these sets did not reveal the fact that the massacre of hundreds of people was going on in the camps. The final means whereby it was hoped that the Phalangists' operations in the camps would be revealed was by placing a Phalangist liaison officer on the roof of the forward command post and a liaison officer from the Mossad in the Phalangist headquarters. The obtaining of information from these two sources was likewise based upon unfounded assumptions. As to the Phalangist officer, there was no reason to believe that on his own initiative, he would tell the I.D.F. officers about the Phalangist operations, for he knew that the I.D.F. would vigorously oppose them if word of such operations came to its attention. While Phalangist liaison officer G. did tell of 300 dead, this was evidently a slip of the tongue on his part, for he immediately tried to play down the assessment by decreasing the number of casualties to 120. No information was received from the Mossad liaison officer; and the hope that he would be able to supply information of this sort was based on the unrealistic expectation that the Phalangist commanders would let him in on all the information that came in about the Phalangists' actions, even if it was a report on an action they knew the I.D.F. would vigorously oppose.

We asked the witnesses why an I.D.F. liaison officer was not attached to the Phalangist force that entered the camps, and we received the reply that there were two reasons: first, the point was that the I.D.F. should not enter the refugee camps, and the presence of an I.D.F. liaison officer would contradict that point; second, there was fear for the life of any such liaison officer, for obvious reasons. We are prepared to accept this explanation and have no criticism of the fact that this step was not adopted. On the other hand, no explanation was given for failing to provide special briefings to the I.D.F. units that were in the vicinity of the camps — something which should have been done, considering the importance of the matter.

The claim that every possible step was taken to obtain detailed information on the excesses of the Phalangists — in the event that such excesses would take place — is not congruent with the claim that such excesses were not foreseen at all.

But we do not wish to go into this logical contradiction, as in any case it is clear that the steps which were adopted fell far short of satisfying the need to know what was going on in the camps; and in fact, the truth about what was happening there only came out after the Phalangists left the camps.

We find that the Chief of Staff did not consider the danger of acts of vengeance and bloodshed being perpetrated against the population of the refugee camps in Beirut; he did not order the adoption of the appropriate steps to avoid this danger; and his failure to do so is tantamount to a breach of duty that was incumbent upon the Chief of Staff.

The other matter for which a notice was sent to the Chief of Staff under Section 15(A) was that when reports reached him about acts of killing or actions that deviated from usual combat operations, he did not check the veracity of these reports and the scope of these actions and did not order the cessation of the operations, the removal of the Phalangists from the camps as quickly as possible, and the adoption of steps to protect the population of the camps. In a meeting with the Phalangist commanders on the morning of 17.9.82, he approved the continuation of their operations until the morning of 18.9.82 and ordered that they be provided with assistance for that purpose.

As related in the description of the events in this report, the Chief of Staff first heard of the excesses perpetrated by the Phalangists when Major General Drori contacted him by phone on Friday morning. The Chief of Staff did not ask Major General Drori at that time what he knew about the excesses and what moved him to halt the Phalangist operation; and one should not take him to task for this, because he had decided to go to Beirut and preferred to clarify the matter during a personal visit, rather than try to clear it up in a phone conversation. On the other hand, it is difficult to understand or justify the Chief of Staff's actions after he reached Beirut, and especially during the meeting with the Phalangist commanders. Upon reaching Beirut, the Chief of Staff heard from Major General Drori what the latter knew about the Phalangist actions; he contented himself with this report and asked no question about this matter either of Major General Drori or of Brigadier General Yaron. If it is still possible to comprehend this reticence as stemming from the Chief of Staff's expectation that he would hear more exact details during his meeting with the Phalangist commanders, what took place at that meeting raises questions to which we have not found a reasonable answer. The Chief of Staff did not raise with the Phalangist commanders any question about the aberrant operations or the grave actions that might have been perpetrated in the camps. It is clear from his testimony that he thought that if any such actions had been perpetrated, the Phalangist commanders would have told him about them on their own initiative. There was no real basis for this naive belief. It is impossible to understand how the Chief of Staff concluded, from the fact that the Phalangist commanders told him nothing about the operations against the civilian population in the camps, that the suspicions that had arisen about those actions had no basis in reality.

The outstanding impression that emerges from the Chief of Staff's testimony is that his refraining from raising the issue of the Phalangists' excesses against the population in the camps stemmed from a fear of offending their honor; but this fear was out of place and should not have been a cause for the lack of any clarification of what had happened, when the Chief of Staff had gotten reports that should have served as a warning about the grave harm caused to the population in the camps and when, as a result of these reports, Major General Drori had issued an order to halt the advance of the Phalangists. Not only did the Chief of Staff not raise the subject of the Phalangists' behavior in the camps at the meeting which was called to clarify what was happening in the camps, but he expressed his satisfaction with the Phalangist operation and agreed to their request to provide them with tractors so they could complete their operations by Saturday morning. It is difficult to avoid the conclusion that this conduct on the Chief of Staff's part during the meeting at the Phalangists' headquarters stemmed from his disregard of the suspicions that the Phalangists were perpetrating acts of slaughter, and this disregard went so deep that even the information that had arrived in the meanwhile and reached the Chief of Staff did not shake it.

It emerges from the Chief of Staff's testimony that after the meeting with the Phalangists, he felt assured that everything was proceeding properly, that nothing out of the ordinary had happened that would require the immediate removal of the Phalangists from the camps, and that there was nothing wrong with — and perhaps there was benefit to be derived from — their completing their operation through Saturday morning. It is impossible to reconcile what we heard from the Chief of Staff regarding this matter with what he told the Minister of Defense in a phone conversation when he returned to Israel. We have already established above that in this conversation, the Chief of Staff told the Minister of Defense things about the conduct of the Phalangists that could have led the Minister of Defense to understand that the Phalangists had perpetrated the murder of civilians in the camps. But even if we go by the Chief of Staff's version of that conversation, according to which he said only that the Phalangists had "overdone it," it is difficult to reconcile this statement with the absence of all suspicion on his part regarding what had happened in the camps and the possibility of further similar actions.

Likewise, after the meeting, the Chief of Staff did not issue any order to Major General Drori or Brigadier General Yaron to prevent the entry of additional Phalangist forces or to send in or replace [Phalangist] forces, because he did not have the impression that there was any reason to stop them.

In our opinion, after the Chief of Staff received the information from Major General Drori in a telephone conversation that the Phalangists had "overdone it" and Major General Drori had halted their operation, this information should have alerted him to the danger that acts of slaughter were being perpetrated in the camps and made him aware of his obligation to take appropriate steps to clarify the matter and prevent the continuation of such actions if the information proved to be of substance. Toward that end, the Chief of Staff should have held a detailed clarification [session] with Major General Drori, Brigadier General Yaron, and other officers of the division, as well as with the Phalangist commanders, immediately upon his arrival in Beirut. If, as a result of this clarification, he was not satisfied that excesses had not been committed in the camps, he should have ordered the immediate removal of the Phalangist forces from the camp, admonished the Phalangist commanders about the aberrant actions, and demanded that they issue immediate orders to their forces to refrain from any act that would cause harm to civilians while they were still in the camp. None of these things were done by the Chief of Staff. On the contrary, the Phalangist commanders could have gotten the impression from the Chief of Staff's words and from his agreement to supply them with tractors that they could continue their operations in the camp without interference until Saturday morning and that no reports of excesses had reached the I.D.F. — and if they had reached the I.D.F., they had not roused any sharp reaction.

We determine that the Chief of Staff's inaction, described above, and his order to provide the Phalangist forces with tractors, or a tractor, constitute a breach of duty and dereliction of the duty incumbent upon the Chief of Staff.

Director of Military Intelligence Major General Yehoshua Saguy

In the notice sent to the Director of Military Intelligence, Major General Yehoshua Saguy, nonfulfillment of duty was ascribed to him because he did not give sufficient attention to the decision regarding sending the Phalangists into the camps and did not warn after the murder of Bashir Jemayel of the danger of acts of revenge and bloodshed by these forces against the Palestinian population in West Beirut, and especially in the refugee camps.

The Director of Military Intelligence testified that he did not know at all about the decision regarding the sending of the Phalangists into the camps and did not hear about the role assigned to the Phalangists in connection with the entry into Beirut until he discovered the matter in the cable regarding the 300 killed on Friday morning (17.9.82). We find it difficult to accept this claim. The decision regarding the sending of the Phalangists into the camps was discussed on the roof of the forward command post on Wednesday morning, 15.9.82, in conversations between the Minister of Defense, the Chief of Staff and Major General Drori; and we find it hard to believe that a decision discussed in these conversations did not at all reach the Director of Military Intelligence, who was present on the roof of the forward command post. According to the description of the detailed discussions which were held that morning on the roof of the forward command post, the Director of Military Intelligence had ample opportunities to hear on that occasion about the plans regarding the participation of the Phalangists in the entry to Beirut and about the role assigned to them. If indeed the Director of Military Intelligence did not hear then about the plan to send the Phalangists into the camps, then the only reason that can be given for this is that he was completely indifferent to what was being said and what was happening at that time on the roof of the forward command post, and showed no interest in the subjects which by virtue of his position should have interested him.

From the forward command post the Director of Military Intelligence traveled together with the Defense Minister to the meeting at Phalangist headquarters; and there the Defense Minister said that the Phalangist forces would enter West Beirut — though he apparently did not say explicitly that they would enter the camps. Regarding this meeting, Major General Saguy testified that it seems to him that it was said that the Phalangists should participate in something, but he does not remember exactly (p. 1561). After that meeting as well, the Director of Military Intelligence evinced no special interest in the question of what would be the role of the Phalangists in the entry into Beirut. He spent a considerable amount of time with the Defense Minister and did not find it necessary to pose any question to him regarding this matter. An additional meeting in which the Director of Military Intelligence could have, if he had wanted to, obtained information on the plans regarding the roles of the Phalangists in West Beirut took place at a gas station, after the condolence call in Bikfaya, when Major General Drori reported to the Defense Minister on the course of events during the I.D.F.'s entry into Beirut and showed him maps. This opportunity was also missed, for some reason, by the Director of Military Intelligence. An additional discussion in which the Director of Military Intelligence participated and in which the entry of the Phalangists into the camps was explicitly mentioned was in the meeting at the Defense Minister's office on Thursday, 16.9.82, at 10:00 A.M. According to Major General Saguy he did not pay attention to things said at that meeting on the sending of the Phalangists into the camps. The inattention [displayed] in this meeting as well is surprising and inexplicable. Major General Saguy was present at the beginning of the Cabinet meeting on Thursday evening and left the meeting a short time after it had begun. It has not been explained why Major General Saguy did not demonstrate sufficient interest in the role of the Phalangists in the entry into West Beirut and left the place without even trying to ascertain from anyone present there who knew what was happening in Beirut what the plan was for involving the Phalangists. To all this it should be added that already on Wednesday, 15.9.82, the assistant for research to the Director of Military Intelligence heard at a meeting in the office of the Deputy Chief of Staff about the plan that the Phalangists would enter the camps (p. 7 in exhibit 130).

We cannot believe that no information about the plan to send the Phalangists into the camps reached the Dirrector [sic] of Military Intelligence until Friday morning, keeping in mind that he was present at a number of meetings in which this plan was mentioned and he had ample opportunities to ascertain the role given to the Phalangists. Even if we were to unreservedly accept Major Saguy's testimony in this matter, his statements would have been surprising. The Director of Military Intelligence, who is required

to provide an intelligence assessment regarding the Phalangists, knows that
the I.D.F. is entering Beirut, knows that in the past there had been complaints about the noninvolvement of the Phalangists in the fighting, hears,
at the latest on Wednesday morning during the meeting at Phalangist headquarters, that these forces will cooperate with the I.D.F. in the entry into
West Beirut, he does not demonstrate any interest and does not raise any
question as to the role assigned them and does not make any comment to
the Defense Minister or the Chief of Staff on this matter in the meetings in
which he participated. The picture received according to the testimony of
Major General Saguy himself is of indifference and a conspicuous lack of
concern, of shutting of eyes and ears to a matter regarding which it was
incumbent on the director of the intelligence arm of the I.D.F. to open his
eyes and listen well to all that was discussed and decided.

The only explanation which can be found for the aforementioned behavior of the Director of Military Intelligence apparently lies in the fact that the
approach of the Director of Military Intelligence to the Phalangists and to
cooperation between Israel and these forces was much more skeptical than
the sympathetic approach of the Mossad, and that he knew that the Defense
Minister, Chief of Staff and perhaps also the Prime Minister accept the Mossad's approach, and Military Intelligence's approach had been rejected in
favor of the Mossad's approach. Therefore, the Director of Military Intelligence was satisfied with Intelligence reports compiled and sent on his behalf, in which, according to his claim, there is sufficient warning of the dangers to be expected from cooperation with the Phalangists.

In our opinion, the Director of Military Intelligence did not fulfill his
duty by [providing only] these situation evaluations. The verbal warning following the murder of Bashir, about which the Defense Minister testified,
was given rather weakly. According to Major General Saguy's testimony (pp.
105-106), he said in a telephone conversation with the Defense Minister on
the night of 14.9.82, when it became clear that Bashir had been killed, that
there were two possibilities: one, that there would be acts of revenge on the
part of the Phalangists; and two, that they would fall apart. It is difficult to
view these vague statements as a substantial warning. On 15.9.82, at about
18:00 hours, Intelligence Branch prepared a document (exhibit 26) bearing
the title, "Main Emphases for Situation Assessment," and the only thing said
there regarding the danger of acts of revenge by the Phalangists is that the
I.D.F.'s entry into West Beirut could "be received by some of the parties
involved, and perhaps even among some of the Muslim elements, as a development which might contribute, at least temporarily, to stability in the
city, and provide them with protection from possible acts of revenge by the
Phalangists" (paragraph 1-a in exhibit 26). This document cannot be considered a clear warning of the danger of involving the Phalangists in the
I.D.F.'s entry into Beirut or an indication of the need to take special precaution in order not to enable the Phalangists to carry out acts of revenge
against the Palestinians. In an additional Intelligence document which was

issued on 15.9.82 and bears the title "The Murder of Bashir Jemayel — Main Implications," it was said that "the assassination creates conditions for heightening the polarization between the rival Lebanese power elements, for mutual settling of accounts, and for deterioration, which, in the absence of a stabilizing element, is liable to develop into a general civil war" (paragraph 4, exhibit 25). Neither can this be considered a substantial warning which draws attention to the dangers of acts of revenge by the Phalangists entering West Beirut with the I.D.F. or in its wake.

The director of Military Intelligence said in his testimony that for the issue of sending the Phalangists into the camps to have been discussed and clarified properly, situation-assessment discussions ought to have been held to examine the various topics (which he enumerated in his testimony, p. 1587) connected with the Phalangists' entry into the camps. In his opinion, such a clarification could have been made within a short time; and had it emerged in such a discussion that it were possible to ensure the coordination with — and the command by — the I.D.F. "all the way," he would have supported the entry of the Phalangists, and not the I.D.F., into the camps. We accept these statements of his; but it appears to us that the director of Military Intelligence should have demonstrated sufficient interest in the matter in order to ascertain the role assigned the Phalangists, if for some reason he had not heard about it in the meetings in which he had participated; and it was incumbent upon him to demand that a clarification or discussion be held regarding those topics which he raised in his testimony before us. The fact which the director of Millitary Intelligence and his representatives point out, namely that the combat morals of the Phalangists and the massacres carried out in the past during the civil war in Lebanon were known to everyone, did not exempt the director of Military Intelligence from the fulfillment of his duties, especially when the issue was cooperation with the Phalangists after the murder of Bashir Jemayel — and this, even if there had not been an organized discussion of this matter.

Less so is there any satisfactory explanation for the lack of substantial action by the director of Military Intelligence in connection with the entry of the Phalangists into the camps, after he had heard on Friday morning not only about the entry of the Phalangist into the camps, but also about the killing of 300 persons in this operation. All he did was give an order to check the veracity of this report, and nothing else. He made no attempt to contact the Chief of Staff or the Defense Minister, to make them aware of the danger in the very operation of the Phalangists in the camps, especially after receipt of the report of the killing of 300 persons. Indeed, this report was unconfirmed, and he thought that it was from an Operations and not Intelligence source; but it contained information which could have confirmed his fears regarding actions by the Phalangists. In his testimony, the director of Military Intelligence explained why he had made no attempt to warn at that stage of the danger in the situation which had been created. His remarks on this matter are as follows:

"I am labelled as one who has always opposed the Phalangists, not from today, [but] for four years already. In the morning, I read that the Phalangists were inside the camps; and I know that this is as per the Defense Minister's orders — since I have the Duda'i document in hand — and that it is under the command of the I.D.F. So what could I say now? Why did you send it [sic] in without asking me? Or should I act insulted? No, I simply step aside in this matter. That's all."

We believe that in these remarks Major General Saguy revealed the main reason why he "stepped aside" regarding the whole issue; and these remarks of his explain not only his inaction after receiving the report on Friday, but also his behavior at previous stages, as we have described. In our opinion, it was the duty of the director of Military Intelligence, as loing as he occupies the post, to demonstrate alertness regarding the role of the Phalangists in the entry into Beirut after Bashir's assassination, to demand an appropriate clarification, and to explicitly and expressly warn all those concerned of the expected danger even prior to receipt of the report on Friday, and certainly after receipt of the report. The fear that his words would not receive sufficient attention and be rejected does not justify total inaction. This inaction constitutes breach of the duty incumbent on the director of Military Intelligence in this capacity.

Head of the Institute for Intelligence and Special Projects (Mossad)

The head of the Mossad was sent a notice under Section 15(A) of the law in which it is stated that he is liable to be harmed if the commission determines that he did not pay appropriate attention to the decision taken regarding the roles to be played by the Phalangists during the I.D.F.'s entry into West Beirut, and did not warn after the murder of Bashir Jemayel of the danger of bloodshed by these forces against the Palestinian population.

The head of the Mossad testified that he first learned of the role given to Phalangists to enter the camps, only at the cabinet meeting on Thursday 16.9.82. On Friday, 15.9.82, he received cables from the Mossad representative in Beirut (exhibits 161 and 162) in which it was reported to him about the meetings of the Chief of Staff and Defense Minister with the Phalangist elite; but in neither of these documents is there any report of the role given the Phalangists in the camps, but rather there is general mention in them that the Phalangists will enter West Beirut after the I.D.F. and will assist the I.D.F. in its operations. In a third cable (exhibit 163), sent on Thursday at 12:00, it was stated that there had been a coordination meeting with the G.O.C. to prepare the Phalangists "for operations to clear the city of terrorists." In an additional cable sent at that time (exhibit 164) it was said that the Phalangists would start work at the Burj el-Barajneh camp.

Apparently, the Mossad was not explicitly informed of the Phalangists' entry into the camps, and the head of the Mossad did not know of the decision which had been made on this matter. The testimony of the head of the Mossad should therefore be accepted, that only at the cabinet meeting of Thursday evening did he hear of the decision regarding the role of the Phalangists and of their entry into the camps, which by then had already taken place.

In the aforementioned circumstances it does not appear to us that the head of the Mossad was obligated, before knowing of the decision regarding the role of the Phalangists, to offer at his initiative an assessment regarding the situation which was liable to develop, if the Phalangists would be given the opportunity to take revenge on the Palestinians and attempt to carry out their plans for them in West Beirut. The head of the Mossad was present at the cabinet meeting until its conclusion. He heard what was said there, but did not himself give a situation assessment regarding the entry of the Phalangists into the camps, and did not express any reservation about this entry. He spoke at that meeting about the Mossad's assessment regarding the situation created after the murder of Bashir, but his remarks did not explicitly deal with the issue of the Phalangists' entry into the camps or with the problems which could ensue therefrom. A certain hint of the danger of irregular actions by the Phalangists can be found in the following remarks made by the head of the Mossad at that meeting (p. 26 in exhibit 122):

"When we learned of the death of Bashir — and this was close to midnight — we thought that there could be two phenomena: one, that the whole forest would catch fire, and the Phalangist forces themselves, which were suddenly left without a commander, [and] with a desire for revenge, could also have taken uncontrolled action; and on the other hand, those Palestinians and Lebanese organizations which were in West Beirut, when they suddenly learned that the leader of the Phalangists is dead and possibly the Phalangists have been weakened following this, it was possible that they would start up — i.e., there was definitely the possibility that a situation of total conflagration would flare up in the city."

These remarks should not be considered an unequivocal warning of the danger entailed in the entry of the Phalangists into the camps, an entry about which the head of the Mossad made no comment in the situation assessment which he gave at the cabinet meeting. The head of the Mossad did not express any reservation about the entry of the Phalangists into the camps. In his first testimony he said that had he been asked at that meeting about the entry of the Phalangists into the camps, he would have recommended this "with the warning that they not carry out a massacre" and with the belief that such a warning would be effective — and this, according to the Mossad's experience with certain operations carried out together with the Phalangists in the past (p. 173). In his additional testimony, the head of the Mossad said that the data which the Mossad had at the time of the cabinet meeting did not indicate and did not warn of the possibility of atrocities in the camps.

The data which he presented (p. 1428) were that according to the reports received, despite the murder of Bashir, the military commander of the Phalangists was in control of his forces; and in addition, according to the information which the Mossad had, the murder of Bashir was carried out not by the Palestinians but by the Mourabitoun. This last argument is far from convincing. It is not at all certain that the Phalangists knew at that time who carried out the assassination; and even if they had known this, it is most doubtful whether this would have moderated their actions against the Palestinians, whom they considered the source of all the tragedies which had befallen Lebanon, and who had cooperated with the Mourabitoun in the fighting against the Phalangists.

The question is whether this inaction by the head of the Mossad constitutes breach of a duty incumbent upon the head of the Mossad.

The answer to this question is not easy. As mentioned above, the view of the Mossad, which had been expressed for a fairly long period prior to the I.D.F.'s entry into Lebanon, as well as afterwards, was that there should be greater cooperation with the Phalangists. The view prevalent in the Mossad, as expressed in various documents, was that the Phalangists are a trustworthy element which can be relied upon, and this despite the Phalangists' past regarding their attitude to the Palestinians and their statements on the way to solve the Palestinian problem once they reach power. The head of the Mossad himself noted in part of his testimony mentioned above, that this approach of the Mossad was influenced by the development of subjective feelings by representatives of the Mossad, who were in constant contact with the leaders of the Phalangists. We do not believe that the head of the Mossad can be held responsible for the existence of such a "conception." He assumed the position of head of the Mossad only on 12.9.82 — that is, two days before the murder of Bashir. He had previously been the deputy head of the Mossad and was acquainted with the Mossad's affairs; but the responsibility for the way in which the Mossad operated was not his. The entry of the Phalangists into the camps did not contradict the Mossad's situation assessment; and therefore it is difficult to expect that the head of the Mossad would have reservations about this decision when he heard about it at the Cabinet meeting on 16.9.82. In this matter as well, it should be taken into account that he had then been serving as head of the Mossad for only four days, and that this was the first Cabinet meeting in which he participated in this capacity.

It appears to us, that even in the situation described above, the head of the Mossad was obligated to express his opinion at the Cabinet meeting on the entry of the Phalangists and deal in this expression of opinion with the dangers involved in the Phalangists' operations — especially after he had heard Minister David Levy's remarks. In consideration of all the aforementioned circumstances, it is our opinion that this inaction of the head of ths [sic] Mossad should not be considered serious.

G.O.C. Northern Command Major General Amir Drori

In the notification sent to G.O.C. Northern Command Amir Drori, it was stated that he is liable to be harmed if the commission determines that he did not take appropriate or sufficient steps to prevent the continuation of the Phalangists' actions in the refugee camps when he received reports of acts of killing or acts which deviate from regular combat operations which were carried out in the camps.

On Thursday night, the division intelligence officer transmitted the report of 300 killed to the Northern Command, but this report did not reach Major General Drori and he did not hear a thing about what was happening in the camps until Friday morning.

We have enumerated above the differences between the versions of Major General Drori and Brigadier General Yaron regarding the circumstances surrounding Major Drori's visit to the forward command post, the conversation which preceded this visit, and the conversation which took place during the visit. According to the testimony of Major General Drori, the visit was made at his initiative, without his knowing that any problem had arisen regarding the camps, while according to Brigadier General Yaron's version, Major General Drori's appearance was the result of a conversation in which Brigadier General Yaron reported his uneasy feelings regarding what was being done in the camps. We do not find that the differing versions on this subject are important in the matter before us.

Neither was there a uniform version regarding the reports transmitted to Major General Drori during his meeting at the forward command post. Colonel Duvdevani said in his statement that he had told Major General Drori about 100 killed in the Phalangists' operations; while according to Major General Drori's testimony, he did not hear in this visit about killing in the camps or about a specific number of killed. From Brigadier General Yaron's remarks it is apparent that he did not report to Major General Drori about the reports of the 300 killed and the 45 persons who had been captured by the Phalangists, since he had thought that these reports were unsubstantiated. Regarding the things Major General Drori heard from Brigadier General Yaron, Major General Drori's version differs only in unimportant details from Brigadier General Yaron's version. It appears to us that it is not possible to determine with sufficient certainly that clear reports were given to Major General Drori about killing in the camps. We believe, however, that in his testimony before us, Major General Drori belittled the importance and significance of the things about which he had heard in the meeting at the forward command post, as well as the impression these had made on him. It should be noted that Major General Drori was aware that the Phalangists were liable to act in an uncontrolled way, and this not necessarily from his conversation with an officer connected with the Lebanese Army on Thursday evening, but mainly from his knowledge of the Phalangists, based on his constant contact with them. There is therefore no room for doubt that after the conversations which he held on the roof of the forward command post on Friday morning, he was aware that the continuation of the Phalangists' actions in ths [sic] refugee camps posed a danger. Three actions which he took are evidence of this. The first — the order he gave regarding cessation of the Phalangists' actions; the second — a telephone report to the Chief of Staff that the Phalangists "had overdone it" and that he had ordered their operation stopped; and the third — the continuation of his efforts to impress upon the commander of the Lebanese Army that this army enter the camps instead of the Phalangists. Here we should mention that in this persuasion effort, Major General Drori told the commander of the Lebanese Army, "You know what the Lebanese are capable of doing to each other." These remarks, in the context in which they were made, in a section of Major General Drori's testimony as cited above, show that Major General Drori had realized the gravity of the matter and the need to make efforts to terminate the Phalangists' operations in the camps.

Taking into consideration that it has not been proved that Major General Drori had [received] explicit reports about acts of killing and about their extent, it appears to us that he acted properly, wisely, and responsibily [sic], with sufficient alertness at this stage. He heard from the Chief of Staff that the latter was to arrive in Beirut in the afternoon hours and could rely on the fact that this visit by the Chief of Staff, which was to take place within a few hours, would lead to positive results regarding the Phalangists' activity in the camps.

In the notification as per Section 15(A) of the law, Major General Drori was informed that he is liable to be harmed if it is determined that he did not warn the Chief of Staff when the latter arrived in Beirut on 17.9.82 of the danger posed to the population in the camps from the continued activity or continued presence of the Phalangists in the camps, and did not try — at a meeting with the Phalangist commanders, or shortly thereafter — to prevent the continuation of such activity.

According to the testimony of Major General Drori, it was clear that he was satisfied with an absolutely passive role regarding the issue of the Phalangists in the camps, from the time the Chief of Staff arrived in Beirut and later. Major General Drori did not emphasize to the Chief of Staff before the meeting with the Phalangist commanders that it was necessary to end the Phalangists' presence in the camps or take some kind of action which could ensure that the Phalangists' actions against the non-combatant populace would stop. This refraining from bringing the importance and seriousness of the matter to the attention of the Chief of Staff was explained by Major General Drori by the fact that after the meeting on the roof of the forward command post with Brigadier General Yaron, the acuteness of his sense of imminent danger diminished, for two reasons. The first reason was that a few hours had gone by before the Chief of Staff arrived, and no additional reports had come in. The second reason which calmed Major General Drori was that at his meeting with the commander of the Lebanese Army, he had not heard anything about irregular occurences in the camps, despite the fact that the Lebanese Army was deployed around the camps, including at the places where the Phalangists had entered, and Lebanese

Army personnel should have known if something unusual had happened in the camps (Major General Drori's testimony, pp. 1611-1615).

These reasons for the diminished sense of the matter's importance are not convincing. It is difficult to consider the lack of additional reports a calming factor, when only few hours are involved and when Major General Drori made no special efforts, while on the roof of the forward command post and while speaking with the officers there, to investigate and testify the details of the reports reaching him, and did not give orders to conduct special checks on what was going on in the camps. He also did not speak during the meeting on the roof of the forward command post with the Phalangists' liaison officer, who was present there. At the meeting with the commander of the Lebanese Army, Major General Drori did not ask whether the commander had any reports on events in the camps, but drew his conclusion which reduced his alertness solely from the fact that this commander did not "volunteer" any information.

We described above what happened at the meeting with the Phalangist commanders, in which the subject of the Phalangist forces' behavior in the camps did not come up at all. In our opinion, even though the Chief of Staff conducted the meeting for the Israeli side, it was Major General Drori's duty to at least make an attempt to raise the issue at this meeting. He also made no attempt to persuade the Chief of Staff to raise the matter at the meeting with the Phalangists, but was satisfied with sitting idly by. Major General Drori is a senior commander with a very important task, who bears heavy responsibility for events on a wide front. A commander at such a level and rank should be expected to take the initiative when he sees that the Chief of Staff does not intend to deal with the issue which was the main cause of his coming to Beirut and holding a meeting with the Phalangist staff. If this passive behavior by Major General Drori was the result of a significant decline in his alertness during the time which had gone by since ordering a halt to the Phalangists' operations, then we have already said above that this reduced alertness was not at all justified. Also, after the conclusion of the meeting with the Phalangist commanders, Major General Drori did nothing about the behavior of the Phalangists and did not raise the matter for discussion with the Chief of Staff. The Phalangists' request that the I.D.F. supply them with tractors should have increased the suspicion that actions which are difficult to describe as combat operations were being carried out in the camps; and apparently this suspicion arose, since the order was to provide the Phalangists with only one tractor and remove the I.D.F. markings from it. We cannot find justification for Major General Drori's disengagement from any treatment of the subject of Phalangist behavior, from the moment the Chief of Staff arrived in Beirut and until after the departure of the Phalangists from the camps.

We determine that it was the duty of the G.O.C. to warn the Chief of Staff when the latter arrived in Beirut on 17.9.82 and during the rest of the Chief of Staff's stay in Beirut, that the population in the camps is endangered by the continued presence of the Phalangist forces in the camps, and that they should be removed from there immediately — or that at least steps be taken to ensure the safety of the population in the camps or to reduce the danger they face to the barest possible minimum. Major General Drori's refraining from any action regarding the danger facing the civilian population from the Phalangist forces, from the time the Chief of Staff arrived in Beirut and until Saturday, 18.9.82, constitutes, in our opinion, a breach of the duty which was incumbent on Major General Drori.

Division Commander Brigadier General Amos Yaron

The first issue specified in the notice sent to Brigadier General Amos Yaron under section 15(A) of the law is that Brigadier General Yaron did not properly evaluate and did not check reports that reached him concerning acts of killing and other irregular actions of the Phalangists in the camps, did not pass on that information to the G.O.C. and to the Chief of Staff immediately after it had been received on 16.9.82, and did not take the appropriate steps to stop the Phalangists' actions and to protect the population in the camps immediately upon receiving the reports.

We determined in the specification of the facts that Brigadier General Yaron received reports of acts of killing in the evening and night hours of 16.9.82. He received the first report from Lieutenant Elul, and from it it should have been clear to him that the Phalangists were killing women and children in the camps. Brigadier General Yaron heard an additional report that same evening from the division intelligence officer concerning the fate of the group of 45 people who were in the Phalangists' hands. A third report was delivered by the Phalangists' liaison officer, G., about 300 killed, a number which was later reduced to 120. Even if we suppose that the first and second report were considered by Brigadier General Yaron to be about the same event, nevertheless, from all the reports, it became known to Brigadier General Yaron that the Phalangists were perpetrating acts of killing which went beyond combat operations, and were killing women and children as well. That evening he was satisfied with reiterating the warnings to the Phalangists' liaison officer and to Elie Hobeika not to kill women and children; but beyond that he did nothing to stop the killing. He did not pass on the information that he had received to Major General Drori that evening nor on the following day in the morning call, nor when they met before noon. When Brigadier General Yaron heard from the division intelligence officer, in the briefing on 16.9.82, about the report indicating the danger that women and children were being killed, he interrupted him — and it appears from the transcript of the conversation that took place then that Brigadier General Yaron wished to play down the importance of the matter and to cut off the clarification of the issue at that briefing. Brigadier General Yaron testified that he was, indeed, aware that the Phalangists' norms of behavior during wartime are different from those of the I.D.F.

and that there is no sense in arguing with them to change their combat ethics; but since in previous Phalangist operations conducted jointly with the I.D.F. they had not behaved aberrantly, he trusted that his reiterated warnings not to kill women and children would suffice, the Phalangist commanders' promises would be kept, and the steps that he had taken in order to obtain information on the Phalangists' operations would enable him to follow their actions. We are not prepared to accept this explanation. We have already determined that the means of supervision over what the Phalangists were doing in the camps could not ensure the flow of real and immediate information on their actions. It is difficult to understand how Brigadier General Yaron relied on these warnings and assurances, when he knew about the Phalangists' combat ethics. He also did not take into account the influence of the assassination of Bashir on the fanning of the Phalangists' feelings of revenge. Already shortly after the Phalangists' entrance into the camps, he started receiving reports which should have clarified to him the gravity of the danger of a massacre being perpetrated in the camps and which should have spurred him to take immediate steps, whether on his own cognizance or by authorization from the G.O.C. or the Chief of Staff, to prevent the continuation of operations of these kinds. No action was taken by Brigadier General Yaron, and neither did he see to conveying the information in his possession to his superiors.

An additional explanation by which Brigadier General Yaron tried to justify his behavior was that in the situation which existed that night, the reports about 300, or fewer, killed did not seem to him sufficiently important to spur him to check whether they were true, since on that night, in his role as division commander, he had combat problems which were much more important than the matter of the Phalangists in the camps (testimony of Brigadier General Yaron on p. 699). We cannot accept this explanation either. If Brigadier General Yaron could find the time to hold a briefing, he could also have issued orders to pass on the reports and to take appropriate measures such as were called for by the information received.

Perhaps it is possible to find an explanation for Brigadier General Yaron's refraining from any substantial reaction to the serious information which had reached him Thursday evening in that he was interested that the Phalangists continue to operate in the camps so that I.D.F. soldiers would not have to engage in fighting in that area. Brigadier General Yaron had no reservations about admitting the Phalangists into the camps; he testified that he was happy with this decision and explained his position in that "we have been fighting here for four months already and there is a place where they can take part in the fighting, the fighting serves their purposes as well, so let them participate and not let the I.D.F. do everything" (p. 695). It is possible to show understanding for this feeling, but it does not justify a lack of any action on the part of Brigadier General Yaron, considering the reports that had reached him.

During Friday as well, Brigadier General Yaron did not act properly with regard to the Phalangist operation in the camps. When he met with Major General Drori, he was obligated to report all the information that had reached him, but he did not do so. As a result of this failure, Major General Drori was not apprised of all the information that had reached the division by that time. A number of times, Brigadier General Yaron approached the Phalangist officers who were at the forward command post, including Elie Hobeika and repeated the admonition not to do harm to women and children; but other than this he did not take any initiative and only suggested that the Phalangists be ordered not to advance — and an order to this effect was issued by Major General Drori. This order might have been regarded as enough of a precaution by Major General Drori, who had not heard about instances of killing; but Brigadier General Yaron should have known that halting the advance did not ensure an end to the killing.

The notice sent to Brigadier General Yaron under Section 15(A) also speaks of the failure to provide any warning to the Chief of Staff when the latter reached Beirut on 17.9.82, as well as of Brigadier General Yaron's granting the Phalangists permission to send a new force into the camps without taking any steps that would bring a stop to the excesses. When the Chief of Staff came to Beirut, Brigadier General Yaron did not tell him everything he had heard and did not make any suggestion to him about the continuation of the Phalangist operation in the camps. From the time he saw the Chief of Staff (after his arrival in Beirut) until the Chief of Staff left Beirut, no warning was heard from Brigadier General Yaron — not even a significant comment regarding the danger of a massacre. Brigadier General Yaron was not oblivious to this danger. We have evidence that on Friday he had spoken to the Phalangist liaison officer charging that his men were killing women and children (statement No. 23 by Colonel Agmon), but he did not express this awareness clearly in his meetings with Major General Drori and the Chief of Staff.

Brigadier General Yaron's inaction regarding the continuation of the Phalangist operation in the camps was epitomized by the fact that he did not issue any order to prevent them from replacing forces on Friday and did not impose any supervision on the movement of the Phalangist forces to and from the camps, despite the fact that the order halting the operation was not rescinded.

We have already cited Brigadier General Yaron's statement at the Senior Command Meeting in which he admitted with laudable candor that this was an instance of "insensitivity" on his part and on the part of others concerned. As we have already stated above, Brigadier General Yaron's desire was to save I.D.F. soldiers from having to carry out the operation in the camps, and this appears to be the main reason for his insensitivity to the dangers of the massacre in the camps. This concern of a commander for the welfare of his men would be praiseworthy in other circumstances; but considering the state of affairs in this particular instance, it was a thoroughly mistaken judgment on the part of Brigadier General Yaron, and a grave error was committed by a high-ranking officer of an I.D.F. force in this sector.

We determine that by virtue of his failings and his actions, Brigadier General Yaron committed a breach of the duties incumbent upon him by virtue of his position.

Mr. Avi Duda'i, Personal Aide to The Minister of Defense

The sole issue regarding which the notice was sent to Mr. Duda'i was "that on 17.9.82, during the morning hours or before noon, Mr. Duda'i received a report about killings that had been perpetrated by the Lebanese Forces in the refugee camps, and did not pass this report on to the Minister of Defense."

In his testimony, Mr. Duda'i denied that any report on what was happening in the camps was given him on 17.9.82. Yet Lieutenant Colonel Gai, an officer in the National Security Unit, testified before us that on Friday morning, 17.9.82, he was in the office of the director of Military Intelligence, where he met one of the officers who works in the office, Captain Moshe Sinai, who told him (according to Lt. Col. Gai) "as a piece of gossip" that about 300 persons had been killed in the camps in Beirut, and that, at around 11.00-11.30 that same day, he — Lt.Col. Gai — in one of his telephone conversations with Duda'i, told Duda'i what he had heard from Captain Sinai (testimony by Gai, pp. 921-923). In his second round of testimony, too, Gai stood by his story that he had passed this report on to Duda'i; except that according to his testimony, the report was not given at about 11.00 but rather at a later hour, between 12.30 — when Duda'i arrived at the Foreign Ministry, whence he spoke with Gai — and 15. 00 hours.

Lieutenant Colonel Hevroni, bureau chief of the director of Military Intelligence, testified that he had been with Duda'i at the Sde Dov airfield for a meeting that the Defense Minister had summoned there, [and] afterwards had come to Jerusalem with Duda'i for a meeting at the Foreign Minister's office which had lasted until 15.00 hours; and during that same period of time, Duda'i asked him what was happening regarding Gai's and Sinai's story — and the reply was that there was no verification of this report. It was clear to Hevroni from this conversation that Duda'i had gotten the report which Gai had received from Sinai (testimony of Hevroni, pp. 876-877). We also heard additional testimony which was intended to show that post factum, Duda'i admitted, in the presence of Gai and the witness Colonel Kniazher (called Zizi), that Gai had told him about the report on Friday; but from Colonel Kniazher's testimony (pp. 1466-1468) it turns out that Gai wasn't present at the time he spoke with Duda'i, and Duda'i wasn't present at the time that Kniazher spoke with Gai (p. 1466); and there is no evidence in Kniazher's testimony that Duda'i had heard about the report from Gai on 17.9.82.

As has been said, an investigation was held in the director of Military Intelligence's bureau after the event, as a result of which an investigative report was drawn up (exhibit 29). In Paragraph 6 of this report, it is stated that the visit by Lt. Col. Gai between the hours of 7.30-8.00 was intended to clarify what had happened to two Military Intelligence documents which had not yet reached the Defense Minister.

From the testimonies we have heard, it becomes apparent that Gai's visit in the morning hours was for the purpose of receiving reports from Military Intelligence about that attack on the tank which had occurred in West Beirut. Gai did pay two visits to the director of Military Intelligence's bureau that same day, but this second visit was at about 11.00 hours and was carried out on an order that Duda'i transmitted by phone from Sde Dov to Gai, so that the latter would clarify the matter of the documents. This inaccuracy would indeed appear tiny, but it has a certain significance in that it fits in with testimonies that on that same Friday morning, Duda'i complained to those who work in his office, including Gai, that there were defects in the reporting of what was happening in Lebanon and that reports weren't reaching the Defense Ministry. Here it should be noted that on that same day, the Defense Minister's military adjutant was not in the office because he was on vacation, and Duda'i was taking his place.

In paragraph 13 of exhibit 29, it is said "that in retrospect (in reconstruction) it turned out that Lt. Col. Gai — after receiving the report from the bureau chief of the director of Military Intelligence — looked into the matter on the morning of 17 September with Operations Branch, after he, too, had gotten the impression that an operations report/occurrence was at issue; and in the investigation, he was told that Operations did not know about such an action by the Phalangists." In his testimony, Gai said that these statements were inaccurate, and that he had only inquired at Operations if there was anything new from Beirut and had received a negative reply. In paragraph 14 of exhibit 29, it is said that in a second update between minister's aide Avi Duda'i and Lt. Col. Gai, Duda'i reported that he had spoken with the bureau chief of the Director of Military Intelligence, who had told him that the report had not received verification from Military Intelligence personnel who had looked into the matter." What is said here was not confirmed by Lt. Col. Gai's testimony; and as mentioned, Duda'i denied receiving any report. The rather obvious general trend of exhibit 29 regarding the report to Gai is: to show that report on the contents of the cable on the 300 killed was conveyed from the Director of Military Intelligence's bureau to the Defense Minister's bureau. According to Lt. Col. Gai's testimony, the conversation between him and Captain Sinai cannot be viewed as more than "an exchange of gossip," and it is difficult to treat such a conversation as a proper act of conveying an important report.

Captain Sinai gave a statement to the staff investigators (No. 112) in which he said that he had read the cable (Appendix A, exhibit 29) in front of Lt. Col. Gai, and that the latter had reacted to it with the words, "Listen, that's very interesting" — and, as far as Sinai recalls, he said, "I spoke with the minister during the night, and I'll go talk with him in a little while; the story is very interesting, and the minister will be very happy to hear the report." According to Sinai, this is more or less the version he heard from Gai. We find it difficult to attribute importance to this statement. In his statement, Sinai gave exact details concerning a search for the two documents which preceded the conversation between Gai and himself, and at present it is already clear that he erred in this, because the search for the documents was not conducted in the early hours of the morning, but rather close to the hour of noon. It is not reasonable [to suppose that] if Gai did indeed receive Sinai's report as an interesting or important report, he would not immediately convey it to Duda'i, who on that same morning complained several times about a lack of reporting on what was happening in Lebanon and inquired after such reports from time to time.

It is our opinion that it cannot be determined that Gai did indeed pass on the contents of the above report to Duda'i on Friday. The doubt stems not only from contradictions revealed in the witnesses' statements, but also from [the fact] that the witnesses who told about the conveying of the report have an interest in showing that they fulfilled their obligation in transmitting the report from the director of Military Intelligence's bureau to the Defence Minister's aide. It is also difficult to treat Gai's testimony as testimony by someone who is a disinterested party in the matter, since it is his interest to show, after all that happened, that he did not keep the contents of the report he'd heard from Sinai to himself. Gai also did not give a satisfactory explanation as to why, according to his version, he had told Duda'i about this report only in the afternoon, despite the fact that Duda'i was constantly asking whether reports had come in from Lebanon and was complaining about a lack of reports. In view of the entire body of evidence, we do not determine the Duda'i indeed received the report about the 300 people killed on Friday, 17.9.82, and it therefore cannot be determined that he refrained from fulfilling an obligation which was incumbent upon him, as was stated in the notice of [possible] harm which was sent to him.

The Functioning of Establishments

Thus far we have dealt with the findings and conclusions regarding the course of events, and the responsibility for them of those persons whose actions had a decisive effect on the course of events. As we noted, we decided not to discuss the activities of other persons who were close to the course of events but who played a secondary role. All these persons, whether they had central or secondary roles, operated within organizational frameworks whose functioning was flawed.

In this section of the report we wish to dwell briefly on the flaws in the functioning of these organizational establishments. We shall devote only a few comments to this important topic, with the aim of pointing to a number of flaws which seem to us worrisome, and to bring about a situation in which all the responsible authorities — civil and military — will take all the requisite measures so that the reasons and causes for these flaws will be examined and analyzed, the lessons therefrom learned, and so that what requires amending will indeed be amended. As in this entire report, we shall deal only with the functioning of the various establishments from the time the decision was taken on the entry of the Phalangists into the camps until their departure. Within this framework, too, we shall offer our opinion only regarding outstanding matters which are especially noteworthy. Unquestionably, there were many establishments that functioned properly, even excellently; but in the nature of things our attention is directed toward those establishments in which were revealed flaws that are relevant to the subject of the commission's scrutiny. Hence, the major part of our attention is directed to two key topics which concern us: one is the flaws in the course of decision-taking by the policy-making institutions; the other is the flaws in the manner of handling the information which was received.

The decision on the entry of the Phalangists into the refugee camps was taken on Wednesday (15.9.82) in the morning. The Prime Minister was not then informed of the decision. The Prime Minister heard about the decision, together with all the other ministers, in the course of a report made by the Chief of Staff at the Cabinet session on Thursday (16.9.82) when the Phalangists were already in the camps. Thereafter, no report was made to the Prime Minister regarding the excesses of the Phalangists in the camps, and the Prime Minister learned about the events in the camps from a BBC broadcast on Saturday (18.9.82) afternoon. This state of affairs is unsatisfactory on two planes: first, the importance of the decision on the entry of the Phalangists, against the backdrop of the Lebanese situation as it was known to those concerned, required that the decision on having the Phalangists enter the camps be made with the prior approval of the Prime Minister. Moreover, once the decision had been taken without the Prime Minister's participation, orderly processes of government required that the decision be made known to him at the earliest possible moment. It is not proper procedure for the Prime Minister to hear about this decision in an incidental manner along with the other Cabinet ministers during a Cabinet session, when the Phalangists were already in the camps.

Second, once the decision was taken, orderly processes of government required that the Prime Minister be informed of any excesses committed. What the Defense Minister, the Chief of Staff and the General of Command knew on Friday and on Saturday morning, the Prime Minister ought also to have known. It is inconceivable that the Prime Minister should receive his information about this from a foreign radio station.

As we have seen, the decision on the Phalangists' entry into the camps took final shape on Wednesday morning (15.9.82) on the roof of the divisional forward command post. When this decision was taken its ramifications were not examined, nor were its advantages and disadvantages weighed. This is explicable in that the decision was taken under pressure of time. Nonetheless, enough time existed before the Phalangists' entry on Thursday evening (16.9.82) to carry out a situation appraisal in which the decision, its manner of execution and its possible results could be examined.

No such deliberation in fact took place. The discussion held by the Defense Minister on Thursday morning (exhibit 27), in which he said, "I would move the Phalangists into the camps," cannot be regarded as a situation appraisal in the usual sense of the term. The Chief of Staff told us that on Wednesday he ordered his deputy to hold a consultation among branch heads. Such a discussion did in fact take place in the late afternoon hours (exhibit 130), but it was a briefing and not a situation appraisal. The issue of the Phalangists' entry was mentioned in that discussion in a general manner, but the decision was not presented in detail, no examination was made of the security measures to be taken, and no evaluation was made of the possible ramifications of the decision.

The way in which decisions are to be taken and the appropriate bodies to that end have been laid down in the procedures. These formats ought to be exploited in order to enhance the prospect that when decisions are taken, all the information at hand, the various positions, the pros and cons, and the possible ramifications of the decision will be taken into account.

Experience and intuition are very valuable, but it is preferable that they not constitute the sole basis on which decisions are taken.

The absence of the required staff discussion regarding the entry of the Phalangists into the camps was accompanied by another inevitable flaw. The information about the decision was not transmitted in an orderly fashion to all the parties who should have known about it. We have already seen that the Prime Minister was unaware of the decision. The Foreign Minister, too, learned of the Phalangists' entry only in the Cabinet session. We have already cited the account of the director of Military Intelligence that he, too, did not learn about the decision until Friday morning. Although we have stated that we find it difficult to accept that account, this cannot justify the absence of an orderly report about the decision being made to all the various staff elements.

Thus, for example, it emerged that the Command Intelligence officers were first briefed by the Command Intelligence Officer about the fact that the Phalangists would enter the camps on Thursday, some two hours after the operation had already commenced. According to the testimony of the Military Intelligence/Research officers whose task it is to prepare situation appraisals, they received no prior information about the decision to have the Phalangists enter the camps.

As a result, that department was unable to prepare its own appraisals, as would have been expected of it prior to the Phalangists' entry into the camps. This also had a certain effect on the manner in which that department functioned at the stage when it received the report about the 300 killed (Section 6, Appendix B).

The head of the Mossad learned of the decision only at the Cabinet session. Despite the fact that Mossad personnel were in Beirut when the events occurred, and maintained ongoing contacts with the Phalangist commanders, no report was received from them regarding the special role of the

Phalangists in the camps prior to their entry, not did they collect any data at all on events in the camps after the Phalangists had entered.

This is not a satisfactory state of affairs. Orderly processes require that the decision on the entry of the Phalangists be reported in an orderly and documented manner to the various bodies that should know about it, so that they can direct their activities and assessments accordingly.

The military establishments are based, inter alia, on diverse channels of reporting. An examination of the events on the dates relevant here indicates the existence of considerable flaws in these channels of reporting. Matters that should have been reported were not reported at all, or were reported late and in fragmentary fashion. For example, the report about the behavior of the Phalangists in the field was not transmitted to Divisional Intelligence. For its part, the latter did not relay the reports about the 45 civilians — which was brought to its attention already on Thursday evening — to Command Intelligence. As for Command Intelligence, despite the fact that it received a report from the Division regarding the 300 killed, it did not convey it to General Staff/Military Intelligence. The transmission of the report to Military Intelligence was the result of the fine initiative of Intelligence Officer A.

We find a similar picture also in the Operations Branch channels. Operations Branch Command did not receive an orderly report of what was happening in the field. As we have seen, already on Thursday evening and Friday morning — and throughout Friday — reports were collected by a considerable number of soldiers and officers who were near the camps. Only some of those reports — and those in fragmentary fashion — were brought to the attention of the Divisional Operations elements. Divisional Operations for its part did not relay the information it had in an orderly fashion to Command Operations elements. Thus, for example, the reports in the possession of Divisional Operations about the 300 killed (or the 120 killed) were not transmitted at all to Command Operations. The latter did not report (not even on the actual entry of the Phalangists into the camps) to Operations Branch/Operations. Thus, for example, the report about the 300 killed was received already on Thursday evening in Command Intelligence. For some reason that report was not conveyed (neither in its telephone form nor in the form of the subsequent cable) to the knowledge of the Command Intelligence Officer. The report was not transmitted to Command Operations, and *ipso facto* was not brought to the knowledge of the G.O.C., either that evening or the following day. Similarly, no orderly report was made regarding the decision of the G.O.C. Northern Command about halting the operations of the Phalangists. These flaws in the reporting require examination and analysis, since in the absence of an orderly and proper report the decision-makers at the various levels lack the information required for their decisions.

The reports that were received via the various channels were also not always handled according to the standing procedures, the result being that the reports sometimes became worthless. Sometimes, reports received were not recorded in the designated log books; reports that were relayed were sometimes transmitted with important omissions, which prevented their being handled properly. Reports that were dealt with (such as the handling of the report about the 300 killed within the framework of Military Intelligence/Research) were at times handled superficially, with a fruitless internal runaround and without exhausting the various possibilities for verification and examination. Other Intelligence means employed sometimes failed to produce the information that was expected of them (see Section 5, Appendix B). Reports that were received and which required a preliminary evaluation to determine their significance and possible implications were not dealt with properly and in the meantime were rendered worthless due to a protracted process of examining their authenticity.

In the course of the testimony we heard, we often came across conversations — whether face-to-face or over the telephone or radio — between highly responsible personnel. Contradictions were often evident in the testimony about these conversations — not out of any intention to conceal the truth, but as a natural result of flaws in human memory. There is no satisfactory explanation of why no notes were taken of these conversations. The Prime Minister held many conversations with the Defense Minister and the Chief of Staff, including the conversations in which the decision was taken to seize key positions in West Beirut. It is not surprising, therefore, if a certain difference exists between the Prime Minister's version of a guideline issued by him, and that of the Chief of Staff regarding the guideline he received.

The Defense Minister and the Chief of Staff held a conversation on Tuesday evening in which a number of important decisions were taken. This conversation was not recorded in any form.

We believe that it is desirable to determine guidelines in this matter in order to prevent a situation in which important decisions are not documented. Precisely because human memory is often faulty, it is desirable to determine a proper method and procedure for recording those conversations which, according to criteria to be determined, it is important to keep on record.

Recommendations and Closing Remarks

RECOMMENDATIONS

With regard to the following recommendations concerning a group of men who hold senior positions in the Government and the Israel Defense Forces, we have taken into account [the fact] that each one of these men has to his credit [the performance of] many public or military services rendered with sacrifice and devotion on behalf of the State of Israel. If nevertheless we have reached the conclusion that it is incumbent upon us to recommend certain measures against some of these men, it is out of the recognition that the gravity of the matter and its implications for the underpinnings of public morality in the State of Israel call for such measures.

The Prime Minister, The Foreign Minister,
and the Head of the Mossad

We have heretofore established the facts and conclusions with regard to the responsibility of the Prime Minister, the Foreign Minister, and the head of the Mossad. In view of what we have determined with regard to the extent of the responsibility of each of them, we are of the opinion that it is sufficient to determine responsibility and there is no need for any further recommendations.

G.O.C. Northern Command Major General Amir Drori

We have detailed above our conclusions with regard to the responsibility of G.O.C. Northern Command Major General Amir Drori. Major General Drori was charged with many difficult and complicated tasks during the week the I.D.F. entered West Beirut, missions which he had to accomplish after a long period to difficult warfare. He took certain measures for terminating the Phalangists' actions, and his guilt lies in that he did not continue with these actions. Taking into account these circumstances, it appears to us that it is sufficient to determine the responsibility of Major General Drori without recourse to any further recommendation.

The Minister of Defense, Mr. Ariel Sharon

We have found, as has been detailed in this report, that the Minister of Defense bears personal responsibility. In our opinion, it is fitting that the Minister of Defense draw the appropriate personal conclusions arising out of the defects revealed with regard to the manner in which he discharged the duties of his office — and if necessary, that the Prime Minister consider whether he should exercise his authority under Section 21-A(a) of the Basic Law: the Government, according to which "the Prime Minister may, after informing the Cabinet of his intention to do so, remove a minister from office."

The Chief of Staff, Lt.-Gen. Rafael Eitan

We have arrived at grave conclusions with regard to the acts and omissions of the Chief of Staff, Lt-Gen. Rafael Eitan. The Chief of Staff is about to complete this term of service in April, 1983. Taking into account the fact that an extension of his term is not under consideration, there is no [practical] significance to a recommendation with regard to his continuing in office as Chief of Staff, and therefore we have resolved that it is sufficient to determine responsibility without making any further recommendation.

The Director of Military Intelligence,
Major General Yehoshua Saguy

We have detailed the various extremely serious omissions of the Director of Military Intelligence, Major General Yehoshua Saguy, in discharging the duties of his office. We recommend that Major General Yehoshua Saguy not continue as Director of Military Intelligence.

Division Commander Brigadier General, Amos Yaron

We have detailed above the extent of the responsibility of Brigadier General Amos Yaron. Taking into account all the circumstances, we recommend that Brigadier General Amos Yaron not serve in the capacity of a field commander in the Israel Defense Forces, and that this recommendation not be reconsidered before three years have passed.

In the course of this inquiry, shortcomings in the functioning of [several] establishments have been revealed, as described in the chapter dealing with this issue. One must learn the appropriate lessons from these shortcomings, and we recommend that, in addition to internal comptrol in this matter, an investigation into the shortcomings and the manner of correcting them be undertaken by an expert or experts, to be appointed by a Ministerial Defense Committee. If in the course of this investigation it be found that certain persons bear responsibility for these shortcomings, it is fitting that the appropriate conclusions be drawn in their regard, whether in accordance with the appropriate provisions of the military legal code, or in some other manner.

CLOSING REMARKS

In the witnesses' testimony and in various documents, stress is laid on the difference between the usual battle ethics of the I.D.F. and the battle ethics of the bloody clashes and combat actions among the various ethnic groups, militias, and fighting forces in Lebanon. The difference is considerable. In the war the I.D.F. waged in Lebanon, many civilians were injured and much loss of life was caused, despite the effort the I.D.F. and its soldiers made not to harm civilians. On more than one occasion, this effort caused I.D.F. troops additional casualties. During the months of the war, I.D.F. soldiers witnessed many sights of killing, destruction, and ruin. From their reactions (about which we have heard) to acts of brutality against civilians, it would appear that despite the terrible sights and experiences of the war and despite the soldier's obligation to behave as a fighter with a certain degree of callousness, I.D.F. soldiers did not lose their sensitivity to atrocities that were perpetrated on non-combatants either out of cruelty or to give vent to vengeful feelings. It is regrettable that the reaction by I.D.F. soldiers to such deeds was not always forceful enough to bring a halt to the despicable acts. It seems to us that the I.D.F. should continue to foster the [consciousness of] basic moral obligations which must be kept even in war conditions, without prejudicing the I.D.F.'s combat ability. The circumstances of combat require the combatants to be tough — which means to give priority to sticking to the objective and being willing to make sacrifices — in order to attain the objectives assigned to them, even under the most difficult conditions. But the end never justifies the means, and basic ethical and human values must be maintained in the use of arms.

Among the responses to the commission from the public, there were those who expressed dissatisfaction with the holding of an inquiry on a subject not directly related to Israel's responsibility. The argument was advanced that in previous instances of massacre in Lebanon, when the lives of many more people were taken than those of the victims who fell in Sabra and Shatilla, world opinion was not shocked and no inquiry commissions were established. We cannot justify this approach to the issue of holding an inquiry, and not only for the formal reason that it was not we who decided to hold the inquiry, but rather the Israeli Government resolved thereon. The main purpose of the inquiry was to bring to light all the important facts relating to the perpetration of the atrocities; it therefore has importance from the perspective of Israel's moral fortitude and its functioning as a democratic state that scrupulously maintains the fundamental principles of the civilized world.

We do not deceive ourselves that the results of this inquiry will convince or satisfy those who have prejudices or selective consciences, but this inquiry was not intended for such people. We have striven and have spared no effort to arrive at the truth, and we hope that all persons of good will who will examine the issue without prejudice will be convinced that the inquiry was conducted without any bias.

PUBLICATION OF THE REPORT

In accordance with Section 20(a) of the Commissions of Inquiry Law, this report and the attached Appendix A will be published after the report is submitted to the Government. Appendix B to this report will not be published, since we are convinced that this is necessary to protect the security of the state and its foreign relations.

Transcripts from the commission hearings which were conducted in open session have already been made public. In accordance with regulation 8(b) of the Commission of Inquiry Regulations (Rules of Procedure) 1969, we resolve that the right to examine the transcripts from those sessions which were held in camera, as well as Appendix B to the report, will be given to all members of the cabinet, all members of the Knesset Defense and Foreign Affairs Committee, the General Staff of the Israel Defense Forces, and any person or class of persons which may be determined by the Ministerial Defense Committee. Similarly, the right to examine Appendix B is given to those persons who received a notice in accordance with section 15(a) of the law, and to their representatives who appeared before the commission.

This report was signed on 7 February 1983.

> Yitzhak Kahan
> Commission Chairman
> Aharon Barak
> Commission Member
> Yona Efrat
> Commission Member

Reprinted from *The Jerusalem Post*, 9 February 1983.

271. Security Council Resolution 529 Renewing the U.N.

Interim Force in Lebanon Mandate, January 18, 1983*

---

* S.C. Res. 529, 38 U.N. SCOR (2411th mtg.) at 1, U.N. Doc. S/INF/39 (1982). *See also* subsequent resolutions, S.C. Res. 536, 38 U.N. SCOR (2456th mtg.) at 3, U.N. Doc. S/INF/39 (1983) and S.C. Res. 538, 38 U.N. SCOR (2480th mtg.) at 4, U.N. Doc. S/INF/39 (1983).

The Security Council,

Recalling its resolutions 425 (1978) and 426 (1978), and all subsequent resolutions on the United Nations Interim Force in Lebanon,

Recalling further its resolutions 508 (1982) and 509 (1982),

Having taken note of the letter of the Permanent Representative of Lebanon to the President of the Security Council and to the Secretary-General of 13 January 1983,[3] and of the statement he made at the 2411th meeting of the Council,

Having studied the report of the Secretary-General[4] and taking note of his observations,

Responding to the request of the Government of Lebanon,

1. *Decides* to extend the present mandate of the United Nations Interim Force in Lebanon for a further interim period of six months, that is, until 19 July 1983;

2. *Calls upon* all parties concerned to co-operate with the Force for the full implementation of the present resolution;

3. *Requests* the Secretary-General to report to the Security Council on the progress made in this respect.

Adopted at the 2411th meeting by 13 votes to none, with 2 abstentions (Poland, Union of Soviet Socialist Republics).

[3] *Ibid.* [*Official Records of the Security Council, Thirty-eighth Year, Supplement for January, February and March 1983*], document S/15557, annex I.

[4] *Ibid.*, document S/15557.

272. Excerpts from the Lebanese Government Statement
on the Lebanese Agreement with Israel, Beirut,

May 16, 1983*

* 12 J. Palestine Stud. 255 (Summer 1983).

... In this agreement we accepted conditions which we would have preferred not to have accepted. However, in return, we have taken the territory and people of the south and, for the first time in the history of the Israeli-Arab wars, we have secured the recovery of the land without establishing peace or normal relations. [applause] All the conditions are temporary, acceptable, and reasonable compared with the dangers that existed and that would have continued to exist. Despite the fact that Lebanon, during the negotiations phase, has been an occupied, divided, and weak country, it nevertheless has a strong will, a clear vision, and a young political leadership that has, for the first time in the history of Lebanon, the consensus of all Lebanese families despite the circumstances in the areas in which they live, the occupation under which they are suffering, and the daily tragedies resulting from this occupation.

Therefore, at a time when Lebanon, the negotiator, accepted what is regarded to be reasonable, it very proudly and willfully said no to everything that was unacceptable. Thus, as an example and not strictly speaking, we said no to holding the negotiations in the city of Jerusalem, the holy city which Lebanon believes to belong to the three religions and which Lebanon has requested be put under international supervision. We said no to political negotiations at ministerial level, no to the establishment of early warning stations, no to observation posts that ensure the continued presence of over 1,000 Israeli soldiers in southern Lebanon, no to the appointment of Israeli liaison officers in every Lebanese Army unit in the security zone and the consequent foreign military control over our young Army this entails as well as the violation of the Lebanese dignity which has refused and continues to refuse to be harmed or violated despite all the sufferings and tragedies.

We said no to giving Israel the right to approve of the Lebanese officers operating in the brigade that is present south of the Az-Zahrani River. We said no to reciprocal political recognition between the two countries, no to considering Al-Baruk as part of the security zone, despite the fact that it, like the rest of the Lebanese areas, is enjoying only Lebanese security so that it may not be said that Israel, through the verification committees, overlooks the Syrian, Turkish, Iraqi, Jordanian, and Egyptian territories from the top of Al-Baruk mountain.

We said no to Israel's imposition of a certain officer to be responsible for the southern brigade, no to Israel's demand to have the right to pursue across the Lebanese territory any group which enters Israel from Lebanon to carry out hostile actions there and then sneaks into Lebanon, because this condition would give the Israeli army the excuse to enter our territory whenever it wished and in the numbers it deemed appropriate.

These conditions were not merely fleeting ideas put forward during the negotiations, but they were serious conditions which we discussed for months.

At the time of signing this agreement, we must speak frankly to our brothers in the Arab world and assure them that this agreement, like the armistice agreement, absolutely does not affect Lebanon's Arab relations, particularly its relations with Syria, other than to increase its strength and prosperity.

Our future role in the Arab League, in our capacity as an independent and free country, will be much stronger than our role in our capacity as a divided and occupied country. Our role as a member of the [Arab] collective defense treaty in our capacity as a sovereign, strong, and unified country will be much stronger than our role in our capacity as a country divided by the others and dependent on their will.

If Egypt, which concluded peace with Israel, has not withdrawn from the collective defense treaty, then why should anyone think that Lebanon, which has concluded an agreement mainly of a security nature, is about to withdraw from this treaty or other major Arab commitments? Lebanon is determined to discharge all its obligations within the Arab League and within the collective defense treaty. In addition, Lebanon will abide by all the ethical and patriotic charters, which are more important than any provisions.

I say to all those who expect a leading role from Lebanon, a support role during the crisis, or a creative role in the future of the Arab society: "Give Lebanon an opportunity. Permit it to exist. Let it find its own way with its own mind, people, institutions, and leadership.

We said during the negotiations that we were holding discussions with Israel and the United States while watching over the interests of Syria, the Arab state which shouldered more than any other state the burdens of the military mobilization in defense of the national Arab national rights. We can say by evicting Israel from Lebanon that we are providing real security for Syria. By forbidding Israel from using Lebanese land as a passage to attack Syria, we are easing many of the risks which Syria might confront in its military equation with Israel. . . .

We did not negotiate to regain one area of Lebanon only but to regain all Lebanon. When the whole is the target, we cannot tarry, procrastinate, or take risks. We entered these negotiations having in front of us 60 years' experience between the Zionist movement and the Palestinians and between Israel and its neighboring Arab states [sentence is heard]. We know much that is happening in lands occupied by Israel. We know much about the Israeli appetite after the occupation. We know what happened in the West Bank, Gaza sector, and the Golan Heights. Therefore, in view of our historic responsiblity [sic] to the rising Lebanese generations, we have no right to lose the south as other Arab areas have been lost to satisfy empty slogans, hollow words, and haughty stands.

We fear lest the south may become like the [West] Bank not on the basis of what has happened in the past but on the basis of what is happening and what is being said and planned now. We began hearing a few weeks ago statements by some Israelis to the effect that the south is part of the land of Israel. We began hearing serious slogans about the south. This is not the time to discuss them because we do not want to open wounds, which we ought to dress, or open cards [as heard] which all of us hope to close forever. We have seen with our eyes airports and utilities constructed in the south. We have seen the military barracks being built as though they will be permanent. We have read about the national guard and the logistics bases. We began to read, think, and see, and we were disturbed.

The Israeli occupation of the south is not, as some believe, a process of repentance ['amaliyyat 'add asabi'] as far as we are concerned because Israel reaps enormous economic profits from the occupation. If Israel manages to control the south as it controlled Sinai in the past and as it is controlling the West Bank, then the gains which it will reap from the occupation of our land will be no less than $2 billion annually. Let nobody forget that Israel needs the Al-Litani River which could secure for it 50 percent of the waters it will need in the near future.

In line with its political ideology, Israel wants land, agriculture, and water. The Lebanese south, which is the most fertile land in Lebanon, can be lost and become a part of Israel overnight if we do not resort to wisdom and courage at the appropriate time.

The West Bank has become an area for exporting workers to Israel. The south could become the same. The West Bank is now fully dependent on Israel's exports and the south could become the same. The plans and studies to divert the Al-Litani waters through canals and tunnels passing near Marj'Uyun and then to Bet Neqofa village in Northern Israel, where they will be connected with the existing Israeli irrigation system, are now complete. What remains is an order for implementation. Israel cannot fully exploit the Al-Litani waters if it does not keep the area it is occupying now in order to defend the course of this river and obtain the waters from the area nearest to the sea. It is impossible to effectively benefit from the Al-Litani's present course which is 2-km from the Israeli border.

Rumors spread, in the course of the Israeli occupation, about the establishment of sectarian statelets on the body of the one Lebanese family. We have read in the papers and in the memoranda about the benefits of dividing the Lebanese homeland into homelands including a Druze homeland, a Shi'ite homeland, and a Christian homeland. These rumors went beyond Lebanon to speak about the establishment of an 'Alawite homeland. Others might consider these rumors with indifference and pay no attention to them. However, we, who witnessed the tragedies of division and what others can do among the members of the Lebanese family, cannot disregard the rumors. We have felt some of its reality and we have been burned by some of its fire.

I want to tell you now my opinion which frankly might displease some of those who have firm stands on Lebanon. I do not believe in the inevitabilty [*sic*] of the annexation of the south to Israel. It is true that at the peace conference in Paris, the Zionist movement presented several maps of the future Israel which take Israel's northern border to the Al-Litani River and even to the Al-Awwali River.

Some of you remember the correspondence exchanged among the senior Israeli politicians and the arguments at the Knesset which every now and then were about Lebanon. In 1967, Israel did not try to occupy the south although it could find suitable excuses to do so. Israel did not try to occupy the south in 1973, although it could find strategic reason for this. However, it invaded the south in 1972 and later occupied it in June 1982. If we do not resort to rationality now and sign this agreement, before Israel changes its mind, and oust the Israeli army from Lebanon, Israel will find its presence in Lebanon profitable and it will take Lebanon's obstinacy as an excuse for remaining in Lebanon permanently. . . .

273. Agreement between the Government of the State of

Israel and the Government of the Republic of Lebanon,

May 17, 1983*

* Text provided by the U.S. Department of State, *reprinted in* 22 Int'l Legal Materials 708 (1983).

The Government of the State of Israel and the Government of the Republic of Lebanon:

Bearing in mind the importance of maintaining and strengthening international peace based on freedom, equality, justice, and respect for fundamental human rights;

Reaffirming their faith in the aims and principles of the Charter of the United Nations and recognizing their right and obligation to live in peace with each other as well as with all states, within secure and recognized boundaries;

Having agreed to declare the termination of the state of war between them;

Desiring to ensure lasting security for both their States and to avoid threats and the use of force between them;

Desiring to establish their mutual relations in the manner provided for in this Agreement;

Having delegated their undersigned representative plenipotentiaries, provided with full powers, in order to sign, in the presence of the representative of the United States of America, this Agreement;

Have agreed to the following provisions:

ARTICLE 1

1. The Parties agree and undertake to respect the sovereignty, political independence and territorial integrity of each other. They consider the existing international boundary between Israel and Lebanon inviolable.

2. The Parties confirm that the state of war between Israel and Lebanon has been terminated and no longer exists.

3. Taking into account the provisions of paragraphs 1 and 2, Israel undertakes to withdraw all its armed forces from Lebanon in accordance with the Annex of the present Agreement.

ARTICLE 2

The Parties, being guided by the principles of the Charter of the United Nations and of international law, undertake to settle their disputes by peaceful means in such a manner as to promote international peace and security, and justice.

ARTICLE 3

In order to provide maximum security for Israel and Lebanon, the Parties agree to establish and implement security arrangements, including the creation of a Security Region, as provided for in the Annex of the present Agreement.

ARTICLE 4

1. The territory of each Party will not be used as a base for hostile or terrorist activity against the other Party, its territory, or its people.

2. Each Party will prevent the existence or organization of irregular

forces, armed bands, organizations, bases, offices or infrastructure, the aims and purposes of which include incursions or any act of terrorism into the territory of the other Party, or any other activity aimed at threatening or endangering the security of the other Party and safety of its people. To this end all agreements and arrangements enabling the presence and functioning on the territory of either Party of elements hostile to the other Party are null and void.

3. Without prejudice to the inherent right of self-defense in accordance with international law, each Party will refrain:

a. from organizing, instigating, assisting, or participating in threats or acts of belligerency, subversion, or incitement or any aggression directed against the other Party, its population or property, both within its territory and originating therefrom, or in the territory of the other Party.

b. from using the territory of the other Party for conducting a military attack against the territory of a third state.

c. from intervening in the internal or external affairs of the other Party.

4. Each Party undertakes to ensure that preventive action and due proceedings will be taken against persons or organizations perpetrating acts in violation of this Article.

ARTICLE 5

Consistent with the termination of the state of war and within the framework of their constitutional provisions, the Parties will abstain from any form of hostile propaganda against each other.

ARTICLE 6

Each Party will prevent entry into, deployment in, or passage through its territory, its air space and, subject to the right of innocent passage in accordance with international law, its territorial sea, by military forces, armament, or military equipment of any state hostile to the other Party.

ARTICLE 7

Except as provided in the present Agreement, nothing will preclude the deployment on Lebanese territory of international forces requested and accepted by the Government of Lebanon to assist in maintaining its authority. New contributors to such forces shall be selected from among states having diplomatic relations with both Parties to the present Agreement.

ARTICLE 8

1. a. Upon entry into force of the present Agreement, a Joint Liaison Committee will be established by the Parties, in which the United States of America will be a participant, and will commence its functions. This Committee will be entrusted with the supervision of the implementation of all areas covered by the present Agreement. In matters involving security arrangements, it will deal with unresolved problems referred to it by the Security Arrangements Com-

mittee established in subparagraph c. below. Decisions of this Committee will be taken unanimously.

b. The Joint Liaison Committee will address itself on a continuing basis to the development of mutual relations between Israel and Lebanon, *inter alia* the regulation of the movement of goods, products and persons, communications, etc.

c. Within the framework of the Joint Liaison Committee, there will be a Security Arrangements Committee whose composition and functions are defined in the Annex of the present Agreement.

d. Subcommittees of the Joint Liaison Committee may be established as the need arises.

e. The Joint Liaison Committee will meet in Israel and Lebanon, alternately.

f. Each Party, if it so desires and unless there is an agreed change of status, may maintain a liaison office on the territory of the other Party in order to carry out the above-mentioned functions within the framework of the Joint Liaison Committee and to assist in the implementation of the present Agreement.

g. The members of the Joint Liaison Committee from each of the Parties will be headed by a senior government official.

h. All other matters relating to these liaison offices, their personnel, and the personnel of each Party present in the territory of the other Party in connection with the implementation of the present Agreement will be the subject of a protocol to be concluded between the Parties in the Joint Liaison Committee. Pending the conclusion of this protocol, the liaison offices and the above-mentioned personnel will be treated in accordance with the pertinent provisions of the Convention on Special Missions of December 8, 1969, including those provisions concerning privileges and immunities. The foregoing is without prejudice to the positions of the Parties concerning that Convention. [Convention appears at 9 I.L.M. 129 (1970).]

2. During the six-month period after the withdrawal of all Israeli armed forces from Lebanon in accordance with Article 1 of the present Agreement and the simultaneous restoration of Lebanese governmental authority along the international boundary between Israel and Lebanon, and in the light of the termination of the state of war, the Parties shall initiate, within the Joint Liaison Committee, *bona fide* negotiations in order to conclude agreements on the movement of goods, products and persons and their implementation on a non-discriminatory basis.

ARTICLE 9

1. Each of the two Parties will take, within a time limit of one year as of entry into force of the present Agreement, all measures necessary for the abrogation of treaties, laws and regulations deemed in conflict with the pres-

ent Agreement, subject to and in conformity with its constitutional procedures.

2. The Parties undertake not to apply existing obligations, enter into any obligations, or adopt laws or regulations in conflict with the present Agreement.

ARTICLE 10

1. The present Agreement shall be ratified by both Parties in conformity with their respective constitutional procedures. It shall enter into force on the exchange of the instruments of ratification and shall supersede the previous agreements between Israel and Lebanon.

2. The Annex, the Appendix and the Map attached thereto, and the Agreed Minutes to the present Agreement shall be considered integral parts thereof.

3. The present Agreement may be modified, amended, or superseded by mutual agreement of the Parties.

ARTICLE 11

1. Disputes between the Parties arising out of the interpretation or application of the present Agreement will be settled by negotiation in the Joint Liaison Committee. Any dispute of this character not so resolved shall be submitted to conciliation and, if unresolved, thereafter to an agreed procedure for a definitive resolution.

2. Notwithstanding the provisions of paragraph 1, disputes arising out of the interpretation or application of the Annex shall be resolved in the framework of the Security Arrangements Committee and, if unresolved, shall thereafter, at the request of either Party, be referred to the Joint Liaison Committee for resolution through negotiation.

ARTICLE 12

The present Agreement shall be communicated to the Secretariat of the United Nations for registration in conformity with the provisions of Article 102 of the Charter of the United Nations.

Done at Kiryat Shmona and Khaldeh this seventeenth day of May, 1983, in triplicate in four authentic texts in the Hebrew, Arabic, English and French languages. In case of any divergence of interpretation, the English and French texts will be equally authoritative.

For the Government of the
State of Israel

For the Government of the
Republic of Lebanon

Witnessed by:

For the Government of the
United States of America

Annex
SECURITY ARRANGEMENTS

1. *Security Region*

   a. A Security Region in which the Government of Lebanon undertakes to implement the security arrangements agreed upon in this Annex is hereby established.

   b. The Security Region is bounded, as delineated on the Map [I.L.M. page 735] attached to this Annex, in the north by a line constituting "Line A", and in the south and east by the Lebanese international boundary.

2. *Security Arrangements*

   The Lebanese authorities will enforce special security measures aimed at detecting and preventing hostile activities as well as the introduction into or movement through the Security Region of unauthorized armed men or military equipment. The following security arrangements will apply equally throughout the Security Region except as noted:

   a. The Lebanese Army, Lebanese Police, Lebanese Internal Security Forces, and the Lebanese auxiliary forces (ANSAR), organized under the full authority of the Government of Lebanon, are the only organized armed forces and elements permitted in the Security Region except as designated elsewhere in this Annex. The Security Arrangements Committee may approve the stationing in the Security Region of other official Lebanese armed elements similar to ANSAR.

   b. Lebanese Police, Lebanese Internal Security Forces, and ANSAR may be stationed in the Security Region without restrictions as to their numbers. These forces and elements will be equipped only with personal and light automatic weapons and, for the Internal Security Forces, armored scout of commando cars as listed in the Appendix.

   c. Two Lebanese Army brigades may be stationed in the Security Region. One will be the Lebanese Army Territorial Brigade stationed in the area extending from the Israeli-Lebanese boundary to "Line B" delineated on the attached Map. The other will be a regular Lebanese Army brigade stationed in the area extending from "Line B" to "Line A". These brigades may carry their organic weapons and equipment listed in the Appendix. Additional units equipped in accordance with the Appendix may be deployed in the Security Region for training purposes, including the training of conscripts, or, in the case of operational emergency situations, following coordination in accordance with procedures to be established by the Security Arrangements Committee.

   d. The existing local units will be integrated as such into the Lebanese
      Army, in conformity with Lebanese Army regulations. The existing
      local civil guard shall be integrated into ANSAR and accorded a
      proper status under Lebanese law to enable it to continue guarding
      the villages in the Security Region. The process of extending Leb-
      anese authority over these units and civil guard, under the super-
      vision of the Security Arrangements Committee, shall start imme-
      diately after the entry into force of the present Agreement and
      shall terminate prior to the completion of the Israeli withdrawal
      from Lebanon.
   e. Within the Security Region, Lebanese Army units may maintain
      their organic anti-aircraft weapons as specified in the Appendix.
      Outside the Security Region, Lebanon may deploy personal, low,
      and medium altitude air defense missiles. After a period of three
      years from the date of entry into force of the present Agreement,
      the provision concerning the area outside the Security Region may
      be reviewed by the Security Arrangements Committee at the re-
      quest of either Party.
   f. Military electronic equipment in the Security Region will be as spec-
      ified in the Appendix. Deployment of ground radars within ten ki-
      lometers of the Israeli-Lebanese boundary should be approved by
      the Security Arrangements Committee. Ground radars throughout
      the Security Region will be deployed so that their sector of search
      does not cross the Israeli-Lebanese boundary. This provision does
      not apply to civil aviation or air traffic control radars.
   g. The provision mentioned in paragraph e. applies also to anti-air-
      craft missiles on Lebanese Navy vessels. In the Security Region,
      Lebanon may deploy naval elements and establish and maintain na-
      val bases or other shore installations required to accomplish the na-
      val mission. The coastal installations in the Security Region will be
      as specified in the Appendix.
   h. In order to avoid accidents due to misidentification, the Lebanese
      military authorities will give advance notice of all flights of any kind
      over the Security Region according to procedures to be determined
      by the Security Arrangements Committee. Approval of these flights
      is not required.
   i. (1) The forces, weapons and military equipment which may be sta-
         tioned, stocked, introduced into, or transported through the Se-
         curity Region are only those mentioned in this Annex and its
         Appendix.
      (2) No infrastructure, auxiliary installations, or equipment capable
         of assisting the activation of weapons that are not permitted by
         this Annex or its Appendix shall be maintained or established in
         the Security Region.

(3) These provisions also apply whenever a clause of this Annex relates to areas outside the Security Region.

3. *Security Arrangements Committee*

   a. Within the framework of the Joint Liaison Committee, a Security Arrangements Committee will be established.

   b. The Security Arrangements Committee will be composed of an equal number of Israeli and Lebanese representatives, headed by senior officers. A representative of the United States of America will participate in meetings of the Committee at the request of either Party. Decisions of the Security Arrangements Committee will be reached by agreement of the Parties.

   c. The Security Arrangements Committee shall supervise the implementation of the security arrangements in the present Agreement and this Annex and the timetable and modalities, as well as all other aspects relating to withdrawals described in the present Agreement and this Annex. To this end, and by agreement of the Parties, it will:

      (1) Supervise the implementation of the undertakings of the Parties under the present Agreement and this Annex.

      (2) Establish and operate Joint Supervisory Teams as detailed below.

      (3) Address and seek to resolve any problems arising out of the implementation of the security arrangements in the present Agreement and this Annex and discuss any violation reported by the Joint Supervisory Teams or any complaint concerning a violation submitted by one of the Parties.

   d. The Security Arrangements Committee shall deal with any complaint submitted to it not later than 24 hours after submission.

   e. Meetings of the Security Arrangements Committee shall be held at least once every two weeks in Israel and in Lebanon, alternately. In the event that either Party requests a special meeting, it will be convened within 24 hours. The first meeting will be held within 48 hours after the date of entry into force of the present Agreement.

   f. *Joint Supervisory Teams*

      (1) The Security Arrangements Committee will establish Joint Supervisory Teams (Israel-Lebanon) subordinate to it and composed of an equal number of representatives from each Party.

      (2) The teams will conduct regular verification of the implementation of the provisions of the security arrangements in the Agreement and this Annex. The teams shall report immediately any confirmed violations to the Security Arrangements Committee and ascertain that violations have been rectified.

      (3) The Security Arrangements Committee shall assign a Joint Supervisory Team, when requested, to check border security ar-

rangements on the Israeli side of the international boundary in accord with Article 4 of the present Agreement.

(4) The teams will enjoy freedom of movement in the air, sea, and land as necessary for the performance of their tasks within the Security Region.

(5) The Security Arrangements Committee will determine all administrative and technical arrangements concerning the functioning of the teams including their working procedures, their number, their manning, their armament, and their equipment.

(6) Upon submission of a report to the Security Arrangements Committee or upon confirmation of a complaint of either Party by the teams, the respective Party shall immediately, and in any case not later than 24 hours from the report or the confirmation, rectify the violation. The Party shall immediately notify the Security Arrangements Committee of the rectification. Upon receiving the notification, the teams will ascertain that the violation has been rectified.

(7) The Joint Supervisory Teams shall be subject to termination upon 90 days notice by either Party given at any time after two years from the date of entry into force of the present Agreement. Alternative verification arrangements shall be established in advance of such termination through the Joint Liaison Committee. Notwithstanding the foregoing, the Joint Liaison Committee may determine at any time that there is no further need for such arrangements.

g. The Security Arrangements Committee will ensure that practical and rapid contacts between the two Parties are established along the boundary to prevent incidents and facilitate coordination between the forces on the terrain.

4. It is understood that the Government of Lebanon may request appropriate action in the United Nations Security Council for one unit of the United Nations Interim Force in Lebanon (UNIFIL) to be stationed in the Sidon area. The presence of this unit will lend support to the Government of Lebanon and the Lebanese Armed Forces in asserting governmental authority and protection in the Palestinian refugee camp areas. For a period of 12 months, the unit in the Sidon area may send teams to the Palestinian refugee camp areas in the vicinity of Sidon and Tyre to surveil and observe, if requested by the Government of Lebanon, following notification to the Security Arrangements Committee. Police and security functions shall remain the sole responsibility of the Government of Lebanon, which shall ensure that the provisions of the present Agreement shall be fully implemented in these areas.

5. Three months after completion of the withdrawal of all Israeli forces from Lebanon, the Security Arrangements Committee will conduct a full-scale review of the adequacy of the security arrangements delineated in this Annex in order to improve them.

6. *Withdrawal of Israeli Forces*
   a. Within 8 to 12 weeks of the entry into force of the present Agreement, all Israeli forces will have been withdrawn from Lebanon. This is consistent with the objective of Lebanon that all external forces withdraw from Lebanon.
   b. The Israel Defense Forces and the Lebanese Armed Forces will maintain continuous liaison during the withdrawal and will exchange all necessary information through the Security Arrangements Committee. The Israel Defense Forces and the Lebanese Armed Forces will cooperate during the withdrawal in order to facilitate the reassertion of the authority of the Government of Lebanon as the Israeli armed forces withdraw.

Appendix

In accordance with the provisions of the Annex, the Lebanese Armed Forces may carry, introduce, station, stock, or transport through the Security Region all weapons and equipment organic to each standard Lebanese Armed Forces brigade. Individual and crew-served weapons, including light automatic weapons normally found in a mechanized infantry unit, are not prohibited by this Appendix.

1. Weapon systems listed below presently organic to each brigade in the Security Region are authorized in the numbers shown:

TANKS

— 40 tanks
— 4 medium tracked recovery vehicles

ARMORED CARS

— 10 AML-90/Saladin/etc.

ARMORED PERSONNEL CARRIERS

— 127 M113A1/VCC-L, plus 44 M113 family vehicles

ARTILLERY/MORTARS

— 18 155MM towed howitzers (also 105MM/122MM)
— 12 120MM mortars
— 27 81MM mortars (mounted on M-125 tracked mortar carriers)

ANTI-TANK WEAPONS

— 112 RPG
— 30 anti-tank weapons (106MM recoilless rifle/TOW/MILAN)

AIR DEFENSE WEAPONS

— 12 40MM or less guns (not radar-guided)

2. Brigade Communications Equipment:

— 482 AN/GRC-160
— 74 AN/VRC-46
— 16 AN/VRC-47
— 9 AN/VRC-49
— 43 GRA-39
— 539 TA-312
— 27 SB-22
— 8 SB-993
— 4 AN/GRC-106

3. Brigade Surveillance Equipment:

— Mortar locating radars
— Artillery locating radars
— Ground surveillance radars
— Night observation devices
— Unattended ground sensors

4. In accordance with the provisions of the Annex, armored vehicles for the Internal Security Forces will be as follows:

— 24 armored wheeled vehicles with guns up to 40MM

5. In accordance with the provisions of the Annex, there will be no limitations on the coastal installations in the Security Region, except on the following four categories:

— Coastal sea surveillance radars: 5
— Coastal defense guns: 15 40MM or less
— Coastal air defense guns: 15 40MM or less (not radar-guided)
— Shore-to-sea missiles: None

6. The Lebanese Army Infantry Brigade and Territorial Brigade in the Security Region are each organized as follows:

1 Brigade Headquarters and Headquarters Company	Off: 14	Enl: 173
3 Infantry Battalions	Off: 31 ea	Enl: 654 ea
1 Artillery Battalaion	Off: 39	Enl: 672
1 Tank Battalion 3 Tank Companies 1 Reconnaissance Company	Off: 37	Enl: 579
1 Logistics Battalion	Off: 26	Enl: 344
1 Engineer Company	Off: 6	Enl: 125
1 Anti-Tank Company	Off: 4	Enl: 117

Agreed Minutes

ART. 4.4   Lebanon affirms that Lebanese law includes all measures necessary to ensure implementation of this paragraph.

ART. 6   Without prejudice to the provisions of the Annex regarding the Security Region, it is agreed that non-combat military aircraft of a foreign state on non-military missions shall not be considered military equipment.

ART. 6   It is agreed that, in the event of disagreement as to whether a particular state is "hostile" for purposes of Article 6 of the Agreement, the prohibitions of Article 6 shall be applied to any state which does not maintain diplomatic relations with both Parties.

ART. 8.1.b   It is agreed that, at the request of either Party, the Joint Liaison Committee shall begin to examine the question of claims by citizens of either Party on properties in the territory of the other Party.

ART. 8.1.h   It is understood that each Party will certify to the other if one of its personnel was on official duty or performing official functions at any given time.

ART. 8.2   It is agreed that the negotiations will be concluded as soon as possible.

ART. 9   It is understood that this provision shall apply *mutatis mutandis* to agreements concluded by the Parties pursuant to Article 8, paragraph 2.

ART. 11   It is agreed that both parties will request the United States of America to promote the expeditious resolution of disputes arising out of the interpretation or application of the present Agreement.

ART. 11   It is agreed that the phrase "an agreed procedure for a definitive resolution" means an agreed third-party mechanism which will produce a resolution of the dispute which is binding on the Parties.

ANNEX   It is agreed that, in that portion of Jabal Baruk shown on the
PARA 1.b   map attachment to the Annex, only civilian telecommunications installations, such as television facilities and radars for air traffic control purposes, may be emplaced. The restrictions on weapons and military equipment that are detailed in the Appendix to the Annex will also apply in that area.

ANNEX   The Government of Lebanon affirms its decision that the Ter-
PARA 2.d   ritorial Brigade established on April 6, 1983, mentioned in subparagraph c, will encompass the existing local units which had been formed into a near brigade-sized unit, along with Lebanese Army personnel from among the inhabitants of the Security Region, in conformity with Lebanese Army regulations.

This brigade will be in charge of security in the area extending from the Israeli-Lebanese boundary to "Line B" delineated on the Map attachment to the Annex. All the Lebanese Armed Forces and elements in this area, including the Lebanese Police, Lebanese Internal Security Forces and ANSAR, will be subordinated to the brigade commander. The organization of the existing local units will be adapted, under the supervision of the Security Arrangements Committee, in conformity with the Table of Organization for the Territorial Brigade as shown in the Appendix.

ANNEX   1. An area extending from:

PARA 2.g   33 degrees 15 minutes N
              35 degrees 12.6 minutes E; to

              33 degrees 05.5 minutes N
              35 degrees 06.1 minutes E; to

1 Anti-Air Artillery Company	Off: 4	Enl: 146
TOTAL: 4,341	Off: 223	Enl: 4,118

2. If the Joint Supervisory Teams uncover evidence of a violation or a potential violation, they will contact the proper Lebanese authorities through the Security Arrangements Supervision Centers created pursuant to the Agreed Minute to paragraph 3.f.(5) of the Annex, in order to assure that Lebanese authorities take appropriate neutralizing and preventive action in a timely way. They will ascertain that the action taken rectified the violation and will report the results to the Security Arrangements Committee.

3. The Joint Supervisory Teams will commence limited activities as early as possible following the coming into force of the Agreement for the purpose of monitoring the implementation of the Israel Defense Forces withdrawal arrangements. Their other supervisory and verification activities authorized in the Annex will commence with the final withdrawal of the Israeli armed forces.

4. Joint Supervisory Teams will conduct daily verifications if necessary during day and night. Verifications will be carried out on the ground, at sea, and in the air.

5. Each Joint Supervisory Team will be commanded by a Lebanese officer, who will recognize the joint nature of the teams when making decisions in unforeseen situations, during the conduct of the verification mission.

6. While on a mission, the Joint Supervisory Team leader at his discretion could react to any unforeseen situation which could require immediate action. The team leader will report

any such situation and the action taken to the Security Arrangements Supervision Center.

7. The Joint Supervisory Teams will not use force except in self-defense.

8. The Security Arrangements Committee will decide *inter alia* on the pattern of activity of the Joint Supervisory Teams, their weaponry and equipment, their mode of transport, and the areas in which the teams will operate on the basis of the rule of reason and pragmatic considerations. The Security Arrangements Committee will determine the overall pattern of activity with a view to avoiding undue disruption to normal civilian life as well as with a view to preventing the teams from becoming targets of attack.

9. Up to a maximum of eight Joint Supervisory Teams will function simultaneously.

ANNEX
PARA 3.f.5

1. Two Security Arrangements Supervision Centers will be set up by the Security Arrangements Committee in the Security Region. The exact locations of the Centers will be determined by the Security Arrangements Committee in accord with the principle that the Centers should be located in the vicinity of Hasbaya and Mayfadun and should not be situated in populated areas.

2. Under the overall direction of the Security Arrangements Committee, the purpose of each Center is to:

   a) Control, supervise, and direct Joint Supervisory Teams functioning in the sector of the Security Region assigned to it.

   b) Serve as a center of communications connected to the Joint Supervisory Teams and appropriate headquarters.

   c) Serve as a meeting place in Lebanon for the Security Arrangements Committee.

   d) Receive, analyze, and process all information necessary for the function of the Joint Supervisory Teams, on behalf of the Security Arrangements Committee.

3. Operational Arrangements:

   a) The Centers will be commanded by Lebanese Army Officers.

   b) The Centers will function 24 hours a day.

   c) The exact number of personnel in each Center will be decided by the Security Arrangements Committee.

   d) Israeli personnel will be stationed in Israel when not engaged in activities in the Centers.

   e) The Government of Lebanon will be responsible for providing security and logistical support for the Centers.

    f) The Joint Supervisory Teams will ordinarily commence their missions from the Centers after receiving proper briefing and will complete their missions at the Centers following debriefing.

    g) Each Center will contain a situation room, communications equipment, facilities for Security Arrangements Committee meetings, and a briefing and debriefing room.

ANNEX
PARA 3.g

In order to prevent incidents and facilitate coordination between the forces on the terrain, "practical and rapid contacts" will include direct radio and telephone communications between the respective military commanders and their staffs in the immediate border region, as well as direct face-to-face consultations.

274. European Parliament Resolution on Lebanon, May 19, 1983*

* 26 O.J. Eur. Comm. (No. C 161) 118 (1983).

The European Parliament,

A. convinced that a return to peace in Lebanon will only be possible following the withdrawal of all uninvited foreign forces from Lebanese territory,
B. convinced also that the establishment of full sovereignty over the entire territory of the country by the Government of Lebanon is the primary prerequisite for a return to peace.

1. Supports the efforts of the Lebanese Government to exercise its rights to secure the withdrawal of foreign forces, especially since the treaty regulating the withdrawal of Israeli troops has been signed and ratified by the Lebanese and Israeli Governments and Parliaments;

2. Reiterates its demand that all foreign troops in Lebanon present without the approval of the Lebanese Government be withdrawn immediately;

3. Recognizes with appreciation the difficult and dangerous role being played by the members of the multinational force, including troops from Community Member States, stationed in Lebanon, and calls for their presence to be maintained, if necessary in increased number, for as long as may be required;

4. Urges the governments of the Member States to show the utmost generosity in providing technical and material assistance to help make good war damage sustained by Lebanon;

5. Calls on the Commission to continue to supply emergency aid to Lebanon for as long as it is needed;

6. Instructs its President to forward this resolution to the Council, the Commission, the governments of the Member States and to the Government of Lebanon.

275. PFLP-DFLP Joint Communiqué on the Developments on Palestinian and Arab Levels, Damascus, June 6, 1983*

* 13 J. Palestine Stud. 224 (Autumn 1983).

One year after the beginning of the Zionist invasion of Lebanon, the imperialist-Zionist attack against the Palestinians and other peoples in the area is still continuing with the aim of spreading complete American dominance and influence throughout the Arab world.

By encouraging and supporting the Zionist invasion of Lebanon, American imperialism was trying to break the impasse with regard to the Camp David agreements and the autonomy plan for the West Bank. This was to be achieved by liquidating the PLO, dealing a severe blow to the Lebanese national forces, weakening Syria and the Arab national liberation movement, creating a rift in the alliance with the socialist countries, especially the Soviet Union, and transforming Lebanon into an American-Zionist protectorate. The achievement of such objectives would have concluded the second phase of the Camp David plan and opened the way to the third phase of pushing the Jordanian regime to negotiate with the Zionist enemy as stipulated by the Reagan plan that aimed at liquidating the national cause and the independent representation of the Palestinian people.

The heroic steadfastness of the forces of the Palestinian revolution, together with that of the Lebanese national forces and the Syrian forces, has foiled the enemy's aim of liquidating the PLO. On the contrary, this steadfastness has enhanced its position and strengthened its role on both Arab and international levels. At the same time, it prompted American imperialism and its local allies to launch a political campaign in the hope of achieving the aims that were not achieved by the invasion, in spite of all the destruction and the massacres that accompanied it.

It was within this context that the Reagan plan was proposed, its aims being the liquidation of the PLO and the rights of the Palestinian people. And it was for these aims that this plan won such widespread support from the Arab reactionary regimes which started exerting pressures on the PLO and the national Arab states to accept the plan. By exerting such pressures, the Arab reactionary forces aim at exploiting the complicated and difficult circumstances faced by the Palestinian revolution and the Lebanese national forces in order to drag the whole area into the American sphere of influence, impose concessions in favor of the Reagan plan and adopt the Lebanese-Zionist defeatist agreement.

The Palestine National Council, in its latest session held in Algiers in February 1983, adopted resolutions that affirmed Palestinian national unity and solidified it on clear and sound political bases. It asserted the PLO's adherence to the Palestinian political plan and to the decisions taken at previous sessions. It reiterated the PLO's insistence on its role as the sole legitimate representative of the Palestinian people and its utter rejection of delegating this representation or sharing it with any other party. The PNC also asserted the PLO's complete adherence to the inalienable national rights of the Palestinian people including the right to return to their homeland, self-determination and the establishment of their independent state on their national land.

The PNC clearly rejected the Reagan plan because it ignored the rights of our people, and called for a solution based on the PLO's Interim Political Program and Arab and international resolutions that are consistent with our inalienable national rights.

Adherence to the latest PNC resolutions and their implementation on all organizational and political levels are the only means to enhance Palestinian national unity and independence of decision, and the only means to block the way once and for all to all sorts of attempts, maneuvers and pressures that aim at making the Reagan plan acceptable by introducing superficial changes that do not affect the core and the aims of the plan. Commitment to these resolutions is the only means of confronting all schemes aimed at dividing the Palestinian people inside and outside the occupied homeland, including the current attempts by the Jordanian regime at forming a political force called the "Popular alliance" to be the alternative to the PLO. Solidifying Palestinian national unity on the bases defined by the latest session of the PNC will certainly lead to the failure of such organizations similar to the failure of the Village League system.

The prompt application of democratic reform within the framework of the PLO organs and institutions requires enforcing the democratic forces among the Palestinian revolution's forces and restricting the role of the bureaucratic groups that have bourgeois aspirations. This reform should be implemented within the framework of national unity and with adherence to the principle of internal democratic dialogue that will enhance the role of the Palestinian national revolution and its national decisions.

The national political climate and the great and continuous struggle of the masses in the occupied territories against the occupiers and their agents and against the reactionary bourgeois symbols that preach the American "solutions" require that the PLO leadership promptly revive the leading instrument of struggle in the occupied territories, i.e., the Palestinian National Front. They also call for the enhancement of unity of popular associations and unions and the various national organizations that are active inside the occupied homeland, and for the necessary measures to be taken to stop the formation of parallel institutions and unions that will adversely affect the unity of Palestinian struggle and frustrate the role of the national institutions.

The Zionist-Lebanese agreement that was announced last May imposes on Lebanon very crucial concessions which affect its sovereignty, unity, independence and its Arab national identity. This agreement falls within the framework of the continued American imperialist assault on our region and the attempts at implementing the second phase of the Camp David plan that would pave the way for the Jordanian regime to negotiate with the Zionist enemy a settlement that would lead to the liquidation of the Palestinian national rights and to the destruction of the PLO, the sole legitimate representative of the Palestinian people.

This agreement carries great dangers to Lebanon and great threats to

Syria, the PLO and all peoples of the region. Consequently, the forces of confrontation and the nationalist Arab countries are faced with the urgent task of foiling the implementation of this agreement and imposing the unconditional Israeli withdrawal from Lebanon in accordance with Security Council resolutions 508 and 509. The first step in performing these tasks is to consolidate the alliance between the various Lebanese nationalist forces, the PLO and Syria. In this context, the Lebanese nationalist forces are faced with the task of promptly forming a wide national front in order to develop political and armed resistance to the occupying forces.

The PLO is also requested to intensify its struggle against the agreement because it will greatly endanger the Palestinian cause and the interests of our people in Lebanon. The PLO should reject the withdrawal of its forces from the Beqaa and from North Lebanon, and should secure the interests of the Palestinians in Lebanon on the political, social and security levels.

The insistence by the United States and the Zionist entity on implementing the agreement could entail preparations for a new war of aggression. This situation faces Syria, the PLO, and the Lebanese national forces with the necessity of making serious preparations to confront this aggression and foil its aims. All Arab national forces and countries are expected to give real support to the forces of confrontation. All these forces have also the task of consolidating and developing their strategic relations with the socialist countries, especially the Soviet Union.

Citing the resolutions of the Arab summits, the Arab states should take all measures of economic and political boycott against the Lebanese authorities until they annul the agreement.

On the first anniversary of the Zionist-imperialist invasion of Lebanon, we call for consolidating our struggle in order to foil the Reagan plan and the Lebanese-Zionist agreement. We call for full alert and awareness in facing all possible aggressions by the Zionist-American enemy. Let us intensify our armed struggle against the occupation and confront all attempts at dividing the Palestinian ranks. Let us struggle to enhance and strengthen Palestinian national unity with the framework of the PLO and on democratic bases in accordance with the resolution of the consequent sessions of the Palestine National Council.

276. European Parliament Resolution on the Unfreezing of the Financial Relations between the European Community and the State of Israel, June 9, 1983*

* 26 O.J. Eur. Comm. (No. C 184) 97 (1983).

The European Parliament,

A. Whereas the Agreement of 17 May 1983 between Israel and Lebanon is a vital element of the Lebanese and Middle-East peace process;

B. Desiring an early implementation of this Agreement, which should involve the withdrawal of all foreign troups whose presence is not explicitly requested by the legitimate Lebanese authorities;

C. Stressing the substantial contribution made by several Member States to Unifil and to the multinational forces stationed in Lebanon;

D. Whereas the Agreement reached between Israel and the Lebanese Government creates favourable conditions for reopening the discussions on the financial protocol between the EEC and Israel which have been frozen since the entry of Israeli troops into Lebanon in June 1982;

1. Calls on the Council and Commission to unfreeze the financial relations between the EEC and Israel immediately;

2. Instructs its President to forward this resolution to the Council, the Commission and the Ministers for Foreign Affairs meeting in political cooperation.

277. Lebanon Emergency Assistance Act of 1983,

June 27, 1983*

* S. Res. 639, Pub. L. No. 98-43, 97 Stat. 214 (codified in scattered sections of 22 U.S.C.).

An Act

To authorize supplemental assistance to aid Lebanon in rebuilding its economy and armed forces, and for other purposes.

Be it enacted by the Senate and House of Representatives of the United States of America in Congress assembled,

SHORT TITLE

SECTION 1. This act may be cited as the "Lebanon Emergency Assistance Act of 1983".

ECONOMIC SUPPORT FUND

SEC. 2. (a) It is hereby determined that the national interests of the United States would be served by the authorization and appropriation of additional funds for economic assistance for Lebanon in order to promote the economic and political stability of that country and to support the international effort to strengthen a sovereign and independent Lebanon.

(b) Accordingly, in addition to amounts otherwise authorized to be appropriated for the fiscal year 1983 to carry out the provisions of chapter 4 of part II of the Foreign Assistance Act of 1961, there are authorized to be appropriated $150,000,000 to carry out such provisions with respect to Lebanon.

(c) Amounts authorized by this section may be appropriated in an appropriation Act for any fiscal year (including a continuing resolution) and shall continue to be available beyond that fiscal year notwithstanding any provision of that appropriation Act to the contrary.

MILITARY SALES AND RELATED PROGRAMS

SEC. 3. (a) In order to support the rebuilding of the armed forces of Lebanon, the Congress finds that the national security interests of the United States would be served by the authorization and appropriation of additional funds to provide training for the Lebanese armed forces and by the authorization of additional foreign military sales guaranties to finance procurements by Lebanon of defense articles and defense services for its security requirements.

(b) In addition to amounts otherwise made available for the fiscal year 1983 to carry out the provisions of chapter 5 of part II of the Foreign Assistance Act of 1961, there are authorized to be appropriated for the fiscal year 1983 $1,000,000 to carry out such provisions with respect to Lebanon.

(c) In addition to amounts otherwise made available for the fiscal year 1983 for loan guaranties under section 24(a) of the Arms Export Control Act, $100,000,000 of loan principal are authorized to be so guaranteed during such fiscal year for Lebanon.

UNITED STATES ARMED FORCES IN LEBANON

SEC. 4. (a) The President shall obtain statutory authorization from the Congress with respect to any substantial expansion in the number or role in

Lebanon of United States Armed Forces, including any introduction of United States Armed Forces into Lebanon in conjunction with agreements providing for the withdrawal of all foreign troops from Lebanon and for the creation of a new multinational peace-keeping force in Lebanon.

(b) Nothing in this section is intended to modify, limit, or suspend any of the standards and procedures prescribed by the War Powers Resolution of 1973.

Approved June 27, 1983.

278. Statement by the EEC Foreign Ministers on the Situation in Lebanon, September 12, 1983*

* 16 Bull. Eur. Comm. (No. 9) 82 (1983).

'The situation in Lebanon is more critical than at any other time in the last 16 months. The number of innocent victims increases every day.

The international community must do all it can to help put an end to this tragedy before it leads to the disintegration of Lebanon.

The Ten appeal for an immediate ceasefire leading to the cessation of violence and pressure in Lebanon, and to national reconciliation.

They call upon all parties to respect the independence, sovereignty and territorial integrity of Lebanon and the authority of its government.

They stress the need for early progress towards the complete withdrawal of all foreign forces from Lebanon, except as the Lebanese Government may request otherwise.

They are ready to work for these objectives, jointly and individually.

They are convinced that the abnormal situation in Lebanon, so long as it continues, is a further obstacle to the achievement of a just and lasting settlement in the Middle East as a whole.'

279. European Parliament Resolution on the Situation in
Lebanon, September 15, 1983*

---

* 26 O.J. Eur. Comm. (No. C 277) 127 (1983).

The European Parliament,

A. having regard to the resumption of hostilities in Lebanon,

B. deploring the attacks perpetrated against soldiers of the multinational peace-keeping force whose sole aim in going to Lebanon was to help restore peace,

C. appalled by the rise in the number of deaths in recent weeks, among soldiers of the multinational force and others,

1. Supports the Lebanese Government in its efforts to liberate Lebanon and restore national sovereignty throughout Lebanese territory;

2. Appeals urgently for hostilities to be ended and immediate efforts made to reach a negotiated solution;

3. Condemns the bombing of Beirut international airport, the Christian areas of the Lebanese capital and the mountains, and all attacks on the multinational peace-keeping force;

4. Urges the governments of all countries involved in the multinational force, and all the Governments of the Member States of the EEC, to increase their active support for the Lebanese Government;

5. Requests the Presidency of the Council to convene a meeting of the Ten on the problem of Lebanon as a matter of extreme urgency, so that the United Nations may propose an immediate and general ceasefire and suitable accompanying measures;

6. Instructs its President to forward this resolution to the Foreign Ministers meeting in Political Cooperation, the Council and the Commission.

280. Multinational Force in Lebanon Resolution, October 12, 1983*

---

* S.J. Res. 159, 97 Stat. 805 (1983).

Joint Resolution

Providing statutory authorization under the War Powers Resolution for continued United States participation in the multinational peacekeeping force in Lebanon in order to obtain withdrawal of all foreign forces from Lebanon.

Resolved by the Senate and House of Representatives of the United States of America in Congress assembled,

SHORT TITLE

SECTION 1. This joint resolution may be cited as the "Multinational Force in Lebanon Resolution".

FINDINGS AND PURPOSE

SEC. 2. (a) The Congress finds that—

(1) the removal of all foreign forces from Lebanon is an essential United States foreign policy objective in the Middle East;

(2) in order to restore full control by the Government of Lebanon over its own territory, the United States is currently participating in the multinational peacekeeping force (hereafter in this resolution referred to as the "Multinational Force in Lebanon") which was established in accordance with the exchange of letters between the Governments of the United States and Lebanon dated September 25, 1982;

(3) the Multinational Force in Lebanon better enables the Government of Lebanon to establish its unity, independence, and territorial integrity;

(4) progress toward national political reconciliation in Lebanon is necessary; and

(5) United States Armed Forces participating in the Multinational Force in Lebanon are now in hostilities requiring authorization of their continued presence under the War Powers Resolution.

(b) The Congress determines that the requirements of section 4(a)(1) of the War Powers Resolution became operative on August 29, 1983. Consistent with section 5(b) of the War Powers Resolution, the purpose of this joint resolution is to authorize the continued participation of United States Armed Forces in the Multinational Force in Lebanon.

(c) The Congress intends this joint resolution to constitute the necessary specific statutory authorization under the War Powers Resolution for continued participation by United States Armed Forces in the Multinational Force in Lebanon.

AUTHORIZATION FOR CONTINUED PARTICIPATION OF UNITED STATES ARMED FORCES IN THE MULTINATIONAL FORCE IN LEBANON

SEC. 3. The President is authorized, for purposes of section 5(b) of the War Powers Resolution, to continue participation by United States Armed Forces in the Multinational Force in Lebanon, subject to the provisions of section 6 of this joint resolution. Such participation shall be limited to performance of the functions, and shall be subject to the limitations, specified in the agreement establishing the Multinational Force in Lebanon as set forth in the exchange of letters between the Governments of the United States and Lebanon dated September 25, 1982, except that this shall not preclude such protective measures as may be necessary to ensure the safety of the Multinational Force in Lebanon.

REPORTS TO THE CONGRESS

SEC. 4. As required by section 4(c) of the War Powers Resolution, the President shall report periodically to the Congress with respect to the situation in Lebanon, but in no event shall he report less often than once every three months. In addition to providing the information required by that section on the status, scope, and duration of hostilities involving United States Armed Forces, such reports shall describe in detail—

(1) the activities being performed by the Multinational Force in Lebanon;

(2) the present composition of the Multinational Force in Lebanon, including a description of the responsibilities and deployment of the armed forces of each participating country;

(3) the results of efforts to reduce and eventually eliminate the Multinational Force in Lebanon;

(4) how continued United States participation in the Multinational Force in Lebanon is advancing United States foreign policy interests in the Middle East; and

(5) what progress has occurred toward national political reconciliation among all Lebanese groups.

STATEMENTS OF POLICY

SEC. 5. (a) The Congress declares that the participation of the armed forces of other countries in the Multinational Force in Lebanon is essential to maintain the international character of the peacekeeping function in Lebanon.

(b) The Congress believes that it should continue to be the policy of the United States to promote continuing discussions with Israel, Syria, and Lebanon with the objective of bringing about the withdrawal of all foreign troops from Lebanon and establishing an environment which will permit the Lebanese Armed Forces to carry out their responsibilities in the Beirut area.

(c) It is the sense of the Congress that, not later than one year after the date of enactment of this joint resolution and at least once a year thereafter, the United States should discuss with the other members of the Security Council of the United Nations the establishment of a United Nations peacekeeping force to assume the responsibilities of the Multinational Force in Lebanon. An analysis of the implications of the response to such discussions for the continuation of the Multinational Force in Lebanon shall be included in the reports required under paragraph (3) of section 4 of this resolution.

DURATION OF AUTHORIZATION FOR UNITED STATES PARTICIPATION IN THE MULTINATIONAL FORCE IN LEBANON

SEC. 6. The participation of United States Armed Forces in the Multinational Force in Lebanon shall be authorized for purposes of the War Powers Resolution until the end of the eighteen-month period beginning on the date of enactment of this resolution unless the Congress extends such authorization, except that such authorization shall terminate sooner upon the occurrence of any one of the following:

(1) the withdrawal of all foreign forces from Lebanon, unless the President determines and certifies to the Congress that continued United States Armed Forces participation in the Multinational Force in Lebanon is required after such withdrawal in order to accomplish the purposes specified in the September 25, 1982, exchange of letters providing for the establishment of the Multinational Force in Lebanon; or

(2) the assumption by the United Nations or the Government of Lebanon of the responsibilities of the Multinational Force in Lebanon; or

(3) the implementation of other effective security arrangements in the area; or

(4) the withdrawal of all other countries from participation in the Multinational Force in Lebanon.

INTERPRETATION OF THIS RESOLUTION

SEC. 7. (a) Nothing in this joint resolution shall preclude the President from withdrawing United States Armed Forces participation in the Multinational Force in Lebanon if circumstances warrant, and nothing in this joint resolution shall preclude the Congress by joint resolution from directing such a withdrawal.

(b) Nothing in this joint resolution modifies, limits, or supersedes any provision of the War Powers Resolution or the requirement of section 4(a) of the Lebanon Emergency Assistance Act of 1983, relating to congressional authorization for any substantial expansion in the number or role of United States Armed Forces in Lebanon.

CONGRESSIONAL PRIORITY PROCEDURES FOR AMENDMENTS

SEC. 8. (a) Any joint resolution or bill introduced to amend or repeal this Act shall be referred to the Committee on Foreign Affairs of the House of Representatives or the Committee on Foreign Relations of the Senate, as the case may be. Such joint resolution or bill shall be considered by such committee within fifteen calendar days and may be reported out, together with its recommendations, unless such House shall otherwise determine pursuant to its rules.

(b) Any joint resolution or bill so reported shall become the pending business of the House in question (in the case of the Senate the time for debate shall be equally divided between the proponents and the opponents) and shall be voted on within three calendar days thereafter, unless such House shall otherwise determine by the yeas and nays.

(c) Such a joint resolution or bill passed by one House shall be referred to the committee of the other House named in subsection (a) and shall be reported out by such committee together with its recommendations within fifteen calendar days and shall thereupon become the pending business of such House and shall be voted upon within three calendar days, unless such House shall otherwise determine by the yeas and nays.

(d) In the case of any disagreement between the two Houses of Congress with respect to a joint resolution or bill passed by both Houses, conferees shall be promptly appointed and the committee of conference shall make and file a report with respect to such joint resolution within six calendar days after the legislation is referred to the committee of conference. Notwithstanding any rule in either House concerning the printing of conference reports in the Record or concerning any delay in the consideration of such reports, such report shall be acted on by both Houses not later than six calendar days after the conference report is filed. In the event the conferees are unable to agree within forty-eight hours, they shall report back to their respective Houses in disagreement.

Approved October 12, 1983.

281. Excerpt from the Final Statement of the Geneva Conference on Lebanese National Dialogue, Geneva, November 4, 1983*

---

* 13 J. Palestine Stud. 217 (Winter 1984).

... The discussion [of the Conference] which focused on cooperation to liberate Lebanese territory from Israeli occupation and ensure Lebanon's full and absolute sovereignty over all its territory, along with determination to lay the foundations of a strong state based on justice, was held in the context of comprehensive national accord. The Conference also committed itself to strengthen Lebanon's Arab relations and international friendships.

The discussions which were held in a spirit of national responsibility, an atmosphere of complete frankness and related to all the subjects under review, led to the following:

I. Unanimous agreement on a formula defining Lebanon's identity, as follows:

Lebanon is a sovereign, free and independent country. Its land, people and institutions are united within the frontiers defined in the Lebanese Constitution and which are internationally recognized. Lebanon is part of the Arab nation and its identity is Arab. It is a founding and active member of the League of Arab States and abides by all the commitments entered into by it, and the state must embody these principles in all fields and areas of its activity without exception.

II. Unanimous agreement that, in view of the circumstances that accompanied the signing of the agreement of May 17, 1983, and because of the international complications that could result from the continuation of the present situation, the conference should request the President of the Lebanese Republic, Sheikh Amin Gemayel, to take measures and make the necessary international contacts with a view to ending the Israeli occupation and securing Lebanon's full and absolute sovereignty over all its territory and in all national fields.

III. It was agreed to strengthen the Security Committee in order that it may supervise the maintenance of security and take the necessary arrangements, receive and investigate complaints and ensure the proper implementation of decisions.

IV. To facilitate the work of the Conference, it was agreed that the conferees shall submit their reform proposals in all fields to the Secretariat General so that it may collate and coordinate them and prepare them for discussion at future sessions.

282. European Community Statement on the Events in the

North of Lebanon, November 9, 1983*

* 16 Bull. Eur. Comm. (No. 11) 68 (1983).

'The Ten are deeply concerned at the fighting in the north of Lebanon, which is causing intolerable suffering and large-scale loss of life, particularly among the civilian population of the region, Palestinians and Lebanese alike.

The Ten, who have frequently expressed their opposition to the use or threat of force in the Middle East, appeal to all those concerned to put an immediate halt to the fighting and let reason and moderation prevail.

This fresh outbreak of violence highlights more than ever the urgent need to seek a negotiated settlement of the region's problems, in accordance with the principles which the Ten set out in the conclusions of the European Council on 29 June 1982[1] and in subsequent statements. In particular, self-determination for the Palestinian people, with all that this implies, remains a fundamental issue which must be dealt with in the context of a fair and lasting overall solution to the conflict.'

[1] Bull. EC 6-1982, point 1.5.4.

283. White House Statement on the Situation in Northern
Lebanon, November 10, 1983*

* 84 U.S. Dep't State Bull. No. 2082, at 69 (January 1984).

We're revolted that once again the people of Lebanon have been subjected to terror and injury, this time around Tripoli by the radical and brutal behavior of Palestinian factions and their supporters. It is tragic that once again the civilian population of Lebanon is victim to hostilities not of their making and over which they are unable to exercise influence and control.

We urge the governments in the area to bring their influence to bear constructively to end the fighting. We suggest that all governments be open to any suggestions from appropriate international organizations for humanitarian and relief efforts to relieve the suffering. As a first specific step to assist, the United States is in the process of contributing $1 million to the International Red Cross to be used for relief activities in Lebanon.

284. European Parliament Resolution on the Situation in
Tripoli, Lebanon, November 17, 1983*

* 26 O.J. Eur. Comm. (No. C 342) 51 (1983).

The European Parliament,

A. wishing the Palestinian civilians and the fighters surrounded in Tripoli by Syrian and Libyan forces in particular to have the right to humanitarian treatment in accordance with the Geneva conventions,
B. aware of the need for Europe to make its voice heard in the face of the massacre of civilian populations,
C. supporting the efforts to establish negotiations and secure peace being made by various Arab countries and France,

   1. Calls on the European governments who played a decisive part in the Beirut agreement to intervene again and instigate urgently a further international initiative;

   2. Calls on the Foreign Ministers meeting in political cooperation to provide diplomatic support for the efforts at mediation;

   3. Instructs its President to forward this resolution to the Council and to the Foreign Ministers meeting in political cooperation.

285. Security Council Resolution 542 Requesting a Cease-Fire in Northern Lebanon, November 23, 1983*

* S.C. Res. 542, 38 U.N. SCOR (2501st mtg.) at 4, U.N. Doc. S/INF/39 (1983).

The Security Council,

Having considered the situation prevailing in northern Lebanon,

Recalling the statement made on this question by the President of the Security Council on 11 November 1983,[21]

Deeply concerned by the intensification of the fighting, which continues to cause great suffering and loss of human life,

1. *Deplores* the loss of human life caused by the events taking place in northern Lebanon;

2. *Reiterates its call* for the strict respect for the sovereignty, political independence and territorial integrity of Lebanon within its internationally recognized boundaries;

3. *Requests* the parties concerned immediately to accept a cease-fire and scrupulously to observe the cessation of hostilities;

4. *Invites* the parties concerned to settle their differences exclusively by peaceful means and to refrain from the threat or use of force;

5. *Pays tribute* to the work done by the United Nations Relief and Works Agency for Palestine Refugees in the Near East and by the International Committee of the Red Cross in providing emergency humanitarian assistance to the Palestinian and Lebanese civilians in Tripoli and its surroundings;

6. *Calls upon* the parties concerned to comply with the provisions of the present resolution;

7. *Requests* the Secretary-General to follow the situation in northern Lebanon, to consult with the Government of Lebanon, and to report to the Security Council, which remains seized of the question.

Adopted unanimously at the 2501st meeting.

[21] Document S/16142, incorporated in the record of the 2496th meeting.

286. Joint Statement by the Popular and Democratic Fronts for the Liberation of Palestine on Proposed Five-Point Palestinian Initiative for Ending the Tripoli Fighting and Protecting Palestinian National Unity, Damascus, November 23, 1983*

* 13 J. Palestine Stud. 198 (Spring 1984).

The proposed initiative stipulates the following:

1. Full adherence to the ceasefire, the halting of military activity in the North, the issue by both parties to the conflict of a clear declaration of commitment not to resort to arms and acceptance of the principle of democratic dialogue in this dispute.

2. The formation of a Palestinian commission to observe the ceasefire, the Joint Command declaring its readiness to place its resources at the disposal of this observation commission.

3. The elimination of armed concentrations in North Lebanon, in accordance with the following principles: (a) The re-deployment of all Palestinian fighters in their original positions; (b) The re-deployment of all forces of the Palestine revolution in positions in which they will be able to perform their duty in the struggle against Israeli occupation; (c) Reaffirmation of the right of all sections of the revolution to enjoy a presence in all the Palestinian camps in the Lebanese arena, and commitment by all parties to honor this right; (d) The evacuation of Palestinian fighters from the city of Tripoli and steps to ensure that all Lebanese nationalist forces can once again exercise their self-evident right to enjoy a presence and to engage in military and political activity in the city, in full freedom.

4. An immediate start on a dialogue between the two parties of Fateh to solve its crisis on the basis of the principles set out in the memorandum of the delegation of the Central Council, in conformity with a detailed schedule for the implementation of these principles to be agreed on by both parties following the dialogue between them, with the participation of a Palestinian arbitration committee consisting of the President of the Palestine National Council, the members of the PLO Executive Committee and the Secretaries General of all sections of the revolution.

5. In view of the crisis within Fateh, the committee consisting of the President of the National Council, the Executive Committee and the Secretaries General shall hold an intensive working session to study the situation of the PLO and discuss the proposals that have been put forward to rectify and improve this situation, including the program of unity and democratic reform proposed by the Joint Command of the Popular and Democratic Fronts, in response to the call of the National Council to hold such a meeting to decide the reforms.

287. European Parliament Resolution on the Situation in
Lebanon, December 15, 1983*

* 27 O.J. Eur. Comm. (No. C 10) 70 (1984).

The European Parliament,

A. having regard to its previous resolutions on the situation in the Middle East,

B. deeply concerned by the aggravation of the crisis in this region and, in particular, in the Lebanon,

1. Resolves to send immediately to the Lebanon, Syria, Israel, Jordan and Egypt a delegation at the highest level headed by its President to examine the possibilities for finding a solution and to report back to it with a view to tabling an emergency resolution on all of the problems currently affecting the Lebanon;

2. Instructs its President to forward this resolution to the Council, the Commission and the governments of the abovementioned countries.

288. President Reagan's Statements on the Increased Violence in Lebanon, February 6–7, 1984*

* 84 U.S. Dep't State Bull. No. 2084, at 47 (March 1984) (notes omitted).

President's Statement, Feb. 6, 1984

Once more the news from Lebanon is filled with scenes of indiscriminate killing and suffering. I know that men and women of good will throughout the world share my deep concern over the renewed violence. They join me in deploring the continued shelling of innocent civilians and the actions of those who would destroy the legitimate Government of Lebanon.

I call on the Government of Syria, which occupies Lebanese territory from which much of the shelling of civilian centers originates and which facilitates and supplies instruments for terrorist attacks on the people of Lebanon, to cease this activity.

President Gemayel is now hard at work trying to form a new government. I welcome his efforts to stop the fighting and to resume the talks in Geneva aimed at achieving national reconciliation. He has set forth a specific agenda of reforms and reconciliation and demonstrated again his openness to a dialogue on all the issues. He has demonstrated a strong desire to bring all factions together to develop equitable and durable political and economic arrangements for his country.

All responsible Lebanese political leaders should take this opportunity to bring into being the more broadly representative government they say they want and which we have continually supported. I urge all parties to answer President Gemayel's call. It is time for all Lebanese to rise above their confessional or factional affiliation and join together as citizens of one nation, united and sovereign.

The commitment of the United States to the unity, independence, and sovereignty of Lebanon remains firm and unwavering. We will continue to support the Government and the people of Lebanon in their efforts to achieve these goals. With good will and hard work, the dream of a rebuilt and reunited Lebanon can still be made a reality. We remain committed to help in that task.

President's Statement, Feb. 7, 1984

The bloodshed we have witnessed in Lebanon over the last several days only demonstrates once again the length to which the forces of violence and intimidation are prepared to go to prevent a peaceful reconciliation process from taking place. If a moderate government is overthrown because it had the courage to turn in the direction of peace, what hope can there be that other moderates in the region will risk committing themselves to a similar course? Yielding to violence and terrorism today may seem to provide temporary relief, but such a course is sure to lead to a more dangerous and less manageable future crisis.

Even before the latest outbreak of violence, we had been considering ways of reconcentrating our forces and the nature of our support in order to take the initiative away from the terrorists. Far from deterring us from this course, recent events only confirm the importance of the decisive new steps I want to outline for you now. Thus after consultation with our MNF [multinational forces] partners and President Gemayel and at his request, we are prepared to do the following.

First, to enhance the safety of Americans and other MNF personnel in Lebanon, I have authorized U.S. naval forces, under the existing mandate of the MNF, to provide naval gunfire and air support against any units firing into greater Beirut from parts of Lebanon controlled by Syria, as well as against any units directly attacking American or MNF personnel and facilities. Those who conduct these attacks will no longer have sanctuary from which to bombard Beirut at will. We will stand firm to deter those who seek to influence Lebanon's future by intimidation.

Second, when the Government of Lebanon is able to reconstitute itself into a broadly based, representative government, we will vigorously accelerate the training, equipping, and support of the Lebanese Armed Forces, on whom the primary responsibility rests for maintaining stability in Lebanon. We will speed up delivery of equipment; we will improve the flow of information to help counter hostile bombardments; and we will intensify training in counterterrorism to help the Lebanese confront the terrorist threat that poses such a danger to Lebanon, to Americans in Lebanon, and, indeed, to peace in the Middle East.

Third, in conjunction with these steps, I have asked Secretary of Defense Weinberger to present to me a plan for redeployment of the Marines from Beirut Airport to their ships offshore. This redeployment will begin shortly and will proceed in stages. U.S. military personnel will remain on the ground in Lebanon for training and equipping the Lebanese Army and protecting the remaining personnel. These are conditional functions that U.S. personnel perform in many friendly countries. Our naval and Marine forces offshore will stand ready, as before, to provide support for the protection of American and other MNF personnel in Lebanon and thereby help ensure security in the Beirut area as I have described.

These measures, I believe, will strengthen our ability to do the job we set out to do and to sustain our efforts over the long term. They are consistent with the compromise joint resolution worked out last October with the Congress with respect to our participation in the multinational force.

289. European Parliament Resolution on the Situation in Lebanon, February 16, 1984*

* 27 O.J. Eur. Comm. (No. C 77) 70 (1984).

The European Parliament,

A. gravely concerned by the danger of still greater loss of life in the Lebanon,

B. recognizing the desirability of the formation of a government of national unity,

C. noting the interest of the Syrian and United States Governments in the French proposal to replace the multinational force with a United Nations force,

1. Calls on the Foreign Ministers meeting in Political Cooperation to consider this proposal as soon as possible;

2. Stresses that for a United Nations force to be of any use, it would have to be capable of resisting attacks on itself and on the civilian population entrusted to its protection;

3. Calls on the Community and the Member States to provide as much assistance as possible to the civilian victims of violence;

4. Instructs its President to forward this resolution to the Commission, the Council and the Foreign Ministers meeting in Political Cooperation.

290. Statement by the EEC Foreign Ministers on Lebanon,

February 27, 1984*

* 17 Bull. Eur. Comm. (No. 2) 94 (1984).

'The Ten:

(i) express concern at the recent events in Lebanon which have been characterized by a renewal of armed confrontation and a struggle between the Lebanese political forces and which threaten to perpetuate the division of the country and the presence of foreign troops in its territory;

(ii) call on all the parties concerned to reach a lasting and effective cease-fire agreement;

(iii) hope that the international community will urgently fulfil its responsibilities in regard to peacekeeping, in particular by installing in the Beirut conurbation with the agreement of all the parties concerned a United Nations force which would take up position following the departure of the Multinational Force on the basis of the mandate to be entrusted to it by the Security Council;

(iv) recall that the re-establishment of the territorial integrity and sovereignty of the Lebanese State requires Lebanese reconciliation as a precondition and indicate their firm conviction that the process initiated during the Geneva conference should be resumed under conditions corresponding to the aspirations of all the political and religious interests;

(v) note that this objective involves also the withdrawal of all foreign troops except those whose presence is agreed to by the Lebanese Government;

(vi) consider that the various Lebanese movements should be able to agree on a definition of the external status of their country which takes into account both its position in the Arab world and the desire of its population to no longer be exposed to the consequences of a conflict which has already caused it so much suffering.

The Ten subsequently dealt with the unresolved problems of the Middle East with which the events in Lebanon are closely linked, without prejudice to the discussion of this subject which the European Council could have on 19-20 March.'

291. Question to the Foreign Ministers of EEC Concerning
Unilateral Withdrawal by the USA from the Multinational
Peace-keeping Force in Lebanon, March 12, 1984—
Answer, June 6, 1984*

* 27 O.J. Eur. Comm. (No. C 177) 13 (1984).

WRITTEN QUESTION NO 2205/83
by Mr Pietro Lezzi (S-I)
to the Foreign Ministers of the 10 Member States of the European
Communities meeting in political cooperation
(12 March 1984)
(84/C 177/21)

Subject: Unilateral withdrawal by the USA from the multinational peace-keeping force in Lebanon

What do the Foreign Ministers meeting in political cooperation think of the USA's unilateral decision to withdraw the marines from the multinational peace-keeping force in Lebanon and the intensification of the American naval bombardment, which inevitably causes grief and destruction among the population and seriously endangers the lives of French and Italian soldiers who, true to the spirit of their mission in Lebanon, remain in Beirut to protect the Palestinian refugee camps which is, in the opinion of *The Times*, an admirable example of honourable behaviour?

Faced with the deteriorating situation, what steps do the Ministers intend to take to promote the idea of bringing in United Nations troops to help Lebanon extricate itself from the chaotic and explosive situation it is in at present? Lebanon's integrity and unity must be resolutely defended in order to remedy the twists and turns of US policy and the serious consequences that would ensue if Europe had no role in Lebanon, the Middle East and the Mediterranean?

ANSWER
(6 June 1984)

The Ten have on various occasions expressed the wish that the Multinational Force should be able to carry out its peace mission in Lebanon with the agreement of all the parties concerned and in accordance with the principles behind its creation:

– they followed with great concern the events in Lebanon last February, which resulted in the successive departure of the various contingents of the Multinational Force. As the obligations of each of the countries taking part were governed by a bilateral agreement concluded with the Lebanese Government, they have no opinion to give regarding the implementation of the US/Lebanon agreement by the United States;

– when those events took place they expressed the wish that the international community should, as a matter of urgency, assume its responsibilities for restoring peace in Lebanon by installing in Beirut, with the agreement of all the parties concerned, a United Nations force which would take up its position on the departure of the Multinational Force. They deeply regretted that this solution came to nothing;

— the Ten continue to attach prime importance to the restoration of Lebanon's independence, sovereignty, unity and territorial integrity. They hope that the Lebanese Government and all political forces will continue their effort to consolidate national unity and establish lasting peace throughout the country.

292. Statement by the EEC Foreign Ministers on Lebanon, March 19–20, 1984*

* 17 Bull. Eur. Comm. (No. 3) 79 (1984).

The ten Heads of State or Government recall the fundamental importance of the re-establishment of Lebanon in its independence, sovereignty, unity and territorial integrity. The Ten hope that, following the Lausanne Conference, progress towards reconciliation in Lebanon will prove possible. They hope that the Lebanese Government and all political forces will continue their efforts to bring about national unity and establish a lasting peace throughout the country by reaching a just solution to its internal problems which respects Lebanese sovereignty and the desire of the population of that country to escape from the suffering inflicted on it by the Middle East conflict. They underline the need to initiate without delay processes which will lead to the withdrawal of foreign forces from Lebanese territory.

They express the hope that the international community will shortly be in a position to give the Lebanese Government any help it requests in order to maintain peace in the country.

They undertake to participate actively at the appropriate time in the work of reconstructing Lebanon.

293. President Reagan's Letter to the Congress Reporting on the Withdrawal of U.S. Marines from Lebanon, March 30, 1984*

---

* 84 U.S. Dep't State Bull. No. 2086, at 68 (May 1984).

Since the date of my last report to you on the participation of United States Armed Forces in the Multinational Force (MNF) in Lebanon, I have decided that the U.S. will terminate its participation in the MNF. In accordance with my desire that Congress be kept informed on these matters, and consistent with Section 4 of the Multinational Force in Lebanon Resolution, I am hereby providing a final report on our participation in the MNF.

U.S. foreign policy interests in Lebanon have not changed, and remain as stated in my last report to Congress on February 13. The U.S. is committed to the goals of the restoration of a sovereign, independent and united Lebanon, the withdrawal of all foreign forces, and the security of Israel's northern border. However, the continuation of our participation in the MNF is no longer a necessary or appropriate means of achieving these goals. We have discussed our decision with the Government of Lebanon and the other MNF participants, and the other MNF countries have made similar decisions.

The U.S. military personnel who made up the U.S. MNF contingent were earlier redeployed to U.S. ships offshore. Likewise, the MNF personnel of other national contingents have either already departed Lebanon or are in the process of departing.

As you know, prior to their earlier redeployment to ships offshore, U.S. MNF personnel had come under intermittent hostile fire as a result of continued fighting in the Beirut area, including the round of serious fighting that occurred in late February. On February 25-26, and again on February 29, U.S. warships returned fire against artillery and rocket positions in Syrian-controlled territory that had fired on U.S. military and diplomatic locations and on U.S. reconnaissance flights.

During the overall course of our participation in the MNF, U.S. forces suffered a total of 264 killed (of which 4 non-MNF personnel were killed in the April 1983 bombing of the U.S. Embassy), and 137 wounded in action. (Three of these were wounded in the period since my last report to Congress on February 13.) The estimated cost of U.S. participation in the MNF for FY 1984 was a total of $14.6 million for the U.S. Marine Corps deployment, $44.9 million for U.S. Navy support, and $243,000 for U.S. Army support.

These were heavy burdens and grievous losses for our country. We owe a great debt of gratitude to those military and diplomatic personnel of the United States and other MNF countries who served their countries so proudly to give the people of Lebanon a chance to achieve peace and national reconciliation.

The United States has not abandoned Lebanon. The U.S. Embassy in Beirut remains in full and active operation and a Marine detachment of approximately 100 personnel drawn from the Marine unit afloat remains to provide additional external security for our diplomatic mission. In addition, a limited number of U.S. military personnel (equipped with personal weapons for self-defense) will remain to provide military training and security assistance liaison to the Lebanese Armed Forces. These personnel will not be part of any multinational force; they will be deployed under the authority of the Foreign Assistance and Arms Export Control Acts, and my Constitutional authority with respect to the conduct of foreign relations and as Commander-in-Chief of U.S. Forces. I do not intend or expect, under present circumstances, that these personnel will become involved in hostilities; nonetheless, U.S. naval and air forces in the Mediterranean area, including the U.S. Marines redeployed from Lebanon, are available to protect our military and diplomatic personnel should that need ever arise.

I appreciate the support for this vital effort that Congress provided last October in adopting the Multinational Force in Lebanon Resolution. I hope that Congress will support the programs of economic and security assistance that are essential for the future of Lebanon and the Middle East. I will keep Congress informed on events in Lebanon, and on the U.S. role in encouraging peace and stability in the area.

Sincerely,

RONALD REAGAN

294. European Parliament Resolution on the Situation in
Lebanon, April 12, 1984*

* 27 O.J. Eur. Comm. (No. C 127) 82 (1984).

The European Parliament,

A. appalled by the continuing violence in Lebanon which since September 1983 alone has driven a third of the population from their homes,

B. repeating its demand for the withdrawal of all foreign forces from Lebanese territory whose presence is not desired by the Lebanese Government,

1. Calls on the Governments of the Member States to recognize publicly their continuing responsibility to assist in the search for a peaceful settlement;

2. Urges the Governments of Member States and the Commission to do all in their power to assist the civilian victims of the conflict especially through the provision of medical teams and equipment;

3. Calls attention to the fact that the relations of the Member States and of the Community with other States in the area are bound to be affected by their policies and actions towards Lebanon;

4. Instructs its President to forward this resolution to the Council, the Commission, the Foreign Ministers meeting in political cooperation and the Lebanese Government.

295. Statement by the Council of Ministers of Lebanon on the Decision to Abrogate the May 17 Agreement, Beirut, March 5, 1984*

* 13 J. Palestine Stud. 205 (Summer 1984).

At the invitation of the President of the Republic, Shaykh Amin Gemayel, the Prime Minister, Mr. Shafiqal-Wazzan and the Ministers met at the Presidential Palace in the morning of Monday March 5, 1984. They reviewed the current situation at the security and political levels, including the talks held in Damascus between their Excellencies Presidents Gemayel and Assad, which talks showed that there was agreement on numerous points and principles that could form the prelude to the solution of the crisis which besets the country.

His Excellency the President made it clear that a whole series of vital and constitutional issues presuppose the existence of a government with full powers to confront the tasks required of it. For this reason, he requested the Prime Minister to withdraw the resignation of his government, especially as no decree had been issued accepting its resignation, and he sent him a letter to this effect.

As a result of consultations, and in view of the fateful and exceptional circumstances through which the country is passing, which require the taking of fundamental decisions, not to mention the fact that President Gemayel had been obliged to leave the country for reasons connected with the higher and fateful interests of the country within the framework of attending the conference on national dialogue, and in conformity with Article 62 of the Lebanese Constitution, the Prime Minister acceded to the request of the President of the Republic that he withdraw the resignation of his government for a short time. He assured His Excellency the President of his desire that he may rapidly succeed in forming a new government of National unity. Mr. al-Wazzan sent President Gemayel a letter to this effect.

A session of the Council of Ministers was then convened and there was an exhaustive discussion of issues connected with the current situation in the country and the dangers that threaten it at all levels. The Council of Ministers discussed the outcome of the talks in Damascus of the President of the Republic and the Foreign Minister, the aim of which was that Lebanon might recover its unity, pursue the course of salvation, recover full sovereignty over its territory and achieve the desired reforms. The Council also reconsidered the May 17 Agreement of 1983 which Lebanon had believed might be a means of securing Israel's withdrawal from its territory, once the withdrawal from Beirut had been completed. Lebanon had not ratified this Agreement so that it was only a plan not a ratified agreement.

The Prime Minister pointed out that Lebanon had not ratified this agreement, and that he considered it as abrogated, this view having been clearly expressed in all the discussions of the Council of Ministers during the last few months. There was all the more reason for this in view of Israel's actions which have run counter to its undertakings to withdraw. The Prime Minister had, moreover, informed the Secretary General of the Arab League of this view in September 1983, affirming that the Agreement was abrogated.

The Foreign Minister also pointed out that the letter sent by Lebanon to the American side that participated in the Agreement, in reply to the letter from the Israeli side stipulating Syrian and Palestinian withdrawal, had affirmed Lebanon's right to suspend or abrogate the Agreement, while reserving its right to secure [Israel's] withdrawal in such ways as it saw fit.

Inasmuch as the new developments that have taken place in the Lebanese arena require the abandonment of this method that had been employed to achieve this end, and consequently, the abrogation of the Agreement and continued efforts to secure withdrawal in all other ways likely to prove successful until such time as all the territory of Lebanon is completely liberated, the Council of Ministers, after examining Articles 56 and 57 of the Lebanese Constitution, which stipulate that the President of the Republic should either promulgate or return, within a specified period of time, a law submitted to him by the Chamber of Deputies.

And inasmuch as the President of the Republic did not promulgate the law passed by the Chamber of Deputies on June 14, 1983, authorizing the Chamber to ratify the Agreement concluded between the representatives of the Lebanese government and Israel, with the participation of the US as witness to the Agreement, and the President of the Republic did not return the law to the Chamber of Deputies within the specified period; the Council of Ministers, at its session of March 5, 1984, with the President of the Republic in the chair, decided the following:

1. To repeal the decision of the Council of Ministers of May 14, 1983 approving the above-mentioned agreement which was signed on May 17, 1983 by the representatives of the Lebanese government and Israel and witnessed by the US, to abrogate this unratified agreement and regard it as null and void, and to invalidate any result it may have had.

2. To inform the signatories of the Agreement of this decision.

3. That the Lebanese government shall take the necessary steps with a view to making security arrangements and measures to ensure sovereignty, security and stability in South Lebanon, to prevent infiltration across the southern frontier and to secure the withdrawal of Israeli forces from all the territory of Lebanon.

296. Security Council Resolution 549 Renewing the U.N.

Interim Force in Lebanon Mandate, April 19, 1984*

---

* S.C. Res. 549, 39 U.N. SCOR (2530th mtg.) at 6, U.N. Doc. S/INF/40 (1984). *See also* subsequent resolutions, S.C. Res. 555, 39 U.N. SCOR (2559th mtg.) at 8, U.N. Doc. S/INF/40 (1984), S.C. Res. 561, 40 U.N. SCOR (2575th mtg.) (1985) and S.C. Res. 575, 40 U.N. SCOR (2623rd mtg.) (1985).

The Security Council,

Recalling its resolutions 425 (1978), 426 (1978), 501 (1982), 508 (1982), 509 (1982) and 520 (1982), as well as all it resolutions on the situation in Lebanon,

Having studied the report of the Secretary-General on the United Nations Interim Force in Lebanon of 9 April 1984[18] and taking note of the observations expressed therein,

Taking note of the letter of the Permanent Representative of Lebanon to the Secretary-General of 9 April 1984,[19]

Responding to the request of the Government of Lebanon,

1. *Decides* to extend the present mandate of the United Nations Interim Force in Lebanon for a further interim period of six months, that is, until 19 October 1984;

2. *Reiterates* its strong support for the territorial integrity, sovereignty and independence of Lebanon within its internationally recognized boundaries;

3. *Re-emphasizes* the terms of reference and general guidelines of the Force as stated in the report of the Secretary-General of 19 March 1978,[20] approved by resolution 426 (1978), and calls upon all parties concerned to co-operate fully with the Force for the full implementation of its mandate;

4. *Reiterates* that the Force should fully implement its mandate as defined in resolutions 425 (1978), 426 (1978) and all other relevant resolutions;

5. *Requests* the Secretary-General to continue consultations with the Government of Lebanon and other parties directly concerned on the implementation of the present resolution and to report to the Council thereon.

Adopted at the 2530th meeting by 13 votes to none, with 2 abstentions (Ukrainian Soviet Socialist Republic, Union of Soviet Socialist Republics).

[18] *Ibid.,* [*Official Records of the Security Council, Thirty-ninth Year, Supplement for April, May and June 1984*], document S/16472.

[19] *Ibid.,* document S/16471.

[20] *Ibid., Thirty-third Year, Supplement for January, February and March 1978*, document S/12611.

297. Statement by the EEC Foreign Ministers on Demarche on Lebanon, February 12, 1985*

* 18 Bull. Eur. Comm. (No. 2) 69 (1985).

'The Ten welcome Israel's decision to withdraw its forces from Lebanon, thus bringing an end to its prolonged occupation of the Lebanese territory, in accordance with the resolutions of the Security Council. They consider that the parties concerned should do all that is in their power to promote an orderly, complete withdrawal.

The Ten urge the Lebanese and Israeli Governments to show flexibility in establishing reasonable security arrangements for the territory to be returned by Israel and to do everything possible to prevent new acts of violence in the whole of the area of Israeli withdrawal.

The Ten believe that an orderly, complete and coordinated withdrawal of Israeli forces, together with appropriate security arrangements for both Lebanon and Israel, is in the interests of all the countries in the region. The Ten also look to the Syrian Government to facilitate such a process that they view as a major step towards the restoration of stability in Lebanon and the recovery of its entire territory, which will lead to a reduction in tension in the area as a whole.

Leaders of the different communities in Lebanon should play their full part in the above process, taking into consideration the existing risk of renewed instability and suffering to all communities, particularly in the areas to be evacuated.

The Ten continue to support UN efforts to bring about the orderly withdrawal of Israeli forces. They also think that the United Nations, and in particular the Secretary-General, in accordance with Resolution 523 (1982), will be able to play a valuable role in the zones to be evacuated, especially as regards ensuring the safety of the inhabitants of the region, guaranteeing Lebanon's territorial integrity and re-establishing international peace and security.'

298. Statement by the EEC Foreign Ministers on Lebanon, April 29, 1985*

* 18 Bull. Eur. Comm. (No. 4) 59 (1985).

'The Ten continue to view with concern the deterioration of the situation in Lebanon and in particular its consequences for the civilian population in the south, which continues to be subjected to unjustifiable acts of violence. Following the Israeli Government's decision to withdraw its forces, they look for the early, orderly and complete withdrawal of those forces from that region in accordance with the relevant resolutions of the UN Security Council, as well as of those other forces which are not there at the request of the Lebanese Government. The Ten consider it important that appropriate security arrangements be reached between the Israeli and the Lebanese Governments.

The Ten appeal to all the parties concerned, both within Lebanon and outside, to act in such a way as to facilitate the process of restoring the sovereignty, unity, territorial integrity and independence of Lebanon, a process which has been seriously compromised by the recent worsening of the political and security situation. The Ten reaffirm their support for Unifil. The Ten call on all parties to respect Unifil's role, avoiding all incidents, cooperating fully with the force and ensuring the safety of its personnel.

They are deeply concerned at the suffering of the Lebanese people and at the kidnappings involving foreign nationals.'

299. European Parliament Resolution on the Situation in
Lebanon, May 9, 1985*

---

* 28 O.J. Eur. Comm. (No. C 141) 456 (1985).

The European Parliament,

A. having regard to its previous resolutions calling for a return to peace in Lebanon and respect for this sovereign country's integrity,

B. deeply shocked by the violence and continued fighting in south Lebanon, especially the sufferings of the Christian communities,

1. Calls, in view of the mounting threat to the existence of the Christian community, for UNIFIL's mandate to be extended so that it can afford complete protection to the civilian population;

2. Condemns any foreign interference in Lebanon's internal affairs;

3. Calls on the Member States of the EEC to take any steps needed to encourage the withdrawal of all foreign forces and the re-establishment of peace, unity and Lebanese sovereignty;

4. Requests the Commission and the governments of the Member States, in view of this tragic situation, to make preparations for taking in civilian refugees and for providing them with material aid;

5. Instructs its President to forward this resolution to the Council, the Commission, the Foreign Ministers meeting in Political Cooperation, the Lebanese Government and the Secretary-General of the United Nations.

300. European Parliament Resolution on the Situation in
Lebanon, May 9, 1985*

* 28 O.J. Eur. Comm. (No. C 141) 457 (1985).

The European Parliament,

A. whereas the people of Lebanon of all creeds are entitled to peace and security,

B. whereas the massacre of Christians in Lebanon by Shiite and Druze militias armed and directed by the Syrian Government amounts to genocide,

1. Is alarmed at the fate of the Christian community in Lebanon;

2. Deplores the inaction of Western countries committed to the cause of human rights and the unacceptable situation prevailing in Lebanon as a result;

3. Calls on the Council as a matter of urgency to make representations to the Syrian Government and the Government of Lebanon to halt the genocide of the Christian population;

4. Calls on the EEC Member States to take whatever steps are necessary to restore peace, unity and national sovereignty in Lebanon, notably by sending a UN international force;

5. Calls on the Commission to send urgent humanitarian aid to help the afflicted population, notably in the region of Jezzine, which is ravaged by famine;

6. Instructs its President to forward this resolution to the Council, Commission and to the governments of the Member States of the European Community.

301. Security Council Resolution 564 Expressing Concern Over the Continuing Violence in Lebanon and Calling for Respect for U.N. Agencies and the Lebanese Government, May 31, 1985*

* S.C. Res. 564, 40 U.N. SCOR (2582nd mtg.) (1985).

The Security Council,

Recalling the statement made by its President on 24 May 1985 (S/17215) on behalf of its members on the heightened violence in certain parts of Lebanon,

Alarmed at the continued escalation of violence involving the civilian population, including Palestinians in refugee camps, resulting in grievous casualties, and material destruction on all sides,

1. *Expresses* anew its deepest concern at the heavy costs in human lives and material destruction affecting the civilian population in Lebanon, and calls on all concerned to end acts of violence against the civilian population in Lebanon and in particular in and around Palestinian refugee camps;

2. *Reiterates* its calls for respect for the sovereignty, independence and territorial integrity of Lebanon;

3. *Calls on* all parties to take necessary measures to alleviate the suffering resulting from acts of violence, in particular by facilitating the work of United Nations agencies, especially the United Nations Relief and Works Agency for Palestine Refugees in the Near East, and non-governmental organizations, including the International Committee of the Red Cross, in providing humanitarian assistance to all those affected and emphasizes the need to ensure the safety of all the personnel of these organizations;

4. *Appeals to* all interested parties to co-operate with the Lebanese Government and the Secretary-General with a view to ensuring the implementation of this resolution, and requests the Secretary-General to report to the Security Council;

5. *Reaffirms* its intention to continue to follow closely the situation.

302. Lebanese Leaders' Statement of National Accord, Damascus, July 8, 1985*

* 15 J. Palestine Stud. 203 (Autumn 1985).

A meeting was held in Vice President 'Abd al-Halim Khaddam's office on 8 July. It was attended by Mufti Hasan Khalid, mufti of the Republic of Lebanon; Shaykh Muhammad Mahdi Shams al-Din, deputy leader of the Higher Islamic Shi'ite Council; Shaykh Muhammad Abu Shaqra, spiritual leader of the Druze community; Shaykh 'Abd al-Amir Qabalan, the Ja'farite mufti; Husayn al-Husayni, speaker of the Lebanese Chamber of Deputies; Rashid Karami, Lebanese prime minister; 'Adil 'Usayran, Lebanese defense minister; Dr. Salim al-Huss, minister of education; Nabih Birri, minister of justice and leader of the Amal movement; Walid Jumblatt, minister of public works and tourism and leader of the Progressive Socialist party; Dr. Nazih al-Bizri, deputy for Sidon; engineer Mustafa Sa'd, leader of the Nasirite Popular Organization in Sidon; and Dr. Husayn al-Quwwatli, secretary general of the mufti's office. Faruq al-Shar', [Syrian] minister of foreign affairs, and 'Isam al-Na'ib, minister of state for foreign affairs, also attended the meeting.

After detailed discussions, the conferees agreed to the following:

National Accord

Concerning the subject of national accord, it was agreed to work seriously and effectively to achieve national accord with the aim of restoring the country's unity on the basis of the following principles:

1. To continue resistance against the Israeli occupation and to support the Lebanese resistance, considering it a radiant phenomenon in contemporary Arab and Islamic history. To work for the fulfillment of UN Security Council resolutions, particularly resolution 425.

2. To achieve full equality in rights and duties among all Lebanese and to achieve the principle of equal opportunity.

3. To set up a truly democratic system which achieves true participation in ruling and in running the country's affairs and which ends all forms of discrimination between one faction and another in governmental affairs.

4. To end all forms of partition on the ground, to restore the state's unity, and the unity of its institutions.

5. To draft a new constitution to unite Lebanon, to confirm its identity and its national and pan-Arab role, to constitute a framework for equality in citizens' rights and duties, to maintain national balance in the government, to organize its institutions, to define these institutions' authorities, to organize these authorities to prevent any tyranny over them, and to end forever the state of factional structure to replace it with national unity.

6. To rebuild the army in a manner enabling it to play its pan-Arab role against the Israeli enemy and assume its national role of defending the country's unity and stability, to immediately begin its reorganization, and to ratify the compulsory military service law.

7. To reject all forms of factional security, with respect to the Lebanese or

Palestinians, from the premise of unified security for a united country, a security that would be imposed on all those residing on Lebanese territory, whether they are Lebanese or non-Lebanese. Any factional control of security would constitute a violation of the country's sovereignty and territorial integrity.

8. To agree on a comprehensive security plan as follows:

a. A single security organ to be agreed upon;

b. The imposition of law and public order;

c. The collection of all kinds of weapons and the dissolution of armed organizations.

9. To reassess educational, developmental, and social policies in accordance with bases which would entrench national unity and would eliminate the causes of division which Lebanon experiences from time to time.

10. To form a committee comprising Husayn al-Husayni, Rashid Karami, Salim al-Huss, and ministers Nabih Birri and Walid Jumblatt to contact Lebanese figures and forces for discussing ways to achieve this national draft project for the settlement of the Lebanese crisis.

Security Situation

To tackle the security situation in Beirut, it was agreed:

1. To withdraw all armed elements from the streets and quarters into barracks which the coordination committee would determine; to remove all armed manifestations; and to remove placards and flags, as well as the political slogans and posters on the walls.

2. To confine party offices to their main offices and to close all other offices and return the buildings to their owners.

3. To lift political immunity for transgressions and violations and those who commit them.

4. To entrust the internal public security forces with the task of assuming their role in controlling security in West Beirut and to facilitate the return of evacuees.

5. To form a special army force, whose tasks will be supported by those of the internal public security forces when requested. This force will be chosen by agreement between the prime minister and the defense minister and will be under their command.

6. The area covered by these measures and arrangements includes West Beirut, the camps, the airport, and the road leading to it.

7. To bolster the Beirut Airport's security organ and to withdraw all party factions and armed elements from the airport and around it.

8. To form a coordination committee to supervise and follow up implementation of these decisions. The committee will consist of three members appointed by the prime minister in agreement with the defense minister,

two Amal movement members, two members of the Lebanese National Democratic Front, and two Syrian observers.

In conclusion, the meeting thanks the Syrian Command under President Hafiz al-Asad for taking the initiative to call for this meeting and for the efforts it has been exerting to extricate Lebanon from its ordeal and safeguard its unity, Arab character, and freedom.

303. European Parliament Resolution on the Situation in
Lebanon, October 10, 1985*

---

* 28 O.J. Eur. Comm. (No. C 288) 106 (1985).

The European Parliament,

A. having regard to the desperate situation created in Lebanon by the civil war and armed intervention from outside,

B. deeply affected by the thousands of deaths among the civilian population, in particular among the Christian community, the ruthless resettlements, the razing of towns and villages and the dispersal of families,

C. appalled at the massacres perpetrated on a section of the Lebanese population, on account of its religion alone, whether it be Christian, Jewish or Moslem,

D. alarmed by the recent murders of hostages in Lebanon,

1. Calls on the Council to take an immediate diplomatic initiative with a view to ending the systematic massacre of the religious communities, the taking and murdering of hostages;

2. Requests the Commission to implement emergency measures to convey the necessary relief and supplies to the communities affected before the winter (medicines, shelter, food, hospitals, schools, etc.);

3. Urges the Foreign Ministers meeting in Political Cooperation to consider what action might be taken to save the hostages still in detention;

4. Instructs its President to forward this resolution to the Council, the Commission and the Foreign Ministers meeting in Political Cooperation.

304. General Assembly Resolution 40/229 on Assistance for the Reconstruction and Development of Lebanon, December 17, 1985*

* G.A. Res. 40/229 (1985).

The General Assembly,

Recalling its resolutions 33/146 of 20 December 1978, 34/135 of 14 December 1979, 35/85 of 5 December 1980, 36/205 of 17 December 1981, 37/163 of 17 December 1982, 38/220 of 20 December 1983 and 39/197 of 17 December 1984 on assistance for the reconstruction and development of Lebanon,

Recalling also Economic and Social Council resolutions 1980/15 of 29 April 1980 and 1985/56 of 25 July 1985 and decisions 1983/112 of 17 May 1983 and 1984/174 of 26 July 1984,

Noting with deep concern the continuing heavy loss of life and the additional destruction of property, which have caused further extensive damage to the economic and social structures of Lebanon,

Also noting with concern the serious economic situation in Lebanon,

Welcoming the determined efforts of the Government of Lebanon in undertaking its reconstruction and rehabilitation programme,

Reaffirming the urgent need for further international action to assist the Government of Lebanon in its continuing efforts for reconstruction and development,

Considering that filling the vacant post of United Nations Co-ordinator of Assistance for the Reconstruction and Development of Lebanon would help the normal operations of international assistance to Lebanon,

Taking note of the report of the Secretary-General[230] and of the statement made on 12 November 1985 by the Under-Secretary-General for Political and General Assembly Affairs,[231]

1. *Expresses its appreciation* to the Secretary-General for his report[232] and for the steps he has taken to mobilize assistance to Lebanon;

2. *Commends* the Under-Secretary-General for Political and General Assembly Affairs for his co-ordination of system-wide assistance for Lebanon, as well as the staff of the Office of the United Nations Co-ordinator of Assistance for the Reconstruction and Development of Lebanon for their invaluable efforts in the discharge of their duties;

3. *Expresses its appreciation* for the relentless efforts undertaken by the Government of Lebanon in the implementation of the initial phase of reconstruction of the country, despite adverse circumstances, and for the steps it has taken to remedy the economic situation;

4. *Requests* the Secretary-General to continue and intensify his efforts to mobilize all possible assistance within the United Nations system to help the Government of Lebanon in its reconstruction and development efforts;

5. *Invites* the Secretary-General to consider arranging, under the terms of resolution 33/146, for the United Nations Co-ordinator of Assistance for the

---

[230] A/40/434 and Add.1.

[231] See *Official Records of the General Assembly, Fortieth Session, Second Committee,* 31st meeting, paras. 34-41.

[232] A/40/434 and Add.1.

Reconstruction and Development of Lebanon to resume his functions in Lebanon;

6. *Requests* the organs, organizations and bodies of the United Nations system to intensify their programmes of assistance and to expand them in response to the needs of Lebanon, and to take the necessary steps to ensure that their offices in Beirut are adequately staffed at the senior level;

7. *Also requests* the Secretary-General to report to the General Assembly at its forty-first session on the progress achieved in the implementation of the present resolution.

C. Israeli Security and Palestinian Autonomy

305. General Assembly Resolution ES-7/6 on the Question of Palestine, August 19, 1982*

* G.A. Res. ES-7/6, ES-7 U.N. GAOR Supp. (No. 1) at 9, U.N. Doc. A/ES-7/14/Add. 1 (1982).

The General Assembly,

Having considered the question of Palestine at its resumed seventh emergency special session,

Having heard the statement of the Palestine Liberation Organization, the representative of the Palestinian people,[13]

Guided by the purposes and principles of the United Nations, in particular the respect for the principle of equal rights and self-determination of peoples,

Aware of the functions of the Security Council during its meetings relevant to the situation in the Middle East, in particular since 4 June 1982,

Expressing its deep regret that the Security Council has, so far, failed to take effective and practical measures in accordance with the Charter of the United Nations to ensure implementation of its resolutions 508 (1982) of 5 June 1982 and 509 (1982) of 6 June 1982,

Alarmed that the situation in the Middle East has further worsened as a result of Israel's acts of aggression against the sovereignty of Lebanon and the Palestinian people in Lebanon,

Guided further by the purposes and principles of the United Nations, in particular to take effective collective measures for the prevention and removal of threats to the peace and for the suppresion [*sic*] of acts of aggression,

Mindful of the humanitarian principles and provisions of the Geneva Conventions of 1949[14] and Additional Protocol I thereto[15] and the obligations arising from the regulations annexed to the Hague Conventions of 1907,[16]

Reaffirming its conviction that the question of Palestine is the core of the Arab-Israeli conflict and that no comprehensive, just and lasting peace in the region will be achieved without the full exercise by the Palestinian people of its inalienable rights in Palestine,

Reaffirming once again that a just and comprehensive settlement of the situation in the Middle East cannot be achieved without the participation on an equal footing of all the parties to the conflict, including the Palestine Liberation Organization as the representative of the Palestinian people,

Expressing its indignation at the continuation and intensification of military activities by Israel within Lebanon, particularly in and around Beirut,

Recalling all its resolutions relevant to the question of Palestine,

Recalling Security Council resolutions 508 (1982) of 5 June 1982, 509 (1982) of 6 June 1982, 511 (1982) of 18 June 1982, 512 (1982) of 19 June 1982, 513 (1982) of 4 July 1982, 515 (1982) of 29 July 1982, 516 (1982) of

---

[13] A/ES-7/PV.25, p. 7.

[14] United Nations, *Treaty Series*, vol. 75, Nos. 970-973.

[15] A/32/144, annex I.

[16] Carnegie Endowment for International Peace, *The Hague Conventions and Declarations of 1899 and 1907* (New York, Oxford University Press, 1915).

1 August 1982, 517 (1982) of 4 August 1982 and 518 (1982) of 12 August 1982,

1. *Reiterates* its affirmation of the fundamental principle of the inadmissibility of the acquisition of territory by force;

2. *Calls* for the free exercise in Palestine of the inalienable rights of the Palestinian people to self-determination without external interference and to national independence;

3. *Reaffirms* its rejection of all policies and plans aiming at the resettlement of the Palestinians outside their homeland;

4. *Demands* that Israel respect and carry out the provisions of the previous resolutions of the General Assembly relating to the occupied Palestinian and other Arab territories, including Jerusalem, as well as the provisions of Security Council resolution 465 (1980) of 1 March 1980, in which the Council, *inter alia*:

(*a*) Determined that all measures taken by Israel to change the physical character, demographic composition, institutional structure or status of the Palestinian and other Arab territories occupied since 1967, including Jerusalem, or any part thereof had no legal validity and that Israel's policy and practices of settling parts of its population and new immigrants in those territories constituted a flagrant violation of the Geneva Convention relative to the Protection of Civilian Persons in Time of War, of 12 August 1949,[17] and also constituted a serious obstruction to achieving a comprehensive, just and lasting peace in the Middle East;

(*b*) Strongly deplored the continuation and persistence of Israel in pursuing those policies and practices and called upon the Government and people of Israel to rescind those measures, to dismantle the existing settlements and in particular to cease, on an urgent basis, the establishment, construction and planning of settlements in the Arab territories occupied since 1967, including Jerusalem;

5. *Demands also* that Israel carry out the provisions of Security Council resolutions 509 (1982), 511 (1982), 512 (1982), 513 (1982), 515 (1982), 516 (1982), 517 (1982) and 518 (1982);

6. *Urges* the Secretary-General, with the concurrence of the Security Council and the Government of Lebanon and pending the withdrawal of Israel from Lebanon, to undertake effective measures to guarantee the safety and security of the Palestinian and Lebanese civilian population in South Lebanon;

7. *Condemns* Israel for its non-compliance with resolutions of the Security Council, in defiance of Article 25 of the Charter of the United Nations;

8. *Urges once again* the Security Council, in the event of continued failure by Israel to comply with the demands contained in its resolutions 465 (1980), 508 (1982), 509 (1982), 515 (1982) and 518 (1982), to meet in order

[17] United Nations, *Treaty Series*, vol. 75, No. 973, p. 287.

to consider practical ways and means in accordance with the relevant provisions of the Charter;

9. *Requests once again* the Secretary-General to delegate a high-level commission to investigate and make an up-to-date assessment of the extent of loss of human life and material damage and to report, as soon as possible, on the result of this investigation to the General Assembly and the Security Council;

10. *Requests* the Secretary-General and organizations of the United Nations system, in co-operation with the International Committee of the Red Cross and other non-governmental organizations, to investigate the strict application by Israel of the provisions of the Geneva Conventions of 1949 and other instruments in the case of those detained;

11. *Calls once again upon* the Secretary-General to initiate contacts with all the parties to the Arab-Israeli conflict in the Middle East, including the Palestine Liberation Organization, the representative of the Palestinian people, with a view to convening an international conference, under the auspices of the United Nations, to find concrete ways and means of achieving a comprehensive, just and lasting solution, conducive to peace in conformity with the principles of the Charter and relevant resolutions;

12. *Decides* to adjourn the seventh emergency special session temporarily and to authorize the President of the latest regular session of the General Assembly to resume its meetings upon request from Member States.

31st plenary meeting
19 August 1982

306. General Assembly Resolution ES-7/8 on an

International Day of Innocent Children Victims of

Aggression, August 19, 1982*

* G.A. Res. ES-7/8, ES-7 U.N. GAOR Supp. (No. 1) at 13, U.N. Doc. A/ ES-7/14/Add.1 (1982).

The General Assembly,

Having considered the question of Palestine at its resumed seventh emergency special session,

Appalled by the great number of innocent Palestinian and Lebanese children victims of Israel's acts of aggression,

Decides to commemorate 4 June of each year as the International Day of Innocent Children Victims of Aggression.

31st plenary meeting
19 August 1982

307. Security Council Resolution 524 Calling for
Implementation of Security Council Resolution 338 (1973)
and Renewing the U.N. Disengagement Observer Force
Mandate, November 29, 1982*

* 37 U.N. SCOR (2403rd mtg.) at 12, U.N. Doc. S/INF/38 (1982). *See also* subsequent resolutions, S.C. Res. 531, 38 U.N. SCOR (2445th mtg.) at 2, U.N. Doc. S/INF/39 (1983), S.C. Res. 543, 38 U.N. SCOR (2502nd mtg.) at 5, U.N. Doc. S/INF/39 (1983), S.C. Res. 551, 39 U.N. SCOR (2544th mtg.) at 7, U.N. Doc. S/INF/40 (1984), S.C. Res. 557, 39 U.N. SCOR (2563rd mtg.) at 9, U.N. Doc. S/INF/40 (1984), S.C. Res. 563, 40 U.N. SCOR (2581st mtg.) (1985), and S.C. Res. 576, 40 U.N. SCOR (2630th mtg.) (1985).

The Security Council,

Having considered the report of the Secretary-General on the United Nations Disengagement Observer Force,[48]

Decides:

(*a*) To call upon the parties concerned to implement immediately Security Council resolution 338 (1973);

(*b*) To renew the mandate of the United Nations Disengagement Observer Force for another period of six months, that is, until 31 May 1983;

(*c*) To request the Secretary-General to submit, at the end of this period, a report on the developments in the situation and the measures taken to implement resolution 338 (1973).

Adopted unanimously at the 2403rd meeting.

[48] *Official Records of the Security Council, Thirty-seventh Year, Supplement for October, November and December 1982*, document S/15493.

308. House of Representatives Concurrent Resolution 322 on Israel-U.S. Response to Any Illegal Activity by United Nations General Assembly, December 1, 1982*

* H.R. Con. Res. 322, 96 Stat. 2673 (1982).

Whereas the United Nations was founded on the principle of universality; and

Whereas the charter stipulates that United Nations members may be suspended by the General Assembly only "upon the recommendation of the Security Council"; and

Whereas any move by the General Assembly that would illegally deny Israel its credentials in the Assembly would be a direct violation of these provisions of the charter: Now, therefore, be it

Resolved by the House of Representatives (the Senate concurring), That if Israel is illegally expelled, suspended, denied its credentials, or in any other manner denied its right to participate in the General Assembly of the United Nations or any specialized agency of the United Nations, it is the sense of Congress that the United States should—

(1) suspend its participation in the General Assembly or such United Nations agency; and

(2) withhold its assessed contribution to the United Nations or to the specialized agency involved until this illegal action is reversed.

SEC. 2. It is the sense of the Congress that the Secretary of State should communicate to the member states of the General Assembly of the United Nations what the Congress has herein resolved.

Agreed to December 1, 1982.

309. General Assembly Resolution 37/86 on the Question of Palestine, December 10 and 20, 1982*

* G.A. Res. 86, 37 U.N. GAOR Supp. (No. 51) at 34, U.N. Doc. A/37/51 (1982).

A

The General Assembly,

Recalling its resolutions 3376 (XXX) of 10 November 1975, 31/20 of 24 November 1976, 32/40 of 2 December 1977, 33/28 of 7 December 1978, 34/65 of 29 November and 12 December 1979, ES-7/2 of 29 July 1980, 35/169 of 15 December 1980, 36/120 of 10 December 1981, ES-7/4 of 28 April 1982, ES-7/5 of 26 June 1982 and ES-7/9 of 24 September 1982,

Having considered the report of the Committee on the Exercise of the Inalienable Rights of the Palestinian People,[68]

1. *Expresses its appreciation* to the Committee on the Exercise of the Inalienable Rights of the Palestinian People for its efforts in performing the tasks assigned to it by the General Assembly;

2. *Endorses* the recommendations of the Committee contained in paragraphs 114 to 119 of its report and draws the attention of the Security Council to the fact that action on the Committee's recommendations, as endorsed by the General Assembly in its resolution 31/20, is long overdue;

3. *Requests* the Committee to keep the situation relating to the question of Palestine under review and to report and make suggestions to the General Assembly or the Security Council, as appropriate;

4. *Authorizes* the Committee to continue to exert all efforts to promote the implementation of its recommendations, to send delegations or representatives to international conferences where such representation would be considered by it to be appropriate, and to report thereon to the General Assembly at its thirty-eighth session and thereafter;

5. *Requests* the United Nations Conciliation Commission for Palestine, established under General Assembly resolution 194 (III) of 11 December 1948, as well as other United Nations bodies associated with the question of Palestine, to co-operate fully with the Committee and to make available to it, at its request, the relevant information and documentation which they have at their disposal;

6. *Decides* to circulate the report of the Committee to all the competent bodies of the United Nations and urges them to take the necessary action, as appropriate, in accordance with the Committee's programme of implementation;

7. Requests the Secretary-General to continue to provide the Committee with all the necessary facilities for the performance of its tasks.

99th plenary meeting
10 December 1982

---

[68] *Official Records of the General Assembly, Thirty-seventh Session, Supplement No. 35* (A/37/35 and Corr.1).

B

The General Assembly,

Having considered the report of the Committee on the Exercise of the Inalienable Rights of the Palestinian People,[68]

Noting, in particular, the information contained in paragraphs 103 to 111 of that report,

Recalling its resolutions 32/40 B of 2 December 1977, 33/28 C of 7 December 1978, 34/65 D of 12 December 1979, 35/169 D of 15 December 1980 and 36/120 B of 10 December 1981,

1. *Takes note with appreciation* of the action taken by the Secretary-General in compliance with General Assembly resolution 36/120 B;

2. *Requests* the Secretary-General to ensure that the Division for Palestinian Rights of the Secretariat continues to discharge the tasks detailed in paragraph 1 of General Assembly resolution 32/40 B, paragraph 2 (*b*) of resolution 34/65 D and paragraph 3 of resolution 36/120 B, in consultation with the Committee on the Exercise of the Inalienable Rights of the Palestinian People and under its guidance;

3. *Also requests* the Secretary-General to provide the Division for Palestinian Rights with the necessary resources to carry out its tasks as urged in paragraph 109 of the Committee's report;

4. *Further requests* the Secretary-General to ensure the continued co-operation of the Department of Public Information and other units of the Secretariat in enabling the Division for Palestinian Rights to perform its tasks and in covering adequately the various aspects of the question of Palestine;

5. *Invites* all Governments and organizations to lend their co-operation to the Committee and the Division for Palestinian Rights in the performance of their tasks;

6. *Takes note with appreciation* of the action taken by Member States to observe annually on 29 November the International Day of Solidarity with the Palestinian People and the issuance by them of special postage stamps for the occasion.

99th plenary meeting
10 December 1982

C

The General Assembly,

Recalling its resolutions 3236 (XXIX) and 3237 (XXIX) of 22 November 1974 and all other United Nations resolutions, including resolution ES-7/2 of 29 July 1980, pertinent to the question of Palestine,

Recalling also its resolutions 36/120 C of 10 December 1981, in which it decided to convene an International Conference on the Question of Palestine for a comprehensive effort to seek effective ways and means to enable the Palestinian people to attain and to exercise their rights, and ES-7/7 of

19 August 1982, in which it decided to convene the Conference at the head-quarters of the United Nations Educational, Scientific and Cultural Organization, in Paris, from 16 to 27 August 1983,

Convinced that a comprehensive, just and lasting peace in the Middle East can be established, in accordance with the Charter and the relevant resolutions of the United Nations, through a just solution to the problem of Palestine on the basis of the attainment of the legitimate rights of the Palestinian people,

Convinced that the Conference will provide a unique opportunity to heighten awareness of the underlying causes of the question of Palestine and to contribute actively and constructively to a solution of the question on the basis of relevant United Nations resolutions,

Stressing the need to assure the participation of all Member States in the Conference and their support for its preparation,

Taking note with appreciation of the report of the Preparatory Committee for the International Conference on the Question of Palestine,[69]

1. *Reiterates* the responsibility of the United Nations to strive for a lasting peace in the Middle East through a just solution of the problem of Palestine;

2. *Endorses* the recommendations of the Preparatory Committee for the International Conference on the Question of Palestine, contained in paragraph 32 of its report,[69] concerning the preparatory activities for the Conference, the objectives, the documentation, the draft provisional agenda and the draft provisional rules of procedure of the Conference, the participation in the Conference and the organization of work of the Preparatory Committee;

3. *Calls upon* all organizations of the United Nations system to continue to extend their fullest support to the Conference and to its preparation;

4. *Urges* all Member States to promote heightened awareness of the importance of the Conference and to intensify preparations at the national, subregional and regional levels in order to ensure its success;

5. *Calls upon* all Member States to contribute to the achievement of Palestinian rights and to support modalities for their implementation, and to participate in the Conference and the regional preparatory meetings preceding it;

6. *Decides* to consider the results of the Conference at its thirty-eighth session.

99th plenary meeting
10 December 1982

D

The General Assembly,

Recalling its resolutions relevant to the question of Palestine, in particular resolutions 181 (II) of 29 November 1947, 194 (III) of 11 December 1948,

[69] *Ibid., Supplement No. 49* (A/37/49 and Corr.1).

3210 (XXIX) of 14 October 1974, 3236 (XXIX) of 22 November 1974 and ES-7/2 of 29 July 1980,

Recalling the resolutions of the Security Council relevant to Palestine,

Having heard the statement of the representative of the Palestine Liberation Organization,[70]

1. *Takes note* of the declaration of the Palestine Liberation Organization of 19 April 1981 of its intention to pursue its role in the solution of the question of Palestine on the basis of the attainment by the Palestinian people of its inalienable rights in Palestine, in accordance with the relevant resolutions of the United Nations;

2. *Reaffirms* the principle of the inadmissibility of the acquisition of territory by force;

3. *Reaffirms once again* that a comprehensive, just and lasting peace in the Middle East cannot be established without the unconditional withdrawal of Israel from the Palestinian and the other Arab territories occupied since 1967, including Jerusalem, and without the exercise and attainment by the Palestinian people of its inalienable rights in Palestine, in accordance with the principles of the Charter and the relevant resolutions of the United Nations;

4. *Requests* the Security Council to discharge its responsibilities under the Charter and recognize the inalienable rights of the Palestinian Arab people, including the right to self-determination and the right to establish its independent Arab State in Palestine;

5. *Reiterates* its request that the Security Council take the necessary measures, in execution of the relevant United Nations resolutions, to implement the plan which, *inter alia*, recommends that an independent Arab State shall come into existence in Palestine;

6. *Requests* the Secretary-General to report on the progress made in implementing the present resolution as soon as possible.

99th plenary meeting
10 December 1982

E

The General Assembly,

Having considered the report of the Committee on the Exercise of the Inalienable Rights of the Palestinian People,[68]

Expressing its extreme concern that no just solution to the problem of Palestine has been achieved and that this problem therefore continues to aggravate the Middle East conflict, of which it is the core, and to endanger international peace and security,

Recalling its previous relevant resolutions, particularly resolutions 181 (II) of 29 November 1947, 194 (III) of 11 December 1948, 3236 (XXIX) of 22

---

[70] *Ibid., Thirty-seventh Session, Plenary Meetings,* 84th meeting, paras. 110-153.

November 1974, ES-7/2 of 29 July 1980, 36/120 D of 10 December 1981 and ES-7/9 of 24 September 1982,

Recalling, in particular, the principles relevant to the question of Palestine that have been accepted by the international community, including the right of all States in the region to existence within internationally recognized boundaries, and justice and security for all the peoples, which requires recognition and attainment of the legitimate rights of the Palestinian people,

Recognizing the necessity of participation by all parties concerned in any efforts aimed at the attainment of a just and lasting solution,

1. *Reaffirms* the inalienable legitimate rights of the Palestinian people, including the right to self-determination and the right to establish, once it so wishes, its independent State in Palestine;

2. *Declares* all Israeli policies and practices of, or aimed at, annexation of the occupied Palestinian and other Arab territories, including Jerusalem, to be in violation of international law and of the relevant United Nations resolutions;

3. *Demands*, in conformity with the fundamental principle of the inadmissibility of the acquisition of territory by force, that Israel should withdraw completely and unconditionally from all the Palestinian and other Arab territories occupied since June 1967, including Jerusalem, with all property and services intact;

4. *Urges* the Security Council to facilitate the process of Israeli withdrawal;

5. *Recommends* that, following the withdrawal of Israel from the occupied Palestinian territories, those territories should be subjected to a short transitional period under the supervision of the United Nations, during which period the Palestinian people would exercise its right to self-determination;

6. *Urgently calls* for the achievement of a comprehensive, just and lasting peace, based on the resolutions of the United Nations and under its auspices, in which all parties concerned, including the Palestine Liberation Organization, the representative of the Palestinian people, participate on an equal footing;

7. *Recommends* that the Security Council should take early action to promote a just and comprehensive solution to the question of Palestine;

8. *Requests* the Secretary-General to report to the General Assembly at its thirty-eighth session on the progress made in implementing the present resolution.

112th plenary meeting
20 December 1982

310. General Assembly Resolution 37/120 on the U.N.
Relief and Works Agency for Palestine Refugees in the
Near East, December 16, 1982*

* G.A. Res. 120, 37 U.N. GAOR Supp. (No. 51) at 103, U.N. Doc. A/37/
51 (1982).

A

WORKING GROUP ON THE FINANCING OF THE UNITED NATIONS RELIEF AND
WORKS AGENCY FOR PALESTINE REFUGEES IN THE NEAR EAST

The General Assembly,

Recalling its resolutions 2656 (XXV) of 7 December 1970, 2728 (XXV) of
15 December 1970, 2791 (XXVI) of 6 December 1971, 2964 (XXVII) of 13
December 1972, 3090 (XXVIII) of 7 December 1973, 3330 (XXIX) of 17
December 1974, 3419 D (XXX) of 8 December 1975, 31/15 C of 23 November 1976, 32/90 D of 13 December 1977, 33/112 D of 18 December 1978,
34/52 D of 23 November 1979, 35/13 D of 3 November 1980 and 36/146 E
of 16 December 1981,

Recalling also its decision 36/462 of 16 March 1982, whereby the General
Assembly took note of the special report of the Working Group on the Financing of the United Nations Relief and Works Agency for Palestine Refugees in the Near East[34] and adopted the recommendations contained
therein,

Having considered the report of the Working Group on the Financing of
the United Nations Relief and Works Agency for Palestine Refugees in the
Near East,[35]

Taking into account the report of the Commissioner-General of the United
Nations Relief and Works Agency for Palestine Refugees in the Near East,
covering the period from 1 July 1981 to 30 June 1982,[36] and his special
report issued on 28 September 1982,[37]

Gravely concerned at the critical financial situation of the United Nations
Relief and Works Agency for Palestine Refugees in the Near East, which
has already reduced the essential minimum services being provided to the
Palestine refugees and which threatens even greater reductions in the future,

Emphasizing the urgent need for extraordinary efforts in order to maintain, at least at their present minimum level, the activities of the United
Nations Relief and Works Agency for Palestine Refugees in the Near East,

1. *Commends* the Working Group on the Financing of the United Nations
Relief and Works Agency for Palestine Refugees in the Near East for its
efforts to assist in ensuring the Agency's financial security;

2. *Takes note with approval* of the report of the Working Group;

3. *Requests* the Working Group to continue its efforts, in co-operation with
the Secretary-General and the Commissioner-General of the United

[34] A/36/866 and Corr.1.

[35] A/37/591.

[36] *Official Records of the General Assembly, Thirty-seventh Session, Supplement No. 13* (A/37/13).

[37] A/37/479.

Nations Relief and Works Agency for Palestine Refugees in the Near East, for the financing of the Agency for a further period of one year;

4. *Requests* the Secretary-General to provide the necessary services and assistance to the Working Group for the conduct of its work.

108th plenary meeting
16 December 1982

B

ASSISTANCE TO PERSONS DISPLACED AS A RESULT OF THE JUNE 1967 AND SUBSEQUENT HOSTILITIES

The General Assembly,

Recalling its resolution 36/146 D of 16 December 1981 and all previous resolutions on the question,

Taking note of the report of the Commissioner-General of the United Nations Relief and Works Agency for Palestine Refugees in the Near East, covering the period from 1 July 1981 to 30 June 1982,[36] and his special report covering the period from 6 June to 31 August 1982,[37]

Concerned about the continued human suffering resulting from the hostilities in the Middle East,

1. *Reaffirms* its resolution 36/146 D and all previous resolutions on the question;

2. *Endorses*, bearing in mind the objectives of those resolutions, the efforts of the Commissioner-General of the United Nations Relief and Works Agency for Palestine Refugees in the Near East to continue to provide humanitarian assistance as far as practicable, on an emergency basis and as a temporary measure, to other persons in the area who are at present displaced and in serious need of continued assistance as a result of the June 1967 and subsequent hostilities;

3. *Strongly appeals* to all Governments and to organizations and individuals to contribute generously for the above purposes to the United Nations Relief and Works Agency for Palestine Refugees in the Near East and to the other intergovernmental and non-governmental organizations concerned.

108th plenary meeting
16 December 1982

C

UNIVERSITY OF JERUSALEM FOR PALESTINE REFUGEES

The General Assembly,

Recalling its resolution 36/146 G of 16 December 1981,
Having examined with appreciation the report of the Secretary-General[38]

[38] A/37/599.

concerning the establishment of a university at Jerusalem in pursuance of paragraphs 5 and 6 of resolution 36/146 G,

Having also examined with appreciation the report of the Commissioner-General of the United Nations Relief and Works Agency for Palestine Refugees in the Near East, covering the period from 1 July 1981 to 30 June 1982,[36]

1. *Commends* the constructive efforts made by the Secretary-General, the Commissioner-General of the United Nations Relief and Works Agency for Palestine Refugees in the Near East, the Council of the United Nations University and the United Nations Educational, Scientific and Cultural Organization, which worked diligently towards the implementation of General Assembly resolution 36/146 G;

2. *Further commends* the close co-operation of the competent educational authorities concerned;

3. *Emphasizes* the need for strengthening the educational system in the Arab territories occupied since 5 June 1967, including Jerusalem, and specifically the need for the establishment of the proposed university;

4. *Endorses* the various steps recommended in the report of the Secretary-General, including the creation of a voluntary fund to be administered by the Department of Technical Co-operation for Development of the Secretariat, in order to provide graduate and post-doctoral fellowships for a highly trained core faculty of the proposed university;

5. *Requests* the Secretary-General to continue to take all necessary measures, including the conduct of a functional feasibility study, for establishing the University of Jerusalem in accordance with the recommendations contained in the report of the Secretary-General;

6. *Calls upon* Israel as the occupying Power to co-operate in the implementation of the present resolution and to remove the hindrances which it has put in the way of establishing the University of Jerusalem;

7. *Requests* the Secretary-General to report to the General Assembly at its thirty-eighth session on the progress made in the implementation of the present resolution.

108th plenary meeting
16 December 1982

D

OFFERS BY MEMBER STATES OF GRANTS AND SCHOLARSHIPS FOR HIGHER
EDUCATION, INCLUDING VOCATIONAL TRAINING, FOR PALESTINE REFUGEES

The General Assembly,

Recalling its resolution 212 (III) of 19 November 1948 on assistance to Palestine refugees,

Recalling also its resolutions 35/13 B of 3 November 1980 and 36/146 H of 16 December 1981,

Cognizant of the fact that the Palestine refugees have, for the last three decades, lost their lands and means of livelihood,

Having examined with appreciation the report of the Secretary-General[39] on offers of grants and scholarships for higher education for Palestine refugees and on the scope of the implementation of resolution 36/146 H,

Having also examined the report of the Commissioner-General of the United Nations Relief and Works Agency for Palestine Refugees in the Near East, covering the period from 1 July 1981 to 30 June 1982,[36] dealing with this subject,

Noting that fewer than one per thousand of the Palestine refugee students have the chance to continue higher education, including vocational training,

Noting also that over the past several years the number of scholarships offered by the United Nations Relief and Works Agency for Palestine Refugees in the Near East has dwindled to half of what it was because of the Agency's recurring budgetary difficulties,

1. *Urges* all States to respond to the appeal contained in General Assembly resolution 32/90 F of 13 December 1977 in a manner commensurate with the needs of Palestine refugees for higher education and vocational training;

2. *Strongly appeals* to all States, specialized agencies and non-governmental organizations to augment the special allocations for grants and scholarships to Palestine refugees in addition to their contributions to the regular budget of the United Nations Relief and Works Agency for Palestine Refugees in the Near East;

3. *Expresses its appreciation* to all Governments, specialized agencies and non-governmental organizations that responded favourably to General Assembly resolution 36/146 H;

4. *Invites* the relevant United Nations agencies to continue, within their respective spheres of competence, to expand assistance for higher education to Palestine refugee students;

5. *Appeals* to all States, specialized agencies and the United Nations University to contribute generously to the Palestinian universities in the territories occupied by Israel since 1967;

6. *Also appeals* to all States, specialized agencies and other international bodies to contribute towards the establishment of vocational training centres for Palestine refugees;

7. *Requests* the United Nations Relief and Works Agency for Palestine Refugees in the Near East to act as recipient and trustee for such special allocations and scholarships and to award them to qualified Palestine refugee candidates;

8. *Requests* the Secretary-General to report to the General Assembly at its thirty-eighth session on the implementation of the present resolution.

108th plenary meeting
16 December 1982

[39] A/37/427.

E

Palestine Refugees in the Gaza Strip

The General Assembly,

Recalling Security Council resolution 237 (1967) of 14 June 1967,

Recalling also General Assembly resolutions 2792 C (XXVI) of 6 December 1971, 2963 C (XXVII) of 13 December 1972, 3089 C (XXVIII) of 7 December 1973, 3331 D (XXIX) of 17 December 1974, 3419 C (XXX) of 8 December 1975, 31/15 E of 23 November 1976, 32/90 C of 13 December 1977, 33/112 E of 18 December 1978, 34/52 F of 23 November 1979, 35/13 F of 3 November 1980 and 36/146 A of 16 December 1981,

Having considered the report of the Commissioner-General of the United Nations Relief and Works Agency for Palestine Refugees in the Near East, covering the period from 1 July 1981 to 30 June 1982,[36] and the report of the Secretary-General of 17 September 1982,[40]

Recalling the provisions of paragraph 11 of its resolution 194 (III) of 11 December 1948 and considering that measures to resettle Palestine refugees in the Gaza Strip away from the homes and property from which they were displaced constitute a violation of their inalienable right of return,

Alarmed by the reports received from the Commissioner-General that the Israeli occupying authorities persist in their policy of demolishing, on punitive grounds, shelters occupied by refugee families,

1. *Reiterates its demand* that Israel desist from the removal and resettlement of Palestine refugees in the Gaza Strip and from the destruction of their shelters;

2. *Requests* the Secretary-General, after consulting with the Commissioner-General of the United Nations Relief and Works Agency for Palestine Refugees in the Near East, to report to the General Assembly, before the opening of its thirty-eighth session, on Israel's compliance with paragraph 1 above.

108th plenary meeting
16 December 1982

F

Resumption of the Ration Distribution to Palestine Refugees

The General Assembly,

Recalling its resolution 36/146 F of 16 December 1981 and all previous resolutions on the question, including resolution 302 (IV) of 8 December 1949,

Having considered the report of the Commissioner-General of the United Nations Relief and Works Agency for Palestine Refugees in the Near East,

---

[40] A/37/425 and Corr.1.

covering the period from 1 July 1981 to 30 June 1982,[36] and his special report covering the period from 6 June to 31 August 1982,[37]

Deeply concerned at the interruption by the United Nations Relief and Works Agency for Palestine Refugees in the Near East, owing to financial difficulties, of the general ration distribution to Palestine refugees in all fields in the occupied Palestinian territories, Jordan and the Syrian Arab Republic,

1. *Calls upon* all Governments, as a matter of urgency, to make the most generous efforts possible to meet the needs of the United Nations Relief and Works Agency for Palestine Refugees in the Near East, particularly in the light of the interruption by the Agency of the general ration distribution to Palestine refugees in all fields, and therefore urges noncontributing Governments to contribute regularly and contributing Governments to consider increasing their regular contributions;

2. *Requests* the Commissioner-General of the United Nations Relief and Works Agency for Palestine Refugees in the Near East to resume on a continuing basis and as soon as possible the interrupted general ration distribution to Palestine refugees in all fields.

108th plenary meeting
16 December 1982

G

POPULATION AND REFUGEES DISPLACED SINCE 1967

The General Assembly,

Recalling Security Council resolution 237 (1967) of 14 June 1967,

Recalling also General Assembly resolutions 2252 (ES-V) of 4 July 1967, 2452 A (XXIII) of 19 December 1968, 2535 B (XXIV) of 10 December 1969, 2672 D (XXV) of 8 December 1970, 2792 E (XXVI) of 6 December 1971, 2963 C and D (XXVII) of 13 December 1972, 3089 C (XXVIII) of 7 December 1973, 3331 D (XXIX) of 17 December 1974, 3419 C (XXX) of 8 December 1975, 31/15 D of 23 November 1976, 32/90 E of 13 December 1977, 33/112 F of 18 December 1978, 34/52 E of 23 November 1979, ES-7/ 2 of 29 July 1980, 35/13 E of 3 November 1980 and 36/146 B of 16 December 1981,

Having consdiered the report of the Commissioner-General of the United Nations Relief and Works Agency for Palestine Refugees in the Near East, covering the period from 1 July 1981 to 30 June 1982,[36] and the report of the Secretary-General of 20 September 1982,[41]

1. *Reaffirms* the inalienable right of all displaced inhabitants to return to their homes or former places of residence in the territories occupied by Israel since 1967 and declares once more that any attempt to restrict, or to

---

[41] A/37/426.

attach conditions to, the free exercise of the right of return by any displaced person is inconsistent with that inalienable right and inadmissible;

2. *Considers* any and all agreements embodying any restriction or condition for the return of the displaced inhabitants as null and void;

3. *Strongly deplores* the continued refusal of the Israeli authorities to take steps for the return of the displaced inhabitants;

4. *Calls once more upon* Israel:

(a) To take immediate steps for the return of all displaced inhabitants;

(b) To desist from all measures that obstruct the return of the displaced inhabitants, including measures affecting the physical and demographic structure of the occupied territories;

5. *Requests* the Secretary-General, after consulting with the Commissioner-General of the United Nations Relief and Works Agency for Palestine Refugees in the Near East, to report to the General Assembly before the opening of its thirty-eighth session on Israel's compliance with paragraph 4 above.

108th plenary meeting
16 December 1982

H

REVENUES DERIVED FROM PALESTINE REFUGEE PROPERTIES

The General Assembly,

Recalling its resolutions 35/13 A to F of 3 November 1980, 36/146 C of 16 December 1981 and all its previous resolutions on the question, including resolution 194 (III) of 11 December 1948,

Taking note of the report of the Secretary-General of 28 September 1982,[42]

Taking note also of the report of the United Nations Conciliation Commission for Palestine, covering the period from 1 October 1981 to 30 September 1982,[43]

Recalling that the Universal Declaration of Human Rights[44] and the principles of international law uphold the principle that no one shall be arbitrarily deprived of one's private property,

Considering that the Palestinian Arab refugees are entitled to their property and to the income derived from their property, in conformity with the principles of justice and equity,

Recalling, in particular, its resolution 394 (V) of 14 December 1950, in which it directed the United Nations Conciliation Commission for Palestine, in consultation with the parties concerned, to prescribe measures for the protection of the rights, property and interests of the Palestinian Arab refugees,

[42] A/37/488 and Corr.1.
[43] A/37/497, annex.
[44] Resolution 217 A (III).

Taking note of the completion of the programme of identification and evaluation of Arab property, as announced by the United Nations Conciliation Commission for Palestine in its twenty-second progress report,[45] of 11 May 1964, and of the fact that the Land Office had a schedule of Arab owners and file of documents defining the location, area and other particulars of Arab property,

1. *Requests* the Secretary-General to take all appropriate steps, in consultation with the United Nations Conciliation Commission for Palestine, for the protection and administration of Arab property, assets and property rights in Israel, and to establish a fund for the receipt of income derived therefrom, on behalf of their rightful owners;

2. *Calls once again upon* the Governments concerned, especially Israel, to render all facilities and assistance to the Secretary-General in the implementation of the present resolution;

3. *Requests* the Secretary-General to report to the General Assembly at its thirty-eighth session on the implementation of the present resolution.

108th plenary meeting
16 December 1982

I

Special identification cards to all Palestine refugees

The General Assembly,

Recalling its resolution 36/146 F of 16 December 1981 and all previous resolutions on the question,

Recalling, in particular, its resolutions 194 (III) of 11 December 1948 and 302 (IV) of 8 December 1949,

Recognizing the concern of the United Nations with the problem of the Palestine refugees,

1. *Reiterates its regret* that paragraph 11 of General Assembly resolution 194 (III) has not thus far been implemented;

2. *Requests* the Secretary-General, in co-operation with the Commissioner-General of the United Nations Relief and Works Agency for Palestine Refugees in the Near East, to issue identification cards to all Palestine refugees and their descendants, irrespective of whether they are recipients or not of rations and services from the Agency, as well as to all displaced persons and to those who have been prevented from returning to their homes as a result of the 1967 hostilities, and their descendants;

3. *Requests* the Secretary-General to report to the General Assembly at its thirty-eighth session on the implementation of the present resolution.

108th plenary meeting
16 December 1982

[45] *Official Records of the General Assembly, Nineteenth Session, Annex No. 11,* document A/5700.

J

PROTECTION OF PALESTINE REFUGEES

The General Assembly,

Recalling Security Council resolutions 508 (1982) of 5 June 1982, 509 (1982) of 6 June 1982, 511 (1982) of 18 June 1982, 512 (1982) of 19 June 1982, 513 (1982) of 4 July 1982, 515 (1982) of 29 July 1982, 517 (1982) of 4 August 1982, 518 (1982) of 12 August 1982, 519 (1982) of 17 August 1982, 520 (1982) of 17 September 1982 and 523 (1982) of 18 October 1982,

Recalling General Assembly resolutions ES-7/5 of 26 June 1982, ES-7/6 of 24 August 1982, ES-7/8 of 19 August 1982 and ES-7/9 of 24 September 1982,

Having considered the report of the Commissioner-General of the United Nations Relief and Works Agency for Palestine Refugees in the Near East, covering the period from 1 July 1981 to 30 June 1982,[36] and his special report covering the period from 6 June to 31 August 1982,[37]

Referring to the humanitarian principles of the Geneva Convention relative to the Protection of Civilian Persons in Time of War, of 12 August 1949,[46] and to the obligations arising from the regulations annexed to the Hague Convention of 1907,

Deeply distressed at the sufferings of the Palestinians resulting from the Israeli invasion of Lebanon,

1. *Urges* the Secretary-General, in consultation with the United Nations Relief and Works Agency for Palestine Refugees in the Near East, and pending the withdrawal of Israeli forces from the Palestinian and other Arab territories occupied by Israel since 1967, including Jerusalem, to undertake effective measures to guarantee the safety and security and the legal and human rights of the Palestine refugees in the occupied territories;

2. *Calls upon* Israel, the occupying Power, to release forthwith all detained Palestine refugees, including the employees of the United Nations Relief and Works Agency for Palestine Refugees in the Near East;

3. *Also calls upon* Israel to desist forthwith from preventing those Palestinians registered by the United Nations Relief and Works Agency for Palestine Refugees in the Near East as refugees in Lebanon from returning to their camps in Lebanon;

4. *Further calls upon* Israel to allow the resumption of health, medical, educational and social services rendered by the United Nations Relief and Works Agency for Palestine Refugees in the Near East to the Palestinians in the refugee camps in southern Lebanon;

5. *Requests* the Commissioner-General of the United Nations relief and Works Agency for Palestine Refugees in the Near East to co-ordinate his activities in rendering those services with the Government of Lebanon, the host country;

[46] United Nations, *Treaty Series*, vol. 75, No. 973, p. 287.

6. *Urges* the Commissioner-General to provide housing, in consultation with the Government of Lebanon, to the Palestine refugees whose houses were demolished or razed by the Israeli forces, in order to protect them from the severity of the weather;

7. *Requests* the Commissioner-General, in consultation with the Government of Lebanon, to prepare a report on the totality of the damage caused to the Palestine refugees and their property and to the Agency's facilities, as well as those of other international bodies, as a result of the Israeli aggression;

8. *Requests* the Secretary-General, in consultation with the Commissioner-General, to report to the General Assembly before the opening of its thirty-eighth session on the implementation of the present resolution.

108th plenary meeting
16 December 1982

K

ASSISTANCE TO PALESTINE REFUGEES

The General Assembly,

Recalling its resolution 36/146 F of 16 December 1981 and all previous resolutions on the question, including resolution 194 (III) of 11 December 1948,

Taking note of the report of the Commissioner-General of the United Nations Relief and Works Agency for Palestine Refugees in the Near East, covering the period from 1 July 1981 to 30 June 1982,[36]

1. *Notes with regret* that repatriation or compensation of the refugees as provided for in paragraph 11 of General Assembly resolution 194 (III) has not been effected, that no substantial progress has been made in the programme endorsed by the Assembly in paragraph 2 of its resolution 513 (VI) of 26 January 1952 for the reintegration of refugees either by repatriation or resettlement and that, therefore, the situation of the refugees continues to be a matter of serious concern;

2. *Expresses its thanks* to the Commissioner-General and to all the staff of the United Nations Relief and Works Agency for Palestine Refugees in the Near East, recognizing that the Agency is doing all it can within the limits of available resources, and also expresses its thanks to the specialized agencies and private organizations for their valuable work in assisting the refugees;

3. *Reiterates its request* that the headquarters of the United Nations Relief and Works Agency for Palestine Refugees in the Near East should be relocated to its former site within its area of operations as soon as practicable;

4. *Notes with regret* that the United Nations Conciliation Commission for Palestine has been unable to find a means of achieving progress in the implementation of paragraph 11 of General Assembly resolution 194 (III) and requests the Commission to exert continued efforts towards the implemen-

tation of that paragraph and to report to the Assembly as appropriate, but not later than 1 October 1983;

5. *Directs attention* to the continuing seriousness of the financial position of the United Nations Relief and Works Agency for Palestine Refugees in the Near East, as outlined in the report of the Commissioner-General;

6. *Notes with concern* that, despite the commendable and successful efforts of the Commissioner-General to collect additional contributions, this increased level of income to the United Nations Relief and Works Agency for Palestine Refugees in the Near East is still insufficient to cover essential budget requirements in the present year and that, at currently foreseen levels of giving, deficits will recur each year;

7. *Calls upon* all Governments as a matter of urgency to make the most generous efforts possible to meet the anticipated needs of the United Nations Relief and Works Agency for Palestine Refugees in the Near East, particularly in the light of the budgetary deficit projected in the report of the Commissioner-General, and therefore urges noncontributing Governments to contribute regularly and contributing Governments to consider increasing their regular contributions.

108th plenary meeting
16 December 1982

311. General Assembly Resolution 37/123 on the Situation
in the Middle East, December 16 and 20, 1982*

* G.A. Res. 123, 37 U.N. GAOR Supp. (No. 51) at 36, U.N. Doc. A/37/51
(1982). *See also* subsequent resolution, G.A. Res. 180, 38 U.N. GAOR Supp.
(No. 47) at 49, U.N. Doc. A/38/47 (1983).

A

The General Assembly,

Having discussed the item entitled "The situation in the Middle East",
Taking note of the reports of the Secretary-General,[71]
Recalling Security Council resolution 497 (1981) of 17 December 1981,
Reaffirming its resolutions 36/226 B of 17 December 1981 and ES-9/1 of 5 February 1982,

Recalling its resolution 3314 (XXIX) of 14 December 1974, in which it defined an act of aggression, *inter alia*, as "the invasion or attack by the armed forces of a State of the territory of another State, or any military occupation, however temporary, resulting from such invasion or attack, or any annexation by the use of force of the territory of another State or part thereof" and provided that "no consideration of whatever nature, whether political, economic, military or otherwise, may serve as a justification for aggression",

Reaffirming the fundamental principle of the inadmissibility of the acquisition of territory by force,

Reaffirming once more the applicability of the Geneva Convention relative to the Protection of Civilian Persons in Time of War, of 12 August 1949,[72] to the occupied Palestinian and other Arab territories, including Jerusalem,

Noting that Israel's record and actions establish conclusively that it is not a peace-loving Member State and that it has not carried out its obligations under the Charter of the United Nations,

Noting further that Israel has refused, in violation of Article 25 of the Charter, to accept and carry out the numerous relevant decisions of the Security Council, the latest of which was resolution 497 (1981), thus failing to carry out its obligations under the Charter,

1. *Strongly condemns* Israel for its failure to comply with Security Council resolution 497 (1981) and General Assembly resolutions 36/226 B and ES-9/1;

2. *Declares once more* that Israel's decision of 14 December 1981 to impose its laws, jurisdiction and administration on the occupied Syrian Golan Heights constitutes an act of aggression under the provisions of Article 39 of the Charter of the United Nations and General Assembly resolution 3314 (XXIX);

3. *Declares once more* that Israel's decision to impose its laws, jurisdiction and administration on the occupied Syrian Golan Heights is null and void and has no legal validity and/or effect whatsoever;

4. *Declares* all Israeli policies and practices of, or aimed at, annexation of

---

[71] A/37/169 and Add.1-3-S/14953 and Add.1-3. For the printed text, see *Official Records of the Security Council, Thirty-seventh Year, Supplement for April, May and June 1982,* documents 5/14953 and Add.1; and *ibid., Supplement for October, November and December 1982,* documents S/14953/Add.2 and 3.

[72] United Nations, *Treaty Series,* vol. 75, No. 973, p. 287.

the occupied Palestinian and other Arab territories, including Jerusalem, to be in violation of international law and of the relevant United Nations resolutions;

5. *Determines once more* that all actions taken by Israel to give effect to its decision relating to the occupied Syrian Golan Heights are illegal and invalid and shall not be recognized;

6. *Reaffirms its determination* that all the provisions of the Hague Convention of 1907[73] and the Geneva Convention relative to the Protection of Civilian Persons in Time of War, of 12 August 1949, continue to apply to the Syrian territory occupied by Israel since 1967, and calls upon the parties thereto to respect and ensure respect of their obligations under these instruments in all circumstances;

7. *Determines once more* that the continued occupation of the Syrian Golan Heights since 1967 and their effective annexation by Israel on 14 December 1981, following Israel's decision to impose its laws, jurisdiction and administration on that territory, constitute a continuing threat to international peace and security;

8. *Strongly deplores* the negative vote by a permanent member of the Security Council which prevented the Council from adopting against Israel, under Chapter VII of the Charter, the "appropriate measures" referred to in resolution 497 (1981) unanimously adopted by the Council;

9. *Further deplores* any political, economic, financial, military and technological support to Israel that encourages Israel to commit acts of aggression and to consolidate and perpetuate its occupation and annexation of occupied Arab territories;

10. *Firmly emphasizes once more* its demands that Israel, the occupying Power, rescind forthwith its decision of 14 December 1981 to impose its laws, jurisdiction and administration on the Syrian Golan Heights, which has resulted in the effective annexation of that territory;

11. *Reaffirms once more* the overriding necessity of the total and unconditional withdrawal by Israel from all the Palestinian and other Arab territories occupied since 1967, including Jerusalem, which is an essential prerequisite for the establishment of a comprehensive and just peace in the Middle East;

12. *Determines once more* that Israel's record and actions confirm that it is not a peace-loving Member State, that it has persistently violated the principles contained in the Charter and that it has carried out neither its obligations under the Charter nor its commitment under General Assembly resolution 273 (III) of 11 May 1949;

13. *Calls once more upon* all Member States to apply the following measures:

[73] Carnegie Endowment for International Peace, *The Hague Conventions and Declarations of 1899 and 1907* (New York, Oxford University Press, 1915), p. 100.

(a) To refrain from supplying Israel with any weapons and related equipment and to suspend any military assistance that Israel receives from them;

(b) To refrain from acquiring any weapons or military equipment from Israel;

(c) To suspend economic, financial and technological assistance to and co-operation with Israel;

(d) To sever diplomatic, trade and cultural relations with Israel;

14. *Reiterates its call* to all Member States to cease forthwith, individually and collectively, all dealings with Israel in order totally to isolate it in all fields;

15. *Urges* non-member States to act in accordance with the provisions of the present resolution;

16. *Calls upon* the specialized agencies and other international organizations to conform their relations with Israel to the terms of the present resolution.

108th plenary meeting
16 December 1982

B

The General Assembly,

Recalling the relevant provisions of the Universal Declaration of Human Rights,[74]

Recalling also the Constitution of the United Nations Educational, Scientific and Cultural Organization[75] and all other relevant international instruments concerning the right to cultural identity in all its forms,

Having learned that the Israeli army, during its occupation of Beirut, seized and took away the archives and documents of every kind concerning Palestinian history and culture, including cultural articles belonging to Palestinian institutions—in particular the Palestine Research Centre—archives, documents, manuscripts and materials such as film documents, literary works by major authors, paintings, *objets d'art* and works of folklore, research works and so forth, serving as a foundation for the history, culture, national awareness, unity and solidarity of the Palestinian people,

1. *Condemns* those acts of plundering the Palestinian cultural heritage;

2. *Calls upon* the Government of Israel to make full restitution, through the United Nations Educational, Scientific and Cultural Organization, of all the cultural property belonging to Palestinian institutions, including the archives and documents removed from the Palestine Research Centre and arbitrarily seized by the Israeli forces.

108th plenary meeting
16 December 1982

---

[74] Resolution 217 A (III).
[75] See *Manual of the General Conference*, 1981 edition (Paris, UNESCO, 1981).

C

The General Assembly,

Recalling its resolution 36/120 E of 10 December 1981, in which it determined that all legislative and administrative measures and actions taken by Israel, the occupying Power, which had altered or purported to alter the character and status of the Holy City of Jerusalem, in particular the so-called "Basic Law" on Jerusalem and the proclamation of Jerusalem as the capital of Israel, were null and void and must be rescinded forthwith,

Recalling Security Council resolution 478 (1980) of 20 August 1980, in which the Council, *inter alia*, decided not to recognize the "Basic Law" and called upon those States that had established diplomatic missions at Jerusalem to withdraw such missions from the Holy City,

1. *Deplores* the transfer by some States of their diplomatic missions to Jerusalem in violation of Security Council resolution 478 (1980);

2. *Calls upon* those States to abide by the provisions of the relevant United Nations resolutions, in conformity with the Charter of the United Nations.

108th plenary meeting
16 December 1982

D

The General Assembly,

Recalling its resolution 95 (I) of 11 December 1946,

Recalling also its resolution 96 (I) of 11 December 1946, in which it, *inter alia*, affirmed that genocide is a crime under international law which the civilized world condemns, and for the commission of which principals and accomplices—whether private individuals, public officials or statesmen, and whether the crime is committed on religious, racial, political or any other grounds—are punishable,

Referring to the provisions of the Convention on the Prevention and Punishment of the Crime of Genocide, adopted by the General Assembly on 9 December 1948,[76]

Recalling the relevant provisions of the Geneva Convention relative to the Protection of Civilian Persons in Time of War, of 12 August 1949,[72]

Appalled at the large-scale massacre of Palestinian civilians in the Sabra and Shatila refugee camps situated at Beirut,

Recognizing the universal outrage and condemnation of that massacre,

Recalling its resolution ES-7/9 of 24 September 1982,

1. *Condemns* in the strongest terms the large-scale massacre of Palestinian civilians in the Sabra and Shatila refugee camps;

2. *Resolves* that the massacre was an act of genocide.

108th plenary meeting
16 December 1982

[76] Resolution 260 A (III).

E

The General Assembly,

Having heard the address by the President of the Lebanese Republic on 18 October 1982,[77]

Taking note of the decision of the Government of Lebanon calling for the withdrawal from Lebanon of all non-Lebanese troops and forces which are not authorized by the Government to deploy therein,

Bearing in mind Security Council resolutions 508 (1982) of 5 June 1982 and 509 (1982) of 6 June 1982,

1. *Calls* for strict respect of the territorial integrity, sovereignty, unity and political independence of Lebanon and supports the efforts of the Government of Lebanon, with regional and international endorsement, to restore the exclusive authority of the Lebanese State throughout its territory up to the internationally recognized boundaries;

2. *Requests* the Secretary-General to report to the General Assembly on the implementation of the present resolution.

108th plenary meeting
16 December 1982

F

The General Assembly,

Having discussed the item entitled "The situation in the Middle East",

Reaffirming its resolutions 36/226 A and B of 17 December 1981 and ES-9/1 of 5 February 1982,

Recalling Security Council resolutions 425 (1978) of 19 March 1978, 497 (1981) of 17 December 1981, 508 (1982) of 5 June 1982, 509 (1982) of 6 June 1982, 511 (1982) of 18 June 1982, 512 (1982) of 19 June 1982, 513 (1982) of 4 July 1982, 515 (1982) of 29 July 1982, 516 (1982) of 1 August 1982, 517 (1982) of 4 August 1982, 518 (1982) of 12 August 1982, 519 (1982) of 17 August 1982, 520 (1982) of 17 September 1982 and 521 (1982) of 19 September 1982,

Taking note of the report of the Secretary-General of 12 October 1982,[78]

Welcoming the world-wide support extended to the just cause of the Palestinian people and the other Arab countries in their struggle against Israeli aggression and occupation in order to achieve a comprehensive, just and lasting peace in the Middle East and the full exercise by the Palestinian people of its inalienable national rights, as affirmed by previous resolutions of the General Assembly relating to the question of Palestine and the situation in the Middle East,

---

[77] *Official Records of the General Assembly, Thirty-seventh Session, Plenary Meetings,* 35th meeting, paras. 2-18.

[78] A/37/525-S/15451. For the printed text, see *Official Records of the Security Council, Thirty-seventh Year, Supplement for October, November and December 1982,* document S/15451.

Gravely concerned that the Arab and Palestinian territories occupied since 1967, including Jerusalem, still remain under Israeli occupation, that the relevant resolutions of the United Nations have not been implemented and that the Palestinian people is still denied the restoration of its land and the exercise of its inalienable national rights in conformity with international law, as reaffirmed by resolutions of the United Nations,

Reaffirming the applicability of the Geneva Convention relative to the Protection of Civilian Persons in Time of War, of 12 August 1949,[72] to all the occupied Palestinian and other Arab territories, including Jerusalem,

Reiterating all relevant United Nations resolutions which emphasize that the acquisition of territory by force is inadmissible under the Charter of the United Nations and the principles of international law and that Israel must withdraw unconditionally from all the Palestinian and other Arab territories occupied by Israel since 1967, including Jerusalem,

Reaffirming further the imperative necessity of establishing a comprehensive, just and lasting peace in the region, based on full respect for the Charter and the principles of international law,

Gravely concerned also at recent Israeli actions involving the escalation and expansion of the conflict in the region, which further violate the principles of international law and endanger international peace and security,

Welcoming the Arab peace plan adopted unanimously at the Twelfth Arab Summit Conference, held at Fez, Morocco, on 25 November 1981 and 9 September 1982,[79]

Bearing in mind the address made, on 26 October 1982, by His Majesty King Hassan II of Morocco,[80] in his capacity as President of the Twelfth Arab Summit Conference,

1. *Condemns* Israel's continued occupation of the Palestinian and other Arab territories, including Jerusalem, in violation of the Charter of the United Nations, the principles of international law and the relevant resolutions of the United Nations, and demands the immediate, unconditional and total withdrawal of Israel from all these occupied territories;

2. *Reaffirms its conviction* that the question of Palestine is the core of the conflict in the Middle East and that no comprehensive, just and lasting peace in the region will be achieved without the full exercise by the Palestinian people of its inalienable national rights and the immediate, unconditional and total withdrawal of Israel from all the Palestinian and other occupied Arab territories;

3. *Reaffirms further* that a just and comprehensive settlement of the situation in the Middle East cannot be achieved without the participation on an equal footing of all the parties to the conflict, including the Palestine Liberation Organization, the representative of the Palestinian people;

---

[79] See A/37/696-S/15510, annex.

[80] *Official Records of the General Assembly, Thirty-seventh Session, Plenary Meetings*, 44th meeting, paras. 83-92.

4. *Declares once more* that peace in the Middle East is indivisible and must be based on a comprehensive, just and lasting solution of the Middle East problem, under the auspices of the United Nations, which ensures the complete and unconditional withdrawal of Israel from the Palestinian and other Arab territories occupied since 1967, including Jerusalem, and which enables the Palestinian people, under the leadership of the Palestine Liberation Organization, to exercise its inalienable rights, including the right to return and the right to self-determination, national independence and the establishment of its independent sovereign State in Palestine, in accordance with the resolutions of the United Nations relevant to the question of Palestine, in particular General Assembly resolutions ES-7/2 of 29 July 1980, 36/120 A to F of 10 December 1981, 37/86 A to D of 10 December 1982 and 37/86 E of 20 December 1982;

5. *Rejects* all agreements and arrangements in so far as they violate the recognized rights of the Palestinian people and contradict the principles of just and comprehensive solutions to the Middle East problem to ensure the establishment of a just peace in the area;

6. *Deplores* Israel's failure to comply with Security Council resolutions 476 (1980) of 30 June 1980 and 478 (1980) of 20 August 1980 and General Assembly resolutions 35/207 of 16 December 1980 and 36/226 A and B of 17 December 1981, determines that Israel's decision to annex Jerusalem and to declare it as its "capital" as well as the measures to alter its physical character, demographic composition, institutional structure and status are null and void and demands that they be rescinded immediately, and calls upon all Member States, the specialized agencies and all other international organizations to abide by the present resolution and all other relevant resolutions, including Assembly resolutions 37/86 A to E;

7. *Condemns* Israel's aggression and practices against the Palestinian people in the occupied Palestinian territories and outside these territories, particularly Palestinians in Lebanon, including the expropriation and annexation of territory, the establishment of settlements, assassination attempts and other terrorist, aggressive and repressive measures, which are in violation of the Charter and the principles of international law and the relevant international conventions;

8. *Strongly condemns* the imposition by Israel of its laws, jurisdiction and administration on the occupied Syrian Golan Heights, its annexationist policies and practices, the establishment of settlements, the confiscation of lands, the diversion of water resources and the imposition of Israeli citizenship on Syrian nationals, and declares that all these measures are null and void and constitute a violation of the rules and principles of international law relevant to belligerent occupation, in particular the Geneva Convention relative to the Protection of Civilian Persons in Time of War, of 12 August 1949;

9. *Considers* that the agreements on strategic co-operation between the United States of America and Israel signed on 30 November 1981 would

encourage Israel to pursue its aggressive and expansionist policies and practices in the Palestinian and other Arab territories occupied since 1967, including Jerusalem, would have adverse effects on efforts for the establishment of a comprehensive, just and lasting peace in the Middle East and
would threaten the security of the region;

10. *Calls upon* all States to put an end to the flow to Israel of any military,
economic and financial aid, as well as of human resources, aimed at encouraging it to pursue its aggressive policies against the Arab countries and the
Palestinian people;

11. *Requests* the Secretary-General to report to the Security Council periodically on the development of the situation and to submit to the General
Assembly at its thirty-eighth session a comprehensive report covering the
developments in the Middle East in all their aspects.

112th plenary meeting
20 December 1982

312. General Assembly Resolution 37/134 on Assistance to the Palestinian People, December 17, 1982*

* G.A. Res. 134, 37 U.N. GAOR Supp. (No. 51) at 111, U.N. Doc. A/37/ 51 (1982).

The General Assembly,

Recalling its resolution ES-7/5 of 26 June 1982,

Recalling also Security Council resolution 512 (1982) of 19 June 1982,

Recalling further Economic and Social Council resolution 1982/48 of 27 July 1982,

Expressing its deep alarm at the Israeli invasion of Lebanon, which claimed the lives of a very large number of civilian Palestinians,

Horrified by the Sabra and Shatila massacre,

Noting with deep concern the dire need of the Palestinian victims of the Israeli invasion for urgent humanitarian assistance,

Noting the need to provide economic and social assistance to the Palestinian people,

1. *Condemns* Israel for its invasion of Lebanon, which inflicted severe damage on civilian Palestinians, including heavy loss of human life, intolerable suffering and massive material destruction;

2. *Endorses* Economic and Social Council resolution 1982/48;

3. *Calls upon* Governments and relevant United Nations bodies to provide humanitarian assistance to the Palestinian victims of the Israeli invasion of Lebanon;

4. *Requests* the relevant programmes, agencies, organs and organizations of the United Nations system to intensify their efforts, in co-operation with the Palestine Liberation Organization, to provide economic and social assistance to the Palestinian people;

5. *Also requests* that United Nations assistance to the Palestinians in the Arab host countries should be rendered in co-operation with the Palestine Liberation Organization and with the consent of the Arab host Government concerned;

6. *Requests* the Secretary-General to report to the General Assembly at its thirty-eighth session, through the Economic and Social Council, on the progress made in the implementation of the present resolution.

109th plenary meeting
17 December 1982

313. General Assembly Resolution 37/222 on the Living Conditions of the Palestinian People in the Occupied Palestinian Territories, December 20, 1982*

* G.A. Res. 222, 37 U.N. GAOR Supp. (No. 51) at 149, U.N. Doc. A/37/51 (1982).

The General Assembly,

Recalling the Vancouver Declaration on Human Settlements, 1976,[177] and the relevant recommendations for national action[178] adopted by Habitat: United Nations Conference on Human Settlements,

Recalling also resolution 3, entitled "Living conditions of the Palestinians in occupied territories", contained in the recommendations for international co-operation adopted by Habitat: United Nations Conference on Human Settlements,[179]

Recalling further its resolution 36/73 of 4 December 1981,

1. *Takes note* of the report of the Secretary-General on the living conditions of the Palestinian people in the occupied Palestinian territories;[180]

2. *Takes note* of the statement made by the observer of the Palestine Liberation Organization;[181]

3. *Expresses its alarm* at the deterioration in the living conditions of the Palestinian people in the Palestinian territories occupied since 1967 as a result of the Israeli occupation;

4. *Affirms* that the Israeli occupation is contradictory to the basic requirements for the social and economic development of the Palestinian people in the occupied West Bank and Gaza Strip;

5. *Affirms also* that the exercise by the Palestinian people of their right to self-determination is a prerequisite for their social and economic development in the Palestinian territories occupied since 1967;

6. *Calls upon* the Israeli occupation authorities to give United Nations bodies and experts access to the Palestinian territories occupied since 1967;

7. *Recognizes* the need for a comprehensive report on the social and economic conditions of the Palestinian people in the Palestinian territories occupied since 1967;

8. *Requests* the Secretary-General to prepare and submit to the General Assembly at its thirty-eighth session, through the Economic and Social Council, a comprehensive report on the living conditions of the Palestinian people in the occupied Palestinian territories.

113th plenary meeting
20 December 1982

[177] *Report of Habitat: United Nations Conference on Human Settlements, Vancouver, 31 May–11 June 1976* (United Nations publication, Sales No. E.76.IV.7 and corrigendum), chap. I.

[178] *Ibid.*, chap. II.

[179] *Ibid.*, chap. III.

[180] A/37/238.

[181] *Official Records of the General Assembly, Thirty-seventh Session, Second Committee,* 31st meeting, para. 86.

314. European Parliament Resolution on the Situation in the Middle East, January 11, 1983*

* 26 O.J. Eur. Comm. (No. C 42) 15 (1983).

The European Parliament,

A. desiring a comprehensive, just and lasting peace settlement in the Middle East,

B. desiring a solution to the problems of the Lebanon that will ensure the independence, sovereignty and integrity of that country and the security and further development of the different communities living there,

C. having regard to resolutions 242 and 338 of the United Nations Security Council,

D. recalling its resolution of 11 October 1978 on the result of the conference at Camp David and its resolution of 26 April 1979 on the signing of the peace treaty between Egypt and Israel and the contribution of the Community to a comprehensive peace settlement ([1]),

E. having regard to the statement on the Middle East by the European Council on 13 June 1980 in Venice,

F. welcoming the participation of four EEC Member States in the Sinai multinational peace-keeping force and the participation of two Member States in the international peace-keeping force in Lebanon,

G. noting the Fahd Plan, made public for the first time on 7 August 1981,

H. recalling its resolutions of 12 October 1978, 10 April 1981, 22 April 1982, 17 June 1982, 16 September 1982 and 15 October 1982, on the Lebanon ([2]),

I. having regard to various statements on Lebanon by the European Council and the Foreign Affairs Ministers meeting in Political Cooperation,

J. taking the view that the *de facto* annexation by Israel of East Jerusalem and the Golan Heights, the settlement policy pursued in the Gaza Strip and on the West Bank and the policy of dismissing elected mayors in the West Bank are not compatible with progress towards a comprehensive peace settlement,

K. believing that recent events in the area, such as the Israeli invasion of Lebanon, the Israeli siege of West Beirut and the war between Iraq and Iran have made the need for a political solution of the Arab-Israeli conflict even more urgent,

L. deploring the assassination of President Beshir Gemayel, President of the Lebanese Republic, the subsequent entry of Israeli forces into West Beirut, and the massacres in the Palestinian camps in September 1982,

M. extremely worried by the resumption of fierce fighting in Northern Lebanon and to the east of Beirut which threatens to jeopardize any possible developments in the negotiations commenced on 28 December 1982 between the Lebanese and Israeli governments,

N. having regard to the motions for resolutions tabled by Mrs Charzat and others on the situation in the Middle East (Doc. 1-101/80), by Mr Lalor

[1] OJ No C 261, 6. 11. 1978 and OJ No C 127, 21. 5. 1979, p. 59.

[2] OJ No C 261, 6. 11. 1978, p. 38, OJ No C 101, 4. 5. 1981, p. 112, OJ No C 125, 17. 5. 1982, p. 79, OJ No C 182, 19. 7. 1982, p. 52, OJ No C 267, 11. 10. 1982, p. 42 and OJ No C 292, 8. 11. 1982, p. 111.

on the situation in Southern Lebanon (Doc. 1-99/80/rev.), by Mr Fanti and others on the expulsion of Palestinian mayors (Doc. 1-774/80), by Mr d'Ormesson and others on Lebanon (Doc. 1-819/80), by Mr van Aerssen and Mr Blumenfeld on the stabilization and extension of peace efforts in the Middle East (Doc. 1-601/81), by Mr Kyrkos on the decision taken by the Israeli Knesset to annex the Golan heights (Doc. 1-892/81), by Mr Ephremidis and others on the annexation of the Golan Heights by Israel (Doc. 1-902/81), by Mr Segre and Mr Cardia on the annexation of the Golan Heights by the State of Israel (Doc. 1-906/81), by Mr Marshall and others on the Israeli annexation of the Golans (Doc. 1-956/81), by Mr Kyrkos on the occupied Arab territories on the West Bank and in the Gaza Strip (Doc. 1-158/82), by Mr Romualdi and others on the Israeli invasion of Southern Lebanon (Doc. 1-333/82) and by Mr Glinne and others on the imposition of martial law in the territories occupied by Israel (Doc. 1-59/82),

O. having regard to the report of the Political Affairs Committee (Doc. 1-786/82),

1. Is convinced that resolutions 242 and 338 of the United Nations Security Council constitute a good and workable framework for a comprehensive peace settlement in the Middle East;

2. Is also convinced that the Camp David agreements can and must be one of the basic elements on which to build a settlement of the Arab-Israeli conflict;

3. Notes, however, that a new initiative will be necessary if the negotiations on autonomy in the Camp David context fail;

4. Considers the Venice Declaration as a useful contribution towards such a settlement;

5. Is of the opinion that any European initiative should follow in the footsteps of Camp David, and should therefore be coordinated with the United States;

6. Appreciates the proposals made on 1 September 1982 by President Reagan as a means of giving a new impetus to the Camp David process;

7. Urges the European Council and the Foreign Ministers meeting in Political Cooperation to start from the following principles:

7.1. the use of force and annexation is unacceptable as a means of gaining control of territory,

7.2. Israel must withdraw from the occupied territories immediately and end the occupation of territories held since 1967,

7.3. the sovereignty, territorial integrity and independence of every State in the region, including Israel, must be upheld together with their right to live in peace within secure and recognized boundaries,

7.4. self-determination for the Palestinian people to be implemented by a procedure compatible with the right of Israel to existence and security as part of a comprehensive peace settlement, including the option of a possible Palestinian State;

8. Takes the view that the Fahd Plan in the form adopted by the Arab Summit at Fez in September 1982 contains new, important and usable elements;

9. Believes that the Franco-Egyptian draft resolution could play a useful role in establishing common ground for a settlement of the problems of the region;

10. Considers that the Palestinians themselves should decide by whom they are to be represented, and that the PLO can only be accepted as a legitimate participant in the negotiations when all paragraphs of its charter calling explicitly or implicitly for the destruction of Israel are formally deleted;

11. Considers it essential for Israel and the Palestinian people, including the PLO, to hold talks with each other and to initiate a process leading to mutual acceptance and recognition;

12. Urges the European Council and the Foreign Ministers meeting in Political Cooperation to consult with the United States on Lebanon with a view to securing:
  (a) the withdrawal of all foreign troops;
  (b) the stationing in Beirut and other parts of the country of an international peace force in which the EEC Member States would participate, preferably to replace UNIFIL;
  (c) the disbanding of the militias;
  (d) the re-establishment of an effective Lebanese police force and Lebanese armed forces;
  (e) the rebuilding of the Lebanese society in a manner that does justice to all sections of the population;

13. Takes the view that any contribution from the European Community and its Member States to a comprehensive settlement must include the following:
  13.1. an offer to make Member State contingents available to a peacekeeping force, possibly under UN auspices, to ensure observance of military and security provisions;
  13.2. offers of economic, financial and technical aid to all States in the area and to the Palestinian people as participants in the settlement;

14. Considers that, in the meantime, the European Community and its Member States must continue supplying humanitarian aid, particularly to Lebanon;

15. Takes the view that the authority of any comprehensive peace settlement will ultimately depend on a UN Security Council follow-up resolution to resolution 242, making explicit reference to the State of Israel and to the right to self-determination of the Palestinian people;

16. Instructs its President to forward this resolution to the Commission, the Council and Foreign Ministers meeting in Political Cooperation, to the parliaments of the Member States of the Community and to the Secretary-General of the United Nations Organization.

315. Statement by the Conference of Palestinian Resistance Groups Meeting in Tripoli, Libya, January 16, 1983*

---

* 12 J. Palestine Stud. 245 (Spring 1983).

From 29 Rabi al-Awwal to 2 Rabi ath-Thani 1982 corresponding to January 10-16, 1983, the PFLP, the DFLP, the PFLP-General Command, the organization of the Popular Liberation War Vanguard-Saiqa Forces, the Popular Struggle Front, and the revolutionary command of the Socialist Peoples Libyan Arab Jamahi-riyah (SPLAJ) met in Tripoli in the SPLAJ to evalute [sic] the results of the imperialist-Zionist-reactionary invasion of Lebanon, and what the Arab patriotic and revolutionary states and forces are called upon to do to discharge the tasks of standing up to the front of the enemies and its plots and the Zionist train of death which is supplied with US weapons and technology and which is backed by reactionary Arab oil money with the aim of destroying the Arab nation one state at a time. This has been made clear after the reaffirmation that the Zionist state is the basic element in implementing the aims of international imperialism, particularly US imperialism, in the Arab homeland, and after exposing the truth about the imperialist-Arab reactionary alliance and by regarding the struggle which is taking place between our Arab nation and the Zionists as a struggle for existence.

Proceeding from all this we confirm our rejection of all forms of recognition, negotiation and making peace with the expansionist Zionist state. The nature of this struggle confirms that what has been taken by force cannot be recovered except by force, and that the armed struggle is the major means in our struggle to recover our national rights to the liberation of Palestine and all the occupied Arab areas.

The crisis of the Arab liberation movement is basically ideological, social, organizational and populist. This crisis manifested itself in the inability of the groups of this movement to shoulder their role of mobilizing the mass against the Zionist-imperialist-reactionary onslaught. This calls for a courageous critical reexamination at regional and pan-Arab levels to ensure the participation of the masses in the struggle against the enemy.

The unity of the progressive forces should be based on a frontal and broad program which develops in the course of the struggle to unified ideological foundations and the building of a single Arab movement. Proceeding from this, the groups of the Palestine Resistance which have been in conference affirm the importance and the necessity of joint action and struggle to consolidate Palestinian national unity on the bases of adhering to the Palestine Charter, the political program of the PLO and the resolutions of the [Palestine] National Councils. This is in order to confront and foil all the capitulationist and liquidationary schemes. In the context of confronting the perils which surround the Palestine Revolution, we affirm the following stances and issues;

I. Concerning ideological problems:

(a) The participants agree that the crisis of the Arab liberation movement is basically an ideological, social, organizational and populist crisis, and agree to hold an intellectual conference of progressive pan-Arab and revolutionary Arab intellectuals for this purpose.

(b) To hold a conference of the groups of the Pan-Arab liberation movement in order to produce a broad vanguard program which develops in the course of struggle to unified ideological foundations and the building of a single Arab movement.

(c) To form a preparatory committee for the conference.

II. The participants have agreed to discuss the operation of the organizational and military structure of the militant experiment in the light of a critical reexamination of the experience of past years and on the basis of their conviction in the pan-Arabism of the battle and specifically, the pan-Arabism of *fida'i* action against the Zionist enemy.

III. The participants affirm the following:

1. That the struggle with the Zionist enemy is a struggle for existence and that the pan-Arab existence contradicts the Zionist existence in Palestine, and therefore, the participants declare: No negotiation, no recognition and no reconciliation (Arabic: *sulh*) with the Zionist enemy.

2. To adhere to the Palestinian National Charter, the resolutions of the Palestine National Councils, the political program and the Tripoli unity document.

3. To adhere to the rifle and the armed struggle as the way to liberate Palestine.

4. To reject the Fez summit as a way, a course of action, and decision on the grounds that Arab reaction, which hindered the convening of the Arab summit throughout the period of the invasion of Lebanon and the battle of Beirut, had at the Fez summit in September 1982 worked to exploit the results of that battle and benefited from the broad defect in the balances of forces in the area in order to adopt a number of resolutions which sought to drag the Arab states and the PLO into joining the capitulationist schemes, particularly the Reagan scheme. The line of Arab reaction as manifested at the Fez summit meeting calls for the recognition of the Zionist enemy. It seeks to reach a compromise with the Reagan scheme, make the liquidationary Camp David agreements universal and disown the Arab summit resolutions which affirm the Palestinian people's right to return, to self-determination and national independence, and which recognize the PLO as the sole and legitimate representative of the Palestinian people.

5. To reject the Reagan plan because, in its aim and contents, it denies the inalienable rights of the Palestinian Arab people and it is aimed at liquidating the Palestinian issue and at ending the Arab-Israeli conflict to enable the United States to spread its domination over the Arab area. It is also hostile to our people's right to return, to self-determination and the establishment of their national and independent state on their national soil. It denies the PLO its position as the sole legitimate representative of the Palestinian people. It [the plan] constitutes an American interpretation of the Camp David

agreements and therefore the groups in conference call on all the patriotic Arab forces to confront and foil it.

6. To reject the autonomy scheme whether in the form of Camp David or in the form of the Reagan plan, and also the scheme of civilian administration which the Zionist occupation is trying to impose; and to confront all attempts to find a substitute, and the participation of leaderships and cadres as a substitute, for the PLO.

7. To adhere to Palestinian national unity within the framework of the PLO on the basis of a commitment to the National Charter and the political program and the resolution of the National Councils adopted during their successive sessions.

8. To adhere to the firm, national and legitimate rights of the Palestinian people which have been confirmed by the resolutions of the Arab summit conferences, the foremost being the right of return, self-determination and an independent state and the PLO being the sole and legitimate representative.

9. To safeguard the Palestinian national decision within the framework of deepening our national and pan-Arab aims and to reject all attempts to encroach on the independent national decision and attempts to drag the PLO into making concessions in favour of the Reagan plan or giving powers to any Arab quarter to act for the Palestinian people and its sole legitimate representative.

10. To struggle against the attempts to drag the PLO into recognizing the expansionist state of the Zionist enemy and to stand up to any Arab attempts to recognize the enemy.

11. Proceeding from our firm adherence to the national and firm rights of our people and to the PLO as the sole legitimate representative, we reject all forms of giving the Jordanian regime powers to act for our people or participate together with elements from the West Bank and Gaza sector. On that basis we reject any joint framework of Palestinian-Jordanian action which contradicts the previous articles. We affirm that any unity relations to be established with any Arab country by our people will take place after the emergence of the independent state on Palestinian national soil and on a voluntary basis.

12. To struggle for the freedom of Palestinian political, organizational and informational action in Jordan in implementation of National Council and the Arab summit decisions.

13. Proceeding from the Palestine National Council resolutions concerning the Camp David agreements and what they entail, we affirm our adherence to these resolutions, which reject relations with the Egyptian regime and say that its isolation should continue and that it should be besieged until the Camp David policy and its consequences are overthrown, including the attempts to make the Egyptian regime act for the Palestinan people.

14. To continue the strengthening of the militant relations with the masses of fraternal Egypt under the leadership of their patriotic and pro-

gressive forces, to strengthen their struggle to overthrow Camp David and to do what is required to restore Egypt to the Arab nation.

15. To denounce the calls of the Iraqi regime to lift the siege from the Mubarak regime, the [Iraqi] regime's abandonment of the Baghdad summit resolutions, and the [Iraqi] regime's calls for recognition of the Zionist enemy and direct Palestinian-Israeli negotiations; and to call on the Palestine Revolution forces and the pan-Arab liberation movement to boycott the Iraqi regime and strengthen their relations with the Iraqi patriotic and progressive forces.

16. To call on all Arab states, especially the patriotic and progressive states and the Arab patriotic and progressive forces, to reject the Lebanese-Israeli negotiations and their results. They are aimed at making Lebanon join Camp David, at imposing a capitulationist treaty on it and normalizing relations with it. All this affects Lebanon's independence and the unity of its territory and does the greatest harm to the struggle of the fraternal Lebanese people and their resistance to Israeli occupation. It would lead to the isolation of Lebanon from its Arab context and its transformation into a US-Israeli sphere of influence.

17. To support the Lebanese masses and their patriotic forces and to call on all Arab and international patriotic and progressive states and forces to support the Lebanese national and armed resistance against Israeli occupation and to consolidate the patriotic Lebanese-Palestinian-Syrian alliance on the basis of the joint struggle against Israeli occupation and its surrender terms.

18. To work for safeguarding the Palestinians' security, political and social rights in Lebanon in accordance with Lebanon's Arab commitments to the Palestinian issue.

19. To consolidate relations between the Palestine Revolution and Syria in view of Syria being the security confrontation line on the joint struggle base against the Camp David accords and all the capitulatory solutions, headed by the Reagan plan, for the sake of safeguarding national rights for the liberation of occupied Arab territories and securing the Palestinian peoples right of return and self-determination, the establishment of its independent national state, and to denounce all attempts aimed at destroying Palestinian-Syrian relations.

20. To consolidate the fateful alliance between the SPLAJ and the Palestine Revolution on the basis of the pan-Arab program of struggle and against all the schemes of capitulationist solutions and the attempt to bring the Arab nation to its knees, and to stand alongside it against the imperialist Zionist-reactionary conspiracy.

21. To consolidate relations between the Palestine Revolution and the Arab patriotic states on the basis of the struggle against imperialism, Zionism and Arab reaction and against the Camp David accords and all capitulationist plans, headed by the Reagan plan and the negotiations of the *fait accompli* taking place in Lebanon.

22. To make efforts to rebuild the steadfastness front on scientific bases that would ensure it could carry out its pan-Arab duties, and transforming it from a political front, as it clearly was in the war in Lebanon, into a front that carries out the mobilization of its political, military and economic energies to confront the imperialist, Zionist, reactionary onslaught and guarantee that its resolutions are put into practice.

23. To consolidate and develop the Palestine Revolution's relations with the pan-Arab liberation movement.

24. To struggle to open the Arab borders to Palestinian *fida'i* action in the direction of the occupied Arab territory to resist Zionist occupation.

25. On the basis of the possibility of defeating the Zionist enemy through a popular war of liberation, we call on the Lebanese patriotic forces to raise the pace of the armed struggle against him so that it can be turned into a popular war of liberation.

26. To (strengthen) and develop the struggle against US imperialism, international Zionism and Arab reaction, and against the attempts to impose US domination on the region.

27. To maintain and consolidate the Palestine Revolution's alliances with the Soviet Union, the socialist countries and all the forces of liberation, progress and democracy in the world.

28. To act so as to regroup the forces of the Palestine Revolution and reorganize and strengthen them in Syria for the sake of continuing the armed struggle.

29. The participants in the meeting denounce all the contacts made which took place with any Jewish, Zionist parties.

30. The participants in the meeting support the position of the Islamic revolution in Iran, since it is an ally of the Arab patriotic and progressive forces in their struggle against imperialism, Zionism and Arab reaction.

316. European Parliament Resolution on the Situation in the Middle East, May 19, 1983*

* 26 O.J. Eur. Comm. (No. C 161) 119 (1983).

The European Parliament,

— having regard to its resolutions on the Middle East and in particular that of 11 January 1983 (¹),
— having regard to the Council Decision of 9 June 1982,
— having regard to the European Council's most recent declaration on the Middle East of 22 March 1983,
— having regard to the dramatic escalation of the situation in the Middle East following the assassination of Mr Sartawi,
— having regard to the efforts of King Hussein of Jordan,
— having regard to the horrifying attack on the American Embassy in Beirut,
— whereas Israel is continuing and intensifying its policy of settlement in the West Bank and the Gaza Strip,
— having regard to the desperate plight of Palestinian refugees in Lebanon and its effect on their health,

1. Condemns all violent attacks on persons and property which can only aggravate the situation;

2 Calls on the Foreign Ministers of the Community meeting in Luxembourg at the end of May 1983 to take a decision reaffirming the Community's vital role in finding a solution to the political problems of the Middle East and to take steps to implement their recommendations, that is, to use every available means in the context of the common foreign and external economic policy to urge Israel to call an immediate halt to its settlement policy in the West Bank and the Gaza Strip in order to avoid placing further pressure of time on the negotiations;

3. Urges the Community to take part in the Conference on the Palestinian question called by the UN General Assembly;

4. Calls on the Council of Ministers and the European Council to use all their influence to find a solution to the crisis in the Middle East so that children and young people are no longer the victims of political conflicts in this part of the world;

5. Instructs its President to forward this resolution to the Foreign Ministers meeting in Political Cooperation, the Council and the Commission.

¹ OJ NO C 42, 14. 2. 1983, p. 11; Penders report Doc. 1-786/82.

317. Question to the Foreign Ministers of EEC on Peace in
the Middle East, May 25, 1983—Answer,
September 14, 1983*

* 26 O.J. Eur. Comm. (No. C 288) 15 (1983).

WRITTEN QUESTION No 832/83
by Mr Gérard Israël (DEP—F)
to the Foreign Ministers of the 10 Member States meeting in political
cooperation
(25 May 1983)

Subject: Peace in the Middle East

In his speech of 5 July 1983 before the European Parliament the President of the Council recalled that one aspect of the position adopted by the Ten was the need to associate the PLO with the peace negotiations.

Will the Foreign Ministers of the Ten make it clear which faction of the PLO was meant?

Answer by the Ministers for Foreign Affairs of the 10 Member States of
the European Community meeting in political cooperation
(14 September 1983)

It is not for the Ten to stipulate which PLO representatives should attend any peace negotiations held.

318. European Parliament Resolution on an Aid
Programme for Palestinian Refugees, June 9, 1983*

---

* 26 O.J. Eur. Comm. (No. C 184) 96 (1983).

The European Parliament,

A. Whereas the 60 000 or more Palestinian refugees living in southern Lebanon are facing a hopeless personal situation and conditions of both moral and material discomfort;

B. Having regard also to the extremely difficult living conditions experienced by the Palestinian refugees in the camps of Sabra and Shatila in Beirut and in all the other refugee camps in Lebanon;

C. Whereas any measures aimed at the social integration of these people, particularly the children and young people, represent a genuine and necessary contribution to peace and security in the Near East;

1. Calls on the Commission to launch an immediate aid programme to meet these needs, administered by the Lebanese Government and with special emphasis on the following aspects:

   (a) social and medical assistance for the families living in refugee camps;

   (b) educational assistance for children and young people (by means of finance for the building of teaching premises and the provision of suitable teaching materials);

   (c) suitable and immediately usable aid for vocational training for young people;

2. Calls on the Commission to inform the European Parliament within two months of the adoption of this resolution of the humanitarian aid measures it has implemented to assist the Palestinian refugees in southern Lebanon and in all the other refugee camps in Lebanon;

3. Instructs its President to forward this resolution to the Council, the Commission and the Ministers for Foreign Affairs meeting in political co-operation.

319. The Palestinian People's Legal Right to Exercise Self-Determination, June 20, 1983*

* Report to the U.N. International Conference on the Question of Palestine, Geneva, U.N. Doc. A/Conf. 114/7.

The Palestinian People's Legal Right to Exercise Self-determination*

CONTENTS

I. THE SOURCES OF INTERNATIONAL LAW

The basic rights of the Palestinian people and their right to constitute a State of their own are based on the customary law and the treaty law which together form the structure of the world legal order.

* Paper prepared for the International Conference on the Question of Palestine by Dr. W Thomas Mallison and Sally V. Mallison, George Washington University, at the request of the Preparatory Committee. The views expressed are those of the authors.

Customs are the more historic method of international law making as compared with treaties. In 1625 when Grotius wrote his classic treatise, *De Jure Belli ac Pacis*[1] custom stood as the almost unique method of prescribing international law. While conventions or treaties are created by the explicit agreement of States, customary law is based upon implicit agreement. Article 38 of the Statute of the International Court of Justice merely purports to specify the sources of law which shall be applied by the Court. It is, nevertheless, widely accepted as describing the sources which are available generally in international law. The first paragraph of the article lists treaties, customs and general principles as the main sources.[2] Custom is specified to be "international custom as evidence of a general practice accepted as law". This carefully worded provision does not require evidence of a universal practice. The historic customary law making process demonstrates that the rules which are regarded as legally established are based upon the assent of a substantial majority of States.[3] It has not been considered necessary that universal assent be obtained. General principles are specified as being "the general principles of law recognized by civilized nations." The requirements here are not a combination of State practice and assent as in customary law, but rather a combination of State articulation or formulation along with assent.[4]

Although much international law is based upon pre-existing state practice, the community of States has the legal capacity and authority to formulate legal rules or principles through a multilateral conference or otherwise, even in the absence of pre-existing practice. The United Nations Charter is a multilateral treaty by which States created the United Nations as a separate factual participant and legal subject of international law.[5] The principles set forth in the Charter are binding on all those States which have accepted it as a treaty and become member States.[6] The provisions of the

---

[1] *De Jure Belli ac Pacis* in J. B. Scott (ed.), *Classics of International Law* (Kelsey transl., Carnegie Endowment for International Peace, 1925).

[2] International Court of Justice Statute, Art. 38 (1) a, b and c. Subsection "d" lists judicial decisions and legal writings as subsidiary sources.

[3] In the famous case of *The Paquete Habana*, 175 U.S. 677 (1900), the United States Supreme Court based its holding concerning the immunity of coastal fishing boats from capture on such assent. The same point is made by legal writers. See, e.g., Professor Brierly, who states: "It would hardly ever be practicable, and all but the strictest of positivists admit that it is not necessary to show that every state has recognized a certain practice . . . [as creating customary law]." J. L. Brierly, *The Law of Nations* 61 (6th ed., Waldock, 1963).

[4] Professor Brierly has accurately characterized general principles as "a dynamic element in international law." (*Ibid.*, at 63). It has also been pointed out that international arbitral tribunals employed general principles of law before the establishment of the International Court of Justice. (1 Oppenheim, *International Law: Peace* 30 (8th ed., Lauterpacht, 1955)).

[5] Advisory Opinion on *Reparation for Injuries Suffered in the Service of the United Nations*, [1949] I.C.J. Rep., 174.

[6] See, *inter alia*, United Nations Charter, Arts. 27 and 103.

Charter are designed to operate in the context of the contemporary international law decision-making process. Following the ratification and implementation of the Charter, States retain their pre-existing law making competence. The Security Council (in subject-matter restricted to international peace and security) and the General Assembly (concerning a wide range of subjects) are institutions which facilitate the making of international law. The widespread use and reliance upon resolutions of the General Assembly and Security Council which are intended to have law making effect provide convincing indication that the matters relied upon constitute, at the least, important evidence of the existence of particular rules or principles of international law.[7] Authoritative international law writers have found the State practice requirement for customary law making in the collective acts of States as well as in their individual acts.[8] The General Assembly is a collective meeting of the States of the world community which comprise its membership. Its authority is derived directly from the member States which have the same legal authority to develop and make international law in the General Assembly as they do outside of it.[9] The advantageous feature of such activity in the Assembly is that it can be done more rapidly and efficiently than the same activity in a less institutionalized environment. The States of the world community since the early years of the United Nations have in fact used the General Assembly as an instrument to express consensus on major international legal issues by majorities substantially in excess of the two-thirds vote required by the Charter for important questions.[10] It is a matter of legal theory as to the precise allocation of authority between the powers derived from the Charter and those derived directly from the member States. The crucial point is that drawing on both sources of authority, the great majority of the member States have adopted the practice of expressing consensus on legal issues through the General Assembly.

II. SELF-DETERMINATION AND THE RIGHT TO CONSTITUTE A STATE

A. The historical development

The practice of self-determination preceded the development of the principle or right in international law. The American Revolution and the subsequent Latin American revolutions against European colonialism provide pre-eminent historic examples. President Woodrow Wilson first articulated self-determination as a norm to be applied in the post-First World War settlement when he included it among his Fourteen Points. Point V concerning "colonial claims" provided that "the interests of the populations concerned

---

[7] E.g., General Assembly resolution 2625 (1970), which is analysed in section II C above.

[8] R. Higgins, *The Development of International Law Through the Political Organs of the United Nations* 2 (1963). See also the distinguished dissenting opinion of Judge Tanaka in *Ethiopia v. South Africa; Liberia v. South Africa*, [1966] I.C.J. Rep. 248, at 291-93.

[9] Higgins, *op. cit.*

[10] See e.g. General Assembly resolution 1514 (1960) considered in section II C above. The two-thirds requirement appears in United Nations Charter, Art. 18 (2).

must have equal weight with the equitable claims of the Government whose title is to be determined".[11] Point XII provided that "the other (non-Turkish) nationalities which are now under Turkish rule should be assured an undoubted security of life and an absolutely unmolested opportunity of autonomous development . . ."[12] Professor Kissinger has accurately described the situation as it existed at the peace settlement.

> In 1919, the Austro-Hungarian Empire disintegrated not so much from the impact of the war as from the nature of the peace, because its continued existence was incompatible with national self-determination, the legitimizing principle of the new international order.[13]

The principle of self-determination was reflected in the provisions of the League of Nations Covenant.[14] At the present time the only examples of peoples who were placed under the mandates system and who have not been permitted to exercise self-determination are the Palestinians and the Namibians (South-West Africans).

B. The United Nations Charter provisions
1. Grants of constitutive authority

One of the major purposes of the United Nations which is specified in Article 1 of the Charter is the development of friendly relations based upon respect for "the principle of equal rights and self-determination of peoples . . ." It is important to be aware that this specification of equal rights and self-determination is a right "of peoples". This is a major departure from the once widely recognized legal theory that international law accorded rights only to States and Governments and not to peoples.[15]

It is sometimes contended by those who oppose self-determination for others that the Charter only states that self-determination is a principle and not a right. This view is not persuasive because of the Charter's repeated emphasis upon self-determination and the practice of the world community in implementing it. In addition, the carefully drafted and equally authentic French text states, "*du principe de l'égalité de droits des peuples et de leur droit à disposer d'eux-memes . . .*".[16] By using the word "*droit*" in connection with self-determination, the French text removes any possible ambiguity. Article 55 of the Charter re-emphasizes the importance of self-determination. Article 73 (b) concerning Non-Self-Governing Territories provides that members assuming responsibility for such territories are required to "develop self-

[11] [1918] *Foreign Rels U.S.*, vol. 1, Supplement 1, pp. 15-16 (1933).

[12] *Ibid.*

[13] H. A. Kissinger, *A World Restored: Metternich, Castlereagh and the Problems of Peace, 1812-1822* p. 145 (Sentry ed., undated).

[14] League of Nations Covenant, Art. 22 (1).

[15] The contrast between the contemporary and older theories of international law is emphasized in McDougal, "Perspectives for an international law of human dignity", *Proc. Am. Soc. Int'l L.* 107 (1959).

[16] United Nations Charter, Art. 1 (2).

government, to take due account of the political aspirations of the people, and to assist them in the progressive development of their free political institutions . . ."

2. Limitations on constitutive authority

The United Nations is also committed to human rights on a non-discriminatory basis as indicated clearly in Article 55[17] of the Charter, which provides in relevant part:

> With a view to the creation of conditions of stability and well-being which are necessary for peaceful and friendly relations among nations based on respect for the principle of equal rights and self-determination of peoples, the United Nations shall promote:
>
> . . .
>
> c. universal respect for, and observance of human rights and fundamental freedoms for all without distinction as to race, sex, language or religion.

Article 56, in which all members pledge themselves to implement the purposes set forth in Article 55, is regarded as making the provisions of Article 55 into legal rights. Consistent with these Charter provisions, the General Assembly is required to impose basic human rights standards upon States which it authorizes.

The right of self-determination cannot be interpreted as including a comprehensive right to secede from a State by any group which regards itself as having national characteristics.[18] If self-determination were so misconstrued[19] it would not have received the existing support of the community of States along with a prominent place in the Charter. At least by implication, the Charter also contains a limitation upon self-determination in its prohibition of the threat or use of force against the "territorial integrity" of States. The negotiating history demonstrates that in the committee considering self-determination it was regarded as implying "the right of self-government of peoples and not the right of secession."[20]

---

[17] McDougal and Reisman (eds.), *International Law in Contemporary Perspective* 160 (1981) lists Article 55 of the Charter as a grant of constitutive authority rather than as a limitation upon it.

[18] See J. A. Perkins, *The Prudent Peace: Law as Foreign Policy* 75 (1981).

[19] Zionist legal writers oppose self-determination as law. See e.g., Blum, "Reflections on the changing concept of self-determination", 10 *Israel L. Rev.* 509 (1975), which states at p. 511: "Consequently, any attempt to convert self-determination into a legally recognized right amounts to an attempt to legitimize revolution and to absorb it into the existing legal system." See also M. Pomerance, *Self-Determination in Law and Practice: The New Doctrine in the United Nations* (1982).

[20] Six *U.N. Conf. Int'l Org. Docs.* 296, Summary report of the sixth meeting of Committee I/1, Doc. 343 I/1/16 (15 May 1945).

C. World community development of the Law of the Charter

General Assembly resolution 1514 (XV) of 14 December 1960, entitled "Declaration on the Granting of Independence to Colonial Countries and Peoples,"[21] is a landmark in the development of the right of self-determination. The first two operative paragraphs of this resolution provide:

1. The subjection of peoples to alien subjugation, domination and exploitation constitutes a denial of fundamental human rights, is contrary to the Charter of the United Nations and is an impediment to the promotion of world peace and co-operation.

2. All peoples have the right to self-determination; by virtue of that right they freely determine their political status and freely pursue their economic, social and cultural development.

The vote on this resolution was 90 votes in favour to none opposed, with 9 abstentions. Since there were no opposing votes, the resolution must be interpreted as reflecting the stated legal views of the then full membership of the United Nations. In view of the increasing implementation of self-determination since 1960, there can be no doubt but that the present membership of the United Nations provides full support for the views expressed in the 1960 resolution. Subsequent applications of the self-determination principle of resolution 1514 to Algeria, Angola and to Zimbabwe (Rhodesia) indicate the view of the General Assembly that a right of self-determination is established in law,[22] and the entire course of action taken by the United Nations since 1960 is consistent with this basic principle.

General Assembly resolution 2625 (XXV) of 24 October 1970 entitled "Declaration on Principles of International Law Concerning Friendly Relations and Co-operation Among States in Accordance with the Charter of the United Nation,"[23] provides further development of the right of self-determination. There are four principal bases for the authoritativeness of this resolution.[24] First, it is based on the Charter, and therefore its principles were already binding on the member nations through their adherence to the Charter. Second, it was developed and adopted by consensus and the negotiating history indicates that a number of Governments regard it as binding international law on the theory that the unanimity of acceptance gives it authority as law either under Article 38 (1) (c) of the Statute of the International Court of Justice concerning "general principles of law recognized by civilized nations", or as a "subsequent agreement between the parties regarding the interpretation of the treaty or the application of its provisions" in accordance with Article 31 (3) (a) of the Vienna Convention on

---

[21] *Official Records of the General Assembly, Fifteenth Session, Supplement No. 16*, pp. 66-67.

[22] General Assembly resolutions 1573 (XV) re Algeria, 1603 (XV) re Angola, and 1747 (XVI) re Zimbabwe (Rhodesia).

[23] *Official Records of the General Assembly, Twenty-fifth Session, Supplement No. 28*, pp. 121-124.

[24] The first of three of these bases are set forth in Perkins, *op. cit.*, p. 66.

the Law of Treaties.[25] The third basis for the authority of resolution 2625 is that it was developed to provide a statement of law, not of policy or aspirations. The title itself and the final paragraph, which provides that "[t]he principles of the Charter which are embodied in this Declaration constitute basic principles of international law", are further indication of the intent of the Member States that this resolution be a binding statement of international law.

The Declaration considers a number of principles. Under the heading of the "principle of equal rights and self-determination of peoples" the first paragraph states:

> By virtue of the principle of equal rights and self-determination of peoples enshrined in the Charter of the United Nations, all peoples have the right freely to determine, without external interference, their political status and to pursue their economic, social and cultural development, and every State has the duty to respect this right in accordance with the provisions of the Charter.

The conjoining of "equal rights" and "self-determination" both in the Charter and in the Declaration means that the peoples who have not yet achieved self-determination have the same equal right to it as did those who exercised it previously.

There is a further significant basis for the high degree of legal authority of both the 1960 Declaration on Decolonization and the 1970 Declaration on International Law and Friendly Relations. It is that their substantive provisions concerning self-determination and independence have been implemented in the practice of States. This practice is manifested by the exercise of self-determination since the establishment of the United Nations, which has resulted in more than tripling its membership. The practice of States is the same requisite element in making customary law which has existed for centuries prior to the establishment of the United Nations.[26] It is probable, therefore, that if the legal formulations of self-determination had not been developed beyond those in the Charter, the practice of States would have made self-determination a doctrine of customary law without either the 1960 or 1970 resolutions.[27] In the present situation, self-determination is law because of the Charter, the development of the Charter in the subsequent resolutions, and the assent and practice of States which have made it customary law.

The opponents of self-determination usually contrast the law of the Charter, including the relevant resolutions of the General Assembly, with the

[25] United Nations document A/CONF.39/27, 8 Int'l Legal Mats. 679 (1969).

[26] See note 3 above.

[27] G. Arangio-Riuz [Ruiz], *The United Nations Declaration on Friendly Relations and the System of the Sources of International Law* (1979) considers several theoretical bases for General Assembly resolution 2625 (XXV) but gives inadequate attention to the practice of States in implementing self-determination and independence.

traditional law which existed prior to 1945.[28] General Assembly resolutions concerning the right of self-determination which have been adopted by consensus or by large majorities have been subjected to particular criticism as being politically motivated.[29] One of the main weaknesses of their arguments is that the law of self-determination has been developed and implemented by precisely the same methods of assent and practice which characterized law making in the pre-1945 traditional law. The making of customary international law has always been based upon the political consensus of a substantial majority of the community of States. Professor Higgins has stated: "Customary international law is therefore perhaps the most 'political' form of international law, reflecting the consensus of the great majority of States."[30] Such political decision was the basis for the abolition of the slave trade in the nineteenth century.[31]

III. APPLICATION OF THE LAW TO THE PALESTINIAN PEOPLE

A. Specification of self-determination through international legal process

Critics of the right of self-determination as enunciated in the Charter and in the 1960 and 1970 resolutions point out the imprecision in these formulations. In particular, they emphasize that there is no precise definition of the "self" which qualifies as a national group of people entitled to self-determination. One such critic, Professor Julius Stone, has written:

If, indeed, the references to "self-determination" in the Charter and in General Assembly declarations have established some legal (as distinct from political) principle, the legal criteria for identifying a "people" having this entitlement—the "self" entitled to "determine" itself—remain at best speculative.[32]

It seems probable that Professor Stone's difficulty arises from his confusing of the basic legal doctrines of the Charter and the 1960 and 1970 resolutions with the subsequent legal instruments which specify the identity of the people qualifying for self-determination. It is as much of a mistake to look for specifications in these general constitutional formulations as it is to look for specifics in the constitution of a State. The general principles of the con-

---

[28] See e.g. J. Stone, *Israel and Palestine: Assault on the Law of Nations* (1981).

[29] *Ibid.* at 27-44, 69-75, and *passim*. A different method of constituting a State was set forth by Prof. Blum in response to a question from Senator Abourezk concerning the consistency of the establishment of the State of Israel with the United Nations Charter: "No State is established under the Charter or in violation of the Charter, simply because, as far as international law is concerned, states are born out of wedlock so to speak. States are not born in conformity with the existing legal framework." *The Colonization of the West Bank Territories by Israel*, Hearings before the Subcommittee on Immigration and Naturalization of the U.S. Senate Judiciary Committee, 95th Cong., 1st. Sess., 24 at 38 (1977).

[30] Higgins, *op. cit.*, p. 1.

[31] Oppenheim, *op. cit.*, pp. 732-735.

[32] "Hopes and loopholes in the 1979 definition of aggression," 71 *American Journal of International Law*, 224, 235 (1977).

stitutional doctrines are made specific by the subsequent legislative and judicial application of them.

There are at least two major issues which must be resolved in an application of the right of self-determination. In addition to the determination of the "people" which qualifies as a "self", a decision must be made concerning the territory in which self-determination is to be exercised. These issues are considered in the balance of the present section.

B. *The recognition of the Palestinians as a people*

Along with other Arab peoples, the Palestinians were under the rule of the Ottoman Empire until the First World War which led to the League of Nations Mandate for Palestine of 24 July 1922.[33] During the period of the Mandate, the British Government recognized the existence of the Palestinians as a people distinct from the European Zionist immigrants by negotiating with their leadership and by adopting the White Paper of 1939[34] restricting Zionist immigration in response to Palestinian demands. The United Nations accorded the Palestinians *de jure* recognition of their status as a people with national rights in the provisions of the Palestine Partition Resolution of 29 November 1947[35] authorizing them to establish "the Arab State". From the time of that resolution in 1947 until 1969, the United Nations dealt with the Palestinians in their *de facto* role as individuals who were refugees and war victims. The United Nations actions were designed to implement their individual right of return and achieve their elementary human rights under the humanitarian law of armed conflict. Again in 1969, the General Assembly recognized Palestinians as a people having rights as an entity under the United Nations Charter.

The first preambular paragraph of General Assembly resolution 2535 B (XXIV) of 10 December 1969[36] recognizes "that the problem of the Palestine Arab refugees has arisen from the denial of their inalienable rights under the Charter of the United Nations and the Universal Declaration of Human Rights . . ." The first operative paragraph provides further recognition by the United Nations of the Palestinians as a people with a national identity by reaffirming "the inalienable rights of the people of Palestine". This recognition of status as a national entity has been reaffirmed by all subsequent resolutions of the General Assembly which deal with the subject. General Assembly resolution 2672 C (XXV) of 8 December 1970[37] follows the pattern of resolution 2535 B in a preambular paragraph which reaf-

---

[33] The text of the Mandate of 24 July 1922 is in *Official Records of the United Nations, Second Session, Supplement No. 11*, (A/364, Add.1) pp. 18-22.

[34] British Statement of Policy, CMD. 6019, in Jewish Agency for Palestine, *Book of Documents Submitted to the General Assembly of the United Nations Relating to the Establishment of the National Home for the Jewish People* 100 (Tulin, ed., 1947).

[35] General Assembly resolution 181 (II) concerning the future Government of Palestine, dated 29 November 1947.

[36] *Official Records of the General Assembly, Twenty-fourth Session, Supplement 30*, pp. 25-26.

[37] *Ibid., Twenty-fifth Session, Supplement 28*, p. 36.

firms the inalienable rights of "the people of Palestine". General Assembly resolution 3236 (XXIX) of 22 November 1974,[38] which contains the basic provisions concerning the rights of self-determination and independence, follows the consistent pattern by referring to "the Palestinian people".

Because the Palestinian people do not have a Government to represent them, it is necessary that they have a representative body with juridical status to act on their behalf. General Assembly resolution 3210 (XXIX) of 14 October 1974[39] concerns the status of the people by providing that "the Palestinian people is the principal party to the question of Palestine". It also concerns the status of their representation by inviting the Palestine Liberation Organization (PLO) as "the representative of the Palestinian people" to participate in plenary meetings of the General Assembly concerning the question of Palestine. In resolution 3237 (XXIX) of 22 November 1974[40] the General Assembly invited the PLO to participate in the sessions and work of the General Assembly, without limitation of subject-matter, in the capacity of observer. The same resolution further recognized the juridical status of the PLO by stating that it is entitled to participate as an observer in "the work of all international conferences convened under the auspices of other organs of the United Nations".

The PLO has been recognized as a public body and national liberation movement with the objective of self-determination for the Palestinian people by more than 100 States.[41] It maintains offices which are similar or equivalent to diplomatic missions in more than 60 States.[42] The PLO has not claimed status as a government in exile. Consequently, the Palestinians have a relationship to the PLO similar to the French people's relationship to the Free French Authority when France was under Nazi military occupation. The attempted destruction of the infrastructure of the PLO in Lebanon by the Israeli armed attack in the summer of 1982 has not altered its legal status as a public body representing the Palestinian people, and the attempted further dispersal of the Palestinians has not changed their status as a national entity.

It provides useful clarification to contrast the Palestinian people with "the Jewish people" transnational entity claimed by the State of Israel.[43] The Zi-

[38] *Ibid., Twenty-ninth Session, Supplement 31*, p. 4.

[39] *Ibid.*, p. 3.

[40] *Ibid., Twenty-ninth Session, Supplement 31*, p. 4.

[41] Kassim, "The Palestine Liberation Organization's claim to status: a juridical analysis under international law", 9 *Denver Journal of International Law and Policy*, 1 at 19 (1980).

[42] *Ibid.*

[43] The "Jewish people" nationality claims are analysed in W. T. Mallison, "The Zionist-Israel juridical claims to constitute 'the Jewish people's nationality entity and to confer membership in it: appraisal in public international law' ", *George Washington Law Review*, 983 (1964) and reprinted as a monograph in 1964. The contrasting view that the claims are lawful is by the authoritative Zionist lawyer, Professor N. Feinberg: "The recognition of the Jewish people in international law", in *The Jewish Yearbook of International Law*, 1 (1948).

onist "Jewish people" concept was developed by the Zionist Organization/ Jewish Agency prior to the establishment of the State of Israel. Before the rise of Zionist nationalism, "the Jewish people" referred simply to voluntary adherents of the religion of Judaism, the oldest of the monotheistic religions of universal moral values. The Zionists have attempted to impress their own secular meaning upon the term internationally and have given it a domestic, juridical definition through various Israeli statutes. "The Jewish people" concept within the State of Israel accords its members certain privileges and rights on a discriminatory basis which are denied to other Israelis. The same term applied to persons outside the State of Israel imposes upon them a juridical link with the State of Israel whether they desire it or not. For example, in the Eichmann case the Israeli court held that "the connection between the Jewish people and the State of Israel constitutes an integral part of the law of nations".[44] In spite of this Israeli municipal pronouncement, recognition of "the Jewish people" concept by the General Assembly or the Security Council would constitute a violation of the Charter because of its discriminatory characteristics. The United States Government has explicitly rejected the concept as a valid concept of international law in a letter from Assistant Secretary of State Phillips Talbot addressed to Rabbi Elmer Berger.[45] Consistent with the Charter requirements, "the Palestinian people" must comprise all Palestinians on a non-discriminatory basis. If it did not do so, it could not be recognized by the United Nations without violation of the Charter. In summary, "the Palestinian people" includes individuals of diverse religious identifications today as it did before the rise of Zionist nationalism.

C. The development of Palestinian national rights

Palestinian national rights have been developed by the community of States utilizing multilateral action through the League of Nations and the United Nations over a considerable period of time.

1. The League of Nations Covenant

Article 22 of the League of Nations Covenant created the mandates system for colonies and territories which were formerly under the sovereignty of Germany and Turkey. Article 22 (1) stated that:

> there should be applied the principle that the well-being and development of such peoples form a sacred trust of civilization and that securities for the performance of this trust should be embodied in this Covenant.

---

[44] *Attorney General of the Government of Israel v. Adolf Eichmann*, 36 Int'l L. Rep. 5 at 53 (1961).

[45] After referring to United States non-discrimination among its citizens based upon religious identification, it stated: "Accordingly, it should be clear that the Department of State does not regard the 'Jewish people' concept as a concept of international law." 8 M. Whiteman, *Digest of International Law* 34 at 35 (1967).

Article 22 (4) provided in full:

> Certain communities formerly belonging to the Turkish Empire have reached a stage of development where their existence as independent nations can be provisionally recognized subject to the rendering of administrative advice and assistance by a Mandatory until such time as they are able to stand alone. The wishes of these communities must be a principal consideration in the selection of the Mandatory.

The Palestine community was in no way excepted from this provisional recognition of "their existence as independent nations". Unfortunately, the wishes of the Palestinian community were not given the consideration specified in the Covenant with the result that Great Britain, which had issued the Balfour Declaration in 1917,[46] was selected as the mandatory power. The Balfour Declaration provided that the British Government "viewed with favour" the Jewish national home enterprise and would use "best endeavours to achieve it". In response to the views of British Jews, and particularly those of Edwin Montagu, who was a member of the British Cabinet, the Government did not accept the Zionist claim of legal right to Palestine. The prefatory clause of the Declaration was subordinated by unequivocal wording to the two safeguards protecting the rights of indigenous Palestinians and of Jews outside of Palestine.

2. The League of Nations Mandate for Palestine

The Palestine Mandate[47] was authorized by Article 22 of the League of Nations Covenant and was subject to its limitations. For example, the provisional granting of independence to Palestine in the Covenant could not be withdrawn by the Mandate. In the same way, the Mandate was juridically limited by the "sacred trust of civilization" for the benefit of the inhabitants of the mandated territory. In short, the purpose of the Mandate, like that of the Covenant, was to lead Palestine to independence as an undivided whole.

Article 2 of the Mandate provided for the establishment of the "Jewish national home" in Palestine referred to in the Balfour Declaration, and at the same time provided for "the development of self-governing institutions" as well as the safeguarding of "the civil and religious rights of all the inhabitants of Palestine" irrespective of race and religion. Article 4 recognized the World Zionist Organization/Jewish Agency "as a public body" which was to be "subject always to the control of the [mandatory] administration". If the Organization/Agency had remained under the control of the mandatory administration and that administration had adhered to the provisions of the Mandate, it seems probable that Palestine would have achieved independence as a unit. A "Jewish national home" as opposed to a Zionist national

---

[46] W. T. Mallison, "The Balfour Declaration: an appraisal in international law", in I. Abu-Lughod (ed.), *The Transformation of Palestine*, 61 (1971).

[47] See note 33 above.

State could well have been consistent with such undivided Palestinian independence.

The Mandate, consistent with the Covenant, contained several provisions designed to protect the rights of the indigenous Palestinians on their way to independence. The second preambular paragraph repeated the substance of the Balfour Declaration including its first safeguard clause which provided that "it being clearly understood that nothing shall be done which might prejudice the civil and religious rights of existing non-Jewish communities in Palestine". The second safeguard clause protecting the rights of Jews "in any other country" than Palestine was also included. Article 15 provided for freedom of religion and added that "no discrimination of any kind shall be made between the inhabitants of Palestine on the ground of race, religion or language." Combined with article 7, which directed the enactment of a nationality law, it required a single nationality law status for all Palestinians. The Palestine Mandate was approved by the Council of the League of Nations on 24 July 1922. The United States was not a Member of the League of Nations, but it agreed to the terms of the Mandate for Palestine in the Anglo-American Convention on Palestine of 1924.[48]

3. The Palestine partition resolution

(a) *The background*

The Palestine partition resolution 181[49] must be analysed with an awareness of the circumstances which brought about United Nations action. The British Government policy of promoting Zionist immigration, at least until the White Paper of 1939, had brought about the dangerous conflict situation in Palestine. This conflict arose from Palestinian resistance to the increasing determination of the European colonists under Zionist leadership to secure their overriding political objective of creating the "national home", which was later changed to a national State, for "the Jewish people".[50] This was to be done without regard for the rights of the native Palestinians, including the Palestinian Jews who opposed Zionism from the beginning.[51]

---

[48] 44 U.S. Stat. 2184 (1924).

[49] See note 35 above.

[50] The earlier Zionist stated position is reflected in the official history by a member of the Executive of the World Zionist Organization: "It has been said, and is still being obstinately repeated by anti-Zionists again and again that Zionism aims at the creation of an independent 'Jewish State.' But this is wholly fallacious. The 'Jewish State' was never a part of the Zionist programme." 1 N. Sokolow, *History of Zionism*, author's introduction at pp. xxiv-xxv (1919).

The later Zionist position is reflected in this official interpretation: "The phrase [in the Balfour Declaration] 'the establishment in Palestine of a National Home for the Jewish people' was intended and understood by all concerned to mean at the time of the Balfour Declaration that Palestine would ultimately become a 'Jewish Commonwealth' or a 'Jewish State,' if only Jews came and settled there in sufficient numbers." See note 34 above.

[51] See e.g., the strong criticism of the Zionists and their programme written by Joseph Hayyim Sonnenfeld, one of the pre-eminent leaders of the Palestinian Jewish community

After it was too late to control the effects of Zionist policies, notwithstanding the provisions of the League of Nations Mandate for Palestine designed to protect Palestinian rights, the British Government concluded that the Mandate was unworkable because of the irreconcilability of the native Palestinians' aspiration for self-determination with the political objectives of the Zionists. In 1946 and 1947 the violence between the European immigrants and the native Palestinians, as well as Zionist attacks on the Mandatory Government, were increasing sharply. Great Britain indicated that it planned to terminate its role as the Mandatory Power and it requested a special meeting of the General Assembly to deal with the problem.

General Assembly resolution 181 was adopted on 29 November 1947 with the full authority of a two-thirds vote as required by the Charter for important questions. It provided for the establishment of two independent States in Palestine, referred to as "the Jewish State" and "the Arab State", which were to be linked in an economic union. A special international régime was provided for the City of Jerusalem which was not to be a part of either State. The territorial division of Palestine was extremely favourable to the Zionist cause.

The native Palestinians had no significant military force following their decisive defeat by the British Army during the Palestinian rebellion of 1936-1939. In contrast, the Zionist Organization/Jewish Agency had effective regular military forces in the Hagana and the Palmach.[52] The principal Zionist terrorist organizations, the Irgun and the Stern Gang, worked effectively with the Zionist regular forces in achieving political and territorial objectives by military means, although there were some disagreements on tactics.[53] According to reliable Zionist historical sources, attacks on Palestinian civilians both inside and outside the boundaries allocated for "the Jewish State" took place before the alleged "invasion" by the Arab regular armies beginning 15 May 1948.[54] As a result of the intensive armed conflict that followed, the *de facto* boundaries of "the Jewish State" were even more favourable to the Zionist cause than were the partition boundaries prescribed by the General Assembly.

The human rights provisions of the partition resolution qualify the au-

---

in 1898, in E. Marmorstein, *Heaven at Bay: The Jewish Kulturkampf in the Holy Land* 79-80 (1969).

[52] See, in Anglo-American Committee of Inquiry, *Report to the United States Government and His Majesty's Government in the United Kingdom*, the descriptions of the Hagana and the Palmach in chap. 9, entitled "Public security", at pp. 45-46 (1946).

[53] See the description of the Irgun and the Stern Gang; *ibid.*, p. 47. Military co-operation between the Irgun and the Zionist regular forces is described in M. Begin, *The Revolt* (1948, new ed. 1972) chap. 29, entitled "The conquest of Jaffa", and *passim*.

[54] E.g., the implementation of "Plan D" involving attacks upon Palestinians throughout the Palestine Mandate prior to the "invasion" by the Arab armies is described in Netanel Lorch [formerly chief of the Historical Division of the Israeli General Staff], *One Long War: Arab Versus Jews Since 1920*, pp. 40-48 under heading "Jewish forces take the initiative" (1976).

thority to establish each of the two States by providing a reciprocal system of rights and obligations in which the exercise of the right to create a state is conditioned upon the obligation to implement human rights. Among the most important human rights provisions of the Partition Plan is section 10 (d) of part I B, which states:

> The Constituent Assembly of each State shall draft a democratic constitution for its State and choose a provisional government to succeed the Provisional Council of Government appointed by the Commission. The constitutions of the States shall embody chapters 1 and 2 of the Declaration provided for in section C below and include *inter alia* provisions for: . . .
>
> (d) Guaranteeing to all persons equal and non-discriminatory rights in civil, political, economic and religious matters and the enjoyment of human rights and fundamental freedoms, including freedom of religion, language, speech and publication, education, assembly and association.

These provisions for human rights are explicit and there cannot be any accurate interpretation of the partition resolution which circumvents them. They are not surprising in view of the human rights provisions of the United Nations Charter. In addition to the basic Charter provisions of Articles 55 and 56, Article 1 (3) specifies as one of the major purposes of the United Nations, "promoting and encouraging respect for human rights and for fundamental freedoms for all without distinction as to race, sex, language or religion".

(b) *The juridical status*

(i) *Claims of invalidity*

There is a single claim which underlies several of the charges that the partition resolution violates particular articles of the Palestine Mandate. It is that the Mandate was in effect when the General Assembly acted in November 1947 and that there was no authority to deprive the native Palestinians of rights and protections which were secured to them at the time by the Mandate.[55]

Article 5 of the Mandate is one of several articles that placed obligations upon the Mandatory Power which made it a trustee for the Palestinians. It is contended that its provision against ceding Palestinian territory to "the control of the Government of any foreign Power" was violated by the General Assembly when it ceded the territory allocated to "the Jewish State" to the Zionist Organization/Jewish Agency. The view is that the Jewish Agency may have been a domestic power while it complied with the limitations placed upon it by article 4 of the Mandate which specified that it be "subject

---

[55] Claims concerning the invalidity of the partition resolution are set forth in H. Cattan, *Palestine and International Law: The Legal Aspects of the Arab-Israeli Conflict*, chap. 4 and *passim* (2nd ed., 1976).

always to the control of the Mandatory Administration". However, it is claimed that, at least from the time of the Anglo-American Committee of Inquiry of 1946 when it was characterized as a "shadow Government" which "has ceased to co-operate with the [Mandatory] Administration . . . in the suppression of terrorism",[56] the Jewish Agency was a foreign power controlled by European Zionists and the allocation of control of territory to it as the *de facto* government of "the Jewish State" in the partition resolution was a clear violation of article 5.

Article 6 of the Mandate required the Mandatory Administration to "facilitate Jewish immigration" providing that "the rights and position of other sections of the population are not prejudiced". There are three related claims involved. The first is that the immigration which took place was not a Jewish immigration, but that it was a politically motivated Zionist immigration. The second claim is that it was not an "immigration" at all as the term is commonly understood in both its factual and its legal aspects. It was rather an invasion by Zionist masses which subverted the Palestinian community under the guise of immigration. The third claim is that, whether it could be termed an immigration or an invasion, it resulted in flagrant violation of "the rights and position of other sections of the population" including depriving them of their homes and their livelihoods. The basic charge of illegality here is that the General Assembly compounded the illegalities of the Mandatory in this respect by acting upon and giving effect to the Zionist "immigration" which was carried out in violation of the Mandate provisions.

Article 1 of the United Nations Charter, dealing with the purposes of the United Nations, sets forth as the second of these the development of friendly relations based upon respect for "equal rights and self-determination of peoples". Article 73 concerning non-self-governing territories provides that members of the United Nations which assume trusteeship responsibilities accept "a sacred trust" and are obligated "to develop self-government". The claim is that, even though these Charter provisions are not explicitly applied to the Palestine Mandate, they are nevertheless *a fortiori* applicable. It would, so the argument goes, be totally beyond the powers of the General Assembly to deal with a League Mandate in disregard of the Charter principle of self-determination which binds the United Nations. The partition resolution, it is claimed, as a partition of the country against the will of the overwhelming majority of the native population, was a flagrant violation of the principle of self-determination and therefore illegal.

(ii) *Claims of validity*

Article 2 (7) of the Charter prohibits the United Nations from intervening "in matters which are essentially within the domestic jurisdiction of any

---

[56] Report of the Anglo-American Committee of Inquiry (see above, note 52) at p. 39. See also [1947] 5 *Foreign Rels. U.S.* (1971) 999-1328, *passim*, and under following headings in index: Terrorism in Palestine, Irgun Zvai Leumi, Stern Gang.

state". Palestine, however, had been regarded as a matter of international concern for some time prior to 1947. This is demonstrated by article 22 (4) of the League Covenant as well as by the Palestine Mandate. In 1947 Palestine, although under a Mandate, was not a state. Consequently, there was no possibility of claiming Palestinian domestic jurisdiction as a bar to action by the General Assembly. In addition, the presence of a large number of recently arrived European immigrants tended to make Palestine a continuing concern to the international community.

There can be no doubt but that the self-determination issue was a central one in the Palestine question. Self-determination is usually conceived as the right of the majority within an established political unit to determine its own future. There was strong evidence that Palestine was an established self-determination unit because of the provisions of the League Covenant and of the Palestine Mandate. The Palestinians and the Zionists in a sense were agreed upon what might be characterized broadly as self-determination for Palestine. Although agreed upon the principle, they had opposite objectives. The Palestinians' objective was self-determination for all the inhabitants of Palestine in a unitary state, whereas the Zionists' objective was self-determination for the European immigrant minority without regard to the rights of the majority population. Both the Palestinians and the Zionists agreed upon the entire area of Palestine as the appropriate unit, but with the central difference that each group wanted it for very different purposes. The existence of the self-determination issue made the Palestine question a particularly appropriate one for action by the General Assembly. From a practical standpoint, there was no alternative forum which could have dealt with the issue so authoritatively.

In 1947 the Zionist terror along with the responding Palestinian violence created a situation in which the most basic human rights were being denied including the right to life itself.[57] This coercion situation made it essential for the United Nations to take immediate steps to protect human rights, and it attempted to do so through the detailed human rights provisions of the partition resolution. The Charter treats the achievement of human rights as a basic principle and this provided additional authority for the General Assembly to act.

Great Britain, as the Mandatory Power, addressed its request for United Nations assumption of responsibility concerning the future government of Palestine to the General Assembly. Chapter XII of the Charter gives the General Assembly comprehensive legal authority over the International Trusteeship system. It also has supervisory authority in law over League of Nations Mandates as the successor to the Assembly of the League of Nations. The International Court of Justice addressed this point with par-

[57] See D. Hirst, *The Gun and the Olive Branch: The Roots of Violence in the Middle East, passim* (1977).

ticular reference to the South-West Africa Mandated Territory in the 1950 Advisory Opinion on the subject:

> The Court has arrived at the conclusion that the General Assembly of the United Nations is legally qualified to exercise the supervisory functions previously exercised by the League of Nations with regard to the administration of the Territory, and that the Union of South Africa is under an obligation to submit to supervision and control of the General Assembly and to render annual reports to it.[58]

(iii) *The continuing validity of the partition resolution*

The adoption of the partition resolution by the two-thirds vote required for important questions gave it a high degree of legal authority. The representative of the Jewish Agency, Mr. Shertok (later the Foreign Minister and the Prime Minister of the Government of Israel), referred to its "binding force" on 27 April 1948:

> With regard to the status of Assembly resolutions in international law, it was admitted that any which touched the national sovereignty of the Members of the United Nations were mere recommendations and not binding. However, the Palestine resolution was essentially different for it concerned the future of a territory subject to an international trust. Only the United Nations as a whole was competent to determine the future of the territory and its decision, therefore, had a binding force.[59]

The State of Israel has placed heavy reliance upon the partition resolution as providing legal authority.[60] Its Declaration of the Establishment of the State of Israel, after referring to General Assembly resolution 181 as "a resolution calling for the establishment of a Jewish State in Eretz-Israel", continues: "This recognition by the United Nations of the right of the Jewish people to establish their State is irrevocable."[61] Another paragraph of the Declaration provides that the State is established "By virtue of our Natural and Historic Right and on the Strength of the Resolution of the United Nations General Assembly".[62] Although the preamble to the Palestine Mandate refers to "the historical connection of the Jewish people with Palestine,"[63] the negotiating history of this wording reveals that the Zionist claim

[58] *International Status of South-West Africa*, Advisory Opinion of 11 July 1950, [1950] I.C.J. Rep. 128 at 137. See also [1955] I.C.J. Rep. 67 at 76 and [1971] I.C.J. Rep. 16 at 43.

[59] United Nations document A/C.1/SR.127, dated 27 April 1948, p. 7.

[60] It is significant that the authoritative Zionist lawyer, Professor N. Feinberg, has argued in favour of the validity of the partition resolution. *The Arab-Israel Conflict in International Law*, (1970), chap. 6.

[61] 1 *Laws of the State of Israel*, p. 3 at para. 9 (auth. transl., 1948).

[62] *Ibid.*, at para. 11.

[63] See note 33 above at para. 3.

of legal right on an historic basis was rejected.[64] Therefore, it appears that the partition resolution is the pre-eminent juridical basis for the State of Israel. Since its extensive military conquests during the intense hostilities of June 1967, the Government of Israel has attempted to deny the continuing validity of the partition resolution.[65]

The Arab States, deeply disturbed by what they initially regarded as the violation of the right of self-determination by the partition resolution, took the position that partition was invalid and voted against it. It is, therefore, significant that they have subsequently relied upon it in presenting legal arguments on behalf of the Palestinians and are now not only supporting the basic principles of the partition resolution, but subsequent General Assembly resolutions which are consistent with those principles as well.

The partition resolution continues to provide legal authority, combined with restrictions upon that authority, for each of two States in Palestine. It is important to recognize that validity in law is not dependent upon subsequent effectuation. Even though there has been little effectuation of many of the specific provisions of the partition resolution, it is not possible to say that this demonstrates its invalidity. The subsequent resolutions of the General Assembly recognizing the Palestinians as a people with national rights are consistent with the basic conception of partition and two States in Palestine.[66] These resolutions are also consistent with the continued existence of the State of Israel as one of the States authorized in the partition resolution. The actions of the General Assembly concerning Palestine have been taken with the affirmative participation of a substantial majority of the States of the world community which comprise the Assembly's membership and thereby constitute a world-wide consensus of support for the continuing validity of the basic principles of the partition resolution.

4. General Assembly resolutions concerning the right of self-determination and statehood of the Palestinian people

The right to establish a State and to exercise sovereignty is based upon the right of self-determination and subject to its limitations. The first direct recognition of this national right of the Palestinian people by the General Assembly was in the Palestine partition resolution provision of authority to establish "the Arab State". The second such recognition was General Assembly resolution 2649 (XXV) of 30 November 1970,[67] which expresses concern

---

[64] Dr. Weizmann states: "The most serious difficulty arose in connection with a paragraph in the Preamble—the phrase which now reads: 'Recognizing the historical connection of the Jews with Palestine'. Zionists wanted to have it read: 'Recognizing the historic rights of the Jews to Palestine'. But Curzon [the British Foreign Secretary] would have none of it . . ." *Trial and Error: The Autobiography of Chaim Weizmann*, p. 348 (1950).

[65] Professor J. Stone, a semi-official spokesman for the Government of Israel, argues the invalidity of the partition resolution. Stone, *op. cit.*, note 28, chap. 4.

[66] E.g., General Assembly resolution 36/120 D of 10 December 1981 specifically reaffirms General Assembly resolution 181 (II).

[67] *Official Records of the General Assembly, Twenty-fifth Session, Supplement 28*, pp. 73-74.

that, because of alien domination many peoples were being denied the right to self-determination. It then condemns those Governments which deny the right to peoples "recognized as being entitled to it, especially the peoples of southern Africa and Palestine".[68] The legal effect of this significant resolution is that the prior resolutions setting forth the basic right of self-determination, resolutions 1514 and 2625 considered above, are now specifically applicable to the Palestinian people.

With the adoption of resolution 2672 C (XXV) on 8 December 1970,[69] the General Assembly moved toward acknowledging the correlation between the right of self-determination and other inalienable rights. The second preambular paragraph recalls resolution 2535 B (XXIV) and the first such paragraph reiterates the language contained in that resolution providing that the Palestine Arab refugee problem had arisen from the denial of their inalienable rights. The two operative paragraphs of resolution 2672 C (XXV) state that the General Assembly:

> 1. *Recongizes* [*sic*] that the people of Palestine are entitled to equal rights and self-determination, in accordance with the Charter of the United Nations;
> 2. *Declares* that full respect for the inalienable rights of the people of Palestine is an indispensable element in the establishment of a just and lasting peace in the Middle East.

In addition to reiterating the specific Palestinian national right of self-determination, this resolution links the achievement of Palestinian inalienable rights to the achievement of peace in the Middle East. Article 1 of the Charter requires the United Nations to bring about peace "in conformity with the principles of justice and international law". It should be clear that neither of these principles is honoured unless Palestinian rights are implemented.

General Assembly resolution 3089 D (XXVIII) of 7 December 1973[70] enunciates the relationship between the rights of self-determination and return by providing in its third operative paragraph that the General Assembly:

> "*Declares* that full respect for and realization of the inalienable rights of the people of Palestine, particularly its right to self-determination, are indispensable for the establishment of a just and lasting peace in the Middle East, and that the enjoyment by the Palestine Arab refugees of their right to return to their homes and property . . . is indispensable . . . for the exercise by the people of Palestine of its right to self-determination."

The necessary legal linkage of return and self-determination is designed to assure Palestinians the practical exercise of national self-determination as

---

[68] *Ibid.*, para. 5.
[69] *Ibid.*, p. 36.
[70] *Ibid.*, *Twenty-eighth Session, Supplement 30*, p. 78.

a "people". It is based on the common sense conception that there can be no self-determination without return to the areas where self-determination may be exercised. An analysis of operative paragraph 3 reveals that while the General Assembly understandably views the achievement of return as a necessary prerequisite to the effective exercise of self-determination, the right of self-determination of Palestinians as a national group was apparently not intended to follow invariably from the return of individual Palestinians. The pertinent wording provides that the "Palestine Arab refugees" are entitled to enjoy "their right to return to their homes and property", while the "people of Palestine" is entitled to exercise "its right to self-determination". The use of "Palestine Arab refugees" when referring to return is apparently meant to stand in contradistinction to the use of "people of Palestine" when reference is made to self-determination.

General Assembly resolution 3236 (XXIX) of 22 November 1974[71] reiterates the customary law of the right of return. It also has pre-eminent importance concerning the right of self-determination. Its fifth preambular paragraph recognizes that "the Palestinian people is entitled to self-determination in accordance with the Charter of the United Nations". The first operative paragraph provides that the General Assembly:

Reaffirms the inalienable rights of the Palestinian people in Palestine, including:
(a) The right to self-determination without external interference;
(b) The right to national independence and sovereignty.

The exact boundaries of the area in Palestine in which these inalienable rights apply must be settled *de jure*. The language of the resolution quoted above includes the "right to national independence and sovereignty" as a particularization of the self-determination right.

In operative paragraph 5, resolution 3236 refers to methods by which rights may be regained. It provides that the General Assembly:

Further recognizes the right of the Palestinian people to regain its rights by all means in accordance with the purposes and principles of the Charter of the United Nations.

Further specification concerning methods is provided in General Assembly resolution 3070 (XXVIII) of 20 November 1973[72] which, after reaffirming the inalienable right to self-determination of all peoples under alien subjugation.[73] provides that the General Assembly:

Also reaffirms the legitimacy of the peoples' struggle for liberation from . . . alien subjugation by all means including armed struggle.[74]

[71] *Ibid., Twenty-ninth Session, Supplement 31*, p. 4.
[72] *Ibid., Twenty-eighth Session, Supplement 30*, p. 78.
[73] *Ibid.*, operative para. 1.
[74] *Ibid.*, operative para. 2.

Since the American Revolution relied upon armed struggle to achieve self-determination about a century and a third before the principle of self-determination was used in the post-First World War peace settlement, it is not surprising that the General Assembly specifies it as a permissible method now. Its permissibility is legally significant as an authoritative General Assembly assertion that armed struggle for self-determination is consistent with the purposes and principles of the United Nations Charter. In a situation such as Palestine where the people has been denied its right of self-determination by armed force, the right to regain it by armed struggle is considered permissible under article 51 of the Charter concerning the inherent right of self-defence.

Subsequent resolutions of the General Assembly, which have also been adopted by large majorities, have reaffirmed the fundamentals of resolution 3236. For example, the last preambular paragraph of resolution 36/120 D of 10 December 1981[75] reaffirmed, *inter alia*, the Palestine partition resolution 181 (II) and resolution 3236 (XXIX). This demonstrates unequivocally the world community's reaffirmation of the continuing validity of the two-state solution. In operative paragraph 2 of resolution 36/120 D the General Assembly:

> *Reaffirms* also the inalienable rights in Palestine of the Palestinian people, including:
> (a) The right to self-determination without external interference, and to national independence and sovereignty;
> (b) The right to establish its own independent sovereign State.

During its seventh emergency special session, the General Assembly adopted resolution ES-7/6 on 19 August 1982.[76] In the second operative paragraph, the General Assembly:

> *Calls* for the free exercise in Palestine of the inalienable rights of the Palestinian people to self-determination without external interference and to national independence.

5. The geographical area to which Palestinian self-determination applies

Where "in Palestine", to use the wording of resolutions 3236 and 36/120 D, may Palestinian national self-determination including independence and sovereignty be exercised? General Assembly resolution 2625 (XXV) dealing with "Principles of International Law concerning Friendly Relations . . ."[77] which has been considered concerning the right of self-determination, also provides basic legal interpretation concerning areas where self-determination may be exercised. Under the heading of the "principle of equal rights and self-determination of peoples" the penultimate paragraph provides:

[75] *Ibid., Thirty-sixth Session, Supplement 51*, p. 27.
[76] Document A/ES-7/14/Add.1.
[77] See note 23 above.

Nothing in the foregoing paragraphs shall be construed as authorizing or encouraging any action which would dismember or impair, totally or in part, the territorial integrity or political unity of sovereign and independent states conducting themselves in compliance with the principle of equal rights and self-determination of peoples as described above and thus possessed of a government representing the whole people belonging to the territory without distinction as to race, creed or colour.

The quoted wording is of particular importance since it is designed to preserve the territorial integrity or political unity of non-discriminatory states which have a government "representing the whole people belonging to the territory".

The only *de jure* boundaries which the State of Israel has ever had are those which were specified for "the Jewish State" in the Palestine partition resolution.[78] Following the Armistice Agreements of 1949, which did not fix *de jure* boundaries, the State of Israel existed within *de facto* boundaries until June 1967. It is probable that those pre-1967 boundaries have received some international assent. Security Council resolution 242 (1967) of 22 November 1967 refers in the first operative paragraph to the principle of "withdrawal of Israel armed forces from territories occupied in the recent conflict". Since there is no statement of withdrawal from territories occupied at a time before 1967, this may amount to an indirect recognition of the pre-June 1967 boundaries. Operative paragraph 1 also refers to the principle of the "territorial integrity and political independence of every State in the area and their right to live in peace within secure and recognized boundaries". As Lord Caradon, the principal author of resolution 242, has stated, "the overriding principle" of resolution 242 is the "inadmissibility of the acquisition of territory by war"[79] and this means Israeli withdrawal from Palestinian and other Arab lands must take place to the pre-June 1967 borders subject to minor variations to be determined, preferably, by an impartial boundary commission.[80]

The Camp David Agreement entitled "A Framework for Peace in the Middle East Agreed at Camp David"[81] of 17 September 1978 is premised upon Israeli withdrawal from the territories occupied since 5 June 1967 because its preamble states that it is based upon "United Nations Security Council resolution 242 (1967), in all its parts". President Reagan's peace plan of 1 September 1982 is also based upon Israeli withdrawal, since it

[78] General Assembly resolution 181 (II), part II B.

[79] Lord Caradon in Caradon, Goldberg, El-Zayyat and Eban, *U.N. Security Council Resolution 242*, p. 1 at 13 (Washington, D.C., Georgetown University, 1981).

[80] Concerning the powers of the Security Council see J. Crawford, *The Creation of States in International Law*, pp. 328-29 (1979).

[81] United States Department of State, Publication No. 8954, Near East and South Asia Series 88, *The Camp David Summit* 6-9 (1978). The inadequacies of this agreement area analysed in F. A. Sayegh, *Camp David and Palestine* (F. A. Sayegh Foundation, 1982).

states that peace cannot be achieved" on "the basis of Israeli sovereignty or permanent control over the West Bank and the Gaza".[82] President Reagan stated in presenting his plan that "UN resolution 242 remains wholly valid".[83] The Declaration of the Arab Summit Conference at Fez on 9 September 1982 also postulated Israeli withdrawal "from all Arab territories occupied in 1967"[84] and apparently recognizes the State of Israel in its pre-1967 boundaries. While the Government of Israel has given verbal assent to resolution 242, subject to its unilateral interpretation, it is continuing its creeping annexation of the occupied territories through the settlement device[85] and has explicitly rejected President Reagan's peace plan.[86]

It is clear that two different national exercises of the right of self-determination cannot take place simultaneously upon precisely the same territory, and the careful wording of resolution 3236 is consistent with this reality. Consequently, those Palestinians who choose to exercise their right of return within the State of Israel cannot exercise Palestinian national self-determination within that State. Since General Assembly resolution 181 (II) established the principle of two States in the area and subsequent resolutions have not departed from this concept, it is clear that it is not the intent of the General Assembly to authorize Palestinian self-determination within the State of Israel. The Palestinian national right of self-determination as recognized in General Assembly resolutions may be exercised "in Palestine" within the *de jure* boundaries of the Palestinian State which are yet to be determined, and outside the *de jure* boundaries of the State of Israel as ultimately determined.

IV. THE URGENT NECESSITY FOR SANCTIONS AND ENFORCEMENT OF THE TWO-STATE SOLUTION FOR PALESTINE WITHIN THE WORLD LEGAL ORDER

Security Council resolution 242 (1967)[87] concerning "a just and lasting peace in the Middle East" has been supplemented by the later resolutions of the General Assembly. In particular, the reference in resolution 242 to "just settlement of the refugee problem"[88] is made more specific by the General Assembly's recognition of the right of return for individual Palestin-

---

[82] Reagan, "A new opportunity for peace in the Middle East", 82 *Department of State Bulletin* No. 23, at p. 25, col. 1 (Sept. 1982).

[83] *Ibid.*

[84] *Washington Post*, 10 Sept. 1982, p. A 21, col. 1.

[85] Mallison and Mallison, *Settlements and the Law: A Juridical Analysis of the Israeli Settlements in the Occupied Territories* (American Educational Trust, 1982).

[86] "Text of Israeli statement rejecting U.S. proposal", *Washington Post*, 3 Sept. 1982, p. A 21, cols. 1-4; E. Walsh, "Begin again rejects U.S. plan", *Washington Post*, 19 Oct. 1982, p. 1, col. 4.

[87] See note 78 above.

[88] The quoted words refer to the Palestinian refugees and not to the Jewish immigration from Arab countries which was solicited by Israel. The Zionist bombings directed at Jews in Baghdad to induce immigration to Israel are described in Hirst, *op. cit.*, pp. 155-64.

ians.[89] In addition, the General Assembly has recognized the national rights of the Palestinian people in carefully formulated terms which do not infringe upon the legitimate rights of the State of Israel.[90] The Israeli national rights which remain inviolate include, among others, the rights to self-determination and to national independence and sovereign equality with other States consistent with international law including the pertinent United Nations resolutions. The Israeli rights do not include, among others, supposed rights to deny self-determination and independence to the Palestinian people and a supposed right to establish Israeli borders on the basis of military conquest and illegal annexations. A limitation which is inherent in the authorization of the two States is that each may exercise its national rights conditioned on, at the least, the requirement of non-obstruction of the national rights of the other.

The essential first step in implementing the United Nations resolutions concerning Palestine is Israeli withdrawal from the territories occupied in 1967. The wasted years of good intentions including General Assembly and Security Council resolutions based upon legally sound and morally just premises but without enforcement cannot now be retrieved.[91] The Israeli attack on the Palestinian people and invasion of Lebanon in the summer of 1982[92] is further evidence that the Zionist aggression will continue until international action is taken to stop it. With each act of aggression it becomes more difficult to implement the United Nations' legal solution to the problem.

The maintenance of public order is a basic task of any legal system, whether domestic or international. The responsibility of a domestic order system is to exercise effective community control over private violence. By analogy, the responsibility of the world legal order is to exercise effective community control of violence and coercion exercised by national states.[93] The Secretary-General of the United Nations has written:

> [O]ur most urgent goal is to reconstruct the Charter concept of collective action for peace and security so as to render the United Nations more capable of carrying out its primary function.[94]

[89] General Assembly resolution 194 (III), para. 11. The General Assembly has reaffirmed the resolution regularly. See, e.g., General Assembly resolution 36/146 F of 16 December 1981.

[90] See note 38 above.

[91] J. Reddaway, "The future of Jerusalem", in "Seek Peace, and Ensue It: Selected Papers on Palestine and the Search for Peace", 127 (Council for the Advancement of Arab-British Understanding, 1982).

[92] This attack-invasion is analysed juridically in the forthcoming Mallison and Mallison, The Palestine Problem in International Law and World Order (to be published by Longman Group, London, 1983).

[93] The world legal order is considered systematically in M. S. McDougal and Associates, Studies in World Public Order (1960).

[94] J. Pérez de Cuéllar, Report of the Secretary-General on the Work of the Organization, p. 6 (1982).

The world legal order must, at the very least, protect peoples and States from coercion and aggression. Such an order is prescribed by the United Nations Charter requirement of peaceful methods of dispute settlement[95] combined with its prohibition upon "the threat or use of force against the territorial integrity or political independence of any state, or in any other manner inconsistent with the Purposes of the United Nations".[96] The Charter also contains the complementary provision which authorizes the use of force only for defensive purposes.[97] It is clear that the Palestinians who have been the victims of organized Zionist terror since the time of the Balfour Declaration and who have been victimized by the Government of Israel's highly institutionalized state terror since 1948 have not received the benefits of the United Nations legal order. In the same way, those Israelis who have been the victims of Palestinian violence have not received the benefits of such a system.[98] The great opportunity which a solution to the Palestine problem presents to the world community acting through the United Nations is to provide Palestinians and Israelis alike with individual and national security. In this era of weapons of mass destruction, the probable alternatives to the achievement of the legal order include further destructive armed conflicts in the Middle East and the danger of a world conflagration of mutual mass destruction as well.[99]

If there is any single point that has been made most clearly in the United Nations dealings with the State of Israel and Zionist nationalism over a period of more than three decades, it is that there will be no solution of the Palestine problem until effective sanctions are applied to the Government of Israel. Because of the continuing Israeli economic crisis, largely caused by the militarization of its foreign policy and its domestic society, there is every reason to believe that economic sanctions[100] would be successful. Such sanctions would immediately raise a new hope within Israel on the part of those patriotic and enlightened Israeli citizens who have been urging their Government to enter into a peaceful settlement based upon law and justice. In the unlikely event that the economic sanctions were unsuccessful, the military sanctions are available under the United Nations Charter.[101] It is necessary to emphasize that sanctions must be conceptualized and applied as a comprehensive process, starting with persuasive measures and leading

[95] United Nations Charter, Art. 2 (3).

[96] *Ibid.*, Art. 2 (4).

[97] *Ibid.*, Art. 51.

[98] Both the Israeli state terror and the Palestinian counter-terror are described and analysed in Hirst, *op. cit.* Primary authority on the state terror is in L. Rokach, *Israel's Sacred Terrorism: A Study Based on Moshe Sharett's Personal Diary* (1980).

[99] Mallison and Mallison, "The Israeli aerial attack on June 7, 1981 upon the Iraqi nuclear reactor: aggression or self-defense?", 15 *Vanderbilt J. Transnational L.* 417, 44-46 (1982).

[100] United Nations Charter, Arts. 39-50.

[101] *Ibid.*

to increasingly coercive ones, rather than as a group of isolated and unrelated episodes.[102]

The main authority to apply sanctions is allocated to the Security Council and its action may be blocked by the negative vote of a single permanent member.[103] The General Assembly may not act while the Security Council is exercising its functions under the Charter concerning any dispute or situation.[104] The General Assembly, nevertheless, may act when the Council is blocked by a great Power negative vote. The first time that the General Assembly acted in such a context was during the Korean War in 1950 when the Soviet Union blocked action by the Security Council. Under the leadership of the United States, the General Assembly adopted the famous "Uniting-for-peace" resolution on 3 November 1950[105] by more than the two-thirds majority required by the Charter for important questions.[106] Thereafter, pursuant to subsequent resolutions of the Assembly, the community of States took effective enforcement action to stop aggression. This method is still available under the Charter and it can be used to overcome a negative vote by any permanent member of the Council.

The application of sanctions to enforce the world community consensus concerning Palestine manifested through the authorized organs of the United Nations is indispensable. No organized community, domestic or international, can achieve a legal order without the ability and the will to use the necessary force and coercion to obtain it. The essential element is that coercion must be in the responsible hands of the community and not in the hands of a militaristic and expansionist state. The central point was made by J. W. Fulbright sometime ago when he wrote, "The crucial distinction is not between coercion and voluntarism, but between duly constituted force applied through law . . . and the arbitrary coercion of the weak by the strong."[107]

One of the objections that will be made to this recommendation for the application of adequate sanctions is the often stated position of the United States Government that it opposes an "imposed settlement".[108] This objection should be clearly understood both in its explicit meaning and in its implication. Its explicit meaning is that an imposed settlement by the world community under law is opposed. Its unexpressed but necessary implication

[102] The past performance and the present potential of such sanctions by the world community are analysed in M. S. McDougal and F. P. Feliciano, *Law and Minimum World Public Order* (1961), chap. 4, entitled "Community sanctioning process and minimum order".

[103] United Nations Charter, Art. 27 (3).

[104] *Ibid.*, Art. 12 (1).

[105] General Assembly resolution 377A (V).

[106] United Nations Charter, Art. 18 (2).

[107] *The Crippled Giant*, (Vintage Books, 1972), p. 108.

[108] E.g. the opposition to such a settlement, as applied to Israel, expressed by Acting U.S. Ambassador to the United Nations, W. J. Vanden Heuvel, in the emergency special session of the General Assembly on Palestine on 24 July 1980. 80 *U.S. Dept. State Bull.* 67 (Sept., 1980).

is that the existing imposed settlement by the military power of the Government of Israel, armed and supported by the United States, is condoned. It is remarkable that the position of the United States applies only to the Israeli-Palestinian conflict. It overlooks the highly successful imposition of a settlement on Japan in the years following the end of the Second World War. It also neglects to mention the imposed settlement in Europe at the end of the same war. No mention of historic settlements would be complete without reference to the peace which the Congress of Vienna imposed on France beginning in 1815.[109] The justice involved in that settlement, including the protection of legitimate French national interests, resulted in less coercion being required than would otherwise have been necessary. Both justice and coercion are typically required in peace settlements and where justice is used less, coercion must be used more.[110] The absence of elementary justice in the unilateral military settlement now imposed upon Palestine leads to the great and increasing use of coercion.

An analogous situation to the one which has existed in Palestine since 1967 arose in 1957 following the Anglo-French-Israeli aggression against Egypt. Pursuant to resolutions of the General Assembly, the British and French armed forces were withdrawn from territory acquired by war. Then, as now, the Government of Israel refused to withdraw. The President of the United States at the time was a man who, like one of the founders of the United Nations, President Franklin D. Roosevelt, was committed to the principles of the United Nations Charter and to the maintenance of its legal order system. On 20 February 1957, in the face of continued Israeli defiance of the United Nations, President Dwight D. Eisenhower stated in an address which was heard and reported on a world-wide basis:

> We are approaching a fateful moment when either we must recognize that the United Nations is unable to restore peace in this area or the United Nations must renew with increased vigor its efforts to bring about Israeli withdrawal.[111]

*   *   *

This raises a basic question of principle. Should a nation which attacks and occupies foreign territory in the face of United Nations disapproval be allowed to impose conditions on its own withdrawal?

If we agree that armed attack can properly achieve the purposes of the assailant, then I fear we will have turned back the clock of international order. We will, in effect, have countenanced the use of force as a

---

[109] See note 13 above.

[110] S. P. Tillman, *The United States in the Middle East: Interests and Obstacles* (1982), chap. 7, entitled "Conclusion: on peace and how to get it".

[111] 36 *U.S. Dept. State Bull.* 387 at 388 (Mar. 11, 1957).

means of settling international differences and through this gaining national advantages.[112]

* * *

The United Nations must not fail. I believe that—in the interests of peace—the United Nations has no choice but to exert pressure upon Israel to comply with the withdrawal resolutions.[113]

The Israeli withdrawal followed.

When the other member States of the United Nations act without hesitancy to assert leadership in achieving a peaceful settlement for Palestine and Israel, it will have a significant impact upon the United States Government in bringing it back, sooner rather than later, to its principled advocacy and practical support for self-determination for all national groups including the Palestinian people. With the concurrence of the United States in the enforcement process, as in 1957, it will be possible to effectuate the Palestinian people's right to its own sovereign State[114] and to bring peace with justice to Palestinians and Israelis alike.

[112] *Ibid.* at 389.

[113] *Ibid.* at 390.

[114] Whatever sovereignty has meant historically, it now means national independence and statehood under law including the legal order established by the United Nations Charter.

320. The Status of Jerusalem, June 22, 1983*

* Report to the U.N. International Conference on the Question of Palestine, Geneva, U.N. Doc. A/Conf. 114/9.

THE STATUS OF JERUSALEM*

CONTENTS

I. Historical background

As it has been a holy city exalted through the entire history of monotheism, temporal rule over Jerusalem has been closely linked with the religious domination of Palestine.

The earliest known people of Palestine were the Canaanites among whom, according to Jewish, Christian and Moslem tradition, Abraham came from Ur. His descendants followed Moses from captivity in Egypt, and after their return, the Jewish tribes were united in about 1000 B.C. under David, who conquered Jerusalem from the Jebusites. His son, the great Solomon, built the first Temple of Jerusalem on Mount Moriah.

Solomon's death was followed by the division of the kingdom into two— Israel and Judah, Jerusalem being the capital of the latter. Early in the eighth century B.C., Israel was destroyed by the Assyrians and the Israelites carried away as captives. In 587 B.C., Nebuchadnezzar destroyed Jerusalem and the Temple of Solomon, carrying the inhabitants of Judah into captivity in Babylon. Afte [*sic*] Cyrus' conquest of Babylon, the Jews returned to Palestine and rebuilt the Temple of Jerusalem *circa* 530 B.C.

In 332 B.C., the Macedonians conquered Palestine. A Jewish uprising led to the destruction of the second Temple *circa* 170 B.C. A partial reappear-

* Paper prepared for the International Conference on the Question of Palestine by a consultant, at the request of the Preparatory Committee.

ance of Jewish rule was ended by the Roman conquest in 63 B.C. Under Roman suzerainty Herod became king of Judea in 40 B.C., rebuilding the Temple in Jerusalem a second time. From 70 A.D., Titus ruled Palestine, sacking Jerusalem and destroying the Temple, of which only the Western Wall survived. In 135 A.D., Hadrian expelled the Jews from Palestine into the Diaspora.

From *circa* 400 A.D., Palestine was ruled by the Byzantine Empire until the Islamic *Fath* (spread) in 637 A.D., the Caliph Omar entering Jerusalem in 638. Arab Moslem rule remained until 1517, with only a brief interruption lasting between 1099 and 1187 when the Crusaders conquered it. It was in 1187 that Salah-El-Din the Great returned Jerusalem to Moslem rule and it so remained for eight centuries, becoming part of the Ottoman Empire in 1517.

The history of rule over Jerusalem shows sharply differing attitudes of the rulers towards religions other than their own. The Babylonians, Macedonians and Romans destroyed the Jewish Temples. Hadrian forbade Jews to enter Jerusalem, but eventually they were able to perform an annual pilgrimage to Jerusalem to continue the tradition of worshipping at the ruins of the Temples. After the Moslem *Fath* (spread), eventually Jews were allowed to return to Jerusalem and to establish their synagogues. Although Moslem holy places were built on Mount Moriah and the site called the Haram Al-Sherif, becoming one of the three most holy places in Islam, the Jews were permitted to worship at the Western Wall. The Crusaders at first dealt with the Jews harshly, but later showed more tolerance for Judaism. After the Moslem reconquest in 1187, Salah-El-Din allowed Jews to return to Palestine and gave them freedom of worship. Moslem rule over Palestine and Jerusalem lasted nearly 13 centuries, except for the Christian interregnum. It was ended by the British occupation in 1917, and the subsequent status of Palestine as a League of Nations Mandate.*

II. Jerusalem under the British Mandate

The League of Nations Mandate for Palestine, granted to Great Britain in 1922, incorporated the Balfour Declaration of 1917, and had as its principal object "the establishment in Palestine of a national home for the Jewish people". This Mandate was granted without reference to the wishes of the people of Palestine required by the League's Covenant, but since Palestine was holy to Moslems and Christians also, and since the people of Palestine were overwhelmingly Moslem and Christian Arabs, the Mandate assumed full responsibility for "preserving existing rights" in all the Holy Places. Article 13 read:

---

* This historical background is extracted from the report of an international commission appointed in 1930 with the approval of the League of Nations (see note 1 under "Notes and references").

All responsibility in connexion with the Holy Places . . . including that of preserving existing rights and of securing free access . . . is assumed by the Mandatory who shall be responsible solely to the League of Nations . . . nothing in this Mandate shall be construed as conferring upon the Mandatory authority to interfere with the fabric or the management of purely Moslem sacred shrines, the immunities of which are guaranteed.

Article 14 read:

A Special Commission shall be appointed by the Mandatory to study, define and determine the rights and claims in connexion with the Holy Places and the rights and claims relating to the different religious communities in Palestine.

Within a few years the increase in the Jewish population through mass immigration had resulted in political tensions in Palestine between the Arabs and Jews, part of which was friction between the Jews and Moslem Arabs which soon developed over the Holy Places in Jerusalem.

In 1929 there was a serious outbreak of violence over the Western Wall (or the Wailing Wall) of the ruins of the ancient Jewish Temples, the holiest site for Jewish worship, situated in the Haram Al-Sherif, for Moslems the holiest place in Jerusalem. An international commission appointed under article 14 of the Mandate with the approval of the Council of the League of Nations investigated the claims of the two religious communities in Jerusalem.

Its award on the fundamental question of religious rights was:

To the Moslems belong the sole ownership of and the sole proprietary right to the Western Wall, seeing that it forms an integral part of the Haram-al-Sherif area . . .

To the Moslems there also belongs the ownership of the Pavement in front of the Moghrabi (Moroccan) Quarter opposite the Wall . . .

Such appurtenances of worship . . . as the Jews may be entitled to place near the Wall either in conformity with the present Verdict or by agreement come to between the Parties shall under no circumstances be considered as, or have the effect of, establishing for them any sort of proprietary right to the Wall or to the adjacent Pavement.[1]

Thus the League of Nations Mandate's reference to "existing rights", presumably meaning the customary rights that had prevailed under the Ottoman Empire, was elaborated by the International Commission.

---

[1] British Government: *Report of the Commission appointed by His Majesty's Government in the United Kingdom of Great Britain and Northern Ireland, with the approval of the Council of the League of Nations, to determine the rights and claims of Moslems and Jews in connection with the Western or Wailing Wall at Jerusalem*, (London, H.M.S.O., 1931) p. 57. (Note: The members of the Commission were from Sweden, Switzerland and the Netherlands).

In its report the Commission noted that in presenting their case for the right of worship at the Western Wall, the Jews "do not claim any property right to the Wall". Its award prescribed certain subsidiary entitlements and obligations for both religious communities. This was made into law on 8 June 1931,[2] and remained law until the end of the Mandate.

The massive immigration under the Zionist Organization's policies was swelled by European Jews seeking refuge from Nazi persecution. The augmented Jewish proportion of Palestine's population brought mounting Jewish-Arab hostility which culminated in the Palestinian rebellion of 1937-1939.

The Royal Commission of enquiry commenting on Jewish-Arab animosity, stated, *inter alia*:

> . . . Nor is the conflict in its essence an interracial conflict, arising from any old instinctive antipathy of Arabs towards Jews. There was little or no friction . . . between Arabs and Jews in the rest of the Arab world until the strife in Palestine . . . [where] . . . there is no common ground between them. The Arab community is predominantly Asian in character, the Jewish community predominantly European . . . .[3]

Citing "the force of circumstance", the Royal Commission proposed the partition of Palestine into an Arab State and a Jewish State. In view of the sanctity of Jerusalem and Behtlehem to all three faiths, the Commission held the Holy Places to be, in words taken from the League's Covenant, "a sacred trust of civilization". It proposed that a Jerusalem-Bethlehem enclave encompassing all the Holy Places, with a corridor to the sea terminating at Jaffa, be endowed with an international status under a new mandate subject to the League's supervision.[4] (See map at annex I.)

This first plan for the partition of Palestine and the internationalization of Jerusalem was superseded by political and military events. After the Second World War, Great Britain declared it was unable to resolve the conflict in Palestine and brought the problem to the United Nations.

III. The international régime for Jerusalem under the partition resolution

When the Palestine question was taken up by the United Nations, in 1947, the country itself was ravaged by conflict. Because of its religious significance and symbolism, Jerusalem inevitably became a particular centre of convergence of the Jewish-Arab confrontation.

A large number of Jewish immigrants had settled in a new expanded western sector of Jerusalem, the ancient eastern sector, including the walled

[2] Palestine Government: *Official Gazette of the Government of Palestine*, Jerusalem, 8 June 1931.

[3] British Government: Palestine Royal Commission: *Report Cmd. 5479*, (London, H.M.S.O., 1937) pp. 131, 370.

[4] *Ibid.*, pp. 381-382.

city, remaining predominantly Arab. The United Nations Special Committee on Palestine (UNSCOP), appointed by the General Assembly to present proposals on Palestine, estimated there were about 100,000 Jews and 105,000 Arabs (and others) in Jerusalem.[5]

Because of the special position of Jerusalem, UNSCOP unanimously recommended that the sanctity of the Holy Places be guaranteed by special provisions, and that "existing rights" in Palestine be preserved:

> A. The sacred character of the Holy Places shall be preserved and access to the Holy Places for the purposes of worship and pilgrimage shall be ensured in accordance with existing rights . . .
>
> B. Existing rights in Palestine of the several religious communities shall neither be impaired nor denied;
>
> . . .
>
> D. Specific stipulations concerning the Holy Places . . . and the rights of religious communities shall be inserted in the constitution or constitutions of any independent Palestinian State or States which may be created.[6]

The minority report recommended an independent, unified, federal State in Palestine. Jerusalem, which would have separate municipalities for the Arab and Jewish sectors, was to be its capital. Elaborating the unanimous recommendation cited above, the minority report proposed a functional form of internationalization:

> In the interest of preserving, protecting and caring for Holy Places . . . in Jerusalem, Bethlehem, Nazareth and elsewhere in Palestine, a permanent international body for the supervision and protection of the Holy Places in Palestine shall be created . . . by the United Nations . . . .[7]

The majority report recommended the partition of Palestine into an Arab State and a Jewish State, and the territorial internationalization of the Jerusalem area as an international enclave in the Arab State in Palestine (see maps at annexes II and III). These recommendations were approved by the General Assembly in its resolution 181 (II) on 29 November 1947. Often referred to as the "partition resolution", it envisaged a demilitarized Jerusalem as a *corpus separatum* under the aegis of the United Nations Trusteeship Council, which would draft a statute for Jerusalem and appoint a Governor. A legislature would be elected by universal adult suffrage. The Statute would remain in force for 10 years, and then be re-examined by the Trusteeship Council, with citizen participation through a referendum.

The principal clauses relating to Jerusalem read:

---

[5] United Nations: *Official Records of the General Assembly, Second Session, Supplement No. 11* (A/364, UNSCOP report), vol. I, p. 54.

[6] *Ibid.*, p. 44.

[7] *Ibid.*, p. 63.

The City of Jerusalem shall be established as a corpus separatum under a special international régime and shall be administered by the United Nations . . . Trusteeship Council . . .

. . .

The Trusteeship Council shall . . . elaborate and approve a detailed Statute of the City . . .

. . .

. . . A Governor of the City of Jerusalem shall be appointed by the Trusteeship Council and shall be responsible to it.

. . .

. . . The City of Jerusalem shall be demilitarized; its neutrality shall be declared and preserved . . .

. . . the Governor shall organize a special police force of adequate strength, the members of which shall be recruited outside of Palestine

. . .

. . . A Legislative Council, elected by adult residents of the city irrespective of nationality on the basis of universal and secret suffrage and proportional representation, shall have powers of legislation and taxation. No legislative measures shall, however, conflict or interfere with the provisions which will be set forth in the Statute of the City . . .

. . . The Statute shall provide for the establishment of an independent judiciary system, including a court of appeal. All the inhabitants of the City shall be subject to it.

. . . *Holy Places* (a) Existing rights in respect of Holy Places and religious buildings or sites shall not be denied or impaired. (b) Free access to the Holy Places and religious buildings or sites and the free exercise of worship shall be secured in conformity with existing rights . . . .

The principle of upholding "existing rights" in the Holy Places thus was maintained in the partition resolution.

Other articles stipulated that the provisions cited above

. . . shall be under the guarantee of the United Nations, and no modification shall be made in them without the assent of the General Assembly . . .

Any dispute relating . . . to this declaration . . . shall be referred, at the request of either party, to the International Court of Justice, unless the parties agree to another mode of settlement.

The Arab States and the Arab Higher Committee for Palestine, however, rejected the resolution, on the grounds that the United Nations was exceeding its competence by proposing the partitioning of Palestine.* The Zionist Organization, which had insisted that a Jewish State should be established

---

* For further elaboration on the basis of the Arab position on the partition plan, consult *The Origins and Evolution of the Palestine Problem*, Part II (United Nations Publication, Sales No. E.78.I.20), pp. 33-36.

in Palestine in its entirety, reluctantly accepted the partition formula. The plan was never fully implemented.

IV. The de facto division of Jerusalem, 1948

In actuality Palestine's fate was being determined not by international agreement but by armed force. Several months before the British finally withdrew from Palestine on 15 May 1948, a virtual state of war existed between the Palestinian Arabs and Zionist military organizations such as the *Haganah* and the *Irgun*. With the entry of forces from bordering Arab countries following the proclamation of the State of Israel on 14 May 1948, full-scale war broke out, being ended by a United Nations-negotiated truce on 16 November 1948, with Israeli forces having decisively defeated the Arab troops. Israeli territorial control expanded deep into the territories allotted to the Arab State, and into the western sector of the Jerusalem enclave destined for internationalization under the partition resolution. Eastern Jerusalem, including the Walled City and the "West Bank", became united with Jordan.

This division of Jerusalem was confirmed by an Israel-Jordan cease-fire agreement of 30 November 1948 (which allowed convoys to an Israeli contingent in occupation of Mount Scopus in the Jordanian sector).

The *de facto* division of the city was further formalized by an Israel-Jordan Armistice Agreement of 3 April 1949. This agreement had no effect on the partition resolution's provisions for the internationalization of Jerusalem.

V. Reaffirmation of the principle of the internationalization of Jerusalem

Both the Israel-Jordan agreements were concluded through the United Nations Mediator for Palestine, appointed by the General Assembly. The first Mediator, Count Bernadotte, before his assassination by an Israeli terrorist group, had reiterated the importance of internationalization:

> The City of Jerusalem . . . should be treated separately and should be placed under effective United Nations control with maximum feasible local autonomy for the Arab and Jewish communities, with full safeguards for the protection of the Holy Places and sites, and free access to them, and for religious freedom.[8]

Another General Assembly resolution, 194 (III) of 11 December 1948, again reaffirmed the principles of internationalization and "existing rights", resolving:

> . . . that Holy Places—including Nazareth—religious buildings and sites in Palestine should be protected and free access to them assured, in accordance with existing rights and historical practice; . . .

[8] *Official Records of the General Assembly, Third Session, Supplement No. 11* (A/648, Progress report of the United Nations Mediator on Palestine), p. 18.

The resolution established a Conciliation Commission for Palestine (CCP), which was instructed, *inter alia*:

> . . . to present to the fourth regular session of the General Assembly detailed proposals for a permanent international régime for the Jerusalem area which will provide for the maximum local autonomy for distinctive groups consistent with the special international status of the Jerusalem area . . .

The resolution contained far-reaching provisions for the wider Palestine issue, and the Arab States did not accept it. Israel, on the other hand, also ignored the United Nations resolution and moved to absorb into its jurisdiction that part of Jerusalem it had occupied. In September 1948 the Israeli Supreme Court was established in New Jerusalem; in February 1949 the Knesset assembled and the President took the oath of office in he [*sic*] city.

Israel's intentions towards Jerusalem became a major focus of the United Nations discussion on Israel's application for membership.

The representative of Israel gave an assurance that:

> The Government of Israel advocated the establishment by the United Nations of an international régime for Jerusalem concerned exclusively with the control and protection of Holy Places, and would co-operate with such a régime.
>
> It would also agree to place under international control Holy Places in parts of its territory outside Jerusalem, and supported the suggestion that guarantees would be given for the protection of the Holy Places in Palestine and for free access thereto.[9]

Delegates, however, raised sharp questions on a statement in a report from the Conciliation Commission for Palestine that on the subject of Jerusalem the Israeli Prime Minister had declared that:

> For historical, political and religious reasons, the State of Israel could not accept the establishment of an international régime for the city of Jerusalem.[10]

The representative of Israel said that this statement had been taken out of context and that in actual fact Israel would:

> make proposals [to] the General Assembly for defining the future juridical status of Jerusalem . . . [which] would differentiate between the powers of an international régime with respect to the Holy Places and the aspiration of the Government of Israel to become recognized as the sovereign authority in Jerusalem . . .[11]

---

[9] *Official Records of the General Assembly, Third Session*, Part II, *Ad Hoc* Political Committee, 45th meeting, p. 236.

[10] *Ibid.*, 46th meeting, p. 254.

[11] *Ibid.*

Israel's assurances in regard of the implementation of General Assembly resolutions 181 (II) and 194 (III) were specifically mentioned in the General Assembly's resolution admitting Israel to the United Nations.[12] It is relevant to note that Israel gave these assurances even though both resolutions had not been accepted by the Arab States, and it can therefore be argued that Israel's assurances were not contingent on reciprocal Arab action. Between them these resolutions maintained the principle of the internationalization of Jerusalem and the maintenance of "existing rights" and historical practice.

Nevertheless, the Knesset proclaimed Jerusalem the capital of Israel on 23 January 1950 and by 1951 Israeli ministries had moved into the New City.

Jordan also took steps to extend its jurisdiction to the West Bank and the Old City in Jerusalem despite the disapproval of the Arab League.[13]

VI. The proposals of the Conciliation Commission for Palestine for an international régime for Jerusalem

The United Nations was continuing its efforts to establish an international régime in Jerusalem. The Conciliation Commission for Palestine (CCP) established by resolution 194 (III), composed of representatives of France, Turkey and the United States of America, set up a Special Committee on Jerusalem. Discussions with Arab and Israeli authorities brought indications that the Arab countries, notwithstanding their initial rejection of resolutions 181 (II) and 194 (III), supported the principle of the internationalization of the city of Jerusalem, but that this was no longer acceptable to Israel. The CCP reported:

> During the Commission's conversations in Beirut with the Arab delegations, the latter showed themselves, in general, prepared to accept the principle of an international régime for the Jerusalem area, on condition that the United Nations should be in a position to offer the necessary guarantees regarding the stability and permanence of such a régime.
>
> From the beginning, however, the Government of Israel, while recognizing that the Commission was bound by General Assembly resolu-

---

[12] General Assembly resolution 273 (III) of 11 May 1949.

[13] On 24 April 1950 a general election was held to choose a new Jordanian Parliament with equal representation from the East and the West Banks. Both houses of the Parliament meeting in Amman adopted a resolution formally uniting the Hashemite Kingdom of Jordan and those areas of Arab Palestine where the Arab legion had entered during the war with Israel and which had remained under Jordanian control since the armistice between Israel and Jordan. Article 2 of the resolution provides: "Emphasis on the preservation of the complete Arab rights in Palestine and on the defence of those rights with all the legitimate means, with full justice and with no prejudice to the final settlement of its just cause within the framework of the national aspirations, Arab co-operation and international justice."

tion 194 (III), declared itself unable to accept the establishment of an international régime for the city of Jerusalem; it did, however, accept without reservation an international régime for, or the international control of, the Holy Places in the City.[14]

Faced with these positions and the *de facto* partition of Jerusalem, where the original United Nations aim of territorial internationalization faced resistance, the CCP inclined toward the idea of a limited internationalization of only the Holy Places, as proposed by Israel. Though the principle was akin to that presented in the UNSCOP minority report, a critical differentiation was that this earlier plan envisaged a united Palestine with Jerusalem as its capital, while the CCP sought to apply it in a partitioned Palestine and a divided Jerusalem. Unlike the Trusteeship Council, which had been charged solely with drafting a statute for an internationalized Jerusalem, the CCP's mandate covered the wider Palestine issue. In its discussions with the CCP Israel had made clear its desire to annex all the additional area it had occupied during the 1948 war, with the additional incorporation of the Gaza strip, while disclaiming any such intentions towards the West Bank.[15] These demands, although rejected by the Arab States, presented the CCP with a situation where the actual line of control between Israel and Jordan in Palestine ran through Jerusalem, and the CCP's proposals for the city seemed to conform to this situation. A CCP report summarized its proposals, detailed in a draft Instrument, as follows:

> The principal aim of the draft Instrument was to reconcile the requirement of the General Assembly for 'maximum local autonomy in Jerusalem' with the interests of the international community in a special status for the City. To this end, the draft Instrument provided that the Jerusalem area should be divided into an Arab and a Jewish zone, within which the local authorities were empowered to deal with all matters not of international concern. These were specifically reserved to the authority of the United Nations Commissioner.
>
> The United Nations Commissioner, to be appointed by and responsible to the General Assembly, was charged with ensuring the protection of and free access to the Holy Places; supervising the permanent demilitarization and neutralization of the Jerusalem area; and ensuring the protection of human rights and of the rights of distinctive groups. The draft Instrument provided for the establishment of a General Council, composed of representatives from the Arab and Jewish zones, and presided over by the Commissioner, to co-ordinate matters of common interest to the two parts of the City. The Council would in practice have only advisory and consultative functions with the authorities of the

[14] *Official Records of the General Assembly, Fifth Session, Supplement No. 18* (A/1367/Rev.1) p. 10.

[15] *Ibid.*, pp. 19-20.

Arab and Jewish zones of the City. The draft Instrument also provided for an international tribunal and a mixed tribunal, which were not, however, designed to function as substitutes for the judicial organization already established in the two zones. The international tribunal would ensure that the provisions of the plan were respected by the United Nations authorities in Jerusalem and by the authorities of the two parts of the area; the mixed tribunal would ensure impartial treatment for Arabs called to justice in the Jewish part of the Jerusalem area or for Jews called to justice in the Arab part, eventualities which would be likely to occur when normal intercourse between the two parts and visits and pilgrimages to the Holy Places situated on either side of the demarcation line were resumed. The draft Instrument also contained detailed provisions for the protection of, and free access to, the Holy Places, religious buildings and sites inside the Jerusalem area and authorized the United Nations Commissioner to supervise the implementation of undertakings which might be made by the States concerned regarding Holy Places, religious buildings and sites of Palestine situated outside the Jerusalem area.[16]

These CCP proposals, giving the appearance of conforming to a fait accompli of a divided Jerusalem, brought reactions strong enough to lead the CCP to issue an explanatory statement.[17] This failed to remove the impression that the proposals would consolidate the division of Jerusalem. In effect, the General Assembly's requirement that Jerusalem be a *corpus separatum* under an international régime was not met. The CCP proposals were not debated in the General Assembly and, in effect, lapsed.

VII. The Trusteeship Council's draft statutes for Jerusalem

The Trusteeship Council had been charged by the General Assembly specifically to prepare a statute for an internationalized Jerusalem in terms of resolution 181 (II) and its efforts were directed to this end.

The Council had prepared, in April 1948, a draft statute for the internationalization of Jerusalem,[18] but the actuality of the situation had made impossible any consideration of the implementation of the Council's proposals. In December 1949 the Geneal Assembly, referring to its two previous major resolutions, reiterated the principle of the internationalization of Jerusalem and requested the Trusteeship Council to finalize a statute, specifying that the Council "shall not allow any actions taken by any interested government or governments to divert it from adopting and implementing the statute of Jerusalem".[19] Israel, by then a United Nations member, voted

---

[16] *Ibid.*, pp. 10-11. The detailed instrument appears in document A/973.
[17] Document A/973 Add.I.
[18] Document T/118/Rev.2 of 31 April 1948.
[19] General Assembly resolution 303 (IV) of 4 December 1949.

against this resolution, its assurances regarding the principle of internationalization notwithstanding.

The Trusteeship Council invited views from Israel and Jordan, which were summarized as follows:

> The representative of the Hashemite Kingdom of Jordan stated that his Government desired to reiterate . . . that it would not discuss any plan for the internationalization of Jerusalem. The representative of Israel stated that, while opposed to the internationalization of the Jerusalem area proposed in the draft Statute, his Government remained willing to accept the principle of direct United Nations responsibility for the Holy Places, to participate in discussions on the form and content of a Statute for the Holy Places, and to accept binding declarations or agreements ensuring religious freedom and full liberty for the pursuit of religious education and the protection of religious institutions.[20]

On 4 April 1950 the Council approved a statute[21] still conforming to the territorial internationalization plan of the partition resolution of 29 November 1947. Jordan, still not a United Nations Member, refused further comment and Israel maintained that, in the changed circumstances since that resolution, it would accept an international régime only for the Holy Places within the Walled City and its immediate environs.[22]

Faced with this situation the Trusteeship Council's proposals lapsed for all practical purposes.

VIII. The interregnum in Jerusalem, 1950-1967

By 1950 certain features of the Palestine issue directly affecting the question of the status of Jerusalem were clear.

The General Assembly had reaffirmed the principle of the maintenance of "existing rights" and of an internationalized *corpus separatum* status for Jerusalem, despite its *de facto* division between Israeli occupation and Jordan. The ultimate determination of the status of the city was unaffected by the Israel-Jordan armistice agreement of 1949. The change in the position of the Arab States (in the CCP talks) to accept the internationalization of Jerusalem had little effect on Israel's determination to hold its territorial gains in the city. These developments combined to prolong the partition of Jerusalem.

After Israel declared Jerusalem its capital, the Old City being part of the West Bank was united with Jordan in accordance with the Act of Unity of 24 April 1950. However, the Jordanian legislation indicated that this move

[20] *Official Records of the General Assembly, Fifth Session, Supplement No. 9* (A/1286: Question of an international régime for the Jerusalem area and protection of the Holy Places) p. 2.
[21] *Ibid.*, p. 19.
[22] *Ibid.*, pp. 2, 32-33.

did not prejudice the final settlement of the Palestine issue.[23] In 1955 Jordan became a Member of the United Nations.

The division of Jerusalem from 1950 to 1967 between two hostile States, in place of the internationalization called for by the General Assembly, brought certain consequences.

The armistice agreement between Israel and Jordan included the principle of free access to the Holy Places, for which detailed arrangements were to be finalized by a special committee. The Arab Governments issued the following statement:

> The Governments of Egypt, the Hashemite Kingdom of Jordan, Lebanon and Syria undertake to guarantee freedom of access to the Holy Places, to religious buildings and sites situated in the territory placed under their authority by the final settlement of the Palestine problem, or pending that settlement, in the territory at present occupied by them under Armistice Agreements, and pursuant to this undertaking will guarantee rights of entry and of transit to ministers of religion, pilgrims and visitors, without distinction as to nationality or faith, subject only to considerations of national security, all the above in conformity with the *status quo* prior to 14 May 1948.[24]

However, in the discussions conducted by the Conciliation Commission for Palestine, territorial questions became directly linked with the question of the return of refugees, and the failure to resolve one led to the inability to resolve the other. The CCP's efforts to mediate the impasse were fruitless.

As the division of Jerusalem became protracted, and its two parts became progressively more integrated into two hostile countries, the political barriers consolidated. The psychological rift also deepened as an essentially Arab society continued its traditions in East Jerusalem, while West Jerusalem progressively became more Europeanized.

United Nations efforts to secure the internationalization of Jerusalem faded after 1950, and the international acquiescence in the *status quo* of a divided Jerusalem was ended by the Israeli occupation of East Jerusalem in 1967. (See map at annex IV.)

IX. The effects of the 1967 war on the status of Jerusalem

Israel's occupation of East Jerusalem in June 1967, brought serious repercussions for the status of Jerusalem. With West Jerusalem already declared by Israel as its capital, Israeli actions immediately following Israel's military success were a clear indication of the Israeli intention, presumably pre-planned, to hold the entire city. For instance when Israeli forces con-

---

[23] *New York Times*, 25 April 1950.
[24] Document S/PV.2126, 14 March 1979, pp. 33-35.

solidated their positions in the Old City, a senior military commander declared on 7 June 1967: "The Israeli Defence Forces have liberated Jerusalem. We have reunited the torn city, the capital of Israel. We have returned to this most sacred shrine, never to part from it again."[25]

The immediate extension, through legislative measures, of Israeli jurisdiction to "Eretz Israel" and to the newly occupied parts of the city[26] confirmed this intent of annexation. Possession was further consolidated by more concrete measures, in particular the razing of the historic Maghrabi quarter before the Wailing Wall to construct a plaza.

Israel's failure to respond to United Nations demands to refrain from consolidating its seizure of Jerusalem brought further evidence of Israel's intentions. Israel refused to accept the Security Council's resolution that the Geneva Conventions of 1949 were applicable in areas under military occupation.[27] Israel's refusal to heed two resolutions of the General Assembly specifically directed to the status of Jerusalem left little doubt of Israeli intent of annexation.

Resolution 2253 (ES-V) of 4 July 1967 read:

The General Assembly,

Deeply concerned at the situation prevailing in Jerusalem as a result of the measures taken by Israel to change the status of the City,

1. Considers that these measures are invalid;

2. Calls upon Israel to rescind all measures already taken and to desist forthwith from taking any action which would alter the status of Jerusalem.

Resolution 2254 (ES-V) of 14 July 1967 read:

The General Assembly,

. . .

Taking note with the deepest regret and concern of the non-compliance by Israel with resolution 2253 (ES-V),

1. Deplores the failure of Israel to implement General Assembly resolution 2253 (ES-V);

2. Reiterates its call to Israel in that resolution to rescind all measures already taken and to desist forthwith from taking any action which would alter the status of Jerusalem;

3. Requests the Secretary-General to report to the Security Council and the General Assembly on the situation and on the implementation of the present resolution.

The references in these resolutions to "the status of Jerusalem" could mean only the status defined in the fundamental General Assembly resolu-

[25] General Dayan. *Facts on File*, vol. XXVII, 7 June 1967.

[26] The Law and Administration Ordinance (Amendment No. 11) Law, 5727-1967 and the Municipalities Ordinance (Amendment No. 6) Law 5727.

[27] Security Council resolution 237 (1967) of 14 June 1967.

tion on the partition of Palestine, i.e., a *corpus separatum* under an international régime.

Both resolutions had received overwhelming support, with no dissent,[28] but were ignored by Israel, which moved its Supreme Court to East Jerusalem, among other measures to extend Israeli law to the newly occupied territories.

The Secretary-General's report was based on information gathered by his Personal Representative in Jerusalem, Ambassador Thalmann of Switzerland, whose terms of reference were limited only to obtaining information. Excerpts from the report presented in September 1967 describe Israeli aims:

> 33. In the numerous conversations which the Personal Representative had with Israel leaders, including the Prime Minister and the Minister for Foreign Affairs, it was made clear beyond any doubt that Israel was taking every step to place under its sovereignty those parts of the city which were not controlled by Israel before June 1967. The statutory bases for this had already been created, and the administrative authorities had started to apply Israel laws and regulations in those parts of the city . . .
>
> 35. The Israel authorities stated unequivocally that the process of integration was irreversible and not negotiable.[29]

X. Security Council actions in relation to Jerusalem

The Security Council also censured Israel and called for the rescinding of all measures taken that affected the status of Jerusalem. Resolution 242 (1967) emphasized the inadmissibility of acquisition of territory by force and called for the withdrawal of Israeli forces from territories occupied during the June 1967 conflict. Both elements were directly applicable to the situation in Jerusalem and might suggest that withdrawal by Israel to the June 1967 lines in Jerusalem would comply with the Council's requirements. But in addition, the Security Council further passed a number of resolutions specifically directed to the status of Jerusalem. Resolution 252 (1968) of 21 May 1968 reads, in part:

> The Security Council,
> Recalling General Assembly resolutions 2253 (ES-V) of 4 July 1967 and 2254 (ES-V) of 14 July 1967,
> . . .
> Noting that since the adoption of the above-mentioned resolutions Israel has taken further measures and actions in contravention of those resolutions,

---

[28] Resolution 2253 (ES-V): 99 votes in favour, 0 against, 20 abstentions; resolution 2254 (ES-V): 99 votes in favour, 0 against, 18 abstentions.

[29] Document S/8146, 12 September 1967, (Report of the Secretary-General under General Assembly resolution 2254 (ES-V) relating to Jerusalem), paras. 26, 27, 28, 33, 35.

Bearing in mind the need to work for a just and lasting peace,

Reaffirming that acquisition of territory by military conquest is inadmissible,

1. Deplores the failure of Israel to comply with the General Assembly and resolutions mentioned above;

2. Considers that all legislative and administrative measures and actions taken by Israel, including expropriation of land and properties thereon, which tend to change the legal status of Jerusalem are invalid and cannot change that status;

3. Urgently calls upon Israel to rescind all such measures already taken and desist forthwith from taking any further action which tends to change the status of Jerusalem;.

Resolution 267 (1969) of 3 July 1969 reads:

The Security Council,

Noting that since the adoption of the above-mentioned resolutions Israel has taken further measures tending to change the status of the City of Jerusalem,

Reaffirming the established principle that acquisition of territory by military conquest is inadmissible,

1. Reaffirms its resolution 252 (1968);

2. Deplores the failure of Israel to show any regard to the resolutions of the General Assembly and the Security Council mentioned above;

3. Censures in the strongest terms all measures taken to change the status of the City of Jerusalem;

4. Confirms that all legislative and administrative measures and actions taken by Israel which purport to alter the status of Jerusalem, including expropriation of land and properties thereon, are invalid and cannot change that status;

5. Urgently calls once more upon Israel to rescind forthwith all measures taken by it which may tend to change the status of the City of Jerusalem, and in future to refrain from all actions likely to have such an effect;

6. Requests Israel to inform the Security Council without any further delay of its intentions with regard to the implementation of the provisions of the present resolution;

. . . .

These references to "the legal status of Jerusalem" by the Security Council again could mean only the status of the internationalized *corpus separatum* defined in the partition resolution, thus maintaining the validity of this status.

Following the outbreak of a major fire in August 1969, evidently by arson, in the Al-Aqsa Mosque, one of the holiest places in Islam, the Security Council took the strong step of condemning Israel for flouting United

Nations resolutions on Jerusalem. Resolution 271 (1969) of 15 September 1969 reads:

> The Security Council,
>
> Grieved at the extensive damage caused by arson to the Holy Al-Aqsa Mosque in Jerusalem on 21 August 1969 under the military occupation of Israel,
>
> Mindful of the consequent loss to human culture,
>
> Having heard the statements made before the Council reflecting the universal outrage caused by the act of sacrilege in one of the most venerated shrines of mankind,
>
> Recalling its resolutions . . . and the earlier General Assembly resolutions . . . concerning measures and actions by Israel affecting the status of the City of Jerusalem,
>
> Reaffirming the established principle that acquisition of territory by military conquest is inadmissible,
>
> 1. Reaffirms its resolutions 252 (1968) and 267 (1969);
>
> 2. Recognizes that any act of destruction or profanation of the Holy Places, religious buildings and sites in Jerusalem or any encouragement of, or connivance at, any such act may seriously endanger international peace and security;
>
> 3. Determines that the execrable act of desecration and profanation of the Holy Al-Aqsa Mosque emphasizes the immediate necessity of Israel's desisting from acting in violation of the aforesaid resolutions and rescinding forthwith all measures and actions taken by it designed to alter the status of Jerusalem;
>
> 4. Calls upon Israel scrupulously to observe the provisions of the Geneva Conventions and international law governing military occupation and to refrain from causing any hindrance to the discharge of the established functions of the Supreme Moslem Council of Jerusalem, including any co-operation that Council may desire from countries with predominantly Moslem population and from Moslem communities in relation to its plans for the maintenance and repair of the Islamic Holy Places in Jerusalem;
>
> 5. Condemns the failure of Israel to comply with the aforementioned resolutions and calls upon it to implement forthwith the provisions of these resolutions . . .

Yet another Security Council resolution reaffirmed the earlier resolutions on the status of Jerusalem, and declared Israeli actions and legislation in respect of Jerusalem "totally invalid". Resolution 298 (1971) of 25 September 1971 reads in part:

> The Security Council,
>
> Recalling its resolutions . . . and the earlier General Assembly resolutions concerning measures and action by Israel designed to change the status of the Israeli-occupied section of Jerusalem,

Having considered the letter of the Permanent Representative of Jordan on the situation in Jerusalem and the reports of the Secretary-General, and having heard the statements of the parties concerned on the question,

Reaffirming the principle that acquisition of territory by military conquest is inadmissible,

Noting with concern the non-compliance by Israel with the above-mentioned meetings,

Noting with concern also that since the adoption of the above-mentioned resolutions Israel has taken further measures designed to change the status and character of the occupied section of Jerusalem;

1. Reaffirms its resolutions 252 (1968) and 267 (1969);

2. Deplores the failure of Israel to respect the previous resolutions adopted by the United Nations concerning measures and actions by Israel purporting to affect the status of the City of Jerusalem;

3. Confirms in the clearest possible terms that all legislative and administrative actions taken by Israel to change the status of the City of Jerusalem, including expropriation of land and properties, transfer of population and legislation aimed at the incorporation of the occupied section, are totally invalid and cannot change that status;

4. Urgently calls upon Israel to rescind all previous measures and actions and to take no further steps in the occupied section of Jerusalem which may purport to change the status of the City or which would prejudice the rights of the inhabitants and the interests of the international community, or a just and lasting peace.

The sweeping language of this resolution appears to confirm an intent to maintain the status of Jerusalem as a *corpus separatum*.

Israel's official reaction to this resolution clearly reflected its intentions regarding the status of Jerusalem:

> The Government of Israel considers that there was no justification whatever for raising the issue of Jerusalem in the Security Council, nor for the resolution adopted. The Government of Israel will not enter into any discussion with any political organ on the basis of this resolution. Israel's policy on Jerusalem will remain unchanged. Israel will continue to ensure the development of the city for the benefit of all its inhabitants, the respect of the religious rights of all communities, and the scrupulous protection of the Holy Places of all faiths and the freedom of access to them. This policy has contributed to the development of fruitful relations between all sections of the population.[30]

Bearing in mind the specific status of Jerusalem and the need for protection and preservation of the unique and spiritual dimension of the Holy Places in Jerusalem, in June 1980, in reaction to proposed legislative action taken by Israel to make a united Jerusalem its capital, the Security Council

[30] Government of Israel: press release of 28 September 1971.

considered the status of Jerusalem and adopted resolution 476 (1980), by which the Security Council deplored the persistence of Israel, in changing the physical character, demographic composition, institutional structure and the status of the Holy City. The Security Council was gravely concerned at the legislative steps initiated in the Israeli Knesset with the aim of changing the character and the status of Jerusalem. Operative paragraphs of the resolution read as follows:

The Security Council,

1. Reaffirms the overriding necessity to end the prolonged occupation of Arab territories occupied by Israel since 1967, including Jerusalem;

2. Strongly deplores the continued refusal of Israel, the occupying Power, to comply with the relevant resolutions of the Security Council and the General Assembly;

3. Reconfirms that all legislative and administrative measures and actions taken by Israel, the occupying Power, which purport to alter the character and status of the Holy City of Jerusalem have no legal validity and constitute a flagrant violation of the Fourth Geneva Convention relative to the Protection of Civilian Persons in Time of War and also constitute a serious obstruction to achieving a comprehensive, just and lasting peace in the Middle East;

4. Reiterates that all such measures which have altered the geographic, demographic and historical character and status of the Holy City of Jerusalem are null and void and must be rescinded in compliance with the relevant resolutions of the Security Council;

5. Urgently calls on Israel, the occupying Power, to abide by this and previous Security Council resolutions and to desist forthwith from persisting in the policy and measures affecting the character and status of the Holy City of Jerusalem;

6. Reaffirms its determination in the event of non-compliance by Israel with this resolution, to examine practical ways and means in accordance with relevant provisions of the Charter of the United Nations to secure the full implementation of this resolution.

After the enactment of the "Basic Law" by Israel, the Security Council adopted resolution 478 (1980). In this resolution, the Security Council called upon those States that had established diplomatic missions in Jerusalem to withdraw their missions from the Holy City. As a result, 13 countries withdrew their missions from Jerusalem.

Resolution 478 (1980) reads in part:

The Security Council,

Recalling its resolution 476 (1980),

Reaffirming again that the acquisition of territory by force is inadmissible,

Deeply concerned over the enactment of a "basic law" in the Israeli

Knesset proclaiming a change in the character and status of the Holy
City of Jerusalem, with its implications for peace and security,

Noting that Israel has not complied with resolution 476 (1980),

Reaffirming its determination to examine practical ways and means,
in accordance with the relevant provisions of the Charter of the United
Nations, to secure the full implementation of its resolution 476 (1980),
in the event of non-compliance by Israel,

1. Censures in the strongest terms the enactment by Israel of the "basic law" on Jerusalem and the refusal to comply with relevant Security
Council resolutions;

2. Affirms that the enactment of the "basic law" by Israel constitutes
a violation of international law and does not affect the continued application of the Geneva Convention relative to the Protection of Civilian
Persons in Time of War, of 12 August 1949, in the Palestinian and
other Arab territories occupied since June 1967, including Jerusalem;

3. Determines that all legislative and administrative measures and actions taken by Israel, the occupying Power, which have altered or purport to alter the character and status of the Holy City of Jerusalem, and
in particular the recent "basic law" on Jerusalem, are null and void and
must be rescinded forthwith;

4. Affirms also that this action constitutes a serious obstruction to
achieving a comprehensive, just and lasting peace in the Middle East;

5. Decides not to recognize the "basic law" and such other actions by
Israel that, as a result of this law, seek to alter the character and status
of Jerusalem and calls upon:

(a) All Member States to accept this decision;

(b) Those States that have established diplomatic missions at Jerusalem to withdraw such missions from the Holy City;.

United Nations resolutions since 1969, emanating mainly from the General Assembly, have been in terms dealing wtih the wider Middle East situation arising out of the continued Israeli occupation of Arab territories since
June 1967,[31] basing themselves on provisions of Security Council resolution
242 (1967).

The mission of the Secretary-General's Special Representative, appointed
in compliance with Security Council resolution 242 (1967) to negotiate a
Middle East agreement, was deeply concerned with the status of Jerusalem
as one of the most fundamental questions in the Middle East dispute, and
its failure left the issue unresolved.

[31] These include Security Council resolution 338 (1973) of 22 October 1973 and the
following General Assembly resolutions: 2628 (XXV) of 7 December 1970, 2799 (XXVI)
of 13 December 1971, 2949 (XXVII) of 8 December 1972, 3414 (XXX) of 5 December
1975, 31/61 of 9 December 1976, 32/20 of 25 November 1977, 33/29 of 7 November 1978.
The status of the inhabitants of East Jerusalem is also referred to in the General Assembly
resolutions since 1970 approving the reports of the Special Committee to Investigate Israeli Practices Affecting the Human Rights of the Population of the Occupied Territories.

In resolution 35/169 E, of 15 December 1980, the General Assembly also censured in the strongest terms the enactment by Israel of the "Basic Law" on Jerusalem which constituted a violation of International Law and did not affect the continued application of the Geneva Convention of 1949 in the Palestinian and other Arab territories occupied since June 1967, including Jerusalem. The General Assembly further determined that all legislative and administrative measures and actions taken by Israel, which altered or purported to alter the character and status of Jerusalem, particularly the "Basic Law" and the proclamation of Jerusalem as the capital of Israel, were null and void and must be rescinded forthwith.

The operative paragraphs of resolution 35/169 E read:

The General Assembly,

1. Censures in the strongest terms the enactment by Israel of the "Basic Law" on Jerusalem;

2. Affirms that the enactment of the "Basic Law" by Israel constitutes a violation of international law and does not affect the continued application of the Geneva Convention relative to the Protection of Civilian Persons in Time of War, of 12 August 1949, in the Palestinian and other Arab territories occupied since June 1967, including Jerusalem;

3. Determines that all legislative and administrative measures and actions taken by Israel, the occupying Power, which have altered or purport to alter the character and status of the Holy City of Jerusalem, and, in particular, the recent "Basic Law" on Jerusalem and the proclamation of Jerusalem as the capital of Israel, are null and void and must be rescinded forthwith;

4. Affirms also that this action constitutes a serious obstruction to achieving a comprehensive, just and lasting peace in the Middle East;

5. Decides not to recognize that "Basic Law" and such other actions by Israel that, as a result of this law, seek to alter the character and status of Jerusalem and calls upon all States, specialized agencies and other international organizations to comply with the present resolution and other relevant resolutions and urges them not to conduct any business which is not in conformity with the provisions of the present resolution and the other relevant resolutions.

In resolution 36/120 E of 10 December 1981, the General Assembly deplored the persistence of Israel in changing the physical character, the demographic composition, the institutional structure and the status of the Holy City of Jerusalem. It determined once again that all legislative and administrative measures and actions taken by Israel, which have altered or purport to alter the character and status of the Holy City of Jerusalem, and, in particular, the so-called "Basic Law" and the proclamation of Jerusalem as the capital of Israel, were null and void and must be rescinded forthwith.

Despite the fact that the United Nations had condemned these actions and declared such actions null and void, Israel has persisted in its policy of establishing settlements in the occupied Palestinian and other Arab territories, including Jerusalem. It annexed the Holy City, and has proceeded with the enlargement of the municipal boundaries of the Holy City by the incorporation of considerable areas of land. By the end of 1982 Israel, in pursuance of the construction of settlements, has established 26 such settlements in the areas bounded by the city/district of Jerusalem. Moreover, hundreds of buildings have been expropriated thus rendering homeless at least 6,500 inhabitants.

Since 1967, Israelis have committed various acts of desecration against both Muslim and Christian Holy Places.

For example, Israeli attacks on the Haram Al-Sherif of the Al-Aqsa Mosque and the Dome of the Rock also began during the latter part of 1967, by early 1968 excavation work around the Al-Aqsa Mosque from the West and South, which, as a result of the extension of the excavations through a tunnel, penetrated underneath the Mosque and later by attempts of infiltration, on the pretext of holding prayers in the Mosque while the real purpose has been to impose the Jewish fait accompli on the Haram Al-Sherif. Assaults have also been carried out by setting fire to the Mosque on 21 August 1969 and through armed intrusion in April 1982 and the attempt to blow up the Mosque in March 1983.

XI. Jerusalem and the rights of the Palestinian people

A development of fundamental importance during this period has been the recognition and endorsement by the General Assembly of the inalienable rights of self-determination, national independence and sovereignty of the Palestinian people. Thus any Middle East settlement necessarily would have to take into account the General Assembly's call for the establishment in the West Bank and Gaza of a Palestinian national entity. An integral part of any such settlement would involve agreement on the status of Jerusalem.

The Committee on the Exercise of the Inalienable Rights of the Palestinian People in 1976 considered the question of the status of Jerusalem. In its report, it stated:

> The members of the Committee stressed the special significance of the city of Jerusalem and its holy shrines to three major religions of the world—Islam, Judaism and Christianity. The international status of the city of Jerusalem, as provided for in General Assembly resolution 181 (II), was recalled.
>
> A suggestion was made that the administration of the city of Jerusalem should consist of two main organs: (a) a 45-member legislative body in which the three main religious communities of the city would be equally represented; (b) an executive organ led by a United Nations commissioner appointed by the Secretary-General with the consent of the Security Council.

Several delegations were of the view that the question of the city of Jerusalem was beyond the mandate of the Committee. According to one view, during the first phase of the proposed programmes of implementation of the inalienable rights of the Palestinian people, Jerusalem should be restored to the situation which had prevailed before the war of June 1967. Its future status could be considered after the establishment of an independent Palestinian entity.

It was felt in the Committee that any solution of the delicate problem of Jerusalem should be sought within the framework of the inalienable rights of the Palestinian people and the religious characteristics of the city . . .[32]

The Committee thus appears to take the view that the question of the future status of Jerusalem would have to be approached in the framework of an overall Middle East settlement, in which the establishment of an independent Palestinian entity would be a central element.

XII. Conclusions

The foregoing survey of the course of the question of the internationalization of Jerusalem in the United Nations leads to the following conclusions regarding the principal elements of the present state of the issue.

(a) During the period 1950-1967, despite the international acquiescence in the division of the City of Jerusalem, the General Assembly continued to uphold the principle of the internationalization of Jerusalem as a *corpus separatum* in terms of its resolutions 181 (II) and 194 (III).

(b) The resolutions of the General Assembly and Security Council in relation to Jerusalem following the occupation of the entire city of Jerusalem by Israel in June 1967 also maintained this original principle of internationalization. Further, they required Israel to withdraw from territories occupied during the conflict, and to rescind all measures taken, as well as to refrain from taking further measures, to alter the status of Jerusalem. Thus, it would appear that the United Nations since 1947 has maintained the principle that the legal status of Jerusalem is that of a *corpus separatum* under an international régime.

(c) Israel's rejection of these resolutions, which have declared its actions and legislation in Jerusalem invalid and illegal, in no way deprives the resolutions of their own validity.

(d) Israel's actions and legislation have not been acquiesced in by the majority of the international community. This was reflected in the action of 13 countries, who withdrew their missions from Jerusalem following the adoption of resolution 478 (1980).

(e) The question of the status of Jerusalem can be finally resolved only in

---

[32] United Nations: *Official Records of the General Assembly, Thirty-first Session, Supplement No. 35* (A/31/35) p. 8.

the context of a general Middle East settlement, which would need to take into account the General Assembly's resolutions on the rights of the Palestinian people.

These factors, *inter alia*, would be of importance in the resolution of the status of the City of Jerusalem and of the Holy Places.

ANNEX I

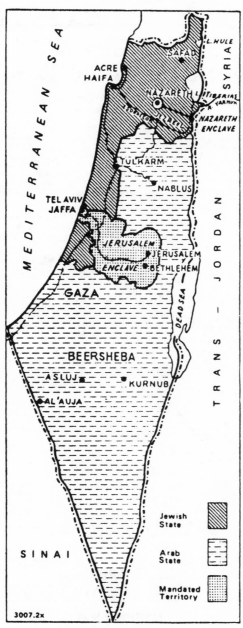

PALESTINE PARTITION PLAN - 1937

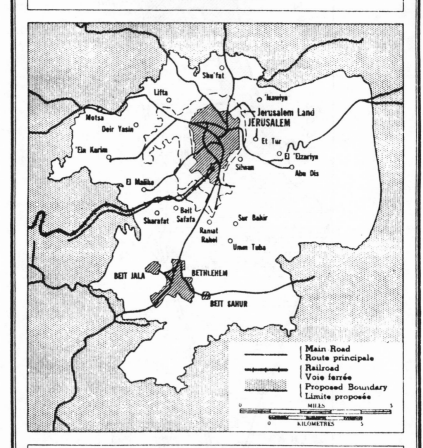

CITY OF JERUSALEM
BOUNDARIES PROPOSED
**BY THE AD HOC COMMITTEE
ON THE PALESTINIAN QUESTION**

VILLE DE JERUSALEM
LIMITES PROPOSEES
**PAR LA COMMISSION AD HOC
CHARGEE DE LA QUESTION PALESTINIENNE**

JERUSALEM – LINES BEFORE HOSTILITIES OF JUNE 1967

JERUSALEM - LINES BEFORE HOSTILITIES OF JUNE 1967

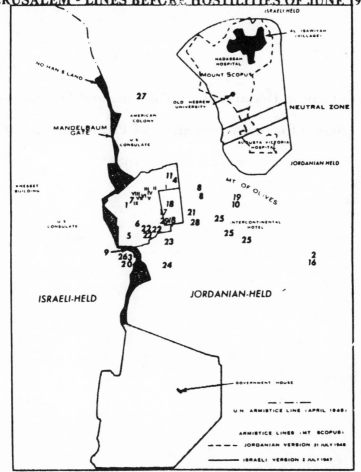

CHRISTIAN	MUSLIM	JEWISH
1 BASILICA OF THE HOLY SEPULCHRE		
2 BETHANY		
3 CENACLE		
4 CHURCH OF ST ANNE		
5 CHURCH OF ST JAMES THE GREAT		
6 CHURCH OF ST MARK		
7 DEIR AL SULTAN		
8 TOMB OF THE VIRGIN AND GARDEN OF GETHSEMANE		21 TOMB OF DAVID NEBI DAOUD
9 HOUSE OF CAIPHAS AND PRISON OF CHRIST		21 TOMB OF ABSALOM
10 SANCTUARY OF THE ASCENSION AND MOUNT OF OLIVES		22 ANCIENT AND MODERN SYNAGOGUES
11 POOL OF BETHESDA		23 BATH OF RABBI ISHMAEL
12 EIN KARIM		24 BROOK SILOAM
13 BASILICA OF THE NATIVITY BETHLEHEM		25 CEMETARY ON MOUNT OF OLIVES
14 MILK GROTTO BETHLEHEM	16 TOMB OF LAZARUS	26 TOMB OF DAVID
15 SHEPHERDS FIELD BETHLEHEM	17 EL BURAK ESH SHARIF	27 TOMB OF SIMON THE JUST
1 TO IX INCLUSIVE	18 HAREM AL SHARIF MOSQUE OF UMAR AND MOSQUE OF ASKAI	28 TOMB OF ZACHARIAH AND OTHER TOMBS N KIDRON VALLEY
STATIONS OF THE CROSS	19 MOSQUE OF THE ASCENSION	29 WAILING WALL
		30 RACHAEL S TOMB

* HOLY PLACE TO WHICH THE STATUS QUO APPLIES
** HOLY PLACES IN INTERNATIONAL AREA OF JERUSALEM NOT SHOWN ON THIS MAP

321. Geneva Declaration on Palestine and Programme of

Action for the Achievement of Palestinian Rights,

September 16, 1983*

* Report to the U.N. International Conference on the Question of Palestine, Geneva, U.N. Doc. A/Conf. 114/41.

A. *Geneva Declaration on Palestine*

In pursuance of General Assembly resolutions 36/120 C of 10 December 1981, ES-7/7 of 19 August 1982 and 37/86 C of 10 December 1982, an International Conference on the Question of Palestine was convened at the United Nations office at Geneva from 29 August to 7 September 1983 to seek effective ways and means to enable the Palestinian people to attain and to exercise their inalienable rights. The Conference was opened by the Secretary-General of the United Nations, Javier Pérez de Cuéllar and presided over by the Minister of Foreign Affairs of Senegal, Moustapha Niassé.

1. The Conference, having thoroughly considered the question of Palestine in all its aspects, expresses the grave concern of all nations and peoples regarding the international tension that has persisted for several decades in the Middle East, the principal cause of which is the denial by Israel, and those supporting its expansionist policies, of the inalienable legitimate rights of the Palestinian people. The Conference reaffirms and stresses that a just solution of the question of Palestine, the core of the problem, is the crucial element in a comprehensive, just and lasting political settlement in the Middle East.

2. The Conference recognizes that, as one of the most acute and complex problems of our time, the question of Palestine—inherited by the United Nations at the time of its establishment - requires a comprehensive, just and lasting political settlement. This settlement must be based on the implementation of the relevant United Nations resolutions concerning the question of Palestine and the attainment of the legitimate, inalienable rights of the Palestinian people, including the right to self-determination and the right to the establishment of its own independent state in Palestine and should also be based on the provision by the Security Council of guarantees for peace and security among all States in the region, inclusing [*sic*] the independent Palestinian State, within secure and internationally recognized boundaries. The Conference is convinced that the attainment by the Palestinian people of their inalienable rights, as defined by General Assembly resolution 3236 (XXIX) of 22 November 1974, will contribute substantially to the achievement of peace and stability in the Middle East.

3. The Conference considers the role of the United Nations in the achievement of a comprehensive, just and lasting peace in the Middle East to be essential and paramount. It emphasizes the need for respect for, and application of the provisions of the Charter of the United Nations, the resolutions of the United Nations relevant to the question of Palestine and the observance of the principles of international law.

4. The Conference considers that the various proposals, consistent with the principles of international law, which have been presented on this question, such as the Arab peace plan adopted unanimously at the Twelfth Arab Summit Conference held at Fez, Morocco, in September 1982, should serve

as guidelines for concerted international effort to resolve the question of Palestine. These guidelines include the following:

(a) The attainment by the Palestinian people of its legitimate inalienable rights, including the right to return, the right to self-determination and the right to establish its own independent state in Palestine;

(b) The right of the Palestine Liberation Organization, the representative of the Palestinian people, to participate on an equal footing with other parties in all efforts, deliberations and conferences on the Middle East;

(c) The need to put an end to Israel's occupation of the Arab territories, in accordance with the principle of the inadmissibility of the acquisition of territory by force, and, consequently, the need to secure Israeli withdrawal from the territories occupied since 1967, including Jerusalem;

(d) The need to oppose and reject such Israeli policies and practices in the occupied territories, including Jerusalem, and any *de facto* situation created by Israel as are contrary to international law and relevant United Nations resolutions, particularly the establishment of settlements, as these policies and practices constitute major obstacles to the achievement of peace in the Middle East;

(e) The need to reaffirm as null and void all legislative and administrative measures and actions taken by Israel, the occupying Power, which have altered or purported to alter the character and status of the Holy City of Jerusalem, including the expropriation of land and property situated thereon, and in particular the so-called "Basic Law" on Jerusalem and the proclamation of Jerusalem as the capital of Israel;

(f) The right of all States in the region to existence within secure and internationally recognized boundaries, with justice and security for all the people, the *sine qua non* of which is the recognition and attainment of the legitimate, inalienable rights of the Palestinian people as stated in paragraph (a) above.

5. In order to give effect to these guidelines, the Conference considers it essential that an international peace conference on the Middle East be convened on the basis of the principles of the Charter of the United Nations and the relevant resolutions of the United Nations, with the aim of achieving a comprehensive, just and lasting solution to the Arab-Israeli conflict, an essential element of which would be the establishment of an independent Palestinian State in Palestine. This peace conference should be convened under the auspices of the United Nations, with the participation of all parties to the Arab-Israeli conflict, including the Palestine Liberation Organization, as well as the United States of America, the Union of Soviet Socialist Republics, and other concerned States, on an equal footing. In this context the Security Council has a primary responsibility to create appropriate institutional arrangements on the basis of relevant United Nations resolutions in order to guarantee and to carry out the accords of the International Peace Conference.

6. The International Conference on the Question of Palestine emphasizes

the importance of the time factor in achieving a just solution to the problem of Palestine. The Conference is convinced that partial solutions are inadequate and delays in seeking a comprehensive solution do not eliminate tensions in the region.

B. Programme of Action for the Achievement of Palestinian Rights

The International Conference on the Question of Palestine agreed that no effort should be spared to seek effective ways and means to enable the Palestinian people to attain and exercise their rights in Palestine in accordance with the Charter of the United Nations, the Universal Declaration of Human Rights[1] and the principles of international law. The Conference, taking into consideration the Geneva Declaration on Palestine (sect. A above), recommended the following Programme of Action.

I

The International Conference on the Question of Palestine recommends that all States, individually or collectively, consistent with their respective constitutions and their obligations under the Charter of the United Nations and in conformity with the principles of international law:

1. Recognize the great importance of the time factor in solving the question of Palestine;

2. Intensify efforts for the establishment of an independent Palestinian State within the framework of a comprehensive, just and lasting settlement to the Arab-Israeli conflict in accordance with the Charter of the United Nations, the relevant United Nations resolutions and the guidelines of the Geneva Declaration on Palestine;

3. Consider the continued presence of Israel in the occupied Palestinian and other Arab territories, including Jerusalem, as exacerbating instability in the region and endangering international peace and security;

4. Oppose and reject, as a serious and continuing obstacle to peace, the expansionist policies pursued by Israel in the Palestinian and other Arab territories occupied since 1967, including Jerusalem, and in particular the alteration of those territories and all the measures taken in violation of the Geneva Convention relative to the Treatment of Prisoners of War[2] and the Geneva Convention relative to the Protection of Civilian Persons in Time of War,[3] both of 12 August 1949, and of the Hague Regulations of 1907,[4] such as the establishment and expansion of settlements, the transfer of Israeli civilians into those territories and the individual and mass transfers therefrom of the Arab Palestinian population;

[1] General Assembly resolution 217 A (III).

[2] United Nations, *Treaty Series*, vol. 75, No. 972, p. 135.

[3] *Ibid.*, No. 973, p. 187.

[4] Carnegie Endowment for International Peace, *The Hague Conventions and Declarations of 1899 and 1907* (New York, Oxford University Press), 1915, p. 100.

5. Refrain from providing Israel with assistance of such a nature as to encourage it militarily, economically and financially to continue its aggression, occupation and disregard of its obligations under the Charter and the relevant resolutions of the United Nations;

6. Not encourage migration to the occupied Arab territories until Israel has put a definitive end to the implementation of its illegal policy of establishing settlements in the Palestinian and other Arab territories occupied since 1967;

7. Fully comply with the relevant resolutions of the United Nations and its specialized agencies on the Holy City of Jerusalem, including those which reject Israel's annexation of Jerusalem and its declaration of that city as its capital;

8. Undertake universal efforts to protect the Holy Places and urge Israel to take measures to prevent their desecration;

9. Consider ways and means of meeting the threat that Israel poses to the regional security in Africa in view of Israel's disregard of United Nations resolutions, and its close collaboration with the *apartheid* régime in the economic, military and nuclear fields, thereby contributing to the continued illegal occupation of Namibia and enhancing the régime's repressive and aggressive capacity;

10. Encourage, through bilateral and multilateral contacts, all States, including Western European and North American States which have not done so, to welcome all peace initiatives based on the recognition of the inalienable rights of the Palestinian people, which were also welcomed by Chairman Yasser Arafat in his address to the International Conference on the Question of Palestine;

11. Seek and develop ways and means to enable the Palestinian people to exercise sovereignty over their national resources;

12. Express concern that Israel debars Palestinians from economic activity and access to national resources on Palestinian teritory [*sic*], in consistent violation of General Assembly resolutions on the right of the Palestinians to permanent sovereignty over their national resources;

13. Declare null and void, and counter such measures and practices applied by Israel in the occupied Palestinian and other Arab territories, including Jerusalem, as the annexation and the expropriation of land, water resources, and property and the alteration of the demographic, geographic, historical and cultural features thereof;

14. Undertake measures to alleviate the economic and social burdens borne by the Palestinian people as a result of the continued Israeli occupation of their territories since 1967;

15. Consider contributing or increasing special contributions to the proposed budgets, programmes and projects of the relevant organs, funds and agencies of the United Nations system that have been requested to provide humanitarian, economic and social assistance to the Palestinian people, with particular reference to:

(a) General Assembly resolution 33/147 of 20 December 1978, and the appeal of the Governing Council of the United Nations Development Programme at its thirtieth session, for additional special contributions amounting to at least $8 million during the third programming cycle (1982-1986) aimed at helping to meet the economic and social needs of the Palestinian people;[5]

(b) The proposed programme budget of the United Nations Conference on Trade and Development (UNCTAD) for the biennium 1984/1985 regarding the establishment within UNCTAD of a special economic unit, as requested by UNCTAD at its sixth session at Belgrade;

(c) Establishing a special legal aid fund to assist Palestinians in securing their rights under conditions of occupation, in accordance with the Geneva Convention relative to the Protection of Civilian Persons in Time of War;

16. Ensure that the United Nations Relief and Works Agency for Palestine Refugees in the Near East can meet the essential needs of the Palestinians without interruption or any diminution in the effectiveness of its services;

17. Review the situation of Palestinian women in Israeli occupied territories and, in view of their special hardships, urge the Preparatory Committee of the World Conference to Review and Appraise the Achievements of the United Nations Decade for Women, to be held at Nairobi in 1985, to include this item on the agenda of the Conference;

18. Review, if they have not yet done so, in conformity with their national legislation, their economic, cultural, technical and other relations with Israel, and the agreements governing them with the aim of ensuring that these regulations and agreements will not be interpreted or construed as implying in any way recognition of any modification of the legal status of Jerusalem and of the Palestinian and other Arab territories occupied by Israel since 1967, or an acceptance of Israel's illegal presence in those teritories [sic];

19. Recognize that the process of enabling the Palestinian people to exercise its inalienable rights in Palestine is a significant contribution to the restoration of the rule of law in international relations;

20. Assure the observance of the stipulations provided in General Assembly resolution 181 (II) guaranteeing to all persons equal and non-discriminatory rights in civil, political, economic and religious matters and the enjoyment of human rights and fundamentl [sic] freedoms, including freedom of religion, speech, publication, education, assembly and association;

21. Express concern that the laws applicable in the occupied Arab territories have been totally eclipsed by a plethora of military orders that have been designed to establish a new "legal régime" in violation of the Hague

---

[5] See *Official Records of the Economic and Social Council, 1983, Supplement No. 9* (E/1983/20).

Regulations of 1907, and the Geneva Convention relative to the Protection of Civilian Persons in Time of War;

22. Act in accordance with their obligations under existing international law, in particular with regard to the Geneva Conventions of 1949 which require States Parties to respect and to ensure respect for those conventions in all circumstances, and in particular ensure the respect by Israel for the Geneva Conventions of 1949 in the occupied Palestinian and other Arab territories;

23. Express concern that the Palestinians and other Arabs in the occupied territories are deprived of juridical and other kinds of protection, that they are victims of repressive legislation, involving mass arrests, acts of torture, destruction of houses, and the expulsion of people from their homes, acts which constitute flagrant violations of human rights;

24. Recognize the necessity that Palestinian and Lebanese prisoners detained by Israel be accorded the status of prisoners of war in accordance with the Geneva Convention relative to the Treatment of Prisoners of War of 1949,[2] if combatants, or in accordance with the Geneva Convention relative to the Protection of Civilian Persons in Time of War of 1949,[3] if civilians;

25. Strive for the adoption of international measures so that Israel will implement in the West Bank and Gaza the provisions of the Hague Regulations of 1907 and the Geneva Convention relative to the Protection of Civilian Persons, in the light of Security Council resolution 465 (1980);

26. Recognize, if they have not yet done so, the Palestine Liberation Organization as the representative of the Palestinian people and establish with it appropriate relations;

27. Encourage, in conformity with their national legislations, the formation of national committees in support of the Palestinian people;

28. Encourage the observances of 29 November as the International Day of Solicarity [sic] with the Palestinian People, in a most effective and meaningful way;

29. Request the General Assembly at its thirty-eighth session to designate a Year of Palestine, to be observed at the earliest possible time, taking into consideration the factors necessary to ensure its effective preparation for the purpose of galvanizing world-wide public opinion and support for further implementation of the Geneva Declaration on Palestine and the Programme of Action.

II

The International Conference on the Question of Palestine stresses the obligation of all Member States, under the Charter of the United Nations to enable the United Nations through an expanded and more effective role to fulfil its responsibility for achieving a solution to the question of Palestine. To this end:

A

States participating in the Conference invite the Security Council, as the organ with primary responsibility for the maintenance of international peace and security:

1. To suppress continuing and growing acts of agression [*sic*] and other breaches of peace in the Middle East which endanger peace and security in the region and the world as a whole;

2. To take prompt, firm and effective steps and actions to establish an independent sovereign Palestinian State in Palestine through the implementation of the relevant United Nations resolutions, by facilitating the organization of the international peace conference on the Middle East, as called for in paragraph 6 of the Geneva Declaration on Palestine, and by creating in this context the appropriate institutional arrangements on the basis of relevant United Nations resolutions in order to guarantee and carry out the accords of the international peace conference, including the following:

(a) Taking measures consistent with the principle of the inadmissibility of the acquisition of territory by force to ensure Israel's withdrawal from the Palestinian and other Arab territories occupied since 1967, including Jerusalem, within a specific time-table;

(b) Undertaking effective measures to guarantee the safety and security and legal and human rights of the Palestinians in the occupied territories pending the withdrawal of the Israeli forces from the Palestinian and other Arab territories occupied by Israel since 1967, including Jerusalem;

(c) Subjecting those territories, following the withdrawal of Israel, to a short transitional period, under the supervision of the United Nations, during which period the Palestinian people would exercise its right to self-determination;

(d) Facilitating the implementation of the right to return of the Palestinians to their homes and property;

(e) Supervising elections to the constituent assembly of the independent Palestinian State in which all Palestinians shall participate, in the exercise of their right to self-determination;

(f) Providing, if necessary, temporary peace-keeping forces in order to facilitate the implementation of subparagraphs (a)-(e) above.

B

Meanwhile the Security Council is also invited:

1. To take urgent action to bring about an immediate and complete cessation of such Israeli policies in the occupied territories, and in particular, the establishment of settlements as have been determined by the Security Council to have no legal validity and as a serious obstruction to achieving a comprehensive, just and lasting peace in the Middle East;

2. To consider urgently the reports of the Commission established under its resolution 446 (1979) of 22 March 1979, which examined the situation

concerning settlements in the Arab territories occupied since 1967, including Jerusalem, and to reactivate the above-mentioned Commission;

3. To initiate action to terminate Israel's exploitative policies which go against the indigenous economic development of the occupied territories, and to compel Israel to lift its restrictions on water use and well-drilling by Palestinian farmers as well as its diversion of West Bank water resources into the Israeli water grid systems;

4. To keep under its constant attention the actions committed by Israel against the Palestinian people in violation of the stipulations provided for in relevant General Assembly resolutions, in particular the stipulations of resolution 181 (II) of 29 November 1947 guaranteeing to all persons equal and non-discriminatory rights and freedoms;

5. To consider, in the event of Israel's persistent non-compliance with the relevant United Nations resolutions which embody the will of the international community, appropriate measures in accordance with the Charter of the United Nations, to ensure Israel's compliance with these resolutions.

C

1. Taking into account the recommendations of the five regional preparatory meetings of the International Conference on the Question of Palestine[6] and United Nations resolutions concerning economic and social assistance to the Palestinian people, the Secretary-General of the United Nations is requested to convene a meeting of the specialized agencies and other organizations associated with the United Nations, as well as representatives of the Palestine Liberation Organization and of those countries which are hosts to Palestinian refugees, and other potential sources of assistance, to develop a co-ordinated programme of economic and social assistance to the Palestinian people and to ensure its implementation.

2. The meeting should also look into the most effective inter-agency machinery to co-ordinate and sustain and intensify United Nations assistance to the Palestinian people.

D

The dissemination of accurate and comprehensive information worldwide, and the role of non-governmental organizations and institutions, remains of vital importance in heightening awareness of and support for the inalienable rights of the Palestinian people to self-determination and to the establishment of an independent sovereign Palestinian State. To these ends:

1. The Department for Public Information of the United Nations, in full co-operation and constant consultations with the Committee on the Exercise of the Inalienable Rights of the Palestinian People should:

(a) Co-ordinate all information activities of the United Nations system

---

[6] African region, A/CONF.114/1; Latin American region, A/CONF.114/2; Western Asian region, A/CONF.114/3; Asian region, A/CONF.114/4; European region, A/CONF.114/5.

on Palestine through the Joint United Nations Information Committee (JUNIC);

(b) Expand publications and audio and visual coverage of the facts and of developments pertaining to the question of Palestine;

(c) Publish newsletters and articles in its respective publications on Israeli violations of human rights of the Arab inhabitants in the occupied territories and organize fact-finding missions for journalists to the area;

(d) Organize regional encounters for journalists;

(e) Disseminate appropriate information on the results of the International Conference on the Question of Palestine;

2. Relevant organizations of the United Nations systems should organize meetings, symposia and seminars on topics within their terms of reference and relating to specific problems of the Palestinian people by establishing closer liaison with non-governmental organizations, the media and other groups interested in the question of Palestine.

III

The International Conference on the Question of Palestine, convinced of the important role of world-wide public opinion in resolving the Question of Palestine, and in the implementation of the Declaration and Programme of Action, urges and encourages:

1. Intergovernmental and non-governmental organizations to increase awareness by the international community of the economic and social burdens borne by the Palestinian people as a result of the continued Israeli occupation and its negative effects on the economic development of the West Asian region as a whole;

2. Non-governmental organizations and professional and popular associations to intensify their efforts to support the rights of the Palestinian people in every possible way;

3. Organizations such as those of women, teachers, workers, youths and students to undertake exchanges and other programmes of joint action with their Palestinian counterparts;

4. Women's associations, in particular, to investigate the conditions of Palestinian women and children in all occupied territories;

5. The media and other institutions to disseminate relevant information to increase public awareness and understanding of the question of Palestine;

6. Institutions of higher education to promote the study of the question of Palestine in all its aspects;

7. Various jurists' associations to establish special investigative commissions to determine the violations by Israel of the Palestinians' legal rights and to disseminate their findings accordingly;

8. Jurists to initiate with their Palestinian counterparts consultations, research and investigations on the juridical aspects of problems affecting the southern African and Palestinian struggles, in particular the detention of

political prisoners and the denial of prisoner-of-war status to detained members of the national liberation movements of southern Africa and Palestine;

9. Parliamentarians, political parties, trade unions, organizations for solidarity and intellectuals particularly in Western Europe and North America, to join their counterparts in other parts of the world in giving their support, where it has not been done, to an initiative which would express the desire of the international community to see the Palestinian people at last living in their own independent homeland in peace, freedom and dignity.

322. Excerpts from the Fateh Central Committee
Statement on the Problems Facing the Palestinian Cause
and the PLO, Kuwait, October 16, 1983*

* 13 J. Palestine Stud. 212 (Winter 1984).

. . .There have been several Arab attempts to bring about a split within Fateh since 1966, the last being the attempt made in Lebanon in 1978. All these moves have failed because those who wanted to cause a split have been unable to secure direct outside protection. However, the rebel dissidence that took place in the Beqaa in May did enjoy direct protection in complicated circumstances—the circumstances that resulted from the departure from Beirut. For this reason, the harm done by this divisive operation was not restricted to the containment of Fateh and the consequent domination of the PLO, and thus the control of Palestinian national decision-making. On the contrary, its destructive effects have expanded, whether consciously or unconsciously in this particular stage, to the point where they coincide with the goals of American-Zionist policy which is utterly hostile to the people of Palestine, their just cause and their heroic struggle. The butcher Sharon embodied this fact when he described the rebel dissidence as being one of the fruits of the invasion which he called Operation "Peace for Galilee." The American Secretary of State Shultz took the same stand when he stated in New Delhi that he was pleased by what was happening in the Beqaa. The same applied to all the hostile media, whether Western or Zionist, when they saw what was happening in the Beqaa as the collapse of the PLO and of Yasser Arafat's leadership. These events in the Beqaa have been rejected by the Palestinian people everywhere, both in the occupied territories and the diaspora, who are fully aware of the danger of containment they represent. They have wrung the conscience of this heroic people, threatened all the achievements of their struggle and led to the undermining of the confidence seized by their struggle when the world recognized the PLO as the sole legitimate representative of the Palestinian people, and it took its seat at the UN and international and regional institutions. This dissident movement was the instrument for the achievement of what the Zionist invasion of Lebanon had failed to achieve, what American attempts had been unable to achieve and what Arab attempts at containment had been unable to perform. All efforts should have been directed towards the rebuilding of the institutions of the PLO and Fateh, to reorganization and replanning, to confronting the requirements of the new stage so that Palestinian armed struggle might continue in occupied Palestine, to activating Palestinian political struggle in the internabonal arena and to exploiting the consequences of international sympathy aroused by the magnificent Palestinian resistance to the Zionist invasion. But all these efforts have been diverted to maintaining the identity of Palestinian struggle in the Palestinian and Arab arenas, and to thwarting the plan to achieve containment and to take over Palestinian legality, the independence of Palestinian national decision-making and the role of the PLO as the sole representative of the Palestinian people.

Dealings with the Rebel Dissident Movement

The dangers of the rebel dissident movement have been leading to these destructive effects, and the people of Palestine were aware of these dangers as soon as they arose. The movement should have been ended by democratic dialogue. But the dissidents rejected such dialogue at the level of the Central Committee and the administrative and military cadres, and in doing so, they enjoyed outside protection. Fateh's Revolutionary Council met, in implementation of the decision it took at its previous meeting in Aden, to discuss the Movement's internal situation, but it found itself confronted with the rebel dissident movement in the Beqaa. The tendency of the Revolutionary Council at that meeting was to take the necessary decisions as regards the dissidents in conformity with the Movement's internal regulations. But the Revolutionary Council decided to condemn this rebel dissident movement and commissioned the Central Committee to take such measures as it saw fit for dealing with and ending the dissidence. After this the Central Committee observed that the vigilant Palestinian people quite clearly condemned the dissidence; Palestinian and Arab delegations arrived to mediate with a view to arranging a meeting with the dissidents that would initiate a democratic dialogue to end the split. This showed beyond all possibility of doubt the position occupied by Fateh in the hearts of our people and the masses of the Arab nation. For these reasons, and because of the policy pursued by Fateh since its inception of avoiding a resort to arms in the Palestinian arena, the Central Committee thought it best to delay taking its decisions until such time as Palestinian and Arab mediation had produced results. If it put an end to the dissident movement and ensured the return to lawfulness of those responsible for it, that was what we wanted and were working for; if this did not happen, the movement's internal regulations could provide it with the means necessary to confront the situation. In addition, the mediation would disclose the facts more clearly. This is what happened. At the same time, we made every possible effort to reach an understanding with Syria on a dialogue to discover the various aspects of the disagreement, if there was one, with the aim of restoring normal relations with it. But we have to record, with regret, that none of the mediation, whether Palestinian, Arab or international, has succeeded so far. The last such mediation was that undertaken by the 18-member committee set up in accordance with the decision of the Central Council. We accepted this, in spite of the Palestinian blood shed by the dissidents in the Beqaa. Despite the praiseworthy efforts made by this honorable committee, it hastened to announce its views before a final understanding was reached. In spite of that, we studied its views with the necessary attention and submitted to it a clear, practical proposal that could lead to the ending of the dissidence if there was good will. Our proposal was as follows:

1. The formation of a joint committee of dissidents and Fateh Central

Committee to study organizational, military and financial affairs and to find out where reform was needed and what measures were required to achieve it.

2. The Central Committee undertakes to implement the recommendations of the joint committee, one by one, as soon as they are made.

3. As regards the political statement called for by the 18-member committee, Fateh Revolutionary Council has already issued it on the basis of commitment to the decisions of the National Council which rejects President Reagan's initiative. It is regrettable that, when the 18-member committee resumed its mediation, the situation exploded again in a variety of ways, one being the military clash that took place in Damascus over the forcible occupation of the movement's offices. Mr. Ibrahim Bakr was unable to meet Abu Ammar, Abu Jihad and Abu al-Hawl in Tripoli and returned to Amman, and those members of the committee who were present issued their latest statement from Amman on October 12, 1983. In this statement they declared that they would continue to perform their task if there were positive moves. We have a number of remarks to make about this latest statement, but we shall not raise this matter now. We shall only point out that the statement called for a halt of the overt and covert information campaigns against Syria, without mentioning the Syrian information campaigns. An Arab attempt is now being made to overcome the dissidence crisis, and the results of this attempt should be known during this week. In the light of this the Central Committee will hold a special meeting at the end of this month so that we may disclose to the people of Palestine and to the Arab nation what they ought to know, and the attitude that should be adopted . . .

The Political Situation

The Central Committee also discussed the general political situation, including the setback suffered by the Palestinian cause as a result of the dissident movement and official Arab silence about it. The Central Committee also discussed recent events in Lebanon and their repercussions on the Palestinian cause and the Middle East conflict as a whole, and decided to affirm that it maintains its previous attitude as regards:

1. Rejection of the Camp David accords and their consequences, including rejection of the autonomy conspiracy and resistance to it by all available means.

2. Rejection of President Reagan's initiative and refusal even to discuss any initiative from whatever quarter that is not based on the right of the Palestinian people to return, to self-determination and to establish an independent state.

3. Commitment to the political and organizational decisions of the Palestine National Council.

4. Rejection of the Lebanese-Israeli agreement, the success of which is to be seen as a conspiracy against the cause of Palestine through the success of

the policy of the US and the Zionist enemy—that of imposing the policy of an American-Israeli peace on the Arab nation by force, under the slogan of a bogus peace that will lead to the eventual liquidation of the Palestinian cause.

The Central Committee also decided:

1. To salute and express appreciation of the Palestinian people in all the occupied territories and in the diaspora for protecting and guarding the PLO by insisting that it is the sole legitimate representative of the people of Palestine, and that its unity must be maintained. They have also insisted that Palestinian national decision-making must be independent, and rejected any dissident activity in the Palestinian arena and any interference in the internal affairs of Fateh and the PLO.

2. To call on the Arab masses to declare their support for the PLO, to maintain its unity and that of Fateh, and to reject any attempt to contain the PLO and to subject it to any quarter except the people of Palestine, and in any way, including that of dissidence, as happened recently in the Beqaa.

3. From its concern for the safety of its position, for Arab solidarity and for the safety of the Palestinian advance, Fateh declares its determination to put an end to the information campaigns. This must also apply to all the other parties, including certain Arab parties.

4. It also declares its commitment to give no opportunity for the outbreak of Palestinian-Palestinian or Palestinian-Arab infighting except in cases of immediate self-defense.

5. The Movement declares its commitment to support the Lebanese nationalist movement and all Lebanese forces that are resisting the Zionist occupation of Lebanon and are seeking to evict it from Lebanese territory within the framework of national accord that will protect Lebanon's sovereignty and Arab affiliation.

6. Fateh affirms that it will maintain relations of friendship with the socialist camp, headed by the USSR, and salutes its unchanging attitude to the PLO and its legitimate leadership and its continuing support for the struggle of the Palestinian people. . . .

323. General Assembly Resolution 38/58 on the Question of Palestine, December 13, 1983*

* G.A. Res. 58, 38 U.N. GAOR Supp. (No. 47) at 46, U.N. Doc. A/38/47 (1983).

A

The General Assembly,

Recalling its resolutions 3376 (XXX) of 10 November 1975, 31/20 of 24 November 1976, 32/40 of 2 December 1977, 33/28 of 7 December 1978, 34/ 65 A and B of 29 November 1979 and 34/65 C and D of 12 December 1979, ES-7/2 of 29 July 1980, 35/169 of 15 December 1980, 36/120 of 10 December 1981, ES-7/4 of 28 April 1982, ES-7/5 of 26 June 1982, ES-7/9 of 24 September 1982 and 37/86 of 10 December 1982,

Having considered the report of the Committee on the Exercise of the Inalienable Rights of the Palestinian People,[100]

1. *Expresses its appreciation* to the Committee on the Exercise of the Inalienable Rights of the Palestinian People for its efforts in performing the tasks assigned to it by the General Assembly;

2. *Endorses* the recommendations of the Committee contained in paragraphs 94 to 98 of its report and draws the attention of the Security Council to the fact that action on the Committee's recommendations, as repeatedly endorsed by the General Assembly, at its thirty-first session and subsequently, is long overdue;

3. *Requests* the Committee to keep under review the situation relating to the question of Palestine as well as the implementation of the Programme of Action for the Achievement of Palestinian Rights[101] adopted by the International Conference on the Question of Palestine and to report and make suggestions to the General Assembly or the Security Council, as appropriate;

4. *Requests* the United Nations Conciliation Commission for Palestine, established under General Assembly resolution 194 (III) of 11 December 1948, as well as other United Nations bodies associated with the question of Palestine, to co-operate fully with the Committee and to make available to it, at its request, the relevant information and documentation which they have at their disposal;

5. *Authorizes* the Committee to continue to exert all efforts to promote the implementation of its recommendations, to send delegations or representatives to international conferences where such representation would be considered by it to be appropriate, and to report thereon to the General Assembly at its thirty-ninth session and thereafter;

6. *Decides* to circulate the report of the Committee to all the competent bodies of the United Nations and urges them to take the necessary action, as appropriate, in accordance with the Committee's programme of implementation;

---

[100] *Official Records of the General Assembly, Thirty-eighth Session, Supplement No. 35* (A/38/ 35).

[101] *Report on the International Conference on the Question of Palestine, Geneva, 29 August-7 September 1983* (United Nations publication, Sales No. E.83.I.21), chap. I, sect. B.

7. *Requests* the Secretary-General to continue to provide the Committee with all the necessary facilities for the performance of its tasks.

95th plenary meeting
13 December 1983

B

The General Assembly,

Having considered the report of the Committee on the Exercise of the Inalienable Rights of the Palestinian People,[100]

Noting, in particular, the information contained in paragraphs 86 to 91 of that report,

Recalling its resolutions 32/40 B of 2 December 1977, 33/28 C of 7 December 1978, 34/65 D of 12 December 1979, 35/169 D of 15 December 1980, 36/120 B of 10 December 1981 and 37/86 B of 10 December 1982,

1. *Notes with appreciation* the action taken by the Secretary-General in compliance with General Assembly resolution 37/86 B;

2. *Requests* the Secretary-General to ensure that the Division for Palestinian Rights of the Secretariat continues to discharge the tasks detailed in paragraph 1 of General Assembly resolution 32/40 B, paragraph 2(*b*) of resolution 34/65 D and paragraph 3 of resolution 36/120 B, in consultation with the Committee on the Exercise of the Inalienable Rights of the Palestinian People and under its guidance;

3. *Also requests* the Secretary-General to provide the Division for Palestinian Rights with the necessary resources to accomplish its tasks and to expand its work programme, *inter alia,* through:

(*a*) Closer contacts with the media and wider dissemination of the Division's information material, particularly where information on the question of Palestine is inadequate;

(*b*) Increased contacts with non-governmental organizations and the convening of symposia and meetings for non-governmental organizations in different regions in order to heighten awareness of the facts relating to the question of Palestine;

4. *Further requests* the Secretary-General to ensure the continued co-operation of the Department of Public Information and other units of the Secretariat in enabling the Division for Palestinian Rights to perform its tasks and in covering adequately the various aspects of the question of Palestine;

5. *Invites* all Governments and organizations to lend their co-operation to the Committee on the Exercise of the Inalienable Rights of the Palestinian People and the Division for Palestinian Rights in the performance of their tasks;

6. *Notes with appreciation* the action taken by Member States to observe annually on 29 November the International Day of Solidarity with the Pal-

estinian People and the issuance by them of special postage stamps for the occasion.

95th plenary meeting
13 December 1983

C

The General Assembly,

Recalling its resolution 36/120 of 10 December 1981, in which it decided to convene, under the auspices of the United Nations, an International Conference on the Question of Palestine on the basis of its resolution ES-7/2 of 29 July 1980,

Recalling also its resolution 37/86 C of 10 December 1982 in which it, *inter alia*, reiterated the responsibility of the United Nations to strive for a lasting peace in the Middle East through a just solution of the problem of Palestine,

Having considered the report of the International Conference on the Question of Palestine,[102] held at Geneva from 29 August to 7 September 1983,

Convinced that the Conference, in adopting by acclamation the Geneva Declaration on Palestine[103] and the Programme of Action for the Achievement of Palestinian Rights,[101] made an important and positive contribution to the attainment of a comprehensive, just and durable peace in the Middle East through a just solution of the problem of Palestine, the core of the Arab-Israeli conflict,

Conscious of the importance of the time factor in achieving a just solution of the problem of Palestine,

1. *Takes note with satisfaction* of the report of the International Conference on the Question of Palestine;

2. *Endorses* the Geneva Declaration on Palestine, adopted by acclamation on 7 September 1983;

3. *Welcomes and endorses* the call for convening an International Peace Conference on the Middle East in conformity with the following guidelines:

(*a*) the attainment by the Palestinian people of its legitimate inalienable rights, including the right to return, the right to self-determination and the right to establish its own independent State in Palestine;

(*b*) The right of the Palestine Liberation Organization, the representative of the Palestinian people, to participate on an equal footing with other parties in all efforts, deliberations and conferences on the Middle East;

(*c*) The need to put an end to Israel's occupation of the Arab territories, in accordance with the principle of the inadmissibility of the acquisition of territory by force, and, consequently, the need to secure Israeli withdrawal from the territories occupied since 1967, including Jerusalem;

(*d*) The need to oppose and reject such Israeli policies and practices in the

[102] United Nations publication, Sales No. E.83.I.21.
[103] *Ibid.*, chap. I, sect. A.

occupied territories, including Jerusalem, and any *de facto* situation created by Israel as are contrary to international law and relevant United Nations resolutions, particularly the establishment of settlements, as these policies and practices constitute major obstacles to the achievement of peace in the Middle East;

(*e*) The need to reaffirm as null and void all legislative and administrative measures and actions taken by Israel, the occupying Power, which have altered or purported to alter the character and status of the Holy City of Jerusalem, including the expropriation of land and property situated thereon, and in particular the so-called "Basic Law" on Jerusalem and the proclamation of Jerusalem as the capital of Israel;

(*f*) The right of all States in the region to existence within secure and internationally recognized boundaries, with justice and security for all the people, the *sine qua non* of which is the recognition and attainment of the legitimate, inalienable rights of the Palestinian people as stated in subparagraph (*a*) above;

4. *Invites* all parties to the Arab-Israeli conflict, including the Palestine Liberation Organization, as well as the United States of America, the Union of Soviet Socialist Republics and other concerned States, to participate in the International Peace Conference on the Middle East on an equal footing and with equal rights;

5. *Requests* the Secretary-General, in consultation with the Security Council, urgently to undertake preparatory measures to convene the Conference;

6. *Invites* the Security Council to facilitate the organization of the Conference;

7. *Also requests* the Secretary-General to report on his efforts no later than 15 March 1984;

8. *Decides* to consider at its thirty-ninth session the report of the Secretary-General on the Conference.

95th plenary meeting
13 December 1983

D

The General Assembly,

Having considered the report on the International Conference on the Question of Palestine,[102] held at Geneva from 29 August to 7 September 1983,

Taking note of the Programme of Action for the Achievement of Palestinian Rights,[101]

Bearing in mind its resolution 38/145 of 19 December 1983 on assistance to the Palestinian people,

Urges the meeting of specialized agencies and other organizations of the United Nations system to be convened in 1984, referred to in General Assembly resolution 38/145, to take into account the recommendations of the five regional preparatory meetings of the International Conference on the Question of Palestine[104] and the United Nations resolutions concerning economic and social assistance to the Palestinian people in developing a co-ordinated programme of economic and social assistance to the Palestinian people, and to ensure the implementation of that programme.

95th plenary meeting
13 December 1983

E

The General Assembly,

Having considered the report of the International Conference on the Question of Palestine,[102] held at Geneva from 29 August to 7 September 1983,

Convinced that the world-wide dissemination of accurate and comprehensive information and the role of non-governmental organizations and institutions remain of vital importance in heightening awareness of and support for the inalienable rights of the Palestinian people to self-determination and to the establishment of an independent sovereign Palestinian State,

Requests that the Department of Public Information of the Secretariat, in full co-operation and co-ordination with the Committee on the Exercise of the Inalienable Rights of the Palestinian People, should:

(*a*) Disseminate all information on the activities of the United Nations system relating to Palestine;

(*b*) Expand publications and audio-visual coverage of the facts and developments pertaining to the question of Palestine;

(*c*) Publish newsletters and articles in its relevant publications of Israeli violations of the human rights of the Arab inhabitants of the occupied territories, and organize fact-finding missions to the area for journalists;

(*d*) Organize regional encounters for journalists;

(*e*) Disseminate appropriate information on the results of the International Conference on the Question of Palestine.

95th plenary meeting
13 December 1983

---

[104] *Ibid.*, chap. II, paras. 10 and 11.

324. General Assembly Resolution 38/79 on the Report of the Special Committee to Investigate Israeli Practices Affecting the Human Rights of the Population of the Occupied Territories, December 15, 1983*

* G.A. Res. 79, 38 U.N. GAOR Supp. (No. 47) at 94, U.N. Doc. A/38/47 (1983). *See also* subsequent resolution, G.A. Res. 95, 39 U.N. GAOR Supp. (No. 51) at 102, U.N. Doc. A/39/51 (1984).

A

The General Assembly,

Having heard the statement of the representative of the Palestine Liberation Organization relative to the fate of Ziad Abu Eain,[4]

Taking note of the report of the International Committee of the Red Cross of 13 December 1983,[5]

1. *Condemns* Israel for the fact that one prisoner, Ziad Abu Eain, who had been registered before embarkation by delegates of the International Committee of the Red Cross at Tel Aviv Airport, was taken at the last minute by the Israeli authorities;

2. *Demands* the immediate release of Ziad Abu Eain, as well as the other prisoners who were duly registered to be freed from Insar Camp and other military command posts in southern Lebanon but have not in fact been released, and the securing of their transfer to Algiers in conformity with the agreement reached through the good offices of the International Committee of the Red Cross;

3. *Requests* the Secretary-General to report on the implementation of the present resolution.

95th plenary meeting
15 December 1983

B

The General Assembly,

Recalling its resolutions 3092 A (XXVIII) of 7 December 1973, 3240 B (XXIX) of 29 November 1974, 3525 B (XXX) of 15 December 1975, 31/106 B of 16 December 1976, 32/91 A of 13 December 1977, 33/113 A of 18 December 1978, 34/90 B of 12 December 1979, 35/122 A of 11 December 1980, 36/147 A of 16 December 1981 and 37/88 A of 10 December 1982,

Recalling also Security Council resolution 465 (1980) of 1 March 1980 in which, *inter alia*, the Council affirmed that the Geneva Convention relative to the Protection of Civilian Persons in Time of War, of 12 August 1949,[6] is applicable to the Arab territories occupied by Israel since 1967, including Jerusalem,

Considering that the promotion of respect for the obligations arising from the Charter of the United Nations and other instruments and rules of international law is among the basic purposes and principles of the United Nations,

Bearing in mind the provisions of the Geneva Convention,

---

[4] *Official Records of the General Assembly, Thirty-eighth Session, Special Political Committee,* 40th meeting, para. 1.

[5] See A/38/735.

[6] United Nations, *Treaty Series*, vol. 75, No. 973, p. 287.

Noting that Israel and those Arab States whose territories have been occupied by Israel since June 1967 are parties to that Convention,

Taking into account that States parties to that Convention undertake, in accordance with article 1 thereof, not only to respect but also to ensure respect for the Convention in all circumstances,

1. *Reaffirms* that the Geneva Convention relative to the Protection of Civilian Persons in Time of War, of 12 August 1949, is applicable to Palestinian and other Arab territories occupied by Israel since 1967, including Jerusalem;

2. *Condemns once again* the failure of Israel as the occupying Power to acknowledge the applicability of that Convention to the territories it has occupied since 1967, including Jerusalem;

3. *Strongly demands* that Israel acknowledge and comply with the provisions of that Convention in Palestinian and other Arab territories it has occupied since 1967, including Jerusalem;

4. *Urgently calls upon* all States parties to that Convention to exert every effort in order to ensure respect for and compliance with its provisions in Palestinian and other Arab territories occupied by Israel since 1967, including Jerusalem.

95th plenary meeting
15 December 1983

C

The General Assembly,

Recalling its resolutions 32/5 of 28 October 1977, 33/113 B of 18 December 1978, 34/90 C of 12 December 1979, 35/122 B of 11 December 1980, 36/147 B of 16 December 1981 and 37/88 B of 10 December 1982,

Recalling also Security Council resolution 465 (1980) of 1 March 1980,

Expressing grave anxiety and concern at the present serious situation in the occupied Palestinian and other Arab territories, including Jerusalem, as a result of the continued Israeli occupation and the measures and actions taken by the Government of Israel, the occupying Power, designed to change the legal status, geographical nature and demographic composition of those territories,

Considering that the Geneva Convention relative to the Protection of Civilian Persons in Time of War, of 12 August 1949,[6] is applicable to all Arab territories occupied since June 1967, including Jerusalem,

1. *Determines* that all such measures and actions taken by Israel in the Palestinian and other Arab territories occupied since 1967, including Jerusalem, are in violation of the relevant provisions of the Geneva Convention relative to the Protection of Civilian Persons in Time of War, of 12 August 1949, and constitute a serious obstruction of efforts to achieve a just and lasting peace in the Middle East and therefore have no legal validity;

2. *Strongly deplores* the persistence of Israel in carrying out such measures,

in particular the establishment of settlements in the Palestinian and other occupied Arab territories, including Jerusalem;

3. *Demands* that Israel comply strictly with its international obligations in accordance with the principles of international law and the provisions of the Geneva Convention;

4. *Demands once more* that the Government of Israel, the occupying Power, desist forthwith from taking any action which would result in changing the legal status, geographical nature or demographic composition of the Palestinian and other Arab territories occupied since 1967, including Jerusalem;

5. *Urgently calls upon* all States parties to the Geneva Convention to respect and to exert every effort in order to ensure respect for and compliance with its provisions in all Arab territories occupied by Israel since 1967, including Jerusalem.

95th plenary meeting
15 December 1983

D

The General Assembly,

Guided by the purposes and principles of the Charter of the United Nations and by the principles and provisions of the Universal Declaration of Human Rights,[7]

Bearing in mind the provisions of the Geneva Convention relative to the Protection of Civilian Persons in Time of War, of 12 August 1949,[6] as well as of other relevant conventions and regulations,

Recalling all its resolutions on the subject, in particular resolutions 32/91 B and C of 13 December 1977, 33/113 C of 18 December 1978, 34/90 A of 12 December 1979, 35/122 C of 11 December 1980, 36/147 C of 16 December 1981 and 37/88 C of 10 December 1982, and also those adopted by the Security Council, the Commission on Human Rights, in particular its resolution 1983/1 of 15 February 1983,[8] and other United Nations organs concerned and by the specialized agencies,

Having considered the report of the Special Committee to Investigate Israeli Practices Affecting the Human Rights of the Population of the Occupied Territories,[9] which contains, *inter alia*, public statements made by officials of the Government of Israel,

1. *Commends* the Special Committee to Investigate Israeli Practices Affecting the Human Rights of the Population of the Occupied Territories for its efforts in performing the tasks assigned to it by the General Assembly and for its thoroughness and impartiality;

---

[7] Resolution 217 A (III).
[8] See *Official Records of the Economic and Social Council, 1983, Supplement No. 3* (E/1983/13 and Corr.1), chap. XXVII.
[9] See A/38/409.

2. *Deplores* the continued refusal by Israel to allow the Special Committee access to the occupied territories;

3. *Demands* that Israel allow the Special Committee access to the occupied territories;

4. *Reaffirms* the fact that occupation itself constitutes a grave violation of the human rights of the civilian population of the occupied Arab territories;

5. *Condemns* the continued and persistent violation by Israel of the Geneva Convention relative to the Protection of Civilian Persons in Time of War, of 12 August 1949, and other applicable international instruments, and condemns in particular those violations which that Convention designates as "grave breaches" thereof;

6. *Declares once more* that Israel's grave breaches of that Convention are war crimes and an affront to humanity;

7. *Strongly condemns* the following Israeli policies and practices:

(*a*) Annexation of parts of the occupied territories, including Jerusalem;

(*b*) Imposition of Israeli laws, jurisdiction and administration on the Syrian Golan Heights, which has resulted in the effective annexation of the Syrian Golan Heights;

(*c*) Establishment of new Israeli settlements and expansion of the existing settlements on private and public Arab lands, and transfer of an alien population thereto;

(*d*) Evacuation, deportation, expulsion, displacement and transfer of Arab inhabitants of the occupied territories and denial of their right to return;

(*e*) Confiscation and expropriation of private and public Arab property in the occupied territories and all other transactions for the acquisition of land involving the Israeli authorities, institutions or nationals on the one hand and the inhabitants or institutions of the occupied territories on the other;

(*f*) Excavation and transformation of the landscape and the historical, cultural and religious sites, especially at Jerusalem;

(*g*) Pillaging of archaeological and cultural property;

(*h*) Destruction and demolition of Arab houses;

(*i*) Collective punishment, mass arrests, administrative detention and ill-treatment of the Arab population;

(*j*) Ill-treatment and torture of persons under detention;

(*k*) Interference with religious freedoms and practices as well as family rights and customs;

(*l*) Interference with the system of education and with the social and economic development of the population in the occupied Palestinian and other Arab territories;

(*m*) Interference with the freedom of movement of individuals within the occupied Palestinian and other Arab territories;

(*n*) Illegal exploitation of the natural wealth, resources and population of the occupied territories;

8. *Strongly condemns* the arming of Israeli settlers in the occupied territories to commit acts of violence against Arab civilians and the perpetration

of acts of violence by these armed settlers against individuals, causing injury and death and wide-scale damage to Arab property;

9. *Reaffirms* that all measures taken by Israel to change the physical character, demographic composition, institutional structure or status of the occupied territories, or any part thereof, including Jerusalem, are null and void, and that Israel's policy of settling parts of its population and new immigrants in the occupied territories constitutes a flagrant violation of the Geneva Convention and of the relevant resolutions of the United Nations;

10. *Demands* that Israel desist forthwith from the policies and practices referred to in paragraphs 7, 8 and 9 above;

11. *Calls upon* Israel, the occupying Power, to take immediate steps for the return of all displaced Arab and Palestinian inhabitants to their homes or former places of residence in the territories occupied by Israel since 1967;

12. *Urges* the international organizations and the specialized agencies, in particular the International Labour Organisation, to examine the conditions of Arab workers in the occupied Palestinian and other Arab territories, including Jerusalem;

13. *Reiterates its call* upon all States, in particular those States parties to the Geneva Convention, in accordance with article 1 of that Convention, and upon international organizations and the specialized agencies not to recognize any changes carried out by Israel in the occupied territories and to avoid actions, including those in the field of aid, which might be used by Israel in its pursuit of the policies of annexation and colonization or any of the other policies and practices referred to in the present resolution;

14. *Requests* the Special Committee, pending the early termination of Israeli occupation, to continue to investigate Israeli policies and practices in the Arab territories occupied by Israel since 1967, to consult, as appropriate, with the International Committee of the Red Cross in order to ensure the safeguarding of the welfare and human rights of the population of the occupied territories and to report to the Secretary-General as soon as possible and whenever the need arises thereafter;

15. *Requests* the Special Committee to continue to investigate the treatment of civilians in detention in the Arab territories occupied by Israel since 1967;

16. *Condemns* Israel's refusal to permit persons from the occupied territories to appear as witnesses before the Special Committee and to participate in conferences and meetings held outside the occupied territories;

17. *Requests* the Secretary-General:

(*a*) To provide all necessary facilities to the Special Committee, including those required for its visits to the occupied territories, with a view to investigating the Israeli policies and practices referred to in the present resolution;

(*b*) To continue to make available additional staff as may be necessary to assist the Special Committee in the performance of its tasks;

(*c*) To ensure the widest circulation of the reports of the Special Committee, and of information regarding its activities and findings, by all means available through the Department of Public Information of the Secretariat and, where necessary, to reprint those reports of the Special Committee which are no longer available;

(d) To report to the General Assembly at its thirty-ninth session on the tasks entrusted to him in the present paragraph;

18. *Requests* the Security Council to ensure Israel's respect for and compliance with all the provisions of the Geneva Convention relative to the Protection of Civilian Persons in Time of War, of 12 August 1949, in Palestinian and other Arab territories occupied since 1967, including Jerusalem, and to initiate measures to halt Israeli policies and practices in those territories;

19. *Decides* to include in the provisional agenda of its thirty-ninth session the item entitled "Report of the Special Committee to Investigate Israeli Practices Affecting the Human Rights of the Population of the Occupied Territories".

98th plenary meeting
15 December 1983

E

The General Assembly,

Recalling Security Council resolutions 468 (1980) of 8 May 1980, 469 (1980) of 20 May 1980 and 484 (1980) of 19 December 1980 and General Assembly resolutions 36/147 D of 16 December 1981 and 37/88 D of 10 December 1982,

Deeply concerned at the expulsion by the Israeli military occupation authorities of the Mayors of Hebron and Halhul and of the Sharia Judge of Hebron,

Recalling the Geneva Convention relative to the Protection of Civilian Persons in Time of War, of 12 August 1949,[6] in particular article 1 and the first paragraph of article 49, which read as follows:

"Article 1
The High Contracting Parties undertake to respect and to ensure respect for the present Convention in all circumstances.
Article 49
Individual or mass forcible transfers, as well as deportations of protected persons from occupied territory to the territory of the occupying Power or to that of any other country, occupied or not, are prohibited, regardless of their motive . . . ",

Reaffirming the applicability of the Geneva Convention to the Palestinian and other Arab territories occupied by Israel since 1967, including Jerusalem,

1. *Demands once more* that the Government of Israel, the occupying Power, rescind the illegal measures taken by the Israeli military occupation author-

ities in expelling and imprisoning the Mayors of Hebron and Halhul and in expelling the Sharia Judge of Hebron and that it facilitate the immediate return of the expelled Palestinian leaders so that they can resume the functions for which they were elected and appointed;

2. *Requests* the Secretary-General to report to the General Assembly as soon as possible on the implementation of the present resolution.

98th plenary meeting
15 December 1983

F

The General Assembly,

Deeply concerned that the Arab territories occupied since 1967 have been under continued Israeli military occupation,

Recalling Security Council resolution 497 (1981) of 17 December 1981 and General Assembly resolutions 36/226 B of 17 December 1981, ES-9/1 of 5 February 1982 and 37/88 E of 10 December 1982,

Recalling its previous resolutions, in particular resolution 3414 (XXX) of 5 December 1975, 31/61 of 9 December 1976, 32/20 of 25 November 1977, 33/28 and 33/29 of 7 December 1978, 34/70 of 6 December 1979 and 35/122 of 11 December 1980, in which it, *inter alia*, called upon Israel to put an end to its occupation of the Arab territories and to withdrawal from all those territories,

Reaffirming once more the illegality of Israel's decision of 14 December 1981 to impose its laws, jurisdiction and administration on the occupied Syrian Golan Heights, which has resulted in the effective annexation of that territory,

Reaffirming that the acquisition of territory by force is inadmissible under the Charter of the United Nations and that all territories thus occupied by Israel must be returned,

Recalling the Geneva Convention relative to the Protection of Civilian Persons in Time of War, of 12 August 1949,[6]

1. *Strongly condemns* Israel, the occupying Power, for its refusal to comply with the relevant resolutions of the General Assembly and the Security Council, particularly Council resolution 497 (1981), in which the Council, *inter alia*, decided that the Israeli decision to impose its laws, jurisdiction and administration on the occupied Syrian Golan Heights was null and void and without international legal effect and demanded that Israel, the occupying Power, should rescind forthwith its decision;

2. *Condemns* the persistence of Israel in changing the physical character, demographic composition, institutional structure and legal status of the occupied Syrian Arab Golan Heights;

3. *Determines* that all legislative and administrative measures and actions taken or to be taken by Israel, the occupying Power, that purport to alter the character and legal status of the Syrian Arab Golan Heights are null and

void and constitute a flagrant violation of international law and of the Geneva Convention relative to the Protection of Civilian Persons in Time of War, of 12 August 1949, and have no legal effect;

4. *Strongly condemns* Israel for its attempts and measures to impose forcibly Israeli citizenship and Israeli identity cards on the Syrian citizens in the occupied Syrian Arab Golan Heights and calls upon it to desist from its repressive measures against the population of the Syrian Arab Golan Heights;

5. *Calls once again upon* Member States not to recognize any of the legislative or administrative measures and actions referred to above;

6. *Requests* the Secretary-General to submit to the General Assembly at its thirty-ninth session a report on the implementation of the present resolution.

98th plenary meeting
15 December 1983

G

The General Assembly,

Bearing in mind the Geneva Convention relative to the Protection of Civilian Persons in Time of War, of 12 August 1949,[6]

Deeply shocked by the most recent atrocities committed by Israel, the occupying Power, against educational institutions in the occupied Palestinian territories,

1. *Reaffirms* the applicability of the Geneva Convention relative to the Protection of Civilian Persons in Time of War, of 12 August 1949, to the Palestinian and other Arab territories occupied by Israel since 1967, including Jerusalem;

2. *Condemns* Israeli policies and practices against Palestinian students and faculties in schools, universities and other educational institutions in the occupied Palestinian territories, especially the policy of opening fire on defenceless students, causing many casualties;

3. *Condemns* the systematic Israeli campaign of repression against and closing of universities in the occupied Palestinian territories, restricting and impeding the academic activities of Palestinian universities by subjecting the selection of courses, textbooks and educational programmes, the admission of students and the appointment of faculty members to the control and supervision of the military occupation authorities, in clear contravention of the Geneva Convention;

4. *Demands* that Israel, the occupying Power, comply with the provisions of that Convention, rescind all actions and measures against all educational institutions, ensure the freedom of those institutions and refrain forthwith from hindering the effective operation of the universities and other educational institutions;

5. *Requests* the Secretary-General to submit a report on the implementation of the present resolution before the end of 1984.

98th plenary meeting
15 December 1983

H

The General Assembly,

Recalling Security Council resolution 471 (1980) of 5 June 1980, in which the Council condemned the assassination attempts against the Mayors of Nablus, Ramallah and Al Bireh and called for the immediate apprehension and prosecution of the perpetrators of those crimes,

Recalling also General Assembly resolutions 36/147 G of 16 December 1981 and 37/88 G of 10 December 1982,

Recalling once again the Geneva Convention relative to the Protection of Civilian Persons in Time of War, of 12 August 1949,[6] in particular article 27, which states, *inter alia*:

"Protected persons are entitled, in all circumstances, to respect for their persons . . . They shall at all times be humanely treated, and shall be protected especially against all acts of violence or threats thereof . . . ",

Reaffirming the applicability of that Convention to the Arab territories occupied by Israel since 1967, including Jerusalem,

1. *Expresses deep concern* that Israel, the occupying Power, has failed for three years to apprehend and prosecute the perpetrators of the assassination attempts;

2. *Demands once more* that Israel, the occupying Power, inform the Secretary-General of the results of the investigations relative to the assassination attempts;

3. *Requests* the Secretary-General to submit to the General Assembly at its thirty-ninth session a report on the implementation of the present resolution.

98th plenary meeting
15 December 1983

325. General Assembly Resolution 38/166 on the Living

Conditions of the Palestinian People in the Occupied

Palestinian Territories, December 19, 1983*

* G.A. Res. 166, 38 U.N. GAOR Supp. (No. 47) at 134, U.N. Doc. A/38/ 47 (1983).

The General Assembly,

Recalling the Vancouver Declaration on Human Settlements, 1976,[86] and the relevant recommendations for national action[87] adopted by Habitat: United Nations Conference on Human Settlements,

Recalling also resolution 3, entitled "Living conditions of the Palestinians in occupied territories", contained in the recommendations for international co-operation adopted by Habitat: United Nations Conference on Human Settlements,[88]

Recalling further its resolution 37/222 of 20 December 1982,

Taking note of resolution 6/2 adopted by the Commission on Human Settlements on 4 May 1983,[89]

Gravely alarmed by the continuation of the Israeli settlement policies, which have been declared null and void and a major obstacle to peace,

1. *Takes note* of the report of the Secretary-General on the living conditions of the Palestinian people in the occupied Palestinian territories;[90]

2. *Takes note also* of the statement made on 1 November 1983 by the observer of the Palestine Liberation Organization,[91]

3. *Rejects* the Israeli plans and actions intended to change the demographic composition of the occupied Palestinian territories, particularly the increase and expansion of the Israeli settlements, and other plans and actions creating conditions leading to the displacement and exodus of Palestinians from the occupied Palestinian territories;

4. *Expresses its alarm* at the deterioration in the living conditions of the Palestinian people in the Palestinian territories occupied since 1967 as a result of the Israeli occupation;

5. *Affirms* that the Israeli occupation is contradictory to the basic requirements for the social and economic development of the Palestinian people in the occupied West Bank and the Gaza Strip;

6. *Calls upon* the Israeli occupation authorities to give United Nations experts access to the occupied Palestinian territories;

7. *Recognizes* the need for a comprehensive report on the impact of the Israeli settlements on the living conditions of the Palestinian people in the occupied Palestinian territories;

8. *Requests* the Secretary-General to prepare and submit to the General Assembly at its thirty-ninth session, through the Economic and Social Coun-

---

[86] *Report of Habitat: United Nations Conference on Human Settlements, Vancouver, 31 May-11 June 1976* (United Nations publication, Sales No. E.76.IV.7 and corridendum), chap. 1.

[87] *Ibid.*, chap. II.

[88] *Ibid.*, chap. III.

[89] See *Official Records of the General Assembly, Thirty-eighth Session, Supplement No. 8* (A/38/8), annex 1.

[90] A/38/278-E/1983/77.

[91] *Official Records of the General Assembly, Thirty-eighth Session, Second Committee*, 24th meeting, paras. 1-5.

cil, a comprehensive report on the current and future impact of the Israeli settlements on the living conditions of the Palestinian people in the occupied Palestinian territories, including a comparison between the living conditions of the latter and those of the residents of the Israeli settlements.

102nd plenary meeting
19 December 1983

326. European Parliament Resolution on a Middle East Peace Initiative, February 16, 1984*

* 27 O.J. Eur. Comm. (No. C 77) 71 (1984).

The European Parliament,

A. concerned at the extremely delicate position throughout the Middle East engendered by the situation in Lebanon,

B. equally concerned at the lack of progress in resolving the Israeli-Palestinian problem which is at the heart of difficulties in the Middle East,

C. asserting that this instability in the Middle East endangers world peace, particularly at this time,

D. convinced it is a European responsibility to play an active part in securing peace in the region,

E. convinced that there is a basis for a possible solution in

   — the respective UN Security Council Resolutions 242 and 338,
   — the European Parliament's resolution of 11 January 1983 on the situation in the Middle East (¹),
   — The Venice Declaration by the EC Member States of June 1980,
   — the resolution of the 12th Arab Summit in Fez of 10 September 1982, which is also supported by the Islamic World Conference Summit of Casablanca,
   — the Franco-Egyptian initiative, which is now accepted by the 10 EC Member States in the framework of European Political Cooperation,

F. considering that the Palestinian leadership now appears inclined to make progress on the basis of the above resolutions and initiatives and that this opportunity must not be missed,

G. certain that delay to any progress until after the US elections in November 1984 is highly dangerous and cannot be countenanced,

    1. Calls on the Foreign Ministers meeting in Political Cooperation to take an immediate initiative to bring all reasonable pressure to bear on the various parties to negotiate a lasting settlement, possibly within the framework of the UN;

    2. Instructs its President to submit this resolution to the Council, the EC Members States' Foreign Ministers meeting in Political Cooperation, to all other parties concerned, including specifically the Israeli Government and the PLO, and the Secretary-General of the United Nations Organization.

¹ OJ No C 42, 11. 2. 1983, p. 11; Penders report Doc. 1-786/82.

327. State Department Statement Before the Senate

Foreign Relations Committee Opposing Moving

the U.S. Embassy to Jerusalem,

February 23, 1984*

---

* 84 U.S. Dep't State Bull. No. 2085, at 65 (April 1984).

I appreciate the opportunity to discuss with the committee the Administration's position on S. 2031. As you know, this bill provides for the U.S Embassy and Ambassador's residence in Israel to be moved to the city of Jerusalem.

This committee has already received Secretary Schultz's letter expressing the strong opposition of the Administration to this bill. Before I outline the reasons for our opposition, let me take a few moments to provide the context in which this proposal arises.

The United States has been and remains Israel's staunchest supporter. In 1948 when Israel proclaimed its independence, the United States was the first country to extend it recognition. We quickly established diplomatic relations and established our embassy at Israel's seat of government, Tel Aviv. There our embassy has remained, during the Administrations of eight Presidents. Dating from well before the establishment of the State of Israel, we have maintained a consulate general in Jerusalem which reports directly to the Department. This is in accord with arrangements in special circumstances elsewhere, such as Hong Kong.

Why has it been consistent with U.S policy, during Democratic and Republican Administrations, to retain our embassy in Tel Aviv? In short, because the location of our embassy is intimately related to the efforts of the United States to secure a just and lasting peace in the Middle East. In this regard, U.S. efforts have stressed peace through negotiations. Our willingness to resist attempts to settle the Arab-Israeli conflict through force or through unilateral actions has preserved our ability to play a constructive role in settling the conflict. Moving our embassy to Jerusalem would inevitably convey a message that the United States accepted the position of one party to the issue, when, in fact, a resolution of that issue—that is, a resolution of the issue that can stand the test of time—can only be found in the framework of a final settlement reached through negotiations.

The status of Jerusalem is an integral part of the Arab-Israeli conflict. While we fully understand the depth of attachment of Israelis to the city of Jerusalem, we have a responsibility to bear in mind the special significance which the city holds as well for Jews, Moslems, and Christians throughout the world. That is a compelling fact that cannot be lightly put aside. We would not have achieved the Camp David accords if the United States had adopted the position of either party on the question of Jerusalem. This explains President Carter's separate letter attached to the Camp David accords which reaffirmed the U.S. position that the status of Jerusalem be resolved through negotiations. That position continues to be U.S. policy today.

Our policy on this issue has been resolute for more than three decades. In 1949, when the Israelis began moving their government to Jerusalem, we informed them that we could not accept a unilateral claim to the city. Again, in 1960, we informed Jordan of our opposition to its intention to make the eastern part of the city Jordan's second capital. And in 1967, when Israel occupied the eastern sector, we opposed Israeli actions to place all of

Jerusalem under Israeli law, jurisdiction, and administration. Most recently, President Reagan stated in his September 1, 1982, Middle East peace initiative that "... we remain convinced that Jerusalem must remain undivided, but its final status should be decided through negotiations."

A change in the U.S. position on the status of Jerusalem would seriously undermine our ability to play an effective role in the Middle East peace process. Indeed, moving our embassy to Jerusalem would widely be perceived as an effort by the United States to preempt negotiations altogether by prejudging a crucial issue. In short, to move our embassy to Jerusalem now would almost certainly gravely damage the prospects for a negotiated settlement; at a minimum, it would seriously compromise the ability of the United States to continue to play a constructive role in bringing the parties to the negotiating table.

In addition, the proposed legislation would be a direct interference in the President's constitutional authority to conduct foreign affairs. As stated in Secretary Schultz's letter, we are concerned that, regardless of its merits, the bill raises serious constitutional questions of a separation of powers nature. The President historically has been responsible for conducting diplomatic relations on behalf of the United States, including the determination of where and through what means to conduct such relations. Legislation directing him to relocate an embassy would be in direct conflict with this principle. By further seeking to compel him to recognize all of Jerusalem as part of Israel, it would impair his ability to determine the recognition policy of the United States. In seeking to force the President's hand, the proposed legislation, in our view, would exceed the proper scope of legislative action.

I am told, although I find it hard to credit, that some have argued that in retaining our embassy in Tel Aviv, we raise doubts concerning American recognition of Israel as a sovereign state. That argues in the face of too many years of history to be taken seriously. The United States and Israel have, since 1948, shared a special friendship, special closeness—a special relationship, if you will—that is known as such throughout the world. There cannot be any doubt about our commitment to Israel.

Some proponents of this legislation apparently also argue that U.S. policy is not in accord with reality, that Jerusalem is Israel's capital, and that by failing to locate our embassy there we are denying Israel a sovereign prerogative. But this begs the fundamental question, at least from the perspective of the United States. It is the essence of the Jerusalem issue—or at least America's decades-old position thereon—that it should not be resolved by the unilateral actions of any party.

It has also been suggested that conducting diplomatic relations through our embassy in Tel Aviv imposes practical impediments, since many Israeli Government offices are now located in Jerusalem. That is, no doubt, true. But we have been able to manage and will continue to be able to do so. In any event, I doubt that even the strongest of S.2031's proponents would argue that their principal purpose for putting the legislation forward is to improve the efficiency of our diplomatic establishment in Israel.

I have spoken here on behalf of the Administration of which I am a part. But were I speaking simply on my own behalf, I would take no different a line. It is because I care about my country's relationship with Israel and my country's ability to continue to play a crucial role in the search for that which the people of Israel so richly deserve—peace—that I oppose this legislation.

I cannot deny the frustration many Americans and most Israelis must feel because of our position. Nor do I, or this Administration, take the frustration lightly. We regret it.

But in the last analysis, it is a just and lasting peace for Israel that will bring with it a solution to this vexing problem of the status of Jerusalem. It is the calling, and the commitment, of the United States to help bring about that just and lasting peace. Indeed, I believe we are indispensable to the achievement of such a result. And, therefore, I must oppose passage of S.2031.

328. Statement by the EEC Foreign Ministers on the Middle East, March 19–20, 1984*

* 17 Bull. Eur. Comm. (No. 3) 79 (1984).

Middle East

Following decades of confrontation in the Middle East, the need for a settlement guaranteeing peace among all the States of the region is universally recognized. The Ten consider that this settlement should include the right to existence and security of all these States, including Israel.

Likewise, all the parties concerned have conceded that a settlement must take account of the legitimate rights of the Palestinian people. In the view of the Ten, this entails acceptance of the right of the Palestinian people to self-determination, with all that this implies.

Finally, it has been universally acknowledged that all the problems which exist between Israel and its neighbours must be resolved in accordance with the principles recognized by the international community, including non-recourse to the use of force and non-acquisition of territory by force. For the Ten, this means that, in accordance with Resolutions 242 and 338 of the Security Council, Israel must put an end to the territorial occupation which it has maintained since the conflict of 1967.

The Ten call on all parties to draw the consequences from these principles and to start the negotiations which are necessary for their implementation.

A negotiated settlement will require the continuing and independent expression of the will of the Palestinian people; the PLO must be associated with the negotiations.

In the Ten's view, furthermore, a process of negotiation presupposes mutual recognition of the existence and the rights of the parties in the conflict.

The Ten express their concern at the collapse of the hopes engendered in September 1982 by certain converging and promising peace initiatives and they declare that the absence of all progress towards a negotiated solution since then exacerbates antagonisms and entrenches the positions of those who favour confrontation.

They note, however, that certain recent developments, such as the meeting of the Islamic Conference in Casablanca and the resumption of the dialogue between Jordan and the Palestinians, have been encouraging. They request all parties to make sincere efforts to re-examine their positions with a view to reducing the gap between them, taking particularly into account elements contained in the Reagan Plan and in the Fez Declaration. They also call upon all parties to renounce the use or threat of force and upon the Government of Israel to put an end to its policy of establishing settlements in the occupied territories.

They undertake to support any constructive step which might be initiated by the parties.

They recall that the United Nations Security Council can play a significant role in the pursuit of a solution to the Middle East conflict negotiated between the parties.

They stress their wish to develop the activity of the European Community on behalf of the populations of the occupied territories.

The governments of the Ten, both individually and collectively through the channel of the presidency, will maintain such contacts with the authorities and personalities of the region as could be useful in bringing the various positions closer together and contributing to the removal of the obstacles which stand in the way of a process of negotiation.

329. Ministry of Defense Statement on Commission of
Inquiry Findings Regarding Murder of Commandos
(4/12/84), Jerusalem, May 28, 1984*

---

1. Maj. Gen. Meir Zorea has submitted to the Minister of Defense the report of the commission of inquiry he chaired, which investigated the causes of the deaths of the terrorists who had hijacked an Egged passenger bus on April 12, 1984, held the passengers hostage and threatened to blow up the bus with its passengers.

2. The Minister of Defense appointed a commission of inquiry after the suspicion surfaced that two of the terrorists who had hijacked the bus remained alive after the IDF force stormed and regained control of the bus and were killed only afterward.

3. During the course of the inquiry, in which testimony was heard from dozens of witnesses, the commission ordered the exhumation of the terrorists' bodies and their examination by a pathologist from the Institute of Forensic Medicine and Abu Kabir in order to determine the causes of death.

4. On the basis of all the evidence before it, the commission determined that two of the terrorists (Jamal Mahmoud Issa Kablan and Mohammed Subhi Mahmoud Barakeh) were killed at an early stage of the strike force's assault on the bus as a result of the attacking force's gunfire. The two other terrorists (Majdi Ahmad Ali abu-Juma'a and Subhi Shehadeh Hassan Abu-Juma'a) were hurt during the retaking of the bus and died at a later stage.

5. From the testimony heard by the commission it has been determined that during the operation to retake the bus, the two captured terrorists were dealt severe blows to the head and body, delivered by weapons in order to stun and prevent any possibility of their detonating the bomb that was aboard the bus at the time. The commission has determined that these blows were an operational necessity, designed to prevent a possible threat to human life.

6. Immediately after the two terrorists were dazed, they were taken off the bus and escorted by security forces personnel to an adjacent field in order to conduct a preliminary interrogation and obtain immediate verification as to the possibility of the existence of booby traps on the bus and/or additional terrorists who might present an immediate danger.

7. During the stage following their removal from the bus, the two terrorists were dealt severe blows by men on the scene.

8. One of the terrorists died of a skull fracture as a result of a blow dealt to the back of the head by a blunt instrument during the time between his removal from the bus, at the earliest, and his evacuation from the site, at the latest. The second terrorist died of a skull fracture as the result of a blow dealt to the back of the head by a blunt instrument during the time between the retaking of the bus by the strike force and his evacuation from the site, at the latest.

9. The commission had determined that no order was issued to the security forces from which it may have been inferred that the two surviving terrorists were to be killed or injured, and no one claims that he received an order to that effect or that he could have construed any order to mean that.

10. The commission has also determined that during the briefings and

operational orders prior to the retaking of the bus, the question of the safety and treatment of terrorists who might be captured by security forces was not dealt with. Neither were orders pertaining to this matter issued after the two terrorists had been captured on the bus. Finally, no arrangements were made to guard the interrogation site with the aim of securing it or preventing unauthorized persons from entering the area.

11. In addition, the commission arrived at findings and recommendations on both the individual and institutional levels.

12. The commission's findings reveal allegations that some security forces personnel may have broken the law. Therefore, an investigation shall be conducted into these allegations on the basis of which it shall be determined what legal proceedings shall be undertaken. The investigation shall be carried out by the CID and the Israeli police force in conjunction with the State Attorney's office. Similarly, disciplinary measures will be taken against a number of other members of the security forces who did not fulfill duties that were incumbent upon them in this case.

13. The findings on the institutional level, relating to the establishment of procedures regarding the detention of terrorists captured by security forces, are, for the most part, acceptable to the Minister of Defense, and he will take steps to have them implemented.

14. The Minister of Defense regards with utmost gravity—and condemns most forcefully—the behavior which led to the deaths of the two terrorists who had been captured on the bus, behavior which is in clear contradistinction to the basic rules and norms incumbent on all, and especially on the security forces. Not even the special circumstances of this case justify such behavior; therefore, legal action shall be taken, in accordance with the evidence uncovered by the investigation, against those suspected of illegal acts or behavior. Furthermore, all possible steps will be taken to ensure that there be no recurrence of a similar incident.

15. The report itself has been classified by the commission as "top secret" because of certain details appearing in it. This announcement contains the primary findings cleared for publication.

330. Excerpts from the Aden-Algiers Agreement between
Fateh Central Committee and the Palestinian Democratic
Alliance, Aden, June 27, 1984*

* 14 J. Palestine Stud. 200 (Autumn 1984).

I. The Occupied Territory

Providing all support to the struggle of our people in the occupied territories against the Israeli occupation, its repressive and terrorist measures and its escalating practice of seizing land, establishing settlements and expelling the inhabitants in preparation for the annexation of the occupied territories.

—Maintaining the unity of national ranks and unified national stand without allowing external problems and difficulties to have repercussions on our people in the occupied territory.

—Reviving the Palestine National Front in the occupied areas on the basis of the resolutions of the sixteenth session of the Palestine National Council and empowering it to lead political and mass struggle against Israeli occupation.

—Adhering to the policy of supporting the steadfastness and struggle of our people and their nationalist forces in the occupied areas, in accordance with the recommendations of the National Front on the expenditure of funds to support steadfastness.

—Serious action to unify popular institutions, such as trade unions, etc. . . . and resolute opposition to all attempts to cause splits and divisions in their ranks.

—Resistance to suspect attempts to bypass the PLO as the sole legitimate representative of the Palestinian people and to contain our people; confrontation of measures aimed at destroying nationalist institutions in the occupied areas and confrontation of the blockade that is intended to force our people to accept plans for the seizure of land.

—Affirming the unity of all nationalist, democratic and progressive Palestinian forces in the territories occupied in 1948 and providing them with all kinds of support within the framework of the national unity of our people.

—Escalating armed and mass struggle against Zionist occupation for the liberation of our occupied land and the recovery of our national rights to return, to self-determination and to establish an independent Palestinian state under the leadership of the PLO, the sole legitimate representative of the Palestinian people.

II. The Visit to Cairo and Palestinian-Egyptian Relations

Affirmation that the visit to Cairo was an infringement of the resolutions of the Palestine National Council and confrontation of its harmful effects, affirming that the PLO is not bound by any of its political consequences or commitments, and passing judgment on it within the framework of the PLO's legitimate institutions.

—Continuing PLO commitment to the resolutions of the Baghdad summit on relations with the Egyptian regime [. . .] and the immediate halting of all political contacts with that regime.

—Reaffirming the resolutions of the sixteenth session of the Palestine National Council on relations with Egyptian nationalist forces and determining relations with the Egyptian regime on basis of its relinquishing the Camp David policy.

III. Jordan

Establishing relations between the PLO and the Jordanian regime on the basis of the constraints mentioned in the resolutions of the Palestine National Council, in particular those adopted at its sixteenth session.

—Taking no joint political action with Jordan regarding a solution of the Palestine problem that could prejudice the PLO's position as sole representative of the Palestinian people.

—Rejecting any solution of the Palestine problem on the basis of the Reagan plan, a compromise territorial solution, the Jordanian option (the Zionist Labour Party's plan) or any plan that prejudices the inalienable national rights of our people to return, to self-determination and to establish an independent state under the leadership of the PLO, their sole legitimate representative. Opposition to any Jordanian attempts to join in these solutions.

—Rejection of the Jordanian step of reviving the parliament as being an infringement of the resolutions of the 1974 Rabat summit, aimed at impairing the right of the PLO to act as the sole representative of the Palestinian people, and thus bypassing it.

IV. The Bloody Events in the Palestinian Arena during the Past Year

Those attending the meeting discussed . . . the grave bloody events that have taken place . . . in the past year affirmed the following:

a. Resort to arms and the use of force with the aim of imposing compulsory solutions of disagreements within the ranks of the revolution conflict with the resolutions of the Palestine National Council affirming the principles of democratic dialogue, and impair the progress and unity of the Palestinian revolution.

b. Rejection of all attempts to split the PLO and divide its ranks and to manufacture alternative leaderships, affirmation of the unity of the Organization and the legitimacy of its institutions.

c. On these bases, this issue will be discussed at the coming Palestine National Council session.

V. Palestinian-Syrian Relations

Establishing relations between the PLO and Syria on national and pan-Arab basis, with a view to the following:

a. Joint action in the struggle against the Israeli enemy and against imperialist and Zionist plans and for the liberation of the occupied Arab territories and the recovery of the rights of the Palestinian people to return, to self-determination and to establish an independent Palestinian state under the leadership of the PLO, their sole legitimate representative.

b. Rejection of American plans, and first and foremost Camp David, the self-government plan and the Reagan plan, and all plans that impair the right of the Palestinian people to return, to self-determination and to establish an independent state, or prejudice the role of the PLO as sole legitimate representative of the Palestinian people, without deputation, delegation or sharing of representation. . . . .

e. Mutual respect for the principles of independence, equality and non-interference in internal affairs.

f. Measures leading to the strengthening of mutual confidence and enabling the Palestinian revolution, side by side with Syria and the Lebanese nationalist forces, to perform its role of resisting the Zionist-imperialist enemy, and solving all pending problems that hinder this.

g. Regarding the Soviet-Syrian statement affirming the unity of the PLO on a nationalist, progressive and anti-imperialist basis, and the need for an early solution of the disagreements within the Palestinian revolution, as one of the principal bases for surmounting the crisis of the revolution and the PLO and for rectifying their relations with Syria.

VI. Lebanon

Strengthening the Lebanese Nationalist-Palestinian-Syrian alliance; developing relations with Lebanese nationalist and progressive forces and supporting their struggle against Zionist occupation, American influence and the Phalangist plan for hegemony, and to safeguard the independence, unity, Arab character and democratic development of Lebanon.

—Organizing relations with the Lebanese nationalist forces with a view to protecting the security of our masses and our camps in Lebanon; maintaining the civil and social rights of our people and insisting on their national rights as regards organization, political action, the bearing of arms and joining the ranks of the revolution, and safeguarding the rights of the PLO and its institutions in Lebanon.

—Joint action together with the Lebanese nationalist forces to escalate armed struggle against Zionist occupation troops.

—the abrogation of the May 17 agreement was an important victory for the struggle of the Lebanese people and supports the struggle of our people and all the Arab peoples against Camp David and the imperialist plan to dominate the area. It was an important stage on the road of continuing national resistance aimed at securing the unconditional ending of the present occupation of Lebanon and its presence [there].

—Joint action by all Palestinian nationalist forces to organize the affairs of our camps, steer them clear of conflicts and maintain their unity through popular committees and mass organizations, and to stimulate all the PLO's institutions in Lebanon.

—Providing support to reinforce the steadfastness of our people in Lebanon through social and mass organizations and through the committee set up by the Central Committee for this purpose. . . .

The Document on Organization

I. The Palestine National Council

1. Expansion of the National Council's office.

2. Recognition of the Palestine Communist Party as a section of the National Council, the number of its representatives being determined through subsequent consultations.

3. Amendment of the National Council's basic regulations to include all the powers agreed on.

II. The Central Council

1. Shall be directly elected from the National Assembly in accordance with rules defining the principles of its formation.

2. The Council shall have powers of decision.

3. The Council shall have the power to call the Executive Committee to account for its implementation of the decisions of the National Council, and also the right to suspend a maximum of one third of its members.

4. The Council shall set up effective permanent committees composed of members of the National Council, on the basis of a front.

5. Internal rules shall be drawn up to regulate the activities of the Central Committee, these rules being regarded as part of the basic regulations.

III. The Executive Committee

1. All nationalist sectors and forces recognized by the Palestine National Council shall be represented on the Executive Committee.

2. The Executive Committee shall elect deputies to its chairmen and define their power and tasks in its internal regulations.

3. A secretariat general shall be formed to a collective working leadership responsible for day to day decisions on all organizational, political, financial, and military problems during the period between two meetings of the Executive Committee; the number of its members is not to exceed one third the number of the members of the Executive Committee.

4. The Executive Committee shall appoint specialist committees from its members to supervise political affairs and affairs in the occupied homeland (including the policy of support for steadfastness) and Lebanon.

5. The Executive Committee shall draw up a schedule of internal rules to govern the activities of the Executive Committee, which shall become part of the basic regulations.

6. Popular Federation: (a) Maintaining the unity of the popular federa-

tions, encouraging them in the performance of their role as regards relations with the masses and adhering to the principle of action on the basis of a front within their ranks. (b) Reunification of the popular federations in conformity with their internal rules and regulations.

IV. The PLO's Departments and Institutions

1. Reorganizing the PLO's departments, institutions and offices on the basis of a front, due respect being paid to competence.

2. The Executive Committee shall set up a special committee to study the situation of the departments, institutions and offices, to ensure their increased effectiveness and the correct performance of their tasks in conformity with paragraph (1) above, and submit its recommendations thereon to the Executive Committee. . . .

331. Excerpts from the Final Communiqué of the Seventeenth Session of the Palestine National Council, Tunis, December 5, 1984*

* 14 J. Palestine Stud. 257 (Winter 1985).

The convening of the PNC has embodied the patriotic Palestinian identity, the independence of Palestinian national decision-making, the freedom of the Palestinian will and the legitimacy of the Palestinian Revolution, which finds its expression in the PLO leader of our people and symbol of our struggle.

The Executive Committee was formed, thus granting the work of the PLO and its institutions the efficiency and effectiveness on all levels and in all fields, including the Arab and international fields.

. . . As a result of all the views and speeches which were presented, including the petition[s] cabled and letters which were received from our people in the occupied homeland and from our friends in the world. . . . Resolutions have included:

1. The concern for the need to achieve Palestinian national unity with independent will and decision-making, faithful and trustworthy [to] the objectives for which our struggle and our Organization have been launched, and for whose sake hundreds of martyrs gave their lives.

Those resolutions have stated the need to continue the dialogue which took place in Aden and Algiers in order to reach national unity.

This dialogue and its consequences can be considered as a positive base to continue the dialogue between the organizations and the national Palestinian forces.

The resolutions of the PNC also stated that the Presidential Bureau of the PNC and the Executive Committee were commissioned to form a committee composed of their members to participate in the follow-up of the global national dialogue in order to enrich it and guarantee its continuity and success in achieving and preserving the Palestinian national unity.

2. The PNC, while considering that the right of self-determination to return and to establish the Palestinian state is the basic approach to any just political move to our cause, reaffirms the resolutions of its previous session relevent [sic] to its position concerning Resolution 242, which does not deal with our cause as the cause of a people and their rights, but as the cause of refugees, thereby denying our national rights.

The PNC reaffirms its rejection of all the plans which do not include these rights, particularly the Camp David accords, the autonomy plan, the Reagan initiative and all plans which do not recognize our national inalienable rights.

Our PNC also declares that its national independent decision-making is linked to the national dimension which considers that any solution to the cause of Palestine can only be achieved in accordance with international legality and on the basis of the UN resolutions relevant to Palestine and within the framework of an international conference in which both superpowers would participate under the auspices of the United Nations and the Security Council in the presence of all parties concerned, including the PLO, on an equal footing. . . .

As for Jordan, the PNC has decided to continue the endeavours to develop relations with Jordan with the objective of coordination for the purpose of achieving our common objectives of the liberation of the Palestinian man and the Palestinian land. This is based on our firm conviction in the one same destiny, on the basis of what the Arabs have agreed upon in Fez and in coordination with the Arab states.

As for fraternal Syria, we value its militant Arab history, its geo-political importance and military capacity. The PNC has taken as a recommendation the need to overcome tensions and bypass the pain, the wounds and the feelings of bitterness with the aim of redressing the relations on a clear and frank basis to include the freedom of will and national Palestinian decision-making, and balance relations within the context of national commitment, away from interference in the internal affairs of either party, in order to mobilize all the potentials for the confrontation of the American-Israeli alliance and of its plans.

As for fraternal Egypt, we highly appreciate and value its place and role. The PNC has clarified the constants in Arab-Egyptian relations and the development in Egyptian policy.

The PNC requested the Executive Committee to follow a policy relying on this basis and which fulfills the requirements of our people in Egypt and the Gaza Strip and to work on enhancing the relations between the two fraternal Egyptian and Palestinian peoples.

As for the Iraq-Iran war which has been going on for over four years, our PNC has urged the Executive Committee and its Chairman, brother Yasser Arafat, to deploy further efforts to halt it immediately, for, by ending it, it will put an end to the flow of Muslim blood and will readjust the balance of forces to the benefit of our nation in confrontation with Zionist aggression.

The PNC reaffirms its resolutions relative to the enhancement and development of relations with the fraternal Arab states in accordance with the resolutions of the 16th session.

The PNC reaffirms the continuation of the support by the Palestinian people and the PLO of the struggle of the Lebanese people for the liberation of their land, their territorial integrity and national sovereignty.

4. The PNC extended to the people of our occupied territory a salute of great pride and high appreciation for their tremendous steadfastness in their confrontation with Zionist occupation and its racist and terrorist practices, this in defence of this freedom and their land, particularly the Holy Places in Jerusalem where al-Masjed al-Aqsa and Al-Haram al-Ibrahimi as well as all the Muslim and Christian sites are being endangered by desecration and judaization.

The council saluted the adherence of our people in the occupied homeland to the PLO and its legitimate leadership which was expressed by demonstrations approving and supporting the converting of the PNC and during which martyrs gave their lives.

Consequently, the PNC decided to name its 17th session the session of the martyrs of the PNC.

The PNC saluted the prisoners and detainees in the enemy's prisons in the occupied homeland and in South Lebanon.

The PNC took a number of resolutions to intensify the steadfastness and resistance of our people in order to achieve the liberation of our land by all legal means, mainly and essentially by the intensification of struggle.

5. The PNC reaffirmed all the resolutions which define the friendly relations between the PLO and the Socialist countries headed by the USSR, the member countries of the Organization of the Islamic Conference, the Non-aligned Movement, People's [Republic of] China, the Organization of African Unity, the Latin American countries, and all countries, forces and movements who are fighting for freedom and independence, justice and peace, against imperialism, racism, particularly the peoples of Namibia and South Africa in their just and common struggle with us against colonialism and racial discrimination.

6. The PNC has decided to review the situation of the institutions of the PLO in a way that will insure their activity and double their effectiveness.

. . .

332. Question to the Commission of the European
Communities on the Arab Boycott of Israel,
December 10, 1984—Answer, April 9, 1985*

* 28 O.J. Eur. Comm. (No. C 135) 17 (1985).

WRITTEN QUESTION NO 1435/84
by Mr Gijsbert de Vries (L–NL)
to the Commission of the European Communities
(*10 December 1984*)
(85/C 135/20)

Subject: The Arab boycott of Israel

On 5 September 1984, the *Guardian* published a report that Shell had cancelled the delivery of several hundred tonnes of polyvinyl chloride to a customer in Tel Aviv because one of its competitors had threatened to 'shout out from the rooftops' that Shell had resumed trade with Israel. According to the *Guardian* 'Shell feared that the inevitable consequence of such publicity would be a dramatic loss of business with the Arab world—and so pulled out'.

The Arab boycott of Israel referred to in this report takes three forms. The Arab countries have no economic relations with the State of Israel (primary boycott); they prohibit all trade with undertakings in non-Arab countries which are suspected of supporting Israel (secondary boycott); they require undertakings from third countries, who wish to enter into relations with Arab countries, not to trade with undertakings subject to a secondary boycott (tertiary boycott).

The 'non-Jewish declarations' also play a part in this matter. These are declarations issued by a third party, an employer for example, stating that a particular employee is not a member of the Jewish faith.

The Arab boycott constitutes an obstacle to one of the most important objectives of the Treaty of Rome: freedom of movement for persons, goods, services and capital. The boycott can be seen as a violation both of the agreements concluded between the Community and Arab countries and of Community rules governing competition. The fact that some Member States have introduced anti-boycott legislation (France, Luxembourg, the Netherlands) whilst others have not, could lead to distortion of trade.

1. Does the Commission not feel that secondary and tertiary boycotts are contrary to the spirit or letter of the agreements concluded between the Community and the Maghreb and Mashreq countries which prohibit discrimination between Member States and their subjects or undertakings?

2. Does the Commission not feel that secondary and tertiary boycotts are contrary to the provisions of Articles 3 (f), 85, 86 or 90 of the EEC Treaty?

Is the Commission prepared to carry out an official investigation into possible instances of contravention of Articles 85 and 86, pursuant to Article 89 of the EEC Treaty?

3. Is it true that national credit insurance companies, such as the NCM in the Netherlands refuse to pay for 'foreseeable' risks, which means that companies suffering losses as a result of their failure to comply with Arab boycott conditions would receive no compensation?

4. Does the Commission share the Dutch Government's view that the issue

of 'non-Israeli' declarations can be curbed by encouraging the issue of positive goods declarations?

Is it true that Bahrain, Iraq, Jordan, Kuwait, North Yemen, Oman, Saudia Arabia and the United Arab Emirates accept positive goods declarations from French exporters?

Does the Commission consider it desirable that national bodies, such as the British Foreign Office, should still be validating signatures appended to negative goods declarations?

5. Does the Commission think that the issue of non-Jewish declarations is contrary to the European Convention on Human Rights and Fundamental Freedoms?

6. Is the Commission considering initiatives pursuant to Article 100 or Article 235 of the EEC Treaty to harmonize the legal and administrative provisions of the Member States banning economic discrimination?

7. Will the Commission submit proposals to the Council along the lines of the Dutch Law on foreign boycotts?

Answer given by Mr Cheysson
on behalf of the Commission
(9 April 1985)

1. As the Commission has already stressed on a number of occasions in statements to Parliament ([1]) or in answers to written questions, secondary and tertiary boycotts including 'non-Israeli declarations' are entirely contrary to the spirit and letter of the agreements concluded by the Community with the Maghreb and Mashreq countries. The clause contained in all these agreements which prohibits discrimination between nationals or undertakings of the Member States constitutes a clear ban on boycotts.

2. The Commission would confirm ([2]) that in so far as the tertiary type of boycott is concerned, it considers that where the conditions for their application are fulfilled the rules of competition contained in the EEC Treaty apply to restrictive or unfair practices resulting from the Arab boycott, notably when such practices may have an appreciable effect on intra-Community trade.

The application of the competition rules with regard to secondary boycotts would appear to be more difficult, if not impossible.

The Commission has already carried out routine investigation in this field on the basis of Council Regulation No 17/62. The facts gathered as a result of this investigation, which was completed in 1982, did not lead to the conclusion that intra-Community trade was appreciably affected by the Arab

[1] See the debate in Parliament, with a contribution by Mr Cheysson, in 1975—Debates of the European Parliament, sitting of 11 May 1975, No. 191.

[2] See the answers to Written Questions No 308/76 by Mr Giraud (OJ No C 305, 27. 12. 1976), No 51/77 by Mrs Dunwoody (OJ No C 233, 29. 9. 1977), No 94/79 by Mr Patijn (OJ No C 164, 2. 7. 1979) and to the oral question by Mr Normanton—Debates of the European Parliament, sitting of 11 April 1978, No. 229.

boycott measures. Consequently, no action was proposed as a result of the investigation.

Should a specific case of possible infringement of the rules of competition be brought to the Commission's knowledge, or if a Community undertaking were to lodge a complaint backed by evidence, the Commission would investigate the matter and take any measures necessary to put a stop to the infringement of the rules in question.

3. The Commission has no exact information on the practice of credit insurance companies, in the Netherlands or elsewhere, as regards the definition of the risks that they will or will not cover.

4, 6 and 7. It is difficult for the Commission to make an accurate assessment of the practices adopted by undertakings in their economic and trade relations with the Arab countries. It would confirm, however, as it has already stated to Parliament (3), that it is willing to look into any complaint presented to it concerning a specific case of discrimination.

Only on the basis of specific cases backed up by a sufficiently detailed body of evidence could the Commission judge whether any action was called for.

On the particular question of harmonizing the Member States' legal and administrative provisions concerning economic discrimination, on the basis of Article 100 or Article 235 of the EEC Treaty, the Commission is still of the opinion (4) that the Treaty provisions and the non-discrimination clause included in the cooperation agreements concluded with a number of Arab countries do not render any particular measures on its part necessary for the present. However, the Commission would point out that for effective measures to be taken against the Arab boycott, all the industrialized countries would first have to adopt legislation declaring such a boycott illegal.

5. It is not within the scope of the Community's powers to determine whether bodies other than the Community are complying with the European Convention on Human Rights and Fundamental Freedoms.

3 See Debates of the European Parliament, sitting of 11 April 1978, No. 229.

4 See answers to Written Questions No 308/76 by Mr Giraud (OJ No C 305, 27. 12. 1976), No 51/77 by Mrs Dunwoody (OJ No C 233, 29. 9. 1977) and No 94/79 by Mr Patijn (OJ No C 164, 2. 7. 1979).

333. General Assembly Resolution 39/49 on the Question
of Palestine, December 11, 1984*

* G.A. Res. 49, 39 U.N. GAOR Supp. (No. 51) at 27, U.N. Doc. A/39/51
(1984).

A

The General Assembly,

Recalling its resolutions 3376 (XXX) of 10 November 1975, 31/20 of 24 November 1976, 32/40 of 2 December 1977, 33/28 of 7 December 1978, 34/65 A and B of 29 November 1979 and 34/65 C and D of 12 December 1979, ES-7/2 of 29 July 1980, 35/169 of 15 December 1980, 36/120 of 10 December 1981, ES-7/4 of 28 April 1982, ES-7/5 of 26 June 1982, ES-7/9 of 24 September 1982, 37/86 A of 10 December 1982 and 38/58 A of 13 December 1983,

Having considered the report of the Committee on the Exercise of the Inalienable Rights of the Palestinian People,[53]

1. *Expresses its appreciation* to the Committee on the Exercise of the Inalienable Rights of the Palestinian People for its efforts in performing the tasks assigned to it by the General Assembly;

2. *Endorses* the recommendations of the Committee contained in paragraphs 155 to 160 of its report and draws the attention of the Security Council to the fact that action on the Committee's recommendations, as repeatedly endorsed by the General Assembly at its thirty-first session and subsequently, is still awaited;

3. *Requests* the Committee to continue to keep under review the situation relating to the question of Palestine as well as the implementation of the Programme of Action for the Achievement of Palestinian Rights[54] adopted by the International Conference on the Question of Palestine and to report and make suggestions to the General Assembly or the Security Council, as appropriate;

4. *Authorizes* the Committee to continue to exert all efforts to promote the implementation of its recommendations, to send delegations or representatives to international conferences where such representation would be considered by it to be appropriate, and to report thereon to the General Assembly at its fortieth session and thereafter;

5. *Requests* the Committee to continue to extend its co-operation to non-governmental organizations in their contribution towards heightening international awareness of the facts relating to the question of Palestine;

6. *Requests* the United Nations Conciliation Commission for Palestine, established under General Assembly resolution 194 (III) of 11 December 1948, as well as other United Nations bodies associated with the question of Palestine, to co-operate fully with the Committee and to make available to it, at its request, the relevant information and documentation which they have at their disposal;

7. *Decides* to circulate the report of the Committee to all the competent bodies of the United Nations and urges them to take the necessary action,

[53] *Official Records of the General Assembly, Thirty-ninth Session, Supplement No. 35* (A/39/35).

[54] *Report of the International Conference on the Question of Palestine, Geneva, 29 August-7 September 1983* (United Nations publication, Sales No. E. 83.I.21), chap. I, sect. B.

as appropriate, in accordance with the Committee's programme of implementation;

8. *Requests* the Secretary-General to continue to provide the Committee with all the necessary facilities for the performance of its tasks.

95th plenary meeting
11 December 1984

B

The General Assembly,

Having considered the report of the Committee on the Exercise of the Inalienable Rights of the Palestinian People,[53]

Noting the particularly relevant information contained in paragraphs 125 to 132 of that report,

Recalling its resolutions 32/40 B of 2 December 1977, 33/28 C of 7 December 1978, 34/65 D of 12 December 1979, 35/169 D of 15 December 1980, 36/120 B of 10 December 1981, 37/86 B of 10 December 1982 and 38/58 B of 13 December 1983,

1. *Notes with appreciation* the action taken by the Secretary-General in compliance with General Assembly resolution 38/58 B;

2. *Requests* the Secretary-General to ensure that the Division for Palestinian Rights of the Secretariat continues to discharge the tasks detailed in paragraph 1 of General Assembly resolution 32/40 B, paragraph 2(*b*) of resolution 34/65 D, paragraph 3 of resolution 36/120 B and paragraphs 2 and 3 of resolution 38/58 B, in consultation with the Committee on the Exercise of the Inalienable Rights of the Palestinian People and under its guidance;

3. *Also requests* the Secretary-General to ensure the continued co-operation of the Department of Public Information and other units of the Secretariat in enabling the Division for Palestinian Rights to perform its tasks and in covering adequately the various aspects of the question of Palestine;

4. *Invites* all Governments and organizations to lend their co-operation to the Committee on the Exercise of the Inalienable Rights of the Palestinian People and the Division for Palestinian Rights in the performance of their tasks;

5. *Notes with appreciation* the action taken by Member States to observe annually on 29 November the International Day of Solidarity with the Palestinian People and the issuance by them of special postage stamps for the occasion.

95th plenary meeting
11 December 1984

C

The General Assembly,

Having considered the report of the Committee on the Exercise of the Inalienable Rights of the Palestinian People,[53]

Noting in particular, the information contained in paragraphs 133 to 142 of that report,

Recalling its resolution 38/58 E of 13 December 1983,

Convinced that the world-wide dissemination of accurate and comprehensive information and the role of non-governmental organizations and institutions remain of vital importance in heightening awareness of and support for the inalienable rights of the Palestinian people to self-determination and to the establishment of an independent sovereign Palestinian State,

1. *Notes with appreciation* the action taken by the Department of Public Information of the Secretariat in compliance with General Assembly resolution 38/58 E;

2. *Requests* that the Department of Public Information, in full co-operation and co-ordination with the Committee on the Exercise of the Inalienable Rights of the Palestinian People, should:

(*a*) Continue the implementation of all parts of General Assembly resolution 38/58 E;

(*b*) Disseminate all information on the activities of the United Nations system relating to Palestine;

(*c*) Expand and update publications and audio-visual material on the facts and developments pertaining to the question of Palestine;

(*d*) Publish newsletters and articles in its relevant publications on Israeli violations of the human rights of the Arab inhabitants of the occupied territories;

(*e*) Organize fact-finding missions to the area for journalists;

(*f*) Organize regional and national encounters for journalists.

95th plenary meeting
11 December 1984

D

The General Assembly,

Recalling its resolution 38/58 C of 13 December 1984, in which it, *inter alia*, endorsed the convening of an International Peace Conference on the Middle East,

Reaffirming paragraph 5 of its resolution 38/58 C, in which it requested the Secretary-General to undertake preparatory measures to convene the Conference,

Having considered the reports of the Secretary-General of 13 March 1984[55] and 13 September 1984,[56] in which he stated that, *inter alia*, "it is clear from

---

[55] A/39/130-S/16409. For the printed text, see *Official Records of the Security Council, Thirty-ninth Year, Supplement for January, February and March 1984*, document S/16409.

[56] A/39/130/Add.1-S/16409/Add.1. For the printed text, see *Official Records of the Security Council, Thirty-ninth Year, Supplement for July, August and September 1984*, document S/16409/Add.1.

the replies of the Governments of Israel and the United States of America that they are not prepared to participate in the proposed Conference",[57]

Reiterating its conviction that the convening of the Conference would constitute a major contribution by the United Nations towards the achievement of a comprehensive, just and lasting solution to the Arab-Israeli conflict,

1. *Takes note* of the reports of the Secretary-General;

2. *Reaffirms* its endorsement of the call for convening the International Peace Conference on the Middle East in conformity with the provisions of General Assembly resolution 38/58 C;

3. *Expresses its regret* at the negative response of the two Governments and calls upon them to reconsider their position towards the Conference;

4. *Urges* all Governments to make additional constructive efforts and to strengthen their political will in order to convene the Conference without delay and for the achievement of its peaceful objectives;

5. *Requests* the Secretary-General, in consultation with the Security Council, to continue his efforts with a view to convening the Conference and to report thereon to the General Assembly not later than 15 March 1985;[58]

6. *Decides* to consider at its fortieth session the report of the Secretary-General on the implementation of the present resolution.

95th plenary meeting
11 December 1984

[57] *Ibid.*, para. 4.

[58] The report was issued under the symbol A/40/168-S/17014. For the printed text, see *Official Records of the Security Council, Fortieth Year, Supplement for January, February and March 1985*, document S/17014.

334. General Assembly Resolution 39/169 on the Living Conditions of the Palestinian People in the Occupied Palestinian Territories, December 17, 1984*

* G.A. Res. 169, 39 U.N. GAOR Supp. (No. 51) at 130, U.N. Doc. A/39/ 51 (1984).

The General Assembly,

Recalling the Vancouver Declaration on Human Settlements, 1976,[35] and the relevant recommendations for national action[36] adopted by Habitat: United Nations Conference on Human Settlements,

Recalling also its resolution 38/166 of 19 December 1983,

Gravely alarmed by the continuation of the Israeli settlement policies, which have been declared null and void and a major obstacle to peace,

Recognizing the need to investigate ways and means of arresting the deterioration in the economy of the occupied Palestinian territories,

1. *Takes note with concern* of the report of the Secretary-General on the living conditions of the Palestinian people in the occupied Palestinian territories;[37]

2. *Takes note also* of the statement made on 29 October 1984 by the Observer of the Palestine Liberation Organization;[38]

3. *Rejects* the Israeli plans and actions intended to change the demographic composition of the occupied Palestinian territories, particularly the increase and expansion of the Israeli settlements, and other plans and actions creating conditions leading to the displacement and exodus of the Palestinians from the occupied Palestinian territories;

4. *Expresses its alarm* at the deterioration, as a result of the Israeli occupation, in the living conditions of the Palestinian people in the Palestinian territories occupied since 1967;

5. *Affirms* that the Israeli occupation is contradictory to the basic requirements for the social and economic development of the Palestinian people in the occupied Palestinian territories;

6. *Requests* the Secretary-General:

(*a*) To organize, in 1985, a seminar on remedies for the deterioration of the economic and social conditions of the Palestinian people in the occupied Palestinian territories;

(*b*) To make the necessary preparations for the seminar providing for the participation of the Palestine Liberation Organization;

(*c*) To invite experts to present papers to the seminar;

(*d*) To invite also relevant intergovernmental and nongovernmental organizations;

(*e*) To report to the General Assembly as its fortieth session, through the Economic and Social Council, on the seminar.

103rd plenary meeting
17 December 1984

---

[35] *Report of Habitat: United Nations Conference on Human Settlements, Vancouver, 31 May-11 June 1976* (United Nations publication, Sales No. E.76.IV.7 and corrigendum), chap. I.

[36] *Ibid.*, chap. II.

[37] A/39/233-E/1984/79.

[38] *Official Records of the General Assembly, Thirty-ninth Session, Second Committee*, 26th meeting, paras. 51-55.

335. General Assembly Resolution 39/223 on Economic Development Projects in the Occupied Palestinian Territories, December 18, 1984*

* G.A. Res. 223, 39 U.N. GAOR Supp. (No. 51) at 170, U.N. Doc. A/39/ 51 (1984).

The General Assembly,

Aware of the Israeli restrictions imposed on the foreign trade of the occupied Palestinian territories,

Aware also of the imposed domination of the Palestinian market by Israel,

Taking into account the need to give Palestinian firms and products direct access to external markets without Israeli interference,

1. *Calls* for the urgent lifting of the Israeli restrictions imposed on the economy of the occupied Palestinian territories;

2. *Recognizes* the Palestinian interest in establishing a seaport in the occupied Gaza Strip to give Palestinian firms and products direct access to external markets;

3. *Calls upon* all concerned to facilitate the establishment of a seaport in the occupied Gaza Strip;

4. *Also calls upon* all concerned to facilitate the establishment of a cement plant in the occupied West Bank and a citrus plant in the occupied Gaza Strip;

5. *Requests* the Secretary-General to report to the General Assembly at its fortieth session, through the Economic and Social Council, on the progress made in the implementation of the present resolution.

104th plenary meeting
18 December 1984

336. Text of Jordanian-Palestinian Accord, February 11, 1985*

---

* 14 J. Palestine Stud. 206 (Spring 1985).

The full text of the joint action agreement recently reached by Jordan and the Palestine Liberation Organization was released to the press in Amman on Saturday, February 23, 1985 by Jordan's Acting Minister of Information Taher Hikmat. Following is the official text of the accord:

Bid for Joint Action

Emanating from the spirit of the Fez Summit resolutions, approved by Arab states, and from United Nations resolutions relating to the Palestine question,

In accordance with international legitimacy, and

Deriving from a common understanding on the establishment of a special relationship between the Jordanian and Palestinian peoples,

The Government of the Hashemite Kingdom of Jordan and the Palestine Liberation Organization have agreed to move together towards the achievement of a peaceful and just settlement of the Middle East crisis and the termination of Israeli occupation of the occupied Arab territories, including Jerusalem, on the basis of the following principles:

1. Total withdrawal from the territories occupied in 1967 for comprehensive peace as established in United Nations and Security Council Resolutions.

2. Right of self-determination for the Palestinian people: Palestinians will exercise their inalienable right of self-determination when Jordanians and Palestinians will be able to do so within the context of the formation of the proposed confederated Arab states of Jordan and Palestine.

3. Resolution of the problem of Palestinian refugees in accordance with United Nations resolutions.

4. Resolutions of the Palestine question in all its aspects.

5. And on this basis, peace negotiations will be conducted under the auspices of an International Conference to which the five Permanent Members of the Security Council and all the parties to the conflict will participate, including the Palestine Liberation Organization, the sole legitimate representative of the Palestine people, within a joint delegation (joint Jordanian-Palestinian Delegation).

337. Communiqué of the Executive Committee of the PLO
on the Plan of Joint Palestinian-Jordanian Action,
February 19, 1985*

* 14 J. Palestine Stud. 205 (Spring 1985).

The Executive Committee of the Palestine Liberation Organization held a series of meetings between the 17th and the 18th of February 1985 under the chairmanship of Yasser Arafat, Chairman of the Executive Committee of the Palestine Liberation Organization.

The Executive Committee discussed the present issues on the agenda and the developments of the political and military situation in the area.

The Executive Committee discussed the Jordanian-Palestinian plan of action which was agreed upon on Monday, February 11th, 1985 between the PLO and the government of the Hashemite Kingdom of Jordan.

The Executive Committee discussed the detailed reports pertaining to the ongoing Palestinian-Jordanian talks which followed the agreement as well as the aide-memoire (explanatory memorandum) which was transmitted.

The Executive Committee of the Palestine Liberation Organization reaffirms that the joint action between the PLO and Jordan is based on the following:

1. Palestinian legitimacy as defined in the resolutions of the Palestine National Council, particularly in its 16th and 17th Sessions.

2. Arab legitimacy as defined in the resolutions of the Arab Summits, particularly the resolutions of the Rabat and Fez Summits.

3. International legitimacy as defined in the United Nations resolutions.

The joint action is based on all the previous resolutions which were approved, and which are:

1. Ending the Zionist occupation of the occupied Arab territories, including Jerusalem.

2. The realization of the inalienable rights of the Palestinian people, including their right to return, to self-determination and to the establishment of their independent state in their national homeland.

3. The rejection of all the plans of capitulation and separate deals, such as the self-rule plan, the Camp David Accords, the Reagan initiative and Security Council Resolution 242 which do not constitute a sound basis for a just solution which guarantees the national rights of the Palestinian people.

4. The rejection of the granting of mandates and representation (al-tafwid w-al-inaba) or the participation in the right of representation to any other party.

The formula for joint Palestinian-Jordanian action aims at establishing a nucleus for common Arab action away from axis-building and for serious and effective action based on total Arab solidarity.

A reaffirmation of the priviledges and specific relations between the Jordanian and the Palestinian people and the common aim of both peoples in conformity with the resolutions of the Palestine National Council are represented in the establishment of a Confederation between the two states of Jordan and Palestine. For the right framework to achieve the required aims is the convening of an international conference under the auspices of the United Nations, to be attended by the permanent members of states in the security council and with the participation of the PLO in its capacity as the sole legitimate representative of the Palestinian people and on an equal footing with the parties concerned in the conflict.

Based upon these foundations from which the joint Palestinian-Jordanian plan of action emanates, the Executive Committee of the Palestine Liberation Organization decided to approve the plan of action affirming that this action must include the parties concerned represented within a joint Arab Delegation, and that this plan of action receive total Arab support.

The Executive Committee of the Palestine Liberation Organization, Tunis, February 19th, 1985.

338. Statement by the EEC Foreign Ministers on the Arab-Israeli Conflict, April 29, 1985*

* 18 Bull. Eur. Comm. (No. 4) 59 (1985).

'The Ten Ministers for Foreign Affairs continue to maintain a close interest in developments in the Middle East. They welcomed recent moves towards a reactivation of the negotiating process in the search for a solution to the Arab-Israeli conflict, notably the Jordan/Palestinian agreement reached on 11 February at the initiative of King Hussein, which contained a commitment to negotiations for peace in accordance with UN resolutions, including resolutions of the Security Council. In the view of the Ten this represents a constructive step forward. They also welcomed the ideas put forward by the President of Egypt.

The Ten consider that these important initiatives reflect a desire for movement towards a peaceful solution. This deserves encouragement and a positive response.

They confirm their conviction that the achievement of a just and lasting solution calls for the participation and the active support of all the parties concerned. The Ten consider that no effort should be spared to maintain and strengthen the present movement in the peace process and to facilitate a dialogue between all the parties to the conflict.

The Ten reconfirm their willingness to contribute to a comprehensive, just and peaceful settlement of the Middle East question on the basis of the principles which they have stated many times in the past and to which they continue to adhere. In particular, they recall the right of all States in the region, including Israel, to existence and security, the right of the Palestinian people to self-determination, with all that this implies. With regard to the association of the PLO with the negotiations, the Ten refer to their well-known positions. In their contacts with all the parties concerned the Ten, both collectively and individually, will work to promote the reconciliation of the various positions.'

339. Excerpts from the Final Communiqué on the Work
of the Emergency Arab Summit Conference, Casablanca,

August 9, 1985*

* 15 J. Palestine Stud. 214 (Autumn 1985).

The summit conference convened in an extraordinary session in Casablanca during the period 7-9 August 1985, at the invitation of His Majesty King Hasan II, king of the Kingdom of Morocco.

In consolidation of the solidarity among the Arab states, and in strengthening the march of joint Arab action on the basis of the principles of the Charter of the Arab League and the league's decisions and the treaties concluded within the league's framework, the conference studied the most important current Arab issues in an atmosphere of fraternity and understanding.

The conference devoted all its attention to the issue of clearing the Arab atmosphere, owing to the significance of this issue. And within this sphere, the conference reaffirms its belief in the necessity of solidarity among the Arab states, particularly in these difficult circumstances which require the mobilization of the efforts of the nation and the disregarding of differences, whatever these may be, among its states in order to face up to the decisive period through which it is passing. The conference declares its full commitment to all clauses of the Charter of Arab Solidarity, which was approved by the third Arab summit, held in Casablanca in September 1965. The conference entrusts the following committees, which consist of a number of member states and the secretary general of the Arab League, to work for solving the differences among some brothers.

A committee which consists of the Kingdom of Saudi Arabia and the Tunisian Republic will strive to bring about reconciliation between the Hashemite Kingdom of Jordan and the Syrian Arab Republic and between the Iraqi Republic and the Syrian Arab Republic. A committee consisting of the Kingdom of Morocco, the United Arab Emirates, and the Islamic Republic of Mauritania will strive to bring about reconciliation between the Iraqi Republic and the Socialist People's Libyan Arab Jamahiriyah, and between the Palestine Liberation Organization and the Socialist People's Libyan Arab Jamahiriyah.

The committees shall submit their reports to the conference chairman, His Majesty King Hasan II. The conference calls on the brothers to respond to these efforts in a true spirit of Arab fraternity. . . .

Within the framework of this discussion of the various developments which the Palestinian issue is going through, the conference heard a detailed explanation from his Majesty King Hussein of the Hashemite Kingdom of Jordan, and brother Yasir Arafat, chairman of the Palestine Liberation Organization, regarding the Jordanian-Palestinian agreement which was signed in 'Amman on 11 February 1985. The conference recorded with full appreciation the detailed explanations submitted by His Majesty King Hussein and brother Yasir Arafat about the compatibility between the Jordanian-Palestinian action plan and the Fez Plan and considers it an action plan for implementing the Arab peace plan for the realization of a peaceful, just, and comprehensive settlement guaranteeing the withdrawal of the Israeli occupation forces from all the occupied Arab territories, at the forefront of which is Holy Jerusalem, and the regaining of the firm national rights of the Palestinian Arab people. And after dealing with this issue in an extensive study, from all aspects, the conference confirms the need to continue the collective Arab adherence to the spirit, principles, and resolutions of the Fez summit conference.

The conference confirms its previous resolutions concerning the Palestinian problem, its backing and support for the PLO in its capacity as sole legitimate representative of the Palestinian Arab people, and its support for its efforts aimed at securing the firm national rights of the Palestinian people. It also confirms the right of the Palestinian people to the independence of its national decision and to not allow any side to interfere in its internal affairs. The conference considers that the holding of an international conference within the framework of the UN facilitates the achievement of peace in the Arab region, with the presence and participation of the U.S.S.R., the United States, and other permanent members of the Security Council, and with the presence and participation of the PLO, the sole legitimate representative of the Palestinian people alongside the other concerned parties.

The conference salutes the steadfastness of the Palestinian Arab people in the occupied Arab areas and their growing struggle against the forces of Israeli occupation, and the conference affirms its commitment to supporting this steadfastness and its development to confront the expansionist plans which seek to Judaize Palestinian territory and render the sons of the Palestinian people homeless.

The conference affirms its condemnation of the terrorist and racist practices of the Israeli occupation authorities in occupied Arab and Palestinian territories, and it appeals to world public opinion to support the Palestinian and Arab people in their resistance to these practices which contradict international laws and human rights. It also appeals to the world community to take practical measures to stand in the way of the Zionist practices.

It affirms previous commitments to giving material political and media support to the PLO—the sole legitimate representative of the Palestinian people, and leader of their struggle to recover their usurped rights. Regarding the suffering endured by the Palestinian camps after the Israeli invasion of Lebanon in 1982 and the massacres and slaughters that ensued; in order to guard against the dangers of displacement and destitution which threaten the Palestinian existence in those camps; and in order to ensure the safety of this existence and the rights of the Palestinian people to work and movement; and to strengthen Lebanese-Palestinian fraternal ties, the conference calls on the Lebanese government and the PLO to cooperate and coordinate between themselves in whatever concerns Palestinian affairs and protects the Palestinian camps in Lebanon, in accordance with the agreements concluded between them.

The conference also stresses that it will strive to implement the resolutions

which the Arab League Council adopted at its emergency session on 8 and
9 June 1985.

The conference expresses extreme concern about the worsening conditions in Lebanon, in a manner which threatens the fate and unity of Lebanese soil and people. The conference affirms that it will assist and support
the Lebanese people and its government to oppose the plans which seek to
dismember and partition Lebanon, and in order to enable Lebanon to eliminate the sectarian sedition which is manipulated by the hostile forces.

The conference also affirms the importance of a stable Lebanon, the need
to preserve its unity and security, and the need to end Israeli occupation of
all its territory.

Committed to the principles in which the Arab nation believes, and inspired by its civilization and deep-rooted origin and ancient traditions, the
conference strongly condemns terrorism in all its shapes, forms, and origins, and foremost Israeli terrorism inside and outside the occupied Arab
areas. It considers that resorting to terrorism does not run parallel with the
lofty ideals of humanity. . . .

340. Senate Joint Resolution 98 Reaffirming the Senate's Condemnation of G.A. Res. 3379 (XXX) Equating Zionism with Racism, August 15, 1985*

* S.J. Res. 98, 99 Stat. 385 (1985).

Whereas, on November 10, 1975, the thirtieth session of the United Nations General Assembly adopted Resolution 3379 which sought to legitimize the lie, first perpetrated at the United Nations General Assembly by representatives of the Union of Socialist Soviet Republics in 1963, that Zionism is a form of racism; and

Whereas Resolution 3379 of the thirtieth United Nations General Assembly directly contravenes the most basic principles and purposes of the United Nations Charter and undermines universal human rights values and principles; and

Whereas that infamous resolution threatens directly the integrity and legitimacy of a member state by singling out for slanderous attack the national movement which gave birth to the State of Israel; and

Whereas the adoption of Resolution 3379 by the thirtieth United Nations General Assembly constituted one of that organization's darkest moments and may fuel the flames of antisemitism and anti-Zionism; and

Whereas the United States Congress sharply condemned the passage of Resolution 3379 ten years ago "in that said resolution encourages antisemitism by wrongly associating and equating Zionism with racism": Now, therefore, be it

Resolved by the Senate and House of Representatives of the United States of America in Congress assembled, That the Congress—

(1) soundly denounces and condemns any linkage between Zionism and racism;

(2) considers UNGA Resolution 3379 to be a permanent smear upon the reputation of the United Nations and to be totally inconsistent with that organization's declared purposes and principles;

(3) unequivocally states that the premise of UNGA Resolution 3379 which equates Zionism with racism is itself clearly a form of bigotry; and

(4) formally repudiates UNGA Resolution 3379, and calls upon the Parliaments of all countries which value freedom and democracy to do the same.

Approved August 15, 1985.

341. The Syrian-Jordanian Joint Communiqué, Damascus, November 13, 1985*

---

* 15 J. Palestine Stud. 199 (Spring 1986).

At the invitation of Dr. 'Abd al-Ra'uf al-Kasm, prime minister of the Syrian Arab Republic, Mr. Zayd al-Rifa'i, prime minister of the Hashimite Kingdom of Jordan, visited Syria from 12 to 13 November 1985, during which a series of meetings were held which dealt with the situation in the region and the bilateral relations between the two brotherly countries.

Others who participated on the Syrian side were Dr. Salim Yasin, deputy prime minister for economic affairs; Faruq al-Shar', foreign minister; Riyadh al-Hajj Khalil, minister of supply and domestic commerce; Dr. Muhammad al-'Imadi, minister of economy and foreign trade; 'Isam al-Na'ib, minister of state for foreign affairs; Dr. Qahtan al-Sayufi, minister of finance; 'Ali al-Tarabulsi, minister of industry; and Dr. Hashim al-Mutawalli, assistant governor of the Syrian Central Bank.

Participating on the Jordanian side were Marwan al-Qasim, president of the Royal Hashimite Diwan; Tahir al-Masri, minister of foreign affairs; Dr. Raja'i al-Mu'ashshir, minister of supply, industry, and commerce; Dr. Hanna 'Awdah, minister of finance; and Husayn al-Qasim, governor of the Central Bank.

President Hafiz al-Asad met Zayd al-Rifa'i and received from him a letter from His Highness King Hussein, King of the Hashimite Kingdom of Jordan. Asad carried with him a letter of reply. During the review of the situation in the region and in the field of the Arab-Israeli conflict, points of view coincided, particularly on the following matters:

1. The necessity of strengthening joint Arab efforts in various fields to achieve a just, comprehensive, and lasting peace and to confront Israeli aggression.

2. Proceeding from the belief of the two sides that the issue of Palestine is the central Arab national issue, the two stressed their rejection of any partial or separate settlement, or of direct talks with Israel.

Likewise, they stressed that a just, comprehensive, and lasting peace can be achieved only through convening an international conference which all concerned parties would attend, under the auspices of the United Nations and in which the Soviet Union and the United States would participate.

3. The two sides affirmed that political forward motion requires the continuation of serious work to build the Arab nation's defense and indigenous capabilities in order to achieve its goals in liberating the land and regaining rights.

4. In the field of bilateral relations between the two brotherly countries, progress was made in economic cooperation and coordination, in completing the implementation of the provisions of the Arab Common Market and lifting all imposed barriers on the exchange of agricultural commodities and industrial products in both countries, and in reaching the stage of a unified market. The two sides agreed on taking all measures necessary to achieve this.

They also agreed on reviving the work of the Joint Higher Council and branch councils emanating from it, as well as supporting joint institutions between the two countries.

Dr. 'Abd al-Ra'uf al-Kasm, the prime minister, will visit the Hashimite Kingdom of Jordan following the invitation of Zayd al-Rifa'i, the Jordanian prime minister, at the soonest possible time.

342. General Assembly Resolution 40/96 on the Question
of Palestine, December 12, 1985*

* G.A. Res. 40/96 (1985).

A

The General Assembly,

Recalling its resolutions 3376 (XXX) of 10 November 1975, 31/20 of 24 November 1976, 32/40 of 2 December 1977, 33/28 of 7 December 1978, 34/65 A and B of 29 November 1979 and 34/65 C and D of 12 December 1979, ES-7/2 of 29 July 1980, 35/169 of 15 December 1980, 36/120 of 10 December 1981, ES-7/4 of 28 April 1982, ES-7/5 of 26 June 1982, ES-7/9 of 24 September 1982, 37/86 A of 10 December 1982, 38/58 A of 13 December 1983 and 39/49 A of 11 December 1984,

Having considered the report of the Committee on the Exercise of the Inalienable Rights of the Palestinian People,[102]

1. *Expresses its appreciation* to the Committee on the Exercise of the Inalienable Rights of the Palestinian People for its efforts in performing the tasks assigned to it by the General Assembly;

2. *Endorses* the recommendations of the Committee contained in paragraphs 163 to 172 of its report and draws the attention of the Security Council to the fact that action on the Committee's recommendations, as repeatedly endorsed by the General Assembly at its thirty-first session and subsequently, is still awaited;

3. *Requests* the Committee to continue to keep under review the situation relating to the question of Palestine as well as the implementation of the Programme of Action for the Achievement of Palestinian Rights[103] adopted by the International Conference on the Question of Palestine and to report and make suggestions to the General Assembly or the Security Council, as appropriate;

4. *Authorizes* the Committee to continue to exert all efforts to promote the implementation of its recommendations, including representation at conferences and meetings and the sending of delegations where such activities would be considered by it to be appropriate, and to report thereon to the General Assembly at its forty-first session and thereafter;

5. *Requests* the Committee to continue to extend its co-operation to nongovernmental organizations in their contribution towards heightening international awareness of the facts relating to the question of Palestine and in creating a more favourable atmosphere for the full implementation of the Committee's recommendations, and to take the necessary steps to expand its contacts with those organizations;

6. *Requests* the United Nations Conciliation Commission for Palestine, established under General Assembly resolution 194 (III) of 11 December 1948, as well as other United Nations bodies associated with the question of Palestine, to co-operate fully with the Committee and to make available to

---

[102] *Official Records of the General Assembly, Fortieth Session, Supplement No. 35* (A/40/35).

[103] *Report of the International Conference on the Question of Palestine, Geneva, 29 August-7 September 1983* (United Nations publication, Sales No. E.83.I.21), chap. I, sect. B.

it, at its request, the relevant information and documentation which they have at their disposal;

7. *Decides* to circulate the report of the Committee to all the competent bodies of the United Nations and urges them to take the necessary action, as appropriate, in accordance with the Committee's programme of implementation;

8. *Requests* the Secretary-General to continue to provide the Committee with all the necessary facilities for the performance of its tasks.

B

The General Assembly,

Having considered the report of the Committee on the Exercise of the Inalienable Rights of the Palestinian People,[104]

Noting the particularly relevant information contained in paragraphs 135 to 150 of that report,

Recalling its resolutions 32/40 B of 2 December 1977, 33/28 C of 7 December 1978, 34/65 D of 12 December 1979, 35/169 D of 15 December 1980, 36/120 B of 10 December 1981, 37/86 B of 10 December 1982, 38/58 B of 13 December 1983 and 39/49 B of 11 December 1984,

1. *Notes with appreciation* the action taken by the Secretary-General in compliance with General Assembly resolution 39/49 B;

2. *Requests* the Secretary-General to ensure that the Division for Palestinian Rights of the Secretariat continues to discharge the tasks detailed in paragraph 1 of General Assembly resolution 32/40 B, paragraph 2 (*b*) of resolution 34/65 D, paragraph 3 of resolution 36/120 B and paragraphs 2 and 3 of resolution 38/58 B, in consultation with the Committee on the Exercise of the Inalienable Rights of the Palestinian People and under its guidance;

3. *Also requests* the Secretary-General to provide the Division for Palestinian Rights with the necessary resources to accomplish its tasks and to expand its work programme particularly through additional meetings for non-governmental organizations, in order to heighten awareness of the facts relating to the question of Palestine and to create a more favourable atmosphere for the full implementation of the recommendations of the Committee on the Exercise of the Inalienable Rights of the Palestinian People;

4. *Also requests* the Secretary-General to ensure the continued co-operation of the Department of Public Information and other units of the Secretariat in enabling the Division for Palestinian Rights to perform its tasks and in covering adequately the various aspects of the question of Palestine;

5. *Invites* all Governments and organizations to lend their co-operation to the Committee on the Exercise of the Inalienable Rights of the Palestinian People and the Division for Palestinian Rights in the performance of their tasks;

6. *Notes with appreciation* the action taken by Member States to observe

[104] *Official Records of the General Assembly, Fortieth Session, Supplement No. 35* (A/40/35).

annually on 29 November the International Day of Solidarity with the Palestinian People and the issuance by them of special postage stamps for the occasion.

C

The General Assembly,

Having considered the report of the Committee on the Exercise of the Inalienable Rights of the Palestinian People,[105]

Noting, in particular, the information contained in paragraphs 151 to 162 of that report,

Recalling its resolutions 38/58 E of 13 December 1983 and 39/49 C of 11 December 1984,

Convinced that the world-wide dissemination of accurate and comprehensive information and the role of non-governmental organizations and institutions remain of vital importance in heightening awareness of and support for the inalienable rights of the Palestinian people to self-determination and to the establishment of an independent sovereign Palestinian State,

1. *Notes with appreciation* the action taken by the Department of Public Information of the Secretariat in compliance with General Assembly resolutions 38/58 E and 39/49 C;

2. *Requests* that the Department of Public Information, in full co-operation and co-ordination with the Committee on the Exercise of the Inalienable Rights of the Palestinian People, should continue its special information programme on the question of Palestine for the biennium 1986-1987 and, in particular, to:

(*a*) Disseminate information on all the activities of the United Nations system relating to the question of Palestine;

(*b*) Continue to update publications on the facts and developments pertaining to the question of Palestine;

(*c*) Publish brochures and booklets on the various aspects of the question of Palestine, including Israeli violations of the human rights of the Arab inhabitants of the occupied territories;

(*d*) Expand its audio-visual material on the question of Palestine, including the production of a new film, special series of radio programmes and television broadcast;

(*e*) Organize fact-finding news missions to the area for journalists;

(*f*) Organize regional and national encounters for journalists.

D

The General Assembly,

Recalling its resolutions 38/58 C of 13 December 1983 and 39/49 D of 11 December 1984, in which it, *inter alia*, endorsed the convening of the International Peace Conference on the Middle East,

[105] *Ibid.*

Reaffirming its resolutions 39/49 D, in which it, *inter alia*, requested the Secretary-General, in consultation with the Security Council, to continue his efforts with a view to convening the Conference,

Having considered the reply of the President of the Security Council to the Secretary-General, dated 26 February 1985, in which he, *inter alia*, states on the subject of the Conference: "in this context, members of the Council invite the Secretary-General to continue consultations on the subject in any manner he deems appropriate in the light of General Assembly resolution 39/49 D",[106]

Having considered again the reports of the Secretary-General of 13 March 1984[107] and 13 September 1984,[108] in which he stated, *inter alia*, that "it is clear from the replies of the Governments of Israel and the United States of America that they are not prepared to participate in the proposed Conference", and regretting the continued negative response of these two Governments and the lack of willingness to reconsider their position towards the Conference,

Having considered the reports of the Secretary-General of 11 March 1985[109] and of 22 October 1985,[110] in which he, *inter alia*, refers to the difficulties experienced in his efforts made last year with a view to convening the Conference,

Having heard the constructive statements made by numerous representatives, including that of the Palestine Liberation Organization,

Taking note of the positive positions of the concerned parties, including the Palestine Liberation Organization, and of other States on the convening of the Conference,[111]

Taking note also of the position of the Palestine Liberation Organization which condemns all acts of terrorism, whether committed by States or individuals, including acts of terrorism committed by Israel against the Palestinian people and the Arab nation,

Reiterating once again its conviction that the convening of the Conference would constitute a major contribution by the United Nations towards the achievement of a comprehensive, just and lasting solution to the Arab-Israeli conflict,

1. *Takes note with appreciation* of the reports of the Secretary-General;[112]

---

[106] A/40/168-S/17014.

[107] A/39/130-S/16409. For the printed text, see *Official Records of the Security Council, Supplement for January, February and March 1984*, document S/16409.

[108] *Ibid.*

[109] A/40/168-S/17014.

[110] A/40/779.

[111] A/39/130/Add.1-S/16409/Add.1. For the printed text, see *Official Records of the Security Council, Supplement for January, February and March 1984*, document S/16409/Add.1.

[112] A/39/130-S/16409, for the printed text, see *Official Records of the Security Council, Supplement for January, February and March 1984*, document S/16409; A/39/130/Add.1-S/16409/Add.1, for the printed text, see *Official Records of the Security Council, Supplement for January, February and March 1984*, document S/16409/Add.1; A/40/168-S/17014; A/40/779.

2. *Reaffirms again* its endorsement of the call for convening the International Peace Conference on the Middle East in conformity with the provisions of General Assembly resolution 38/58 C;

3. *Stresses* the urgent need for additional constructive efforts by all Governments in order to convene the Conference without further delay and for the achievement of its peaceful objectives;

4. *Determines* that the question of Palestine is the root-cause of the Arab-Israeli conflict in the Middle East;

5. *Calls upon* the Governments of Israel and the United States of America to reconsider their positions towards the attainment of peace in the Middle East through the convening of the Conference;

6. *Requests* the Secretary-General, in consultation with the Security Council, to continue his efforts with a view to convening the Conference and to report thereon to the General Assembly not later than 15 March 1986;

7. *Decides to consider* at its forty-first session the report of the Secretary-General on the implementation of the present resolution.

343. General Assembly Resolution 40/161 on the Report of the Special Committee to Investigate Israeli Practice Affecting the Human Rights of the People of the Occupied Territories, December 16, 1985*

* G.A. Res. 40/161 (1985).

A

The General Assembly,

Recalling its resolutions 38/79 A of 15 December 1983 and 39/95 A of 14 December 1984,

Taking note of the report of the International Committee of the Red Cross of 13 December 1983,[3]

Taking note of the report of the Secretary-General of 30 September 1985,[4]

Taking note also of the report of the Special Committee to Investigate Israeli Practices Affecting the Human Rights of the Population of the Occupied Territories,[5]

1. *Calls upon* Israel to release all Arabs arbitrarily detained and/or imprisoned as a result of their struggle for self-determination and for the liberation of their territories;

2. *Notes* the initial release of Ziyad Abu Eain, among others, from prison on 20 May 1985;

3. *Deplores* the Israeli subsequent arbitrary detention of Ziyad Abu Eain and others;

4. *Demands* that the Government of Israel, the occupying Power, rescind its action against Ziyad Abu Eain and others and release them immediately;

5. *Requests* the Secretary-General to report to the General Assembly as soon as possible and not later than the beginning of its forty-first session on the implementation of the present resolution.

B

The General Assembly,

Recalling Security Council resolution 465 (1980) of 1 March 1980, in which, *inter alia*, the Council affirmed that the Geneva Convention relative to the Protection of Civilian Persons in Time of War, of 12 August 1949,[6] is applicable to the Arab territories occupied by Israel since 1967, including Jerusalem,

Recalling also its resolutions 3092 A (XXVIII) of 7 December 1973, 3240 B (XXIX) of 29 November 1974, 3525 B (XXX) of 15 December 1975, 31/106 B of 16 December 1976, 32/91 A of 13 December 1977, 33/113 A of 18 December 1978, 34/90 B of 12 December 1979, 35/122 A of 11 December 1980, 36/147 A of 16 December 1981, 37/88 A of 10 December 1982, 38/79 B of 15 December 1983 and 39/95 B of 14 December 1984,

Considering that the promotion of respect for the obligations arising from the Charter of the United Nations and other instruments and rules of inter-

---

[3] See A/38/735.
[4] A/40/686.
[5] A/40/702.
[6] United Nations, *Treaty Series*, vol. 75, No. 973, p. 287.

national law is among the basic purposes and principles of the United Nations,

Bearing in mind the provisions of the Geneva Convention,

Noting that Israel and the Arab States whose territories have been occupied by Israel since June 1967 are parties to that Convention,

Taking into account that States parties to the Convention undertake, in accordance with article 1 thereof, not only to respect but also to ensure respect for the Convention in all circumstances,

1. *Reaffirms* that the Geneva Convention relative to the Protection of Civilian Persons in Time of War, of 12 August 1949,[7] is applicable to the Palestinian and other Arab territories occupied by Israel since 1967, including Jerusalem;

2. *Condemns once again* the failure of Israel, the occupying Power, to acknowledge the applicability of that Convention to the territories it has occupied since 1967, including Jerusalem;

3. *Strongly demands* that Israel acknowledge and comply with the provisions of that Convention in the Palestinian and other Arab territories it has occupied since 1967, including Jerusalem;

4. *Urgently calls upon* all States parties to that Convention to exert all efforts in order to ensure respect for and compliance with its provisions in the Palestinian and other Arab territories occupied by Israel since 1967, including Jerusalem;

5. *Requests* the Secretary-General to report to the General Assembly at its forty-first session on the implementation of the present resolution.

C

The General Assembly,

Recalling Security Council resolution 465 (1980) of 1 March 1980,

Recalling also its resolutions 32/5 of 28 October 1977, 33/113 B of 18 December 1978, 34/90 C of 12 December 1979, 35/122 B of 11 December 1980, 36/147 B of 16 December 1981, 37/88 B of 10 December 1982, 38/79 C of 15 December 1983 and 39/95 C of 14 December 1984,

Expressing grave anxiety and concern at the present serious situation in the occupied Palestinian and other Arab territories, including Jerusalem, as a result of the continued Israeli occupation and the measures and actions taken by Israel, the occupying Power, designed to change the legal status, geographical nature and demographic composition of those territories,

Confirming that the Geneva Convention relative to the Protection of Civilian Persons in Time of War, of 12 August 1949,[8] is applicable to all Arab territories occupied since June 1967, including Jerusalem,

1. *Determines* that all such measures and actions taken by Israel in the Palestinian and other Arab territories occupied since 1967, including Jeru-

---

[7] *Ibid.*

[8] United Nations, *Treaty Series*, vol. 75, No. 973, p. 287.

salem, are in violation of the relevant provisions of the Geneva Convention relative to the Protection of Civilian Persons in Time of War, of 12 August 1949,[9] and constitute a serious obstacle to the efforts to achieve a comprehensive, just and lasting peace in the Middle East and therefore have no legal validity;

2. *Strongly deplores* the persistence of Israel in carrying out such measures, in particular the establishment of settlements in the Palestinian and other occupied Arab territories, including Jerusalem;

3. *Demands* that Israel comply strictly with its international obligations in accordance with the principles of international law and the provisions of the Geneva Convention;

4. *Demands once more* that Israel, the occupying Power, desist forthwith from taking any action which would result in changing the legal status, geographical nature or demographic composition of the Palestinian and other Arab territories occupied since 1967, including Jerusalem;

5. *Urgently calls upon* all States parties to the Geneva Convention to respect and to exert all efforts in order to ensure respect for and compliance with its provisions in all Arab territories occupied by Israel since 1967, including Jerusalem;

6. *Requests* the Secretary-General to report to the General Assembly at its forty-first session on the implementation of the present resolution.

D

The General Assembly,

Guided by the purposes and principles of the Charter of the United Nations and by the principles and provisions of the Universal Declaration of Human Rights,[10]

Bearing in mind the provisions of the Geneva Convention relative to the Protection of Civilian Persons in Time of War, of 12 August 1949,[11] as well as of other relevant conventions and regulations,

Recalling all its resolutions on the subject, in particular resolutions 32/91 B and C of 13 December 1977, 33/113 C of 18 December 1978, 34/90 A of 12 December 1979, 35/122 C of 11 December 1980, 36/147 C of 16 December 1981, 37/88 C of 10 December 1982, 38/79 D of 15 December 1983 and 39/95 D of 14 December 1984,

Recalling also the relevant resolutions adopted by the Security Council, by the Commission on Human Rights, in particular its resolutions 1983/1 of 15 February 1983,[12] 1984/1 of 20 February 1984,[13] 1985/1 A and B of 19 Feb-

---

9 *Ibid.*

10 General Assembly resolution 217 A (III).

11 United Nations, *Treaty Series*, vol. 75, No. 973, p. 287.

12 See *Official Records of the Economic and Social Council, 1983, Supplement No. 3* (E/1983/ 13 and Corr.1), chap. XXVII.

13 See *Official Records of the Economic and Social Council, 1984, Supplement No. 4* (E/1984/ 14), chap. II, sect. A.

ruary 1985 and 1985/2 of 19 February 1985,[14] and by other United Nations organs concerned and by specialized agencies,

Having considered the report of the Special Committee to Investigate Israeli Practices Affecting the Human Rights of the Population of the Occupied Territories, dated 4 October 1985, which contains, *inter alia*, self-incriminating public statements made by officials of Israel, the occupying Power,[15]

Taking note of the letter dated 29 July 1985 from the Permanent Representative of Jordan addressed to the Secretary-General,[16] concerning the closing down of the Roman Catholic Medical Facility Hospice in Jerusalem,

1. *Commends* the Special Committee to Investigate Israeli Practices Affecting the Human Rights of the Population of the Occupied Territories for its efforts in performing the tasks assigned to it by the General Assembly and for its thoroughness and impartiality;

2. *Deplores* the continued refusal by Israel to allow the Special Committee access to the occupied territories;

3. *Demands* that Israel allow the Special Committee access to the occupied territories;

4. *Reaffirms* the fact that occupation itself constitutes a grave violation of the human rights of the civilian population of the occupied Arab territories;

5. *Condemns* the continued and persistent violation by Israel of the Geneva Convention relative to the Protection of Civilian Persons in Time of War, of 12 August 1949,[17] and other applicable international instruments, and condemns, in particular, those violations which the Convention designates as "grave breaches" thereof;

6. *Declares once more* that Israel's grave breaches of that Convention are war crimes and an affront to humanity;

7. *Reaffirms*, in accordance with the Convention, that the Israeli military occupation of the Palestinian and other Arab territories is of a temporary nature, thus giving no right whatsoever to the occupying Power over the territorial integrity of the occupied territories;

8. *Strongly condemns* the following Israeli policies and practices:

(*a*) Annexation of parts of the occupied territories, including Jerusalem;

(*b*) Imposition of Israeli laws, jurisdiction and administration on the Syrian Golan Heights, which has resulted in the effective annexation of the Syrian Golan Heights;

(*c*) Illegal imposition of levy of heavy and disproportionate taxes and dues;

(*d*) Establishment of new Israeli settlements and expansion of the existing

[14] See *Official Records of the Economic and Social Council, 1985, Supplement No. 2* (E/1985/22).

[15] A/40/702.

[16] A/40/517-S/17371.

[17] United Nations, *Treaty Series*, vol. 75, No. 973, p. 287.

settlements on private and public Arab lands, and transfer of an alien population thereto;

(e) Eviction, deportation, expulsion, displacement and transfer of Arab inhabitants of the occupied territories and denial of their right to return;

(f) Confiscation and expropriation of private and public Arab property in the occupied territories and all other transactions for the acquisition of land involving the Israeli authorities, institutions or nationals on the one hand and the inhabitants or institutions of the occupied territories on the other;

(g) Excavation and transformation of the landscape and the historical, cultural and religious sites, especially at Jerusalem;

(h) Pillaging of archaeological and cultural property;

(i) Destruction and demolition of Arab houses;

(j) Collective punishment, mass arrests, administrative detention and ill-treatment of the Arab population;

(k) Ill-treatment and torture of persons under detention;

(l) Interference with religious freedoms and practices as well as family rights and customs;

(m) Interference with the system of education and with the social and economic and health development of the population in the occupied Palestinian and other Arab territories;

(n) Interference with the freedom of movement of individuals within the occupied Palestinian and other Arab territories;

(o) Illegal exploitation of the natural wealth, resources and population of the occupied territories;

9. *Condemns also* the Israeli repression against and closing of the educational institutions in the occupied Syrian Golan Heights, particularly the prohibition of Syrian textbooks, Syrian educational system, the deprivation of Syrian students from pursuing their higher education in Syrian universities, the denial of the right to return to Syrian students receiving their higher education in Syria, forcing Hebrew on Syrian students, the imposition of courses that promote hatred, prejudice and religious intolerance and the dismissal of teachers, all in clear violation of the Geneva Convention;

10. *Strongly condemns* the arming of Israeli settlers in the occupied territories to commit acts of violence against Arab civilians and the perpetration of acts of violence by these armed settlers against individuals, causing injury and death and wide-scale damage to Arab property;

11. *Reaffirms* that all measures taken by Israel to change the physical character, demographic composition, institutional structure or legal status of the occupied territories, or any part thereof, including Jerusalem, are null and void, and that Israel's policy of settling parts of its population and new immigrants in the occupied territories constitutes a flagrant violation of the Geneva Convention and of the relevant resolutions of the United Nations;

12. *Demands* that Israel desist forthwith from the policies and practices referred to in paragraphs 8, 9 and 10 above;

13. *Calls upon* Israel, the occupying Power, to take immediate steps for the

return of all displaced Arab and Palestinian inhabitants to their homes or former places of residence in the territories occupied by Israel since 1967, in implementation of Security Council resolution 237 (1967) of 14 June 1967;

14. *Urges* the international organizations and the specialized agencies, in particular the International Labour Organisation, to examine the conditions of Arab workers in the occupied Palestinian and other Arab territories, including Jerusalem;

15. *Reiterates its call* upon all States, in particular those States parties to the Geneva Convention, in accordance with article 1 of that Convention, and upon international organizations and the specialized agencies not to recognize any changes carried out by Israel in the occupied territories and to avoid actions, including those in the field of aid, which might be used by Israel in its pursuit of the policies of annexation and colonization or any of the other policies and practices referred to in the present resolution;

16. *Requests* the Special Committee, pending early termination of Israeli occupation, to continue to investigate Israeli policies and practices in the Arab territories occupied by Israel since 1967, to consult, as appropriate, with the International Committee of the Red Cross in order to ensure the safeguarding of the welfare and human rights of the population of the occupied territories and to report to the Secretary-General as soon as possible and whenever the need arises thereafter;

17. *Requests* the Special Committee to continue to investigate the treatment of civilians in detention in the Arab territories occupied by Israel since 1967;

18. *Condemns* Israel's refusal to permit persons from the occupied territories to appear as witnesses before the Special Committee and to participate in conferences and meetings held outside the occupied territories;

19. *Requests* the Secretary-General:

(*a*) To provide all necessary facilities to the Special Committee, including those required for its visits to the occupied territories, with a view to investigating the Israeli policies and practices referred to in the present resolution;

(*b*) To continue to make available additional staff as may be necessary to assist the Special Committee in the performance of its tasks;

(*c*) To ensure the widest circulation of the reports of the Special Committee and of information regarding its activities and findings, by all means available through the Department of Public Information of the Secretariat and, where necessary, to reprint those reports of the Special Committee that are no longer available;

(*d*) To report to the General Assembly at its forty-first session on the tasks entrusted to him in the present paragraph;

20. *Requests* the Security Council to ensure Israel's respect for and compliance with all the provisions of the Geneva Convention relative to the Protection of Civilian Persons in Time of War, of 12 August 1949, in the Pal-

estinian and other Arab territories occupied since 1967, including Jerusalem, and to initiate measures to halt Israeli policies and practices in those territories;

21. *Calls upon* Israel, the occupying Power, to allow the reopening of the Roman Catholic Medical Facility Hospice in Jerusalem in order to continue to provide needed health and medical services to the Arab population in the city;

22. *Decides* to include in the provisional agenda of its forty-first session the item entitled "Report of the Special Committee to Investigate Israeli Practices Affecting the Human Rights of the Population of the Occupied Territories".

E

The General Assembly,

Recalling Security Council resolutions 468 (1980) of 8 May 1980, 469 (1980) of 20 May 1980 and 484 (1980) of 19 December 1980,

Recalling also its resolutions 36/147 D of 16 December 1981, 37/88 D of 10 December 1982, 38/79 E of 15 December 1983 and 39/95 E of 14 December 1984,

Taking note of the report of the Secretary-General of 14 August 1985,[18]

Deeply concerned at the expulsion by the Israeli military occupation authorities of the Mayor of Halhul, the Mayor of Hebron who has since died, the Sharia Judge of Hebron and other Palestinians during 1985,

Alarmed by the decision of the Israeli military occupation authorities on 26 October 1985 to expel four Palestinian leaders,

Recalling the Geneva Convention relative to the Protection of Civilian Persons in Time of War, of 12 August 1949,[19] in particular article 1 and the first paragraph of article 49, which read as follows:

"Article 1

The High Contracting Parties undertake to respect and to ensure respect for the present Convention in all circumstances.

Article 49

Individual or mass forcible transfers, as well as deportations of protected persons from occupied territory to the territory of the occupying Power or to that of any other country, occupied or not, are prohibited, regardless of their motive . . . ",

Reaffirming the applicability of the Geneva Convention to the Palestinian and other Arab territories occupied by Israel since 1967, including Jerusalem,

1. *Strongly condemns* Israel, the occupying Power, for its persistent refusal

---

[18] A/40/541.
[19] United Nations, *Treaty Series*, vol. 75, No. 973, p. 287.

to comply with the relevant Security Council and General Assembly resolutions;

2. *Demands* that the Government of Israel, the occupying Power, rescind the illegal measures taken by the Israeli military occupation authorities in expelling the Mayor of Halhul, the Sharia Judge of Hebron and other Palestinians expelled during 1985, and that it facilitate the immediate return of the expelled Palestinians so that they can, *inter alia*, resume the functions for which they were elected and appointed;

3. *Calls upon* Israel, the occupying Power, to rescind its illegal decision taken on 26 October 1985 and refrain from deporting the four Palestinian leaders;

4. *Further calls upon* Israel, the occupying Power, to cease forthwith the expulsion of Palestinians and to abide scrupulously by the provisions of the Geneva Convention relative to the Protection of Civilian Persons in Time of War, of 12 August 1949;[20]

5. *Requests* the Secretary-General to report to the General Assembly as soon as possible and not later than the beginning of its forty-first session on the implementation of the present resolution.

F

The General Assembly,

Deeply concerned that the Arab territories occupied since 1967 have been under continued Israeli military occupation,

Recalling Security Council resolution 497 (1981) of 17 December 1981,

Recalling also its resolutions 36/226 B of 17 December 1981, ES-9/1 of 5 February 1982, 37/88 E of 10 December 1982, 38/79 F of 15 December 1983 and 39/95 F of 14 December 1984,

Having considered the report of the Secretary-General of 18 September 1985,[21]

Recalling its previous resolutions, in particular resolutions 3414 (XXX) of 5 December 1975, 31/61 of 9 December 1976, 32/20 of 25 November 1977, 33/28 and 33/29 of 7 December 1978, 34/70 of 6 December 1979 and 35/122 E of 11 December 1980, in which it, *inter alia*, called upon Israel to put an end to its occupation of the Arab territories and to withdraw from all those territories,

Reaffirming once more the illegality of Israel's decision of 14 December 1981 to impose its laws, jurisdiction and administration in the Syrian Golan Heights, which has resulted in the effective annexation of that territory,

Reaffirming that the acquisition of territory by force is inadmissible under the Charter of the United Nations and that all territories thus occupied by Israel must be returned,

[20] United Nations, *Treaty Series*, vol. 75, No. 973, p. 287.
[21] A/40/649.

Recalling the Geneva Convention relative to the Protection of Civilian Persons in Time of War, of 12 August 1949,[22]

1. *Strongly condemns* Israel, the occupying Power, for its refusal to comply with the relevant resolutions of the General Assembly and the Security Council, particularly Council resolution 497 (1981), in which the Council, *inter alia*, decided that the Israeli decision to impose its laws, jurisdiction and administration in the occupied Syrian Golan Heights was null and void and without international legal effect and demanded that Israel, the occupying Power, should rescind forthwith its decision;

2. *Condemns* the persistence of Israel in changing the physical character, demographic composition, institutional structure and legal status of the occupied Syrian Arab Golan Heights;

3. *Determines* that all legislative and administrative measures and actions taken or to be taken by Israel, the occupying Power, that purport to alter the character and legal status of the Syrian Golan Heights are null and void and constitute a flagrant violation of international law and of the Geneva Convention relative to the Protection of Civilian Persons in Time of War, of 12 August 1949,[23] and have no legal effect;

4. *Strongly condemns* Israel for its attempts and measures to impose forcibly Israeli citizenship and Israeli identity cards on the Syrian citizens in the occupied Syrian Arab Golan Heights and calls upon it to desist from its repressive measures against the population of the Syrian Arab Golan Heights;

5. *Calls once again upon* Member States not to recognize any of the legislative or administrative measures and actions referred to above;

6. *Requests* the Secretary-General to submit to the General Assembly at its forty-first session a report on the implementation of the present resolution.

G

The General Assembly,

Bearing in mind the Geneva Convention relative to the Protection of Civilian Persons in Time of War, of 12 August 1949,[24]

Deeply concerned at the continued harassment by Israel, the occupying Power, against educational institutions in the occupied Palestinian territories,

Recalling its resolutions 38/79 G of 15 December 1983 and 39/95 G of 14 December 1984,

Taking note of the report of the Secretary-General of 14 August 1985,[25]

Taking note of the relevant decisions adopted by the United Nations Educational, Scientific and Cultural Organization Executive Committee concerning the educational and cultural situation in the occupied territories,

---

[22] United Nations, *Treaty Series*, vol. 75, No. 973, p. 287.
[23] United Nations, *Treaty Series*, vol. 75, No. 973, p. 287.
[24] *Ibid.*
[25] A/40/542.

1. *Reaffirms* the applicability of the Geneva Convention relative to the Protection of Civilian Persons in Time of War, of 12 August 1949,[26] to the Palestinian and other Arab territories occupied by Israel since 1967, including Jerusalem;

2. *Condemns* Israeli policies and practices against Palestinian students and faculties in schools, universities and other educational institutions in the occupied Palestinian territories, especially the policy of opening fire on defenceless students, causing many casualties;

3. *Condemns* the systematic Israeli campaign of repression against and closing of universities and other educational and vocational institutions in the occupied Palestinian territories, restricting and impeding the academic activities of Palestinian universities by subjecting the selection of courses, textbooks and educational programmes, the admission of students and the appointment of faculty members to the control and supervision of the military occupation authorities, in clear contravention of the Geneva Convention;

4. *Demands* that Israel, the occupying Power, comply with the provisions of that Convention, rescind all actions and measures against all educational institutions, ensure the freedom of those institutions and refrain forthwith from hindering the effective operation of the universities and other educational institutions;

5. *Requests* the Secretary-General to report to the General Assembly as soon as possible and not later than the beginning of its forty-first session on the implementation of the present resolution.

[26] United Nations, *Treaty Series*, vol. 75, No. 973, p. 287.

344. General Assembly Resolution 40/165 on the U.N. Relief and Works Agency for Palestine Refugees in the Near East, December 16, 1985*

---

* G.A. Res. 40/165 (1985). *See also* previous resolutions, G.A. Res. 83, 38 U.N. GAOR Supp. (No. 47) at 107, U.N. Doc. A/38/47 (1983) and G.A. Res. 99, 39 U.N. GAOR Supp. (No. 51) at 115, U.N. Doc. A/39/51 (1984).

A

ASSISTANCE TO PALESTINE REFUGEES

The General Assembly,

Recalling its resolution 39/99 A of 14 December 1984 and all previous resolutions on the question, including resolution 194 (III) of 11 December 1948,

Taking note of the report of the Commissioner-General of the United Nations Relief and Works Agency for Palestine Refugees in the Near East, covering the period from 1 July 1984 to 30 June 1985,[110]

1. *Notes with deep regret* that repatriation or compensation of the refugees as provided for in paragraph 11 of General Assembly resolution 194 (III) has not been effected, that no substantial progress has been made in the programme endorsed by the Assembly in paragraph 2 of it resolution 513 (VI) of 26 January 1952 for the reintegration of refugees either by repatriation or resettlement and that, therefore, the situation of the refugees continues to be a matter of serious concern;

2. *Expresses its thanks* to the Commissioner-General and to all the staff of the United Nations Relief and Works Agency for Palestine Refugees in the Near East, recognizing that the Agency is doing all it can within the limits of available resources, and also expresses its thanks to the specialized agencies and private organizations for their valuable work in assisting the refugees;

3. *Expresses its deep appreciation* to the former Commissioner-General, Mr. Olof Rydbeck, for his many years of effective service to the Agency and his dedication to the welfare of the refugees;

4. *Reiterates its request* that the headquarters of the United Nations Relief and Works Agency for Palestine Refugees in the Near East should be relocated to its former site within its area of operations as soon as practicable;

5. *Notes with regret* that the United Nations Conciliation Commission for Palestine has been unable to find a means of achieving progress in the implementation of paragraph 11 of General Assembly resolution 194 (III),[111] and requests the Commission to exert continued efforts towards the implementation of that paragraph and to report to the Assembly as appropriate, but no later than 1 September 1986;

6. *Directs attention* to the continuing seriousness of the financial position of the United Nations Relief and Works Agency for Palestine Refugees in the Near East, as outlined in the report of the Commissioner-General;[112]

7. *Notes with profound concern* that, despite the commendable and successful efforts of the Commissioner-General to collect additional contributions, this increased level of income to the United Nations Relief and Works Agency for Palestine Refugees in the Near East is still insufficient to cover

[110] *Official Records of the General Assembly, Fortieth Session, Supplement No. 13* (A/40/13 and Add.1 and Corr.1).

[111] A/40/580, annex.

[112] *Official Records of the General Assembly, Fortieth Session, Supplement No. 13* (A/40/13 and Add.1 and Corr.1).

essential budget requirements in the present year and that, at currently foreseen levels of giving, deficits will recur each year;

8. *Calls upon* all Governments as a matter of urgency to make the most generous efforts possible to meet the anticipated needs of the United Nations Relief and Works Agency for Palestine Refugees in the Near East, particularly in the light of the budgetary deficit projected in the report of the Commissioner-General, and therefore urges non-contributing Governments to contribute regularly and contributing Governments to consider increasing their regular contributions.

B

WORKING GROUP ON THE FINANCING OF THE UNITED NATIONS RELIEF AND WORKS AGENCY FOR PALESTINE REFUGEES IN THE NEAR EAST

The General Assembly,

Recalling its resolutions 2656 (XXV) of 7 December 1970, 2728 (XXV) of 15 December 1970, 2791 (XXVI) of 6 December 1971, 2964 (XXVII) of 13 December 1972, 3090 (XXVIII) of 7 December 1973, 3330 (XXIX) of 17 December 1974, 3419 D (XXX) of 8 December 1975, 31/15 C of 23 November 1976, 32/90 D of 13 December 1977, 33/112 D of 18 December 1978, 34/52 D of 23 November 1979, 35/13 D of 3 November 1980, 36/146 E of 16 December 1981, 37/120 A of 16 December 1982, 38/83 B of 15 December 1983 and 39/99 B of 14 December 1984,

Recalling also its decision 36/462 of 16 March 1982, whereby it took note of the special report of the Working Group on the Financing of the United Nations Relief and Works Agency for Palestine Refugees in the Near East[113] and adopted the recommendations contained therein,

Having considered the report of the Working Group on the Financing of the United Nations Relief and Works Agency for Palestine Refugees in the Near East,[114]

Taking into account the report of the Commissioner-General of the United Nations Relief and Works Agency for Palestine Refugees in the Near East, covering the period from 1 July 1984 to 30 June 1985,[115]

Gravely concerned at the critical financial situation of the United Nations Relief and Works Agency for Palestine Refugees in the Near East, which has already reduced the essential minimum services being provided to the Palestine refugees and which threatens even greater reductions in the future,

Emphasizing the urgent need for extraordinary efforts in order to maintain, at least at their present minimum level, the activities of the United Nations Relief and Works Agency for Palestine Refugees in the Near East,

1. *Commends* the Working Group on the Financing of the United Nations

---

[113] A/36/866; see also A/37/591.

[114] A/40/736; see also A/40/207 for the special report adopted on 26 March 1985.

[115] *Official Records of the General Assembly, Fortieth Session, Supplement No. 13* (A/40/13 and Add.1 and Corr.1).

Relief and Works Agency for Palestine Refugees in the Near East for its efforts to assist in ensuring the Agency's financial security;

2. *Takes note with approval* of the report of the Working Group;[116]

3. *Requests* the Working Group to continue its efforts, in co-operation with the Secretary-General and the Commissioner-General of the United Nations Relief and Works Agency for Palestine Refugees in the Near East, for the financing of the Agency for a further period of one year;

4. *Requests* the Secretary-General to provide the necessary services and assistance to the Working Group for the conduct of its work.

C

ASSISTANCE TO PERSONS DISPLACED AS A RESULT OF THE JUNE 1967 AND SUBSEQUENT HOSTILITIES

The General Assembly,

Recalling its resolution 39/99 C of 14 December 1984 and all previous resolutions on the question,

Taking note of the report of the Commissioner-General of the United Nations Relief and Works Agency for Palestine Refugees in the Near East, covering the period from 1 July 1984 to 30 June 1985,[117]

Concerned about the continued human suffering resulting from the hostilities in the Middle East,

1. *Reaffirms* its resolution 39/99 C and all previous resolutions on the question;

2. *Endorses*, bearing in mind the objectives of those resolutions, the efforts of the Commissioner-General of the United Nations Relief and Works Agency for Palestine Refugees in the Near East to continue to provide humanitarian assistance as far as practicable, on an emergency basis and as a temporary measure, to other persons in the area who are at present displaced and in a serious need of continued assistance as a result of the June 1967 and subsequent hostilities;

3. *Strongly appeals* to all Governments and to organizations and individuals to contribute generously for the above purposes to the United Nations Relief and Works Agency for Palestine Refugees in the Near East and to the other intergovernmental and non-governmental organizations concerned.

D

OFFERS BY MEMBER STATES OF GRANTS AND SCHOLARSHIPS FOR HIGHER EDUCATION, INCLUDING VOCATIONAL TRAINING, FOR PALESTINE REFUGEES

The General Assembly,

Recalling its resolution 212 (III) of 19 November 1948 on assistance to Palestine refugees,

---

[116] A/40/736; see also A/40/207 for the special report adopted on 26 March 1985.

[117] *Official Records of the General Assembly, Fortieth Session, Supplement No. 13* (A/40/13 and Add.1 and Corr.1).

Recalling also its resolutions 35/13 B of 3 November 1980, 36/146 H of 16 December 1981, 37/120 D of 16 December 1982, 38/83 D of 15 December 1983 and 39/99 D of 14 December 1984,

Cognizant of the fact that the Palestine refugees have, for the last three decades, lost their lands and means of livelihood,

Having examined the report of the Secretary-General of 10 September 1985,[118] on offers of grants and scholarships for higher education for Palestine refugees and on the scope of the implementation of resolution 39/99 D,

Having also examined the report of the Commissioner-General of the United Nations Relief and Works Agency for Palestine Refugees in the Near East, covering the period from 1 July 1984 to 30 June 1985,[119] dealing with this subject,

1. *Urges* all States to respond to the appeal contained in General Assembly resolution 32/90 F of 13 December 1977 in a manner commensurate with the needs of Palestine refugees for higher education and vocational training;

2. *Strongly appeals* to all States, specialized agencies and non-governmental organizations to augment the special allocations for grants and scholarships to Palestine refugees in addition to their contributions to the regular budget of the United Nations Relief and Works Agency for Palestine Refugees in the Near East;

3. *Expresses its appreciation* to all Governments, specialized agencies and non-governmental organizations that responded favourably to General Assembly resolution 39/99 D;

4. *Invites* the relevant specialized agencies and other organizations of the United Nations system to continue, within their respective spheres of competence, to extend assistance for higher education to Palestine refugee students;

5. *Appeals* to all States, specialized agencies and the United Nations University to contribute generously to the Palestinian universities in the territories occupied by Israel since 1967, including, in due course, the proposed University of Jerusalem "Al-Quds" for Palestine refugees;

6. *Also appeals* to all States, specialized agencies and other international bodies to contribute towards the establishment of vocational training centres for Palestine refugees;

7. *Requests* the United Nations Relief and Works Agency for Palestine Refugees in the Near East to act as the recipient and trustee for such special allocations and scholarships and to award them to qualified Palestine refugee candidates;

8. *Requests* the Secretary-General to report to the General Assembly at its forty-first session on the implementation of the present resolution.

[118] A/40/612.
[119] *Official Records of the General Assembly, Fortieth Session, Supplement No. 13* (A/40/13 and Add.1 and Corr.1).

E

PALESTINE REFUGEES IN THE GAZA STRIP

The General Assembly,

Recalling Security Council resolution 237 (1967) of 14 June 1967,

Recalling also General Assembly resolutions 2792 C (XXVI) of 6 December 1971, 2963 C (XXVII) of 13 December 1972, 3089 C (XXVIII) of 7 December 1973, 3331 D (XXIX) of 17 December 1974, 3419 C (XXX) of 8 December 1975, 31/15 E of 23 November 1976, 32/90 C of 13 December 1977, 33/112 E of 18 December 1978, 34/52 F of 23 November 1979, 35/13 F of 3 November 1980, 36/146 A of 16 December 1981, 37/120 E of 16 December 1982, 38/83 E of 15 December 1983 and 39/99 E of 14 December 1984,

Having considered the report of the Commissioner-General of the United Nations Relief and Works Agency for Palestine Refugees in the Near East, covering the period from 1 July 1984 to 30 June 1985,[120] and the report of the Secretary-General of 11 September 1985,[121]

Recalling the provisions of paragraph 11 of its resolution 194 (III) of 11 December 1948 and considering that measures to resettle Palestine refugees in the Gaza Strip away from the homes and property from which they were displaced constitute a violation of their inalienable right of return,

Alarmed by the reports received from the Commissioner-General that the Israeli occupying authorities, in contravention of Israel's obligation under international law, persist in their policy of demolishing shelters occupied by refugee families,

1. *Reiterates strongly its demand* that Israel desist from the removal and resettlement of Palestine refugees in the Gaza Strip and from the destruction of their shelters;

2. *Requests* the Secretary-General, after consulting with the Commissioner-General of the United Nations Relief and Works Agency for Palestine Refugees in the Near East, to report to the General Assembly, before the opening of its forty-first session, on Israel's compliance with paragraph 1 above.

F

RESUMPTION OF THE RATION DISTRIBUTION TO PALESTINE REFUGEES

The General Assembly,

Recalling its resolutions 36/146 F of 16 December 1981, 37/120 F of 16 December 1982, 38/83 F of 15 December 1983, 39/99 F of 14 December 1984 and all previous resolutions on the question, including resolution 302 (IV) of 8 December 1949,

---

[120] *Official Records of the General Assembly, Fortieth Session, Supplement No. 13* (A/40/13 and Add.1 and Corr.1).

[121] A/40/613.

Having considered the report of the Commissioner-General of the United Nations Relief and Works Agency for Palestine Refugees in the Near East, covering the period from 1 July 1984 to 30 June 1985,[122] and the report of the Secretary-General of 18 October 1985,[123]

Deeply concerned at the interruption by the United Nations Relief and Works Agency for Palestine Refugees in the Near East, owing to financial difficulties, of the general ration distribution to Palestine refugees in all fields,

1. *Regrets* that its resolutions 37/120 F, 38/83 F and 39/99 F have not been implemented;

2. *Calls once again upon* all Governments, as a matter of urgency, to make the most generous efforts possible and to offer the necessary resources to meet the needs of the United Nations Relief and Works Agency for Palestine Refugees in the Near East, particularly in the light of the interruption by the Agency of the general ration distribution to Palestine refugees in all fields, and therefore urges non-contributing Governments to contribute regularly and contributing Governments to consider increasing their regular contributions;

3. *Requests* the Commissioner-General of the United Nations Relief and Works Agency for Palestine Refugees in the Near East to resume on a continuing basis the interrupted general ration distribution to Palestine refugees in all fields;

4. *Requests* the Secretary-General, in consultation with the Commissioner-General, to report to the General Assembly at its forty-first session on the implementation of the present resolution.

G

POPULATION AND REFUGEES DISPLACED SINCE 1967

The General Assembly,

Recalling Security Council resolution 237 (1967) of 14 June 1967,

Recalling also General Assembly resolutions 2252 (ES-V) of 4 July 1967, 2452 A (XXIII) of 19 December 1968, 2535 B (XXIV) of 10 December 1969, 2672 D (XXV) of 8 December 1970, 2792 E (XXVI) of 6 December 1971, 2963 C and D (XXVII) of 13 December 1972, 3089 C (XXVIII) of 7 December 1973, 3331 D (XXIX) of 17 December 1974, 3419 C (XXX) of 8 December 1975, 31/15 D of 23 November 1976, 32/90 E of 13 December 1977, 33/112 F of 18 December 1978, 34/52 E of 23 November 1979, ES-7/2 of 29 July 1980, 35/13 E of 3 November 1980, 36/146 B of 16 December 1981, 37/120 G of 16 December 1982, 38/83 G of 15 December 1983 and 39/99 G of 14 December 1985,

---

[122] *Official Records of the General Assembly, Fortieth Session, Supplement No. 13* (A/40/13 and Add.1 and Corr.1).

[123] A/40/766.

Having considered the report of the Commissioner-General of the United Nations Relief and Works Agency for Palestine Refugees in the Near East, covering the period from 1 July 1984 to 30 June 1985,[124] and the report of the Secretary-General of 11 September 1985,[125]

1. *Reaffirms* the inalienable rights of all displaced inhabitants to return to their homes or former places of residence in the territories occupied by Israel since 1967 and declares once more that any attempt to restrict, or to attach conditions to, the free exercise of the right to return by any displaced person is inconsistent with that inalienable right and inadmissible;

2. *Considers* any and all agreements embodying any restriction on or condition for the return of the displaced inhabitants as null and void;

3. *Strongly deplores* the continued refusal of the Israeli authorities to take steps for the return of the displaced inhabitants;

4. *Calls once more upon* Israel:

(*a*) To take immediate steps for the return of all displaced inhabitants;

(*b*) To desist from all measures that obstruct the return of the displaced inhabitants, including measures affecting the physical and demographic structure of the occupied territories;

5. *Requests* the Secretary-General, after consulting with the Commissioner-General of the United Nations Relief and Works Agency for Palestine Refugees in the Near East, to report to the General Assembly before the opening of its forty-first session on Israel's compliance with paragraph 4 above.

H

REVENUES DERIVED FROM PALESTINE REFUGEE PROPERTIES

The General Assembly,

Recalling its resolutions 35/13 A to F of 3 November 1980, 36/146 C of 16 December 1981, 37/120 H of 16 December 1982, 38/83 H of 15 December 1983, 39/99 H of 14 December 1984 and all its previous resolutions on the question, including resolution 194 (III) of 11 December 1948,

Taking note of the report of the Secretary-General of 11 September 1985,[126]

Taking note also of the report of the United Nations Conciliation Commission for Palestine, covering the period from 1 September 1984 to 31 August 1985,[127]

Recalling that the Universal Declaration of Human Rights[128] and the principles of international law uphold the principle that no one shall be arbitrarily deprived of his or her private property,

---

[124] *Official Records of the General Assembly, Fortieth Session, Supplement No. 13* (A/40/13 and Add.1 and Corr.1).

[125] A/40/614.

[126] A/40/616.

[127] A/40/580.

[128] General Assembly resolution 217 A (III).

Considering that the Palestine Arab refugees are entitled to their property and to the income derived from their property, in conformity with the principles of justice and equity,

Recalling, in particular, its resolution 394 (V) of 14 December 1950, in which it directed the United Nations Conciliation Commission for Palestine, in consultation with the parties concerned, to prescribe measures for the protection of the rights, property and interests of the Palestinian Arab refugees,

Taking note of the completion of the programme of identification and evaluation of Arab property, as announced by the United Nations Conciliation Commission for Palestine in its twenty-second progress report,[129] of 11 May 1964, and of the fact that the Land Office had a schedule of Arab owners and file of documents defining the location, area and other particulars of Arab property,

1. *Requests* the Secretary-General to take all appropriate steps, in consultation with the United Nations Conciliation Commission for Palestine, for the protection and administration of Arab property, assets and property rights in Israel, and to establish a fund for the receipt of income derived therefrom, on behalf of the rightful owners;

2. *Calls once again upon* Israel to render all facilities and assistance to the Secretary-General in the implementation of the present resolution;

3. *Calls upon* all other Governments of Member States concerned to provide the Secretary-General with any pertinent information in their possession concerning Arab property, assets and property rights in Israel, which would assist the Secretary-General in the implementation of the present resolution;

4. *Deplores* Israel's refusal to co-operate with the Secretary-General in the implementation of the resolutions on the question;

5. *Requests* the Secretary-General to report to the General Assembly at its forty-first session on the implementation of the present resolution.

I

PROTECTION OF PALESTINE REFUGEES

The General Assembly,

Recalling Security Council resolutions 508 (1982) of 5 June 1982, 509 (1982) of 6 June 1982, 511 (1982) of 18 June 1982, 512 (1982) of 19 June 1982, 513 (1982) of 4 July 1982, 515 (1982) of 29 July 1982, 517 (1982) of 4 August 1982, 518 (1982) of 12 August 1982, 519 (1982) of 17 August 1982, 520 (1982) of 17 September 1982 and 523 (1982) of 18 October 1982,

Recalling General Assembly resolutions ES-7/5 of 26 June 1982, ES-7/6

[129] *Official Records of the General Assembly, Nineteenth Session, Annex No. 11*, document A/5700.

and ES-7/8 of 19 August 1982, ES-7/9 of 24 September 1982, 37/120 J of 16 December 1982, 38/83 I of 15 December 1983 and 39/99 I of 14 December 1984,

Having considered the report of the Secretary-General of 16 October 1985,[130]

Having also considered the report of the Commissioner-General of the United Nations Relief and Works Agency for Palestine Refugees in the Near East, covering the period from 1 July 1984 to 30 June 1985,[131]

Referring to the humanitarian principles of the Geneva Convention relative to the Protection of Civilian Persons in Time of War, of 12 August 1949,[132] and to the obligations arising from the Regulations annexed to the Hague Convention IV of 1907,[133]

Taking into consideration the marked deterioration in the security situation experienced by the refugees living in the Gaza Strip as reported by the Commissioner-General in his statement of 4 November 1985,[134]

Deeply concerned at the lack of security for the Palestine refugees in the Palestinian and other Arab territories occupied since 1967, including Jerusalem, resulting in scores of violent deaths, woundings, kidnappings, disappearances, evictions in the face of threats, explosions and arsons,

Deeply distressed at the sufferings of the Palestinians resulting from the Israeli invasion of Lebanon,

Reaffirming its support for Lebanese sovereignty, unity and territorial integrity, within its internationally recognized boundaries,

1. *Urges* the Secretary-General, in consultation with the United Nations Relief and Works Agency for Palestine Refugees in the Near East, to undertake effective measures to guarantee the safety and security and the legal and human rights of the Palestine refugees in all the territories under Israeli occupation in 1967 and thereafter;

2. *Holds* Israel responsible for the security of the Palestine refugees in the Palestinian and other Arab territories occupied since 1967, including Jerusalem, and calls upon it to fulfil its obligations as the occupying Power in this regard, in accordance with the pertinent provisions of the Geneva Convention relative to the Protection of Civilian Persons in Time of War, of 12 August 1949;[135]

3. *Calls once again upon* Israel, the occupying Power, to release forthwith

[130] A/40/756.

[131] *Official Records of the General Assembly, Fortieth Session, Supplement No. 13* (A/40/13 and Add.1 and Corr.1).

[132] United Nations, *Treaty Series*, vol. 75, No. 973, p. 287.

[133] Carnegie Endowment for International Peace, *The Hague Conventions and Declarations of 1899 and 1907* (New York, Oxford University Press, 1915), p. 100.

[134] See A/SPC/40/SR.22.

[135] *Official Records of the General Assembly, Fortieth Session, Supplement No. 13* (A/40/13 and Add.1 and Corr.1).

all detained Palestinian refugees, including the employees of the United Nations Relief and Works Agency for Palestine Refugees in the Near East;

4. *Urges* the Commissioner-General of the United Nations Relief and Works Agency for Palestine Refugees in the Near East to provide housing, in consultation with the Government of Lebanon, to the Palestine refugees whose houses were demolished or razed by the Israeli forces;

5. *Calls once again upon* Israel to compensate the United Nations Relief and Works Agency for Palestine Refugees in the Near East for the damage to its property and facilities resulting from the Israeli invasion of Lebanon, without prejudice to Israel's responsibility for all damages resulting from that invasion;

6. *Requests* the Secretary-General, in consultation with the Commissioner-General, to report to the General Assembly, before the opening of its forty-first session, on the implementation of the present resolution.

J

PALESTINE REFUGEES IN THE WEST BANK

The General Assembly,

Recalling Security Council resolution 237 (1967) of 14 June 1967,

Recalling also General Assembly resolutions 38/83 J of 15 December 1983 and 39/99 J of 14 December 1984,

Having considered the report of the Secretary-General of 11 September 1985,[136]

Having also considered the report of the Commissioner-General of the United Nations Relief and Works Agency for Palestine Refugees in the Near East, covering the period from 1 July 1984 to 30 June 1985,[137]

Alarmed by Israel's plans to remove and resettle the Palestine refugees of the West Bank and to destroy their camps,

Recalling the provisions of paragraph 11 of its resolution 194 (III) of 11 December 1948 and considering that measures to resettle Palestine refugees in the West Bank away from the homes and property from which they were displaced constitute a violation of their inalienable right of return,

1. *Calls once again upon* Israel to abandon its plans and to refrain from the removal, and from any action that may lead to the removal and resettlement, of Palestine refugees in the West Bank and from the destruction of their camps;

2. *Requests* the Secretary-General, in co-operation with the Commissioner-General of the United Nations Relief and Works Agency for Palestine Refugees in the Near East, to keep the matter under close supervision and to

[136] A/40/615.
[137] *Official Records of the General Assembly, Fortieth Session, Supplement No. 13* (A/40/13 and Add.1 and Corr.1).

report to the General Assembly, before the opening of its forty-first session, on any development regaring [*sic*] this matter.

K

UNIVERSITY OF JERUSALEM "AL-QUDS" FOR PALESTINE REFUGEES

The General Assembly,

Recalling its resolutions 36/146 G of 16 December 1981, 37/120 C of 16 December 1982, 38/83 K of 15 December 1983 and 39/99 K of 14 December 1984,

Having examined the report of the Secretary-General on the question of the establishment of a university at Jerusalem,[138]

Having also examined the report of the Commissioner-General of the United Nations Relief and Works Agency for Palestine Refugees in the Near East, covering the period from 1 July 1984 to 30 June 1985,[139]

1. *Commends* the constructive efforts made by the Secretary-General, the Commissioner-General of the United Nations Relief and Works Agency for Palestine Refugees in the Near East, the Council of the United Nations University and the United Nations Educational, Scientific and Cultural Organization, which worked diligently towards the implementation of General Assembly resolution 38/83 D and other relevant resolutions;

2. *Further commends* the close co-operation of the competent educational authorities concerned;

3. *Emphasizes* the need for strengthening the educational system in the Arab territories occupied since 5 June 1967, including Jerusalem, and specifically the need for the establishment of the proposed university;

4. *Requests* the Secretary-General to continue to take all necessary measures for establishing the University of Jerusalem, "Al-Quds", in accordance with General Assembly resolution 35/13 B of 3 November 1980, giving due consideration to the recommendations consistent with the provisions of that resolution;

5. *Calls upon* Israel, the occupying Power, to co-operate in the implementation of the present resolution and to remove the hindrances which it has put in the way of establishing the University of Jerusalem;

6. *Requests* the Secretary-General to report to the General Assembly at its forty-first session on the progress made in the implementation of the present resolution.

[138] A/40/543.

[139] *Official Records of the General Assembly, Fortieth Session, Supplement No. 13* (A/40/13 and Add.1 and Corr.1).

345. General Assembly Resolution 40/168 on the Situation in the Middle East, December 16, 1985*

* G.A. Res. 40/168 (1985). *See also* previous resolution G.A. Res. 146, 39 U.N. GAOR Supp. (No. 51) at 50, U.N. Doc. A/39/51 (1984).

A

The General Assembly,

Having discussed the item entitled "The situation in the Middle East",

Reaffirming its resolutions 36/226 A and B of 17 December 1981, ES-9/1 of 5 February 1982, 37/123 F of 20 December 1982, 38/58 A to E of 13 December 1983, 38/180 A to D of 19 December 1983 and 39/146 A to C of 14 December 1984,

Recalling Security Council resolutions 425 (1978) of 19 March 1978, 497 (1981) of 17 December 1981, 508 (1982) of 5 June 1982, 509 (1982) of 6 June 1982, 511 (1982) of 18 June 1982, 512 (1982) of 19 June 1982, 513 (1982) of 4 July 1982, 515 (1982) of 29 July 1982, 516 (1982) of 1 August 1982, 517 (1982) of 4 August 1982, 518 (1982) of 12 August 1982, 519 (1982) of 17 August 1982, 520 (1982) of 17 September 1982, 521 (1982) of 19 September 1982 and 555 (1984) of 12 October 1984,

Taking note of the reports of the Secretary-General,[162]

Reaffirming the need for continued collective support for the resolutions adopted by the Twelfth Arab Summit Conference, held at Fez, Morocco, on 25 November 1981 and from 6 to 9 September 1982,[163] reiterating its previous resolutions regarding the Palestinian question, and its support for the Palestine Liberation Organization as the sole, legitimate representative of the Palestinian people, and considering that the convening of an International Conference for Peace in the Middle East, under the auspices of the United Nations, in accordance with the General Assembly resolution 38/58 C and other relevant resolutions related to the question of Palestine, would contribute to the promotion of peace in the region,

Welcoming all efforts contributing towards the realization of the inalienable rights of the Palestinian people through the achievement of a comprehensive, just and lasting peace in the Middle East, in accordance with the United Nations resolutions relating to the question of Palestine and to the situation in the Middle East,

Welcoming the world-wide support extended to the just cause of the Palestinian people and the other Arab countries in their struggle against Israeli aggression and occupation in order to achieve a comprehensive, just and lasting peace in the Middle East and the full exercise by the Palestinian people of its inalienable national rights, as affirmed by previous resolutions of the General Assembly relating to the question of Palestine and to the situation in the Middle East,

Gravely concerned that the Palestinian and other Arab territories occupied since 1967, including Jerusalem, still remain under Israeli occupation, that the relevant resolutions of the United Nations have not been implemented and that the Palestinian people is still denied the restoration of its land and

---

[162] A/40/168-S/17014, A/40/668 and Add.1 and A/40/779-S/17581 and Corr.1.
[163] See A/37/696-S/15510, annex.

the exercise of its inalienable national rights in conformity with international law, as reaffirmed by resolutions of the United Nations,

Reaffirming the applicability of the Geneva Convention relative to the Protection of Civilian Persons in Time of War, of 12 August 1949,[164] to all the occupied Palestinian and other Arab territories, including Jerusalem,

Reaffirming further all relevant United Nations resolutions which stipulate that the acquisition of territory by force is inadmissible under the Charter of the United Nations and the principles of international law and that Israel must withdraw unconditionally from all the Palestinian and other Arab territories occupied by Israel since 1967, including Jerusalem,

Reaffirming also the imperative necessity of establishing a comprehensive, just and lasting peace in the region, based on full respect for the Charter and the principles of international law,

Gravely concerned also at the continuing Israeli policies involving the escalation and expansion of the conflict in the region, which further violate the principles of international law and endanger international peace and security,

Stressing once again the great importance of the time factor in the endeavours to achieve an early comprehensive, just and lasting peace in the Middle East,

1. *Reaffirms its conviction* that the question of Palestine is the core of the conflict in the Middle East and that no comprehensive, just and lasting peace in the region will be achieved without the full exercise by the Palestinian people of its inalienable national rights and the immediate, unconditional and total withdrawal of Israel from all the Palestinian and other occupied Arab territories;

2. *Reaffirms further* that a just and comprehensive settlement of the situation in the Middle East cannot be achieved without the participation on an equal footing of all the parties to the conflict, including the Palestine Liberation Organization, the representative of the Palestinian people;

3. *Declares once more* that peace in the Middle East is indivisible and must be based on a comprehensive, just and lasting solution of the Middle East problem, under the auspices of the United Nations and on the basis of relevant resolutions of the United Nations, which ensures the complete and unconditional withdrawal of Israel from the Palestinian and other Arab territories occupied since 1967, including Jerusalem, and which enables the Palestinian people, under the leadership of the Palestine Liberation Organization, to exercise its inalienable rights, including the right to return and the right to self-determination, national independence and the establishment of its independent sovereign State in Palestine, in accordance with the resolutions of the United Nations relevant to the question of Palestine, in particular General Assembly resolutions ES-7/2 of 29 July 1980, 36/120 A to F of 10 December 1981, 37/86 A to D of 10 December 1982, 37/86 E of

---

[164] United Nations, *Treaty Series*, vol. 75, No. 973, p. 287.

20 December 1982, 38/58 A to E of 13 December 1983 and 39/146 A to C of 14 December 1984;

4. *Considers* the Arab Peace Plan adopted unanimously at the Twelfth Arab Summit Conference, held at Fez, Morocco, on 25 November 1981 and from 6 to 9 September 1982,[165] reiterated by the Extraordinary Summit Conference of the Arab States held at Casablanca from 7 to 9 August 1985,[166] as well as relevant efforts and action to implement the Fez Plan, as an important contribution towards the realization of the inalienable rights of the Palestinian people through the achievement of a comprehensive, just and lasting peace in the Middle East;

5. *Condemns* Israel's continued occupation of the Palestinian and other Arab territories, including Jerusalem, in violation of the Charter of the United Nations, the principles of international law and the relevant resolutions of the United Nations, and demands the immediate, unconditional and total withdrawal of Israel from all the territories occupied since 1967;

6. *Rejects* all agreements and arrangements which violate the inalienable rights of the Palestinian people and contradict the principles of a just and comprehensive solution to the Middle East problem which ensures the establishment of a just peace in the area;

7. *Deplores* Israel's failure to comply with Security Council resolutions 476 (1980) of 30 June 1980 and 478 (1980) of 20 August 1980 and General Assembly resolutions 35/207 of 16 December 1980 and 36/226 A and B of 17 December 1981; determines that Israel's decision to annex Jerusalem and to declare it as its "capital" as well as the measures to alter its physical character, demographic composition, institutional structure and status are null and void and demands that they be rescinded immediately; and calls upon all Member States, the specialized agencies and all other international organizations to abide by the present resolution and all other relevant resolutions and decisions;

8. *Condemns* Israel's aggression, policies and practices against the Palestinian people in the occupied Palestinian territories and outside these territories, including expropriation, establishment of settlements, annexation and other terrorist, aggressive and repressive measures, which are in violation of the Charter and the principles of international law and the relevant international conventions;

9. *Strongly condemns* the imposition by Israel of its laws, jurisdiction and administration on the occupied Syrian Golan Heights, its annexationist policies and practices, the establishment of settlements, the confiscation of lands, the diversion of water resources and the imposition of Israeli citizenship on Syrian nationals, and declares that all these measures are null and void and constitute a violation of the rules and principles of international law relative to belligerent occupation, in particular the Geneva Convention

[165] See A/37/696-S/15510, annex.
[166] A/40/564, annex.

relative to the Protection of Civilian Persons in Time of War, of 12 August 1949;[167]

10. *Considers* that the agreements on strategic co-operation between the United States of America and Israel, signed on 30 November 1981, and the continued supply of modern arms and *matériel* to Israel, augmented by substantial economic aid, including the recently concluded Agreement on the Establishment of a Free Trade Area between the two Governments, have encouraged Israel to pursue its aggressive and expansionist policies and practices in the Palestinian and other Arab territories occupied since 1967, including Jerusalem, and have had adverse effects on efforts for the establishment of a comprehensive, just and lasting peace in the Middle East and would threaten the security of the region;

11. *Calls once more upon* all States to put an end to the flow to Israel of any military, economic, financial and technological aid, as well as of human resources, aimed at encouraging it to pursue its aggressive policies against the Arab countries and the Palestinian people;

12. *Strongly condemns* the continuing and increasing collaboration between Israel and the racist régime of South Africa, especially in the economic, military and nuclear fields, which constitutes a hostile act against the African and Arab States and enables Israel to enhance its nuclear capabilities, thus subjecting the States of the region to nuclear blackmail;

13. *Reaffirms* its call for the convening of an International Peace Conference on the Middle East under the auspices of the United Nations and on the basis of relevant resolutions of the United Nations—as specified in paragraph 5 of the Geneva Declaration on Palestine[168] and endorsed by General Assembly resolution 38/58 C of 13 December 1983;

14. *Requests* the Secretary-General to report to the Security Council periodically on the development of the situation and to submit to the General Assembly at its forty-first session a comprehensive report covering the developments in the Middle East in all their aspects.

B

The General Assembly,

Having discussed the item entitled "The situation in the Middle East",

Taking note of the report of the Secretary-General of 22 October 1985,[169]

Recalling Security Council resolution 497 (1981) of 17 December 1981,

Reaffirming its resolutions 36/226 B of 17 December 1981, ES-9/1 of 5 February 1982, 37/123 A of 16 December 1982, 38/180 A of 19 December 1983 and 39/146 B of 14 December 1984,

Recalling its resolution 3314 (XXIX) of 14 December 1974, in which it

---

[167] United Nations, *Treaty Series*, vol. 75, No. 973, p. 287.

[168] *Report of the International Conference on the Question of Palestine, 29 August-7 September 1983* (United Nations publication, Sales No. E.83.I.21), chap. I, sect. A.

[169] A/40/779-S/17581 and Corr.1.

defined an act of aggression, *inter alia*, as "the invasion or attack by the armed forces of a State of the territory of another State, or any military occupation, however temporary, resulting from such invasion or attack, or any annexation by the use of force of the territory of another State or part thereof" and provided that "no consideration of whatever nature, whether political, economic, military or otherwise, may serve as a justification for aggression",

Reaffirming the fundamental principle of the inadmissibility of the acquisition of territory by force,

Reaffirming once more the applicability of the Geneva Convention relative to the Protection of Civilian Persons in Time of War, of 12 August 1949,[170] to the occupied Palestinian and other Arab territories, including Jerusalem,

Noting that Israel's record, policies and actions establish conclusively that it is not a peace-loving Member State and that it has not carried out its obligations under the Charter of the United Nations,

Noting further that Israel has refused, in violation of Article 25 of the Charter, to accept and carry out the numerous relevant decisions of the Security Council, in particular resolution 497 (1981), thus failing to carry out its obligations under the Charter,

1. *Strongly condemns* Israel for its failure to comply with Security Council resolution 497 (1981) and General Assembly resolutions 36/226 B, ES-9/1, 37/123 A, 38/180 A and 39/146 B;

2. *Declares once more* that Israel's continued occupation of the Golan Heights, and its decision of 14 December 1981 to impose its laws, jurisdiction and administration on the occupied Syrian Golan Heights constitute an act of aggression under the provisions of Article 39 of the Charter of the United Nations and General Assembly resolution 3314 (XXIX);

3. *Declares once more* that Israel's decision to impose its laws, jurisdiction and administration on the occupied Syrian Golan Heights is illegal and therefore null and void and has no validity whatsoever;

4. *Declares* all Israeli policies and practices of, or aimed at, annexation of the occupied Palestinian and other Arab territories, including Jerusalem, to be illegal and in violation of international law and of the relevant United Nations resolutions;

5. *Determines once more* that all actions taken by Israel to give effect to its decision relating to the occupied Syrian Golan Heights are illegal and invalid and shall not be recognized;

6. *Reaffirms its determination* that all relevant provisions of the Regulations annexed to the Hague Convention IV of 1907,[171] and the Geneva Convention relative to the Protection of Civilian Persons in Time of War, of 12 August 1949,[172] continue to apply to the Syrian territory occupied by Israel

---

[170] United Nations, *Treaty Series*, vol. 75, No. 973, p. 287.

[171] Carnegie Endowment for International Peace, *The Hague Conventions and Declarations of 1899 and 1907* (New York, Oxford University Press, 1915), p. 100.

[172] United Nations, *Treaty Series*, vol. 75, No. 973, p. 287.

since 1967, and calls upon the parties thereto to respect and ensure respect of their obligations under these instruments in all circumstances;

7. *Determines once more* that the continued occupation of the Syrian Golan Heights since 1967 and their annexation by Israel on 14 December 1981, following Israel's decision to impose its laws, jurisdiction and administration on that territory, constitute a continuing threat to international peace and security;

8. *Strongly deplores* the negative vote by a permanent member of the Security Council which prevented the Council from adopting against Israel, under Chapter VII of the Charter, the "appropriate measures" referred to in resolution 497 (1981) unanimously adopted by the Council;

9. *Further deplores* any political, economic, financial, military and technological support to Israel that encourages Israel to commit acts of aggression and to consolidate and perpetuate its occupation and annexation of occupied Arab territories;

10. *Firmly emphasizes once more* its demand that Israel, the occupying Power, rescind forthwith its illegal decision of 14 December 1981 to impose its laws, jurisdiction and administration on the Syrian Golan Heights, which resulted in the effective annexation of that territory;

11. *Reaffirms once more* the overriding necessity of the total and unconditional withdrawal by Israel from all the Palestinian and other Arab territories occupied since 1967, including Jerusalem, which is an essential prerequisite for the establishment of a comprehensive and just peace in the Middle East;

12. *Determines once more* that Israel's record, policies and actions confirm that it is not a peace-loving Member State, that it has persistently violated the principles contained in the Charter and that it has carried out neither its obligations under the Charter nor its commitment under General Assembly resolution 273 (III) of 11 May 1949;

13. *Calls once more upon* all Member States to apply the following measures:

(*a*) To refrain from supplying Israel with any weapons and related equipment and to suspend any military assistance that Israel receives from them;

(*b*) To refrain from acquiring any weapons or military equipment from Israel;

(*c*) To suspend economic, financial and technological assistance to and cooperation with Israel;

(*d*) To sever diplomatic, trade and cultural relations with Israel;

14. *Reiterates its call* to all Member States to cease forthwith, individually and collectively, all dealings with Israel in order totally to isolate it in all fields;

15. *Urges* non-member States to act in accordance with the provisions of the present resolution;

16. *Calls upon* the specialized agencies and other international organiza-

tions to conform their relations with Israel to the terms of the present resolution;

17. *Requests* the Secretary-General to report to the General Assembly at its forty-first session on the implementation of the present resolution.

C

The General Assembly,

Recalling its resolutions 36/120 E of 10 December 1981, 37/123 C of 16 December 1982, 38/180 C of 19 December 1983 and 39/146 C of 14 December 1984, in which it determined that all legislative and administrative measures and actions taken by Israel, the occupying Power, which had altered or purported to alter the character and status of the Holy City of Jerusalem, in particular the so-called "Basic Law" on Jerusalem and the proclamation of Jerusalem as the capital of Israel, were null and void and must be rescinded forthwith,

Recalling Security Council resolution 478 (1980) of 20 August 1980, in which the Council, *inter alia*, decided not to recognize the "Basic Law" and called upon those States that had established diplomatic missions at Jerusalem to withdraw such missions from the Holy City,

Having considered the report of the Secretary-General of 22 October 1985,[173]

1. *Determines* that Israel's decision to impose its laws, jurisdiction and administration on the Holy City of Jerusalem is illegal and therefore null and void and has no validity whatsoever;

2. *Deplores* the transfer by some States of their diplomatic missions to Jerusalem in violation of Security Council resolution 478 (1980) and their refusal to comply with the provisions of that resolution;

3. *Calls once again upon* those States to abide by the provisions of the relevant United Nations resolutions, in conformity with the Charter of the United Nations;

4. *Requests* the Secretary-General to report to the General Assembly at its forty-first session on the implementation of the present resolution.

[173] A/40/779-S/17581 and Corr.1.

346. General Assembly Resolution 40/170 on Assistance to the Palestinian People, December 17, 1985*

* G.A. Res. 40/170 (1985). *See also* previous resolutions, G.A. Res. 145, 38 U.N. GAOR Supp. (No. 47) at 118, U.N. Doc. A/38/47 (1983) and G.A. Res. 224, 39 U.N. GAOR Supp. (No. 51) at 170, U.N. Doc. A/39/51 (1984).

The General Assembly,

Recalling its resolution 39/224 of 18 December 1984,

Recalling also Economic and Social Council resolution 1985/57 of 25 July 1985,

Recalling further the Programme of Action for the Achievement of Palestinian Rights, adopted by the International Conference on the Question of Palestine,[2]

Noting the need to provide economic and social assistance to the Palestinian people,

1. *Takes note* of the report of the Secretary-General on assistance to the Palestinian people;[3]

2. *Notes* the meeting on assistance to the Palestinian people that was held at Geneva on 5 and 8 July 1985 in response to General Assembly resolution 39/224;[4]

3. *Expresses its thanks* to the Secretary-General for convening the meeting on assistance to the Palestinian people;

4. *Regards* such a meeting as a valuable opportunity to assess progress in economic and social assistance to the Palestinian people and to explore ways and means of enhancing such assistance;

5. *Draws the attention* of the international community, the United Nations system and intergovernmental and non-governmental organizations to the need to disburse their aid to the occupied Palestinian territories only for the benefit of the Palestinian people;

6. *Requests* the Secretary-General:

(a) To review the progress made in the implementation of the proposed activities and projects described in his report on assistance to the Palestinian people;

(b) To take all necessary steps to finalize the programme of economic and social assistance to the Palestinian people requested in General Assembly resolution 38/145 of 19 December 1983;

(c) To convene in 1986 a meeting of the relevant programmes, organizations, agencies, funds and organs of the United Nations system to consider economic and social assistance to the Palestinian people;

(d) To provide for the participation in the meeting of the Palestine Liberation Organization, the Arab host countries and relevant intergovernmental and non-governmental organizations;

7. *Requests* the relevant programmes, organizations, agencies, funds and organs of the United Nations system to intensify their efforts, in co-operation with the Palestine Liberation Organization, to provide economic and social assistance to the Palestinian people;

[2] *Report of the International Conference on the Question of Palestine, Geneva, 29 August-7 September 1983* (United Nations publication, Sales No. E.83.I.21), chap I, sect. B.

[3] A/40/353-E/1985/115 and Corr.1 and A/40/353/Add.1-E/1985/115/Add.1 and Corr.1.

[4] A/40/353/Add.1-E/1985/115/Add.1 and Corr.1.

8. *Also requests* that United Nations assistance to the Palestinians in the Arab host countries should be rendered in co-operation with the Palestine Liberation Organization and with the consent of the Arab host Government concerned;

9. *Requests* the Secretary-General to report to the General Assembly at its forty-first session, through the Economic and Social Council, on the progress made in the implementation of the present resolution.

347. General Assembly Resolution 40/201 on the Living Conditions of the Palestinian People in the Occupied Palestinian Territories, December 17, 1985*

* G.A. Res. 40/201 (1985).

The General Assembly,

Recalling the Vancouver Declaration on Human Settlements, 1976,[125] and the relevant recommendations for national action[126] adopted by Habitat: United Nations Conference on Human Settlements,

Recalling also its resolution 39/169 of 17 December 1984,

Taking note of Commission of Human Settlements resolution 8/3 of 10 May 1985,[127]

Gravely alarmed by the continuation of the Israeli settlement policies, which have been declared null and void and a major obstacle to peace,

Recognizing the need to identify priority development projects needed for improving the living conditions of the Palestinian people in the occupied Palestinian territories,

1. *Takes note with concern* of the report of the Secretary-General on the living conditions of the Palestinian people in the occupied Palestinian territories;[128]

2. *Takes note also* of the statement made on 25 October 1985 by the Observer of the Palestine Liberation Organization;[129]

3. *Rejects* the Israeli plans and actions intended to change the demographic composition of the occupied Palestinian territories, particularly the increase and expansion of the Israeli settlements, and other plans and actions creating conditions leading to the displacement and exodus of Palestinians from the occupied Palestinian territories;

4. *Expresses its alarm* at the deterioration, as a result of the Israeli occupation, in the living conditions of the Palestinian people in the Palestinian territories occupied since 1967;

5. *Affirms* that the Israeli occupation is contradictory to the basic requirements for the social and economic development of the Palestinian people in the occupied Palestinian territories;

6. *Requests* the Secretary-General:

(*a*) To organize, by April 1987, a seminar on priority development projects needed for improving the living conditions of the Palestinian people in the occupied Palestinian territories, including a comprehensive general housing programme, as recommended in resolution 8/3 of 10 May 1985 of the Commission on Human Settlements;[130]

---

[125] *Report of Habitat: United Nations Conference on Human Settlements, Vancouver, 31 May-11 June 1976* (United Nations publication, Sales No. E.76.IV.7 and corrigendum), chap. I.

[126] *Ibid.*, chap. II.

[127] See *Official Records of the General Assembly, Fortieth Session, Supplement No. 8* (A/40/8 and Corr.1), annex I.

[128] A/40/373-E/1985/99.

[129] *Official Records of the General Assembly, Fortieth Session, Second Committee*, 14th meeting.

[130] See *Official Records of the General Assembly, Fortieth Session, Supplement No. 8* (A/40/8 and Corr.1), annex I.

(b) To make the necessary preparations for the seminar, providing for the participation of the Palestine Liberation Organization;

(c) To invite experts to present papers to the seminar;

(d) To invite also relevant intergovernmental and non-governmental organizations;

(e) To report to the General Assembly at its forty-first session, through the Economic and Social Council, on the preparations for the seminar;

(f) To report to the General Assembly at its forty-second session, through the Economic and Social Council, on the seminar.

348. Israel and the Occupied Territories (excerpt),

February 1986*

* U.S. Dep't State, "The Occupied Territories," in *Country Reports on Human Rights Practices for 1985*, at 1267 (Feb. 1986).

The territories which Israel has occupied since 1967 consist of the West Bank, East Jerusalem, the Golan Heights, and the Gaza Strip. The West Bank and Gaza remain under military goverment. Israel regards East Jerusalem and the Golan Heights as subject to Israeli law, jurisdiction, and administration.

The United States holds the view that Israel's presence in all these territories is that of an occupying power. The United States regards Israel's administration as subject to the Hague regulations of 1907 and the 1949 Fourth Geneva Convention concerning the protection of civilian populations under military occupation.

Israel declares that the Fourth Geneva Convention does not apply to the West Bank and Gaza, but that it voluntarily observes most of the Convention's provisions in these areas. Major differences have arisen in regard to the applicability of these provisions in East Jerusalem and the Golan Heights, the introduction of civilian settlers, and the use of collective punishment. Israel declares that it enforces Jordanian law in the West Bank and British Mandatory regulations in the Gaza Strip. In addition, Israel has issued over 1,000 military orders altering or overriding portions of these laws and uses some British Mandatory ordinances and Ottoman Empire laws on the West Bank.

The complex human rights situation in the occupied territories is largely the result of the fact that since the 1967 war and in the absence of a peace settlement, the territories remain under military administration and there is friction between occupation authorities and the Palestinian population which opposes Israeli control. Among the symptoms of friction are active resistance to the occupation, including episodes of violence, sometimes encouraged by outside extremist groups. Friction also arises from security measures taken by Israel to counteract terrorist acts and threats of terrorism, and to counter other kinds of activities which the Israeli authorities assert endanger security. Another cause of friction is the introduction of civilian Israeli settlers, although settlement activity has slowed. Establishment of new settlements was limited to six by the National Unity Government agreement in late 1984. In 1985 three of these were officially dedicated, one in the Golan Heights and two in the West Bank. Frictions are exacerbated by some Israeli political elements who advocate annexation or permanent Israeli control of the territories, as well as by the refusal of the principal Palestinian organizations to recognize the State of Israel.

Israel implements its policy in the West Bank and Gaza through civil administrations. These were created in 1981 under the control of the Defense Ministry, and are staffed by military as well as civilian personnel. Israel's national police, border police, security service, and the Israel Defense Forces (IDF) all have a role in the administration of the occupied territories. The national police, which includes local Palestinians in its ranks, is seldom the target of criticism. However, there are frequent complaints by West Bankers and Gazans about the actions of the other organizations.

Civil Administration authorities have attempted to reshape local politics, particularly by blocking the influence of the Palestine Liberation Organization (PLO) and by trying to promote an alternate leadership. Israel permitted municipal elections in 1972 and 1976, but after 1980, citing security considerations, postponed further elections and removed numerous elected and appointed officials in the West Bank and Gaza. Threats and intimidation by extremist Palestinians have also inhibited the development of a visible, moderate local leadership. The present Israeli policy is to support the installation of acceptable, non-PLO Palestinian mayors who have local and Jordanian support in place of Israeli military appointees. A new Arab mayor of Nablus took office in December, and there is discussion of installing other Arab mayors.

Israel has allowed the establishment of four universities in the West Bank and one in Gaza where none existed before, but has restricted activities of student and faculty members which it regards as threatening to its security. Israel permits criticism of its policies by the East Jerusalem-based Arabic press but has often censored articles and editorials and restricts the circulation of Arabic publications in the West Bank and Gaza. One Arabic newspaper and one press service were ordered closed during the year and one Jewish settler newspaper was temporarily banned. Broad restrictions on speech and assembly apply in the occupied territories.

Arab and Jewish residents suffered from a marked increase in violent acts in 1985. One or another faction of the PLO as well as a variety of PLO dissident groups claimed responsibility for nearly all acts of violence against the IDF or Israeli civilians. Much of the violence, including the increased use of homemade bombs, knives, guns, and Molotov cocktails, appears, however, to have been spontaneous and local.

Complaints of settler violence continued throughout the year, including unauthorized armed patrols and physical harassment. Israel prosecuted and convicted Jewish settlers for a variety of illegal acts. Twenty-five Jewish settlers were convicted of offenses including membership in a terrorist organization, murder, conspiracy, and other charges in 1985 and were given sentences ranging from four months to life imprisonment. Two IDF officers are currently being tried for their alleged roles in terrorism against Arabs.

Respect for Human Rights

Section 1 Respect for the Integrity of the Person, Including Freedom from:
a. Political Killing
Political killing is not condoned by the Israeli Government. There have been, however, deaths and serious injuries as a result of both terrorist acts and IDF security enforcement measures. A military government spokesman said in October that 660 terrorist incidents had occurred in Israel and the occupied territories since January 1985.
At least 2 unarmed Arab residents of the occupied territories were killed

and 17 wounded by IDF soldiers enforcing security regulations. Members of the IDF also killed at least 4 residents of the occupied territories and wounded at least 5 in armed confrontations. Attacks by Arabs took the lives of at least 4 IDF soldiers, 5 Jewish civilians (in addition to 4 who were killed in Israel) and 4 Arabs, while at least 7 IDF soldiers, 40 Jewish civilians, and 16 Arabs were wounded. During 1985, two Palestinians who had been missing for some time were found dead at the site of explosions.

b. Disappearance

Israeli authorities neither sponsor nor condone disappearances.

c. Torture and Cruel, Inhuman, or Degrading Treatment or Punishment

Torture is forbidden by Israeli law, and there is no evidence that torture is condoned by the Israeli authorities. Israeli border and national policemen have been convicted of abusive use of force against Arab prisoners, and the Israeli Supreme Court has ordered the withdrawal from evidence of confessions by West Bankers on the grounds that they appeared to have been obtained by force.

Palestinian prisoners at a number of West Bank and Israeli prisons conducted hunger strikes throughout the year protesting conditions. The head of occupied territories prisons said inmates at Jenin prison spend 23 hours a day in 30 square-meter cells holding 14 people each. In 1984 Israeli courts convicted two former officials of Farah prison of having abused prisoners. Based on affidavits collected from former prisoners between May 1982 and May 1984, a report prepared by the West Bank organization Law in the Service of Man, and published by the International Commission of Jurists, alleged in January that prisoners at Farah prison are systematically abused. Israel denied the charges of systematic abuse.

d. Arbitrary Arrest, Detention, or Exile

Persons arrested for common crimes in the occupied territories are usually provided the opportunity for bail, access to an attorney, and a clear statement of charges. Individuals may be held in administrative detention without formal charges for up to 18 days. The normal detention period after the filing of charges is 60 days before trial. This period can be extended by a Supreme Court judge for an additional 3 months, and this extension may be renewed at the end of the 3 months.

Persons detained for security investigations are not permitted bail and initially are denied access to an attorney or other outside contact, including consular officers. In some cases, officials have declined initially to confirm a person's detention to consular officers. This denial of notification of arrest to any third party can, under Israeli law, be extended for up to 15 days. It is unclear whether detainees are informed of the specific charges against them. Many of those released from such detention without charges claim ignorance of the reasons for their detention.

A sizable number of Arabs are often detained after terrorist incidents or the dispersal of demonstrations. Such detentions usually do not result in formal charges and are not prolonged. Persons arrested during demonstrations are tried in military courts on security grounds. The security forces can and do detain individuals without prompt notification of their relatives and apparently without the use of warrants.

In May, Israel released 1,150 prisoners, including 879 who had been convicted of security offenses (alleged terrorists, their accomplices, and contacts), in exchange for 3 Israeli military personnel who had been captured in Lebanon. Some of the approximately 400 security prisoners who were released in the occupied territories as the result of this exchange were later rearrested on new security charges. Thirty-one of those released in the occupied territories were served expulsion orders alleging that they were not bona fide residents of the territories. The Government of Israel permitted 10 of the 31 to remain in the territories after they proved to the satisfaction of the Israeli courts that they were pre-1967 residents of the West Bank. Twenty-one others were expelled, drawing a rare public rebuke from the International Committee of the Red Cross (ICRC), which had helped negotiate the original exchange agreement. The ICRC disagreed with the Israeli interpretation of the residency requirements as established in the agreement. Israel maintained that those who had reentered Israel illegally had forfeited their residency rights; the ICRC disagreed.

In August, after a 5-year hiatus, the Israeli Government revived 6-month administrative detention and deportation from the territories. The United States has indicated its belief that these measures are likely to foster further tensions and that they are inconsistent with the Fourth Geneva Convention. Since that time, approximately 100 Palestinians have been placed under administrative detention. Administrative detention must be confirmed by a military judge. The hearing is confidential and the detainee and counsel are not automatically given access to evidence cited as grounds for the detention. Six West Bank Palestinians were deported for alleged security offenses. Where the deportees appealed, the Israeli Supreme Court upheld the deportation orders.

In 1985 at least 25 Arabs were placed under new or renewed orders restricting them to their town of residence for 3 months or more. Such restrictions involve no formal charges and are ordered by regional military commanders without judicial review. Many of those so restricted are political activists, persons who are outspoken critics of Israeli policies, or PLO supporters.

More than 10 West Bank towns and at least 10 refugee camps were placed under curfew at least once during 1985. Complaints about other forms of collective punishment and humiliating treatment at the hands of the security forces, such as the holding of groups of Arab men in town or village squares for long periods, rose sharply in 1985, especially during August and September. Some soldiers were disciplined for improper use of force and for stealing from those they had stopped for questioning or search.

There is no forced labor in the occupied territories.

e. Denial of Fair Public Trial

Jordanian law, as modified by Israeli military orders, remains in force in the West Bank for most criminal and civil matters. British Mandatory law, as modified, prevails in Gaza. The judicial application of these laws, except in security cases, land acquisition, or where jurisdiction has been transferred by military order, has been left in the hands of an Arab judiciary, which acts independently of Israeli authority. Residents of the occupied territories accused of nonsecurity offenses receive public trials in local courts. In East Jerusalem and the Golan Heights, Israeli law applies.

Persons suspected of having committed security offenses, which are not precisely defined under Israeli law, are normally tried in Israeli military courts with a military judge presiding, and are defended by counsel. Israeli residents of the occupied territories accused of security offenses are not tried by military court but by the Israeli district court closest to their residence or the scene of their crime.

Most military trials are open to the public, except for some cases involving serious security offenses. Consular officers normally have no difficulty in attending any court proceeding in which a foreign citizen is involved. Israel asserts jurisdiction with respect to alleged security offenses committed outside of Israel and the occupied territories.

Orders of the Civil Administration may be appealed to the Israeli Supreme Court. Nonjudicial administrative orders of the military government may be appealed to area military commanders and the Supreme Court. No appeal of military court verdicts is possible, although the area commander may exercise the right of commutation. In April, a petition was filed on behalf of two Palestinians to have Israel establish a military appeals court in the occupied territories, contending that such a court is required by international law. The Government has argued that international law does not require an appeals apparatus, that the present system is adequate, and that an appeals court would undermine the military's antiterrorism deterrent measures. As of this date, the Israeli Supreme Court has not yet rendered a decision.

Palestinians complain that due process is denied in the course of Israel's designating as state land areas of the occupied territories regarded by them as community or private land. Complaints include a lack of written notification or that the 30-day period for filing competing claims is too brief to obtain substantiating documentation. Earth-moving work sometimes begins before the 30-day period has elapsed. Israeli authorities respond that extensions are granted upon requests, and that no title is required if the disputed land has been cultivated for at least ten years.

f. Arbitrary Interference with Privacy, Family, Home, or Correspondence

Under occupation regulations, military authorities can and do enter private homes and institutions without prior judicial approval in pursuit of security objectives. A military order permits any soldier to search any person or premise on the West Bank at any time without warrant on the suspicion that a person or organization may be in possession of a proscribed publication.

In 1985, at least 17 houses of West Bank and Gaza residents accused of involvement in security incidents were demolished and 20 were sealed. There is no judicial review of a decision to seal or demolish a house or room and such action is usually taken before the suspect has been put on trial. Houses or rooms used by Israelis suspected or convicted of security offenses in the occupied territories were not demolished or sealed in 1985.

It is widely believed that mail and telephone services in the West Bank and Gaza are monitored. Individuals can be and are questioned on their political views by security officials. Such inquiries can involve overnight detention.

Section 2 Respect for Civil Rights, Including:

a. Freedom of Speech and Press

Freedom of expression is restricted on security grounds. Proscribed acts include flying the Palestinian flag or displaying its colors, displaying Palestinian nationalist slogans, and publicly expressing support for the PLO. The Arabic press, most of which is located in East Jerusalem, remains outspoken in its criticism of Israeli policies and actions. Arrests, prison sentences, land seizures, and other politically sensitive stories are generally reported, but editorials and articles are frequently censored in whole or in part. All items to be printed in Jerusalem's Arabic papers must be submitted to the censor for prior review. Hebrew papers need submit only articles on military security matters to the censors. At least 90 editorials and commentaries from Arabic newspapers were censored during the year. Censorship decisions may be challenged by appeal to the chief censor.

Materials licensed to be published in East Jerusalem are free to circulate there, but require an additional license for distribution in the West Bank and Gaza. Military orders forbid the printing or publishing of anything containing political significance without a prior license. Political significance is not defined in the order.

A permit must be obtained for every publication (book, magazine, or newspaper) imported into the occupied territories. Arabic educational materials, periodicals, and books originating outside Israel are censored or banned for anti-Semitic or anti-Israeli content and for the encouragement of Palestinian nationalism. Possession of banned materials by West Bank or Gaza Arabs is a criminal offense. Restrictions of this kind are usually not applied to Israeli residents. Lawyers have complained of difficulty in obtaining the list of proscribed publications. The number of books explicitly prohibited was reduced from 1,300 to 350 after the present Israeli Government took office.

In September, the Arabic weekly newspaper Al Darb was ordered permanently closed on the charge that it was run and directed by the Democratic Front for the Liberation of Palestine. An appeal has been filed. Also in September, the East Jerusalem press service Al Minar was ordered shut for 6 months. In October, the Arabic weekly magazine Al Biyadar As Siassi was refused permission to distribute in the occupied territories for 2 weeks for failing to submit published material to the censors. The Arabic daily Ashaab was shut down for 3 days in August for printing material not approved by the censor. Five Arab journalists were placed under administrative detention in 1985. In November, the Jewish settler newspaper Aleph Yud was temporarily prevented from publishing due to alleged incitement to violent resistance against what was contended to be the willingness of the Government of Israel to make territorial concessions as part of a peace settlement.

Arabic-language radio and television programs from Jordan, Syria, and other Arab countries, including broadcasts of the Voice of Palestine, are received in the occupied territories without jamming.

Foreign journalists have not reported any difficulties in meeting with inhabitants of the occupied territories. All reports filed by the foreign press, however, are subject to military censorship.

b. Freedom of Peaceful Assembly and Association

The Israeli occupation authorities have permitted a wide range of labor, professional, and fraternal groups organized before 1967 to continue to function. Professional associations are active and frequently take public stands on political issues. No political parties or other groups viewed as primarily political are permitted. Public gatherings, defined as a group of more than ten people, require permission, often withheld from both Arab and Israeli groups, based on the consideration of public order.

There are approximately 40 labor unions in the occupied territories, grouped into 2 rival federations. Fifteen new labor unions have been permitted to register in the West Bank since the beginning of the occupation, but over 100 applications have been turned down and a number of Arab unions have been disbanded by the occupation authorities for alleged security concerns. In 1985, the Israeli authorities refused permission for a union of Arab lawyers on the West Bank to form. Strikes are legal so long as they are not undertaken for political reasons. There were no reports of arrests for labor-organizing activity during 1985. Some union activities, such as cultural exhibitions or May Day festivities, were prohibited during the year on security grounds.

West Bank unions are generally small and confined to urban workers in skilled craft trades. The occupation authorities must approve all candidates for election to union office but such elections are held without other interference. Membership in the Histadrut, the Israeli national labor organization, is open to Arab workers from East Jerusalem and the Golan Heights.

c. Freedom of Religion

Freedom of religious practice exists in the occupied territories. No group or sect is banned on religious grounds. Muslim and Christian holy days are observed without hindrance, and Muslims and Christians operate a variety of private schools and institutions. There has been controversy concerning rights of access to worship inside the Ibrahimi Mosque/Tomb of the Patriarchs, which is also the site of an ancient synagogue. The occupation authorities tolerate the existence of a number of Islamic fundamentalist groups. There has been no reported interference with the publication or distribution of religious publications.

Israel protects Muslim and Christian holy places and usually assures freedom of access to them. On occasion, the authorities have denied both Arab and Jewish groups access to religious sites on religious or security grounds. Israel makes concerted efforts to facilitate travel into Jordan for Muslims wishing to make the Hajj to Mecca. This includes expedited bridge clearance procedures and extended hours of crossing. In 1985, several thousand Muslims from the occupied territories made the pilgrimage. At least 20 were refused permission on security grounds.

In July, a number of suspects in the Jewish terrorist underground trials were convicted and sentenced to prison terms for, among other things, conspiracy to destroy the Dome of the Rock [Mosque] with explosives.

d. Freedom of Movement Within the Country, Foreign Travel, Emigration, and Repatriation

Freedom of movement is generally unrestricted for Arabs within the occupied territories, but certain categories are significantly restricted. Approximately 80,000 Arabs travel daily to Israel to work. All residents over 16 must carry identity documents with them at all times and must show them to military or law enforcement officials whenever requested. Vehicles owned by Arabs of the occupied territories are frequently stopped for security checks, sometimes at unauthorized roadblocks manned by settlers. Palestinians are required to obtain permits to remain overnight in Israel; West Bankers are generally forbidden to remain in Jerusalem after midnight.

Most inhabitants of the occupied territories are permitted to travel abroad and many thousands do so each year. Exit visas are required. The Government of Israel issues laissez passers to residents of the occupied territories upon their request to facilitate foreign travel after a security check. In some cases, restrictions are imposed on reentry. Travel bans are also imposed on some persons suspected of antioccupation activities. Eight West Bank women were prohibited from traveling to the U.N. Conference on Women in Nairobi in August. The leader of a West Bank charitable society was denied permission to travel to the United States in September to attend the Congressional Black Caucus annual conference.

Bans on the travel of residents of particular areas have been employed by Israeli security forces as a form of collective punishment. The residents of at least 10 West Bank towns were prohibited from crossing the Allenby Bridge to Jordan for various periods following terrorist attacks. Bans on Tulkarm and Hebron lasted 1 month and 5 weeks, respectively. OOespite [sic] the formal state of war between Israel and Jordan, two-way travel between the West Bank and Jordan is permitted. Palestinians returning from

Jordan, as well as other Arabs or persons of Arab descent, all of whom are subject to search, complain of unnecessarily harsh or humiliating treatment and harassment. Israel permitted all members of the Jordanian Parliament resident in the West Bank to travel freely to attend parliamentary sessions during 1985.

There are no obstacles to emigration. Israel sometimes refuses to renew the laissez passers of West Bank residents who study or work abroad for a period of time, even though they have not acquired foreign citizenship. Such residents are permitted to return to the West Bank, as tourists only, and are sometimes denied the right to return at all. Entry permits or residency rights are often denied to spouses and children solely because the head of the household has emigrated. Israel also has not permitted the return of many former West Bank residents who happened to be absent at the time the June 1967 war broke out and Israeli occupation began.

Gazans normally do not require prior approval for travel to the West Bank. Under special arrangements concluded between Israel and Egypt, thousands of Gazans regularly cross the border into Egypt, particularly to work or visit relatives in the divided city of Rafah. Israel permits Golan Heights Druze to return after attending school in Syria; it has not, however, permitted the return of other Syrians who fled or were expelled from the area during and after the 1967 war.

Section 3 Respect for Political Rights: The Right of Citizens to Change Their Government

There is no regional self-government in the occupied territories and only limited Arab administration at the town level; most villages retain their traditional leadership. Arab civil servants, institutions, and municipal officials operate under the military government. No indigenous formal political parties or overtly political organizations are permitted.

Municipal elections, held in 1972 and 1976 and scheduled for 1980, were postponed and have not been rescheduled. Of the 23 Arab mayors and municipal councils elected in 1976, 14 of the mayors and at least 4 municipal councils were dismissed by occupation authorities. The mayors of the major towns of Hebron, Nablus, Ramallah, and El Bireh were replaced by Israeli officials. Neither the dismissals nor appointments of alternate officials is subject to judicial review. Bethlehem and Tulkarm are the only major towns governed by elected Arab mayors. Nablus was returned to an Arab mayor, the last duly elected deputy mayor and elected head of the Chamber of Commerce, in December 1985.

Arab residents of East Jerusalem are permitted and encouraged to vote in municipal elections. Approximately 20 percent of those eligible did so in the 1983 elections.

Most Arab residents of the West Bank are Jordanian citizens and as such are represented by 2 senators and 30 members of the Jordanian Parliament.

Section 4 Governmental Attitudes Regarding International and Nongovernmental Investigation of Alleged Violations of Human Rights

A variety of local groups, both Israeli and Palestinian, are concerned with
human rights issues. These groups' publications and statements are allowed
to circulate in the occupied territories.

The Israeli Government normally permits international human rights
groups to visit the occupied territories, and does not interfere with their
investigations. However, two field investigators for Law in the Service of
Man, the West Bank affiliate of the International Commission of Jurists
which is involved in legal assistance on human rights issues, were placed
under administrative arrest in September on security grounds. One was released in December; the other is due to be released in March.

Since 1978 the International Labor Organization has sent factfinding
missions to Israel and the occupied territories. Among its recommendations
it has urged that "the impact of the state of occupation . . . on the exercise
of trade union activities should be reduced to a strict minimum. . . ."

Amnesty International's 1985 Report on Israel and the occupied territories expressed concern regarding due process and the treatment of prisoners. Freedom House has characterized the occupied territories as "partly
free."

Economic, Social, and Cultural Situation

There are between 800,000 to 1 million Palestinians in the West Bank.
Living standards have risen substantially since 1967, although more slowly
than in Israel or Jordan; per capita gross income in 1985 was three times its
1967 level. Much of this increase in income is due to the large number of
West Bankers working in Israel and to remittances from Palestinians working abroad. In 1985, Israel's economic problems continued to affect West
Bank commercial and agricultural sales, tourist trade, and local construction. A large but undetermined portion of the Arab work force is tradition-
ally underemployed or engaged in seasonal work.

Economic life in the occupied territories has become enmeshed in Israeli
regulations, some used politically. Israeli restrictions on the export to Israel
of West Bank and Gaza products, especially agricultural products, limits local market opportunities. While Jordan imposes market-protection limits on
West Bank produce, export to Jordan is sometimes banned by Israel as punishment for a security incident. Construction of new factories is also restricted for political as well as economic reasons. Some localities from which
security offenders have been arrested have been declared off-limits to development projects. While Israel is concerned that funds from the PLO or
other hostile sources might be brought into the occupied territories under
the guise of development, Arabs contend that even projects which are fully
funded by proven local sources have not been approved.

The Israeli Government has indicated that it would review favorably several long-standing Arab proposals and in October the Civil Administration approved a large number of projects which had previously been rejected. Several municipalities have been permitted to import funds held in Jordanian banks and private import of funds has been liberalized.

The taking of land by Israeli authorities for settlements, military use, and in connection with major road plans, and the reclassification of communal areas as state land, significantly affects the lives and economic activities of Palestinians. According to come calculations, Palestinians have been precluded from use of an area approaching 50 percent of the West Bank land and 15 percent of the Gaza Strip, of which about one half is presently vacant and barren. There are currently more than 150 nonmilitary settlements in the West Bank (excluding unilaterally expanded Jerusalem) and Gaza, with a total population of about 40,000, although the growth of settlements slowed considerably in 1985. The scarcity of water in most parts of the West Bank constrains agricultural and urban development. A disproportionate amount is allocated for settlers' use.

The United Nations Relief and Works Agency (UNRWA) and the military government meet the basic educational needs of refugee students in the West Bank. Overall adjusted primary school enrollment there was 83 percent in 1984. The West Bank is served by four universities, one college, one community college, and a variety of other educational institutions, all established or upgraded since the beginning of the Israeli occupation. None of the universities receives financial support or other assistance from the occupation authorities. The creation of additional institutions is under consideration by various Arab groups. All teachers at educational institutions in the occupied territories must receive certificates from the Israeli authorities, issuance of which include criteria beyond that of professional competence. In March, 18 teachers were dismissed for political activities. An-Najah University was closed twice during 1985: once for 2 months after occupation authorities seized materials considered inflammatory during a campaign for student council elections and for 3 days in December for allegedly allowing illegal assembly. Bir Zeit University was closed by the authorities for 1 month and Bethlehem University was closed for 1 week when proscribed books were found at book fairs on the campuses. Bethlehem was also closed for 1 day in November following student demonstrations protesting deportations. These measures at times go beyond what might be reasonably justified on security grounds.

The 363 square kilometer Gaza strip has a population of about 500,000 with a per capita income of about $1,100 a year. Gaza's economy advanced marginally in the early 1980's, whereas real gross national product grew at over 10 percent in the late 1960's, and 5 to 6 percent in the late 1970's. Since 1967, infant mortality has declined sharply and health services have improved. Gaza's basic needs for food, clothing, and shelter are largely met. Severe population pressure and inadequate public sanitation remain major problems. Housing is especially crowded in the eight Gaza refugee camps, where approximately 210,000 of the 370,000 refugees registered with UNRWA live. Approximately 35,000 refugees have left the camps to live in Israeli government-sponsored communities. Inadequate classroom space has forced double-shifting at many UNRWA and government schools in recent years. Gaza producers of citrus, the major crop, complain that marketing has suffered from both Israeli and Jordanian restrictions. Israel has reduced water use to allow the water table to rise and inhibit saline intrusion. The fishing industry has shrunk due to restrictions on fishing waters. About 35,000 Gazans commute daily to work in Israel, earning about one-third of Gaza's income. Gaza's Al Azhar University, an affiliate of Al Azhar in Cairo, offers a 4-year program to about 3,300 Gaza students.

The Israeli-occupied portion of the Golan Heights consists of 1,295 square kilometers and has an Arab population of about 15,000, mostly Druze and a small percentage of Alawites. Approximately 7,500 Israeli settlers live in some 32 settlements in the Golan Heights. Druze village councils have complained that they do not receive sufficient funding to provide minimal municipal services, and a third of the estimated 4,000 school children are reported to be studying in substandard classrooms.

Child labor is not permitted and adequate regulations on working conditions are in effect. Histadrut, the Israeli national labor organization, has taken steps to assure that working conditions for Golan Druze are comparable to those of Israelis.

Urban West Bankers are increasingly sophisticated in their social attitudes, including toward the role of women, but the rural majority continues to hold more traditional social values. There are no legal or administrative prohibitions on the employment of women in the occupied territories, although traditional cultural mores and family commitments limit most to homemaking. Most Palestinian women holding jobs outside their homes reside and work in urban areas. Employment of women is concentrated in service industries, education, and health services, with a small number working in journalism, law, and other professions.

Although women legally have equal access to public education, custom and family pressures limit the number of women in West Bank schools. Even so, female school enrollment is quite high by Middle Eastern standards. A little over 45 percent of the primary and secondary school students are female. While female enrollment at the postsecondary level varies between roughly 30 to 45 percent at coeducational West Bank colleges and universities, a number of teacher and vocational training centers are all male or all female.

There is a wide range of women's cooperative groups for health care, child care, handicraft production, vocational training, and other services. The West Bank-wide Society for the Preservation of the Family is active in supporting women's needs.

349. Text of Joint Communiqué Issued by Israel and Morocco, July 24, 1986*

His Majesty King Hassan II on July 22-23, 1986, received at his palace at Ifrane Mr. Shimon Peres, Prime Minister of Israel. In the talks, marked with frankness and devoted essentially to the study of the Fez plan, the Moroccan sovereign and the Israeli Prime Minister analyzed in depth the situation in the Middle East and the conditions in form and in substance likely to contribute efficiently to the establishment of peace in this region.

His Majesty King Hassan II gave a presentation of the Fez plan, explaining his views concerning the merits of each of its elements and suggesting that this plan has a double merit of on the one hand constituting the sole document which is objectively valid to serve as a basis for a just and durable peace and on the other hand being the object of an Arab consensus in contrast to any other plan or peace proposal.

In his turn, Mr. Shimon Peres clarified his observations on the Fez plan putting forth observations pertaining to conditions he deems necessary for the installation of peace.

As the meeting was of a purely exploratory nature aiming at no moment at engaging in negotiations, His Majesty King Hassan II will inform the Arab leaders and Prime Minister Mr. Shimon Peres his Government on the points of view developed during these talks.

350. Memorandum to British Prime Minister Margaret
Thatcher from Palestinian Leaders in the Occupied
Territories, May 27, 1986*

---

* 16 J. Palestine Stud. 212 (Autumn 1986).

We welcome British Prime Minister Mrs. Margaret Thatcher to Palestine, particularly to East Jerusalem, the West Bank, and the Gaza Strip, which are under Israeli occupation. We would like to point out some issues that concern our people and their legitimate struggle.

The British government, in contrast to the various U.S. administrations that have striven and continue to strive to play the role of peacemaker in the region without possessing the neutrality that would render them suitable for this role, has shown its desire to seek a just solution to the Palestinian-Israeli conflict. This desire was evident in a British attempt last autumn to meet with PLO officials in London. In addition, Britain, as one of the large countries to sign the Venice Declaration, has explicitly recognized the Palestinian people's right to self-determination.

Furthermore, the British government, as is clear from its political positions and official statements, holds the view that Jewish settlement in the West Bank and Gaza Strip is an illegal act that constitutes an obstacle on the road to a solution. At the same time, we believe that due to Britain's mandate period in Palestine, during which the Palestinian problem was rendered practically insolvable, Britain bears an historical responsibility to resolve this problem at the current time. Allow us to present a number of other points:

1. The sons of the Palestinian people in the occupied lands are part of the entire Palestinian people, one-third of whom live here and two-thirds in the diaspora. Any solution to the Palestinian problem should deal with the entire people, and not only with the residents of the occupied lands.

2. The Palestinian problem is a political and national problem epitomized by the Palestinian people's insistence on attaining their national rights, foremost of which is the right to self-determination and the establishment of an independent state on their national soil, as well as the right to choose a representative without coercion or tutelage.

3. Our people, both inside and outside the occupied land, have affirmed on more than one occasion that they have chosen the PLO as their sole legitimate representative. In making this choice, the Palestinian people believe they are practicing one of their basic rights which has been recognized by the majority of the world's nations. The Palestinian people expect the rest of the world's freedom-loving nations to recognize the reality of their representation by the PLO.

4. Dealing with and engaging in a direct dialogue with the PLO is an inevitable condition for progress on the correct path to peace. In order for peace efforts to advance, we urge the British government to launch a dialogue with representatives of the PLO, without preconditions.

5. We support the PLO leadership headed by Yasir Arafat as representing the hopes and aspirations of the Palestinian people, and call on others to deal with this leadership on all issues that concern the Palestinian problem.

6. Our people call for the immediate convening of an international conference to discuss the reasons for the Israeli-Palestinian conflict and the

ways to solve it. We demand that this conference be attended by the five permanent member countries of the Security Council, as well as all parties to the conflict, including the PLO, which must participate in the conference on an equal footing. Our people affirm that no political solution can be achieved except through an international conference.

7. We denounce the escalation of acts of international violence during the past few months; in this context we support the position of the PLO's official leadership, as stipulated in the Cairo Declaration.

8. We condemn the recent air raid on sister Libya. U.S. policy epitomized by the strike against Libya, which, unfortunately, gained Britain's support, will fan the fires of hatred and conflict if no efforts are made to correct the basic causes for misdeeds in the world.

Therefore, proceeding from the basis of the unforgettable injustice that has befallen us, we call upon you to exert urgent efforts to prepare conditions leading to a durable and just peace in the region. At the same time, we call upon you to pressure the Israeli government to end its repressive practices in the occupied territories. We make special mention of the settlement there, confiscation of land, violation of human rights, and efforts to stifle the national spirit of our Palestinian people.

351. Fateh Revolutionary Council Statement, Tunis, June 19, 1986*

* 16 J. Palestine Stud. 201 (Autumn 1986).

The Fateh Revolutionary Council held its three-day ordinary meetings as of 15 June 1986. During these meetings, the council discussed the Fateh movement's internal and organizational situation and devoted the larger part of its discussions to the situation in Lebanon and the aggression against the Palestinian camps in Beirut. The council also reviewed the general political and military situation in the occupied territory and Lebanon, as well as Palestinian relations on domestic, Arab, and international levels.

On the domestic level, the council made a comprehensive assessment of the movement's domestic, organizational, and administrative situation. The council also reviewed a series of decisions which should be implemented. It has been decided to submit these decisions to the Central Committee during its next session in order to submit the results of these discussions to the Revolutionary Council during a special session for this purpose.

The Revolutionary Council also endorsed the Executive Committee's decision to expel 'Atallah 'Atallah and Ghazi 'Atallah from the movement for violating the movement's bylaws.

On the political level, the most prominent feature of the present stage is the escalation of the comprehensive U.S.-Zionist onslaught against our Arab nation, its national militant forces, and its basic issues, particularly the Palestine cause. This comprehensive escalation was expressed frankly and blatantly with the aim of deepening the state of division and fragmentation in our Arab homeland. There have also been negative effects because of some Arab parties' involvement in certain policies and practices obstructing the emergence of a united Arab stand adopted by the Arab masses and national forces in their struggle to confront this U.S.-Zionist onslaught and abort its conspiratorial objectives.

The political and military events which have taken place in the Arab arena are clear signs of the U.S.-Zionist concentrated attempts to strike at the PLO, surround it, and create agent alternatives. One of these signs, for example, is the British prime minister's visit to the Zionist entity and the definite trends emerging from that visit—trends directly declared by the British prime minister when she launched a rancorous campaign against the PLO and made a suspect call for creating a fabricated alternative to represent the Palestinian people.

This suspect trend was completed by the desperate U.S.-Zionist attempt to make the fighting against the PLO the major topic of their destructive efforts in the area by using so-called terrorism as an excuse to recruit new parties to the comprehensive plot against the Arab nation, the Palestinian issue, and pan-Arab security.

The objective of fighting the PLO and the brutality of U.S.-Zionist attempts to this end are well known to us. What we consider tragic and suspect is the appearance of a number of proposals and practices made and carried out by Arab hands which converge practically and identically with this U.S.-Zionist objective. While the United States and Israel consider striking at the PLO and liquidating the Palestinian people's national rights as the main priorities of the U.S. move, we notice at this time a series of measures adopted by the Jordanian government which directly and seriously encroach on national Palestinian and basic Arab principles defining correct stands toward the Palestinian issue, the Palestinian people's national rights, and the national Palestinian struggle led by the PLO.

This is in addition to many official Jordanian statements directly presenting courses contradicting Arab summit resolutions, as well as many executive measures which affirm suspicions about the convergence of these measures with the U.S.-Zionist policy to liquidate the Palestinian people's inalienable and national rights and strike at Palestinian representation.

These executive measures were included in the restrictive policy carried out by official Jordanian apparatuses against Palestinian citizens in the occupied territory and in Jordan. These measures were also included in the compulsory attempts of polarization carried out by these apparatuses exploiting Palestinian citizens' needs and daily interests. These apparatuses also restored to deportation, deprivation, threats, and economic attacks in a way that reminds us of similar measures adopted by the occupation authorities within the framework of their policy to strike at national Palestinian steadfastness in the occupied territory and entrenching the Zionist fait accompli.

At a time when the PLO, together with all free and honest Jordanian people, affirm their rejection of and resistance to the heresy of an alternative country and resettlement, the Jordanian authorities made a serious decision which we believe embodies a very serious step in this rejected trend. This decision is the approval of a law in accordance with which Palestinians will be represented in the Jordanian Parliament. Meanwhile, the situation of Palestinians in Jordan has its own firm bases to which Arabs and the international community adhere, and they firmly reject merging the Palestinians constitutionally through the fraternal and guest countries' institutions because this will create a danger to the Palestinian cause and the national identity of the Palestinian people in the diaspora.

At a time when we sense these negative, dangerous phenomena, the aggression against the camps in Beirut is escalating in a criminal, bloody attempt to physically annihilate Palestinians who live on Lebanese territory—an attempt falling within the context of new-yet-old conspiracies in which some Arab sides are involved as part of cheap deals with the United States at several stages. It is also no longer a secret that the multiphase aggression against the camps coincides with every plot represented by initiating suspect plans to impose capitulation on the Palestinian people and the Arab nation. As these events and signs coincide with conspiratorial U.S. and Zionist proposals, such as administrative self-rule in the West Bank and Gaza—and in the Gaza Strip alone as a prelude to spreading the experience to the West Bank—it would be an act of shortsightedness, ignorance of facts, and a disavowal of responsibility to see these events as connected to the Palestinian position or the PLO's position. In essence, they are the center of conspiracy against the future of the entire region and the Arab nation's future, interests, rights, and destiny.

The Fateh Revolutionary Council believes that the Palestinian position, which should be represented by the PLO at this stage within its local, Arab, and international arenas, should be extremely clear and decisive with regard to the following bases:

1. On the Palestinian level:

A. All studies, and responsible and programmed efforts need to be directed toward strengthening our great masses' steadfastness in the occupied land, solidifying the tool of national confrontation of the occupation and its policies and plans, supporting the confrontation to further strengthen, escalate, and double its effectiveness on both political and military levels. Here, the Fateh Revolutionary Council records with great pride our people's steadfastness and creative struggle against the occupation—a struggle epitomizing the most brilliant phenomena in our Arab reality and epitomizing the source of the central power of the PLO, the Palestinian people's legitimate sole representative and the only leader of their national struggle.

B. Any step by any side against the Palestinian people's inalienable national rights and their national struggle under the PLO, as well as any step to harm the Palestinian affiliation to the Palestinian homeland, to the Palestinian identity, and to the Palestinian national identity inside and outside the occupied land will be confronted decisively, because the most prominent historical, political, and militant duties of the PLO are to protect the bases of the Palestine question and the Palestinian people's gains, which have been achieved by our people's great steadfastness, by the blood of their righteous martyrs, and by their absolute commitment to Palestine—land and homeland[.]

C. Every effort needs to exerted to strengthen the unity of the Palestinian revolution's goals by achieving Palestinian unity within the framework of the PLO. The Fateh Revolutionary Council fully appreciates the efforts of the Palestinian leadership on this level and also highly appreciates the brotherly initiative launched by struggler President Chadli Bendjedid, as well as the honest support epitomized by the Soviet friends and comrades and all friends and brothers in this regard. The Revolutionary Council stresses the need to continue efforts to achieve the unity of groups on the basis of responsibility, commitment, and enthusiasm in achieving this important national goal.

D. The continuous brutal, bloody aggression against the Palestinian camps in Beirut by conspiring sides of the Amal movement and the [Lebanese] Sixth Brigade, as well as by other formations loyal to known Arab organs, should be confronted strongly by all free honorable people in Lebanon and the Arab nation. The Revolutionary Council records with great pride our masses' steadfastness in the camps and the heroism of our sons in defending the honor and security of the masses in these camps and representing true national unity.

The Revolutionary Council also greets all honest people in the Lebanese nationalist and Islamic forces which reject and condemn this ugly plot and which are working with all their power to put an end to it. The Revolutionary Council also rejects all the unjust proposals based on the pretext there is a Palestinian danger in Lebanon. It draws the attention of our brothers in Lebanon to the danger of this suspect conspiratorial proposal, because what is threatening Lebanon—territory, people, and sovereignty—is the great plot drawn up by the United States, which asked its Zionist agents and others to carry it out to disrupt Lebanon and impose a sectarian balkanization on Lebanon and to spread this disease in the entire Arab region.

Hence, the Revolutionary Council stresses its firm support for a solution guaranteeing Lebanon's Arabism, independence, and territorial integrity. The Fateh Revolutionary Council urges all forces and Arab countries to assume their pan-Arab responsibilities toward supporting the Lebanese people in accordance with Arab summit resolutions.

It also stresses the movement's firm position on the need to end the Iraq-Iran war, which is being exploited by enemies and which dissipates the energies of the Iraqi and Iranian peoples, through peaceful means in the interest of these two peoples, the Arab and Islamic nations, and the Palestine question. The Revolutionary Council appreciates the position of the Soviet Union and socialist countries toward the Palestine question and the PLO despite all attempts to split these relations. The Soviet Union, the Palestinian people's friend, affirms its support for the Palestinian people's national rights and assumes a principled position on these relations. These fraternal relations were crowned in the great meeting between Comrade Gorbachev and Brother Abu 'Ammar [Yasir Arafat] in Berlin during the eleventh congress of the SED. Revolution until victory.

352. Jordan's Five-Year Development Plan for the Occupied Territories, Amman, August 1986*

* 16 J. Palestine Stud. 205 (Autumn 1986).

I. Scope of the Problem:

A. Demography: At the end of 1967, the population of the occupied Arab territories was 1,034,000, distributed as follows:

West Bank	586,000
Arab Jerusalem	67,000
Gaza Strip	381,000

Natural increase of the population between 1967 and 1984 amounted to 640,000, which should have put their number at 1,674,000. However, actual population in residence in the occupied territories at the end of 1984 was only 1,010,000, implying net emigration of 664,000. This emigration was induced by various pressures, including economic pressures.

B. Manpower and Employment: Evidence of economic pressures under occupation is provided by official Israeli statistics of manpower and employment. Aggregate manpower in the occupied territories was:

· In 1970, 195,000, of which 187,000 were employed;
· In 1984, 273,000, of which 262,000 were employed.

However, of total manpower employment, the number employed in economic activities in the occupied territories themselves was 164,000 in 1970, and just about 164,000 in 1984. The balances of 23,000 in 1970 and 98,000 in 1984 were the number of Arab citizens of the occupied territories working inside Israel.

The inescapable conclusion is that any economic development that might have taken place in the occupied territories over fourteen years did not result in any perceptible increase in job opportunities, and the increase in manpower over the years was forced either to emigrate or work for Israeli activities.

C. Output and Growth: The virtual arrest of economic growth in the occupied territories is also shown by relating Gross Domestic Product [GDP] of the West Bank to that of the East Bank of Jordan as it was before the occupation (1965) and after the occupation (1984):

GDP (JD millions)		
	1965	1984
East Bank	95	1,319
West Bank	55	330
Total	150	1,649
% of Total	27%	20%

On per capita basis, comparison of GDP in the three areas was as follows:

	JD millions	%
East Bank	495	100
West Bank	361	73
Gaza Strip	204	41

It should be noted that before 1967, per capita income did not differ to any significant extent between the two banks. If anything, it is believed to have been somewhat higher in the West Bank.

Recent figures of GDP growth for the 1981-84 period give the following overall annual averages:

· West Bank: 2.4 percent, i.e., 0.0 percent per capita [sic];

Gaza Strip: 1.1 percent, i.e., 3.9 percent per capita.

II. Objectives and Investment Criteria:

A. The broad objectives of development efforts in the occupied territories are the following:

1. Limiting the emigration of the population, especially permanent emigration, while also minimizing the temporary emigration motivated by work or study needs.

2. Blunting the pressures and incentives that prompt Arab labor to seek employment in Israeli activities.

3. Upgrading the quality of Arab manpower, fortifying its national and civic consciousness, and equipping it with a wide spectrum of skills and capabilities at all levels.

B. Consistent with these objectives, the following are the criteria that should apply in determining the priorities of economic action and the selection of projects and activities:

1. Effects on job opportunities and durability of employment;

2. Effects on the nexus between the people and the land, e.g., the citizen and the house, the farmer and the land, the workers and the workshop, the student and the institute, the physician and the clinic, etc.;

3. Effects on citizens' resilience and resistance to the pressures and strains exerted by the occupation;

4. Effects on the Arab village and rural life and their attraction as places of work and raising families in competition with urban life and opportunities.

III. Economic Aggregates and Capital Requirements:

A. Manpower projections: The minimum expected increase in manpower over the 1986-90 period is about 60,000; i.e., at the rate of 12,000 a year. This corresponds to a minimum rate of increase in population of only 2 percent but is combined with a modest expected increase in the rate of participation in economic activity by the population [group] of working age.

The overall cost of investment leading to the creation of one job opportunity in the occupied territories is estimated to be $16,000 as a minimum. Accordingly, the investable resources required to secure productive employment of the projected increase in manpower in the next five years, not to mention the reemployment in Arab economic activities of workers losing their jobs in Israel and/or neighboring Arab countries, may be estimated at a minimum of $960 million for the five years, or close to $200 million a year.

B. Resources Gap Projections: Another approach to estimating external capital assistance required for the occupied territories is through the analysis and projection of the resources gap between projected domestic savings and aggregate investment, or between projected foreign exchange earning and import requirements. The gap in 1984, which was a depressed year, was about $935 million. This gap was financed as follows:

	$ millions
Earnings of citizens working in Israel	224
Remittances of citizens working in Arab countries	247
Foreign loans and grants	464
Total	935

It is concluded that foreign assistance of about $450 million and remittances from abroad of about $250 million will be required to keep matters at the far-from-satisfactory status quo. It is to be recalled that in 1984, some significant official development assistance of about $40 million was still being provided by Arab countries. In view of the economic recession in the region, such amounts will not be forthcoming. For similar reasons, remittances of workers in these countries are expected to be sharply reduced to possibly 50 percent of their 1984 level. Accordingly, about $165 million needs to be found just to offset the expected curtailment of these resources. To make an impact on the development of the occupied territories, a study of the various sectors outlined below shows the need for about JD 462 mil-

Table 1: Estimates of Required Public Investments
for the Occupied Territories' Five-Year Program 1986–90

Sector	JD millions	$ millions	Percentage
Agriculture	61.7	172.8	13.4
Industry	22.5	63.0	4.9
Housing	190.0	532.0	41.2
Construction	64.0	179.2	13.9
Education	78.7	220.4	17.0
Health	34.4	96.3	7.5
Social Development	10.2	28.6	2.1
Total	461.5	1,292.2	100.0

lion ($1,292 million) to be provided in the form of external financial assistance in the next five years (see Table 1 above and Table 2 below).

IV. Human Resource Development:

As the physical resources available in the occupied territories are extremely meager, it is imperative that development of the country should depend first and foremost on the human resource base in patterns not dissimilar from those that proved successful in natural resource-deficient countries of the Far East. At the same time, manpower development, through education and training, should be based on an educational doctrine that takes into full account the sociopolitical environment associated with the occupation. One central characteristic of this environment that is of decisive importance as far as economic and development activities are concerned is the absence of a public sector and public institutions favorable to the promotion of those activities. Worse, to the extent that the public sector, namely the military government, concerns itself with those activities, it is actively doing so to influence them in directions contradicting the basic and long-term interests of the Arab community.

Hence, the relevant educational doctrine is the one that prepares manpower to function independently from support by the public sector or private institutions, virtually in a free enterprise, highly competitive situation. Conventional liberal arts and science secondary school certificates and matriculation to university appears highly unsuitable. Elementary and secondary education should shift emphasis to vocational and technical education, albeit with contents that include a spectrum of skills and civic briefings that are conducive to high mobility of the skilled workers across different . . . [sic] . . . vocational school should not overconcentrate on agronomy and animal husbandry but should include accounting and elements of finance (to enable intelligent handling of business on the farm) as well as some mechanical skills (to enable intelligent handling of farm tools and equipment).

With this approach, the development program envisages a massive effort to influence the quality of education not only through building new vocational and specialized schools but also through a broad effort to upgrade existing schools and improve the qualification and training of teachers. The cost of this program over five years is about JD 79 million (about $221 million), of which the teachers' support fund amounts to JD 25 million ($70 million).

V. Agriculture:

The agricultural sector has been hardest hit by the Israeli occupation's policies and practices, particularly in the areas of:

A. Land expropriation, which through various means and excuses diverted 1.2 million dunums of privately owned Arab agricultural land (not to mention land expropriated on account of being state domain) for Israeli settlement or other purposes, while also preventing any expansion in the extent of Arab land available for agriculture;

B. Control of water resources and their diversion to Israeli settlements and other purposes, while restricting the water supply to Arab agriculture and forcibly restricting such supply to its 1967 level;

C. Competition from Israeli agriculture, by employing techniques aimed at undermining Arab production, such as dumping Israeli produce while not allowing Arab produce into the Israeli market.

As in the case of the industrial, housing, and construction sectors, the development of agriculture requires four sets of measures. These are:

1. Procedural and administrative: These include introducing policies and measures to facilitate the marketing of produce in the East Bank and the neighboring Arab markets, and encouraging the growth and development of agro-industries;

2. Institutional and organizational: These include encouraging and supporting agricultural cooperatives, establishing an agricultural guidance/training apparatus, and introducing new techniques and technologies, especially the creation of a marketing company;

3. Financial and investment: These include the creation of an agricultural credit bank or revolving fund, and other forms of financial support;

4. Infrastructural: These are tied to the overall development of infrastructure in the rural areas, including improvement of roads and transportation facilities, public utilities, and health community development schemes.

The cost of envisaged investments in this sector amounts to JD 62 million ($174 million).

Table 2: Summary of Major Public Sector
Development Projects in the Occupied Territories

	Estimates (JD millions)
I: Agricultural Sector	
A. Institutional Structure	
1. Establishing Agricultural Guidance Units in the West Bank and Gaza	53.4
2. Establishing Agricultural Cooperatives	6,000.0
3. Capitalization of Agricultural Credit Bank or Fund	5,000.0
4. Offices and Personnel	45.6
5. Support for Agricultural Research	700.0
6. Establishing a Marketing Company	10,000.0
Subtotal	21,799.0
B. Productive Projects	
1. Land Reclamation	9,000.0
2. Agricultural Service (Roads, Plowing, etc.)	1,580.0
3. Artesian Wells and Irrigation Systems	2,100.0
4. Development of Nurseries	400.0
5. Development of Livestock	9,140.0
6. Construction	3,500.0
7. Agricultural Industries	7,500.0
8. Machinery and Equipment	1,900.0
9. Operational Expenses	4,775.0
Subtotal	39,895.0
Total (A and B)	61,694.0
II: Industrial Sector	
1. Industrial Credit Fund or Bank	6,000.0
2. Training Centers	3,500.0
3. Supervision and Follow-up Units, Surveys and Research	2,750.0
4. Industrial Towns	10,250.0
Total	22,500.0
III: Housing Sector	
1. Urgent Housing Needs	72,000.0
2. Housing Loans and Credits	118,000.0
Total	190,000.0
IV: Nonhousing Construction	
1. Public Utilities	64,000.0
Total	64,000.0

Table 2: *Continued*

	Estimates (JD millions)
V: Education	
1. Open University	5,000.0
2. Kindergartens	3,360.0
3. Teachers' Support Fund	24,900.0
4. Buildings and Utilities	3,112.0
5. Financial Support for Private Schools	2,500.0
6. Vocational Education	8,000.0
7. Support for Community Colleges	5,000.0
8. Universities	25,000.0
9. Administration, Supervision, and Research	1,825.0
Total	78,697.0
VI: Health	
1. New Hospitals	25,000.0
2. Hospitals Maintenance	3,058.0
3. New Equipment and Laboratories	3,281.0
4. Rural Health Centers	2,325.0
5. Technical Training for Physicians, Nurses, and Technicians	736.0
Total	34,400.0
VII: Social Development	
1. Social Care Centers	3,924.0
2. Assistance for Voluntary Societies	3,000.0
3. Assistance for the Poor	3,000.0
4. Social Research Center	250.0
Total	10,174.0
Grand Total	461,465.0

VI. Industry:

Industry's share of GDP declined under occupation to 7 percent in the West Bank and 12 percent in Gaza. The total number of industrial establishments also dropped from its 1967 level. Meanwhile, the occupied territories continue to be open domain to Israeli dumping and monopolistic practices. Israel's sales in the captive markets of the West Bank and Gaza, estimated in 1984 at $320 million, constitute 10.6 percent of its total exports, and 32 percent of imports to the occupied territories. Industrial products constitute 48 percent of such sales.

Development of the industrial sector is envisaged to rest primarily on private initiative, supported by: (a) quality manpower output of the educational and training system; and (b) institutional and administrative measures to remove marketing constraints and provide financial incentives. The objective of such support is to enable citizens of the occupied territories to progressively acquire the capabilities and mobilize the skills to perform the following:

A. Build their dwellings and manufacture the building materials and tools required for building;

B. Increase the value added to agricultural produce by the creation and upgrading of agro-industries;

C. Create/expand manufacturing capabilities in the export industries. Immediate potential appears in: (a) agro-industrial products; (b) tourist-oriented handicraft products; and (c) industries characterized by high intensity in skilled labor and high technology, e.g., engineering design, computer systems design, and software production;

D. Undertake the technical services associated with construction and equipment installation, maintenance, and repair;

E. Manufacture spare parts, complex components, tools, and machine tools associated with each industrialization level that the country attains.

Institutional and administrative measures include:

· Relaxation of restrictions on licensing of industries in the occupied territories and on admission of industrial products produced by the licensed industries. Only the restriction on industries using Israeli-produced equipment and materials should remain;

· Creation and support of institutions servicing the industrial sector with management consulting, feasibility and market studies, quality and specifications control, etc.;

· Provision of intermediate and long-term credit through a specialized institution.

The investment allocation for the sector is estimated at about JD 23 million ($64 million).

VII. Housing and Construction:

The housing and construction sector should perform a pivotal role in achieving the program objectives. Improvement of the quality of life through better housing would help to reduce the pressures on people to migrate. At the same time, the achievement of satisfactory levels of employment requires the maintenance of a high and steady level of building and construction activity.

A review of housing activity since occupation shows that whereas the building of dwellings was progressing at quite a high rate between 1967 and 1976, it completely leveled off, if not actually declined, between 1976 and 1984. Thus, the number of housing units built annually was in the neighborhood of one thousand or less before 1970; it increased at a very fast rate up to a peak of 8,165 units in 1976, but declined afterwards to 5,620 units in 1984.

Projections of housing requirements to meet the needs of new families as well as the replacement of dilapidated dwellings show that a minimum of 8,500 housing units need to be constructed annually over the next five years. It is projected that a large part of this demand will be met by autonomous private investment, and a part will have to be induced and supported by external funding. The proportion that will depend on external support constitutes 35 to 40 percent of the total, and is estimated to cost about JD 190 million ($532 million) over the five years. Assistance to nonresidential construction in various sectors is estimated at JD 64 million ($179 million).

VIII. Health and Social Services:

Health services in the occupied territories are substandard in quality and generally limited to the urban centers. The numbers of hospitals, hospital beds, clinics, laboratories, and specialized support services are all vastly inadequate. The available equipment generally predates 1967 and is sometimes operated by unskilled technicians. There is a general lack of higher specialization, as such qualified physicians tend to emigrate. The areas of public and preventive health and mother and child care also suffer similar limitations.

The development effort aims at providing improved public health standards and better health and medical services through three main means:

A. Introducing a public health care program;

B. Establishing new hospitals, clinics, rural health care units, and providing new equipment and laboratories for existing institutions;

C. Manpower development through the training of medical and paramedical personnel.

In the social development area, the program aims at raising the levels of social consciousness and modifying the conditions and behavioral patterns that limit community development, whether on the human or material levels.

The five-year program allocates JD 34.4 million ($98.3 million) to health services, and JD 10.2 million ($28.6 million) to other social services.

353. PLO Executive Committee Statement, Baghdad, August 10, 1986*

* 16 J. Palestine Stud. 208 (Winter 1987).

During the period 8-10 August 1986, the PLO Executive Committee held a series of meetings in the Iraqi capital, Baghdad, under Brother Abu 'Ammar [Yasir Arafat], PLO Executive Committee chairman and commander in chief of the Palestinian Revolution Forces. These meetings were attended by PNC Speaker Shaykh 'Abd al-Hamid al-Sa'ih. The PLO Executive Committee discussed developments in the Palestinian and Arab arenas and developments at the international level. The committee also discussed a number of administrative issues and made the necessary decisions on them.

The PLO Executive Committee listened to a report by Brother Abu 'Ammar on his visits to several friendly African countries which reiterated their firm and principled support for our people's just cause. The committee valued all that was agreed upon during the successful visits to these friendly countries at all levels, including the resolutions of the recent OAU summit which was convened in Addis Ababa supporting the PLO and the Palestinian people in their just struggle for the recognition of their inalienable rights.

The PLO Executive Committee was also acquainted with the important and successful talks Brother Abu 'Ammar held with Comrade Mikhail Gorbachev, CPSU Central Committee general secretary; Chairman Erich Honecker, general secretary of the Socialist Unity Party of Germany; and PRC State Council Premier Zhao Ziyang.

The PLO Executive Committee reviewed the results of the talks conducted by five Palestinian organizations within the PLO framework on completing the unity of the factions. The committee expressed appreciation for the sense of responsibility the officials in charge of these factions have demonstrated. The PLO Executive Committee was also familiarized with the results of the recent visit by the Palestinian delegation to Moscow and it highly valued the results achieved by the delegation and the Soviet officials, stressing its appreciation for the Soviet stand as voiced by these officials as well as their concern over Palestinian achievements and the support they have provided and will continue to provide for the Algerian initiative announced by President Shadhli Bin Jadid for strengthening Palestinian unity.

The PLO Executive Committee appeals to the other Palestinian organizations to respond to the call for Palestinian unity and to jointly work for serving the cause. In this respect, the PLO Executive Committee expresses appreciation for the stands of our people in the occupied homeland and the diaspora through which our people daily and publicly express their awareness of their national interests and their rallying around the PLO, their sole legitimate representative, and around their legitimate leadership. The committee reaffirmed its pride in the genuine, firm national stand our people in the occupied homeland adopt despite the various practices and attempts seeking to undermine their steadfastness and affiliation. To entrench this stand, the PLO Executive Committee adopted the necessary decisions and steps to continue and expand the support for the steadfastness of our people in the occupied homeland.

The PLO Executive Committee expresses its deep regret over the suspension by some fraternal Arab countries of their contributions in accordance with the Arab summit resolutions. This has restricted the activities of the Palestinian-Jordanian committee for bolstering the steadfastness of the Palestinian people. The PLO Executive Committee stresses that the invigoration of this committee's activities through the Arab countries' resumption of the fulfillment of their contributions to this committee's budget and securing the potentialities that will enable it to pursue the implementation of its programs constitutes a national, pan-Arab duty within the framework of the strategy of struggle against the Zionist enemy. This committee also remains a suitable means to convey support funds to our people or to secure them with development means from any source that may come in view of the experience it has gained over many years and because this was established in accordance with an Arab summit resolution.

What arouses the PLO Executive Committee's attention is what the United States and Israel urge regarding the so-called plan to improve living conditions in the occupied West Bank and the Gaza Strip. Although the PLO Executive Committee gives top priority to securing all Arab and international aid for our people under occupation, to the best of its knowledge it sees in the U.S.-Israeli call an approach to entrench occupation and plan based on the principle of actual normalization in an attempt to harmonize our people's conditions with the occupation and to make people become accustomed to this fact.

Undoubtedly, our people are asking: Why has this plan come now after twenty years of occupation? Why has this plan coincided with the fierce campaign against the Palestinian struggle, against Palestinian national rights, and against the PLO and its legitimate leadership? Our people know full well that this Israeli-U.S. plan comes after their planners hampered all peace efforts in the region on various fabricated pretexts. Our people also realize that the true objective of this plan is to obliterate the Palestinian national identity and its independent decision making, and to continue to strike at the PLO in its capacity as the Palestinian people's sole legitimate representative and as the leader of their struggle which expresses their hopes and national aspirations. This plan is also aimed at implementing autonomy rule or other forms which seek to liquidate the Palestine question. Our people also realize that the U.S.-Israeli plan is based on the conditions of achieving the interests of its planners—interests of whose tragic reflections on them our people are aware.

Our people who enjoy a good awareness and experience will not be deceived by false hopes. Our people will not be affected by the moves of some individuals and the propaganda covers they use to forge facts and spread confusion in an attempt to affect the spirit of resistance in our people. Our people will watch those who publicize this new plan or other similar plans and programs closely, and will foil these plans. U.S. Vice President George

Bush's visit to our occupied territory was one of the prominent signs through which the U.S. administration attempted to publicize this plan.

The PLO Executive Committee has also discussed the dangers against our Palestinian people in Lebanon whether in the besieged camps in Beirut or in southern Lebanon as a result of the threats posed by the Zionist entity and its agents. The committee reiterates its call for the Arab League, the United Nations, and other international organizations to exert every possible effort to alleviate these dangers that are threatening half a million Palestinians in Lebanon with destruction and expulsion. The PLO Executive Committee stresses the need to intensify efforts and contacts to secure the minimum level of security and protection for the sons of the Palestinian people in Lebanon whether through the Arab League, the United Nations, or through giving the PLO the opportunity to carry out this task with full coordination with the Lebanese authorities.

The PLO Executive Committee reviewed Shimon Peres' visit to Morocco. While it rejects and condemns this event, the PLO stresses its call for convening an emergency Arab summit to study this event at the highest Arab level, voice its understanding of its graveness, and stress the importance of confronting it with a pan-Arab responsibility in accordance with the Arab summit conferences' resolutions, foremost of which are the Fez and Casablanca resolutions which affirm that a just and comprehensive solution cannot be achieved through bilateral or individual solutions but on the basis of Arab unanimity, and that any solution to the Middle East problem should be achieved through a UN-sponsored international conference attended by the five permanent UN Security Council member states as well as all parties to the dispute including the PLO and other parties.

The PLO Executive Committee also discussed Jordanian-Palestinian relations and noted with deep regret the recent measures in deporting Brother Abu Jihad [Khalil al-Wazir], head of the Palestinian side to the Palestinian-Jordanian joint committee, and closing twenty-five offices in Amman. These measures endanger Jordanian-Palestinian relations at a time when we are working for the sake of real Arab solidarity based on joint action to confront imperialist and Zionist designs. As it affirms its eagerness to preserve the distinguished relations between the two fraternal Palestinian and Jordanian peoples in accordance with the resolutions of the successive PNC sessions, the Executive Committee believes in the need to continue, strengthen, and promote these relations.

The Executive Committee also discussed relations between the PLO and Syria, stressing the PLO's desire to resume normal relations between the two sides on the basis of mutual respect, independent decisionmaking, and noninterference by either side in the other's domestic affairs; to begin a new phase to deal with a new Arab reality that needs a joint effort in order to create appropriate circumstances for achieving the national goals in line with the Arab interest; and to fight imperialism and world Zionism.

The Executive Committee also highly appreciated President Saddam Husayn's recent peace initiative to end the Iraq-Iran war. The Executive Committee calls on the Iranian leadership to accept the proposed peace initiatives to stop this war which is against the Iranian people, the Iraqi people, and the Arab and Islamic nations. The Palestinian people are the ones who are most harmed by its continuation. Ignoring this fact will affect the Palestine question and will give Israel the opportunity to continue its occupation of Arab and Palestinian lands and Islamic holy places, particularly holy Jerusalem and the al-Aqsa mosque.

354. The Prague Declaration Issued by Fateh, the Democratic Front for the Liberation of Palestine, and the Palestinian Communist Party, Prague, September 6, 1986*

* 16 J. Palestine Stud. 211 (Winter 1987).

During the period 1-5 September 1986, leadership delegations representing the Palestinian National Liberation Movement (Fateh), the Democratic Front for the Liberation of Palestine, and the Palestinian Communist party met in Prague and studied in a spirit of patriotic responsibility the continuing dangers to which the national cause of the Palestinian people is exposed as a result of the intensification of the reactionary American-Israeli onslaught aimed at striking the PLO and eliminating its role as the sole legitimate representative of our Palestinian people in order to eliminate their enduring national rights to return, to self-determination, and to establish an independent state. They also studied the swift steps required to confront this onslaught to establish unity among all the Palestinian patriotic organizations within the framework of the PLO on the basis of adhering to its program and its patriotic line which opposes imperialism, Zionism, and capitulationist solutions.

The conferring parties agreed that the American-Israeli plan to collude with some Arab leaders has reached the stage of extreme danger after the meeting at Ifrane, which the PLO and all Palestinian patriotic forces condemned, and following the subsequent visit of the American Vice President George Bush and the feverish American activity, which aimed at crystallizing the agreement between Israel and the concerned Arab states in the form of a solution that would bypass the role of the PLO as the legitimate and sole representative of our Palestinian people, attack their national rights, and open the way to generalize and Arabize the Camp David plot.

In this framework the conferring parties exposed the Jordanian policy which attempts to bypass the PLO, take over its role and place, and violate the right of our people to self-determination and an independent state. In that framework there has been increased interference in the affairs of the occupied territories in order to create an alternative to the PLO, to encourage some opportunistic elements to depart from Palestinian national consensus, and to provide material support to them under the guise of a so-called development plan which limits and besieges patriotic forces bound to the PLO. This coincides with Israeli measures aimed at implementing a functional partition of the land and appointing municipal officials in the place of the elected patriotic officials. It also coincides with Israeli measures aimed at imposing a civil administration and increasing the repressive grip against our people and their national forces and institutions.

These steps also coincide with false American enticements and actions of some Arab reactionary circles to promote again illusions and false dreams about an American solution. The conferees affirmed the need for all patriotic forces to be watchful and wary of these malicious attempts. This vicious onslaught against our Palestinian people also coincides with campaigns of intimidation and robbery launched by American imperialism to impose its hegemony over our Arab area. Among its most notable actions were the threats and aggression directed against Libya, Syria, and other Arab states.

The conferring parties affirmed that national unity is the most effective weapon in the hands of our people and our revolution to confront and foil these immense dangers which continue to threaten our national existence and future. They agreed on the need to hasten the pursuit of unity among all the patriotic organizations and forces in the framework of the PLO on the basis of the following principles:

(1) Adherence to the political program of the PLO and the decisions of the Palestine National Council (which were the result of consensus among all the patriotic groups, forces, and personalities) and the rejection of any departure from them;

(2) Confirmation of the rejection of partial, unilateral solutions, of liquidation plans like Camp David and the Reagan Plan, of the autonomy plan, and of functional partition; the rejection of Resolution 242 because of its neglect of the national and established rights of the Palestinian people; and the confirmation that the only solution to the Palestinian problem is represented in assuring the right to return, to self-determination, and to establishing an independent state on Palestinian national land;

(3) Working toward holding a fully valid and effective Middle East peace conference in which the PLO would participate on an independent and equal basis with the other parties by virtue of its status as sole, legitimate representative of the Palestinian people and on the basis of UN resolutions that recognize the established national rights of our people as the only framework in which to search for a just solution to the Palestinian question and the Middle East crisis;

(4) Commitment to the PLO as the sole legitimate representative of our Palestinian people, resisting any attempt to create alternatives to it, refusal to delegate its authority, to appoint a proxy, or to have a copartner in Palestinian representation;

(5) Proceeding from these national commitments, Fateh affirmed that the Amman agreement signed on 11 February 1985 is no longer applicable and that this agreement no longer represents a basis of PLO policy, movement, or activity on various Palestinian, Arab, and international fronts. Bilateral relations between the PLO and Jordan are based on the resolutions of the Rabat Summit and on support for the struggle of the Palestinian revolution against Israeli aggression and occupation;

(6) Strengthening the unity of all patriotic forces inside the occupied territories in the struggle against the policy of settlement, the Israeli "iron fist," and plans for autonomy and functional partition; against Jordanian intervention aimed at creating reactionary leadership as an alternative to the PLO; and for the sake of supporting the steadfastness of our people in the occupied territories as represented in their patriotic forces and institutions;

(7) Strengthening PLO relations with all Arab liberation forces on the basis of solidarity of common struggle against Zionist imperialism and capitulationist solutions;

(8) Working to strengthen Arab solidarity on the basis of decisions of the Arab summits which were won through Arab consensus and on the basis of

mobilizing energy to confront Zionist aggression and American hegemonic plots;

(9) Guarding brotherly relations with Syria, proceeding from goals of common national struggle against imperialism and Zionism and on the basis of solidarity in struggle, equality, and mutual respect;

(10) Reinforcing relations of alliance with progressive forces and forces of liberation around the world, especially the Soviet Union and the rest of the socialist countries; and strengthening ties with the states of the non-aligned movement and Islamic and African states in order to fortify their support for the just struggle of our people and their national rights;

(11) Stabilizing the conventions of the PLO as a framework for a broad national front and forming leadership bodies in accordance with the articles of the Aden-Algiers Agreement so that all patriotic forces participate in drafting PLO policy according to its legitimate policies and leadership bodies.

The sides agreed that adhering to these patriotic constants and bases will put an end to the obstacles which obstruct the way to national dialogue aimed at restoring national unity. The conferring parties appealed to all the Palestinian patriotic forces and groups to raise to the level of national responsibility a comprehensive national agreement as a basis for convening a new session of the PNC to regain unity in the framework of the PLO.

In that framework the conferring parties renewed their support for the initiative of Algerian president Shadhli Bin Jadid which calls for a Palestinian national meeting on Algerian soil to restore and firmly implant national unity.

355. The Alexandria Declaration Read by President Husni Mubarak of Egypt and Prime Minister Shimon Peres of Israel, Alexandria, Egypt, September 12, 1986*

* 16 J. Palestine Stud. 196 (Winter 1987).

The meeting between President Husni Mubarak and Israeli Prime Minister Shimon Peres in Alexandria on the 11th and 12th of September marks a new era in bilateral relations between Egypt and Israel as well as in the search for a just and comprehensive peace in the Middle East.

The signing of the compromise of the Taba arbitration reaffirms the importance of dialogue and negotiation as a means for settling international dispute away from the spirit of confrontation and violence. It constitutes a promising model to be followed and built upon.

The Egyptian-Israeli peace treaty reflects a shared commitment to proceed jointly and simultaneously to enforce the structure of peace between the two peoples and the achievement of a comprehensive peace in the region that will bring about a peaceful settlement of the Arab-Israeli conflict including the resolution of the Palestinian question in all its aspects.

President Mubarak and Prime Minister Peres firmly believe that having referred the Taba issue to arbitration, the two countries can now concentrate their efforts on revising the comprehensive peace process. They view with great concern the effects of the stalemate on the process.

They declare 1987 as a year of negotiations for peace.

They call upon all parties concerned to dedicate this year to intensive efforts to achieve the common and noble objective of a just, lasting and comprehensive peace.

President Mubarak and Prime Minister Peres, together with other concerned parties, will continue their efforts toward a solution of the Palestinian problem in all its aspects and the establishment of a comprehensive peace in the region.

I have been asked to inform you that Egypt has appointed a new Ambassador for Israel, Dr. Muhammad Basyuni, and that the government of Israel has accepted this nomination.

356. Statement of Israeli Prime Minister Shimon Peres on Return from Summit with Egyptian President Husni Mubarak in Alexandria, Egypt, September 12, 1986*

* 16 J. Palestine Stud. 213 (Winter 1987).

First of all, I am very happy that we have reached an agreement on the issue of Taba, an issue that was a very serious obstacle on our path. I must thank the Egyptian and Israeli delegations who, with the help of the United States, allowed us to arrive at this agreement without which we would not have been able to make progress.

An Egyptian ambassador, Dr. Basyuni, has been appointed to Israel, as had been agreed from the outset. The summit meeting itself was very intensive and included some seven to eight hours of talks with President Mubarak. I found him to be an open person, in control of the situation, optimistic about his country, and sincerely wanting to make progress in improving relations between our two countries, in promoting peace, and in solving the Palestinian problem.

In my opinion, our main problem was lack of time. Even ten hours would not have been enough to deal with such a complex problem. Finally, toward the end of the summit meeting, we decided to present the picture of the situation as it really is. This picture shows some things are sufficiently ripe to put them in writing—and that is the joint communiqué. On some matters we agreed enough as to state them verbally—and that is what President Mubarak announced. And on some other things we reached a conceptual agreement, but we did not have time to formulate them in writing or verbally.

I would like to address myself to each of these three types of issues. As for the ones we put in writing, you have seen the joint communiqué, although when we started the summit it was not yet clear whether a joint communiqué would be issued. However, a communiqué was issued through the common work of the delegations and their leaders. The communiqué indeed expresses the desire to promote peace, to put an end to the acts of hostility, to solve all the aspects of the Palestinian problem, and to enrich our bilateral relations.

As for the verbal announcement as delivered by President Mubarak, it speaks about the wish to open a peace conference with international participation. Regarding the nature, participants, procedures, and timing of the conference, we actually agreed to set up a preparatory committee that would prepare this conference.

The third part, which we did not have time to formulate, refers to the most difficult problem, that of the Palestinians. On this issue, we decided that the best way to solve the Palestinian problem is through a Jordanian-Palestinian agreement. I suppose that if we could have had a few more hours we would have managed to put this into writing. However, as I said, there was no time. We will continue this dialogue until we arrive at a formulation of this key issue as well.

All in all, we were greeted very cordially and warmly. I think both sides made a very serious effort to meet each other halfway, bearing in mind that both sides harbor the same ambitions, but each of the sides operates under different constraints and has a different public behind it, and this fact cannot be ignored.

Contrary to what several Israeli papers published, this summit had reverberations in the Egyptian media, generous reverberations both on television and in the press. All in all, I think we are returning home with a feeling, as stated in the joint communiqué, that a new leaf has been turned, both in the sphere of the peace efforts and in the sphere of Israeli-Egyptian relations.

357. The Seven Points of the Jordanian Development
Conference, Amman, Jordan, November 10, 1986*

* 16 J. Palestine Stud. 222 (Spring 1987).

The Jordan Development Conference concluded its three-day meeting today and delegates presented the following points:

1. There has been a consensus in the conference on backing Jordan's economic and social development plan for 1986-1990 as well as the economic and social development plan for the occupied West Bank and Gaza Strip.

2. The Jordanian government's decision to allocate at least ten million Jordanian dinars each year for development goals in the West Bank and Gaza demonstrates a clear intention and an honest desire to ensure the success of the program which is designed to sustain the steadfastness of the Arab population in the occupied territories and protect the Arab identity there.

3. Representatives of financial organizations attending the conference have expressed satisfaction with Jordan's development efforts and its fulfillment of its commitments. They voiced full readiness to continue aiding the country's development programs.

4. The measures and investment policies of Jordan have created a suitable climate for attracting Arab and foreign investment funds and provided an incentive for local investments. These measures and policies serve as an example for securing the fundamentals of inter-Arab economic integration.

5. The principle of free movement of Arab labor force which Jordan has largely put into effect is an advance step toward inter-Arab economic integration.

6. Free trade exchange among Arab countries constitutes a basic element in inter-Arab economic integration, and facilitating the exportation of products of the occupied territories to Arab and foreign countries is an important tool in sustaining the steadfastness of the Arab population in the occupied territories and linking their economy with the economies of the Arab world.

7. Jordan's geographic position and the economic policies it has been adopting, which aim at achieving further inter-Arab and international economic cooperation, qualify the country to play a central role in deepening inter-Arab economic relations.

358. European Community Declaration on the Middle East, Brussels, February 23, 1987*

* 16 J. Palestine Stud. 185 (Summer 1987).

The member states of the European Community have particularly important political, historical, geographical, economic, religious, cultural and human links with the countries and peoples of the Middle East. They cannot therefore adopt a passive attitude towards a region which is so close to them nor remain indifferent to the grave problems besetting it. The repercussions of these problems affect the Twelve in many ways.

At the present time, tension and conflict in the Near and Middle East are continuing and worsening. The civilian population is suffering more and more without any prospect of peace. The Twelve would like to reiterate their profound conviction that the search for peace in the Near and Middle East remains a fundamental objective. They are profoundly concerned at the absence of progress in finding a solution to the Israeli-Arab conflict.

Consequently, they have a direct interest in the search for negotiated solutions to bring just, global and lasting peace to the region and good relations between neighbors, and to allow the economic, social and cultural development which has been too long neglected. They have stated the principles on which solutions would be based on several occasions, in particular in their Venice Declaration.

Accordingly, the Twelve would like to state that they are in favor of an international peace conference to be held under the auspices of the United Nations with the participation of the parties concerned and of any party able to make a direct and positive contribution to the restoration and maintenance of peace and to the region's economic and social development. The Twelve believe this conference should provide a suitable framework for the necessary negotiations between the parties directly concerned.

For their part, the Twelve are prepared to play their role with respect to such a conference and will endeavor to make an active contribution, both through the President-in-Office and individually, to bringing the positions of the parties concerned closer to one another with a view to such a conference being convened. In the meantime, the Twelve would request the parties concerned to avoid any action likely to worsen the situation or complicate and delay the search for peace.

Without prejudging future political solutions, the Twelve wish to see an improvement in the living conditions of the inhabitants of the Occupied Territories, particularly regarding their economic, social, cultural, and administrative affairs. The Community has already decided to grant aid to the Palestinian population of the Occupied Territories and to allow certain products from those territories preferential access to the Community market.

359. Cancellation of the Amman Agreement, Algiers, April 19, 1987*

* 16 J. Palestine Stud. 195 (Summer 1987).

On 11 December 1985 the PLO and the government of the Hashimite Kingdom of Jordan signed an agreement for a joint plan of action to achieve the mutual interests of the Jordanian and Palestinian peoples in accordance with the resolutions of the Arab summit in Fez; and following the termination of the work of the seven-member Arab committee as a new instrument of an Arab peace plan in order to secure the attainment of the established national rights of the Palestinian people through ongoing international and Arab efforts.

The agreement was based on resolutions of the PNC, especially those of the sixteenth and seventeenth sessions which affirmed the special, brotherly relations between the two peoples and which called for the establishment of future relations on a confederal basis between the two states (Jordan and Palestine) and for coordination of joint political efforts to thwart separate solutions and settlements and to foil the project for an "alternative homeland."

During the course of the joint work differences arose between the two parties as to the meaning of some of the text of the agreement and the means of implementing it. In addition, there were the pressures brought to bear by the United States and other circles in the aftermath of which Jordan, on 19 February 1986, announced the suspension of political coordination with the PLO and took certain measures which froze the agreement and led to a period of rupture in relations.

Proceeding from its desire for the correct implementation of the resolutions of the PNC related to the special, brotherly relations between the Palestinian and Jordanian peoples and in the light of what practical experience has proven, that the above-mentioned agreement has become an obstacle to the development of these relations, and, since it is no longer standing in practice, the PLO Executive Committee considers it null and void.

At the same time the Executive in the context of its established policy will continue its efforts to find new bases for working with Jordan and other Arab countries in order to achieve a joint struggle in the framework of united Arab action and effective Arab solidarity to liberate occupied Palestinian and Arab land and to build Arab unity taking into consideration the resolutions of Fez in support of an international conference in which the Soviet Union, the United States and other permanent members of the Security Council would participate along with the parties to the Middle East conflict, including the PLO, on an equal footing with the other parties in the framework and under the auspices of the UN.

360. Resolution of the Political Committee of the Eighteenth Session of the PNC, Algiers, April 26, 1987*

---

* 16 J. Palestine Stud. 196 (Summer 1987).

Proceeding from the Palestinian National Charter and in harmony with the PNC resolutions, we emphasize the following principles as a basis for Palestinian national action within the framework of the PLO, the sole legitimate representative of the Arab Palestinian people:

I. On the Palestinian Level

1. Adhering to the Arab Palestinian people's national inalienable rights to repatriation, self-determination, and establishment of an independent state of Palestinian national soil, whose capital is Jerusalem. Commitment to the PLO's political program which is aimed at attaining these rights. Adhering to the PLO as a sole, legitimate representative for our people and rejecting deputization, procuration, and sharing of participation in Palestinian representation. Rejecting and resisting any alternatives to the PLO.

3. Adhering to the PLO's independence and rejecting trusteeship, containment, annexation, and interference in its internal affairs.

4. Continuing struggle in all its armed, popular, and political forms for the sake of attaining our national objectives; liberating Palestinian and Arab lands from Israeli occupation; and confronting the hostile schemes of the imperialist-Zionist alliance in our region, particularly the strategic U.S.-Israeli alliance, as a genuine expression of our people's national liberation movement, which antagonizes imperialism, colonialism, and Zionism.

5. Continued rejection of the Security Council Resolution 242, which is not considered a good basis for a settlement of the Palestine question because it deals with it as if it were an issue of refugees and ignores the Palestinian people's national inalienable rights.

6. Rejecting and resisting all solutions and plans aimed at liquidating our Palestine question, including the Camp David accords, Reagan's autonomy plan, and functional partition in all its forms.

7. Adhering to the Arab summits' resolutions on the Palestine question, particularly the Rabat 1974 summit, and considering the Arab peace plan approved by the Fez 1982 summit and confirmed by the extraordinary Casablanca summit as a framework for Arab action on the international level to achieve a solution to the Palestine question and to regain the occupied Arab territories.

8. Taking into consideration UN Resolutions 35, 38, 48/41 regarding the convocation of an international conference for peace in the Middle East, and UN resolutions on the Palestine question, the PNC supports the convocation of an international conference within the framework of the United Nations and under its auspices to be attended by the permanent member states of the UN Security Council and the parties to the conflict in the region, including the PLO, on equal footing with the other parties. The PNC stresses that the international conference should have full powers. The PNC also expresses support for the proposal to form a preparatory committee, and calls for swift action to form and convene this committee. In this re-

gard, the PNC expresses appreciation for the fifth ICO summit conference in Kuwait, the eighth nonaligned conference in Harare and the coordination committee stemming from it, and the OAU summit in Addis Ababa, which expressed support for the convocation of the international conference, the preparatory committee, and for the efforts to convene this conference.

9. Enhancing the unity of all the national institutions and forces inside the occupied homeland under the PLO, promoting their joint struggle action against the Zionist enemy, the Zionist iron-fist policy, the autonomy plan, functional partition, normalization, the so-called development plan, and the attempts to create alternatives to the PLO, including the establishment of municipal councils, and supporting the steadfastness of our people who are represented by their national forces and institutions.

10. Reinforcing the unity of action regarding reorganizing the situation in our camps in Lebanon; defending these camps; deepening the unity of our people in them under the PLO; insisting upon our people's rights in Lebanon regarding residence, work, movement, and the freedom of political and social action; rejecting the attempts to expel and disarm our people; stressing our people's right to struggle against the Zionist enemy, to protect themselves, and to defend their camps in accordance with the Cairo agreement and its annexes, which organize relations between the PLO and the Lebanese Republic; and contributing along with our Lebanese brothers and their nationalist forces to resisting the Israeli occupation in Lebanon.

11. Protecting our people; taking care of their affairs wherever they reside; insisting upon their rights of residence, mobility, work, education, health, and security in accordance with the Arab League resolutions and the declaration on human rights; guaranteeing the freedom of political action as embodied in Arab brotherhood ties and pan-Arab affiliation; and bolstering their cohesion with their Arab brothers.

II. On the Arab Level

1. Bolstering Arab solidarity on the basis of the Arab summit resolutions and adhering to the charters of the joint Arab action and the Collective Arab Defense Pact to mobilize potential to liberate the occupied Arab territories and to confront Zionist aggression and U.S. schemes to impose control over the Arab nation.

2. Consolidating the relations of alliance with Arab liberation movement forces on the basis of action to attain the objectives of joint pan-Arab struggle against imperialism and Zionism and to reorganize the Arab front, which participates in the Palestinian revolution to enable it to perform its pan-Arab role of supporting and protecting the revolution.

3. Supporting the struggle of the Lebanese people and their nationalist forces against the Israeli occupation of southern Lebanon and for the sake

of Lebanon's unity, Arab affiliation, independence, and for enhancing the Palestinian-Lebanese militant struggle.

Special Resolution

The PNC expresses pride in and appreciation for the fraternal Lebanese people; emphasizes the importance of pursuing the alliance with the heroic Lebanese National Movement under Walid Junblatt and the other nationalist and Islamic leaders and forces with which we have fought and continue to fight to liberate Lebanese territory from the Zionist occupation; and stresses to them that the Palestinian revolution will remain a support for their program and for the continuation of the joint confrontation against the Israeli aggression and occupation, and for Lebanon's unity, Arab character, and independence.

4. Correcting and establishing relations between the PLO and Syria on the basis of the struggle objectives hostile to imperialism and Zionism, and in accordance with Arab summit resolutions, particularly the Rabat and Fez summit resolutions, and on a basis of equality and mutual respect leading to militant Palestinian-Syrian relations as well as close Arab ties.

5. The Iraq-Iran war. Working to halt the Iraq-Iran war because it is a destructive war to the two neighboring Muslim people from which only imperialism and Zionism benefit. This war seeks to exhaust Arab efforts and resources from the principal arena of confronting Zionist aggression, which is backed by U.S. imperialism against the Arab nation and the Islamic countries. While valuing Iraq's peace initiatives seeking to halt this war, establishing relations of good neighborliness between the two countries based on total respect for the sovereignty of each, on the noninterference by either side in the domestic affairs of the other, and with respect to their political and social potential, the PNC stands at fraternal Iraq's side in defending its land and any Arab land that is the target of foreign aggression and invasion. The PNC also condemns Iran's occupation of Iraqi territory and U.S.-Israeli collusion to perpetuate this war through the U.S. and Israeli arms deals to Iran.

6. Jordan. Reaffirming the special and distinctive relations that link the fraternal Palestinian and Jordanian people and working to develop these relations in a manner that will be in line with the pan-Arab interests of the two people and those of our Arab nation; consolidating their joint struggle to enhance Jordan's independence and against the Zionist designs of expansion at the expense of its territory, and for the attainment of the Palestinian people's inalienable rights, including their right to repatriation, self-determination, the establishment of the independent Palestinian state; abiding by the PNC resolutions pertaining to the relationship with Jordan on the basis that the PLO is the Palestinian people's sole and legitimate representative inside and outside the occupied territories, as was affirmed by the 1974 Fez Summit resolution. Reaffirming that any future relationship with Jordan should be based on confederal bases between two independent states; and

stressing adherence to the bases that were approved by the 15th PNC session and the Baghdad Summit resolutions concerning bolstering steadfastness, including the Palestinian-Jordanian Joint Committee.

7. Egypt. While stressing the historic role of Egypt and its great people within the framework of the Arab struggle against the Zionist enemy, the sacrifices of the fraternal Egyptian people and its heroic army in defense of the Palestinian people and their national rights, Egypt's struggle to achieve Arab unity and liberation from colonialism and Zionism, Egypt's struggle to liberate the occupied Arab and Palestinian territories in all circles and arenas, and while also appreciating Egypt's pan-Arab and international position and the importance of Egypt's return [to the Arab fold] and its assumption of its natural role in the Arab arena, the PNC has entrusted the PLO Executive Committee with the task of defining the bases for Palestinian-Egyptian relations in accordance with successive PNC resolutions, especially those of the sixteenth session, which contain certain positions and principles of Palestinian struggle, foremost of which are the right to self-determination, repatriation, and the establishment of an independent Palestinian state and that the PLO is the sole legitimate representative; as well as in light of the Arab summit conferences' resolutions to achieve the Palestinian people's goals and inalienable national rights, which have been stressed by these Arab resolutions in the service of the Palestinian and Arab struggle against the Zionist enemy and its supporters.

III. On the International Level

1. Bolstering relations of alliance with the world liberation movements.

2. Cooperating closely with the Islamic, African, and nonaligned countries, and activating the PLO's action in these countries to promote relations with them and gain further support for the Palestinian struggle.

3. Strengthening militant relations of alliance with the socialist bloc countries, foremost of which is the Soviet Union, as well as with the PRC.

4. Supporting peoples struggling against imperialism and racism for the sake of their national liberation, especially in southern and southwest Africa, Central America, and Latin America; condemning the aggressive alliance between the racist regimes in Tel Aviv and South Africa against the Arab nation and the African peoples; strongly supporting the African frontline countries in their struggle against the Pretoria regime; and strongly supporting the South African and Namibian peoples.

5. Working with all means in the international arena to expose the Zionist racism exercised in our occupied homeland. This racism was confirmed by the historic UN Resolution 3379 in 1975 stating that Zionism is a form of racism; and working to abort the Zionist-imperialist move to cancel this resolution.

6. Working to develop positive positions toward our cause in West European circles, in Japan, in Australia, and in Canada, and strengthening rela-

tions with democratic parties and forces in the capitalist countries that support our established national rights.

7. Joining world peoples in the struggle for world peace and international detente; stopping the arms race; averting the danger of a nuclear war; supporting Soviet initiatives in this regard; and exposing the dangers of Israeli nuclear armament in cooperation with South Africa against the region and world peace.

8. Developing relations with Israeli democratic forces supporting the Palestinian people's struggle against Israeli occupation and expansion and the inalienable national rights of our people, including their rights to repatriation and self-determination as well as the establishment of their independent state; and recognizing the PLO as the sole, legitimate representative of the Palestinian people. Condemning all U.S. imperialist-backed Zionist attempts to drive Jews in a number of countries to emigrate to occupied Palestine, and calling upon all honorable forces to stand up to these feverish propagandist campaigns and their harmful effects.

9. In its eighteenth session, the PNC appreciates the efforts made by the UN Committee to help the Palestinian people exercise their inalienable rights in cooperation with various UN bodies, especially in organizing periodic symposiums and news conferences with a view to educating world public opinion about the true objectives of the Palestinian people's struggle. The PNC appreciates the efforts of nongovernmental bodies throughout the world to bolster the struggle of the Palestinian people to realize their inalienable rights in Palestine.

Resolutions

The PNC would like to express most profound thanks and appreciation to sisterly Algeria—president, government, and people—for Algeria's noble pan-Arab stand on the Palestinian revolution and people in the common pan-Arab battle for liberation and return. Proceeding from the common Arab destiny and common struggle against the usurper Zionist enemy, Arab solidarity, and the camaraderie of struggle between Algeria and Palestine, the PNC proudly recognizes Algeria's pioneering, pan-Arab role of promoting Palestinian national unity on the heroic land of Algeria. The Algerian President Shadhly ben Jadid crowned his genuine pan-Arab initiative on promoting Palestinian national unity by welcoming and playing host to the comprehensive national dialogue in the Algerian capital.

Greatly appreciating these pioneering stands toward our people and revolution, which mark a watershed in the common pan-Arab battle, the PNC would like to stress, on behalf of the Palestinian people and the PLO, that these pioneering Algerian stands are a true expression of Algeria's pan-Arab commitment—president, government, party, and people—to the Palestinian armed revolution and people. The PNC extends heartfelt warm greetings to sisterly Algeria, and promises the country of 1,500,000 martyrs that it will continue the struggle until our people and nation achieve victory and the flag of Palestine flies over Jerusalem. Greetings to the sons of Algeria who have embraced the revolutionaries of Palestine, as they consolidate their unity and close their ranks under the banner of the struggle for a free independent Palestine.

A Statement on Lebanon and the Camps' Steadfastness

The PNC sends greetings of appreciation and pride to our steadfast masses in the camps of Lebanon and to our brave fighters who have honorably and heroically confronted the fierce onslaught waged by the Amal Movement leadership and by those supporting it with the aim of destroying and disarming our camps as a prelude to their evacuation at a time when Israel is carrying out savage raids on our camps to achieve the same objectives.

Our people's steadfastness in these camps has once and for all confirmed the impossibility of liquidating our people, canceling their institutions, or undermining the continuity of their struggle to achieve their constant aims. Moreover, this war aimed to classify the population, which is bound to peddle the schemes of the Zionist-imperialist alliance by establishing sectarian mini-states, and which the nationalist, honorable Lebanese masses and forces continue to resist. Naturally, this was not neglected by the kind masses of the Shi'i sect who were described by Imam Musa al-Sadr as a deprived people in their homeland and for whom he asked to care. Proceeding from its charter and resolutions, the PNC reaffirms its pan-Arab stand on fraternal Lebanon as an Arab country whose sovereignty, independence, and the unity of whose lands and people we respect. The PNC, in fulfillment of its central mission and of the sanguinary cohesion between the Palestinian and Lebanese peoples who have waged together the most honorable battles against the common Zionist enemy, affirms the continuity of our joint struggle to complete the liberation of southern Lebanon along with the Lebanese and all our Arab peoples until Palestine is liberated, until the Palestinian people return to their land, and until Palestinian banners are raised in holy Jerusalem. The PNC views that the civil and national rights of our masses in Lebanon have been confirmed and entrenched through various agreements both at Arab summits and in bilateral relations. The PNC affirms that our people's security in Lebanon, along with their legitimate gains, have been confirmed by the unity of fate shared by the two fraternal peoples. This is an opportunity to extend greetings of joint struggle to all nationalist and Islamic forces. The PNC looks forward to the Syrian forces'—present in the camp areas—shouldering their responsibilities in accordance with the agreements guaranteeing security for our people and their right to protect themselves against any attempts to attack them, besiege our camps, or prevent our people from exercising their right to movement outside these camps in search of their right to an honorable living.

The PNC does not forget the efforts of the honorable foreign friends who supported our people during their tribulation, which had brought great international reaction. The PNC presents to the Executive Committee an urgent recommendation to reconstruct the camps in Lebanon and to compensate for the grave material losses caused by the recent war.

O steadfast kinfolk in Lebanon. O Arab Lebanese people. With your sacrifices you have written legends; by the unity of your stand you have preserved both the cause and the destiny; and the mingling of your blood has laid a solid base for national and pan-Arab unity. Today, the eyes of the whole world are upon you, seeing Palestine and Lebanon in you, and because of your will are determined to continue along the road. O colleagues of martyrs. O colleagues of 'Ali Abu Tawq. O brothers and kinfolk. We support you as you also support us. Tomorrow, the children of Shatila, Rashidiyyah, Burj al-Barajinah, and 'Ayn al-Hilwah will remember the bitter days that deepened our belief in the liberation of Palestine, the Arabism of Lebanon, the unity of the Arabs, and the coming victory, God willing. We support you and we will meet. Glory and immortality to the righteous martyrs. Long live a free, Arab Lebanon! Long live a free, Arab Palestine!

361. Palestinian Memorandum to U.S. Secretary of State
George Shultz, Jerusalem, October 1987*

* 17 J. Palestine Stud. 214 (Winter 1988).

Mr. George Shultz, U.S. secretary of state.

Mr. Minister: Twenty hard years have passed since the Israeli occupation of our homeland, during which over 1.5 million Palestinians have lost their freedom and become a target of an Israeli scheme to return us to the Middle Ages. In pursuit of this impossible goal, the Israeli authorities set out to use all kinds of repressive practices, including building settlements, confiscating land, attempting to extinguish Palestinian nationalism, and violating all human rights conventions.

Your proposal three years ago to improve living conditions for the Palestinians under occupation came as a surprise to our Palestinian people. It is inconceivable that there can be liberal occupation; occupation can only mean the forcible subjugation of one people by another. Occupation and improving living conditions are therefore an impossible combination. Furthermore, from the moment you raised this point the Israeli authorities sought to escalate their repressive measures against our people and institutions. You may familiarize yourself with details of our suffering over the past three years at the U.S. Consulate in Jerusalem.

Mr. Minister, in our opinion continued Israeli occupation, coupled with American support, which is a hallmark of the present administration, robs the United States of moral credibility. U.S. decisionmakers continue to refuse to recognize the basic right of our Palestinian people to self-determination. They also refuse to recognize the PLO as the sole legitimate representative of the Palestinian people who decided and affirmed this representation. Peace efforts in the region will hardly be helped by the continuation of the current American position.

An unchanged American position symbolizes the absence of a will to establish the foundations for a just peace whereby the rights and aspirations of all peoples in the region—above all those of Palestinians—are realized. The United States must reconsider its commitments and policies, particularly the policy of ignoring the PLO and the national rights of the Palestinian people.

It must be recalled that 75 initiatives have been presented since 1948 to resolve the Arab-Israeli dispute. All of them met with failure since they failed to take into account the true political and national dimensions of the Palestinian issue. We have always cherished the hope that a just solution to the Arab-Israeli dispute will be reached.

We would like to call your attention to the following facts that must be taken into consideration when the Arab-Israeli dispute comes up for discussion or negotiation: First, the only road to initiating the peace process is a UN-sponsored international peace conference attended by the five permanent members of the Security Council and all of the parties to the dispute, including the PLO, the sole legitimate representative of the Palestinians, both those under occupation and those in exile.

Second, the Palestinian people reject the current version of the UN Security Council Resolution 242 given the national and political nature of their cause. The national and political side of the Palestinian cause has found expression in the Palestinians' yearning to exercise their right to self-determination, set up a state on their national soil, and choose their own representatives without Israeli or other pressures.

Third, our Palestinian people have made known their support for their sole legitimate representative: namely, the PLO.

Fourth, we call on the U.S. administration to honor the principles and code of the United Nations, of which the United States was a founding member, and specifically, to pressure the Israeli government to treat the Palestinian people according to the laws and conventions drafted by the United States concerning peoples that come under occupation.

Fifth, we believe that occupation and improving living conditions are diametrically opposed; the two are mutually exclusive. Continuing to link them only means encouraging continued occupation.

Sixth, our people would like to stress their abiding commitment to a just and comprehensive peace; the cost of a continuing status quo would be borne by our people. We would like the American people to become acquainted with our thinking since they have only heard the Israeli side of the story.

Seventh, it is hoped that your meeting with the Soviet foreign minister will lay the groundwork for a joint American-Soviet effort promoting the forces of peace and diplomacy rather than those of violence and war.

Eighth, we denounce the decision to close the Palestine Information Office in Washington and view it as the result of pressure from the Zionist lobby in the United States. It is hoped the decision will be reversed to keep our restricted lines of communication open.

362. Memorandum Submitted to French Prime Minister Jacques Chirac by Palestinians from the Occupied Territories, Jerusalem, November 3, 1987*

* 17 J. Palestine Stud. 174 (Spring 1988).

His Excellency Mr. Jacques Chirac, Prime Minister of the Republic of France:

It is our pleasure that we have the opportunity to meet with you and to express to you and to your French government and the French people, our deep appreciation for the sincere efforts you are exerting to convene the international peace conference in the hope that a just, comprehensive, and peaceful settlement can be established in the region.

We also express our appreciation for the courageous stand of the French government to work to maintain a comprehensive and just settlement in a region shattered by instability and lack of peace and security, yet an area that will continue by its critical circumstances to threaten international peace and security.

While we mark the twentieth anniversary of the Israeli occupation of our Arab land and the repercussions that have followed the daily practices of the occupation, as well as the multi-phase measures taken against our land and people, we would like to reiterate the points that were submitted to your foreign minister, Mr. Jean-Bernard Raimond, when we had the honor of meeting him on 2 June 1987. These points include:

1. The PLO is the sole, legitimate representative of our Palestinian people wherever they are located, whether under occupation or in diaspora, and we reject all attempts and plots that are aimed, no matter by whom, at replacing or liquidating this representation by the PLO.

2. Our people in the occupied Arab territories support a just and comprehensive settlement for the Palestinian question and believe that the convening of an international peace conference with the participation of the two superpowers and the remaining permanent members of the UN Security Council, along with all the parties concerned in the conflict, including the PLO, the sole, legitimate representative of the Palestinian people, is the only way to achieve peace in the region.

3. Our Palestinian people stress that no peace or a comprehensive settlement can be achieved in the region and no just solution for the Palestinian problem can be reached without the recognition of the national legitimate rights of the Palestinian people, including their right to self-determination and the establishment of an independent Palestinian state on our soil and the right of the Palestinian people living in diaspora to return to their homeland.

4. Our people stress that UN Security Council resolutions 242 and 338 do not form any adequate basis for reaching a just and comprehensive settlement for the Palestinian problem because both deal with the Palestinian issue as merely a case of refugees and not as a national political question.

5. Our people support the declaration of the European Economic Community of last February and stress the importance of France's positive role in propelling the peace process forward. We hope that this constructive role will continue to achieve a just and comprehensive solution to the Palestinian problem, which is the core issue of the Middle East conflict.

6. Our people under occupation stress that the continuation of the Israelis' daily practices, which over the past twenty years took the form of establishing settlements and violation of human rights by the occupying power, completely contravene the UN Charter and international laws and form a major obstacle on the road to a just and durable peace in the region.

363. Excerpt from the Resolutions of the Arab Summit, Amman, November 11, 1987*

* 17 J. Palestine Stud. 176 (Spring 1988).

Resolution on the Arab-Israeli Conflict:

Their majesties, excellencies, and highnesses the kings, presidents, and amirs of the Arab states, meeting within the framework of the extraordinary Arab summit conference in Amman, the Hashimite Kingdom of Jordan, 8-11 November 1987, considering that the Palestinian question is the Arabs' cause and the crux of the Arab-Israeli conflict and that struggle for the sake of regaining usurped Arab rights in Palestinian territory and other occupied Arab territories is a Pan-Arab responsibility; since the Zionist danger is not only targeted against the confrontation states but threatens the destiny and existence of the whole Arab nation; in view of Israel's continued perpetration of repressive practices in the occupied Arab and Palestinian territories; and in light of its persistent pursuit of its hostile and expansionist policy, decide:

1. To pool the Arab states' capabilities and resources for the sake of reinforcing the capabilities and energies of the states and forces that are confronting Israel on all levels to help end its continued aggression against the Arab nation and regain usurped Arab rights in Palestine and occupied Arab territories.

2. To achieve strategic parity with Israel within the framework of an effective Arab solidarity to confront the Zionist danger, which threatens the Arab nation's destiny and existence, and to force Israel to accept the UN resolutions seeking to establish a just and comprehensive peace in the region.

3. To provide material and moral support to the persistent heroic struggle being waged by the Palestinian people in occupied Palestine, the Golan Heights, and southern Lebanon in their confrontation of Israeli occupation.

4. To urge all Arab parties to abide by Arab summit resolutions stipulating the inadmissibility of any Arab side's unilaterally concluding any solution to the Arab-Israeli conflict, rejecting any peaceful settlement of the Arab-Israeli conflict that does not guarantee full and unconditional Israeli withdrawal from all occupied Palestinian and Arab territories and that does not call for enabling the Palestinian Arab people to exercise their inalienable national rights in accordance with Arab summit resolutions, especially those adopted at the Fez summit in 1982.

5. To condemn the U.S. government's decision to close the Palestine Information Office in Washington.

Resolution on an International Peace Conference:

Their majesties, excellencies, and highnesses the kings, presidents, and amirs of the Arab states, meeting within the framework of the extraordinary Arab summit conference in Amman, the Hashimite Kingdom of Jordan, 8-11 November 1987, out of commitment to the objectives and bases defined by the resolutions of Arab summit conferences concerning the Arab-Israeli conflict; in view of Israel's continued rejection of peace efforts as well as Israel's failure to accept UN resolutions to establish a just and comprehensive peace in the region; proceeding from the Arab nation's determination to pool its resources and capabilities to confront the Zionist challenge to its fate and existence; and out of commitment to the Arab nation's approach to peace defined in the Arab peace plan approved at the 1982 Fez summit with the aim of achieving a just and comprehensive settlement of the Arab-Israeli conflict guaranteeing the return of the occupied Arab and Palestinian territories as well as resolving the Palestine question in all its aspects on the basis of international legitimacy, decide:

The convening of an international conference for peace in the Middle East under UN auspices, called for by the UN secretary general and attended by the five permanent Security Council member states along with all parties to the Arab-Israeli conflict, including the PLO, the sole legitimate representative of the Palestinian people, on an equal footing, is the appropriate way to settle the conflict in a comprehensive, just, and peaceful manner.

This settlement will guarantee the return of occupied Palestinian and Arab territories, the resolution of the Palestine question in all its aspects, and the attainment of the inalienable national rights of the Palestinian Arab people.

364. U.S. Policy toward the Occupied Territories
(excerpt), March 1988*

---

* 88 U.S. Dep't State Bull. No. 2132, at 71 (March 1988). Statement of Richard W. Murphy, U.S. Dep't of State.

I welcome this opportunity to testify on U.S. policy regarding the West Bank and Gaza, territories occupied by Israel since the June 1967 Middle East war.

U.S. policy toward the West Bank and Gaza has two major objectives.

First, we support a resolution of the status of these territories in the context of a lasting peace to be achieved through direct negotiations between Israel and its Arab neighbors.

Second, we want to improve the quality of Palestinian life in the territories.

These two objectives are complementary. An active peace process gives both Israelis and Palestinians in the territories the promise of an end to strife, genuine security, and a brighter future for themselves and their children. The expectation that a just and comprehensive peace is possible and that active efforts are continuing to achieve it preserves hope and encourages movement toward reconciliation. At the same time, practical measures to improve the daily lives of Palestinians help to reinforce efforts toward a comprehensive political settlement while reducing the frustrations that are one cause of extremism and violence. Active efforts for peace and improvements in the quality of life are, therefore, essential to sustain each other.

Security in the West Bank and Gaza

The state of war—now in its 40th year—and the occupation—now in its 21st year—exact a toll on the 1.5 million Palestinians in the territories, and on Israel as well. In the absence of peace and a political agreement, the prevailing atmosphere is one of tension and mutual mistrust. This environment produces protest demonstrations by Palestinians, acts of violence by both Palestinians and Israeli settlers, and harsh security measures by Israeli occupation authorities which are sometimes inconsistent with recognized international standards.

The situation in the occupied territories fluctuates between periods of calm and periods of unrest, but tensions are chronic and appear to be increasing, especially in the refugee camps and among younger Palestinians. Last week's eruption of violent confrontation reminds us of the deep communal conflict and of the unresolved political status of the West Bank and Gaza. At least seven Palestinians and one Israeli have been killed during these latest tragic events, and many more have been wounded.

Israel continues to limit severely Palestinian family reunification, which the United States regards as an important humanitarian issue. In 1986 about 1,400 individuals were allowed to rejoin their families, an increase over the previous 2 years' approval rate. This was encouraging; however, Palestinian sources state that over 10,000 applications, many for entire families, are pending.

The situation in the occupied territories is clearly unsatisfactory to both Palestinians and Israelis. Against this background, the United States, while continuing to encourage Israel and its Arab neighbors to find a way to the negotiating table, pursues a three-part policy toward the West Bank and Gaza.

· We condemn violence and extremism in all forms and from all sides.

· We support programs to improve economic and social conditions for the Palestinians.

· We encourage Israel to assure that its occupation practices are consistent with accepted international standards and the legitimate needs of maintaining security.

In keeping with our close and friendly relationship, we have an active and serious dialogue with Israel on these aspects of our policy.

Economic and Social Conditions

Long-term economic development in the West Bank and Gaza is supported, in principle, by both Israel and Jordan, and certain policies have been adopted by both governments to support growth. However, although the standard of living has risen, the potential of these areas is far from being realized because of the unresolved status of the territories and by various constraints and protectionist policies imposed by Israel and Jordan. As a result, job creation has not kept up with the rapidly growing and increasingly well-educated labor force. About 90,000 Palestinians are now employed in the service or manual labor sectors in Israel. However, there are very few opportunities for Palestinian secondary and college graduates in Israel.

Social problems in the West Bank and Gaza must be viewed in the context of the continuing occupation, the lack of economic development, and the absence of local public institutions. Social services, including secondary health care, sanitation, vocation training, and care of the elderly and handicapped, are largely undertaken by nongovernmental groups. Their funding is often precarious and their activities are subject to control by the occupation authorities. The problem is especially acute in Gaza, where the very rapid population growth rate has made it one of the most densely populated areas in the world and has significantly increased the demand for social services.

U.S. Assistance Programs

U.S. assistance programs to the West Bank and Gaza respond to these economic and social problems. Our assistance flows through separate but mutually reinforcing channels—the direct program, Jordan's development program, and the UN Relief and Works Agency (UNRWA), which provides assistance to over 2 million Palestinian refugees, of whom over 800,000 reside in the West Bank and Gaza.

We have provided over $76 million to fund projects of private voluntary organizations in the West Bank and Gaza since 1975. In addition to health and social services, we have increasingly directed our aid toward longer term development needs, particularly employment creation.

A major impediment to further private voluntary organization activities is our inability to fund the program adequately. For FY 1987, we requested $18 million but were able to provide only $8.5 million. For 1988, taking into account U.S. budget stringencies, we requested $12 million. If funding remains at the 1987 level, it will be very difficult to undertake new projects.

In 1986 King Hussein announced an important new economic development program for the occupied territories. Jordan's program focuses on infrastructure development, education, and agriculture in the territories. We have provided $18.5 million since September 1986 for King Hussein's initiative. Britain, Italy, and West Germany have also pledged support.

Jordan's program is making progress. Municipalities and other local organizations have submitted proposals whose costs far exceed Jordan's current ability to fund them, clearly indicating a willingness by West Bankers and Gazans to work with the Jordanians to improve their social and economic conditions.

To have a major impact, however, Jordan's program needs substantial additional funding. We are requesting an additional $23 million for this year, beyond the $7 million we sought in FY 1988. We continue to encourage our friends to contribute, but they are hesitant to allocate scarce resources to a new, untested program. Our strongest argument with them is that we have enough confidence in King Hussein's initiative for all of us to provide significant funding, even though we face a major budgetary crisis.

We support UNRWA's efforts to sustain decent conditions in the refugee camps. In 1987, UNRWA's expenditures in the territories were approximately $82 million. The United States contributed $67 million to UNRWA's $200 million budget for activities in Lebanon, Syria, and Jordan, as well as the West Bank and Gaza.

Private Sector Development

Economic assistance to the West Bank and Gaza cannot substitute for vigorous private sector growth and development. A variety of trade constraints imposed by Israel and Jordan continue to hamper the marketing of goods produced by Palestinians. These trade barriers protect Israeli and Jordanian commercial interests from Palestinian competition.

We believe artificial constraints should be eliminated, and there has been some modest success. The European Community has granted preferential access to certain commodities from the West Bank and Gaza and has sought Israeli approval to permit these goods to flow more freely to Western Europe. We understand that Israel and the European Community have made some progress in defining how Palestinians will be able to take advantage of these trade concessions. Export growth is critical to the economic future of the territories, and we hope that the sides will work to resolve outstanding issues.

In 1986 the first Arab bank to operate in the territories since 1967 was opened, and a second branch opened this year. Both have attracted sizable deposits, and plans are underway to open a third branch. The provision of Arab banking services in the territories can help create a more normal environment for business expansion.

Ultimately problems in the West Bank and Gaza cannot be fully resolved in the absence of an agreement to end the occupation in a way that is accepted by the Palestinian inhabitants, by Israelis, and by their Arab neighbors. Until then we will seek ways to improve conditions in the territories.

365. Report of the Secretary-General

of the United Nations

to the Security Council regarding the Situation in

the Occupied Territories, January 21, 1988*

* U.N. Doc. S/19443 (Jan. 21, 1988).

Introduction

1. On 22 December 1987 the Security Council adopted resolution 605 (1987), which reads as follows:

"*The Security Council,*

Having considered the letter dated 11 December 1987 from the Permanent Representative of Democratic Yemen to the United Nations, in his capacity as chairman of the Arab Group for the month of December,[1]

Bearing in mind the inalienable rights of all peoples recognized by the Charter of the United Nations and proclaimed by the Universal Declaration of Human Rights,[2]

Recalling its relevant resolutions on the situation in the Palestinian and other Arab territories, occupied by Israel since 1967, including Jerusalem, and including its resolutions 446 (1979), 465 (1980), 497 (1981) and 592 (1986),

Recalling also the Geneva Convention relative to the Protection of Civilian Persons in Time of War, of 12 August 1949,[3]

Gravely concerned and alarmed by the deteriorating situation in the Palestinian and other Arab territories occupied by Israel since 1967, including Jerusalem,

Taking into account the need to consider measures for the impartial protection of the Palestinian civilian population under Israeli occupation,

Considering that the current policies and practices of Israel, the occupying Power, in the occupied territories are bound to have grave consequences for the endeavors to achieve comprehensive, just and lasting peace in the Middle East,

1. *Strongly deplores* those policies and practices of Israel, the occupying Power, which violate the human rights of the Palestinian people in the occupied territories, and in particular the opening of fire by the Israeli army, resulting in the killing and wounding of defenceless Palestinian civilians;

2. *Reaffirms* that the Geneva Convention relative to the Protection of Civilian Persons in Time of War, of 12 August 1949, is applicable to the Palestinian and other Arab territories occupied by Israel since 1967, including Jerusalem;

3. *Calls once again upon* Israel, the occupying Power, to abide immediately and scrupulously by the Geneva Convention relative to the Protection of Civilian Persons in Time of War, of 12 August 1949, and to desist forthwith from its policies and practices that are in violation of the provisions of the Convention;

4. *Calls furthermore for* the exercise of maximum restraint to contribute towards the establishment of peace;

[1] S/19333.
[2] General Assembly Resolution 217 A (III).
[3] United Nations, *Treaty Series*, vol. 75, No. 973, p. 287.

5. *Stresses* the urgent need to reach a just, durable and peaceful settlement of the Arab-Israeli conflict;

6. *Requests* the Secretary-General to examine the present situation in the occupied territories by all means available to him, and to submit a report no later than 20 January 1988 containing his recommendations on ways and means for ensuring the safety and protection of the Palestinian civilians under Israeli occupation;

7. *Decides* to keep the situation in the Palestinian and other Arab territories occupied by Israel since 1967, including Jerusalem, under review."

Resolutions 607 (1988) and 608 (1988), relating to Israel's deportation of Palestinian civilians from the occupied territories, were adopted on 5 and 14 January 1988 respectively. The present report is submitted in accordance with paragraph 6 of resolution 605 (1987).

2. In order to obtain information needed for the preparation of this report, I instructed Mr. Marrack Goulding, Under-Secretary-General for Special Political Affairs, to visit Israel and the occupied Palestinian territories. The purpose of this visit, which took place from 8 to 17 January 1988, was twofold: to examine on the spot the situation in the occupied territories and to explore ways and means I could consider recommending to the Security Council to ensure the safety and protection of the Palestinian population of the territories.

3. Mr. Goulding had meetings with Mr. Shimon Peres, Foreign Minister of Israel, and with Mr. Yitzhak Rabin, Defense Minister, who was accompanied by Mr. Shmuel Goren, Coordinator of Government Operations in the territories, on 11 and 12 January, respectively. Further meetings took place with Mr. Peres on 14 January (in connection with Israel's deportation of Palestinian civilians the previous day) and with Mr. Goren on 17 January.

4. The Israeli Ministers stated that, as had been made clear in the Security Council, they rejected resolution 605 (1987) because the Security Council had no role to play in the security of the occupied territories, for which Israel was exclusively responsible. As was well known, Israel did not accept the applicability of the Fourth Geneva Convention in the territories. They had agreed to meet Mr. Goulding as a representative of the Secretary-General whom they regularly received and not in connection with the report requested from the Secretary-General in resolution 605 (1987). They said that Mr. Goulding was free to travel where he wished, except in areas which were under curfew or had been declared to be closed military areas, and to speak with whom he wished. It was, however, recommended that the Gaza Strip and the West Bank, and especially the refugee camps, be avoided and that contacts with Palestinians take place in Jerusalem.

5. As regards the situation in the occupied territories, the Israeli Ministers agreed that it was a serious one. The Israel Defense Forces (IDF) had been surprised by the extent of the disturbances. As a largely conscript army, trained to defend Israel against external attack, IDF lacked expertise in riot

control. The Government of Israel regretted the civilian casualties that had occurred and was taking steps to minimize such casualties in the future. But the present disorder in the refugee camps could not be tolerated and firm measures would, if necessary, be taken to suppress it. A political solution had to be found to the underlying problem and Israel remained committed to the search for a negotiated settlement. But, meanwhile, law and order had to be restored.

6. As the safety and protection of the residents of the refugee camps was a clear priority, I had of course instructed Mr. Goulding to visit some of the camps. In the event this proved difficult. Throughout the visit almost all the camps in the Gaza Strip were under curfew or had been declared to be closed military areas; the same was true of many of the camps on the West Bank.

7. On 12 January Mr. Goulding, who was accompanied by the Acting Director of Operations in Gaza of the United Nations Relief and Works Agency for Palestine Refugees in the Near East (UNRWA), was denied access by IDF to Jabalia and Beach Camps in the Gaza Strip, on the grounds that the camps were a closed military area and under curfew, respectively. They themselves decided not to pursue a visit to a third camp, Maghazi, when they judged that there was a risk that their visit would lead to a confrontation between IDF, who were deployed in some strength at the camp entrance, and an excited and angry crowd just inside. The following day a successful two-hour visit was made to Rafah camp, also in the Gaza Strip, where Mr. Goulding and his party were welcomed by several hundred of the camp residents. The latter, however, felt provoked when an IDF patrol, including an armored vehicle, approached the health centre where the visiting party was holding its meetings and a brief clash ensued, involving stone-throwing by young residents of the camp and the firing of tear gas and rubber bullets by IDF. Fortunately, there were no casualties. Further visits were paid, in the company of officials of the UNRWA West Bank operations, to Dheisheh Camp, near Bethlehem, and Balata Camp at Nablus, on 14 and 16 January 1988 respectively. The visit to Dheisheh was entirely peaceful and the visitors were able to talk to many of the refugees and tour the camp. The visit to Balata, however, had to be cut short after one hour when an IDF patrol, apparently involved in a separate incident, fired rubber bullets at the crowd accompanying the visitors, who at that point were touring the camp.

8. During these visits to refugee camps and in many meetings with groups and individuals elsewhere in the occupied territories, Mr. Goulding and his colleagues were able to discuss the situation in the territories with about 200 Palestinian men and women, of all ages and from all walks of life, ranging from intellectuals and elected mayors to the most deprived residents of the camps. All rejected the Israeli occupation of the West Bank and the Gaza Strip and insisted that the Palestinian problem was not a problem of refugees but a political problem requiring a political solution. Priority, they said,

had to be given to the negotiation of such a settlement and measures to alleviate the suffering of the civilian population should not be allowed to become a substitute for an urgent solution of the underlying political problem. All complained bitterly about Israeli practices in the occupied territories, especially the behavior of the security forces, and about the Israeli settlements and the obstruction of Palestinian economic development. It was argued that these practices had to be made known to a world which, after 20 years, seemed to have forgotten the occupied territories. There was also much criticism of the failure of the States Members of the United Nations to secure implementation of the dozens of resolutions adopted by the Security Council and the General Assembly, both on the situation in the territories and on the wider political issue of a just and lasting settlement.

9. Section I of the present report contains a brief examination of the situation in the occupied Palestinian territories. Section II discusses possible ways and means of ensuring the safety and protection of the civilian population. Section III contains some concluding remarks.

I. The Situation in the Occupied Palestinian Territories

10. Resolution 605 (1987) was adopted on 22 December 1987, following two weeks of disturbances in the West Bank, including East Jerusalem, and the Gaza Strip during which 18 Palestinians were killed and scores were injured by the Israeli security forces, who themselves suffered injuries from stones and petrol bombs. Since the resolution was adopted, the disturbances have continued and the Palestinian casualties have more than doubled, with further injuries on the Israeli side also.

11. In view of the widespread coverage that these events have received in the international press, it is not necessary to recapitulate in the present report all that has occurred during the past six weeks. It is apparent, however, that measures taken by the Israeli security forces to restore law and order in the occupied territories have not as yet succeeded. The atmosphere in the territories, and especially in the refugee camps, is marked by tension and unrest; commercial strikes are observed in almost all the towns, and most educational institutions remain shut. More than 2,000 Palestinians—many of them under the age of 16 and some as young as 11 or 12—have been detained since mid-December, and others have been placed under house or town arrest. Precise figures have not been published but it appears that several hundred of those detained have since been released. Four Palestinians were deported to Lebanon on 13 January, and five others have received deportation orders which are at present under appeal. Those most acutely affected by the disturbances have been the residents of the refugee camps, particularly those in the Gaza Strip, where normal life has been totally disrupted by curfews and the closing-off of the camps to non-residents, including relief workers.

12. Both Israelis and Palestinians told Mr. Goulding and his colleagues

that these disturbances were not an isolated phenomenon. Although it had earlier been stated in Israel that they were orchestrated from the outset by the Palestine Liberation Organization (PLO) and/or fundamentalist Islamic groups, Israeli Ministers said that they had come to the conclusion that they originated as a spontaneous outburst of protest. That this was the case was certainly the impression gained from the conversations which Mr. Goulding and his colleagues had with Palestinian inhabitants of the occupied territories. The disturbances were a reaction, supported by Palestinians of all age groups and all walks of life, to 20 years of occupation and to the lack of hope that it could be brought to an early end.

13. Without exception, the Palestinians consulted said that they rejected the Israeli occupation and complained bitterly about the practices of the Israeli security forces (which term includes IDF, the Border Police, the civilian police and the General Security Services (GSS), also known as Shin Beth). It was said that, in addition to harsh methods of riot control, random and capricious violence against individuals was normal (e.g. the beating of young bystanders who happened to be present at the scene of a stone-throwing incident or the beating, in front of his pupils, of a school teacher who refused to suspend his class to remove obstacles placed by others in the road outside). Equally common was the complaint (which was also made against officials of the Israeli Civilian Administration in the territories) that Palestinians were treated with a contempt and arrogance that seemed to be deliberately intended to humiliate them and undermine their dignity as human beings. Complaints were also made, especially in the Gaza Strip, about the inhumane manner in which curfews were enforced, e.g. the prevention of UNRWA ambulances from entering camps to collect civilians wounded in earlier disturbances. Another set of complaints related to allegations of routine violence in detention centres, as well as to the whole system of administrative detention. It was said that the purpose of interrogation was normally to extract a confession, for use in subsequent proceedings in the military courts, and that heavy physical and psychological pressure was used for this purpose by GSS, which used techniques (e.g. hooding) that left no permanent physical disfigurement.

14. In the time available, it was not possible to follow up any individual complaint in detail. But the persistence of these complaints and their ready corroboration by foreign observers (including the media) and by Palestinian professional people (some of whom said that they had themselves suffered at the hands of the security forces) give grounds for serious concern.

15. Other subjects of complaint were:

(a) The lack of outlets for political activity (there have been no elections since the municipal elections of 1976) and the tendency of the authorities to classify any expression of nationalist sentiment as "terrorist" activity, with consequent intervention of the security forces;

(b) The taking of land in the occupied territories, especially for Israeli settlements, and the privileged access that these settlements are given to water supplies;

(c) Deportations and other violations of the rights of the individual, including the blocking of family reunions;

(d) Interruption of education through the closing of schools and universities and, especially, the denial of laissez-passers for an adequate period to Palestinian students pursuing higher education in other countries;

(e) Shortcomings in the judicial system, especially the complexity of a system in which the legislation in force comes from such varied sources as the British Mandate, Egyptian and Jordanian laws and military orders (often not published) issued by Israel since 1967, the obstacles placed in the way of the defence, usually on security grounds, and the lack of a fair hearing for Palestinians in the higher Israeli courts;

(f) Heavy taxation, many of the proceeds of which benefit Israel and are not spent in the occupied territories (the budget for which is not published);

(g) Economic discrimination against the territories, with the purpose of hindering their agricultural and industrial development and keeping them as a captive market and source of cheap labour for Israel.

16. As in the case of the security forces' behavior, many examples of the above practices were cited, not only by Palestinians but also by foreign observers. They have also been described in the publications of such research institutions as The West Bank Data Base Project and Al-Haq: Law in the Service of Man.

17. At the four meetings held with Israeli Ministers and officials, the latter rejected the complaints mentioned above, describing almost all of them as politically motivated exaggerations or distortions. They said that there had been great improvements in the economic and social situation in the territories since 1967 especially as regards consumption and social services. They drew a favourable comparison between Israel's record and that of Egypt and Jordan in the 1948-1967 period. They agreed that more needed to be done to enhance the economic and social conditions of the civilian population but said that Israel had been disappointed by the paucity of the international community's response to its invitation to provide funds for the development of the territories.

18. In a conversation on 17 January, Mr. Goren said that the security forces had very strict orders against mistreatment of the civilian population; there were isolated cases in which these orders were not properly observed but such cases were severely dealt with by the Israeli authorities themselves. Mr. Goren offered to investigate any individual case that was brought to his attention. He also offered to take up any specific case of alleged obstruction of UNRWA activities by the security forces, though the latter had orders to co-ordinate on a regular basis with UNRWA over access for food and medical supplies to camps under curfew. On the economic questions, Mr. Goren said that Israel in fact spent more in the territories than it received in tax revenue and that health and education services there were better than the

Palestinians would admit. Israel wanted foreign countries to contribute to the territories' development and would give them a free hand, subject only to security requirements and observance of Israeli procedures.

19. There is thus a conflict of evidence. In almost every case, one side's version of events is at variance with the other's. This illustrates the difficulty of conducting a rigorous examination of the situation in the occupied territories. For reasons it has expressed in the past, Israel has been reluctant to co-operate with bodies previously set up by the United Nations to investigate its practices in the occupied territories, including the commission established by Security Council resolution 446 (1979), and has consistently rejected their findings. But the evidence available from published sources and from conversations with Israelis, Palestinians, and foreign observers confirms that the international community's concern about the situation in the occupied territories is fully justified.

II. Ways and Means for Ensuring the Safety and Protection of the Palestinian Civilians under Israeli Occupation

A. Need for a political settlement

20. Before exploring the ways and means that the Security Council might wish to consider for ensuring the safety and protection of the Palestinian civilians, one point of fundamental importance must be underlined. It is certainly necessary that more should be done to ensure the safety and protection of the civilian population. But such measures can only be palliatives. They cannot cure the underlying problem, which is the continuing occupation by Israel of the territories captured in the 1967 war. It was repeatedly emphasized by all shades of Palestinian opinion that there was no way in which the Israeli occupation could be made acceptable to the Palestinian people of the occupied territories. Equally, members of the Israeli Government stressed the need for a political solution. I strongly share that view. In the long run, the only certain way of ensuring the safety and protection of the Palestinian people in the occupied territories, and of the people of Israel, is the negotiation of a comprehensive, just and lasting settlement of the Arab-Israeli conflict acceptable to all concerned. An urgent effort is required by the international community, led by the Security Council, to promote an effective negotiating process and to help create the conditions necessary for it to succeed.

B. Fourth Geneva Convention

21. A second point to be stressed at this stage is that the Fourth Geneva Convention, whose applicability to the occupied territories has repeatedly been reaffirmed by the Security Council, lays down the civilian population's entitlement to safety and protection. This is clearly stated in the first paragraph of article 27, which reads:

Protected persons are entitled, in all circumstances, to respect for their persons, their honour, their family rights, their religious convictions and practices, and their manners and customs. They shall at all times be humanely treated, and shall be protected especially against all acts of violence or threats thereof and against insults and public curiosity.

The responsibility of the occupying Power is underlined in article 29, which reads:

The Party to the conflict in whose hands protected persons may be is responsible for the treatment accorded to them by its agents, irrespective of any individual responsibility which may be incurred.

22. Israeli violations of provisions of the Fourth Geneva Convention have, since 1970, been frequently alluded to in the annual reports of the International Committee of the Red Cross (ICRC), which is the guardian of the Geneva Conventions of 1949 (see, for instance the ICRC annual report for 1986). They have also been the subject of numerous resolutions of the Security Council, e.g. 452 (1979), 465 (1980), 468 (1980), 469 (1980), 471 (1980), 476 (1980) and 478 (1980). Examples, together with the articles of the Fourth Geneva Convention which they offend, are as follows:

(a) Attempts to alter the status of Jerusalem (article 47);

(b) The establishment of Israeli settlements in the occupied territories (article 49, para. 6);

(c) Deportations of Palestinian civilians from the occupied territories (article 49, para. 1);

(d) Collective punishments, e.g. curfews applied to whole districts (article 33);

(e) Destruction of houses (article 53).

There is also evidence that, in dealing with demonstrations and other disturbances, IDF has used disproportionate force, leading to fatal casualties, which could be avoided if less harsh measures were employed. As noted in paragraph 14 above, there are grounds for serious concern about whether the practices of the Israeli security forces are always consistent with article 32 of the Convention.

23. Israel has consistently taken the position that it does not accept formally the *de jure* applicability of the Fourth Geneva Convention but that it has decided since 1967 to act in *de facto* accordance with "the humanitarian provisions" of that Convention. Israel justifies this position by the argument that the Convention applies only where the Power ousted from the territory in question was a legitimate sovereign and that neither Jordan nor Egypt was the sovereign power, in the West Bank and Gaza Strip respectively, during the years preceding the 1967 war (see, for instance, the Permanent Representative of Israel's statement in the Security Council on 16 December 1987—S/PV.2774, p. 74). Israel also sometimes justifies individual violations of the Fourth Convention (e.g. deportations) by reference to legislation that

was in force in what are now the occupied territories during the British Mandate and/or the period of Egyptian/Jordanian control, from 1948 to 1967.

24. The Israeli position is not accepted by ICRC, nor has it been endorsed by the other High Contracting Parties to the Fourth Geneva Convention. Under that Convention, each Contracting State undertakes a series of unilateral engagements, *vis-à-vis* itself and at the same time *vis-à-vis* the others, of legal obligations to protect those civilians who are found in occupied territories following the outbreak of hostilities. This is why article 1 states that "The High Contracting Parties undertake to respect and to ensure respect for the present Convention *in all circumstances*" (emphasis added). The phrase "in all circumstances" is intended to include declared or undeclared war, recognized or unrecognized state of war, partial or total occupation with or without armed resistance, or even under certain circumstances when the opponent is not a contracting party (see article 2).

25. The Convention becomes automatically applicable upon the outbreak of hostilities and its application in territories occupied by the belligerents is not subject to the requirement that the ousted Power is the legitimate sovereign of the territories lost. Humanitarian considerations are the fundamental basis of the Geneva Conventions and it is for this reason that even in the case of armed conflict not of an international character (e.g. civil war) the Contracting States are legally bound under the Convention to apply, as a minimum, certain provisions of a humanitarian character.

26. Several Security Council and General Assembly resolutions (including resolution 242 (1967)) have declared the inadmissibility of the acquisition of territory by war and insisted on Israel's withdrawal from territories occupied since the 1967 war. The Security Council and the General Assembly have consistently maintained since 1967 that the territories that came under Israeli control during the 1967 war are "occupied territories" within the meaning of the Fourth Geneva Convention. Both the Security Council and the General Assembly have also stated in numerous resolutions that the Fourth Geneva Convention applies to these occupied territories. Accordingly, even though Israel does not accept the *de jure* applicability of the Fourth Geneva Convention, the *opinio juris* of the world community is that it must be applied.

27. The most effective way, pending a political settlement, of ensuring the safety and protection of the civilian population of the occupied territories would thus be for Israel to apply in full the provisions of the Fourth Geneva Convention. To this end, I recommend that the Security Council should consider making a solemn appeal to all the High Contracting Parties to the Fourth Geneva Convention that have diplomatic relations with Israel, drawing their attention to their obligation under article 1 of the Convention to ". . . ensure respect for the present Convention in all circumstances" and urging them to use all the means at their disposal to persuade the Government of Israel to change its position as regards the applicability of the Con-

vention. Meanwhile, Israel could introduce the following measures which are urgently needed:

(a) The dissemination of, and training of IDF personnel in, the rules of international humanitarian law (which is an obligation under the Convention);

(b) Orders to IDF to assist, in all circumstances, the rapid evacuation to medical care of persons wounded in disturbances, and to ensure that the efficient functioning of hospitals and their staff is not interrupted by military activities;

(c) Orders to IDF not to obstruct the delivery of essential food and medical supplies to the civilian population.

C. Different types of "protection"

28. While continuing to insist that responsibility for protection of the civilian population of the occupied territories rests with the occupying Power, the Security Council may wish to consider what other ways and means might be available to the international community, without prejudice to that fundamental principle, in order to help ensure the civilian population's protection. Before addressing that question, it may be appropriate to analyze the different concepts that can be meant by "protection." They seem to be four:

(a) "Protection" can mean physical protection, i.e. the provision of armed forces to deter, and if necessary fight, any threats to the safety of the protected persons;

(b) "Protection" can mean legal protection, i.e., intervention with the security and judicial authorities, as well as the political instances, of the occupying Power, by an outside agency, in order to ensure just treatment of an individual or group of individuals;

(c) "Protection" can also take a less well-defined form, called in this report "general assistance," in which an outside agency intervenes with the authorities of the occupying Power to help individuals or groups of individuals to resist violations of their rights (e.g. land confiscations) and to cope with the day-to-day difficulties of life under occupation, such as security restrictions, curfews, harassment, bureaucratic difficulties and so on;

(d) Finally, there is the somewhat intangible "protection" afforded by outside agencies, including especially the international media, whose mere presence and readiness to publish what they observe may have a beneficial effect for all concerned; in this report this type of protection is called "protection by publicity".

D. Ways and means available to the international community to help ensure the civilian population's protection

29. As regards *physical protection*, several of the Palestinians consulted by Mr. Goulding, especially in the refugee camps, asked that United Nations

forces should be deployed in the occupied territories, either to protect the inhabitants against the Israeli security forces or to replace the latter completely in the populated areas. The latter possibility was mentioned in the Security Council's debate preceding the adoption of resolution 605 (1987). I have given careful thought to both possibilities but they seem to present very real difficulties at this time.

30. First, the Fourth Geneva Convention gives the occupying Power the right to

> subject the population of the occupied territory to provisions which are essential to enable the occupying Power to fulfil its obligations under the present Convention, to maintain the orderly government of the territory, and to ensure the security of the occupying Power, of the members and property of the occupying forces or administration, and likewise of the establishments and lines of communication used by them (article 64, para. 2).

This in effect makes the occupying Power responsible for the maintenance of law and order. It is also, as discussed above, responsible for protecting the civilian population. The introduction of other forces into the occupied territories to provide physical protection would thus detract from the occupying Power's responsibilities under the Fourth Geneva Convention.

31. Secondly, it is a principle of United Nations peace-keeping operations that they require the prior consent of the parties to the conflict concerned. The introduction of United Nations forces into the occupied territories (unless the Security Council had decided to take enforcement action under Chapter VII of the Charter of the United Nations) would thus require the consent of the Government of Israel. That Government has, however, stated that it will not agree to any involvement of United Nations military personnel in the security of the occupied territories.

32. Unless there is a change in Israel's position, the deployment of United Nations forces in the territories is thus not practicable at present. This idea should not, however, be lost sight of. Israel has in the past accepted international forces in other contexts of the Arab-Israeli conflict and these have played a valuable role in the implementation of interim or permanent agreements. Such forces could again be a valuable ingredient in the implementation of a negotiated settlement of the conflict or in transitional arrangements that might be agreed upon for the occupied territories.

33. Reference has also been made to the possible deployment of United Nations military observers in the occupied territories. They would not however be able to provide physical protection and their possible role is therefore discussed in paragraph 42 below.

34. A measure of *legal protection* is nevertheless provided to the population of the occupied territories by ICRC. As is clear from its annual reports, ICRC enjoys co-operation from the occupying Power in its efforts to protect detained persons but the Israeli authorities usually disallow interventions by

ICRC with regard to measures for the maintenance of law and order and aspects of the administration of the occupied territories which violate the provisions of the Fourth Geneva Convention.

35. ICRC is to be commended for its activities in the occupied territories and the High Contracting Parties to the Fourth Geneva Convention may wish to include in the diplomatic initiative put forward in paragraph 27 above an expression of appreciation for the co-operation extended to ICRC by Israel and of hope that this will be maintained and enlarged.

36. The Security Council may also wish to urge Member States to respond generously if ICRC should appeal for funds to finance the extra activities it is undertaking in the occupied territories in response to the recent very large increase in the number of detained persons.

37. I come now to the type of protection described as *general assistance* in paragraph 28 above. Various agencies are already active in this field. As far as the registered refugees are concerned, UNRWA has the leading role and provides a wide variety of assistance and protection (in addition, of course, to its main function of providing education, health and relief services); in the Gaza Strip, in particular, it provides indispensable support to the refugees in their day-to-day efforts to cope with living under occupation. ICRC also assists, especially with the families of detainees; many voluntary agencies, Palestinian and international, also play a part. It was nevertheless argued by many of the Palestinians and foreign relief workers who were consulted that the international community should do more.

38. In the case of the registered refugees, who number 818,983, or about 55 per cent of the Palestinian population of the occupied territories, UNRWA is clearly best placed to provide additional general assistance. UNRWA has been established on the ground for nearly forty years; it knows well the refugees' problems; it is accepted by the Israeli authorities on the basis of an agreement signed in 1967; and it is trusted by the refugees. However, the number of UNRWA international staff in the field has declined over the years. Before the recent disturbances began, there were only 9 international staff in the West Bank (373,586 refugees and 19 camps) and only 6 in the Gaza Strip (445,397 refugees and 8 camps). In paying tribute to the invaluable service that UNRWA Palestinian staff have been rendering to the refugees in very difficult circumstances, I believe that international staff can at present play an especially valuable role. It is usually easier for them to gain access to Israeli authorities in emergency situations; and their mere presence at points of confrontation has a significant impact on how the civilian population (including UNRWA Palestinian staff) is treated by the security forces and helps it psychologically by making it feel less exposed.

39. I have therefore asked the Commissioner-General of UNRWA to examine the addition to UNRWA establishment in the occupied territories of extra international staff, within UNRWA existing administrative structures, to improve the general assistance provided to the refugee population. It

would be for the Commissioner-General to decide the number and location of these additional international staff, in the light of the perceived need and the resources available. I would also urge Member States to respond generously to the appeal the Commissioner-General would have to make for funds to finance these additional staff.

40. It is also essential that Israel should honor UNRWA privileges and immunities in full, especially the right of its personnel to freedom of movement in all circumstances and the inviolability of its premises and installations, and to provide access at all times to responsible officials of the occupying administration. Mr. Goulding and his colleagues were witnesses of painful situations in the Gaza Strip where the curfews imposed by IDF had made it impossible, or at best difficult and dangerous, for UNRWA to evacuate the wounded and sick to hospital or to deliver food to the camps.

41. In making these observations relating to UNRWA, I am conscious of the need not to neglect those Palestinians in the occupied territories who are not registered refugees (about one third of the Palestinian population in Gaza and two thirds in the West Bank). Their economic and social circumstances are in general superior to those of the refugees, especially the camp residents, but they face the same political frustrations as the latter, are equally vulnerable to the security authorities and also suffer from the economic and administrative aspects of the occupation. They benefit from the activities of ICRC (which makes no distinction between refugees and non-refugees) and various voluntary agencies, but are normally excluded from UNRWA mandate. It seems desirable in present circumstances that, as on certain occasions in the past, the Commissioner-General should be permitted to provide humanitarian assistance as far as practicable, on an emergency basis and as a temporary measure, to non-refugees who are in serious need of assistance because of the recent disturbances.

42. Reference has been made in paragraph 33 above to the possible deployment of United Nations military observers. Some of the Palestinians consulted favoured this measure as a way of monitoring (and hopefully restraining) the activities of the Israeli security forces and of providing general assistance to the civilian population. It is true that such observers could provide expert information on military matters (though they would need at least some co-operation from the occupying Power for this purpose). But in other respects, especially their short tours of duty and lack of familiarity with the territories, they are not well placed to provide general assistance of an essentially civilian character. In any case, Israel, whose consent would be necessary, has so far expressed firm opposition to any such proposal.

43. As regards *protection by publicity*, great emphasis was laid by Palestinians on the need to publicize the situation in the occupied territories. It was argued that more publicity should be given and that this would have a beneficial influence both on Israel's practices in the territories and on her readiness to negotiate a political settlement. Recent developments in the territories have in fact been fully reported by the Israeli and international media

and it is of great importance that the latter should continue to have unhindered access to events.

44. Some of the Palestinians consulted suggested that the Secretary-General might appoint a kind of United Nations ombudsman to reside in the occupied territories. Such an appointment could be a valuable step if Israel was ready to co-operate fully with the official concerned and use his or her good offices in handling the many problems to which the occupation gives rise. This idea is in the same category as other possibilities, such as United Nations trusteeship or a United Nations interim administration, which could be of potential value in the future. But the practicability of all these ideas depends on the full consent and co-operation of Israel.

E. Economic and social conditions of the population of the occupied territories

45. Although it is strictly outside the "safety and protection" referred to in paragraph 6 of resolution 605 (1987), I should like to take the opportunity of this report to make two observations relating to the economic and social conditions in which the population of the occupied territories lives.

46. The first relates to the refugee camps. The recent disturbances have attracted world attention to the squalid living conditions in many of the camps, especially in the Gaza Strip, resulting from the lack of such basic amenities as paved roads, sewage, water, lighting and housing of a minimum standard. The Commissioner-General of UNRWA has also referred in his last report[1] to the urgent need to rehabilitate many UNRWA installations, such as schools, health centres and food distribution centres.

47. In the past, the refugees have sometimes expressed reservations about measures to improve the infrastructure of the camps, for fear that these would make the camps more permanent and thus conflict with their insistence on a political settlement in accordance with United Nations resolutions. This matter was therefore discussed with most of the Palestinians consulted. Their reaction was that they would welcome steps to improve conditions in the camps provided that:

(a) It was made absolutely clear that this was a temporary measure, pending a comprehensive political settlement, and not a substitute for such a settlement;

(b) That the work was done by UNRWA.

48. In these circumstances, I have asked the Commissioner-General of UNRWA to prepare urgently proposals for improving the infrastructure of the camps, and to seek the necessary funds. I would again urge Member States to respond generously to such a request.

49. My second observation relates to the wider economic situation in the occupied territories. Reference has been made in paragraph 15 above to the conviction of the Palestinian population that Israeli policy is deliberately to

[1] *Official Records of the General Assembly, Forty-second Session, Supplement No. 13* (A/42/13).

obstruct the economic development of the territories. Many examples were given to corroborate this assertion. Israeli Ministers and officials, however, insisted that it was unfounded and that Israel welcomed foreign assistance for the development of the territories provided only that each project complied with Israel's security requirements, which were overriding, and with Israeli procedures. Many of the Palestinians consulted expressed the hope that a concerted international effort could be undertaken to revive the territories' economy, perhaps initially through an expansion of the existing program of the United Nations Development Programme (UNDP) in the territories. I have asked the Administrator of UNDP to study this possibility.

III. Concluding Remarks

50. The Israeli authorities have stated on numerous occasions in recent weeks that security in the occupied territories remains their exclusive responsibility. The Security Council, for its part, has repeatedly reaffirmed the applicability to the occupied territories of the Fourth Geneva Convention relative to the Protection of Civilian Persons in Time of War of 12 August 1949. While that Convention makes the occupying Power responsible for maintaining law and order, its raison d'être is the safety and protection of the civilian population, for which the occupying Power is no less responsible.

51. My principal recommendation in this area is that that the international community should make a concerted effort to persuade Israel to accept the *de jure* applicability of the Fourth Geneva Convention to the occupied territories and to correct its practices in order to comply fully with that Convention. This report also makes recommendations and describes certain steps which I am taking, within existing arrangements, to improve the safety and protection accorded to the population of the territories by the international community.

52. It cannot be emphasized too strongly, however, that such measures to enhance the safety and protection of the Palestinian people of the territories, urgently required though they are, will neither remove the causes of the tragic events which prompted Security Council resolution 605 (1987) nor bring peace to the region. The unrest of the past six weeks has been an expression of the despair and hopelessness felt by the population of the occupied territories, more than half of whom have known nothing but an occupation that denies what they consider to be their legitimate rights. The result is a tragedy for both sides. Nothing illustrates this more clearly than the daily sight of young unarmed Palestinians in confrontation with Israeli soldiers of their own age.

53. The underlying problem can only be resolved through a political settlement which responds both to the refusal of the Palestinian population of the territories to accept a future under Israeli occupation and to Israel's determination to ensure its security and the well-being of its people. I con-

tinue to believe that this should be achieved through a comprehensive, just and lasting settlement based on Security Council resolutions 242 (1967) and 338 (1973) and taking fully into account the legitimate rights of the Palestinian people, including self-determination. Such a settlement should be negotiated by means of an international conference under United Nations auspices, with the participation of all the parties concerned. The history of the Arab-Israeli conflict, from 1948 onwards, has repeatedly shown that there are many ways in which the United Nations can contribute impartially both to the negotiation of agreements and to their implementation. Allusion has been made in this report to the possible use of United Nations forces or other interim arrangements as progress is made towards a comprehensive settlement.

54. The negotiation of the settlement will, of course, be exceptionally difficult, for it will require all concerned to move from positions to which they are at present very strongly attached. I am conscious of the great complexity of the choices which confront them and I should like to take this opportunity to appeal to them to exercise restraint and to bring about that change of attitudes which will be necessary if a settlement is to be negotiated. Each side must put aside the often justified resentment it feels at past wrongs and understand better the legitimate interests and legitimate grievances of the other. Such understanding is not assisted by invective and abuse nor by sheltering behind the illusion that the other side does not exist. Equally, I appeal to the international community to help, both by reducing the virulence of debates on the Arab-Israel conflict and by consciously acting in a manner which promotes mutual understanding.

55. As stated earlier in this report, I believe that an urgent effort is required by the international community, led by the Security Council, to promote an effective negotiating process. This is what the Charter requires and it is the fundamental recommendation in this report. I remain personally committed to the search for a settlement and will contribute in any way that I can to that objective. In the coming weeks I intend to explore actively with the parties and with the members of the Council, especially its permanent members, how the present impasse in the peace process can be unblocked. After the recent dramatic demonstration of the dangers and suffering inherent in the *status quo*, I hope that all concerned will join in an effort to reinvigorate the search for a comprehensive, just and lasting settlement. This alone will secure the interests of both the Israeli and the Palestinian peoples and enable them to live in peace with each other.

D. Natural Resources in the Occupied Territories

366. General Assembly Resolution 37/122 on Israel's Decision to Build a Canal Linking the Mediterranean Sea to the Dead Sea, December 16, 1982*

---

* G.A. Res. 122, 37 U.N. GAOR Supp. (No. 51) at 107, U.N. Doc. A/37/ 51 (1982). *See also* subsequent resolutions, G.A. Res. 85, 38 U.N. GAOR Supp. (No. 47) at 112, U.N. Doc. A/38/47 (1983), and G.A. Res. 101, 39 U.N. GAOR Supp. (No. 51) at 120, U.N. Doc. A/39/51 (1984).

The General Assembly,

Recalling its resolution 36/150 of 16 December 1981,

Recalling the rules and principles of international law relative to the fundamental rights and duties of States,

Bearing in mind the principles of international law relative to belligerent occupation of land, including the Geneva Convention relative to the Protection of Civilian Persons in Time of War, of 12 August 1949,[46] and reaffirming their applicability to all Arab territories occupied since 1967, including Jerusalem,

Taking note of the report of the Secretary-General,[49]

Recognizing that the proposed canal, to be constructed partly through the Gaza Strip, a Palestinian territory occupied in 1967, would violate the principles of international law and affect the interests of the Palestinian people,

Confident that the canal linking the Mediterranean Sea with the Dead Sea, if constructed by Israel, will cause direct, serious and irreparable damage to Jordan's rights and legitimate vital interests in the economic, agricultural, demographic and ecological fields,

Noting with regret the non-compliance by Israel with General Assembly resolution 36/150,

1. *Deplores* Israel's non-compliance with General Assembly resolution 36/150;

2. *Emphasizes* that the canal linking the Mediterranean Sea with the Dead Sea, if constructed, is a violation of the rules and principles of international law, especially those relating to the fundamental rights and duties of States and to belligerent occupation of land;

3. *Demands* that Israel not construct this canal and cease forthwith all actions and/or plans taken towards the implementation of this project;

4. *Calls upon* all States, specialized agencies, governmental and non-governmental organizations not to assist, directly or indirectly, in preparations for and execution of this project and strongly urges national, international and multinational corporations to do likewise;

5. *Requests* the Secretary-General to monitor and assess, on a continuing basis and through a competent expert organ, all aspects—juridical, political, economic, ecological and demographic—of the adverse effects on Jordan and on the Arab territories occupied since 1967, including Jerusalem, arising from the implementation of the Israeli decision to construct this canal and to forward the findings of that organ on a regular basis to the General Assembly;

[46] United Nations, *Treaty Series*, vol. 75, No. 973, p. 287.

[49] A/37/328-S/15277 and Corr.1. For the printed text, see *Official Records of the Security Council, Thirty-seventh Year, Supplement for April, May and June 1982*, document S/15277.

6. *Requests* the Secretary-General to report to the General Assembly at its thirty-eighth session on the implementation of the present resolution;

7. *Decides* to include in the provisional agenda of its thirty-eighth session the item entitled "Israel's decision to build a canal linking the Mediterranean Sea to the Dead Dea".

108th plenary meeting
16 December 1982

367. General Assembly Resolution 37/135 on Permanent Sovereignty Over National Resources in the Occupied Palestinian and Other Arab Territories, December 17, 1982*

* G.A. Res. 135, 37 U.N. GAOR Supp. (No. 51) at 111, U.N. Doc. A/37/51 (1982). *See also* subsequent resolution, G.A. Res. 144, 38 U.N. GAOR Supp. (No. 47) at 117, U.N. Doc. A/38/47 (1983).

The General Assembly,

Recalling its resolutions 3175 (XXVIII) of 17 December 1973, 3336 (XXIX) of 17 December 1974, 3516 (XXX) of 15 December 1975, 31/186 of 21 December 1976, 32/161 of 19 December 1977, 34/136 of 14 December 1979, 35/110 of 5 December 1980 and 36/173 of 17 December 1981 on permanent sovereignty over national resources in the occupied Palestinian and other Arab territories,

Recalling also its previous resolutions on permanent sovereignty over natural resources, particularly their provisions supporting resolutely the efforts of the developing countries and the peoples of territories under colonial and racial domination and foreign occupation in their struggle to regain effective control over their natural and all other resources, wealth and economic activities,

Bearing in mind the relevant principles of international law and the provisions of the international conventions and regulations, in particular Convention IV of the Hague of 1907,[4] and the fourth Geneva Convention of 12 August 1949,[5] concerning the obligations and responsibilities of the occupying Power,

Bearing in mind also the pertinent provisions of its resolutions 3201 (S-VI) and 3202 (S-VI) of 1 May 1974, containing the Declaration and the Programme of Action on the Establishment of a New International Economic Order, and 3281 (XXIX) of 12 December 1974, containing the Charter of Economic Rights and Duties of States,

Regretting that the report of the Secretary-General on permanent sovereignty over national resources in the occupied Palestinian and other Arab territories, requested in General Assembly resolution 36/173, was not submitted,

1. *Condemns* Israel for its exploitation of the national resources of the occupied Palestinian and other Arab territories;

2. *Emphasizes* the right of the Palestinian and other Arab peoples whose territories are under Israeli occupation to full and effective permanent sovereignty and control over their natural and all other resources, wealth and economic activities;

3. *Reaffirms* that all measures undertaken by Israel to exploit the human, natural and all other resources, wealth and economic activities in the occupied Palestinian and other Arab territories are illegal and calls upon Israel to desist immediately from such measures;

4. *Further reaffirms* the right of the Palestinian and other Arab peoples subjected to Israeli aggression and occupation to the restitution of and full compensation for the exploitation, depletion and loss of and damages to

---

[4] Carnegie Endowment for International Peace, *The Hague Conventions and Declarations of 1899 and 1907* (New York, Oxford University Press), 1915, p. 100.

[5] United Nations, *Treaty Series*, vol. 75, No. 973, p. 287.

their natural, human and all other resources, wealth and economic activities, and calls upon Israel to meet their just claims;

5. *Calls upon* all States to support the Palestinian and other Arab peoples in the exercise of their above-mentioned rights;

6. *Calls upon* all States, international organizations, specialized agencies, business corporations and all other institutions not to recognize, or co-operate with or assist in any manner in, any measures undertaken by Israel to exploit the national resources of the occupied Palestinian and other Arab territories or to effect any changes in the demographic composition, the character and form of use of their natural resources or the institutional structure of those territories;

7. *Requests* the Secretary-General to prepare and submit to the General Assembly at its thirty-eighth session, through the Economic and Social Council, the two reports requested in Assembly resolution 36/173.

109th plenary meeting
17 December 1982

368. Economic Activity and Access to Natural Resources:
Legal Restrictions on Access to Land and Water in Israel,
June 20, 1983*

* Report to the U.N. International Conference on the Question of Palestine, Geneva, U.N. Doc. A/Conf. 114/6.

CONTENTS

INTRODUCTION

The object of this paper is to unveil the structures of legal exclusivity in Israel, as legislated by the Israeli Parliament (Knesset), regarding access to the national resources of land and water inside pre-1967 Israel. Zionism is Irael's [*sic*] system, and the key legal distinction in Zionist legislation in Israel is between "Jew" and "non-Jew". This key distinction in the foundation of the body of Israeli law is, however, constructed as a two-tier structure, which has veiled Israeli separatist legislation for more than three decades.

The first tier, the level at which the distinction between "Jew" and "non-Jew" is rendered openly and explicitly, is contained in the constitutions and articles of association of all institutions of the Zionist movement, such as the World Zionist Organization (WZO), the Jewish Agency for the Land of Israel (JA) and the Jewish National Fund (JNF).

Thus, the Constitution of the Jewish Agency stipulated:

> Land is to be acquired as Jewish property and . . . the title of the lands acquired is to be taken in the name of the JNF to the end that the same shall be held the inalienable property of the Jewish people. The Agency shall promote agricultural colonization based on Jewish labour, and in all works or undertakings carried out or furthered by the Agency, it shall be deemed to be a matter of principle that Jewish labour shall be employed. (Article 3(d) & (e)).

Similarly a Memorandum of Association of the Keren Kayemeth Leisrael (JNF), as incorporated in Israel in 1954, defines the primary object of the Israeli Company:

> To purchase, acquire on lease or in exchange etc. . . . in the prescribed region (which expression shall in this Memorandum mean the State of Israel in any area within the jurisdiction of the Government of Israel)

or any part thereof for the purpose of settling Jews on such lands and properties. (Article 3(a)).

The second tier is the level at which the distinction between "Jew" and "non-Jew" is incorporated into the laws of the State of Israel.

After the establishment of the State of Israel, the exclusivist constitutional stipulation of the WZO, JA and the JNF were incorporated into the body of the Israeli law. Thus, organizations and bodies which prior to 1948 could credibly claim to be voluntary, have been incorporated, following the introduction of the legislation listed below, into the legal, compulsory judicial state machinery. These laws are as follows:

1950: Law of Return
       Absentees' Property Law
       Development Authority Law
1952: World Zionist Organization—Jewish Agency Status Law
1953: Keren Kayemeth Leisrael (Jewish National Fund) Law
       Land Acquisition (Validations of Acts and Compensation) Law
1954: Covenant between the Government of Israel and the Zionist Executive, also known as the Executive of the Jewish Agency for the Land of Israel
1958: Prescription Law
1960: Basic Law: Israel Lands
       Israel Lands Law
       Israel Lands Administration Law
1961: Covenant Between the Government of Israel and the National Fund
1967: Agricultural Settlement (Restriction on Use of Agricultural Land and Water) Law
1980: Lands (Allocation of Rights to Foreigners) Law

Legislated together with the laws listed above were the unlimited powers of the requisition of lands and property; these powers are vested in the Israeli authorities under the various Defence (Emergency) Regulations, 1945 and Ordinances in force since 1948/49. These are, *inter alia*:

* Defence (Emergency) Regulations, 1945
* Emergency (Security Zones) Regulations, 1949
* Requisitioning of Property in Times of Emergency Law, 1949
* Emergency Regulations (Cultivation of Waste Lands) Ordinance, 1949

Through this mechanism an all-encompassing exclusivist system could be legislated in Israel without overtly resorting to explicit and frequent legal categorization of "Jew" vs. "non-Jew".

With the exception of the Law of Return (1950), none of the above laws resort in the text to distinction between "Jew" and "non-Jew". For instance, the Israeli Parliament through its WZO-JA Status Law (1952), committed the State of Israel by law to secure a monopolistic concession in the areas of "settlement projects in Israel" to an organization that is constitutionally restricted to promote and benefit Jewish citizens alone; the organization deemed it a matter of principle that only Jewish labour would be in its employ.

Similarly, Israel Lands Law and Israel Lands Administration Law (1960) are predicated on this same legal duplicity, as articulated by the Minister of Religious Affairs and Chairman of the Constitution, Law and Justice Committee, Zerah Wahrhaftig, when presenting the Basic Law:

> ... [W]hat is it that we want? We want something that is difficult to define. We want to make clear that the Land of Israel belongs to the people of Israel. The "people of Israel" is a concept that is broader than that of the "people resident in Zion", because the people of Israel live throughout the world. On the other hand, every law that is passed is for the benefit of all the residents of the State and all the residents of the state also include people who do not belong to the people of Israel ... Knesset Debates, Session 138-39, Fourth Knesset, 19 July 1960, pp. 1916, 1920).

Thus, without resorting in the legal text to an explicit distinction between "Jew" and "non-Jew", it was made possible in the State of Israel to prohibit non-Jews, and in the first instance the Palestinian Arab native population of the country, from purchase or lease of 92.4 per cent of pre-1967 Israel territory.

The same legal structures apply to access to water resources. The Israeli Parliament legislates laws which to the uninformed seem universal laws, not overtly "Jewish" laws (with few exceptions, notably the Law of Return, 1950). But at all key junctures that determine everyday life and the circumstances of living for the body of the inhabitants under Israeli rule, the legislature endorses covenants that secure monopolistic concessions in administration, development and control to organizations constitutionally committed to promote Jewish interests exclusively. This is separatism. zionism as a form of racism and racial discrimination was pronounced by the United Nations General Assembly in 1975.

LEGAL RESTRICTIONS ON ACCESS TO LAND: JEWISH NATIONAL FUND, ISRAEL LANDS ADMINISTRATION, AND HISTADRUT GENERAL FEDERATION OF WORKERS IN THE LAND OF ISRAEL[1]

The Jewish National Fund

On May 14th, 1948 Israel was declared a "Jewish" State, not a "sovereign, independent" State. Indeed the document popularly known as Israel's

---

[1] Pages 10-19 on the Jewish National Fund (JNF) include slightly edited excerpts from Uri Davis and Walter Lehn, "And the Fund still lives: the role of the Jewish National Fund in the determination of Israel's land policies", *Journal of Palestine Studies*, vol. VII, No. 4, 1978.

"Declaration of Independence" is not officially so identified; it is called the Declaration of the Establishment of the State of Israel. The difference does not reflect a casual oversight.[1a] Those who formulated the draft consciously avoided words that would have specified the sovereignty and independence of the proposed State, emphasizing only its Jewishness.[2]

Immediately after the establishment of the State, the following question was raised:

Is the existence of the [World] Zionist Organization, whose main objective has apparently been realized, still justified? Has the Zionist Organization not ended its historic mission, and have not all its functions been handed over to the newly-born state?[3]

It is from the ensuing debate that we discover why Israel was declared a Jewish and not an independent, sovereign Jewish state:

Berl Locker (Chairman of the Zionist Executive): Today there is a need for a larger and stronger Zionist movement, more so than at any other time . . . The Zionist movement is needed not only for the Jews who ought to come to the country, but for the very existence of the state . . . A Zionist movement and I emphasize the word movement—is necessary, because the destiny of the entire people must be borne by them; it must not be the object of custodianship, not even that of the State of Israel. It is necessary that the Jewish people, for whom the State of Israel was created—and this state was created to be their homeland— themselves and through their strength forge their destiny and be the bearers of their own history . . .[4]

In short, the State of Israel was established as a Jewish state and not as a sovereign, independent Jewish state, because only under the former definition is it a state by, for, and of the "Jewish people" throughout the world;

[1a] I am indebted for this insight to Akivah Orr, who has elaborated this point in his lecture and in his forthcoming book on Israel, *Zionism and Jewish Identity.*

[2] Significantly, the borders of the State were left intentionally undefined, the relevant discussion was summarized by David Ben Gurion: "There was a discussion of this matter in the People's Executive. There was a proposal to determine borders, and there was opposition to this proposal. We decided to *evade* (and I choose this word intentionally) the matter for a simple reason: if the United Nations fulfils all its resolutions and undertakings and maintains the peace and prevents bombardments and uses its powers to execute its own resolutions, then we on our part (and I express the opinion of the people) will honour all the resolutions in their entirety. So far the UN has not done so . . . Therefore, we are not bound by anything, and we left this matter open. We did not say, NO United Nations border; but neither did we say the opposite. We left this matter open for developments". *Ibid.,* p. 19; emphasis in original.

[3] The Executive of the World Zionist Organization, *Problems of the Zionist Organization with the Establishment of the State. Summary of the Debate on Ideological and Organizational Problems of the Movement.* (Jerusalem, 1950, in Hebrew) vol. I, p. 2; mimeographed, Central Zionist Archives (CZA) 11.149.

[4] *Ibid.,* p. 4.

under the latter definition it would be a state by, for, and of its Jewish citizens.

This was the first step in regularizing the legal status of the various Zionist institutions in the newly-established Jewish State of Israel. The Status Law makes the World Zionist Organization (WZO) responsible for "settlement projects in the state" (section 3) and authorizes it to co-ordinate "the activities in Israel of Jewish institutions and organizations active in . . . development and settlement of the country" (4). Prominent among these Jewish institutions—"various bodies" (8), "funds and other institutions" (12) of the WZO—is, of course, the JNF, over which the WZO holds absolute control.[5] In addition the law identifies the Jewish Agency (JA) with the WZO (3 and 7).[6] This takes on added significance when the Constitution of the JA is recalled; article 3 (d) and (e) states:

> Land is to be acquired as Jewish property, and . . . the title to the lands acquired is to be taken in the name of the JNF, to the end that the same shall be held as the inalienable property of the Jewish people.

> The Agency shall promote agricultural colonization based on Jewish labour, and in all works or undertakings carried out or furthered by the Agency, it shall be deemed to be a matter of principle that Jewish labour shall be employed . . .[7]

Thus the activities of the WZO, the JA, and the JNF are essentially specialized functions of one and the same organization recognized as an equal of the Israeli state.

The next step was taken in November 1953 with the adoption of the Keren Kayemeth Leisrael law,[8] which authorized the Minister of Justice "to approve the Memorandum and Articles of Association of a company limited by guarantee to be submitted to him by the Existing Company [the JNF incorporated in England] for the establishment of a body incorporated in Israel with a view to continuing the activities of the Existing Company that had been founded and incorporated in the diaspora" (section 2). The new company's Memorandum and Articles of Association were approved by Minister of Justice Pinhas Rosen on May 9, 1954,[9] thereby establishing an Israeli company called Keren Kayemeth Leisrael.

Shortly after the establishment of the Israeli company in July 1954, the

---

[5] For details of the mechanisms of this control, see Walter Lehn, "The Jewish National Fund", *Journal of Palestine Studies*, vol. 3, No. 4, 1974, p. 82.

[6] Thus Ben Halpern identifies with justice the JA as "another name for the Zionist Organization". *The Idea of the Jewish State*, 2nd ed. (Cambridge, Mass., 1969), p. 195.

[7] *Constitution of the Jewish Agency for Palestine* (London, 1929), pp. 4-5.

[8] Adopted by the Knesset on 23 November 1953; the text of this law, (along with other relevant material) is available in *"Report on the Legal Structure, Activities, Assets, Income and Liabilities of the Keren Kayemeth Leisrael"*, Jewish National Fund (Jerusalem, 1973) pp. 49-51, (hereafter, *Report on the JNF*).

[9] *Ibid.*, p. 55.

Covenant referred to in the WZO-JA (Status) Law[10] was signed by Moshe Sharett for the Government and Nahum Goldmann and Berl Locker for the Zionist Executive. Although the relationships between the Government and the WZO in Israel were clarified by the Covenant, it was still necessary to define the role and activities within Israel of the JNF, the largest and most influential Zionist institution. This initiative was taken by the JNF, whose Board of Directors meeting jointly with the JA Executive on March 13, 1955 adopted a resolution calling for the establishment of a "common institution for national lands".[11] With the backing of the Twenty-fourth Zionist Congress (Jerusalem, 1956), the JNF and the Government eventually agreed on the wording and intent of the "Israel Lands" laws,[12] the role of the JNF in the implementation of these, and the relationship of the JNF to the State. The most significant result was the extension of the JNF's restrictive land-holding and leasing policies to all state lands—now identified as Israel or national lands—a consequence for which the JNF takes credit.

The negotiations between the Government and the JNF were concluded in August 1960 by a memorandum signifying agreement in principle "to observe the regulations of the Covenant to be signed by the Government and the JNF, the formal endorsement of which will be effected after the clarification of certain legal problems relating to the status of the JNF."[13] This new Covenant, signed in Jerusalem on November 28, 1961, details the agreed terms of implementation of the Israel-lands laws adopted by the Knesset in July 1960. It is an agreement "between the State of Israel, represented for this purpose by the Minister of Finance, and the JNF—with the sanction of the WZO—represented for this purpose by the Chairman of the Board of Directors of the JNF".[14]

Nevertheless, despite the extensive legislation, the JNF remained unwilling to transfer its land title to the state. Some insight into the reasons for this may be afforded by the explanation given to the Twenty-third Zionist Congress (Jerusalem, 1951) as to why the JNF, and not the state, should acquire title to the abandoned lands made available through "the triumph of the *Haganah* [pre-state Jewish Army] and the flight of the Arabs". The JNF "will redeem the lands and will turn them over to the Jewish people—

[10] Section 7: "Details of the status of the WZO—whose representation is the Zionist Executive, also known as the Executive of the JA—and the form of its co-operation with the Government shall be determined by a Covenant to be made in Israel between the Government and the Zionist Executive".

[11] *The New Partnership* (Jerusalem, JNF Department of Public Relations, 1960) (in Hebrew). This pamphlet provides a useful and generally accurate calendar of events from 1955-60, detailing the development of the Israel Land Laws and the 1960 agreement between the Government and the JNF.

[12] *Basic Law, Israel Lands*, adopted by the Knesset on 19 July 1960. *Israel Lands Law* (1960) and *Israel Lands Administration Law* (1960), both adopted on 25 July 1960, texts of these laws, *Report on the JNF*, pp. 86-94.

[13] *Ha-aretz*, 2 August 1960.

[14] Preamble to the Covenant, *Report on the JNF*, p. 78, full text of the Covenant, pp. 78-83.

to the people and not the state, which in the current composition of population cannot be an adequate guarantor of Jewish ownership".[15]

As a consequence of the 1960 Israel Lands laws, the 1960 Memorandum of Agreement, and the 1961 Covenant between the Government and the JNF, "the State of Israel adopted the JNF guidelines for all publicly-owned lands, i.e., for over 90 per cent of the area included in Israel's borders at that date".[16] This claim by the JNF appears to be warranted, and in full accord with the entent of the land laws.[17]

Only three JNF agrarian principles are mentioned prominently: (1) "public ownership", (2) "inalienability of the soil", and hence use of the land only through (3) "hereditary leaseholds" which "run for periods of 49 years and can be automatically renewed".[18] Less prominent is another JNF principle, (4) "the stipulation of Jewish labour on JNF land".[19] A fifth principle not made explicit at all and rarely is in Zionist literature: (5) the lessee must be Jewish.

The phrase "over 90 per cent" occurs repeatedly in JNF sources[20] when referring to *public* or *national* or *Israel* lands. Rather different meanings are ascribed to these terms in Zionist usage where "person" is read as "Jewish person", "public" as "Jewish public", "the people" as "the Jewish people", "nation" as "Jewish nation", and "Israel" as the "people of Israel", i.e., the community of adherents to Judaism, to be distinguished from the citizens of the State of Israel, and even from the Jewish citizens of the State of Israel.

More precise figures are given in the *Report* of the Israel Lands Administration for 1961-62:

Land Ownership

Land ownership in Israel is divided into four categories: State, Development Authority, JNF, and private. Private ownership is in turn divided into Jewish and minorities.

---

[15] *Report on the Activities of the Keren Kayemeth Leisrael,* Jewish National Fund, September 1946-August 1951. Submitted to the 23rd Zionist Congress, Jerusalem, August 1951 (Jerusalem, 1951), pp. 32-33.

[16] Efraim Orni, *Agrarian Reform and Social Progress in Israel,* (Jerusalem, JNF, 1974), p. 87.

[17] *Ibid.,* p. 7, similarly p. 27.

[18] *Ibid.,* pp. 28, 36-37. See also Abraham Granott, *The Land System in Palestine: History and Structure,* (London, 1952), p. 319: "The land is leased for forty-nine years, when the lessee is at liberty to renew the lease for a like period. Practically, therefore the period is one of ninety-eight years, the space of three generations, sufficient to allow the passing of the property by inheritance from fathers to children." While not requiring, this certainly invites the interpretation that the 49-year lease is renewable only once, yielding the total of 98 years.

[19] Orni, *op. cit.,* p. 62; cf. also pp. 45, 63.

[20] E.g., Orni, *op. cit.,* pp. 7, 27, 32, 68, 87; similarly in numerous JNF pamphlets, e.g., a JNF calendar-pamphlet. *JNF in Thirty Years of Statehood,* (Jerusalem, 1968). An exception is the JNF pamphlet. *Seventy Years in Facts and Figures* (Jerusalem, 1971), where the figure is "92 per cent of the state's surface prior to June 1967".

State and Development Authority lands	15,205,000	dunams
JNF lands	3,570,000	"
(National lands total)	18,775,000	"
Privately-owned lands	1,480,000	"
TOTAL	20,255,000	"

It follows that national lands concentrated under the administration of the Israel Lands Administration represent 92.6 per cent of the total area of the State.[21]

Based on this information it can be concluded that privately owned lands now represent at most 7.4 per cent of the area of pre-1967 Israel, the majority of which is reported to be owned by Arabs.[22] The Arabs, however, are excluded by law from most of the area of Israel, from the 92.6 per cent designated national lands.[23]

Until the establishment of the State of Israel in 1948 one could present the WZO and its various executive arms, e.g., the Jewish Agency for the Land of Israel and the Jewish National Fund as voluntary confessional associations constitutionally limited to cultivate and promote confessional interests under any given political regime, both within and outside Palestine. It is interesting that in their capacity as voluntary confessional associations, the success of the various Zionist agencies in Palestine was fairly limited. The JNF, for instance, since its incorporation in London in 1907 and throughout its activity from the Ottoman and British Mandate regimes until 1948, failed to puchase any more than 936,000 dunams,[24] namely some 3.5 per cent of 1922 Mandate Palestine or some 5 per cent of pre-1967 Israel territory.

Israel Lands Administration (ILA)

The role of the Israel Lands Administration,[25] according to its official brochure, is restricted to the administration of "national lands". The bro-

---

[21] Israel Lands Administration report (Jerusalem, 1962) in Hebrew, pp. 6-7. The reader unfamiliar with Hebrew needs to be cautioned that the word here translated as "administration" is also sometimes (elsewhere) translated "authority". This can result in serious ambiguity between the Development Authority (set up to administer, including settling the so-called abandoned lands) and the Development Administration (sometimes translated Development Authority) controlled by the JNF, which is responsible for development of all national lands in Israel.

[22] Orni, *op. cit.* pp. 34, 68.

[23] Uzzi Ornan of the Hebrew University has studied this question and concludes that "the principles of the JNF apply to all the lands for which the Israel Lands Administration is responsible". He identifies this area as "95 per cent" of pre-1967 Israel; *Maariv*, 30 January 1974.

[24] Orni, *op. cit.*, p. 66; Walter Lehn, "Zionist land: the Jewish National Fund", *Journal of Palestine Studies*, vol. iii, No. 4 Summer 1974, p. 66.

[25] *Israel Lands Administration*, Jerusalem, 1978, (Hebrew).

chure states that the Israel Lands Administration "is not designed to constitute a supreme and ultimate centre of authority on *all* aspects and problems of lands inside the territory of the State of Israel2 [*sic*]".[26] Such operations as land and housing remained under the authority of appropriate ministries.

Israel Lands Administration is an official body of the Israel Government and its 600 odd employees are employees of the state and are subject to the laws and regulations governing state employment. The brochure calls its status "irregular" in that unlike other government ministries it is governed by an Israel Lands Council appointed by the Government which is "the forum of discussion resolution of principles and the fountain of authority for the activities of the Administration". Further, "*two* Ministers, the Minister of Finance and the Minister of Agriculture *jointly*" are charged with the implementation of both the Israel Lands Law (1960) and the Israel Lands Administration Law (1960).[27]

The Israel Lands Administration is charged with the administration of Israel state domain lands (approximately 11,000,000 dunams), lands appropriated by the Development Authority under the Development Authority (Transfer of Property) Law (1950), which include the majority of the lands previously administered by the Custodian of Absentees' Property as defined under the Absentees' Property Law (1950), and lands purchased from the Custodian of Enemy Property as defined by the Government of Great Britain and the British Mandate High Commissioner (approximately 5,000,000 dunams) and Jewish National Fund Lands (approximately 2,600,000 dunams).[28]

Since the Israel Lands Administration is an official arm of the Government of the State of Israel, its definition of what constitutes the body of lands under "national", i.e., "Jewish" ownership is of supreme significance:

> . . . Over nine tenths of the lands of the State of Israel are under national *ownership*, namely, in the hands of bodies whose lands are administered by the Israel Lands Administration.[29]

The Israel Lands Administration's brochure also outlines land distribution inside the territory of the State of Israel:

> . . . [I]n the Negev, the Arabah and the Jerusalem corridor these lands approximate 100 per cent of the total land area of these regions . . .

---

[26] *Ibid.*, p. 7.

[27] *Ibid.*, p. 23.

[28] The figures are quoted from Tom Segev, "A dunam here and a dunam there", *Haaretz Weekly Supplement*, 31 October 1980. Note the repeated inconsistency in the official figures quoted for the total of JNF lands inside the State of Israel. Israel Lands Administration, report (Jerusalem, 1962) quotes the figure of 3,570,000 dunams as the total of JNF Lands (as against 15,205,000 dunams of State and Development Authority Lands).

[29] *Israel Lands Administration*, Jerusalem, 1978 (Hebrew). p. 25.

[I]n the greater metropolitan areas of Jerusalem, Tel Aviv and Haifa the percentage of these lands is reduced to approximately *one third*, a quarter and even less [of the total land area]. The possibilities for influence by the Israel Lands Administration on the land market in these areas is, therefore, fairly limited.[30]

In other words, the official brochure seems to ignore the legal distinction in ownership between state lands, Development Authority lands, and JNF lands. In the formulation of Israel Lands Administration policy, 92.6 per cent of all pre-1967 Israel lands are regarded as being under "national", namely "Jewish" ownership.

The Israel Lands Administration Law of 1960 and the Covenant between the State of Israel and the JNF distinguish between the Israel Lands Council nominated by the Israel Government under the Israel Lands Administration Law (Article 3) and the Land Reclamation and Development Council constituted under the Covenant (Article 15). In addition the Covenant stipulates the constitution of a separate Land Development Administration (articles 10, 11, 12 and 13).

Israel Lands Council constituted under Israel Lands Administration Law (1960). The number of its membership as determined by the Covenant (1961) is 13: seven appointed by the Government and six by the JNF. The Israel Lands Council is chaired by an Israel Government Minister (Article 9). According to Segev,[31] the number of the members of the Israel Lands Council has been increased to 23 (12 appointed by the Government; 11 by the JNF), and the chairmanship of the Council is vested in the Minister of Agriculture. The Council is mandated to "lay down the land policy in accordance with which the [Israel Lands] Administration shall act; [the Council] shall supervise the activities of the [Israel Lands] Administration and shall approve the draft of its budget, which shall be fixed by Law" (Israel Lands Administration Law (1960), article 3).

Israel Lands Administration constituted under Israel Lands Administration Law (1960) and the Covenant (1961) is accountable to the Israel Lands Council (above) and charged with the administration of all Israel lands, i.e., state lands, Development Authority lands and JNF lands, in the framework of the policies as set by the Council. The costs of the Israel Lands Administration are borne by the Government; the Director of the Israel Lands Administration is appointed by the Government "after consultation with the JNF" (Covenant (1961), article 2).

Land Reclamation and Development Council constituted under the Covenant (1961). Its membership is determined by the Covenant as 13: seven appointed by the JNF and six by the Government. The Land Reclamation and Development Council is chaired by the Chairman of the Board of Directors

[30] *Ibid.*, p. 25.
[31] Segev, *op. cit.*

of the JNF (Covenant, Article 15), and it is mandated to "lay down the development policy in accordance with the agricultural development scheme of the Minister of Agriculture; [the Council] shall approve the budget proposal of the [Land] Development Administration (see below) and the manner in which it carries this Covenant into effect," (Covenant, article 15).

Land Development Administration constituted under the Covenant (1961) as a body exclusively under JNF control to regulate "the reclamation and aforestation of Israel lands". The Director of the Land Development Administration is appointed by the JNF after consultation with the Minister charged by the Government with the implementation of the Covenant (Article 10), namely, the Minister of Agriculture.

Against this legal-administrative setting Tom Segev, feature journalist for the Hebrew daily *Ha-aretz*, observed:

> Once a fortnight, on Sundays, some twenty-five people convene at the Board room of the Israel Lands Administration, many of whom are retired senior army officers, for a meeting that sometimes extends into the night and whose resolutions are worth hundreds of millions of Israeli pounds. These are the Heads of the Districts of the Israel Lands Administration, the Heads of Departments and some other of the Administration senior officials. They convene together in order to endorse leasehold deals . . .

> The Administration does not sell lands, but leases lands to tenants and entrepreneurs who have won public tenders at fees determined by the Government Valuer. This is how, at least, its affairs are supposed to be administered. In reality it is possible to appeal against the assessment of the Government Valuer and there is also place to bargain with him. When the bargaining does not fetch the desired results, it is possible to use contacts and apply pressure.

Tom Segev devotes considerable space in his article to the vulnerability of the system to pressure and corruption. The Israel Lands Administration Council nominates a Committee to determine who will receive Administration lands without tender and who will have to apply through public tender. The right connections with the right people can make the crucial difference.

The Israel Lands Administration administeres the total of 92.6 per cent of the total of 20,255,000 dunams constituting the pre-1967 territory of the state of Israel.[32] Of these some 4,200,000 dunams are classified by the israel Lands Administration as agricultural lands.[33] These agricultural lands are distributed as follows:

[32] Israel Lands Administration report (Jerusalem, 1962), pp. 6-7 (Hebrew).
[33] Letter to Dr. Uri Davis from Mr. Arieh Shapira, Spokesman and Director of Public Enquiries, *Israel Lands Administration*, Spokesman Department, Jerusalem, 17 November 1980.

Under *kibbutz* cultivation 1,460,000
Under *moshav* (co-operative)
  cultivation 1,270,000
Under *moshavah* cultivation
  (private ownership), cities,
  companies, etc. 510,000
Schools and Institutions 60,000
Minorities .... 900,000 (including
  350,000 dunams
  in the Negev
  under Bedouin
  cultivation,
  occupancy and
  ownership)

Just under 79 per cent of the total of agricultural lands inside pre-1967 Israel are under exclusive Israeli Jewish cultivation and ownership. In this context, it is important to note that some 6.5 per cent of the Israeli population, *viz.* the 251,000 Israeli Jewish *kibbutz* and *moshav* members, control 65 per cent of all agricultural lands inside the State of Israel. Sixteen percent of the predominantly Palestinian Arabs of the State of Israel cultivate and own just about 21.5 per cent of all agricultural lands. The reality of the alienation of lands from the native Palestinian Arab population as reflected in the figures above is in fact much worse in that the overwhelming majority of the Palestinian Arabs of Israel are concentrated in the Triangle and the Galilee. The Bedouin population in the Negev consists of 9.5 per cent (58,600 people) against a total population of 617,800 Palestinian Arabs inside the pre-1967 borders of Israel. If the Bedouin population and the 350,000 dunams cultivated by them in the Negev are discounted, it emerges from the above figures that the 14.5 per cent of the Palestinian Arabs of Israel cultivate 13 per cent of all available agricultural lands.[34] These revealing figures place the Zionist notion of agricultural cooperative Jewish socialism against its wider context of Israeli class structure, and the systematic, and by now next to complete, dispossession of the Palestinian Arabs inside Israel from their lands.

Israel Lands, Israel Lands Law and Israel Lands Administration Law, all contracts of leasehold for state lands and Development Authority lands, as well as JNF lands, are issued by the Israel Lands Administration (ILA). The

[34] Israeli-Jewish *kibbutz* population, constituting 2.8 per cent (106,000 people) of the total of the Israeli population (3,836,200 people), controls some 35 per cent of the total of agricultural lands inside pre-1967 Israel. Israeli Jewish *moshav* population constituting 3.8 per cent (145,200 people) of the total of Israeli population controls 30 per cent of the total of agricultural lands. (Based on *Statistical Abstract of Israel, 1980*, table II/9, (Jerusalem, Central Bureau of Statistics), pp. 40-41).

most important legal feature of all ILA contracts of leasehold, or at least contracts of leasehold for agricultural lands, is the stipulation that the Lessee is not the individual Jewish settler or the individual Jewish settlement, but rather the Executive of the Jewish Agency. The Executive of the Jewish Agency grants the individual Jewish settler or the individual Jewish settlement the concession of a Licencee only.

Through this procedure two legal separatist structures secure the exclusion of non-Jews, including Palestinian Arabs especially, from access to Israeli lands.

Until the establishment of the State of Israel in 1948, the JA was legally a private voluntary establishment committed under article 3 (d) and (e) of its Constitution to the following:

> Land is to be acquired as Jewish property, and . . . the title to the land to be taken in the name of the JNF, to the end that the same shall be held as the inalienable property of the Jewish people. The Agency shall promote agricultural colonization based on Jewish labour, and in all works and undertakings carried out or furthered by the Agency, it shall be deemed to be a matter of principle that Jewish labour shall be employed . . . (article 3 (d) and (e)).

This Constitutional principle was given legal recognition by the WZO—JA (Status) Law, 1952. Through this legislation and the subsequent Covenant signed in 1954 between the Government of Israel and the Zionist Executive, also known as the Executive of the Jewish Agency for the Land of Israel, the WZO and the Jewish Agency were given the following concession:

> Organization of *aliyah* [Jewish immigration] from abroad, and transfer of the *olim* [Jewish immigrants] and their property to the country; participation in the absorption of *olim* in the country; youth *aliyah*; agricultural settlement in the country and the purchase of land and its development by the institutions of the Zionist Organization, the JNF and the Foundation Fund; participation in the establishment and expansion of development projects in the country; encouragement of private capital investments in the country; assistance to cultural projects and institutions of higher education in the country; mobilisation of funds to finance these activities; coordination of the activities in Israel of Jewish institutions and organisations which are active in the domains outlined above and are financed by public funding. (*Covenant* (1954), article 1).

It is important to note again that the reasons for the choice of the JA as Lessee are stated explicitly in the Preamble to the Contract, namely,

> Whereas the Agency by force of the Provisions as stipulated in Article 3 of the WZO—JA (Status) Law, 1952, and the Covenant made accord-

ing to this Law is engaged in the settlement of *Jews* on *Israel lands, as defined in the said law* . . . (emphasis added).

Thus through the positing of the JA as Lessee, the exclusion of non-Jews is secured by the laws of the State of Israel, and specifically by the WZO—JA (Status) Law, 1952 and the Israel Lands Law, 1960.

The legal separatist structure of all Israeli Jewish *kibbutz* (collective) and *moshav* (co-operative) agricultural settlements, which, through the various *kibbutz* and *moshav* federations as licensees from the Executive of the JA in the framework of the ILA contracts of leasehold, monopolize and cultivate the majority of the arable lands inside pre-1967 Israel.

The Histadrut: the General Federation of Workers in the Land of Israel

The *Histadrut*[35] was founded in 1920 as the General Federation of Hebrew Workers in the Land of Israel. In 1960 the ninth *Histadrut* Convention made legal provisions to permit membership in the *Histadrut* for Palestinian Arab workers in Israel. The next *Histadrut* Convention in 1966 changed the official name of the *Histadrut* Federation from "The General Federation of Hebrew Workers in the Land of Israel" to "The General Federation of Workers in the Land of Israel". Also, the term "Hebrew" was deleted from Chapter 1, "the Foundations of *Histadrut*", Article 1 of the *Histadrut* Constitution, which otherwise remains identical with the original pre-1966 text unaltered, including its commitment to cultural and social activity inside the workers' public; the imparting of the values of the labour movement; the instruction of the Hebrew language; and publication of literature and press.

The change of the *Histadrut*'s name was strongly debated. Prominent among the opposers of the change was MP Shimon Peres, who represented the Israel Workers List—*Rafi*:[36]

This is clearly a General Federation, this is a Hebrew Federation in Israel. Let us not make it nameless. Let us not make it devoid of identity. Let us not deny its anthems. Let us not manipulate its challenges. This is not a Federation that ends with a question mark. I heard that one of the additional arguments for the change of name is: what will they say in the world? I do not consider the proposed apologetics as necessary. *(The Tenth Histadrut Convention, 3-7 January, 1966, Tel Aviv-Jaffa, Complete Protocols of the Debates*, Ed. Josjeph Olitzki, The General Federation of Workers in the Land of Israel, The Executive Committee, p. 541).

---

[35] The Hebrew term *histadrut* means "federation".

[36] The Israel Workers List-*Rafi* was founded in 1965 following the Ben Gurion split from the Land of Israel Workers Party—*Mapai*. In 1968 it merged back with *Mapai* and Ahdut ha-Avodah ("Labour Union") to form the Israel Labour Party, of which Shimon Peres is at the time of writing (1980) the Chairman.

MP Israel Yeshaayahu, Chairman of the *Histadrut* Permanent Committee, concluded as follows:

> A new reality was created: The *Histadrut* opened its gates to the Arab worker. It is now necessary to change the name in order that it be compatible with the new reality, but thereby the contents and the mission of the *Histadrut* is not altered. (*Ibid.*, p. 547).

Histadrut policy following the name change strongly supports Yeshaayahu's position. It is also significant that the amendment proposed by the Israeli Communist Party (Maki) to alter the name of the *Histadrut* to "the General Federation of Workers in Israel"[37] was turned down. The Israeli victory in the 1967 war gave ample scope to the *Histadrut* to demonstrate that the name change did not entail alteration in the Zionist mission of the *Histadrut*, and that the General Federation of Labour in Israel could effectively accommodate the reality of the post-1967 Israeli occupation, and abandon the Palestinian Arab workers of the West Band [*sic*] and the Gaza Strip to economic exploitation and social and political oppression.[38]

The resolution by the ninth *Histadrut* Convention to "open its gates to the Arab worker" highlights the legal separatist structure of the organization. The name of the *Histadrut* was altered, and the reference to "Hebrew workers" was replaced with the reference "workers" in Article 1, Chapter 1, "The Foundations of the *Histadrut*", of the *Histadrut* Constitution—but that is all. The constitutions of all the subsidiary companies and associations of the *Histadrut* were not amended and remained by deliberate design exclusive to the body of Hebrew workers alone.

Thus the full official name of the holding company of all *Histadrut* agricultural, marketing, service and manufacturing companies and associations, the Workers Company (established 1922), was until 1979 the General Co-operative Company of the Hebrew Workers in the Land of Israel Ltd. Its Constitution begins with a statement of objectives:

1. The objective of the Company is to unite on co-operative foundations the Hebrew workers in the Land of Israel in all professions of labour, both manual labour and spiritual labour.
2. In order to achieve this object the Company will have the following power of activity:

---

[37] There is no record in the Protocols of a New Communist List—*Rakah* amendment proposal.

[38] For details see Emanuel Farajun, *Palestinian Worker in Israel: A Reserve Army of Labour*, The Socialist Organization in Israel—Matzpen, Red Pages, No. 5, Tel Aviv, 1978. Reprinted in *Khamsin: Journal of Revolutionary Socialists of the Middle East*, No. 7, Ithaca Press, London, 1980, and the *Jerusalem Al-Fajr*, vol. i, Nos. 17, 18 and 19, August 1980. Also, Sarah Graham-Brown, *Palestinian Workers and Trade Unions*, Middle East Research and Action Group (MERAG) in conjunction with United Kingdom Palestine Co-ordination, London, Undated (c. 1980).

(a) To engage in the settlement of members in the village and in town; to purchase, rent, receive in exchange or as a gift and purchase in other ways agricultural farms, plantations, estates, lands, houses, real estate and moveable properties; to establish, found, build cities, villages, settlements, residential quarters or participate in the building and the establishment of the same. . . .

(The General Co-operative Company of the Hebrew Workers in the Land of Israel, *Constitution*, mimeo, date unspecified, amendments to the Constitution included as footnotes. Later amendment noted is dated 15-16.41970).

In 1979 the name change from the General Co-operative Company of the Hebrew Workers in the Land of Israel Ltd. to the General Co-operative Company of the Workers in the Land of israel Ltd.[39] was only a change in name. The Company's constitutional objectives remained unchanged. In 1979 the Workers Company produced 21 per cent of the total sale of industrial production in Israel through its industrial plants and corporations, and 75 per cent of the total agricultural production through the *kibbutz* and *moshav* Federations and related agricultural co-operatives.[40]

The principle of the legal exclusion of non-Jews is clearly a constitutional unifying norm through the hierarchy of the *Histadrut* institution's corporations and enterprises. Thus, all *kibbutz* and *moshav* agricultural settlements are incorporated as daughter companies of *Nir*: A Co-operative Company for the Settlement of Hebrew Workers Ltd., which in turn is wholly owned by the *Histadrut* Workers Company.

"Nir" was established in 1924 as the "official legal expression of the authority of the Articultural Federation on the farms and the agricultural plants as part of the Workers Company . . ."[41]

With the introduction of the legal changes that made Arab membership in the *Histadrut* possible by the *Histadrut* convention in 1960, the membership of the Workers Company became *ipso facto* no longer exclusively Jewish, and thereby a legal contradiction was introduced into the heart of the *Histadrut* constitutional structure. The Workers Company, which is legally constituted to "unite on co-operative foundations the Hebrew workers of the land in all professions of labour, both manual labour and spiritual labour", now has non-Jews, namely, Palestine Arabs who are citizens of the State of Israel, as members.

---

[39] The change of name was resolved by the 98th Council of the Workers Company at its meeting on 26th April, 1979 and registered with the Registrar of Co-operative Associations on 9th May 1979.

[40] The Workers Company, Economic Department, *The Workers Company 1979-1980*, Tel Aviv, 1981 pp. 5-6, (Hebrew).

[41] Zvi Magen, *Nir Shitufi: Its History, Development and Tasks*, a Seminary Paper in the Institutional Structure of the Labour Movement in Israel, University of Tel Aviv, The Faculty of Social Sciences, the Department of Labour Studies, 1968, p. 12 (Hebrew).

Non-Jews' membership in Israeli-Jewish *moshavim* and *kubbutzim* is legally barred by two insurmountable obstacles:

1. The *moshav* and *kibbutz* land is constitutionally defined as being in the possession of "the nation", namely, the Jewish people.
2. *Moshav* and *kibbutz* membership require endorsement by Nir: A Co-operative Company for the Settlement of Hebrew Workers Ltd., and *Nir* Ltd. is constitutionally restricted to the promotion of the settlement of Hebrew Workers only.[42]

The WZO and its various executive bodies, e.g., the JA and the JNF, as well as the *Histadrut* aspired to establish a Jewish state in Palestine for the Jewish people worldwide, and hence, unavoidably, pursued various measures and policies to evacuate and deprive the majority of the native Palestinian Arab people of their land, homeland and right of self-determination and sovereignty. Their restructive constitutions, which were legally binding on what were until 1948 technically voluntary organizations, are now incorporated into the legal foundations and the body of law of the State of Israel, thereby establishing a legal apartheid situation of Jew versus non-Jew.

LEGAL RESTRICTIONS ON ACCESS TO WATER: MEKOROT ISRAEL WATER COMPANY AND TAHAL WATER PLANNING FOR ISRAEL COMPANY[43]

Israel water resources are administered by the Israel Water Commission, headed by the Water Commissioner who is subject to the Minister of Agriculture. The Israel Water Commission operates within the framework of Israel Water Law (1959) which states as follows:

> Article Number 1. The Water resources in the State are public property; they are subject to the control of the State and are destined for the requirements of its inhabitants and for the development of the country.
>
> . . .
>
> Article Number 3. Every person is entitled to receive and use water, subject to the provisions of this Law.

The Water Commission administration is divided into a number of Departments of which *Mekorot*, Israel Water Co. and *Tahal*, Water Planning for

---

[42] See also, "Introduction" by the late David Remez, Second Secretary-General of the Histadrut, *ibid.* pp. 9-12, "The Constitution of the Kevutzah", *ibid.* pp. 98-118, and the "Regulations of the Kevutzah or the Kibbutz", *ibid.* p. 252.

[43] Pages 44-49 on Israeli water resources include slightly edited excerpts from Uri Davis, Antonia E. L. Maks and John Richardson, "Israel's water policies", *Journal of Palestine Studies*, vol. IX, No. 2, 1980. Pages 51-54 include slightly edited excerpts from Adnan Abed Elrazik, Riad Amin and Uri Davis, "Problems of Palestinians in Israel" *Journal of Palestine Studies*, vol. VII, No. 3, 1978. (First published in *The Destiny of Arab Students in Institutions of Higher Education in Israel: An Outline Towards a Discussion of the Prospects for an Arab University in the Galilee* (Miftah (Key) Publishers, Kefar Shemaryahu, 1977).

Israel Co., are responsible for the construction of irrigation and water supply projects (Mekorot), and the overall planning and design engineering of Israel water development projects (Tahal). These two agencies control the water supplied to all consumers under Israeli rule in agriculture, industry, and domestic consumption. Mekorot was established in 1936 by the Jewish Agency, the Jewish National Fund and the *Histadrut* General Federation of Workers (then still called the General Federation of Hebrew Workers). Currently the Israeli Government has a 33 per cent share in Mekorot, and the remainder is divided between the *Histadrut* (33 per cent), the Jewish Agency (25 per cent) and the Jewish National Fund (8 per cent). Tahal was established in 1952 as an Israel Government company. The Government has the controlling share (51 per cent), and the remainder is divided equally between the Jewish Agency (24 per cent) and the Jewish National Fund (24 per cent).[44]

In 1976 Israel was consuming 98% of its known renewable proven water resources. Israeli water consumption has increased radically over the thirty years of Israeli history: from 17% in 1949 to 90% in 1968 to 95% in 1978. Future economic development in Israel therefore depends critically on either the tapping of new water resources or the development of new techniques. Additional water supplies are needed not only for the further development of agriculture, but also to meet expected increases in domestic consumption.

Eli El'ad has written:

The estimate is that the future increase in urban population and in standards of living will necessitate the development of some additional 400 million cm water towards 1990. If the needed quantity is not *found* it will be necessary to divert water from production to domestic consumption at the total that is equivalent to one-third (1/3) of the water consumed by agriculture today. Diversion of water from agriculture to domestic consumption will entail economic and social regression as well as injury to the policy of population dispersion. [i.e. Israeli policy of

[44] The Executive of the Zionist Organization and the Executive of the Jewish Agency, *The Companies and Investments Bureau Report to the Twenty Seventh Zionist Congress in Jerusalem*, Jerusalem, 1968. Table 1, pp. 298-99. The Companies and Investments Bureau of the Jewish Agency was established in 1953 to deal with the investments of the World Zionist Organization, the Jewish Agency and the Jewish National Fund. The list of the companies under the administration of the Bureau includes, *inter alia*, and in addition to Mekorot and Tahal, El Al (Israel's national air carrier), Zim (Israel's national navigation company), the Convention Centre (Israel's national hall in Jerusalem), Agrexco (Israel's agricultural export monopoly), the Israel Economic Development Corporation, the Jerusalem Economic Corporation, the Tel Aviv Development Company, the Diur la-Oleh and Amidar Housing Companies, the Jewish Settlement Trust, the Israel Land Development Corporation etc. Again, it cannot be sufficiently underlined that *every aspect of everyday life* inside the State of Israel is governed and regulated by legislation and a corresponding administration predicated upon the legal and official distinction between "Jew" and "non-Jew".

dispersion of its Jewish population from the urban metropolitan centres along the coast into the not as yet completely Judaized periphery both in pre-1967 Israel proper and in the post-1967 Israeli occupied territories].[45]

Israel's national water economy consists of the following water resources: river waters; springs; flood water run-offs; ground water; recycles, purified sewage and irrigation waters. According to Yakobowitz and Prushansky[46] the total renewable fresh water potential in (pre-1967) Israel is estimated, after the development of all available water resources, at 1,610-1,650 million cm per annum as follows:

ground water	950
Jordan river and Lake Kinneret	600
floodwater run offs	60-100
Total	1,610-1,650 million cm p.a.

One-third of pre-1967 Israel annual water consumption of 1,600 million cm originated in the rainfall over the western slopes of the West Bank and was drawn by drilling inside pre-1967 Israel proper from the same water aquifer system that contains the water reserves for the West Bank. However, Israel will need by the sheer weight of the increase in its urban Jewish population *alone* an addition of 400-450 million cm by 1990 for domestic consumption, or an addition of one-third of current Israeli water consumption.

The denial of equal access to the national resource of water to the Palestinian Arab citizens of Israel, like the denial of equal access to water for agricultural irrigation, has been a consistent foundation policy of all Israeli governments since 1948. Consistent with Israel's land policies, where "national lands" have been legislated as "Jewish national lands", the stipulation in the Israel Water Law (1959) that the water resources in the State of Israel are "public property" must be read in the context of the exclusive control of Mekorot and Tahal over the domains of water supply and water development. The water resources inside Israel have been legislated as Jewish public property and mobilized to promote Jewish agricultural colonization of the lands and properties from which the native Palestinian Arab population has been dispossessed.

The massive confiscation of Palestinian Arab lands and the denial of access to irrigation water resources to Palestinian Arab peasants and farmers by the Israeli occupation authorities in the post-1967 occupied territories corresponds closely to the patterns of colonization and dispossession applied inside pre-1967 Israel against the Palestinian Arab population under Israeli rule since 1948. Thus, when we examine the patterns of agricultural

[45] *Ha-aretz*, 27 April 1978, emphasis added.

[46] M. Yakobowitz and Y. Prushansky, *The Water in Israel* (Jerusalem, Israel Information Centre, 1978), p. 21.

cultivation in Jewish and non-Jewish (Arab) farms, inside pre-1967 Israel, as recorded by official Israeli statistics, the following data emerge:

(a) *Cultivated area of field crops by type of locality (thousand dunams) (1973/74)*

Total	2,738.9 (100%)
Total Jewish farms	2,119.8 (77.4%)
Total non-Jewish (Arab) farms	619.1 (22.6%)
Unirrigated total Jewish farms	1,513.1 (71.4% of Jewish total)
Unirrigated total non-Jewish (Arab) farms	610.9 (98.7% of Arab total)
Irrigated total Jewish farms	606.7 (28.6% of Jewish total)
Irrigated total non-Jewish (Arab) farms	8.2 (1.3% of Arab total)

Source: Statistical Abstract of Israel, 1975, table xiii/6.

(b) *Agricultural water consumption by source, use and type of locality (million M³) (1973/74)*

Towns and urban localities	71	
Moshavot	63	
Moshavim	358	
Kibbutzim	526	
Institutions and farms	43	
Others	96	
Total	1157	
Non-Jewish villages	23	(1.98%)

Source: Statistical Abstract of Israel, 1975, table xv/3.

After over two-thirds of their lands have been confiscated, the Arab villages in pre-1967 Israel still cultivate 22.6 per cent of the cultivated area of field crops in the country. Yet official statistics show that they are allocated only 1.98 per cent of the national agricultural water consumption.

The story of the legal measures taken by the Israeli Government and Parliament to alienate the Palestinian Arab population under Israeli rule since 1948 from their lands is now well documented.[48] Over one million dunams of lands were expropriated from their Arab owners and transferred to exclusive Jewish cultivation between 1948 and 1967. The vast majority of the Palestinian Arab village population under Israeli rule has been forced to

[47] *Israel Pocket Library*, "Economy", Jerusalem, 1973, p. 156.

[48] Ibrahim Abu Lughod, *The Transformation of Palestine*, (Evanston, Ill. Northwestern University Press, 1971). Sabri Jiryis, *The Arabs in Israel* (New York, Monthly Review Press, 1976). Fouzi el-Asmar, *To Be an Arab in Israel* (Beirut, Institute of Palestine Studies, 1978). Uri Davis, *Israel: Utopia Incorporated* (London, Zed Press, 1977). Elia Zureik, *The Palestinians in Israel: A Study in Internal Colonialism*, (London, Routledge Kegan Paul, 1979).

become daily commuting wage labourers in Israeli manufacturing, construction and service industries. Very little land has remained under Arab ownership and cultivation.

The Israeli Water Commissioner, with exclusive control of water supplies and water allocation, can exercise his control either through Mekorot and/or Tahal, or directly through the granting of permits to individuals or to village associations to sink wells locally. The denial of access to the national resource of water to non-Jewish, namely, Palestinian Arab population under Israeli rule since 1948 is legally structured and patterned to correspond to their exclusion from access to the national resource of land.

The legal structures regulating the activity of Mekorot and Tahal result in virtually total exclusion of Palestinian Arab peasants and farmers under Israeli rule from access to irrigation water. Thus, Mekorot and Tahal regard it as their national mission to secure running water to every home in every Israeli Jewish settlement. All Israeli Jewish settlements are connected to the national grid of running water supply and are fully electrified by the national Electricity Company before the first Jewish settler family sets foot in the place. On the other hand, the majority of surviving Palestinian Arab villages inside Israel[49] remained for over a decade without supply of running water for domestic consumption.

According to Sabri Jiryis, only 27 of the total of 100 Arab villages inside pre-1967 Israel were connected to the national grid for domestic supply of running water.[50] Improvement in the area of domestic supply of running water was achieved at enormous costs for the communities in question. Ian Lustick offers an accurate summary of the matter at hand in the following:

> [W]hereas Jewish settlements receive electricity, sewage systems, paved roads, waterworks, land development etc. essentially free of charge, Arab villages must collect taxes from their inhabitants in order to make even a down payment on any *one* of these projects. While Arab local councils must use their tax revenues for the installation of basic services and facilities, their Jewish counterparts are free to spend their tax monies on, among other things, better schools and university scholarships.[51]

[49] Of the 500 Palestinian Arab villages inside the territories which fell to Israeli sovereignty in the 1948/49 war only 100 villages survived. Four hundred villages were razed to the ground by the Israeli authorities, having expelled their population in the course of the 1948/49 war, and handed their lands over to the exclusive Jewish cultivation and ownership. The inhabitants of these 400 destroyed villages, originally some 750,000 people, constitute the bulk of the approximately 1,800,000 Palestinian Arab refugees registered with the United Nations Relief and Works Agency (UNRWA). Of the total of the UNRWA registered refugee population, some 500,000 are resident in UNRWA refugee camps since 1948. (Source: Map of UNRWA's Area of Operations, 30 June 1977)

[50] Sabri Jiryis, *The Arabs in Israel*, (New York, Monthly Review Press, 1976), p. 229.

[51] Ian Lustick, *Arabs in the Jewish State*, (Austin, University of Texas Press, 1980), p. 168. Lustick also outlines the parallel structures of radical discrimination regarding the supply of electricity to Arab villages inside Israel. The Israel Electricity Company is the successor of the Palestine Electricity Company which supplied almost all the electric power in Pal-

Not all Arab localities inside pre-1967 Israel were connected to the national grid of domestic supply of running water in 1982. The most glaring case is that of the Palestinian Arab Bedouin localities and encampments in the Negev. Whereas every Jewish locality in the Negev is connected to the national grid, the Bedouin Palestinian Arab Israeli citizens of the Negev are frequently reduced to illegally puncturing the pipelines supplying running water to their Jewish settler neighbours because of the persistent refusal by Mekorot to extend a connection to their locality. The population concerned was estimated in 1979 at 47,300.[52] In other words, some 8 per cent of the total Palestinian Arab population inside pre-1967 Israel of over 600,000[53] are denied domestic supply of running water.

CONCLUSION

It is important to emphasize that these patterns of discrimination and exclusion are not rooted in structures of *de facto* practices which violate the law, but rather in official legislation by the Israeli Parliament which authorizes the Israeli Government to grant monopolistic concession over the national resources of land and water to companies that are committed constitutionally to exclusive Jewish settlement, to the exclusive promotion of Jewish benefits and Jewish interests and to the employment of all their work and undertaking to Jewish labour only.

---

estine prior to 1948 and was until 1954 wholly owned by the Jewish Agency. By 1973 still 44 per cent of the Arab village population inside Israel was still without electricity. The percentage is in fact higher, since the figure excludes Bedouin encampments and villages in the South and North of the country. Even by 1976, 22 per cent of the Arab (urban and village) population inside Israel were not serviced by the Israel Electricity Corporation (Lustick, *Ibid.*, pp. 158, 306n)

[52] Israel Bureau of Statistics, *Statistical Abstract of Israel* (Jerusalem, 1980), table II/4.

[53] *Ibid.*, table II/4.

369. General Assembly Resolution 40/167 on Israel's
Decision to Build a Canal Linking the Mediterranean Sea
to the Dead Sea, December 16, 1985*

---

* G.A. Res. 40/167 (1985).

The General Assembly,

Recalling its resolutions 36/150 of 16 December 1981, 37/122 of 16 December 1982, 38/85 of 15 December 1983 and 39/101 of 14 December 1984,

Taking note of the report of the Secretary-General,[141]

1. *Requests* the Secretary-General to monitor on a continuing basis any new development relating to the proposed canal linking the Mediterranean Sea to the Dead Sea and to report all findings in this regard to the General Assembly;

2. *Decides* to resume consideration of this item in case activities by Israel relating to the said canal are resumed.

[141] A/40/803.

E. Nuclear Proliferation and Associated Issues

370. General Assembly Resolution 37/18 on Armed Israeli Aggression Against the Iraqi Nuclear Installations and Its Grave Consequences for the Established International System Concerning the Peaceful Uses of Nuclear Energy, the Non-Proliferation of Nuclear Weapons and International Peace and Security, November 16, 1982*

* G.A. Res. 18, 37 U.N. GAOR Supp. (No. 51) at 22, U.N. Doc. A/37/51 (1982).

The General Assembly,

Having considered the item entitled "Armed Israeli aggression against the Iraqi nuclear installations and its grave consequences for the established international system concerning the peaceful uses of nuclear energy, the non-proliferation of nuclear weapons and international peace and security",

Recalling the relevant resolutions of the Security Council and the General Assembly,

Taking note of the report of the Secretary-General,[28]

Taking note also of the relevant resolution of the International Atomic Energy Agency and the Commission on Human Rights,

Viewing with deep concern Israel's refusal to comply with those resolutions, particularly Security Council resolution 487 (1981) of 19 June 1981,

Gravely alarmed by the dangerous escalation of Israel's acts of aggression in the region,

Gravely concerned that Israel continues to maintain its threats to repeat such attacks against nuclear installations,

Reiterating its alarm over the information and evidence regarding the acquisition and development of nuclear weapons by Israel,

Recalling the Declaration and the Programme of Action on the Establishment of a New International Economic Order,[29] the Charter of Economic Rights and Duties of States[30] and the Declaration on the Use of Scientific and Technological Progress in the Interests of Peace and for the Benefit of Mankind,[31]

Affirming the need to ensure against the repetition of such an attack on nuclear facilities by Israel or any other State,

1. *Condemns* Israel's refusal to implement resolution 487 (1981), unanimously adopted by the Security Council;

2. *Strongly condemns* Israel for the escalation of its acts of aggression in the region;

3. *Condemns* Israel's threats to repeat such attacks, which would gravely endanger international peace and security;

4. *Demands* that Israel withdraw forthwith its officially declared threat to repeat its armed attack against nuclear facilities;

5. *Considers* the Israeli act of aggression to be a violation and a denial of the inalienable sovereign right of States to scientific and technological progress for achieving social and economic development and raising the standards of peoples and the dignity of the human person, as well as a violation

---

[28] A/37/365 and Add.1-S/15320 and Add.1. For the printed text, see *Official Records of the Security Council, Thirty-seventh Year, Supplement for July, August and September 1982*, documents S/15320 and Add.1.

[29] Resolutions 3201 (S-VI) and 3202 (S-VI).

[30] Resolution 3281 (XXIX).

[31] Resolution 3384 (XXX).

and a denial of inalienable human rights and the sovereign right of States to scientific and technological development;

6. *Requests* the Security Council to consider the necessary measures to deter Israel from repeating such an attack on nuclear facilities;

7. *Calls* for the continuation of the consideration, at the international level, of legal measures to prohibit armed attacks against nuclear facilities, and threats thereof as a contribution to promoting and ensuring the safe development of nuclear energy for peaceful purposes;

8. *Requests* the Secretary-General to prepare, with the assistance of a group of experts,[32] a comprehensive study on the consequences of the Israeli armed attack against the Iraqi nuclear installations devoted to peaceful purposes, and to submit that study to the General Assembly at its thirty-eighth session;

9. *Further requests* the Secretary-General to report to the General Assembly at its thirty-eighth session on the implementation of the present resolution;

10. *Decides* to include in the provisional agenda of its thirty-eighth session the item entitled "Armed Israeli aggression against the Iraqi nuclear installations and its grave consequences for the established international system concerning the peaceful uses of nuclear energy, the non-proliferation of nuclear weapons and international peace and security".

70th plenary meeting
16 November 1982

[32] Subsequently named Group of Experts on the Consequences of the Israeli Armed Attack against the Iraqi Nuclear Installations.

371. General Assembly Resolution 37/75 on the Establishment of a Nuclear-Weapon-Free Zone in the Region of the Middle East, December 9, 1982*

---

* G.A. Res. 75, 37 U.N. GAOR Supp. (No. 51) at 56, U.N. Doc. A/37/51 (1982). *See also* subsequent resolutions, G.A. Res. 64, 38 U.N. GAOR Supp. (No. 47) at 57, U.N. Doc. A/38/47 (1983), G.A. Res. 54, 39 U.N. GAOR Supp. (No. 51) at 59, U.N. Doc. A/39/51 (1984), and G.A. Res. 40/82 (1985).

The General Assembly,

Recalling its resolutions 3263 (XXIX) of 9 December 1974, 3474 (XXX) of 11 December 1975, 31/71 of 10 December 1976, 32/82 of 12 December 1977, 33/64 of 14 December 1978, 34/77 of 11 December 1979, 35/147 of 12 December 1980 and 36/87 of 9 December 1981 on the establishment of a nuclear-weapon-free zone in the region of the Middle East,

Recalling also the recommendations for the establishment of such a zone in the Middle East consistent with paragraphs 60 to 63, in particular paragraph 63 (*d*), of the Final Document of the Tenth Special Session of the General Assembly,[21]

Emphasizing the basic provisions of the above-mentioned resolutions, which call upon all parties directly concerned to consider taking the practical and urgent steps required for the implementation of the proposal to establish a nuclear-weapon-free zone in the region of the Middle East and, pending and during the establishment of such a zone, to declare solemnly that they will refrain, on a reciprocal basis, from producing, acquiring or in any other way possessing nuclear weapons and nuclear explosive devices and from permitting the stationing of nuclear weapons on their territory by any third party, to agree to place all their nuclear facilities under International Atomic Energy Agency safeguards and to declare their support for the establishment of the zone and deposit such declarations with the Security Council for consideration, as appropriate,

Reaffirming the inalienable right of all States to acquire and develop nuclear energy for peaceful purposes,

Emphasizing further the need for appropriate measures on the question of the prohibition of military attacks on nuclear facilities,

Bearing in mind the consensus reached by the General Assembly at its thirty-fifth session that the establishment of a nuclear-weapon-free zone in the region of the Middle East would greatly enhance international peace and security,

Desirous to build on that consensus so that substantial progress can be made towards establishing a nuclear-weapon-free zone in the region of the Middle East,

1. *Urges* all parties directly concerned to consider seriously taking the practical and urgent steps required for the implementation of the proposal to establish a nuclear-weapon-free zone in the region of the Middle East in accordance with the relevant resolutions of the General Assembly and, as a means of promoting this objective, invites the countries concerned to adhere to the Treaty on the Non-Proliferation of Nuclear Weapons;[22]

2. *Calls upon* all countries of the region that have not done so, pending the establishment of the zone, to agree to place all their nuclear activities under International Atomic Energy Agency safeguards;

[21] Resolution S-10/2.
[22] Resolution 2373 (XXII), annex.

3. *Invites* those countries, pending the establishment of a nuclear-weapon-free zone in the region of the Middle East, to declare their support for establishing such a zone, consistent with the relevant paragraph of the Final Document of the Tenth Special Session of the General Assembly, and to deposit those declarations with the Security Council;

4. *Invites further* those countries, pending the establishment of the zone, not to develop, produce, test or otherwise acquire nuclear weapons or permit the stationing on their territories, or territories under their control, of nuclear weapons or nuclear explosive devices;

5. *Invites* the nuclear-weapon States and all other States to render their assistance in the establishment of the zone and at the same time to refrain from any action that runs counter to both the letter and spirit of the present resolution;

6. *Requests* the Secretary-General to report to the General Assembly at its thirty-eighth session on the implementation of the present resolution;

7. *Decides* to include in the provisional agenda of its thirty-eighth session the item entitled "Establishment of a nuclear-weapon-free zone in the region of the Middle East".

98th plenary meeting
9 December 1982

372. General Assembly Resolution 37/82 on Israeli
Nuclear Armament, December 9, 1982*

* G.A. Res. 82, 37 U.N. GAOR Supp. (No. 51) at 67, U.N. Doc. A/37/51
(1982).

The General Assembly,

Recalling its resolutions 35/157 of 12 December 1980 and 36/98 of 9 December 1981 on Israeli nuclear armament,

Recalling also its relevant resolutions on the establishment of a nuclear-weapon-free zone in the region of the Middle East,

Recalling further its resolution 33/71 A of 14 December 1978 on military and nuclear collaboration with Israel,

Recalling its repeated condemnation of the nuclear collaboration between Israel and South Africa,

Recalling Security Council resolution 487 (1981) of 19 June 1981 and taking note of the first special report of the Special Committee against *Apartheid* on recent developments concerning relations between Israel and South Africa,[58]

Noting with grave concern Israel's persistent refusal to adhere to the Treaty on the Non-Proliferation of Nuclear Weapons,[59] despite repeated calls by the General Assembly, the Security Council and the International Atomic Energy Agency, and to place its nuclear facilities under Agency safeguards,

Conscious of the grave consequences which endanger international peace and security as a result of Israel's nuclear-weapon capability and its collaboration with South Africa to develop nuclear weapons and their delivery systems,

Taking note of the report of the Secretary-General on Israeli nuclear armament,[60]

1. *Reaffirms* its demand that Israel renounce, without delay, any possession of nuclear weapons and place all its nuclear activities under international safeguards;

2. *Calls again upon* all States and other parties and institutions to terminate forthwith all nuclear collaboration with Israel;

3. *Requests again* the Security Council to investigate Israel's nuclear activities and the collaboration of other States, parties and institutions in these activities;

4. *Calls upon* all States to submit to the Secretary-General all information in their possession concerning the Israeli nuclear programme or any public or private assistance thereto;

5. *Requests* the Security Council to consider taking effective action so as to prevent Israel from endangering international peace and security by pursuing its policy of aggression, expansion and annexation of territories;

6. *Condemns* Israel's officially declared intention to repeat its armed attack against nuclear facilities;

[58] *Official Records of the General Assembly, Thirty-seventh Session, Supplement No. 22A* (A/37/22/Add.1 and 2), document A/37/22/Add.1.
[59] Resolution 2373 (XXII), annex.
[60] A/37/434.

7. *Requests* the Secretary-General to keep Israeli nuclear activities under constant review and to report thereon as appropriate;

8. *Also requests* the Secretary-General, in co-operation with the Organization of African Unity and the League of Arab States, to follow closely the nuclear and military collaboration between Israel and South Africa and the dangers it constitutes to peace and security and to efforts aimed at the establishment of nuclear-weapon-free zones in Africa and the Middle East;

9. *Decides* to include in the provisional agenda of its thirty-eighth session the item entitled "Israeli nuclear armament".

98th plenary meeting
9 December 1982

373. General Assembly Resolution 38/9 on Armed Israeli Aggression Against the Iraqi Nuclear Installations and Its Grave Consequences for the Established International System Concerning the Peaceful Uses of Nuclear Energy, the Non-Proliferation of Nuclear Weapons and International Peace and Security, November 10, 1983*

* G.A. Res. 9, 38 U.N. GAOR Supp. (No. 47) at 20, U.N. Doc. A/38/47 (1983).

The General Assembly,

Having considered the item entitled "Armed Israeli aggression against the Iraqi nuclear installations and its grave consequences for the established international system concerning the peaceful uses of nuclear energy, the non-proliferation of nuclear weapons and international peace and security",

Recalling the relevant resolutions of the Security Council and the General Assembly,

Taking note of the relevant resolutions of the International Atomic Energy Agency,

Taking note also with appreciation of the report of the Secretary-General,[28]

Viewing with deep concern Israel's continued refusal to comply with those resolutions,

Reiterating its alarm over the information and evidence regarding the acquisition and development of nuclear weapons by Israel,

Recalling Article 2, paragraph 4, of the Charter of the United Nations, which enjoins all Member States to refrain in their international relations from the threat or use of force against the territorial integrity or political independence of any State, or in any other manner inconsistent with the purposes of the United Nations,

Noting that serious radiological effects would result from an armed attack with conventional weapons on a nuclear installation, which could also lead to the initiation of radiological warfare,

1. *Reiterates its condemnation* of Israel's continued refusal to implement Security Council resolution 487 (1981), unanimously adopted by the Council on 19 June 1981;

2. *Notes* that the statements made so far by Israel have not removed apprehensions that its threat to repeat its armed attack against nuclear facilities, as well as any similar action against such facilities, will continue to endanger the role and activities of the International Atomic Energy Agency and other international instruments in the development of nuclear energy for peaceful purposes and in safeguarding against further proliferation of nuclear weapons;

3. *Considers* that any threat to attack and destroy nuclear facilities in Iraq and in other countries constitutes a violation of the Charter of the United Nations;

4. *Reiterates its demand* that Israel withdraw forthwith its threat to attack and destroy nuclear facilities in Iraq and in other countries;

5. *Once again requests* the Security Council to consider the necessary measures to deter Israel from repeating such an attack on nuclear facilities;

6. *Reaffirms is call* for the continuation of the consideration, at the international level, of legal measures to prohibit armed attacks against nuclear facilities, and threats thereof, as a contribution to promoting and ensuring the safe development of nuclear energy for peaceful purposes;

[28] A/38/342.

7. *Expresses its deep appreciation* to the Secretary-General and the Group of Experts on the Consequences of the Israeli Armed Attack against the Iraqi Nuclear Installations for their comprehensive study;[29]

8. *Requests* the Secretary-General to report to the General Assembly at its thirty-ninth session on the implementation of the present resolution;

9. *Decides* to include in the provisional agenda of its thirty-ninth session the item entitled "Armed Israeli aggression against the Iraqi nuclear installations and its grave consequences for the established international system concerning the peaceful uses of nuclear energy, the non-proliferation of nuclear weapons and international peace and security".

52nd plenary meeting
10 November 1983

[29] A/38/337, annex.

374. General Assembly Resolution 38/69 on Israeli
Nuclear Armament, December 15, 1983*

* G.A. Res. 69, 38 U.N. GAOR Supp. (No. 47) at 60, U.N. Doc. A/38/47
(1983). *See also* subsequent resolution, G.A. Res. 147, 39 U.N. GAOR Supp.
(No. 51) at 75, U.N. Doc. A/39/51 (1984).

The General Assembly,

Recalling its previous resolutions on Israeli nuclear armament,

Recalling its relevant resolutions on the establishment of a nuclear-weapon-free zone in the region of the Middle East,

Recalling also its resolution 35/157 of 12 December 1980 on military and nuclear collaboration with Israel,

Recalling its repeated condemnation of nuclear collaboration between Israel and South Africa,

Recalling Security Council resolution 487 (1981) of 19 June 1981 and taking note of the special report of the Special Committee against *Apartheid* on recent developments concerning relations between Israel and South Africa,[24]

Noting with concern Israel's refusal to comply with Security Council resolution 487 (1981),

Further noting with grave concern Israel's persistent refusal to adhere to the Treaty on the Non-Proliferation of Nuclear Weapons,[25] despite repeated calls by the General Assembly, the Security Council and the International Atomic Energy Agency, and to place its nuclear facilities under Agency safeguards,

Conscious of the grave consequences which endanger international peace and security as a result of Israel's development and acquisition of nuclear weapons and Israel's collaboration with South Africa to develop nuclear weapons and their delivery systems,

Taking note of the report of the Secretary-General,[26]

1. *Condemns* Israel's refusal to renounce any possession of nuclear weapons and to place all its nuclear activities under international safeguards;

2. *Requests* the Security Council to take urgent and effective measures to implement its resolution 487 (1981) and to ensure that Israel complies with the resolution and places its nuclear facilities under International Atomic Energy Agency safeguards;

3. *Requests* the International Atomic Energy Agency to suspend any scientific co-operation with Israel which could contribute to Israel's nuclear capabilities;

4. *Reiterates* its condemnation of the Israeli threat, in violation of the Charter of the United Nations, to repeat its armed attack on peaceful nuclear facilities in Iraq and in other countries;

5. *Requests* the Secretary-General to continue to follow closely Israel's nu-

---

[24] *Official Records of the General Assembly, Thirty-eighth Session, Supplement No. 22 A* (A/38/22/Add.1).

[25] Resolution 2373 (XXII), annex.

[26] A/38/199.

clear activities and the nuclear and military colloboration between Israel and South Africa and to report to the General Assembly at its thirty-ninth session thereon, as appropriate;

6. *Decides* to include in the provisional agenda of its thirty-ninth session the item entitled "Israeli nuclear armament".

97th plenary meeting
15 December 1983

375. General Assembly Resolution 39/14 on Armed Israeli Aggression Against the Iraqi Nuclear Installations and Its Grave Consequences for the Established International System Concerning the Peaceful Uses of Nuclear Energy, the Non-Proliferation of Nuclear Weapons and International Peace and Security, November 16, 1984*

* G.A. Res. 14, 39 U.N. GAOR Supp. (No. 51) at 23, U.N. Doc. A/39/51 (1984).

The General Assembly,

Having considered the item entitled "Armed Israeli aggression against the Iraqi nuclear installations and its grave consequences for the established international system concerning the peaceful uses of nuclear energy, the non-proliferation of nuclear weapons and international peace and security",

Recalling the relevant resolutions of the Security Council and the General Assembly,

Taking note of the relevant resolutions of the International Atomic Energy Agency,

Viewing with deep concern Israel's refusal to comply with those resolutions, particularly Security Council resolution 487 (1981) of 19 June 1981,

Noting that Israel's statements contained in its communication of 12 July 1984[38] continue to ignore the safeguards system of the International Atomic Energy Agency and do not specify the Iraqi nuclear installations which were the subject of the Israeli attack and subsequent threats,

Convinced that the Israeli threats to attack nuclear facilities in Iraq and in other countries will continue to endanger peace and security in the region,

1. *Reiterates its condemnation* of Israel's continuing refusal to implement Security Council resolution 487 (1981), unanimously adopted by the Council on 19 June 1981;

2. *Considers* that Israel's statements contained in its communication of 12 July 1984 do not fulfil or, in the view of some, do not completely fulfil the provisions of General Assembly resolution 38/9 of 10 November 1983 which specifically demanded that Israel withdraw forthwith its threat to attack and destroy nuclear facilities in Iraq and in other countries;

3. *Further considers* that any threat to attack and destroy nuclear facilities in Iraq and in other countries constitutes a violation of the Charter of the United Nations;

4. *Demands* that Israel undertake forthwith not to carry out, in disregard of the safeguards system of the International Atomic Energy Agency, any attack on nuclear facilities in Iraq, or on similar facilities in other countries, devoted to peaceful purposes;

5. *Requests* the Security Council to consider the necessary measures to ensure Israel's compliance with Security Council resolution 487 (1981) and to deter Israel from repeating its attack on nuclear facilities;

6. *Reaffirms its call* for the continuation of the consideration, at the international level, of legal measures to prohibit armed attacks against nuclear facilities, as a contribution to promoting and ensuring the safe development of nuclear energy for peaceful purposes;

7. *Requests* the Secretary-General to report to the General Assembly at its fortieth session on the question of the implementation of Security Council resolution 487 (1981) and on the consequences of Israel's non-compliance with that resolution;

[38] A/39/349.

8. *Decides* to include in the provisional agenda of its fortieth session the item entitled "Armed Israeli aggression against the Iraqi nuclear installations and its grave consequences for the established international system concerning the peaceful uses of nuclear energy, the non-proliferation of nuclear weapons and international peace and security".

65th plenary meeting
16 November 1984

376. General Assembly Resolution 40/6 on Armed Israeli Aggression Against the Iraqi Nuclear Installations and Its Grave Consequences for the Established International System Concerning the Peaceful Uses of Nuclear Energy, the Non-Proliferation of Nuclear Weapons and International Peace and Security, November 1, 1985*

* G.A. Res. 40/6 (1985).

The General Assembly,

Having considered the item entitled "Armed Israeli aggression against the Iraqi nuclear installations and its grave consequences for the established international system concerning the peaceful uses of nuclear energy, the non-proliferation of nuclear weapons and international peace and security",

Recalling the relevant resolutions of the Security Council and the General Assembly,

Taking note of the relevant resolutions of the International Atomic Energy Agency,

Viewing with deep concern Israel's refusal to comply with Security Council resolution 487 (1981) of 19 June 1981,

Noting with deep concern the threatening statement made by an Israeli cabinet member on 26 March 1985,[13] in which he stated, *inter alia,* "We are prepared to strike against any nuclear reactor built by Iraq in the future",

Deeply alarmed by Israel's failure to state without ambiguity its acceptance of the internationally recognized criteria for the definition of a peaceful nuclear facility and to acknowledge the effectiveness of the safeguards system of the International Atomic Energy Agency as a reliable means of verifying the peaceful operation of nuclear facilities,

Concerned that armed attacks against nuclear facilities raise fears about the safety of present and future nuclear installations,

Aware that all States developing nuclear energy for peaceful purposes need assurances against armed attacks on nuclear facilities,

1. *Strongly condemns* all military attacks on all nuclear installations dedicated to peaceful purposes, including the military attacks by Israel on the nuclear facilities of Iraq;

2. *Considers* that Israel has not yet committed itself not to attack or threaten to attack nuclear facilities in Iraq or elsewhere, including facilities under International Atomic Energy Agency safeguards;

3. *Requests* the Security Council to take urgent and effective measures to ensure that Israel complies without further delay with the provisions of resolution 487 (1981);

4. *Requests* the International Atomic Energy Agency to consider additional measures effectively to ensure that Israel undertakes not to attack or threaten to attack peaceful nuclear facilities in Iraq or elsewhere, in violation of the Charter of the United Nations and in disregard of the safeguards system of the International Atomic Energy Agency;

5. *Calls upon* Israel urgently to place all its nuclear facilities under International Atomic Energy Agency safeguards in accordance with resolution 487 (1981) adopted unanimously by the Security Council;

6. *Reaffirms* that Iraq is entitled to compensation for the damage it has suffered as a result of the Israeli armed attack on 7 June 1981;

7. *Urges* all Member States to provide necessary technical assistance to

[13] See A/40/283, annex.

Iraq to restore its peaceful nuclear programme and to overcome the damage caused by the Israeli attack;

8. *Calls upon* all States and organizations that have not yet done so to discontinue co-operating with and giving assistance to Israel in the nuclear field;

9. *Requests* the Conference on Disarmament to continue negotiations with a view to an immediate conclusion of the agreement on the prohibition of military attacks on nuclear facilities as a contribution to promoting and ensuring the safe development of nuclear energy for peaceful purposes;

10. *Decides* to include in the provisional agenda of its forty-first session the item entitled "Armed Israeli aggression against the Iraqi nuclear installations and its grave consequences for the established international system concerning the peaceful uses of nuclear energy, the non-proliferation of nuclear weapons and international peace and security".

377. General Assembly Resolution 40/93 on Israeli Nuclear Armament, December 12, 1985*

* G.A. Res. 40/93 (1985).

The General Assembly,

Bearing in mind its previous resolutions on Israeli nuclear armament, the latest of which is 39/147 of 17 December 1984,

Recalling resolution 39/54 of 12 December 1984, in which, *inter alia*, it called upon all countries of the Middle East, pending the establishment of a nuclear-weapon-free zone in the Middle East, to agree to place all their nuclear activities under International Atomic Energy Agency safeguards,

Recalling further Security Council resolution 487 (1981) of 19 June 1981 in which, *inter alia*, the Council called upon Israel urgently to place its nuclear facilities under International Atomic Energy Agency safeguards,

Noting with grave concern Israel's persistent refusal to commit itself not to manufacture or acquire nuclear weapons, despite repeated calls by the General Assembly, the Security Council and the International Atomic Energy Agency and to place its nuclear facilities under Agency safeguards,

Aware of the grave consequences that endanger international peace and security as a result of Israel's development and acquisition of nuclear weapons and Israel's collaboration with South Africa to develop nuclear weapons and their delivery systems,

1. *Takes note* of the report of the United Nations Institute for Disarmament Research of 9 August 1985;[79]

2. *Reiterates* its condemnation of Israel's refusal to renounce any possession of nuclear weapons;

3. *Requests once more* the Security Council to take urgent and effective measures to ensure that Israel complies with the Security Council resolution 487 (1981) and places all its nuclear facilities under International Atomic Energy Agency safeguards;

4. *Reiterates* its request to the Security Council to investigate Israel's nuclear activities and the collaboration of other States, parties and institutions in these activities;

5. *Calls upon* all States and organizations that have not yet done so to discontinue co-operating with and giving assistance to Israel in the nuclear field;

6. *Reaffirms* its condemnation of the continuing nuclear collaboration between Israel and South Africa;

7. *Requests* the Secretary-General to follow closely Israeli nuclear activities and to report thereon as appropriate to the General Assembly.

[79] A/40/520.

F. Continuing Terrorism and Response

378. President Reagan's and Secretary of State Shultz's Remarks Concerning the Bombing of the U.S. Embassy in Beirut, April 18–26, 1983*

* 83 U.S. Dep't State Bull. No. 2075, at 60 (June 1983) [notes omitted].

President's Remarks, Apr. 18, 1983

As you know, our Embassy in Beirut was the target this morning of a vicious, terrorist bombing. And this cowardly act has claimed a number of killed and wounded. It appears that there are some American casualties, but we don't know yet the exact number or the extent of injury.

In cooperation with the Lebanese authorities, we're still verifying the details and identifying the casualties. I commend Ambassador Robert Dillon and his dedicated staff who are carrying on under these traumatic circumstances in the finest tradition of our military and foreign services.

Just a few minutes ago, President Gemayel called me to convey, on behalf of the Lebanese people, his profound regret and sorrow with regard to this incident and asked me to relay the condolences on behalf of the people of Lebanon to the families of those victims. He also expressed his firm determination that we persevere in the search for peace in that region. And I told President Gemayel that I joined him in those sentiments. This criminal attack on a diplomatic establishment will not deter us from our goals of peace in the region. We will do what we know to be right.

Ambassadors Habib and Draper [Philip C. Habib, special representative of the President to the Middle East, and Morris Draper, special negotiator for Lebanon], who are presently in Beirut, will continue to press in negotiations for the earliest possible total withdrawal of all external forces.

We also remain committed to the recovery by the Lebanese Government of full sovereignty throughout all of its territory. The people of Lebanon must be given the chance to resume their efforts to lead a normal life free from violence without the presence of unauthorized foreign forces on their soil. And to this noble end, I rededicate the efforts of the United States.

Secretary's Statement, Apr. 18, 1983

I learned this morning of the terrible bombing tragedy at our Embassy in Beirut today with the greatest shock and horror.

Words alone cannot adequately express my total revulsion at this senseless and inhuman terrorist act, directed against our very dedicated and courageous staff—Lebanese as well as American—in Beirut. Ambassador Dillon, who pulled himself out of the rubble of his office, is directing rescue operations right now. He exemplifies the bravery, coolness, and clearheadedness that typifies the Foreign Service, and I am extremely proud of him and his excellent staff.

We do not yet know the casualty toll of this terrible act. My prayers and grief go out to all those who might be involved and to their families. We are grateful for the concern expressed by President Gemayel and his government, all of whom are working extremely hard to help our people.

Let us rededicate ourselves to our battle against terrorism and violence;

Lebanon has seen far too much of this already and it is long past time for peace and security to prevail.

President's Remarks, Apr. 23, 1983

There can be no sadder duty for one who holds the office I hold than to pay tribute to Americans who have given their lives in the service of their country. I extend also the condolences of ourselves and our people, through Ambassador Turk [Lebanese Government representative], to the families of our loyal Lebanese employees who perished in this tragic event along with their American colleagues.

You here today—the families of these honored dead—I want you to know I speak for all Americans when I say that we share your sorrow and offer you our heartfelt sympathy. We are in your debt and theirs. Your loved ones served their country with talent and energy, courage and commitment. With your sorrow you must feel at the same time a pride—pride in their dedication. And we, your fellow citizens, share in that, also.

These gallant Americans understood the danger they faced, and yet they went willingly to Beirut. And the dastardly deed, the act of unparalleled cowardice that took their lives, was an attack on all of us—on our way of life and on the values we hold dear. We would, indeed, fail them if we let that act deter us from carrying on their mission of brotherhood and peace.

And it is written, "Blessed be the peacemakers." And they truly were peacemakers. They knew the road they traveled was hard and fraught with peril. They walked that road with cool professionalism and a deep sense of purpose. They knew it firsthand how an afflicted mankind looks to us for help—with faith in our strength, our sense of justice, and our decency. And that is the America that your loved ones exemplified. Let our monument to their memory be a preservation of that America.

Let us here in their presence serve notice to the cowardly, skulking barbarians in the world that they will not have their way. Let us dedicate ourselves to the cause of those loved ones, the cause they served so nobly and for which they sacrificed their lives, a cause of peace on earth and justice for all mankind. We thank God for them, and God bless you.

Secretary's Remarks, Apr. 26, 1983

One week ago, all too many of our fellow workers—Lebanese and American—gave their lives in the service of the United States and the ideals for which we stand.

On Saturday evening, at Andrews Air Force Base just outside Washington, I stood by President Reagan's side as the caskets bearing the American dead were returned to their families and their homeland.

The tide of emotion is strong; anger at this murderous violence against innocent people, sorrow for the families bereaved, determination that the noble work in which our diplomats were engaged will go forward. And yet, beyond emotion in that Air Force hangar at Andrews was a profound reminder of our common humanity:

· Our deep feelings for the families who shed their tears and will miss the touch, the warmth, of loved ones;

· Our respect and appreciation for the Foreign Service family, for people who serve the United States around the world, often at hazard, always in the cause of peace and justice; and

· Our pride in our country that has such men and women in its service— a proud calling, a selfless calling.

As our representatives, our diplomats tend to our relationships around the world. They explain our society to others and in return convey the viewpoint of other governments and peoples to our own. In so doing, they foster America's goals of peace, well-being, and freedom.

All of us here today, whatever our nationality or religion, are bound by common devotion to the cause of peace. On behalf of those who fell in Beirut, we offer our prayers. In their honor and memory, we offer our pledge never to flag in pursuit of peace.

379. Secretary of State Shultz's Statement Before the Senate Foreign Relations Committee and the House Foreign Affairs Committee, October 24, 1983*

* 83 U.S. Dep't State Bull. No. 2081, at 44 (December 1983). *See also* Presidential and White House Statements on the Bombing of the Marine Barracks in Beirut, October 23, 1983. 83 U.S. Dep't State Bull. No. 2081, at 40 (December 1983).

I am sorry to have to be here in such tragic circumstances, but I also appreciate the opportunity to come here to discuss our policy in Lebanon in the wake of yesterday's events. This outrage perpetrated against our forces is a brutal reminder, as the President said yesterday, of the bestial nature of those elements in the Middle East that will take over if we are not steadfast and strong.

I want to take this opportunity to pay tribute to the courage and sacrifice of our French ally, as well as to offer my personal sympathy to the families of all those who perished, American and French.

Let me say a few words about the broader issues at stake, and then about the situation in Lebanon.

The Stakes in Lebanon

We are in Lebanon because the outcome in Lebanon will affect our position in the whole Middle East. To ask why Lebanon is important is to ask why the Middle East is important—because the answer is the same.

The United States is involved in the quest for peace in the Middle East because it is a region of vital strategic and economic importance for the free world, because it is an arena of competition between the United States and the Soviet Union, because we have a deep and abiding commitment to Israel and an interest in strengthening the trends of moderation in the Arab world, and because our role of leadership in Middle East diplomacy is a reflection of America's responsibility as a world leader.

The crisis in Lebanon cannot be isolated from the broader Middle East crisis. Indeed, that has been the heart of Lebanon's tragedy in the past 15 years. The contest in Lebanon involves many of the same parties that figure in the broader Middle East drama: moderate elements that yearn to settle their differences peacefully and radical elements that both preach and practice hatred as a matter of policy. The issues at stake in Lebanon are, therefore, some of the same issues at stake in the search for Middle East peace: questions of security, of respect for national sovereignty, and the viability of peaceful solutions.

At stake in Lebanon is the fate of the second moderate Arab country to negotiate a major agreement with Israel. I should not have to elaborate on what it would mean for the overall peace process, and for Israel's long-term security, if the assault on this moderate government should succeed. Indeed, this is a major reason why that assault is taking place.

At stake is the right of a small country like Lebanon to decide for itself how to achieve its sovereign objectives free of outside pressure, threat, or blackmail. This is a basic principle of international law and international morality that is vital not only to the future of the Middle East but to the kind of world we want to live in over the remainder of this century.

If America's efforts for peaceful solutions are overwhelmed by brute force, our role in the world is that much weakened everywhere. Friends who rely on us will be disheartened and will be that much less secure. Moderates in the Arab world whom we are encouraging to take risks for peace will feel it far less safe to do so. Israel's security will ultimately be weakened.

If we are driven out of Lebanon, radical and rejectionist elements will have scored a major victory. The message will be sent that relying on the Soviet Union pays off and that relying on the United States is a fatal mistake. This is, of course, the opposite of the message that we want to convey in our foreign policy.

If we are driven out of Lebanon, it will be a major blow to the American position in the Middle East. If we want the role and influence of a great power, then we have to accept the responsibilities of a great power. If we as Americans decide we do not want the role and influence of a great power, then I shudder to think what kind of world of anarchy and danger our children will inherit.

Our Policy in Lebanon

Let me turn now to the situation in Lebanon. Our goal in Lebanon is a political settlement between the government and the various confessional groups, aiming at a broader based government that can extend its sovereign authority throughout the country. In these circumstances we envisage the withdrawal of all foreign forces, as well as security arrangements to assure the security of Israel's northern border. This process of political accommodation is an urgent task. It should be a priority responsibility of Lebanon's leaders and Lebanon's people. It is also one of our high priorities.

One step toward this goal was the May 17 agreement between Lebanon and Israel. It provides a framework for cooperation between Lebanon and Israel, and it offers the only existing arrangement for assuring Israeli withdrawal while addressing the basic problem of border security that created the Lebanese crisis in the first place. We will continue to defend this agreement, and we look to the day when it will be implemented.

Our goal is a political solution, not a military solution. Yet the presence of our Marines has been a crucial pillar of the structure of stability that is needed to make a political solution possible. Our strategy is built on several such pillars.

· Our Marines are part of a multinational peacekeeping force, including the forces of our British, French, and Italian allies. These units symbolize the broad international support for the legitimate Government of Lebanon.

· Backing up our Marines is a powerful offshore naval force, which has fired in defense of the Marines when they have come under fire. Our allies also have naval assets in the eastern Mediterranean and have used them.

· In the military dimension, the primary responsibility rests on the Lebanese Armed Forces, which we helped to train and equip. The army has proven to be a brave and effective fighting force and is getting stronger by the day. It is more than a match for its Lebanese opponents; its difficulties have come when it was under assault by forces protected, armed, supported, and encouraged by Syria.

· The Lebanese Government has the support of moderate Arabs, which can only be strengthened by a successful effort of national reconciliation.

· Israel, too, remains a key factor in Lebanon, and we need its constructive efforts in support of the Lebanese Government and the process of reconciliation. Israel has leverage with some of the confessional groups, and we hope it will use this leverage in the direction of encouraging political accommodation.

Syria and its surrogates, of course, have been obstructing both our efforts to get foreign forces out and our efforts to promote political accommodation. No one questions Syria's legitimate security concerns with respect to Lebanon. But Syria, unlike Israel, has been unwilling to negotiate with Lebanon over how to reconcile its security concerns with Lebanon's sovereign right to decide its own future. Instead, Syria has declared a kind of "Brezhnev doctrine," whereby countries in its orbit have no sovereign right to make any decisions that displease it.

We acheived a cease-fire on September 26, however, by demonstrating that there were limits beyond which we could not be pushed. The achievement of this cease-fire showed that we have the assets to maintain a stable balance in Lebanon so that the government's opponents cannot steamroll the political negotiations. We must maintain that balance. Pulling our Marines out or reducing their number would only undercut the balance and undermine the chances for an equitable political outcome. This is not President Reagan's policy. The bipartisan support shown in the congressional joint resolution on the war powers issue was an important contribution, dispelling doubts about our staying power and strengthening our hand.

Responsibility for the Bombing

A question I am sure is on your minds is: who is responsible for this bombing outrage? I can say to you now only that we are still sifting the evidence, most of which is from before the bombing, and, therefore, only circumstantially related to the event. I can also read you some press reports of some interesting reactions to yesterday's bombings.

· The president of the Iranian Supreme Court issued a statement yesterday saying that the "Muslim people" of Lebanon have "dealt with the U.S. and France in such a way that they have learned their lesson not to embark on aggression and attacks on oppressed nations."

· A Syrian newspaper—part of Syria's state-controlled press—contained a reference to the bombings of our Marines and French soldiers which attributed the two actions to the so-called Lebanese nationalist resisistance.

Both Iran and Syria, of course, deny any responsibility for the bombing attacks.

Since we don't yet know who is directly responsible for the attack, it would not be fruitful to speculate. But there is a broader point to be made. It is not difficult to detect who are the opponents of stability in Lebanon. The opponents of peace in Lebanon are those who oppose progress toward peace in the Middle East, and it is not a coincidence that these elements have been bitter opponents of the multinational force in Lebanon of which our Marines are a part:

· Syria, which seems determined to make Lebanon a satellite of "Greater Syria";

· The Soviet Union, which arms Syria with the most sophisticated weapons and encourages its hegemonistic policies; and

· Iran, the regime of fanatics with which we have had earlier experience.

Iranian elements in Lebanon operate from behind Syrian lines and are allied with Syria. Syria must bear a share of responsibility for any Iranian actions in Lebanon whether or not Syria knew of any specific terrorist plans. Likewise, the Soviet Union, even though its relations with Iran are strained, has encouraged Syria and contributed to the climate of violence and intimidation which obtains in Lebanon. And the Soviets have been bitterly opposed to the presence of the multinational force.

The Soviet Union, Syria, and Iran—that should tell you something about what is going on in Lebanon, why it is a part of something much larger than Lebanon, and why we have a stake in the outcome.

As the result of our deliberations yesterday and today, the President has decided on a series of steps.

· He has ordered the immediate replacement of our losses and strengthening of our Marine contingent in Beirut, so that there is no gap in the performance of our mission.

· General P.X. Kelley, Commandant of the Marine Corps, has gone to Beirut to study the security situation of our Marines and to make urgent recommendations on ways of improving it.

· We are continuing an intensified intelligence effort to identify the perpetrators of Sunday's massacre.

· I will travel to Europe by the end of this week to consult urgently and intensively with the foreign ministers of our MNF partners—Britain, France, and Italy.

· Ambassador Richard Fairbanks, who was the partner of Ambassador McFarlane in our recent diplomatic efforts in Lebanon, will be in Geneva to lend support and impetus to President Gemayel's efforts at national reconciliation.

President Reagan is determined that we will not be driven out of Lebanon by the enemies of peace. We will stay, and we will carry out our mission. Many millions of people around the world look to the United States as the strongest defender of freedom and peace. We cannot walk away from such responsibilities without paying a moral, political, and strategic price.

380. General Assembly Resolution 38/130 on Measures to Prevent International Terrorism Which Endangers or Takes Innocent Human Lives or Jeopardizes Fundamental Freedoms and Study of the Underlying Causes of Those Forms of Terrorism and Acts of Violence Which Lie in Misery, Frustration, Grievance and Despair and Which Cause Some People to Sacrifice Human Lives, Including Their Own, in an Attempt to Effect Radical Change, December 19, 1983*

---

* G.A. Res. 130, 38 U.N. GAOR Supp. (No. 47) at 266, U.N. Doc. A/38/47 (1983).

The General Assembly,

Recalling its resolutions 3034 (XXVII) of 18 December 1972, 31/102 of 15 December 1976, 32/147 of 16 December 1977, 34/145 of 17 December 1979 and 36/109 of 10 December 1981,

Recalling also the Declaration on Principles of International Law concerning Friendly Relations and Co-operation among States in accordance with the Charter of the United Nations,[15] the Declaration on the Strengthening of International Security,[16] the Definition of Aggression[17] and the Protocols Additional to the Geneva Conventions of 1949,[18]

Deeply concerned about continuing acts of international terrorism which take a toll of innocent human lives,

Convinced of the importance of international cooperation for dealing with acts of international terrorism,

Reaffirming the principle of self-determination of peoples enshrined in the Charter of the United Nations,

Reaffirming the inalienable right to self-determination and independence of all peoples under colonial and racist régimes and other forms of alien domination, and upholding the legitimacy of their struggle, in particular the struggle of national liberation movements, in accordance with the purposes and principles of the Charter and of the Declaration on Principles of International Law concerning Friendly Relations and Co-operation among States in accordance with the Charter of the United Nations,

Taking note of the report of the Secretary-General,[19]

1. *Deeply deplores* the loss of innocent human lives and the pernicious impact of acts of international terrorism on friendly relations among States as well as on international co-operation, including co-operation for development;

2. *Urges* all States, unilaterally and in co-operation with other States, as well as relevant United Nations organs to contribute to the progressive elimination of the causes underlying international terrorism;

3. *Invites* all States to take all appropriate measures at the national level with a view to the speedy and final elimination of the problem of international terrorism, such as the harmonization of domestic legislation with international conventions, the implementation of assumed international obligations and the prevention of the preparation and organization in their territory of acts directed against other States;

4. *Calls upon* all States to fulfil their obligations under international law to refrain from organizing, instigating, assisting or participating in acts of civil

[15] Resolution 2625 (XXV), annex.
[16] Resolution 2734 (XXV).
[17] Resolution 3314 (XXIX), annex.
[18] A/32/144, annexes I and II.
[19] A/38/355 and Add.1-3.

strife or terrorist acts in another State, or acquiescing in organized activities within their territory directed towards the commission of such acts;

5. *Appeals* to all States that have not yet done so to consider becoming parties to the existing international conventions relating to various aspects of the problem of international terrorism;

6. *Urges* all States to co-operate with one another more closely, especially through the exchange of relevant information concerning the prevention and combating of international terrorism, the apprehension and prosecution of the perpetrators of such acts, the conclusion of special treaties and/ or the incorporation into appropriate bilateral treaties of special clauses, in particular regarding the extradition or prosecution of international terrorists;

7. *Re-endorses* the recommendations submitted by the *Ad Hoc* Committee on International Terrorism in its report to the General Assembly at its thirty-fourth session relating to practical measures of co-operation for the speedy elimination of the problem of international terrorism;[20]

8. *Calls upon* all States to observe and implement the recommendations submitted by the *Ad Hoc* Committee;

9. *Requests* the Secretary-General to follow up, as appropriate, the implementation of the present resolution and, in particular, of the recommendations submitted by the *Ad Hoc* Committee and to submit a report to the General Assembly at its fortieth session;

10. *Decides* to include the item in the provisional agenda of its fortieth session.

101st plenary meeting
19 December 1983

[20] *Official Records of the General Assembly, Thirty-fourth Session, Supplement No. 37* (A/34/37), para. 118.

381. Excerpt from the Comprehensive Crime Control Act of 1984 Pertaining to Hostage Taking and Aircraft Sabotage, October 12, 1984*

* The Comprehensive Crime Control Act, Ch. XX, Pub. L. No. 98-473, 98 Stat. 1837, 2186 (1984).

CHAPTER XX—TERRORISM

PART A—HOSTAGE TAKING

SEC. 2001. This part may be cited as the "Act for the Prevention and Punishment of the Crime of Hostage-Taking".

SEC. 2002. (a) Chapter 55 of title 18 of the United States Code is amended by adding at the end the following new section:

"§ 1203. Hostage taking

(a) Except as provided in subsection (b) of this section, whoever, whether inside or outside the United States, seizes or detains and threatens to kill, to injure, or to continue to detain another person in order to compel a third person or a governmental organization to do or abstain from doing any act as an explicit or implicit condition for the release of the person detained, or attempts to do so, shall be punished by imprisonment for any term of years or for life.

(b)(1) It is not an offense under this section if the conduct required for the offense occurred outside the United States unless—

(A) the offender or the person seized or detained is a national of the United States;

(B) the offender is found in the United States; or

(C) the governmental organization sought to be compelled is the Government of the United States.

(2) It is not an offense under this section if the conduct required for the offense occurred inside the United States, each alleged offender and each person seized or detained are nationals of the United States, and each alleged offender is found in the United States, unless the governmental organization sought to be compelled is the Government of the United States.

(C) As used in this section, the term 'national of the United States' has the meaning given such term in section 101(a)(22) of the Immigration and Nationality Act (8 U.S.C. 1101(a)(22)).".

(b) The table of sections at the beginning of chapter 55 of title 18 of the United States Code is amended by adding at the end the following new item:

1203. Hostage taking.

SEC. 2003. This part and the amendments made by this part shall take effect on the later of—

(1) the date of the enactment of this joint resolution; or

(2) the date the International Convention Against the Taking of Hostages has come into force and the United States has become a party to that convention.

PART B—AIRCRAFT SABOTAGE

SHORT TITLE

SEC. 2011. This part may be cited as the "Aircraft Sabotage Act".

SEC. 2012. The Congress hereby finds that—

(1) the Convention for the Suppression of Unlawful Acts Against the Safety of Civil Aviation (ratified by the United States on November 1, 1972) requires each contracting State to establish its jurisdiction over certain offenses affecting the safety of civil aviation;

(2) such offenses place innocent lives in jeopardy, endanger national security, affect domestic tranquility, gravely affect interstate and foreign commerce, and are offenses against the law of nations; and

(3) the purpose of this subtitle is to implement fully the Convention for the Suppression of Unlawful Acts Against the Safety of Civil Aviation and to expand the protection accorded to aircraft and related facilities.

SEC. 2013. (a) Section 31 of title 18, United States Code, is amended—

(1) in the first paragraph by—

(A) striking out "and" before the term "spare part" and inserting "and 'special aircraft jurisdiction of the United States'" after the term "spare part"; and

(B) striking out "Civil Aeronautics Act of 1938" and inserting in lieu thereof "Federal Aviation Act of 1958";

(2) by striking out "and" at the end of the third undesignated paragraph thereof;

(3) by striking the period at the end thereof and inserting in lieu thereof ";"; and

(4) by adding at the end thereof the following new paragraphs:

" 'In flight' means any time from the moment all the external doors of an aircraft are closed following embarkation until the moment when any such door in [sic] opened for disembarkation. In the case of a forced landing the flight shall be deemed to continue until competent authorities take over the responsibility for the aircraft and the persons and property on board; and

" 'In service' means any time from the beginning of preflight preparation of the aircraft by ground personnel or by the crew for a specific flight until twenty-four hours after any landing; the period of service shall, in any event, extend for the entire period during which the aircraft is in flight.".

(b) Section 32 of title 18, United States Code, is amended to read as follows:

"§ 32. Destruction of aircraft or aircraft facilities

(a) Whoever willfully—

(1) sets fire to, damages, destroys, disables, or wrecks any aircraft in the special aircraft jurisdiction of the United States or any civil aircraft used, operated, or employed in interstate, overseas, or foreign air commerce;

(2) places or causes to be placed a destructive device or substance in, upon, or in proximity to, or otherwise makes or causes to be made unworkable or unusable or hazardous to work or use, any such aircraft, or any part or other materials used or intended to be used in connection

with the operation of such aircraft, if such placing or causing to be placed or such making or causing to be made is likely to endanger the safety of any such aircraft;

(3) sets fire to, damages, destroys, or disables any air navigation facility, or interferes by force or violence with the operation of such facility, if such fire, damaging, destroying, disabling, or intefering is likely to endanger the safety of any such aircraft in flight;

(4) with the intent to damage, destroy, or disable any such aircraft, sets fire to, damages, destroys, or disables or places a destructive device or substance in, upon, or in proximity to, any appliance or structure, ramp, landing area, property, machine, or apparatus, or any facility or other material used, or intended to be used, in connection with the operation, maintenance, loading, unloading or storage of any such aircraft or any cargo carried or intended to be carried on any such aircraft;

(5) performs an act of violence against or incapacitates any individual on any such aircraft, if such act of violence or incapacitation is likely to endanger the safety of such aircraft;

(6) communicates information, knowing the information to be false and under circumstances in which such information may reasonably be believed, thereby endangering the safety of any such aircraft in flight; or

(7) attempts to do anything prohibited under paragraphs (1) through (6) of this subsection;

shall be fined not more than $100,000 or imprisoned not more than twenty years or both.

(b) Whoever willfully—

(1) performs an act of violence against any individual on board any civil aircraft registered in a country other than the United States while such aircraft is in flight, if such act is likely to endanger the safety of that aircraft;

(2) destroys a civil aircraft registered in a country other than the United States while such aircraft is in service or causes damage to such an aircraft which renders that aircraft incapable of flight or which is likely to endanger that aircraft's safety in flight;

(3) places or causes to be placed on a civil aircraft registered in a country other than the United States while such aircraft is in service, a device or substance which is likely to destroy that aircraft, or to cause damage to that aircraft which renders that aircraft incapable of flight or which is likely to endanger that aircraft's safety in flight; or

(4) attempts to commit an offense described in paragraphs (1) through (3) of this subsection;

shall, if the offender is later found in the United States, be fined not more than $100,000 or imprisoned not more than twenty years, or both.

(c) Whoever willfully imparts or conveys any threat to do an act which would violate any of paragraphs (1) through (5) of subsection (a) or any of paragraphs (1) through (3) of subsection (b) of this section, with an apparent determination and will to carry the threat into execution shall be fined not more than $25,000 or imprisoned not more than five years, or both.".

(c) Section 101(38)(d) of the Federal Aviation Act of 1958 (49 U.S.C. 1301(38)(d), relating to the definition of the term "special aircraft jurisdiction of the United States", is amended—

(1) in clause (i), by striking out "; or" and inserting in lieu thereof a semicolon;

(2) at the end of clause (ii), by striking out "and" and inserting in lieu thereof "or;"; and

(3) by adding at the end thereof the following new clause:

(iii) regarding which an offense as defined in subsection (d) or (e) of article I, section I of the Convention for the Suppression of Unlawful Acts against the Safety of Civil Aviation (Montreal, September 23, 1971) is committed if the aircraft lands in the United States with an alleged offender still on board; and.

SEC. 2014. (a)(1) Section 901 of the Federal Aviation Act of 1958 (49 U.S.C. 1471) is amended by adding at the end thereof the following new subsections:

"(c) Whoever imparts or conveys or causes to be imparted or conveyed false information, knowing the information to be false and under circumstances in which such information may reasonably be believed, concerning an attempt or alleged attempt being made or to be made, to do any act which would be a crime prohibited by subsection (i), (j), (k), or (l) of section 902 of this Act, shall be subject to a civil penalty of not more than $10,000 which shall be recoverable in a civil action brought in the name of the United States.

(d) Except for law enforcement officers of any municipal or State government or officers or employees of the Federal Government, who are authorized or required within their official capacities to carry arms, or other persons who may be so authorized under regulations issued by the Administrator, whoever while aboard, or while attempting to board, any aircraft in, or intended for operation in, air transporation or intrastate air transportation, has on or about his person or his property a concealed deadly or dangerous weapon, which is, or would be, accessible to such person in flight shall be subject to a civil penalty of not more than $10,000 which shall be recoverable in a civil action brought in the name of the United States.".

(2) That portion of the table of contents contained in the first section of the Federal Aviation Act of 1958 which appears under the side heading

Sec. 901. Civil penalties.

is amended by inserting at the end thereof:

(c) Conveying false information.

(d) Concealed weapons.

(b) Section 901(a)(2) of the Federal Aviation Act of 1958 (49 U.S.C. 1471(a)(2)) is amended by inserting "penalties provided for in subsections (c) and (d) of this section or" after "Secretary of Transportation in the case of".

(c)(1) Section 902(1)(1) of the Federal Aviation Act of 1958 (49 U.S.C. 1472(1)(1) is amended by striking out "$1,000" and inserting in lieu thereof "$10,000".

(2) Section 902(1)(2) of the Federal Aviation Act of 1958 (49 U.S.C. 1472(1)(2)) is amended by striking out "$5,000" and inserting in lieu thereof "$25,000".

(d)(1) Section 902(m) of the Federal Aviation Act of 1958 (49 U.S.C. 1472(m)) is amended to read as follows:

"FALSE INFORMATION AND THREATS

(m)(1) Whoever willfully and maliciously, or with reckless disregard for the safety of human life, imparts or conveys or causes to be imparted or conveyed false information, knowing the information to be false and under circumstances in which such information may reasonably be believed, concerning an attempt or alleged attempt being made or to be made, to do any act which would be a felony prohibited by subsection (i), (j), (k), or (l) of this section, shall be fined not more than $25,000 or imprisoned not more than five years, or both.

(2) Whoever imparts or conveys or causes to be imparted or conveyed any threat to do an act which would be a felony prohibited by subsection (i), (j), (k), or (l) of this section with an apparent determination and will to carry the threat into execution shall be fined not more than $25,000 or imprisoned not more than five years, or both.".

(2) That portion of the table of contents contained in the first section of the Federal Aviation Act of 1958 which appears under the side heading

Sec. 902. Criminal penalties.

is amended by striking out

(m) False information.

and inserting in lieu thereof

(m) False information and threats.

SEC. 2015. This part shall become effective on the date of the enactment of this joint resolution.

382. Excerpt from the International Security and Development Cooperation Act of 1985 Pertaining to International Terrorism and Foreign Airport Security, August 8, 1985*

---

* The International Security and Development Cooperation Act, Title V, Pub. L. No. 99–83, 99 Stat. 190, 219 (1985).

TITLE V—INTERNATIONAL TERRORISM AND FOREIGN AIRPORT SECURITY

PART A—INTERNATIONAL TERRORISM GENERALLY

SEC. 501. ANTI-TERRORISM ASSISTANCE PROGRAM.

(a) AUTHORIZATIONS.—Section 575 of the Foreign Assistance Act of 1961 is amended to read as follows:

"SEC. 575. AUTHORIZATIONS OF APPROPRIATIONS.—(a) There are authorized to be appropriated to the President to carry out this chapter $9,840,000 for fiscal year 1986 and $9,840,000 for fiscal year 1987.

(b) Amounts appropriated under this section are authorized to remain available until expended.".

(b) ITEMS ON THE MUNITIONS LIST.—Section 573(d)(4) of such Act is amended to read as follows:

"(4)(A) Except as provided in subparagraph (B), articles on the United States Munitions List established pursuant to the Arms Export Control Act may not be made available under this chapter.

(B) For fiscal years 1986 and 1987, articles on the United States Munitions List may be made available under this chapter if—

(i) they are small arms in category I (relating to firearms), ammunition in category III (relating to ammunition) for small arms in category I, or articles in category X (relating to protective personnel equipment), and they are directly related to anti-terrorism training being provided under this chapter;

(ii) the recipient country is not prohibited by law from receiving assistance under one or more of the following provisions: chapter 2 of this part, chapter 5 of this part, or the Arms Export Control Act; and

(iii) at least 15 days before the articles are made available to the foreign country, the President notifies the Committee on Foreign Affairs of the House of Representatives and the Committee on Foreign Relations of the Senate of the proposed transfer, in accordance with the procedures applicable to reprogramming notifications pursuant to section 634A of this Act.

(C) The value (in terms of original acquisition cost) of all equipment and commodities provided under subsection (a) of this section, including articles described in subparagraph (B)(i) of this paragraph, may not exceed $325,000 in fiscal year 1986 or $325,000 in fiscal year 1987.".

(c) RESTRICTION.—Section 573 of such Act is amended by adding at the end thereof the following new subsection:

"(f) Funds made available to carry out this chapter may not be used for personnel compensation or benefits.".

(d) EXPIRATION OF AUTHORITY.—Section 577 of such Act is repealed.

SEC. 502. COORDINATION OF ALL UNITED STATES ANTI-TERRORISM ASSISTANCE TO FOREIGN COUNTRIES.

(a) COORDINATION.—The Secretary of State shall be responsible for coordinating all anti-terrorism assistance to foreign countries provided by the United States Government.

(b) REPORTS.—Not later than February 1 each year, the Secretary of State, in consultation with appropriate United States Government agencies, shall report to the appropriate committees of the Congress on the anti-terrorism assistance provided by the United States Government during the preceding fiscal year. Such reports may be provided on a classified basis to the extent necessary, and shall specify the amount and nature of the assistance provided.

SEC. 503. PROHIBITION ON ASSISTANCE TO COUNTRIES SUPPORTING INTERNATIONAL TERRORISM.

(a) PROHIBITION.—Section 620A of the Foreign Assistance Act of 1961 is amended to read as follows:

"SEC. 620A. PROHIBITION ON ASSISTANCE TO COUNTRIES SUPPORTING INTERNATIONAL TERRORISM.—(a) The United States shall not provide any assistance under this Act, the Agricultural Trade Development and Assistance Act of 1954, the Peace Corps Act, or the Arms Export Control Act, to any country which the President determines—

(1) grants sanctuary from prosecution to any individual or group which has committed an act of international terrorism, or

(2) otherwise supports international terrorism.

(b) The President may waive the application of subsection (a) to a country if the President determines that national security or humanitarian reasons justify such waiver. The President shall publish each waiver in the Federal Register and, at least 15 days before the waiver takes effect, shall notify the Committee on Foreign Affairs of the House of Representatives and the Committee on Foreign Relations of the Senate of the waiver (including the justification for the waiver) in accordance with the procedures applicable to reprogramming notifications pursuant to section 634A of this Act.

(c) If sanctions are imposed on a country pursuant to subsection (a) because of its support for international terrorism, the President should call upon other countries to impose similar sanctions on that country.".

(b) CONFORMING AMENDMENT.—Section 3(f) of the Arms Export Control Act is amended by striking out ", credits, and guaranties" and ", credits, or guaranties" each place they appear.

SEC. 504. PROHIBITION ON IMPORTS FROM AND EXPORTS TO LIBYA.

(a) PROHIBITION ON IMPORTS.—Notwithstanding any other provision of law, the President may prohibit any article grown, produced, extracted, or manufactured in Libya from being imported into the United States.

(b) PROHIBITION ON EXPORTS.—Notwithstanding any other provision of law, the President may prohibit any goods or technology, including technical data or other information, subject to the jurisdiction of the United States or exported by any person subject to the jurisdiction of the United States, from being exported to Libya.

(c) DEFINITION.—For purposes of this section, the term "United States", when used in a geographical sense, includes territories and possessions of the United States.

SEC. 505. BAN ON IMPORTING GOODS AND SERVICES FROM COUNTRIES SUPPORTING TERRORISM.

(a) AUTHORITY.—The President may ban the importation into the United States of any good or service from any country which supports terrorism or terrorist organizations or harbors terrorists or terrorist organizations.

(b) CONSULTATION.—The President, in every possible instance, shall consult with the Congress before exercising the authority granted by this section and shall consult regularly with the Congress so long as that authority is being exercised.

(c) REPORTS.—Whenever the President exercises the authority granted by this section, he shall immediately transmit to the Congress a report specifying—

(1) the country with respect to which the authority is to be exercised and the imports to be prohibited;

(2) the circumstances which necessitate the exercise of such authority;

(3) why the President believes those circumstances justify the exercise of such authority; and

(4) why the President believes the prohibitions are necessary to deal with those circumstances.

At least once during each succeeding 6-month period after transmitting a report pursuant to this subsection, the President shall report to the Congress with respect to the actions taken, since the last such report, pursuant to this section and with respect to any changes which have occurred concerning any information previously furnished pursuant to this subsection.

(d) DEFINITION.—For purposes of this section, the term "United States" includes territories and possessions of the United States.

SEC. 506. INTERNATIONAL ANTI-TERRORISM COMMITTEE.

The Congress calls upon the President to seek the establishment of an international committee, to be known as the International Anti-Terrorism Committee, consisting of representatives of the member countries of the North Atlantic Treaty Organization, Japan, and such other countries as may be invited and may choose to participate. The purpose of the Committee should be to focus the attention and secure the cooperation of the governments and the public of the participating countries and of other countries on the problems and responses to international terrorism, by serving as a forum at both the political and law enforcement levels.

SEC. 507. INTERNATIONAL TERRORISM CONTROL TREATY.

It is the sense of the Congress that the President should establish a process by which democratic and open societies of the world, which are those most plagued by terrorism, negotiate a viable treaty to effectively prevent and respond to terrorist attacks. Such a treaty should incorporate an operative definition of terrorism, and should establish effective close intelligence-sharing, joint counterterrorist training, and uniform laws on asylum, extradition, and swift punishment for perpetrators of terrorism. Parties to such a treaty should include, but not be limited to, those democratic nations who are most victimized by terrorism.

SEC. 508. STATE TERRORISM.

It is the sense of the Congress that all civilized nations should firmly condemn the increasing use of terrorism by certain states as an official instrument for promoting their policy goals, as evidenced by such examples as the brutal assassination of Major Arthur D. Nicholson, Junior, by a member of the Soviet armed forces.

PART B—FOREIGN AIRPORT SECURITY
SEC. 551. SECURITY STANDARDS FOR FOREIGN AIR TRANSPORTATION.

(a) SECURITY AT FOREIGN AIRPORTS.—Section 1115 of the Federal Aviation Act of 1958 (49 U.S.C. App. 1515) is amended to read as follows:

"SECURITY STANDARDS IN FOREIGN AIR TRANSPORTATION
ASSESSMENT OF SECURITY MEASURES

SEC. 1115. (a)(1) The Secretary of Transportation shall conduct at such intervals as the Secretary shall deem necessary an assessment of the effectiveness of the security measures maintained at those foreign airports being served by air carriers, those foreign airports from which foreign air carriers serve the United States, those foreign airports which pose a high risk of introducing danger to international air travel, and at such other foreign airports as the Secretary may deem appropriate.

(2) Each such assessment shall be made by the Secretary of Transportation in consultation with the appropriate aeronautic authorities of the foreign government concerned and each air carrier serving the foreign airport at which the Secretary is conducting such assessment.

(3) The assessment shall determine the extent to which an airport effectively maintains and administers security measures. In making an assessment of any airport under this subsection, the Secretary shall use a standard which will result in an analysis of the security measures at such airport based upon, at a minimum, the standards and appropriate recommended practices contained in Annex 17 to the Convention on International Civil Aviation, as those standards and recommended practices are in effect on the date of such assessment.

CONSULTATION WITH THE SECRETARY OF STATE

(b) In carrying out subsection (a), the Secretary of Transportation shall consult the Secretary of State with respect to the terrorist threat which exists in each country. The Secretary of Transportation shall also consult with the Secretary of State in order to determine which foreign airports are not under the de facto control of the government of the country in which they are located and pose a high risk of introducing danger to international air travel.

REPORT OF ASSESSMENTS

(c) Each report to the Congress required by section 315 of this Act shall contain a summary of the assessments conducted pursuant to subsection (a).

NOTIFICATION TO FOREIGN COUNTRY OF DETERMINATION

(d) Whenever, after an assessment in accordance with subsection (a), the Secretary of Transportation determines that an airport does not maintain and administer effective security measures, the Secretary (after advising the Secretary of State) shall notify the appropriate authorities of such foreign government of such determination, and recommend the steps necessary to bring the security measures in use at that airport up to the standard used by the Secretary in making such assessment.

NOTICE AND SANCTIONS

(e)(1) Paragraph (2) of this subsection shall becomes effective—

    (A) 90 days after notification to the foreign government pursuant to subsection (d), if the Secretary of Transporation finds that the foreign government has failed to bring the security measures at the identified airport up to the standard used by the Secretary in making an assessment of such airport under subsection (a); or

    (B) immediately upon the Secretary of Transportation's determination under subsection (d) if the Secretary of Transportation determines, after consultation with the Secretary of State, that a condition exists that threatens the safety or security of passengers, aircraft, or crew traveling to or from such airport.

The Secretary of Transportation shall immediately notify the Secretary of State of any determination made pursuant to subparagraph (B) so that the Secretary of State may comply with the requirement of section 552(a) of the International Security and Development Cooperation Act of 1985 that a travel advisory be issued.

(2) Subject to paragraph (1), if the Secretary of Transportation determines pursuant to this section that an airport does not maintain and administer effective security measures—

    (A) the Secretary of Transportation—

        (i) shall publish the identity of such airport in the Federal Register,

        (ii) shall cause the identity of such airport to be posted and prominently displayed at all United States airports regularly being served by scheduled air carrier operations, and

        (iii) shall notify the news media of the identity of such airport;

    (B) each air carrier and foreign air carrier providing service between the United States and such airport shall provide notice of such determination by the Secretary to any passenger purchasing a ticket for transportation between the United States and such airport, with such notice to be made by written material included on or with such ticket;

(C) the Secretary of Transportation, after consultation with the appropriate aeronautical authorities of the foreign government concerned and each air carrier serving such airport, may, notwithstanding section 1102 of this Act and with the approval of the Secretary of State, withhold, revoke, or impose conditions on the operating authority of any air carrier or foreign air carrier to engage in foreign air transportation utilizing such airport; and

(D) the President may prohibit air carriers and foreign air carriers from providing service between the United States and any other foreign airport which is directly or indirectly served by aircraft flying to or from the airport with respect to which the determination is made under this section.

(3) The Secretary of Transportation shall promptly submit to the Congress a report (with a classified annex if necessary) on any action taken under this subsection, setting forth information concerning the attempts made to secure the cooperation of the foreign government in meeting the standard used by the Secretary in making the assessment of the airport under subsection (a).

LIFTING OF SANCTIONS

(f)(1) The sanctions required to be imposed with respect to an airport pursuant to subsection (e)(2)(A) and (B) may be lifted only if the Secretary of Transportation, in consultation with the Secretary of State, has determined that effective security measures are maintained and administered at that airport.

(2) The Congress shall be notified if any sanction imposed pursuant to subsection (e) is lifted.

AUTHORITY FOR IMMEDIATE SUSPENSION OF AIR SERVICE

(g) Notwithstanding sections 1102 and 1114 of this Act, whenever the Secretary of Transportation determines that—

(1) a condition exists that threatens the safety or security of passengers, aircraft, or crew traveling to or from a foreign airport, and

(2) the public interest requires an immediate suspension of services between the United States and the identified airport,

the Secretary of Transportation shall, without notice or hearing and with the approval of the Secretary of State, suspend the right of any air carrier or foreign air carrier to engage in foreign air transportation to or from that foreign airport and the right of any person to operate aircraft in foreign air commerce to or from that foreign airport.

CONDITIONS OF AUTHORITY

(h) The provisions of this section shall be deemed to be a condition to any authority granted under title IV or title VI of this Act to any air carrier or any foreign air carrier, issued under authority vested in the Secretary of Transportation.".

(b) CONFORMING AMENDMENTS.—

(1) INFORMATION IN SEMIANNUAL REPORTS.—Section 315(a) of the Federal Aviation Act of 1958 (49 U.S.C. App. 1356(a)) is amended by adding at the end thereof the following new sentence: "Each semiannual report submitted by the Administrator pursuant to the preceding sentence shall include the information described in section 1115(c) of this Act.".

(2) CIVIL PENALTIES.—Section 901(a)(1) of the Federal Aviation Act of 1958 (49 U.S.C. App. 1471(a)(1)) is amended by inserting "or 1115(e)(2)(B)" after "1114".

(3) TABLE OF CONTENTS.—That portion of the table of contents contained in the first section of the Federal Aviation Act of 1958 which appears under the center heading

"TITLE XI—MISCELLANEOUS"

is amended by striking out

"Sec. 1115. Security standards in foreign air transportation.".

and inserting in lieu thereof

"Sec. 1115. Security standards in foreign air transportation.

(a) Assessment of security measures.

(b) Consultation with the Secretary of State.

(c) Report of assessments.

(d) Notification to foreign country of determination.

(e) Notice and sanctions.

(f) Lifting of sanctions.

(g) Authority for immediate suspension of air service.

(h) Conditions of authority.".

(c) CLOSING OF BEIRUT INTERNATIONAL AIRPORT.—It is the sense of the Congress that the President is urged and encouraged to take all appropriate steps to carry forward his announced policy of seeking the effective closing of the international airport in Beirut, Lebanon, at least until such time as the Government of Lebanon has instituted measures and procedures designed to prevent the use of that airport by aircraft hijackers and other terrorists in attacking civilian airlines or their passengers, hijacking their aircraft, or taking or holding their passengers hostage.

SEC. 552. TRAVEL ADVISORY AND SUSPENSION OF FOREIGN ASSISTANCE.

(a) TRAVEL ADVISORY.—Upon being notified by the Secretary of Transportation that the Secretary has determined, pursuant to subsection (e)(1)(B) of section 1115 of the Federal Aviation Act of 1958 that a condition exists that threatens the safety or security of passengers, aircraft, or crew travelling to or from a foreign airport which the Secretary of Transporta-

Continuing Terrorism and Response

tion has determined pursuant to that section to be an airport which does not maintain and administer effective security measures, the Secretary of State shall immediately issue a travel advisory with respect to that airport. Any travel advisory issued pursuant to this subsection shall be published in the Federal Register. The Secretary of State shall take the necessary steps to widely publicize that travel advisory.

(b) SUSPENSION OF FOREIGN ASSISTANCE.—The President shall suspend all assistance under the Foreign Assistance Act of 1961 or the Arms Export Control Act to any country in which is located an airport with respect to which section 1115(e)(2) of the Federal Aviation Act of 1958 becomes effective if the Secretary of State determines that such country is a high terrorist threat country. The President may waive the requirements of this subsection if the President determines and reports to the Congress that national security interests or a humanitarian emergency require such waiver.

(c) LIFTING SANCTIONS.—The sanctions required to be imposed pursuant to this section may be lifted only if, pursuant to section 1115(f) of the Federal Aviation Act of 1958, the Secretary of Transportation, in consultation with the Secretary of State, has determined that effective security measures are maintained and administered at the airport with respect to which the Secretary of Transportation had made the determination described in section 1115 of that Act.

(d) NOTIFICATION TO CONGRESS.—The Congress shall be notified if any sanction imposed pursuant to this section is lifted.

SEC. 553. UNITED STATES AIRMARSHAL PROGRAM.

(a) STUDY OF NEED FOR EXPANSION OF PROGRAM.—The Secretary of Transportation, in coordination with the Secretary of State, shall study the need for an expanded airmarshal program on international flights of United States air carriers. The Secretary of Transportation shall report the results of this study to the Congress within 6 months after the date of enactment of this Act.

(b) AUTHORITY TO CARRY FIREARMS AND MAKE ARRESTS.—The Secretary of Transportation, with the approval of the Attorney General and the Secretary of State, may authorize persons, in connection with the performance of their air transportation security duties, to carry firearms and to make arrests without warrant for any offense against the United States committed in their presence, or for any felony cognizable under the laws of the United States, if they have reasonable grounds to believe that the person to be arrested has committed or is committing a felony.

SEC. 554. ENFORCEMENT OF INTERNATIONAL CIVIL AVIATION ORGANIZATION STANDARDS.

The Secretary of State and the Secretary of Transportation, jointly, shall call on the member countries of the International Civil Aviation Organization to enforce that Organization's existing standards and to support United States actions enforcing such standards.

SEC. 555. INTERNATIONAL CIVIL AVIATION BOYCOTT OF COUNTRIES SUPPORTING INTERNATIONAL TERRORISM.

It is the sense of the Congress that the President—
(1) should call for an international civil aviation boycott with respect to those countries which the President determines—
(A) grant sanctuary from prosecution to any individual or group which has committed an act of international terrorism, or
(B) otherwise support international terrorism; and
(2) should take steps, both bilateral and multilateral, to achieve a total international civil aviation boycott with respect to those countries.

SEC. 556. MULTILATERAL AND BILATERAL AGREEMENTS WITH RESPECT TO AIRCRAFT SABOTAGE, AIRCRAFT HIJACKING, AND AIRPORT SECURITY.

The Secretary of State shall seek multilateral and bilateral agreement on strengthening enforcement measures and standards for compliance with respect to aircraft sabotage, aircraft hijacking, and airport security.

SEC. 557. RESEARCH ON AIRPORT SECURITY TECHNIQUES FOR DETECTING EXPLOSIVES.

In order to improve security at international airports, there are authorized to be appropriated to the Secretary of Transportation from the Airport and Airway Trust Fund (in addition to amounts otherwise available for such purpose) $5,000,000, without fiscal year limitation, to be used for research on and the development of airport security devices or techniques for detecting explosives.

SEC. 558. HIJACKING OF TWA FLIGHT 847 AND OTHER ACTS OF TERRORISM.

The Congress joins with all Americans in celebrating the release of the hostages taken from Trans World Airlines flight 847. It is the sense of the Congress that—
(1) purser Uli Derickson, pilot John Testrake, co-pilot Philip Maresca, flight engineer Benjamin Zimmermann, and the rest of the crew of Trans World Airlines flight 847 displayed extraordinary valor and heroism during the hostages' ordeal and therefore should be commended;
(2) the hijackers who murdered United States Navy Petty Officer Stethem should be immediately brought to justice;
(3) all diplomatic means should continue to be employed to obtain the release of the 7 United States citizens previously kidnapped and still held in Lebanon;
(4) acts of international terrorism should be universally condemned; and
(5) the Secretary of State should be supported in his efforts to gain international cooperation to prevent future acts of terrorism.

SEC. 559. EFFECTIVE DATE.

This part shall take effect on the date of enactment of this Act.

383. Department of State Statements on the TWA Hijacking, June 14 and 17, 1985*

* 85 U.S. Dep't State Bull. No. 2101, at 77 (August 1985) (notes omitted).

Department Statement, June 14, 1985

The United States strongly condemns the hijacking of TWA [Trans-World Airlines] Flight #847, as it does all other such acts of terrorism. We call for the immediate safe release of all the passengers and crew members. These lawless acts, which endanger innocent lives, are repugnant, and we do not see how such acts gain sympathy for the cause of those who commit them. At this time, we are working with all appropriate governments and parties to secure the release of the hostages. We have a task force at the State Department working continually on the situation and coordinating U.S. Government efforts on this matter.

Secretary's Statement, June 17, 1985

Hijacking and other forms of terrorism are unacceptable in any civilized society.

We call upon those holding hostages to treat them properly and to release them immediately. The U.S. Government is heavily engaged in efforts to bring about their safe return to their families. In pursuing these efforts, as is well known, we will not make deals with terrorists and will not encourage others to do so.

Our thoughts and prayers are with the hostages and their families, as we all work and wait for their safe release.

384. Security Council Resolution 573 Condemning the Israeli Air Raid on the PLO Headquarters in Tunisia, October 4, 1985*

* S.C. Res. 573, 40 U.N. SCOR (2615th mtg.) (1985).

The Security Council,

Having considered the letter dated 1 October 1985 (S/17509) in which Tunisia made a complaint against Israel following the act of aggression which the latter committed against the sovereignty and territorial integrity of Tunisia,

Having heard the statement by the Minister for Foreign Affairs of Tunisia,

Having noted with concern that the Israeli attack has caused heavy loss of human life and extensive material damage,

Considering that, in accordance with Article 2, paragraph 4, of the Charter of the United Nations, all Members shall refrain in their international relations from the threat or use of force against the territorial integrity or political independence of any State, or in any other manner inconsistent with the purposes of the United Nations,

Gravely concerned at the threat to peace and security in the Mediterranean region posed by the air raid perpetrated on 1 October 1985 by Israel in the area of Hammam-Plage, situated in the southern suburb of Tunis,

Drawing attention to the serious effect which the aggression carried out by Israel and all acts contrary to the Charter cannot but have on any initiative designed to establish an overall, just and lasting peace in the Middle East,

Considering that the Israeli Government claimed responsibility for the attack as soon as it had been carried out,

1. *Condemns* vigorously the act of armed aggression perpetrated by Israel against Tunisian territory in flagrant violation of the Charter of the United Nations, international law and norms of conduct;

2. *Demands* that Israel refrain from perpetrating such acts of aggression or from the threat to do so;

3. *Urgently requests* the States Members of the United Nations to take measures to dissuade Israel from resorting to such acts against the sovereignty and territorial integrity of all States;

4. *Considers* that Tunisia has the right to appropriate reparations as a result of the loss of human life and material damage which it has suffered and for which Israel has claimed responsibility;

5. *Requests* the Secretary-General to report to it on the implementation of this resolution by 30 November 1985 at the latest;

6. *Decides* to remain seized of the matter.

385. European Parliament Resolution on the Israeli Raid in Tunisia, October 10, 1985*

---

* 28 O.J. Eur. Comm. (No. C 288) 109 (1985).

The European Parliament,

A. deeply perturbed by the Israeli raid of 1 October 1985, on Tunisian territory, on the headquarters of the Palestine Liberation Organization, which cost the lives of more than 70 people and injured more than 100, several of them civilians,

B. deploring the attack in Cyprus during Yom Kippur, which claimed three victims,

C. extremely concerned at the hijacking of the liner 'Achille Lauro' by Palestinian terrorists on Monday, 7 October 1985,

D. noting that the PLO has disclaimed all responsibility for the Cyprus attack and the hijacking of the 'Achille Lauro',

1. Endorses the statement of condemnation issued by the Foreign Ministers of the Ten, Spain and Portugal meeting in Political Cooperation in Luxembourg on 1 October 1985;

2. Reaffirms its condemnation of all terrorist acts whether they are perpetrated by individuals, groups or states;

3. Instructs its President to forward this resolution to the Council, the Commission, the Foreign Ministers meeting in Political Cooperation and the governments of the Ten, of Spain and Portugal and to the Secretary-General of the UN.

386. Statement by the Egyptian Ministry of Foreign
Affairs in Reaction to the Interception by U.S. Warplanes
of an *Egypt Air* Plane Carrying the Hijackers of
the *Achille Lauro*, Cairo, October 11, 1985*

---

* 15 J. Palestine Stud. 214 (Winter 1986), as translated by the Associated Press.

The government of the Arab Republic of Egypt was regrettably taken by surprise when American planes intercepted an Egypt Air plane that was carrying hijackers of the Italian ship along with two PLO officials who had participated in negotiations with hijackers. The interception of the plane occurred when it was on its way back to Cairo after the Tunisian authorities denied it access and announced that the airport was closed to it, despite Tunisia's earlier approval for the plane to land at Tunis Airport—approval that had taken several hours to obtain.

Egypt, which always has condemned terror and violence in all forms by air or on land or by sea and which also denounced the hijacking of the Italian ship in line with its well-known and declared principles, negotiated with the hijackers of the ship on humanitarian grounds to save the lives of more than four hundred people who did not include a single Egyptian and who were in grave and certain danger. It did so at the insistence of some countries that had nationals on board the ship. These countries signed a document asking Egypt to negotiate, without their making any specific demands regarding the fate of the hijackers in the event of their surrender.

Egypt ended the hijack peacefully, although the ship was outside its territorial waters and at a time when its information was that there had been no victims of the hijack, as acknowledged by the captain of the ship in the tape recording that was played by the deputy prime minister and foreign minister at his press conference.

It is well known that the world followed with satisfaction Egypt's efforts to save the lives of the hostages. In this connection Egypt received messages of appreciation from most world capitals, and this led Egypt to try to deliver the hijackers to the leadership of the Palestine Liberation Organization for trial in accordance with what Mr. Yasir Arafat had stated and what the American president endorsed at the time. Egypt afforded a full opportunity for all Egyptian bodies of inquiry to obtain the largest possible amount of information about the hijack so that the parties concerned may know the facts and for the sake of revealing the truth.

The Arab Republic of Egypt, in condemning the developments of the incident, reaffirms its oft-stated position that these acts will not serve the peace process. This is in line with the basic position we have always stated: namely, that terror leads to more terror and that violence breeds more violence and that a just and comprehensive peace is the only road to the stability of the Middle East and the security of all its states.

387. Warrant for Arrest and Criminal Complaint of Individuals in the *Achille Lauro* Incident, October 12, 1985*

---

* Filed in U.S. District Court, District of Columbia, October 12, 1985, *reprinted in* 24 Int'l Legal Materials 1556 (1985).

Attachment

Hostage Taking (18 U.S.C. 1203 and 2)

From on or about October 7, 1985, to on or about October 10, 1985, on the high seas in the vicinity of Alexandria, Egypt; Port Said, Egypt; Tartus, Syria, Larnaca, Cyprus, and various other places outside of the United States, the defendants, HALLAH ABDALLA AL-ASAN, MAGED YUSSEF AL-MALAKI, HAMMAD ALI ABDULLA, ABDEL ATIF IBRAHIM FA-TAYER, and ABU EL-ABAS did knowingly, willfully, and unlawfully seize and detain and cause to be seized and detained and threaten to kill, injure and continue to detain nationals of the United States who were passengers on the cruise ship Achille Lauro, en route from Alexandria, Egypt, to Port Said, Egypt, in order to compel a governmental organization, that is, the State of Israel, to do an act, that is, release 50 Palestinians held in Israel, as a condition for the release of the United States nationals on the cruise ship.

Piracy under the Law of Nations

(18 U.S.C. 1651 and 2)

From on or about October 7, 1985, to on or about October 10, 1985, in the Mediterranean Sea, on the high seas, in various locations outside of the United States, the defendants, HALLAH ABDALLA AL-ASAN, MAGED YUSSEF AL-MALAKI, HAMMAD ALI ABDULLA, ABDEL ATIF IB-RAHIM FATAYER, and ABU EL-ABAS did knowingly, willfully, and un-lawfully commit and cause the commission of the crime of piracy as defined by the law of nations, that is, did knowingly, willfully and without legal au-thority from any sovereign power and for private ends seize control of the cruise ship Achille Lauro by force, violence and threat of force and violence.

Conspiracy

(18 U.S.C. 371)

From on or about October 3, 1985, and continuing to on or about Octo-ber 10, 1985, within the nation of Italy, the nation of Egypt, the nation of Syria, the Island of Cyprus, on the high seas, and elsewhere, HALLAH AB-DALLA AL-ASAN, MAGED YUSSEF AL-MALAKI, HAMMAD ALI AB-DULLA, ABDEL ATIF IBRAHIM FATAYER, and ABU EL-ABAS, defen-dants and co-conspirators herein, together with other co-conspirators, did unlawfully, willfully and knowingly conspire, combine and agree together:

a) to seize and detain and threaten to kill, injure and continue to detain, nationals of the United States who were passengers on the cruise ship Achille Lauro in order to compel a governmental organization, that is, the State of Israel, to do an act, that is, release 50 Palestinians held in Israel, as a condition for the release of the United States nationals on the cruise liner, in violation of 18 U.S.C., Section 1203 and 2.

b) To commit the crime of piracy as defined by the law of nations, that is, to seize control, without legal authority from any sovereign power and for private ends, of the cruise liner Achille Lauro by force, violence and threat of force and violence, in violation of 18 U.S.C., Section 1651 and 2.

388. Cairo Declaration on the PLO and Terrorism as Read by PLO Chairman Yasir Arafat, November 7, 1985*

* 15 J. Palestine Stud. 214 (Winter 1986).

The Palestinian people has and continues to struggle to liberate its occupied land, to exercise its right to self-determination, and to establish a state as a necessary condition for achieving a just and lasting peace in the region in which all peoples would coexist, free from acts of terrorism or subjugation.

Despite the political and military changes which the region has witnessed, especially in the last few years, beginning with the Israeli aggression against the PLO in Beirut, Lebanon in 1982 and the Israeli raid on Tunis against the PLO headquarters in 1985, the Palestinian people has continued to struggle and to cling to peace in pursuit of preparing the climate in the region and internationally for a just and peaceful solution.

The PLO has made good progress along this path in very important stages:

· The Arab summit in Fez which was held in 1982 and in which all the Arab parties, including the PLO, chose the peace option with Security Council guarantees and under the auspices of international legitimacy. These decisions were reaffirmed in Casablanca in 1985.

· The Geneva declaration regarding the international conference on Palestine in 1983, which reaffirmed the right of all states in the region to exist within safe and internationally recognized borders, including the right of the Palestinian people to self-determination on its land and to establish a Palestinian state.

· The Palestinian-Jordanian agreement of 11 February 1985, which dealt with the specifics of the special relationship between the Jordanian and Palestinian peoples and which set down their adherence to a single line and a shared vision of goals and means.

· Continued adherence to the framework of an international conference on peace in the Middle East, to be attended by the U.S.S.R., the U.S., and the permanent members of the Security Council, as well as the other concerned parties in the region, including the PLO. And, in the framework of pursuing a just and peaceful solution, and given the PLO's struggle by all legitimate means to regain the established national rights of the Palestinians as well as their political freedom, the PLO condemns all violations of human rights, especially the right to life and security without discrimination on the basis of creed, gender, or color.

As an impetus to the efforts which have been exerted to convene an international peace conference, the PLO announces its criticism and condemnation of all acts of terrorism, whether they be those in which states become involved or those committed by individuals or groups against the innocent and defenseless, wherever they may be.

The PLO reaffirms its declaration issued in 1974 which condemned all operations outside [Palestine] and all forms of terrorism. And it restates the adherence of all its groups and institutions to that declaration. Beginning today, the PLO will take all measures to deter violators.

In view of the fact that this adherence cannot be achieved unilaterally, it is up to the international community to force Israel to stop all of its acts of terrorism both inside and outside [Palestine].

In this context, the PLO stresses its insistence upon the right of the Palestinian people to resist the Israeli occupation of its land by all available means, with the goal of achieving withdrawal from its land. For the right to resist foreign occupation is a legitimate right, not abrogated by the UN Charter, which calls for disavowing the use of force or threatening to use it to settle conflicts, and which considers the resort to force a violation of its principles and goals. The right of the Palestinian people to resist the occupation in the occupied territories has been stressed in numerous UN resolutions and in the rules of the Geneva Convention.

Events underline the certainty that terrorist operations committed outside [Palestine] hurt the cause of the Palestinian people and distort its legitimate struggle for freedom. From another perspective, these events deepen our conviction that terminating the occupation and putting limits on its policies is the one way to achieve peace and security in the region. The PLO implores all peace-loving powers in all parts of the world to stand beside it as it takes this step to participate in ridding the world of the phenomenon of terrorism and in freeing the individual from fear and protecting him from danger. For in the end, our goal is achieving a just, comprehensive, and lasting peace which will safeguard the affirmation of the enduring national rights of the Palestinian people in order to establish a safe society everywhere.

389. Communiqué Issued by the Central Council of the Palestine Liberation Organization, Baghdad, November 25, 1985*

* 15 J. Palestine Stud. 200 (Spring 1986).

After discussing the latest events in the Arab world and on the Palestinian scene, the PLO Central Council decided that:

1. The Council condemns the U.S./Israeli raid on the PLO headquarters in Tunis and its violation of Tunisian sovereignty. It salutes the Tunisian people and their great leader, Mr. Bourguiba.

2. The Central Council of the PLO condemns the U.S. piracy of the Egyptian airliner which it sees as a blow to Egyptian, Italian, and PLO efforts to save the hostages.

The PLO also condemns the hijacking of the Italian liner, the *Achillo Lauro*, as it hails the Italian people and Mr. Craxi and the Egyptian people and government for their position and their firm stand in the face of the U.S.A.

3. The PLO Central Council condemns all forms of terrorism whether undertaken by individuals, groups, or states against the innocent, wherever they may be. This is based on all resolutions taken by the various Palestine National Councils.

4. The Central Council affirms and urges the PLO Executive Committee to continue military operations and all forms of armed struggle against the Israeli occupiers of the Palestinian homeland, as it affirms its continuing support for the Palestinian masses under occupation through all means. The Council further added that the role of all Arabs in this matter should not be forgotten.

5. The Central Council salutes the Lebanese and Palestinian masses in Lebanon who face an Israeli-American plan to disarm the camps and the Palestinian population and to relocate them in other countries. The Council further urges the Executive Committee to work side by side with all nationalist, progressive, and Islamic forces in Lebanon in the face of the conspiracy against the Lebanese and Palestinian peoples. The Council also urges the Executive Committee of the PLO to continue its support for the Palestinian population in Lebanon through all means.

6. The Central Council stresses to all sides the importance of a meeting between all the PLO organizations and the PLO Executive Committee with the shortest possible delay to work for a national Palestinian unity around the PLO. The Council asks the Executive Committee to make the necessary arrangements to decide on the time and place of the meeting. The Council asks that the working paper include all points and problems, without any conditions and according to the democratic decisions of all the Palestine National Councils; it urges all Arab sides to help to reinforce Palestinian national unity.

7. The Central Council supports all efforts by Arabs and other friendly sides to achieve a just and lasting peace and urges all Arabs to form a united front. Thus it urges:

· The ending of the Iraq-Iran war;

· The reintegration of Egypt into the Arab world and outside the Camp David agreement, taking into consideration changes in Egypt towards the

Palestinian cause and in relation to an international conference on the Middle East;

· Unification of Arab states and sides.

8. The Council insists on the continuation of armed struggle and military work alongside political and diplomatic work, as specified by decisions of the various Palestine National Council decisions, the Arab summit meetings in Fez and Casablanca, the Jordanian-Palestinian accord, and the Cairo Declaration, which condemn terrorism and talk about the legitimate and legal right of the Palestinian people to fight occupation by all means. The Council urges the Executive Committee to work to have the Palestinian people represented in an international conference on the Middle East alongside the Soviet Union, the U.S., and all permanent members of the UN Security Council to discuss Israeli withdrawal from the occupied Palestinian territories, the right of Palestinians to return, self-determination, and the establishment of a Palestinian state in the homeland with Jerusalem as its capital, and as part of a confederation with Jordan.

390. General Assembly Resolution 40/61 on Measures to Prevent International Terrorism Which Endangers or Takes Innocent Human Lives or Jeopardizes Fundamental Freedoms and Study of the Underlying Causes of Those Forms of Terrorism and Acts of Violence Which Lie in Misery, Frustration, Grievance and Despair and Which Cause Some People to Sacrifice Human Lives, Including Their Own, in an Attempt to Effect Radical Change, December 9, 1985*

---

* G.A. Res. 40/61 (1985).

The General Assembly,

Recalling its resolutions 3034 (XXVII) of 18 December 1972, 31/102 of 15 December 1976, 32/147 of 16 December 1977, 34/145 of 17 December 1979, 36/109 of 10 December 1981 and 38/130 of 19 December 1983,

Recalling also the Declaration on Principles of International Law concerning Friendly Relations and Co-operation among States in accordance with the Charter of the United Nations,[1] the Declaration on the Strengthening of International Security,[2] the Definition of Aggression[3] and relevant instruments on international humanitarian law applicable in armed conflict,

Further recalling the existing international conventions relating to various aspects of the problem of international terrorism, *inter alia*, the Convention on Offences and Certain Other Acts Committed on Board Aircraft, signed at Tokyo on 14 September 1963,[4] the Convention for the Suppression of Unlawful Seizure of Aircraft, signed at The Hague on 16 December 1970,[5] the Convention for the Suppression of Unlawful Acts against the Safety of Civil Aviation, signed at Montreal on 23 September 1971,[6] the Convention on the Prevention and Punishment of Crimes against Internationally Protected Persons, including Diplomatic Agents,[7] concluded at New York on 14 December 1973 and the International Convention against the Taking of Hostages,[8] concluded at New York on 17 December 1979,

Deeply concerned about the world-wide escalation of acts of terrorism in all its forms, which endanger or take innocent human lives, jeopardize fundamental freedoms and seriously impair the dignity of human beings,

Taking note of the deep concern and condemnation of all acts of international terrorism expressed by the Security Council and the Secretary-General,

Convinced of the importance of expanding and improving international co-operation among States, on a bilateral and multilateral basis, which will contribute to the elimination of acts of international terrorism and their underlying causes and to the prevention and elimination of this criminal scourge,

Reaffirming the principle of self-determination of peoples as enshrined in the Charter of the United Nations,

Reaffirming also the inalienable right to self-determination and independence of all peoples under colonial and racist régimes and other forms of alien domination, and upholding the legitimacy of their struggle, in partic-

---

[1] General Assembly resolution 2625 (XXV), annex.
[2] General Assembly resolution 2734 (XXV).
[3] General Assembly resolution 3314 (XXIX), annex.
[4] United Nations, *Treaty Series*, vol. 704, No. 10106, p. 219.
[5] *Ibid.*, vol. 860, No. 12325, p. 106.
[6] United States Treaties and Other International Agreements, vol. 24, part one (1973), p. 568.
[7] General Assembly resolution 3166 (XXVIII).
[8] General Assembly resolution 34/146.

ular the struggle of national liberation movements, in accordance with the purposes and principles of the Charter and of the Declaration on Principles of International Law concerning Friendly Relations and Co-operation among States in accordance with the Charter of the United Nations,

Mindful of the necessity of maintaining and safeguarding the basic rights of the individual in accordance with the relevant international human rights instruments and generally accepted international standards,

Convinced of the importance of the observance by States of their obligations under the relevant international conventions to ensure that appropriate law enforcement measures are taken in connection with the offences addressed in those conventions,

Expressing its concern that in recent years terrorism has taken on forms that have an increasingly deleterious effect on international relations, which may jeopardize the very territorial integrity and security of States,

Taking note of the report of the Secretary-General,[9]

1. *Unequivocally condemns*, as criminal, all acts, methods and practices of terrorism wherever and by whomever committed, including those which jeopardize friendly relations among States and their security;

2. *Deeply deplores* the loss of innocent human lives which results from such acts of terrorism;

3. *Further deplores* the pernicious impact of acts of international terrorism on relations of co-operation among States, including co-operation for development;

4. *Appeals* to all States that have not yet done so to consider becoming party to the existing international conventions relating to various aspects of international terrorism;

5. *Invites* all States to take all appropriate measures at the national level with a view to the speedy and final elimination of the problem of international terrorism, such as the harmonization of domestic legislation with existing international conventions, the fulfilment of assumed international obligations, and the prevention of the preparation and organization in their respective territories of acts directed against other States;

6. *Calls upon* all States to fulfil their obligations under international law to refrain from organizing, instigating, assisting or participating in terrorist acts in other States, or acquiescing in activities within their territory directed towards the commission of such acts;

7. *Urges* all States not to allow any circumstances to obstruct the application of appropriate law enforcement measures provided for in the relevant conventions to which they are party to persons who commit acts of international terrorism covered by those conventions;

8. *Further urges* all States to co-operate with one another more closely, especially through the exchange of relevant information concerning the prevention and combating of terrorism, apprehension and prosecution or ex-

[9] A/40/455 and Add.1 and 2.

tradition of the perpetrators of such acts, the conclusion of special treaties and/or the incorporation into appropriate bilateral treaties of special clauses, in particular regarding the extradition or prosecution of terrorists;

9. *Urges* all States, unilaterally and in co-operation with other States, as well as relevant United Nations organs, to contribute to the progressive elimination of the causes underlying international terrorism and to pay special attention to all situations, including, *inter alia*, colonialism, racism and situations involving mass and flagrant violations of human rights and fundamental freedoms and those involving alien occupation, that may give rise to international terrorism and may endanger international peace and security;

10. *Calls upon* all States to observe and implement the recommendations of the *Ad Hoc* Committee on International Terrorism contained in its report to the General Assembly at its thirty-fourth session;[10]

11. *Calls upon* all States to take all appropriate measures as recommended by the International Civil Aviation Organization and as set forth in relevant international conventions to prevent terrorist attacks against civil aviation transport and other forms of public transport;

12. *Encourages* the International Civil Aviation Organization to continue its efforts aimed at promoting universal acceptance of and strict compliance with the international air security conventions;

13. *Requests* the International Maritime Organization to study the problem of terrorism aboard or against ships with a view to making recommendations on appropriate measures;

14. *Requests* the Secretary-General to follow up, as appropriate, the implementation of the present resolution and to submit a report to the General Assembly at its forty-second session;

15. *Decides* to include the item in the provisional agenda of its forty-second session.

[10] *Official Records of the General Assembly, Thirty-fourth Session, Supplement No. 37* (A/34/37).

391. Security Council Resolution 579 Condemning Hostage Taking, December 18, 1985*

* S.C. Res. 579, 40 U.N. SCOR (2637th mtg.) (1985).

The Security Council,

Deeply disturbed at the prevalence of incidents of hostage-taking and abduction, several of which are of protracted duration and have included loss of life,

Considering that the taking of hostages and abductions are offences of grave concern to the international community, having severe adverse consequences for the rights of the victims and for the promotion of friendly relations and co-operation among States,

Recalling the statement of 9 October 1985 by the President of the Security Council resolutely condemning all acts of terrorism, including hostage-taking (S/17554),

Recalling also resolution 40/61 of 9 December 1985 of the General Assembly,

Bearing in mind the International Convention against the Taking of Hostages adopted on 17 December 1979, the Convention on the Prevention and Punishment of Crimes against Internationally Protected Persons Including Diplomatic Agents adopted on 14 December 1973, the Convention for the Suppression of Unlawful Acts against the Safety of Civil Aviation adopted on 23 September 1971, the Convention for the Suppression of Unlawful Seizure of Aircraft adopted on 16 December 1970, and other relevant conventions,

1. *Condemns unequivocally* all acts of hostage-taking and abduction;

2. *Calls for* the immediate safe release of all hostages and abducted persons wherever and by whomever they are being held;

3. *Affirms* the obligation of all States in whose territory hostages or abducted persons are held urgently to take all appropriate measures to secure their safe release and to prevent the commission of acts of hotage-taking and abduction in the future;

4. *Appeals* to all States that have not yet done so to consider the possibility of becoming parties to the International Convention against the Taking of Hostages adopted on 17 December 1979, the Convention on the Prevention and Punishment of Crimes against Internationally Protected Persons Including Diplomatic Agents adopted on 14 December 1973, the Convention for the Suppression of Unlawful Acts against the Safety of Civil Aviation adopted on 23 September 1971, the Convention for the Suppression of Unlawful Seizure of Aircraft adopted on 16 December 1970, and other relevant conventions;

5. *Urges* the further development of international co-operation among States in devising and adopting effective measures which are in accordance with the rules of international law to facilitate the prevention, prosecution and punishment of all acts of hostage-taking and abduction as manifestations of international terrorism.

392. Executive Order No. 12543 Prohibiting Trade and Certain Transactions Involving Libya, January 7, 1986*

* 22 Weekly Comp. Pres. Doc. 19 (January 13, 1986).

By the authority vested in me as President by the Constitution and laws of the United States of America, including the International Emergency Economic Powers Act (50 U.S.C. 1701 *et seq.*), the National Emergencies Act (50 U.S.C. 1601 *et seq.*), sections 504 and 505 of the International Security and Development Cooperation Act of 1985 (Public Law 99-83), section 1114 of the Federal Aviation Act of 1958, as amended (49 U.S.C. 1514), and section 301 of title 3 of the United States Code,

I, Ronald Reagan, President of the United States of America, find that the policies and actions of the Government of Libya constitute an unusual and extraordinary threat to the national security and foreign policy of the United States and hereby declare a national emergency to deal with that threat.

I hereby order:

Section 1. The following are prohibited, except to the extent provided in regulations which may hereafter be issued pursuant to this Order:

(a) The import into the United States of any goods or services of Libyan origin, other than publications and materials imported for news publications or news broadcast dissemination;

(b) The export to Libya of any goods, technology (including technical data or other information) or services from the United States, except publications and donations of articles intended to relieve human suffering, such as food, clothing, medicine and medical supplies intended strictly for medical purposes;

(c) Any transaction by a United States person relating to transportation to or from Libya; the provision of transportation to or from the United States by any Libyan person or any vessel or aircraft of Libyan registration; or the sale in the United States by any person holding authority under the Federal Aviation Act of any transportation by air which includes any stop in Libya;

(d) The purchase by any United States person of goods for export from Libya to any country;

(e) The performance by any United States person of any contract in support of an industrial or other commercial or governmental project in Libya;

(f) The grant or extension of credits or loans by any United States person to the Government of Libya, its instrumentalities and controlled entities;

(g) Any transaction by a United States person relating to travel by any United States citizen or permanent resident alien to Libya, or to activities by any such person within Libya, after the date of this Order, other than transactions necessary to effect such person's departure from Libya, to perform acts permitted until February 1, 1986, by Section 3 of this Order, or travel for journalistic activity by persons regularly employed in such capacity by a newsgathering organization; and

(h) Any transaction by any United States person which evades or avoids, or has the purpose of evading or avoiding, any of the prohibitions set forth in this Order.

For purposes of this Order, the term "United States person" means any

United States citizen, permanent resident alien, juridical person organized under the laws of the United States or any person in the United States.

Sec. 2. In light of the prohibition in section 1(a) of this Order, section 251 of the Trade Expansion Act of 1962, as amended (19 U.S.C. 1881), and section 126 of the Trade Act of 1974, as amended (19 U.S.C. 2136) will have no effect with respect to Libya.

Sec. 3. This order is effective immediately, except that the prohibitions set forth in Section 1(a), (b), (c), (d) and (e) shall apply as of 12:01 a.m. Eastern Standard Time, February 1, 1986.

Sec. 4. The Secretary of the Treasury, in consultation with the Secretary of State, is hereby authorized to take such actions, including the promulgation of rules and regulations, as may be necessary to carry out the purposes of this Order. Such actions may include prohibiting or regulating payments or transfers of any property or any transactions involving the transfer of anything of economic value by any United States person to the Government of Libya, its instrumentalities and controlled entities, or to any Libyan national or entity owned or controlled, directly or indirectly, by Libya or Libyan nationals. The Secretary may redelegate any of these functions to other officers and agencies of the Federal government. All agencies of the United States government are directed to take all appropriate measures within their authority to carry out the provisions of this Order, including the suspension or termination of licenses or other authorizations in effect as of the date of this Order.

This Order shall be transmitted to the Congress and published in the *Federal Register*.

Ronald Reagan

The White House,
January 7, 1986.

[*Filed with the Office of the Federal Register, 10:16 a.m., January 8, 1986*]

393. Executive Order No. 12544 Blocking Libyan
Government Property in the United States or Held by
U.S. Persons, January 8, 1986*

* 22 Weekly Comp. Pres. Doc. 37 (January 13, 1986).

By the authority vested in me as President by the Constitution and laws of the United States, including the International Emergency Economic Powers Act (50 U.S.C. 1701 *et seq.*), the National Emergencies Act (50 U.S.C. 1601 *et seq.*) and section 301 of title 3 of the United States Code, in order to take steps with respect to Libya additional to those set forth in Executive Order No. 12543 of January 7, 1986, to deal with the threat to the national security and foreign policy of the United States referred to in that Order,

I, Ronald Reagan, President of the United States, hereby order blocked all property and interests in property of the Government of Libya, its agencies, instrumentalities and controlled entities and the Central Bank of Libya that are in the United States, that hereafter come within the United States or that are or hereafter come within the possession or control of U.S. persons, including overseas branches of U.S. persons.

The Secretary of the Treasury, in consultation with the Secretary of State, is authorized to employ all powers granted to me by the International Emergency Economic Powers Act, 50 U.S.C. 1701 *et seq.*, to carry out the provisions of this Order.

This Order is effective immediately and shall be transmitted to the Congress and published in the *Federal Register*.

Ronald Reagan

The White House,
January 8, 1986.

[*Filed with the Office of the Federal Register, 5 p.m., January 8, 1986*]

394. U.S. Letter to the U.N. Security Council on Libyan Attacks in the Gulf of Sidra, March 25, 1986*

---

* 86 U.S. Dep't State Bull. No. 2110, at 80 (May 1986).

In accordance with Article 51 of the Charter of the United Nations, I wish, on behalf of my government, to report that United States forces have exercised their right of self-defense by responding to hostile Libyan military attacks in international waters in the Gulf of Sidra.

U.S. forces exercised great restraint. It was only after several missiles had been launched by Libya that the U.S. reacted. In the ensuing action, two Libyan naval vessels were disabled in an area where the U.S. fleet was operating. Key components of the missile complex at Sirte from which SA-5 missiles had been fired were also damaged.

The United States Government protests the unjustified attacks against American naval units which were operating in and/or above international waters in the exercise of the freedom of navigation under international law and in accordance with a standard "notification of intent" filed with the International Civil Aviation Organization (ICAO). That notification covered operations to begin at 0000 GMT, March 23 and to conclude at 2359, April 1. Those operations in no way threatened the security of Libya. Similar operations have been conducted many times over the last few years.

The Government of the United States of America views this unjustified attack with grave concern. Any further attacks against United States forces operating in and over international waters off Libya will also be resisted with force if necessary.

In view of the gravity of Libya's action, and the threat that this poses to the maintenance of international peace and security, I ask that you circulate the text of this letter as a document of the Security Council.

Sincerely,

VERNON A. WALTERS

395. President Reagan's Letter to Congress on the United

States Air Strike Against Libya, April 16, 1986*

* 22 Weekly Comp. Pres. Doc. 499 (April 21, 1986).

Dear Mr. Speaker: (Mr. President:)

Commencing at about 7:00 p.m. (EST) on April 14, air and naval forces of the United States conducted simultaneous bombing strikes on headquarters, terrorist facilities and military installations that support Libyan subversive activities. These strikes were completed by approximately 7:30 p.m. (EST).

The United States Air Force element, which launched from bases in the United Kingdom, struck targets at Tripoli Military Air Field, Tarabulus (Aziziyah) Barracks, and Sidi Bilal Terrorist Training Camp. The United States Navy element, which launched from the USS Coral Sea and the USS America, struck targets at Benina Military Air Field and Benghazi Military Barracks. One F-111 with its two crew members is missing. These targets were carefully chosen, both for their direct linkage to Libyan support of terrorist activities and for the purpose of minimizing collateral damage and injury to innocent civilians.

These strikes were conducted in the exercise of our right of self-defense under Article 51 of the United Nations Charter. This necessary and appropriate action was a preemptive strike, directed against the Libyan terrorist infrastructure and designed to deter acts of terrorism by Libya, such as the Libyan-ordered bombing of a discotheque in West Berlin on April 5. Libya's cowardly and murderous act resulted in the death of two innocent people—an American soldier and a young Turkish woman—and the wounding of 50 United States Armed Forces personnel and 180 other innocent persons. This was the latest in a long series of terrorist attacks against United States installations, diplomats and citizens carried out or attempted with the support and direction of Muammar Qadhafi.

Should Libyan-sponsored terrorist attacks against United States citizens not cease, we will take appropriate measures necessary to protect United States citizens in the exercise of our right of self-defense.

In accordance with my desire that Congress be informed on this matter, and consistent with the War Powers Resolution, I am providing this report on the employment of the United States Armed Forces. These self-defense measures were undertaken pursuant to my authority under the Constitution, including my authority as Commander in Chief of United States Armed Forces.

Sincerely,

Ronald Reagan

396. Joint Statement on Terrorism Made at the Tokyo Economic Summit, May 5, 1986*

* 22 Weekly Comp. Pres. Doc. 583 (May 12, 1986).

1. We, the Heads of State or Government of seven major democracies and the representatives of the European Community, assembled here in Tokyo, strongly reaffirm our condemnation of international terrorism in all its forms, of its accomplices and of those, including governments, who sponsor or support it. We abhor the increase in the level of such terrorism since our last meeting, and in particular its blatant and cynical use as an instrument of government policy. Terrorism has no justification. It spreads only by the use of contemptible means, ignoring the values of human life, freedom and dignity. It must be fought relentlessly and without compromise.

2. Recognizing that the continuing fight against terrorism is a task which the international community as a whole has to undertake, we pledge ourselves to make maximum efforts to fight against that scourge. Terrorism must be fought effectively through determined, tenacious, discreet and patient action combining national measures with international cooperation. Therefore, we urge all like-minded nations to collaborate with us, particularly in such international fora as the United Nations, the International Civil Aviation Organization and the International Maritime Organization, drawing on their expertise to improve and extend countermeasures against terrorism and those who sponsor or support it.

3. We, the Heads of State or Government, agree to intensify the exchange of information in relevant fora on threats and potential threats emanating from terrorist activities and those who sponsor or support them, and on ways to prevent them.

4. We specify the following as measures open to any government concerned to deny to international terrorists the opportunity and the means to carry out their aims, and to identify and deter those who perpetrate such terrorism. We have decided to apply these measures within the framework of international law and in our own jurisdictions in respect of any state which is clearly involved in sponsoring or supporting international terrorism, and in particular of Libya, until such time as the state concerned abandons its complicity in, or support for, such terrorism. These measures are:

— refusal to export arms to states which sponsor or support terrorism;
— strict limits on the size of the diplomatic and consular missions and other official bodies abroad of states which engage in such activities, control of travel of members of such missions and bodies, and, where appropriate, radical reductions in, or even the closure of, such missions and bodies;
— denial of entry to all persons, including diplomatic personnel, who have been expelled or excluded from one of our states on suspicion of involvement in international terrorism or who have been convicted of such a terrorist offence;
— improved extradition procedures within due process of domestic law for bringing to trial those who have perpetrated such acts of terrorism;

– stricter immigration and visa requirements and procedures in respect of nationals of states which sponsor or support terrorism;
– the closest possible bilateral and multilateral cooperation between police and security organizations and other relevant authorities in the fight against terrorism.

Each of us is committed to work in the appropriate international bodies to which we belong to ensure that similar measures are accepted and acted upon by as many other governments as possible.

5. We will maintain close cooperation in furthering the objectives of this statement and in considering further measures. We agree to make the 1978 Bonn Declaration more effective in dealing with all forms of terrorism affecting civil aviation. We are ready to promote bilaterally and multilaterally further actions to be taken in international organizations or fora competent to fight against international terrorism in any of its forms.

397. U.S. Orders Closure of Palestine Information Office, September 15, 1987*

---

* 87 U.S. Dep't State Bull. No. 2128, at 43 (November 1987).

The Department of State informed the Palestine Information Office (PIO) this afternoon that the U.S. Government has ordered that it be closed within 30 days.

This action was taken in accordance with the President's constitutional authority for the conduct of foreign affairs and under the authority granted to the Secretary of State under the Foreign Missions Act. The Department has determined that the Palestine Information Office is a "foreign mission" as defined by the Foreign Missions Act.

The Department of Justice has determined that the First Amendment does not preclude the U.S. Government from closing the Palestine Information Office since it is operating as a foreign mission. Nothing in the Department's action with respect to the Palestine Information Office derogates from the constitutionally protected rights of U.S. citizens and permanent residents who are now associated with the PIO.

This action is being taken to demonstrate the U.S. concern over terrorism committed and supported by organizations and individuals affiliated with the Palestine Liberation Organization (PLO). Among our particular concerns are:

· The continued membership on the PLO Executive Committee of Abu al-Abbas, who has been linked directly with the murder of an American citizen;

· The participation in the April Palestine National Congress of groups having a history of involvement with terrorism; for example, the Popular Front for the Liberation of Palestine (PFLP) and the Democratic Front for the Liberation of Palestine (DFLP), both of which rejoined the PLO at the April Palestine National Congress; and

· Contacts between the Abu Nidal organization and the mainline PLO.

The United States fully supports the legitimate rights of the Palestinian people and respects their efforts to achieve these rights through a process of peaceful negotiations. It is important that Palestinian representatives participate in all stages of that process. The rights of the Palestinians in a just and peaceful resolution of the Arab-Israeli conflict are no less important than the right of Israel to live in peace with its neighbors.

However, the United States believes that terrorism, committed purportedly on behalf of the Palestinian people by some groups and individuals associated with the PLO, has done grievous damage to the achievement of legitimate Palestinian rights. Terrorism by a small minority of Palestinians has been a major obstacle to a peaceful Arab-Israeli settlement. Achievement of these legitimate rights is broadly supported by the majority of nations, including the United States, which oppose terrorism and support instead the peaceful settlement of disputes.

The United States does not intend to close the PLO observer mission in New York, which has a special status as an observer to the United Nations.

G. The Shultz Initiative, the Intifadah,

and the Continuing Search for Peace

398. The "London Document" on Peace Concluded
between King Hussein of Jordan and Israeli Foreign
Minister Peres, London, April 1987*

* 17 J. Palestine Stud. 168 (Spring 1988).

Following is the full text of the London document, which is being published verbatim for the first time:

Accord between the government of Jordan, which has confirmed it to the government of the United States, and the Foreign Minister of Israel, pending the approval of the government of Israel. Parts "A" and "B," which will be made public upon agreement of the parties, will be treated as proposals of the United States to which Jordan and Israel have agreed. Part "C" is to be treated with great confidentiality, as commitments to the United States from the government of Jordan to be transmitted to the government of Israel.

A Three-Part Understanding between Jordan and Israel

— Invitation by the UN secretary general: The UN secretary general will sendinvitations [*sic*] to the five permanent members of the Security Council and to the parties involved in the Israeli-Arab conflict to negotiate an agreement by peaceful means based on UN resolutions 242 and 338 with the purpose of attaining comprehensive peace in the region and security for the countries in the area, and granting the Palestinian people their legitimate rights.

— Decisions of the international conference: The participants in the conference agree that the purpose of the negotiations is to attain by peaceful means an agreement about all the aspects of the Palestinian problem. The conference invites the sides to set up regional bilateral committees to negotiate bilateral issues.

— Nature of the agreement between Jordan and Israel: Israel and Jordan agree that: 1) the international conference will not impose a solution and will not veto any agreement reached by the sides; 2) the negotiations will be conducted in bilateral committees in a direct manner; 3) the Palestinian issue will be discussed in a meeting of the Jordanian, Palestinian, and Israeli delegations; 4) the representatives of the Palestinians will be included in the Jordanian-Palestinian delegation; 5) participation in the conference will be based on acceptance of UN resolutions 242 and 338 by the sides and the renunciation of violence and terror; 6) each committee will conduct negotiations independently; 7) other issues will be resolved through mutual agreement between Jordan and Israel.

This document of understanding is pending approval of the incumbent governments of Israel and Jordan. The content of this document will be presented and proposed to the United States.

399. Secretary of State Shultz, Working for Peace and
Freedom (excerpt), May 17, 1987*

---

* U.S. Dep't State Current Policy No. 957 (1987).

International Peace Conference Initiative

Now, let me say a little more, from the standpoint of the United States, what we are for and what we make of all this.

· First of all, we are for a strong Israel and for the strongest permanent link possible between the United States and Israel. We believe, among other things, that the underpinning of movements toward peace is to make it crystal clear to everybody that there is no military solution as far as the enemies of Israel are concerned. They can't get there that way.

· We are for, in the strongest terms, the Treaty of Peace Between Egypt and Israel. With the passage of time and serious efforts on both sides, that relationship, born of Camp David, represents the brightest hope for peace in the Middle East. Egypt is our friend, and we honor the role it has taken for peace and justice. I think we made a further step in the Taba agreement.

· We are for the President's September 1 initiative. It's not a plan; it's an initiative. That is our position, and we will take it to the table as our view; just as we recognize, when we get to those face-to-face negotiations, others will come with their own views and, no doubt, differing views. But that represents the view the United States will take unto that table.

· We are for the effort to achieve real improvement in the quality of life on the West Bank and Gaza. This program has made progress in recent years. It draws sustenance from the diplomatic activity in the peace process and contributes to creating an atmosphere in which negotiations can take place. And we consistently stand for the principle that the only reliable way to achieve peace is through face-to-face negotiations between Israel and its Arab neighbors.

The United States believes it is important to explore all possible approaches to this objective, to see whether any of these approaches, including an international conference, would lead immediately to direct negotiations.

I might say we are also careful not to intervene in domestic Israeli politics. I have the highest regard for and the closest relationship with both Prime Minister Shamir and Foreign Minister Peres and, for that matter, many other Israeli leaders. We are working with all of them to reach an agreed position on recent developments, and I want to say that I know, knowing them all as I do, that all of them are dedicated to peace—*all of them are.*

Now, this Administration remains committed to helping Israel in its quest for peace and security, as we always have. That has been a steady, constant commitment of the United States, and it has helped time after time after time. We are still here—the same steady friends, working together with Israel and you on the basis of the same principles.

But important developments have, in fact, occurred that have led us, consistent with out established policies, to look carefully at the idea of an international conference. I say carefully, cautiously, skeptically, but, nonetheless, with open minds and willing spirits. The answers are worth working through, even if this idea fails, like so many others on which we have worked. No one should ever be able to claim that a failure to advance the cause of peace resulted from the lack of effort on the part of the United States. For any approach to warrant consideration, we would have to insist that, in addition to leading promptly and directly to face-to-face negotiations, it also would not interfere with, impose its will on, or veto work of the bilateral negotiating parties; include Palestinians in the negotiations, only in a Jordanian-Palestinian delegation; and require all of the negotiating participants to accept UNSC [UN Security Council] Resolutions 242 and 338 and to renounce violence and terrorism.

Now, sometimes in our policy about the PLO, we use the words: "and recognize Israel's right to exist." Frankly, I cringe a little bit when anybody says that or when I say it, although it is part of our policy. Of course, Israel has a right to exist. *It exists.* It has a right to prosper. It has a right to peace.

Now, if such a conference were ever to take place, only states would be represented and involved. They should have diplomatic relations with all of the parties that come to the table. And it should be clear that the right of any party to remove itself from the conference or the negotiations is there if such rules or understandings are not observed. Now there recently has been progress toward such a negotiating format, which would offer serious prospects of reaching an agreement between the parties on peace. So as far as we are concerned, we have to, as I said, look this over carefully, skeptically, but look it over. It may be that there is a genuine opportunity to bring about direct talks. If so, we have all been striving for that.

I might say, all across the spectrum of Israeli politics, there is a desire to have direct talks. Everybody is in favor of that. Once direct talks have been achieved, an important psychological obstacle would have been overcome, irrespective of the results. We have to insist that there is no predetermined result or plan, so each party can advocate its preferred approach, including the approach that is represented in the Camp David accords.

As far as the Soviets are concerned, it's impossible to know whether they want to be spoilers or whether they want to be constructive. I must say they couldn't do a lot worse than they're doing now—encouraging the PLO and the radicals to reunite. So we'll have to see about that.

And, of course, I think we also need to remind ourselves, as the statement I made at the outset underlines, that a lack of progress has its own dangers, including increased and deepening bitterness and the continued and potentially explosive tension that we know is there in the region. I believe that as we look at this—as I said, carefully and skeptically—we need to take out an insurance policy in terms of the close working relationship which is there between Israel and the United States; as long as we agree on that basic structure—and we're ready to walk away from the idea or walk away from a conference if it fails—then we can pursue this road without too great a risk. But we can only pursue it if we are able to do so in partnership with the

Government of Israel, and we will make no moves unless we are assured of that.

So let me summarize the present initiative accurately. The President and I are not committed to an international conference, and we are not asking others to commit themselves now to the idea. We believe, however, that Jordan is sincere and that a real opportunity has been presented for progress. We are not interested in disrupting Israeli politics in the process. To the contrary, as I said, we will proceed only with the support of the Government of Israel. We have our own views, however, and we will state them in the same spirit in which we have worked with Israel for many years. We believe the present circumstances clearly call for a fair and thorough effort to develop an acceptable plan, however dubious we may be of the general idea. If no acceptable understanding emerges, so be it. We will try again another way, but let us try. Let us use our ingenuity and courage so that we accomplish whatever progress toward peace is achievable.

Israel has fought many wars in its short history. Let us continue to do everything we can to avoid another while safeguarding forever Israel's security and prosperity.

400. Excerpts from the Speech Given by Israeli Foreign Minister Shimon Peres to the Forty-second Session of the U.N. General Assembly, New York, September 30, 1987*

* 17 J. Palestine Stud. 207 (Winter 1988).

Mr. President, permit me to congratulate you on your assumption of the Presidency of the General Assembly.

Mr. President, I wish to take this opportunity to express our support for the relentless efforts of the emissary of peace and goodwill, Secretary-General Mr. Javier Perez de Cuellar.

In a world grown cynical of the superpowers' increased arms competition, and fearful of the technologies it has unleashed, the people of Israel appreciate the readiness of the United States and the Soviet Union to begin a process of nuclear disarmament. This is not just a technical accord. It is a political dictum: No longer can we find military answers to political problems—what is necessary are political answers to the military menace. . . .

Indeed, two years ago, both Arabs and Israelis announced from this podium support for the current initiative for peace.

Moreover, since then, further progress has been made.

We have rekindled our peace with Egypt and intensified the dialogue with its leaders and people. We found President Mubarak to be a builder of better life for his people and of bridges for comprehensive peace in the region.

At the cedar groves of the mountain of Ifrane, we met courageous leadership: King Hassan of Morocco calling for peace.

Across the Jordan River, rich in history and poor in water, we hear the echo of the voice of King Hussein. An experienced leader who wishes, like us, to bring our peoples out of the darkness of old hostility into the new greenhouses of peace, security and development.

In the West Bank and Gaza we notice an unannounced change. Many Palestinians seem to have concluded that violence leads nowhere, that dialogue should not be postponed. There is a readiness to negotiate in a joint Jordanian-Palestinian delegation.

We have all matured politically with the repeated failure at attempts to produce peace plans for our region; we have realized that none can be acceptable as a precondition for negotiation. For it is the object of negotiation to produce solutions otherwise unattainable. Hence, over the past three years, efforts have focused on the most promising plan: begin negotiations without pre-planning their outcome.

Five months ago these efforts crystallized and found expression in a document worked out with the support of American emissaries, whose tireless and creative efforts should be credited with much of what has been accomplished. It reflected a meeting of minds based on eight principles:

1. The goal is peace; direct negotiations are the way to get there.

2. An international conference is the door to direct negotiations. Once convened it should lead immediately to face-to-face, bilateral negotiations.

3. The conference will not impose a settlement or veto agreements reached bilaterally.

4. Those who attend the conference must accept Security Council Resolutions 242 and 338 and renounce terrorism and violence.

5. Negotiations are to solve the Palestinian problem in all its aspects. This

is to be done in negotiations between the Jordanian-Palestinian delegation and the Israeli delegation.

6. Negotiations will be conducted independently in three bilateral/geographic committees:
  – a Jordanian/Palestinian delegation and an Israeli delegation in one.
  – a Syrian and Israeli delegation in another.
  – a Lebanese and Israeli delegation in the third. All delegations, as well as an Egyptian one, will be invited to participate in a fourth, multilateral committee.

7. Whereas the bilateral committee will be engaged in solving the conflicts of the past, the multilateral committee will deal with charting opportunities for the region's future.

8. The five permanent members are to serve as the matchmakers; entrusted with bringing the parties together, and legitimizing the process whereby the parties negotiate freely and directly, without uninvited—and occasionally divided—external involvement. This is not a ceremonial task, but an essential role for facilitating negotiations.

Mr. President, Israel is united in its search for peace, in our desire to negotiate directly with our neighbors. We differ over how best to move the process forward. An international conference raises opposition in some Israeli quarters, while others see it as an opening.

The Israeli Cabinet is divided on the issue and is yet to make a decision. Much depends on the nature of the conference. Unless the permanent members of the Security Council respect the current consensus—rather than insist on their old preferences—the international conference will remain just a slogan.

We call upon the Soviet Union to credit us with the same good faith in our efforts for peace as we credit it in its readiness to make *glasnost* a way of life. The Soviet Union is not our enemy. It must be aware of our historical and family attachment to our brethren living on its land. We appeal to the new leadership in Moscow to allow the Jewish people to express their identity freely and to allow them to reunite with their destiny in the land of their ancestors.

We call upon the People's Republic of China, the great country that we respect, not to be timid or one-sided in its support for free negotiation.

To both Moscow and Beijing we say candidly, diplomatic relations are not the prize for peace but a channel for communication. Those wishing to participate in bringing peace cannot confine their relations to one side of the rivalry alone.

I would like to address the Palestinian people: The time for recrimination and blame is past. These have brought only violence and terror. Now is the time to turn from violence to dialogue, and travel jointly towards a different destiny. There your children, like ours, will live in self-respect, exercise self-expression and enjoy freedom and peace. We, who have experienced others' domination, do not wish to dominate others. We, who sought justice and security, do not wish to deny them to others. . . .

Mr. President, I welcome the forthcoming visit of Secretary Shultz to our region as an opportunity to negotiate the remaining obstacles.

I am convinced there are no conflicts without hope for solution—only people who have lost hope in their search for solutions. I am convinced that the real conflict today in the Middle East is not between Jew and Moslem; Arab and Israeli; Palestinian and Zionist. The conflict is between "past oriented" leadership and "future oriented" ones; between those resigned to the fatalism of belligerency and those determined to alter this fate. For the future of our children, for a better tomorrow, we must all stand up to the preachers of war. . . .

401. Excerpts from Remarks by Secretary of State Shultz at a News Conference, Jerusalem, October 18, 1987*

* 87 U.S. Dep't State Bull. No. 2129, at 17 (December 1987).

I have received a very warm and personal welcome here in Israel. I want to express my appreciation and the return of that warmth—that goes for the constructive and worthwhile meetings I have had with Prime Minister Shamir, with Foreign Minister Peres, Defense Minister Rabin, and their associates; the meetings at Tel Aviv University and the ceremony at the Weizmann Institute and the luncheon following.

The moving experience of meeting with Ida Nudel and Ilana Friedman, whom I had met with before—both of them under different circumstances—was a genuine joy; but at the same time, they and others whom I met with are continual reminders of the work yet to be done. I hope that my presence here before I go to Moscow makes clear the fact of the importance that the President and, I think, all Americans attach to the issues involved in human rights and Soviet Jewry.

Of course we look forward to the continuing and very rich dialogue between our two countries. Prime Minister Shamir will be in Washington, I think on the 20th, to see the President and will come next year for a more formal visit. And we will be welcoming President Herzog earlier. So there are continuing discussions going on all the time.

Q. Do you think the situation—the peace process—really requires what a local paper here calls "new ideas," or if it requires the Arabs and the Israelis to find their own way to negotiation?

A. Obviously the objective of all our efforts is peace. We believe it's pretty clear—I do, and I think all my friends here do—that the way to get there is through direct negotiations. And how do you bring that about? We continue to scratch our heads about that.

There is a sense in which you have to say so many people who are very well-informed and very bright have worked on these issues for so long that it is improbable that there are any genuinely new ideas. But the situation evolves and you try to arrange these, both substantively and procedurally, to see if you can't find a way for some progress, because the objective of peace is so important and the benefits potentially are so great. I have been doing that with the Prime Minister, whose drive for peace is quite apparent, as well as with the Foreign Minister, who also has a great concern and is consumed by that objective.

That is what I have been doing. I will do that with President Mubarak [of Egypt], with King Hussein [of Jordan], again with Prime Minister Shamir when he is in Washington, and so on. We hope that we gradually get somewhere; and in a way, if you look back a ways, there has been considerable progress.

Q. Do you think your talks with the Israelis have moved things forward at all? Do you see any rearrangements that give any possibility of any future movements?

A. I can't point to any particular thing and say, "Look, we have gone from here to there." But I do feel that we have had some; the discussions are always intense and good on this subject. They have been very thorough, and I believe, at least from my standpoint, it has been very beneficial and constructive. But I can't point to any particular thing at this point that is a big sign of progress.

Q. Would you like to see Prime Minister Shamir relax his objections to an international conference? Do you think that would help make any progress?

A. He is concerned, as we all are, by wanting to find a road to peace. And he is concerned, as we all are, that we find a road that turns out to be fruitful and that doesn't get overwhelmed by risks. So I think he has an assessment of risks that is quite understandable. And we have to keep working at this balance of the risks of doing something, the risks of not doing something—how to minimize the risks connected with any action that we contemplate and keep struggling at it. And that's what we are doing. So I am not trying to talk anybody into or out of any particular thing but just find some avenue that we can all feel more comfortable with.

Q. Do you agree with the Prime Minister, Mr. Shamir, that the main objection to the international conference is that the Soviet Union would be one of the participants and that the Soviet Union could only be a destructive element in the peace process?

A. Of course there are the facts that in the past, the Soviet Union has not been very constructive toward this. And when somebody has made constructive moves like King Hussein's effort to find some reasonable ground with the PLO [Palestine Liberation Organization], and he seemed to be finding that they waited on the other side of the ledger. They don't have diplomatic relations with all of the parties concerned, most particularly Israel. We have these continuing, very deep issues of Soviet Jewry that they need to face up to. So there are problems there. That is something of an obstacle. There are other obstacles, but there are always obstacles.

The question is: How do you deal with them and solve the problems so you get somewhere? I hope at some point the Soviet Union might be in a constructive frame of mind.

Q. When you will be speaking to King Hussein in London, will you be able to give him a definitive answer on the international conference, or will you be able to bring him some kind of an alternative for him to weigh based on your talks?

A. I will have some things to talk to King Hussein about, and I will reserve them for him.

Q. What did you mean by the risks of doing nothing?

A. What I mean by the risks of doing nothing is that if the situation just drifts and people get the feeling that there is no hope, then there tends to be a debilitating process taking place. I think, therefore, having a process that is alive—and to be seen to be alive; it has genuinely to be alive and moving—allows people to believe, at least with some genuine basis, that things can be better. I think that is very important. The risks of people being resigned to feeling that nothing can change for the better are great risks, because it tends to lead them to turn more to violence.

Q. How do you perceive or consider the idea raised by the Prime Minister, Yitzhak Shamir, that a meeting between him and King Hussein without the framework of an international conference would serve the cause of peace better than the conference itself?

A. King Hussein has to judge the manner in which he can productively move forward, and I think we all have to respect the concerns of each party. In the end, of course, it's important that the key people in the area be able to sit down and talk to each other and talk through these problems. That's the way in which they are going to be dealt with. Outsiders really can't do it. But King Hussein has, I think, quite understandable reasons for proceeding with a certain amount of caution, as we have seen.

Q. One example of the frustration you may have been talking about was the refusal today of any of the Palestinian leaders you had invited here to attend. What was your reaction to that, and what do you think their reasoning was?

A. You'll have to ask them about their reasoning. But I think it is too bad for them, because the Palestinians keep saying they want representation, they want to be heard, they want their point of view to be listened to, they have ideas, they have an important role, and, of course, I agree with all of that. And so does everybody. It's right in, for example, the Camp David accords that there are legitimate rights, and so on.

I came here and I have been listening to various people, as you know, and I thought it would be worthwhile to listen to them so they could tell me what their views are, and what their concerns are, and what their ideas are. I think they have missed something in not taking part in an invitation to a dialogue. It's sort of contradictory for them to say they need to be heard, but then when they are offered the chance, not to take advantage of it.

Undoubtedly as far as individual human beings are concerned, as I understand it, a number were threatened. That only reminds us that peace has enemies, and it reminds us of risks that people need to take. But we need to focus on the fact that the enemies of peace are not being constructive here, and the enemies of peace and the purveyors of violence, what have they achieved for the Palestinian people? Nothing.

You can achieve more by dialogue and by constructive work, and there are many things that have been put in place in the last 2 or 3 years that are proving constructive. I just hope the enemies of peace will have some second thoughts and that they will find themselves increasingly in the minority. They are part of the problem that prevents the people that they allegedly, to them, represent. They are part of preventing those people from expressing their views and making their arguments—trying to help me gain more insight into their point of view.

. . . .

Q. Do you think it would be a good idea at this point in time for Prime Minister Shamir and King Hussein to meet? And would you want to put that forward as a proposal when you meet with the King?

A. If you say that you believe as I do that in the end the way to settle these questions is through bilateral negotiations, then that's what you are trying to arrange—a way to meet and to come to grips directly with these problems. And in a sense, that is the question: How do you arrange the scenery so that such a negotiation is possible? We all realize that there are impediments. So you try to deal with those impediments, and in a way, as you discuss the peace process—or as I do—you kind of ratchet back and forth between discussions of substantive issues and discussions of procedural issues and try to find some combination that will work. We haven't found it, but we keep inching along at it. And that's what we are trying to do.

Q. *You've talked about the improvement of the quality of life in the occupied territories, but since you've made this phrase, the Defense Minister, Rabin, has imposed deportations, administrative detentions, and town arrests. We also have the problem of Palestinian family reunification. Can you comment of these human rights violations?*

A. Of course there are problems, as well as advances, and we discussed the problems. We have a very good, strong dialogue with Israel about them, and I think there have been a number that have been addressed in a satisfactory way. There have also been positive things that have taken place that seem to be working, such as the establishment of an Arab bank. It's now accumulating more branches; deposits are coming in; and from the standpoint of the population, it's their bank, so to speak, and it's working. And there are other examples.

There are problems, and there are advances, and you have to work to try to solve the problems and think of new things to do that will move matters along. That's what we're doing. We have a very good dialogue with the Government of Israel on this matter—[U.S.] Ambassador Pickering does—and I might say it's a source of some satisfaction.

I think we should take some pride in the United States at the quality of our Ambassador here, and I say that because wherever I go, people sort of casually, seem to quietly let me know, "Gee, you've sure got a capable ambassador here." And I might say we'll welcome the Israeli Ambassador to Washington. We're well represented in both countries.

Q. *But the human rights issue you didn't address.*

A. I thought I did. I said that we have a strong dialogue; we discuss all these problems and so, on the one hand, you discuss the problems where there are genuine problems and you try to work in a positive way. That's what we are doing.

Q. *Before you came, your aides in Washington and practically all the Israeli papers since you've been here have talked about new ideas being discussed and generated. In your speech today at the Weizmann Institute, you said, "Those who are reluctant to explore new ideas, or even revisit old ones, have an obligation to offer something different as an alternative to the status quo." Is this a description of the kind of reaction that there's been to some ideas that you have been proposing, or could you explain a little bit more of what you had in mind when you said that?*

A. No, it's not a description of what I've run into here at all; quite to the contrary. I find an eagerness to discuss the peace process on all sides. It's really very much akin to something I said earlier in Washington, in one of my talks—I forget which one—addressing this subject. It's just by way of saying that I think all of us who have some responsibilities here need to keep thinking and working and examining new ideas; and being willing to take a look at the old ones again; and, to the extent that we come up with a conclusion that maybe what we're talking about doesn't work, to dig in and try to think of some other ways.

I think that just drifting is not good. That is also a course of action, and it also has its risks and its problems. Doing nothing is not an empty course of action; it has consequences, too. I was just sort of exhorting myself and everybody else to keep working at it, which is what we've been doing. And I have found great receptivity to that effort.

402. Secretary of State Shultz, A Statement for Palestinians, East Jerusalem, February 26, 1988*

* U.S. Dep't of State Current Policy No. 1055 (1988).

I have a statement for Palestinians. Palestinian participation is essential to success in the peace process. I had hoped to carry this message to East Jerusalem this evening and to hear firsthand from leading Palestinians about your aspirations and your point of view. Peacemaking is difficult. Peace has its enemies. Even small steps toward peace can be significant in moving beyond mistrust and hatred. In a small way, I wanted to do that this evening.

All the peoples of this land need to be able to look to a future of dignity, security, and prosperity. New respect for rights and new readiness for political change must replace old recrimination and distrust.

The United States is for positive and rapid change. Fundamental considerations guide our approach.

First, Palestinians and Israelis must deal differently with one another. Palestinians must achieve control over political and economic decisions that affect their lives. Palestinians must be active participants in negotiations to determine their future. Legitimate Palestinian rights can be achieved in a manner which protects Israeli security. Israeli security and Palestinian security are necessary conditions for a better future for Palestinians, as well as for Israelis.

Second, these moves must be part of a broader effort to reach a comprehensive settlement. Israel and the occupied territories do not exist in isolation. Jordan, Syria, Lebanon, and Palestinians living outside the territories have concerns which need to be resolved. In moving toward a comprehensive settlement, Resolutions 242 and 338, in their entirety, must be the basis for negotiations.

Third, what we are seeking must be achieved through negotiations. Negotiations work. Negotiations produce agreements which meet the fundamental concerns of all parties. Experience shows you that you can have an agreement with Israel, and it will be kept by Israel.

Fourth, the start of negotiations must be soon, and the pace of negotiations must be rapid, so that results can be achieved with equal rapidity.

The human resources and potential of Arabs and Israelis are boundless. They have energy and drive which, if not directed against each other, can be marshaled collectively to explore science and technology, literature, and the arts. This region, which nurtured three great world religions, carries within it a powerful and moral force. Islam, Christianity, and Judaism can work together in creating a more durable, moral, and spiritual world for all of us.

Our vision is of Israelis and Palestinians living together in peace in this land; where the rights of each are respected; where the energies of all are directed at peaceful purposes; where security and trust exist. Israelis and Palestinians need to see in each other the embodiment of their own dreams. They will realize that the fulfillment of their own dreams is impossible without the fulfillment of the other side's dreams.

They will see that dreams rooted in reality are dreams which can be fulfilled.

Opportunity knocks loudly on your doors. Now is the time to get to work. We have a workable plan, and we are ready to commit our efforts to it. The time is right, together, to make decisions of historic importance. Let us translate our dreams into the reality of peace, rights, and security for all.

403. Secretary of State Shultz, Middle East Peace Plan, March 18, 1988*

* 88 U.S. Dep't State Bull. No. 2134, at 57 (May 1988).

There are few fixed rules for resolving conflicts. Each conflict has a unique history and unique characteristics. Each party to a conflict has its own dreams, concerns and fears. The task is to find the right inducements to draw the parties off the battlefield and into the negotiating room. The success of negotiations is attributable not to a particular procedure chosen but to the readiness of the parties to exploit opportunities, confront hard choices and make fair and mutual concessions.

In the Arab-Israeli conflict, negotiations work. They provide the means for parties to learn to deal with each other. They produce durable and realistic agreements that meet the fundamental concerns of the parties. Experience shows that Arabs and Israelis can make agreements and keep them.

The United States has launched an initiative designed to produce negotiations—direct, bilateral Arab-Israeli negotiations to achieve comprehensive peace. Our concept is based on all the provisions and principles of U.N. Security Council Resolution 242, which is the internationally accepted framework for negotiations. In the case of the West Bank and Gaza, the initiative involves a two-stage interlocked set of negotiations designed to produce rapid and fundamental change in the way Arabs and Israelis relate to each other.

The United States is a firm and consistent supporter of direct, bilateral negotiations between Israel and all of its neighbors as the means to achieve a comprehensive peace. At the same time, the United States has always been willing to consider any approach that could lead to direct negotiations, including an international conference.

In recent months, some parties have focused on a specific kind of international conference—one that would have an authoritative role or plenipotentiary powers. In January of this year, the United States vetoed a resolution in the U.N. Security Council that called upon the secretary-general to convene such a conference. The United States made clear its belief that this kind of conference would make real negotiations impossible. It would be a vehicle for avoiding meaningful negotiations, not promoting them.

The issue confronting the parties in the Middle East, therefore, is not whether an international conference should or should not be convened. That misses the point. The Arabs require a conference to launch negotiations; without a properly structured conference, there will be no negotiations. But the wrong kind of conference should never be convened. The United States will not attend that kind of conference. No sovereign state would agree to attend the kind of conference that would presume to pass judgment on issues of national security.

The issue is whether the moment is here to negotiate an end to the Arab-Israeli conflict; whether each party is ready and able to confront hard choices and make difficult decisions; and whether the requirements of the parties are amenable to a procedural blend that satisfies minimal demands.

The strength of the American approach is its integrity; no individual aspect of it can be extracted, finessed or ignored without sacrificing its balance. The conference we support launches a series of bilateral negotiations and thereafter may receive reports from the parties on the status of negotiations, in a manner to be agreed by the parties. All conference attendees will be required to accept Security Council Resolutions 242 and 338 and to renounce violence and terrorism. The conference will be specifically enjoined from intruding in the negotiations, imposing solutions or vetoing what had been agreed bilaterally.

The United States is committed to this integral concept for beginning direct, bilateral negotiations. We will not permit any aspect of our proposal to be eroded, compromised or expanded beyond its meaning. In particular, we will not permit a conference to become authoritative or plenipotentiary, or to pass judgments on the negotiations, or to exceed its jurisdiction as agreed by the parties.

The ingredients for a peace process are present. There is an unacceptable and untenable *status quo*. There are competing parties willing to shed illusions and temper dreams to the underlying realities. And there are realistic and achievable ideas on the table that meet the fundamental concerns of everyone.

Our task is also clear. We must act with integrity, resolve and tenacity to bring Arabs and Israelis off the battlefield and into negotiations. The initiative put forward by the United States—two interlocked stages or direct negotiations launched by a properly structured international conference—is realistic and compelling.

This is the moment for a historic breakthrough, and this is the plan. The time for decisions is now.

404. King Hussein, Speech on the West Bank, Amman, July 31, 1988*

* 18 J. Palestine Stud. 279 (Autumn 1988).

In the Name of God, the Compassionate, the Merciful, and peace be upon his faithful Arab Messenger.

Brother Citizens,

I send you my greetings, and I am pleased to address you in your cities and villages, in your camps and dwellings, in your institutions of learning, and in your places of work. I would like to address your hearts and your minds, in all parts of our beloved Jordanian land. This is all the more important at this juncture when we have initiated, after seeking God's assistance, and in light of a thorough and extensive study, a series of measures with the aim of enhancing the Palestinian national orientation, and highlighting the Palestinian identity. Our objective is the benefit of the Palestinian cause and the Arab-Palestinian people.

Our decision, as you know, comes after thirty-eight years of the unity of the two banks, and fourteen years after the Rabat summit resolution, designating the Palestine Liberation Organization (PLO) as the sole legitimate representative of the Palestinian people. It also comes six years after the Fez summit resolution that agreed unanimously on the establishment of an independent Palestinian state in the occupied West Bank and the Gaza Strip, as one of the bases, and results of the peaceful settlement.

We are certain that our decision to initiate these measures does not come as a surprise to you. Many among you have anticipated it, and some of you have been calling for it for some time. As for its contents, it has been, for everyone, a topic for discussion and consideration since the Rabat conference.

Nevertheless, some may wonder: why now? Why today, and not after the Rabat or Fez summits, for instance?

To answer this question, we need to recall certain facts that preceded the Rabat resolution. We also need to recall the factors that led to the debate, over the slogan-objective which the PLO raised, and worked to gain Arab and international support for: namely, the establishment of an independent Palestinian state. This meant, in addition to the PLO's ambition to embody the Palestinian identity on Palestinian national soil, the separation of the West Bank from the Hashemite Kingdom of Jordan.

I have reviewed the facts that preceded the Rabat resolution, as you recall, before the Arab leaders in the Algiers extraordinary summit last June. It may be important to recall that one of the main facts that I stated was the text of the Unity Resolution of the Two Banks, of April 1950. This resolution affirms, "the reservation of all Arab rights in Palestine and the defense of such rights by all legitimate means—without prejudice to the final settlement of the just cause of the Palestinian people, within the scope of the people's aspirations and of Arab cooperation and international justice."

Another of these facts was our proposal of 1972 outlining alternative forms for the relationship between Jordan and the occupied West Bank and Gaza Strip, after the latters' liberation. One of these alternatives was the maintenance of brotherly cooperation between the Hashemite Kingdom of Jordan and an independent Palestinian state, if the Palestinian people so preferred. This means, simply, that we have declared clearly our commitment to the Palestinian people's right to self-determination on their national soil, including their right to establish their independent Palestinian state, more than two years before the Rabat resolution, and we shall adhere to it until the Palestinian people realize their national goals completely, God willing.

The considerations leading to the search to identify the relationship between the West Bank and the Hashemite Kingdom of Jordan, against the background of the PLO's call for the establishment of an independent Palestinian state, are two-fold:

I. The principle of Arab unity, this being a national objective to which all the Arab peoples aspire, and which they all seek to realize.

II. The political reality of the scope of benefit to the Palestinian struggle that accrues from maintaining the legal relationship between the two banks of the kingdom.

Our answer to the question, "Why now?" also derives from these two factors, and the background of the clear and constant Jordanian position on the Palestinian cause, as already outlined.

Regarding the principle of Arab unity, we believe that such unity between two or more Arab peoples is a right of choice for every Arab people. Based on that, we have responded to the wish of the representatives of the Palestinian people for unity with Jordan in 1950. Within this context, we respect the wish of the PLO, the sole, legitimate representative of the Palestinian people, to secede from us in an independent Palestinian state. We say this in all understanding. Nevertheless, Jordan will remain the proud bearer of the message of the great Arab revolt; faithful to its principles; believing in the common Arab destiny; and committed to joint Arab action.

Regarding the political factor, it has been our belief, since the Israeli aggression of June 1967, that our first priority should be to liberate the land and holy places from Israeli occupation.

Accordingly, as is well known, we have concentrated all our efforts during the twenty-one years since the occupation toward this goal. We had never imagined that the preservation of the legal and administrative links between the two banks could constitute an obstacle to the liberation of the occupied Palestinian land. Consequently, during the period before adopting these measures, we did not see a reason to do so, particularly since our position, which calls for, and supports, the Palestinian people's rights to self-determination, was clear beyond equivocation.

Lately, it has transpired that there is a general Palestinian and Arab orientation toward highlighting the Palestinian identity in a complete manner, in every effort or activity related to the Palestinian question and its developments. It has also become clear that there is a general conviction, that maintaining the legal and administrative links with the West Bank, and the ensuing Jordanian interaction with our Palestinian brothers under occupation, through Jordanian institutions in the occupied territories, contradicts this orientation. It is also viewed that these links hamper the Palestinian struggle to gain international support for the Palestinian cause, as the national cause of a people struggling against foreign occupation.

In view of this line of thought, which is certainly inspired by genuine Palestinian will, and Arab determination to support the Palestinian cause, it becomes our duty to be part of this direction, and to respond to its requirements. After all, we are a part of our nation, supportive of its causes, foremost among which is the Palestinian cause. Since there is a general conviction that the struggle to liberate the occupied Palestinian land could be enhanced by dismantling the legal and administrative links between the two banks, we have to fulfill our duty, and do what is required of us. At the Rabat summit of 1974 we responded to the Arab leaders' appeal to us to continue our interaction with the occupied West Bank through the Jordanian institutions, to support the steadfastness of our brothers there. Today we respond to the wish of the Palestine Liberation Organization, the sole, legitimate representative of the Palestinian people and to the Arab orientation to affirm the Palestinian identity in all its aspects. We pray God that this step be a substantive addition to the intensifying Palestinian struggle for freedom and independence.

Brother Citizens,

These are the reasons, considerations, and convictions that led us to respond to the wish of the PLO, and the general Arab direction consistent with it. We cannot continue in this state of suspension, which can neither serve Jordan nor the Palestinian cause. We had to leave the labyrinth of fears and doubts, toward clearer horizons where mutual trust, understanding, and cooperation can prevail, to the benefit of the Palestinian cause and Arab unity. This unity will remain a goal which all the Arab peoples cherish and seek to realize.

At the same time, it has to be understood in all clarity, and without any ambiguity or equivocation, that our measures regarding the West Bank, concern only the occupied Palestinian land and its people. They naturally do not relate in any way to the Jordanian citizens of Palestinian origin in the Hashemite Kingdom of Jordan. They all have the full rights of citizenship and all its obligations, the same as any other citizen irrespective of his origin. They are an integral part of the Jordanian state. They belong to it, they live on its land, and they participate in its life and all its activites [*sic*]. Jordan is not Palestine; and the independent Palestinian state will be established on the occupied Palestinian land after its liberation, God willing. There the Palestinian identity will be embodied, and there the Palestinian struggle shall come to fruition, as confirmed by the glorious uprising of the Palestinian people under occupation.

National unity is precious in any country; but in Jordan it is more than that. It is the basis of our stability, and the spring-board of our development and prosperity. It is the foundation of our national security and the source of our faith in the future. It is the living embodiment of the principles of the Great Arab Revolt, which we inherited, and whose banner we proudly bear. It is a living example of constructive plurality, and a sound nucleus for wider Arab unity.

Based on that, safeguarding national unity is a sacred duty that will not be compromised. Any attempt to undermine it, under any pretext, would only help the enemy carry out his policy of expansion at the expense of Palestine and Jordan alike. Consequently, true nationalism lies in bolstering and fortifying national unity. Moreover, the responsibility to safeguard it falls on every one of you, leaving no place in our midst for sedition or treachery, with God's help, we shall be as always, a united cohesive family, whose members are joined by bonds of brotherhood, affection, awareness, and common national objectives.

It is most important to remember, as we emphasize the importance of safeguarding national unity, that stable and productive societies, are those where orderliness and discipline prevail. Discipline is the solid fabric that binds all members of a community in a solid, harmonious structure, blocking all avenues before the enemies, and opening horizons of hope for future generations.

The constructive plurality which Jordan has lived since its foundation, and through which it has witnessed progress and prosperity in all aspects of life, emanates not only from our faith in the sanctity of national unity, but also in the importance of Jordan's Pan-Arab role. Jordan presents itself as the living example of the merger of various Arab groups on its soil, within the framework of good citizenship, and one Jordanian people. This paradigm that we live on our soil gives us faith in the inevitability of attaining Arab unity, God willing. In surveying contemporary tendencies, it becomes clear that the affirmation of national identity does not contradict the attainment of unitary institutional formats that can enjoin Arabs as a whole. There are living examples within our Arab homeland that attest to this, as there are living examples in foreign regions. Foremost among them is the European Community, which now seeks to realize European political unity, having successfully completed the process of economic complementarity among its members. It is well known that the bonds linking the Arabs are far greater than those linking European nations.

Citizens,

Palestinian Brothers in the Occupied Palestinian Lands,

To dispel any doubts that may arise out of our measures, we assure you that these measures do not mean the abandonment of our national duty, either toward the Arab-Israeli conflict, or towards the Palestinian cause. Nor do they mean relinquishing our faith in Arab unity. As I have stated, these steps were taken only in response to the wish of the Palestine Liberation

Organization, the sole, legitimate representative of the Palestinian people, and the prevailing Arab conviction that such measures will contribute to the struggle of the Palestinian people and their glorious uprising. Jordan will continue its support for the steadfastness of the Palestinian people, and their courageous uprising in the occupied Palestinian land, within its capabilities. I have to mention, that when we decided to cancel the Jordanian development plan in the occupied territories, we contacted, at the same time, various friendly governments and international institutions, which had expressed their wish to contribute to the plan, urging them to continue financing development projects in the occupied Palestinian lands, through the relevant Palestinian quarters.

Jordan, dear brothers, has not, nor will it give up its support and assistance to the Palestinian people, until they achieve their national goals, God willing. No one outside Palestine has had, nor can have, an attachment to Palestine, or its cause, firmer than that of Jordan or of my family. Moreover, Jordan is a confrontation state, whose borders with Israel are longer than those of any other Arab state, longer even than the combined borders of the West Bank and Gaza with Israel.

In addition, Jordan will not give up its commitment to take part in the peace process. We have contributed to the peace process until it reached the stage of a consensus to convene an international peace conference on the Middle East. The purpose of the conference would be to achieve a just and comprehensive peace settlement to the Arab Israeli conflict, and the settlement of the Palestinian problem in all its aspects. We have defined our position in this regard, as everybody knows, through the six principles which we have already made public.

Jordan, dear brothers, is a principal party to the Arab-Israeli conflict, and to the peace process. It shoulders its national responsibilities on that basis.

I thank you and salute you, and reiterate my heartfelt wishes to you, praying God the almighty to grant us assistance and guidance, and to grant our Palestinian brothers victory and success.

May God's peace, mercy, and blessings be upon you.

405. Secretary of State Shultz, The Administration's

Approach to Middle East Peacemaking,

September 16, 1988*

* U.S. Dep't of State Current Policy No. 1104 (1988).

Following is an address by Secretary Shultz before the Washington Institute for Near East Policy, Wye Plantation, Queenstown, Maryland, September 16, 1988.

Decision time is approaching in the Middle East. In Israel and Lebanon, within the Palestinian community, and in the gulf, choices will be made that will have a profound impact on the politics of the region and on the chances of settling conflicts peacefully. These decisions must be based on a dispassionate and cold look at reality.

For nearly 9 months, the United States has highlighted a simple but far-reaching reality in the Arab-Israeli conflict: The status quo between Arabs and Israelis does not work. It is not viable. It is dangerous. It contains the seeds of a worsening conflict that threatens to inflict even greater losses on all sides in the future.

The Arab-Israeli conflict is not static. Today potentially far-reaching changes are taking place. But the fundamental nature of the conflict and the principles for resolving it have not changed. Indeed, continuity and constancy appear even more important in the process of resolving this conflict. The challenge facing the next Administration will be to shape change by building on the fundamental constants. This will serve U.S. interests and enhance the prospects for peace.

What is the shape of the Middle East today?

· The Palestinian uprising in the West Bank and Gaza has not altered the fundamental nature of the Arab-Israeli conflict. It's a reminder that comprehensive peace requires peace between Israelis and Palestinians. And it's a reminder that the status quo serves the interests of no party.

· Jordan's disengagement from the West Bank hasn't ended Jordan's involvement in the peace process. Jordan has its own interests to pursue. Jordan's border with Israel is the longest of any, and much of its population is related by family ties to residents of the West Bank and Gaza. The shaping of Jordan's role in negotiations and in a settlement are among the key issues that need to be assessed by all parties.

· Israel's upcoming elections only highlight the intense and continuing debate within that country about peace. People are taking a hard look at the prospects for peace, and they are asking hard questions: Should Israel trade land for peace? Will continued occupation affect the democratic and Jewish nature of the State of Israel? What should Israelis do about Palestinian rights? Are other Arabs ready to accept Israel as a neighbor and make peace?

· The options before the Palestinians also have not changed. Palestinians are grappling with tough choices. Should they renounce terrorism and violence and choose a political course toward peace? How should they move beyond empty slogans toward realistic and responsible positions to give new life to the peace process?

· Elsewhere in the region, change and constancy are key words. In Lebanon, a new president is scheduled to be elected amidst hopes that this will give a push to the process of national reconciliation. All Lebanese recognize the dangers that would result from a failure to elect a president according to the constitution.

· Iran and Iraq are now negotiating under UN auspices to bring an end to 8 years of bloody and destructive war in the gulf. The results of these talks will have a profound influence on the entire region.

· Ballistic missiles and chemical weapons continue to proliferate. The use of chemical weapons by both sides in the gulf war and Iraq's use of these weapons against the Kurds are grim reminders of the dangers these weapons pose to the conduct of international relations.

· In Afghanistan, Soviet troops are withdrawing. The people of Afghanistan look forward to the end of Soviet intervention.

Continuity in the Midst of Change

So, the fact of change is less important than the uses made of change. The Arab-Israeli conflict does not stand still. But there are enduring realities that point to a mehod [sic] for resolving the conflict.

The Arab-Israeli conflict is *not* intractable. Negotiations *can* bring about peace. No matter what new situations or difficulties Arabs and Israelis face as they approach negotiations, one thing is certain once they get there: They will confront some enduring realities that shape the rules of the negotiations *and* the outlines of a fair settlement that negotiations can be expected to produce.

What are the principles that underlie a comprehensive settlement of the Arab-Israeli conflict?

The existence, security, and well-being of Israel are the first principles of any settlement. Israel has the right to exist, and it has the right to exist in security. We will do our utmost to ensure it.

The requirements of security need to be understood clearly. These include military hardware, defensible geographic positions, and technological know-how. The United States has cooperated with Israel on these elements, and that cooperation will continue. But these are not the only critical components of Israel's security.

Real security results from resolving political differences that continue to fuel conflict. The location of borders is important, but more important is what crosses those borders: ideas, goods, people, instead of armies and weapons. Borders need to be secure and recognized, but political differences between neighbors also need to be resolved through compromise.

Palestinian political rights must also be recognized and addressed. Palestinians want more than the basic necessities of life. They want, and they are entitled to, political participation and influence over political and economic decisions that affect their lives. This can occur if opportunities for peace and dialogue are seized.

A third enduring reality is that the history, security, and destiny of Israelis, Jordanians, Palestinians, and Egyptians are inextricably bound together. Jordan is a vibrant and heterogeneous society with a strong national identity of its own. It is not a Palestinian state. An enduring settlement must reflect the reality that strong, open relations will need to exist among Israeli, Palestinian, Jordanian, and Egyptian peoples.

A critical and enduring reality is that negotiations work. Ten years ago, Egypt and Israel forged a treaty of peace that has survived enormous strains. They continue to demonstrate that dialogue and negotiations resolve differences between peoples far better than war and violence.

Translating Principles Into a Negotiated Settlement

American efforts to bring about negotiations are rooted in these enduring principles. Our approach seeks a comprehensive and durable settlement grounded in UN Security Council Resolutions 242 and 338. It calls for direct negotiations, launched, if required, through an international conference. It requires acceptance of 242 and 338 and renunciation of violence and terrorism.

As regards the West Bank and Gaza, our approach highlights the need for a transitional period to help the parties adjust to working with each other to implement an agreement. It recognizes the relationship in time and substance between the transitional period and the final status agreement. It affirms the right of Palestinians to participate actively in every stage of negotiations. And it reflects the strategic reality of Jordanian-Palestinian interdependence.

This has been the American approach to negotiations. The purposes of this effort have been clear.

First, the objective is comprehensive peace between Israel and all its neighbors, achieved through negotiations based on UN Security Council Resolutions 242 and 338. This will require the exchange of territory for peace. It will require recognition that sovereignty cannot be defined in absolute terms. Today, borders are porous. Openness is required for the free movement of ideas, people, and goods. There will need to be a border demarcation but not a wall established between peoples.

The territorial issue needs to be addressed realistically. Israel will never negotiate from or return to the lines of partition or to the 1967 borders. But it must be prepared to withdraw—as Resolution 242 says—"from territories occupied in the recent conflict." Peace and security for all sides are at stake.

Second, peace between Israel and its neighbors will need time and growing mutual good will to succeed. In the case of the West Bank and Gaza, this means there must be a transitional period. All sides need to deal with one another gradually in the light of an agreement freely negotiated. All need time to adjust to a new situation. Palestinians need to achieve rapid control over political and economic decisions that affect their lives. Israelis need time to adjust to a new situation—one in which Palestinians, not Israeli military government officials, administer the West Bank and Gaza.

The concept of transition is vital and far reaching. Many of its elements have already been worked through and accepted by Israel. These transitional arrangements are extensive and dramatic. They can be implemented quickly.

Such transitional arrangements will benefit from the interplay with final status negotiations. Each party needs to know the principles that will define the final settlement. As those principles are hammered out in negotiations, they will enhance the transitional arrangements themselves. Each element strengthens the other. This is the essence and benefit of interlock between transitional arrangements and final status.

Direct negotiations are at the heart of this negotiating process. No party should be expected to trust its vital national security interests to any mechanism except direct talks. How better to engage an adversary, take his measure, assess intentions, and probe for openings than to square off across the table? Direct talks work.

In the Arab-Israeli conflict, an international conference may also be necessary to ease the entry of the parties into direct negotiations. This conference would also be in a position, at the right time, to deal with important regionwide issues such as economic development, joint resource sharing, and humanitarian concerns. But only the right kind of conference should take place—one that helps launch and support direct negotiations without interfering in them.

Palestinian participation is required at every stage of the negotiations. Palestinians have a vital stake in the outcome of negotiations. They must have a say in the negotiations themselves, and they must approve the outcome.

Participation involves responsibilities, however. There are no free rides. All parties must demonstrate their desire to make peace. They must be creative and reliable; they must adhere to internationally accepted principles and norms. For Palestinians, this means acting credibly and pursuing goals that are achievable.

No participant in a peace process can wave the flag of justice in one hand and brandish the weapons of terrorism in the other. All participants must renounce violence and terrorism. Each must agree to negotiate on the accepted international basis of Security Council Resolutions 242 and 338.

There are also no free rides for outside parties that want to play a role in settling the conflict. Both the United States and the Soviet Union consider a settlement of the conflict to be in their national interest. But the Soviets will need to confront some difficult choices.

There is no longer any excuse for the Soviets to avoid such important steps as resuming full diplomatic relations with Israel; nor is there justification for preventing Jews who wish to emigrate from doing so. The sooner these things are done, the better for the peace process.

Effective Policies in a Period of Change

The challenge of Arab-Israeli peacemaking in a time of change is to find the right mix of fundamental realities and creative ideas. The question is how to assess some of these ideas at this time.

· Peace cannot be achieved through the creation of an independent Palestinian state or through permanent Israeli control or annexation of the West Bank and Gaza. At the same time, each party is free to bring any position it chooses to the negotiating table. Israelis are free to argue for annexation; Palestinians are free to argue for independence. The United States will not support either of these positions during negotiations.

· The status of the West Bank and Gaza cannot be determined by unilateral acts of either side but only through a process of negotiations. A declaration of independent Palestinian statehood or government-in-exile would be such a unilateral act. Palestinians need to decide whether to remain a part of the problem in the Middle East or become a part of the solution. History need not repeat itself. Practical, realistic steps by Palestinians are required.

· An attempt by Israel to transfer Palestinians from the West Bank and Gaza would also be a unilateral act to determine the status of those territories. The United States would oppose this vigorously. Such a policy does not provide a solution to the problem, nor does it bring negotiations any closer.

· It is also not acceptable to shift the focus from what Palestinians or Israelis need to do to advance the peace process to what the United States should do. This applies to those who urge that the United States should support Palestinian self-determination.

The United States cannot accept "self-determination" when it is a codeword for an independent Palestinian state or for unilateral determination of the outcome of negotiations. To expect the PLO [Palestine Liberation Organization] to accept Resolutions 242 and 338 as the basis for negotiation is not to ask it to make a concession. Those resolutions lay out basic principles which the international community has decided must be reflected in a peace settlement. In addition to these, the legitimate rights of the Palestinian people—including political rights—must also be addressed. It is through acceptance of these principles, not through any action by the United States, that the Palestinians can participate fully in determining their own future.

Conditioning the Environment for Negotiations

In the Arab-Israeli conflict, there is no objective reality and no immutable set of circumstances that cannot be shaped by decisions for peace. During the period ahead, such decisions are required. Israelis and Palestinians themselves must condition the environment for negotiations. They can start down the road to accommodation and reconciliation. Violence has distracted people from establishing achievable objectives. Political debate must replace violence.

Concrete actions on the ground are required. Palestinians must renounce terrorism and violence. They must accept the right of Israel to exist in peace and present themselves as a viable negotiating partner. They cannot murder or threaten other Palestinians who maintain contact with Israeli authorities.

For its part, Israel has the responsibility to maintain law and order in the West Bank and Gaza. But Israel must also find a way to respond to expressions of Palestinian grievances. It cannot claim there is no one to talk to, while suppressing political expression and arresting or deporting those who speak out—even those who speak in moderate terms.

There must also be actions on the regional level. The peace treaty between Egypt and Israel is a strategic anchor of the entire peace process; it must constantly be enhanced. Relations between Israel and other Arab states must start down the road to normalization. Relations between people don't need to await the formality of a treaty. Israelis and Arabs should find ways to talk to each other now, even before treaty relations exist.

The conditions under which refugees live in the region must also be addressed. Poverty is no ally of peace. The continuing existence of refugees does not make the case for Palestinian nationalism stronger. Palestinian refugees can live in better conditions even while the search for peace continues. Arabs and Israelis, together with the international community, must shoulder this responsibility.

Finally, there must be a change of attitude throughout the region. The way people think affects the way they act. Cynicism, skepticism, and pessimism about peace must be shaken. The conflict must be seen to be resolvable. Once there is the will for and belief in a settlement, the benefits of peace will be seen to outweigh the real but transitory risks of achieving it.

So fundamental realities persist, even in the midst of change. The goals of the peace process have not changed, nor have the principles of negotiations.

Indeed, the only thing that needs to change is the willingness of people in the Middle East to move the peace process forward. Israelis, Palestinians, Jordanians, Syrians, and Lebanese can make peace happen. The Egyptians are more than ready to do their part. So are we. And so are others around the world. The opportunities today are greater than before, and so are the risks of doing nothing. To make peace, the parties must exploit the new opportunities created by the current ferment. And they should start now.

Published by the United States Department of State · Bureau of Public Affairs

Office of Public Communication · Editorial Division · Washington, D.C. · September 1988

Editor: Cynthia Saboe · This material is in the public domain and may be reprinted without permission; citation of this source is appreciated.

406. General Assembly Resolution 43/21 on the Uprising (Intifadah) of the Palestinian People, November 3, 1988*

* G.A. Res. 43/21, UNGA Doc. A/RES/43/21 (1988).

43/21. *The uprising (intifadah) of the Palestinian people*

The General Assembly,

Aware of the uprising (*intifadah*) of the Palestinian people since 9 December 1987 against Israeli occupation, which has received significant attention and sympathy from world public opinion,

Deeply concerned at the alarming situation in the Palestinian territories occupied since 1967, including Jerusalem, as well as in the other occupied Arab territories, as a result of the continued occupation by Israel, the occupying Power, and of its persistent policies and practices against the Palestinian people,

Reaffirming that the Fourth Geneva Convention relative to the Protection of Civilian Persons in Time of War, of 12 August 1949,[1] is applicable to all the Palestinian and other Arab territories occupied by Israel since 1967, including Jerusalem,

Recalling its relevant resolutions as well as Security Council resolutions 605 (1987) of 22 December 1987, 607 (1988) of 5 January 1988 and 608 (1988) of 14 January 1988,

Recognizing the need for increased support and aid for, and solidarity with the Palestinian people under Israeli occupation,

Conscious of the urgent need to resolve the underlying problem through a comprehensive, just and lasting settlement, including a solution to the Palestinian problem in all its aspects,

1. *Condemns* Israel's persistent policies and practices violating the human rights of the Palestinian people in the occupied Palestinian territories, including Jerusalem, and, in particular, such acts as the opening of fire by the Israeli army and settlers that result in the killing and wounding of defenceless Palestinian civilians, the beating and breaking of bones, the deportation of Palestinian civilians, the imposition of restrictive economic measures, the demolition of houses, collective punishment and detentions, as well as denial of access to the media;

2. *Strongly deplores* the continuing disregard by Israel, the occupying Power, of the relevant decisions of the Security Council;

3. *Reaffirms* that the occupation by Israel of the Palestinian territories since 1967, including Jerusalem, in no way changes the legal status of those territories;

4. *Demands* that Israel, the occupying Power, abide immediately and scrupulously by the Fourth Geneva Convention relative to the Protection of Civilian Persons in Time of War, of 12 August 1949, and desist forthwith from its policies and practices that are in violation of the provisions of the Convention;

5. *Calls upon* all the High Contracting Parties to the Convention to take appropriate measures to ensure respect by Israel, the occupying Power, for

[1] United Nations, *Treaty Series*, vol. 75, No. 973.

the Convention in all circumstances in conformity with their obligation under article 1 thereof;

6. *Invites* Member States, the organizations of the United Nations system, governmental, intergovernmental and non-governmental organizations, and the mass communications media to continue and enhance their support for the Palestinian people;

7. *Urges* the Security Council to consider the current situation in the occupied Palestinian territories, taking into account the recommendations contained in the report of the Secretary-General;[2]

8. *Also requests* the Secretary-General to examine the present situation in the occupied Palestinian territories by all means available to him and to submit periodic reports thereon, the first such report no later than 17 November 1988.

45th plenary meeting
3 November 1988

[2] S/19443.

407. Palestine National Council, "Palestinian Declaration of Independence," November 15, 1988*

* 18 J. Palestine Stud. 213 (Winter 1989).

In the name of God, the Compassionate, the Merciful.

Palestine, the land of the three monotheistic faiths, is where the Palestinian Arab people was born, on which it grew, developed, and excelled. The Palestinian people was never separated from or diminished in its integral bonds with Palestine. Thus the Palestinian Arab people ensured for itself an everlasting union between itself, its land, and its history.

Resolute throughout that history, the Palestinian Arab people forged its national identity, rising even to unimagined levels in its defense as invasion, the design of others, and the appeal special to Palestine's ancient and luminous place on that eminence where powers and civilizations are joined . . . All this intervened thereby to deprive the people of its political independence. Yet the undying connection between Palestine and its people secured for the land its character and for the people its national genius.

Nourished by an unfolding series of civilizations and cultures, inspired by a heritage rich in variety and kind, the Palestinian Arab people added to its stature by consolidating a union between itself and its patrimonial land. The call went out from temple, church, and mosque to praise the Creator, to celebrate compassion, and peace was indeed the message of Palestine. And in generation after generation, the Palestinian Arab people gave of itself unsparingly in the valiant battle for liberation and homeland. For what has been the unbroken chain of our people's rebellions but the heroic embodiment of our will for national independence? And so the people were sustained in the struggle to stay and to prevail.

When in the course of modern times a new order of values was declared with norms and values fair for all, it was the Palestinian Arab people that had been excluded from the destiny of all other peoples by a hostile array of local and foreign powers. Yet again had unaided justice been revealed as insufficient to drive the world's history along its preferred course.

And it was the Palestinian people, already wounded in its body, that was submitted to yet another type of occupation over which floated the falsehood that "Palestine was a land without people." This notion was foisted upon some in the world, whereas in Article 22 of the Covenant of the League of Nations (1919) and in the Treaty of Lausanne (1923), the community of nations had recognized that all the Arab territories, including Palestine, of the formerly Ottoman provinces were to have granted to them their freedom as provisionally independent nations.

Despite the historical injustice inflicted on the Palestinian Arab people resulting in their dispersion and depriving them of their right to self-determination, following upon UN General Assembly Resolution 181 (1947), which partitioned Palestine into two states, one Arab, one Jewish, yet it is this resolution that still provides those conditions of international legitimacy that ensure the right of the Palestinian Arab people to sovereignty and national independence.

By stages, the occupation of Palestine and parts of other Arab territories by Israeli forces, the willed dispossession and expulsion from their ancestral homes of the majority of Palestine's civilian inhabitants was achieved by organized terror; those Palestinians who remained, as a vestige subjugated in its homeland, were persecuted and forced to endure the destruction of their national life.

Thus were principles of international legitimacy violated. Thus were the Charter of the United Nations and its resolutions disfigured, for they had recognized the Palestinian Arab people's national rights, including the Right of Return, the Right to Independence, the Right to Sovereignty over territory and homeland.

In Palestine and on its perimeters, in exile distant and near, the Palestinian Arab people never faltered and never abandoned its conviction in its rights of return and independence. Occupation, massacres, and dispersion achieved no gain in the unabated Palestinian consciousness of self and political identity, as Palestinians went forward with their destiny, undeterred and unbowed. And from out of the long years of trial in evermounting struggle, the Palestinian political identity emerged further consolidated and confirmed. And the collective Palestinian national will forged itself in a political embodiment, the Palestine Liberation Organization, its sole, legitimate representative, recognized by the world community as a whole, as well as by related regional and international institutions. Standing on the very rock of conviction in the Palestinian people's inalienable rights, and on the ground of Arab national consensus, and of international legitimacy, the PLO led the campaigns of its great people, molded into unity and powerful resolve, one and indivisible in the triumphs, even as it suffered massacres and confinement within and without its home. And so Palestinian resistance was clarified and raised into the forefront of Arab and world awareness, as the struggle of the Palestinian Arab people achieved unique prominence among the world's liberation movements in the modern era.

The massive national uprising, the *intifadah*, now intensifying in cumulative scope and power on occupied Palestinian territories, as well as the unflinching resistance of the refugee camps outside the homeland, have elevated consciousness of the Palestinian truth and right into still higher realms of comprehension and actuality. Now at last the curtain has been dropped around a whole epoch of prevarication and negation. The Intifadah has set siege to the mind of official Israel, which has for too long relied exclusively upon myth and terror to deny Palestinian existence altogether. Because of the Intifadah and its revolutionary irreversible impulse, the history of Palestine has therefore arrived at a decisive juncture.

Whereas the Palestinian people reaffirms most definitely its inalienable rights in the land of its patrimony:

Now by virtue of natural, historical, and legal rights and the sacrifices of successive generations who gave of themselves in defense of the freedom and independence of their homeland;

In pursuance of resolutions adopted by Arab summit conferences and relying on the authority bestowed by international legitimacy as embodied in the resolutions of the United Nations Organization since 1947;

And in exercise by the Palestinian Arab people of its rights to self-determination, political independence, and sovereignty over its territory;

The Palestine National Council, in the name of God, and in the name of the Palestinian Arab people, hereby proclaims the establishment of the State of Palestine on our Palestinian territory with its capital Jerusalem (Al-Quds Ash-Sharif).

The State of Palestine is the state of Palestinians wherever they may be. The state is for them to enjoy in it their collective national and cultural identity, theirs to pursue in it a complete equality of rights. In it will be safeguarded their political and religious convictions and their human dignity by means of a parliamentary democratic system of governance, itself based on freedom of expression and the freedom to form parties. The rights of minorities will duly be respected by the majority, as minorities must abide by decisions of the majority. Governance will be based on principles of social justice, equality and nondiscrimination in public rights on grounds of race, religion, color, or sex under the aegis of a constitution which ensures the role of law and on independent judiciary. Thus shall these principles allow no departure from Palestine's age-old spiritual and civilizational heritage of tolerance and religious co-existence.

The State of Palestine is an Arab state, an integral and indivisible part of the Arab nation, at one with that nation in heritage and civilization, with it also in its aspiration for liberation, progress, democracy, and unity. The State of Palestine affirms its obligation to abide by the Charter of the League of Arab States, whereby the coordination of the Arab states with each other shall be strengthened. It calls upon Arab compatriots to consolidate and enhance the emergence in reality of our State, to mobilize potential, and to intensify efforts whose goal is to end Israeli occupation.

The State of Palestine proclaims its commitment to the principles and purposes of the United Nations, and to the Universal Declaration of Human Rights. It proclaims its commitment as well to the principles and policies of the Non-Aligned Movement.

It further announces itself to be a peace-loving state, in adherence to the principles of peaceful co-existence. It will join with all states and peoples in order to assure a permanent peace based upon justice and the respect of rights so that humanity's potential for well-being may be assured, an earnest competition for excellence be maintained, and in which confidence in the future will eliminate fear for those who are just and for whom justice is the only recourse.

In the context of its struggle for peace in the land of love and peace, the State of Palestine calls upon the United Nations to bear special responsibility for the Palestinian Arab people and its homeland. It calls upon all peace- and freedom-loving peoples and states to assist it in the attainment of its objectives, to provide it with security, to alleviate the tragedy of its people, and to help to terminate Israel's occupation of the Palestinian territories.

The State of Palestine herewith declares that it believes in the settlement of regional and international disputes by peaceful means, in accordance with the UN Charter and resolutions. Without prejudice to its natural right to defend its territorial integrity and independence, it therefore rejects the threat or use of force, violence, and terrorism against its territorial integrity, or political independence, as it also rejects their use against the territorial integrity of other states.

Therefore, on this day unlike all others, 15 November, 1988, as we stand at the threshold of a new dawn, in all honor and modesty we humbly bow to the sacred spirits of our fallen ones, Palestinian and Arab, by the purity of whose sacrifice for the homeland our sky has been illuminated and our land given life. Our hearts are lifted up and irradiated by the light emanating from the much blessed *intifadah*, from those who have endured and have fought the fight of the camps, of dispersion, of exile, from those who have borne the standard of freedom, our children, our aged, our youth, our prisoners, detainees, and wounded, all those whose ties to our sacred soil are confirmed in camp, village, and town. We render special tribute to that brave Palestinian woman, guardian of sustenance and life, keeper of our people's perennial flame. To the souls of our sainted martyrs, to the whole of our Palestinian Arab people, to all free and honorable peoples everywhere, we pledge that our struggle shall be continued until the occupation ends, and the foundation of our sovereignty and independence shall be fortified accordingly.

Therefore, we call upon our great people to rally to the banner of Palestine, to cherish and defend it, so that it may forever be the symbol of our freedom and dignity in that homeland, which is a homeland for the free, now and always.

In the name of God, the Compassionate, the Merciful.

"Say: 'O God, Master of the Kingdom, Thou givest the Kingdom to whom Thou wilt, and seizest the Kingdom from whom Thou wilt. Thou exaltest whom Thou wilt, and Thou abasest whom Thou wilt; in Thy hand is the good; Thou art poweful over everything."

Sadaqa Allahu al-'Azim

408. U.S. Department of State, Statement on the Determination by the Secretary of State on the Visa Application of Mr. Yasir Arafat, November 26, 1988*

---

* Internal document, U.S. Dep't of State, November 26, 1988.

November 26, 1988
Department of State
Statement on the Determination
by the Secretary of State
on the Visa Application of Mr. Yassir Arafat

The 1947 United Nations Headquarters Agreement obligates the United States to provide certain rights of entry, transit, and residence to persons invited to the United Nations headquarters district in New York City.

The Congress of the United States conditioned the entry of the U.S. into the UN headquarters Agreement on the retention by the U.S. government of the authority to bar the entry of aliens associated with or invited by the United Nations "in order to safeguard its own security."

In this regard, U.S. law excludes members of the PLO from entry into the United States by virtue of their affiliation in an organization which engages in terrorism. The Secretary of State is vested by law with the discretion to recommend to the Attorney General that the prohibition against a particular PLO member be waived.

The United Nations General Assembly in 1974 invited the Palestine Liberation Organization to participate as an observer at the General Assembly. The United States acknowledged that this UN invitation obligates the U.S. to accord PLO observers entry, transit, and residence; therefore, visa waivers have been issued to such individuals as a routine practice. As a result, a PLO Observer Mission has been in operation at the UN since 1975. The PLO therefore has had, and continues to have, ample opportunity to make its positions known to the membership of the United Nations.

On November 24, 1988 we received an application from Mr. Yassir Arafat, Chairman of the PLO, for a visa to attend the United Nations General Assembly session in New York City as an invitee. The Secretary of State has decided not to recommend a waiver of ineligibility in this case; the visa application therefore is not approved.

The U.S. Government has convincing evidence that PLO elements have engaged in terrorism against Americans and others. This evidence includes a series of operations undertaken by the Force 17 and the Hawari organizations since the PLO claimed to foreswear the use of terrorism in the Cairo Declaration of November, 1985. As Chairman of the PLO Mr. Arafat is responsible for actions of these organizations which are units of Fatah, an element of the PLO of which he also is Chairman and which is under his control. The most recent sign of Mr. Arafat's associations with terrorism was the presence at the Algiers session of the Palestine National Council this month of Abu Abbas, a member of the Executive Committee of the PLO who has been convicted by the Italian judicial system of the murder of an American citizen, Mr. Leon Klinghoffer.

In summary, we find that:

- The PLO through certain of its elements has employed terrorism against Americans.
- Mr. Arafat, as Chairman of the PLO, knows of, condones, and lends support to such acts; he therefore is an accessory to such terrorism.
- Terrorism and those involved in it are a serious threat to our national security and to the lives of American citizens.
- The Headquarters Agreement, contained in Public Law 80-357, reserves to us the right to bar the entry of those who represent a threat to our security.

The United States firmly believes that Palestinian political rights must be recognized and addressed. A comprehensive settlement of the Arab-Israeli conflict is achievable through the peace process that already has brought significant progress. Palestinian participation is required at every stage of the negotiations required to achieve peace, justice, and security. Participation requires responsibilities, however. All parties must demonstrate their desire to make peace; they must adhere to internationally accepted principles and norms. No participant in a peace process can wave the flag of justice in one hand and brandish the weapons of terrorism in the other. All participants must renounce violence and terrorism.

The outcome of the PNC session in Algiers produced signs that there are Palestinians who are trying to move the PLO in a constructive way. That is encouraging and should continue. It is unfortunate that the blight of terrorism still afflicts the Palestinian cause and leaves no alternative to decisions such as the Secretary has taken today.

409. Excerpts from the Speech Given by Yasir Arafat to the Forty-third Session of the U.N. General Assembly, December 13, 1988*

---

* *New York Times*, December 14, 1988, at A12.

I am both proud and happy to meet with you today, here in Geneva, after an arbitrary American decision barred me from going to you there.

I extend deep gratitude to all nations, forces and international organizations and personalities who backed our people and supported its national rights . . . I also thank the Western European nations and Japan for their latest stands toward our people and I invite them to take further steps to positively evolve their resolutions in order to open the way for peace and a just settlement in our region, the Middle East.

. . .

We set out in the Palestine Liberation Organization to look for realistic and attainable formulas that would settle the issue on the basis of possible rather than absolute justice while securing the rights of our people to freedom, sovereignty and independence; insuring for everyone peace, security and stability; and sparing Palestine and the Middle East wars and battles that have been going on for 40 years.

. . .

Israel's response to all this has been the escalation of its settlement and annexation schemes; the fanning of the flames of conflict with more destruction, devastation and bloodshed; and the expansion of the confrontation fronts to include brotherly Lebanon.

. . .

American Government

It is painful and regrettable that the American Government alone should continue to back these aggressive and expansionist schemes as well as Israel's continued occupation of Palestinian and Arab territories, its crimes, and its iron-fist policy against our children and women.

It is painful and regrettable too that the American Government should continue refusing to recognize the right of six million Palestinians to self-determination, a right which is sacred to the American people and other peoples on this planet.

. . .

Our people does not want a right which is not its own or which has not been vested in it by international legitimacy and international law. It does not seek its freedom at the expense of anyone else's freedom, nor does it want a destiny which negates the destiny of another people. Our people refuses to be better or worse than any other people. Our people wants to be the equal of all other peoples, with the same rights and obligations.

. . .

While we greatly appreciate the free American voices that have explained and supported our position and resolutions, we note that the U.S. Administration remains uncommitted to even-handedness in its dealings with the parties to the conflict.

. . .

Rejection of Terrorism

The Palestine National Council has also reaffirmed its rejection of terrorism in all its forms, including state terrorism, emphasizing its commitment to its past resolutions in this regard, and to the resolution of the Arab summit in Algiers in 1988, and to U.N. Resolutions 42-159 of 1987 and 61-40 of 1985, and to what was stated on this subject in the Cairo Declaration of 7 November 1985.

This position, Mr. President, is clear and free of all ambiguity. And yet, I, as chairman of the Palestine Liberation Organization, hereby once more declare that I condemn terrorism in all its forms, and at the same time salute those sitting before me in this hall who, in the days when they fought to free their countries from the yoke of colonialism, were accused of terrorism by their oppressors, and who today are the faithful leaders of their peoples, stalwart champions of the values of justice and freedom.

. . .

The United Nations bears a historic, extraordinary responsibility toward our people and their rights. More than 40 years ago, the United Nations, in its Resolution 181, decided on the establishment of two states in Palestine, one Palestinian Arab and the other Jewish. Despite the historic wrong that was done to our people, it is our view today that the said resolution continues to meet the requirements of international legitimacy which guarantee the Palestinian Arab people's right to sovereignty and national independence.

. . .

The Palestinian Plan

In my capacity as chairman of the P.L.O. executive committee, presently assuming the functions of the provisional government of the state of Palestine, I therefore present the following Palestinian peace initiative:

First: That a serious effort be made to convene, under the supervision of the secretary-general of the United Nations, the preparatory committee of the international conference for peace in the Middle East—in accordance with the initiative of President Gorbachev and President Mitterrand, which President Mitterrand presented to your Assembly toward the end of last September and which was supported by many states—to pave the way for the convening of the international conference, which commands universal support except from the government of Israel.

Second: In view of our belief in international legitimacy and the vital role of the United Nations, that actions be undertaken to place our occupied Palestinian land under temporary United Nations supervision, and that international forces be deployed there to protect our people and, at the same time, to supervise the withdrawal of the Israeli forces from our country.

Third: The P.L.O. will seek a comprehensive settlement among the parties concerned in the Arab-Israeli conflict, including the state of Palestine, Israel and other neighbors, within the framework of the international conference for peace in the Middle East on the basis of Resolutions 242 and 338 and so as to guarantee equality and the balance of interests, especially our people's rights in freedom, national independence, and respect the right to exist in peace and security for all.

. . .

I come to you in the name of my people, offering my hand so that we can make true peace, peace based on justice. I ask the leaders of Israel to come here under the sponsorship of the United Nations, so that, together, we can forge that peace . . . And here, I would address myself specifically to the Israeli people in all their parties and forces, and especially to the advocates of democracy and peace among them. I say to them: Come let us make peace.

410. Statement by Yasir Arafat on Peace in the Middle
East, December 14, 1988*

* *New York Times*, December 15, 1988, at A19.

Let me highlight my views before you. Our desire for peace is a strategy and not an interim tactic. We are bent on peace come what may, come what may.

Our statehood provides salvation to the Palestinians and peace to both Palestinians and Israelis.

Self-determination means survival for the Palestinians and our survival does not destroy the survival of the Israelis as their rulers claim.

Yesterday in my speech I made reference to United Nations Resolution 181 as the basis for Palestinian independence. I also made reference to our acceptance of Resolution 242 and 338 as the basis for negotiations with Israel within the framework of the international conference. These three resolutions were endorsed by our Palestine National Council session in Algiers.

'I Repeat for the Record'

In my speech also yesterday, it was clear that we mean our people's rights to freedom and national independence, according to Resolution 181, and the right of all parties concerned in the Middle East conflict to exist in peace and security, and, as I have mentioned, including the state of Palestine, Israel and other neighbors, according to the Resolution 242 and 338.

As for terrorism, I renounced it yesterday in no uncertain terms, and yet, I repeat for the record. I repeat for the record that we totally and absolutely renounce all forms of terrorism, including individual, group and state terrorism.

Between Geneva and Algiers, we have made our position crystal clear. Any more talk such as "The Palestinians should give more"—you remember this slogan?—or "It is not enough" or "The Palestinians are engaging in propaganda games and public-relations exercises" will be damaging and counterproductive.

Enough is enough. Enough is enough. Enough is enough. All remaining matters should be discussed around the table and within the international conference.

Ending the Uprising

Let it be absolutely clear that neither Arafat, nor any for that matter, can stop the intifada, the uprising. The intifada will come to an end only when practical and tangible steps have been taken towards the achievement of our national aims and establishment of our independent Palestinian state.

In this context, I expect the E.E.C. to play a more effective role in promoting peace in our region. They have a political responsibility, they have a moral responsibility, and they can deal with it.

Finally, I declare before you and I ask you to kindly quote me on that: We want peace. We want peace. We are committed to peace. We are committed to peace. We want to live in our Palestinian state, and let live. Thank you.

411. Statement by President Reagan on American Relations with the Palestine Liberation Organization, December 14, 1988*

* *New York Times*, December 15, 1988, at A18.

Text of Reagan Statement

Special to The New York Times

WASHINGTON, Dec. 14—Following is the text of a statement by President Reagan on American relations with the Palestine Liberation Organization, as issued tonight by the White House:

The Palestine Liberation Organization today issued a statement in which it accepted United Nations Security Council Resolutions 242 and 338, recognized Israel's right to exist, and renounced terrorism. These have long been our conditions for a substantive dialogue. They have been met. Therefore, I have authorized the State Department to enter into a substantive dialogue with P.L.O. representatives. The Palestine Liberation Organization must live up to its statements. In particular, it must demonstrate that its renunciation of terrorism is pervasive and permanent.

The initiation of a dialogue between the United States and P.L.O. representatives is an important step in the peace process, the more so because it represents the serious evolution of Palestinian thinking toward realistic and pragmatic positions on the key issues. But the objective of the United States remains, as always, a comprehensive peace in the Middle East. In that light, we view this development as one more step toward the beginning of direct negotiations between the parties, which alone can lead to such a peace.

The United States' special commitment to Israel's security and well-being remains unshakable. Indeed, a major reason for our entry into this dialogue is to help Israel achieve the recognition and security it deserves.

412. Remarks by Secretary of State Shultz Outlining New
U.S. Position toward the Palestine Liberation Organization,
December 14, 1988*

* *New York Times*, December 15, 1988, at A18.

The Palestine Liberation Organization today issued a statement in which it accepted U.N. Security Council Resolutions 242 and 338 recognized Israel's right to exist in peace and security and renounce terrorism. As a result, the United States is prepared for a substantive dialogue with P.L.O. representatives.

I am designating our Ambassador to Tunisia as the only authorized channel for that dialogue. The objective of the United States remains as always, a comprehensive peace in the Middle East. In that light, I view this development as one more step toward the beginning of direct negotiations between the parties which alone can lead to such a peace.

Nothing here may be taken to imply an acceptance or recognition by the United States of an independent Palestinian state. The position of the U.S. is that the status of the West Bank and Gaza cannot be determined by unilateral acts of either side, but only through a process of negotiations. The United States does not recognize the declaration of an independent Palestinian state.

It is also important to emphasize that the United States commitment to the security of Israel remains unflinching.

QUESTIONS AND ANSWERS

Ambiguities Removed

Q. Mr. Secretary, what was it today that changed your mind?

A. I didn't change my mind, they changed their—they made their statement clear so that it doesn't have the ambiguities in it that earlier statements had, which tended to allow various people to give different interpretations of what was meant.

Q. What was different about it today?

A. It was clear. It was not encumbered.

Q. Mr. Secretary, what about the P.L.O.'s record which only two weeks— you decided the terrorism record—you called Arafat an accomplice or accessory to terrorism. You denied him a visa. Are you expunging the P.L.O. record and saying let bygones be bygones?

A. No, when we have our dialogue you can be sure that the first item of business on our agenda in that dialogue will be the subject of terrorism. And we'll make it clear that our position about the importance of the renunciation of terrorism is central.

Kissinger Promise

Q. What can the dialogue do about people who are already dead and what has your statement have—how does your statement bear on the promise Kissinger made the Israelis?

A. The promise that Kissinger made the Israelis, which had to do with 242 and 338 and with the recognition of Israel's right to exist—since that time we have added our insistence on a renunciation of terrorism. Those conditions have been U.S. conditions for a dialogue with the P.L.O. going back to 1975. Our position has not changed. We have stayed with that position consistently. And now today we have an acceptance of those conditions in a clear-cut way.

Q. Mr. Secretary, have you told the State of Israel of your intentions, and can you tell us what their response was?

A. Everybody has been put on notice repeatedly for—since 1975, in effect, that if the P.L.O. meets our conditions, then we're prepared for a substantive dialogue. That is well known. Of course we have had communications with Israel, as we have had with other states, and we have been engaged in the last hour or so of trying to call people to tell them explicitly what we are prepared to do now that there is this statement. But I don't want to try to speak for others. I'm only speaking for the United States.

Q. Do you have reason to believe that the Israelis would be willing to sit down with the P.L.O.?

A. No, I don't have any reason to believe that. But all I'm telling you is what the U.S. policies are, and this policy has been in place for—since 1975. And it has been consistently adhered to. And now that we see a change in the posture of the P.L.O., all we're doing is following through on that policy. Our policy remains unchanged.

Q. Mr. Secretary, do you see this as a symbol meeting—at the beginning of a process in which a series of meetings and aimed at what result? Is it going to be a series of meetings, or where do you want it to go?

A. The meetings are not an end in themselves. Our object is a comprehensive peace, and so our object in any dialogue that we have with the P.L.O. will emphasize our desire for that, and our views of what it takes to get there. I made a speech last September on behalf of the United States and set out our views as a supplement to the views contained in the initiative that we worked on earlier this year. So our object is not a dialogue. Our object is peace. And we will be talking to the P.L.O., as to others, in an effort to move things along to that objective.

Q. Mr. Secretary, Secretary Kissinger was at the White House this morning. Was that why he was there?

A. No, it wasn't. However, I did talk to Secretary Kissinger since we got the, got word of this development.

P.L.O. Leadership

Q. Mr. Secretary, your statement at the American Colony was addressed specifically to Palestinians resident in the West Bank and Gaza and not, specifically not to the P.L.O. Does this dialogue with the P.L.O. now mean that the United States is prepared to address that sort of statement to the P.L.O. leadership as well as to other Palestinians?

A. That was a statement to Palestinians that I made in Jerusalem last spring, as I remember. Do you have the date of it in mind? I forget. It's been some while ago.

Anyway, I sought a meeting with Palestinians and I went to their turf, so to speak. And they would not meet. And of course the word we got was that they were afraid to meet because they were afraid they would be killed if they did. So I went and I made a statement that you referred to, saying here is what I would have told you if you had come. And we issued that statement as a statement of our efforts toward peace and of our recognition which has been consistent. And it's obviously so that if you're going to get to a peaceful settlement in the Middle East you have to include Palestinians in the process from the beginning and at the end. That is clear enough and that was basically what I said.

Q. As a result of this Mr. Secretary, are you going to be willing to talk with Mr. Arafat before you leave office?

A. What I am doing is authorizing our Ambassador in Tunisia to make himself available for a direct dialogue. And we are making it clear that this is the only authorized channel of communication. So anybody else who is representing themselves as a channel, is not a channel. This is the authoritative channel representing the United States Government.

Now what may evolve from this remains to be seen. But I think that when it comes to any genuine substantive discussion, we are in a transition phase and it is basically for the next Administration to decide what they do.

Response for President

Q. When will the first meeting be held?

A. I don't—we have seen this P.L.O. statement. I'm making this response on behalf of the President. I might say the President, the Vice President agree with this and I'm authorizing now the Ambassador in Tunis to undertake this dialogue. But when there will be a meeting, I don't know.

Q. Mr. Secretary, now that the United States has recognized the P.L.O. as a legitimate partner for negotiations, do you feel that there's any reason for Israel not to negotiate with the P.L.O.?

A. What we are doing as a result of the P.L.O.'s meeting our conditions is establishing a substantive dialogue with them. We hope that that dialogue may help bring about direct negotiations that will lead to peace. How those negotiations are structured, who is there to speak on behalf of the Palestinians, is a subject that's a difficult one; we've worked on it a long time, and I imagine it will continue to be difficult. But at any rate, we'll have a dialogue with the P.L.O. and that dialogue will be designed to find answers to those questions.

Israel Policies

Q. Now that the P.L.O. has recognized Israel's right to exist and the U.N. resolutions, and renounced terrorism, do you feel there is any reason that Israel should not now talk to the P.L.O.?

A. Israel has its own views and own policies, and Israel has always made it clear that these conditions that are U.S. conditions are not necessarily theirs. So I am not in any way speaking for Israel; it's totally for Israel to make its own decisions about what it wants to do and there's nothing to be inferred judgmentally about what they should do. I'm only saying that for the period since 1975, the U.S. has had a position in effect that if the P.L.O. meets these conditions we will have a substantive dialogue, and since they have met the conditions, we are carrying through on our policy. And that's the sum and substance of it.

Q. Mr. Secretary, would the incumbent Administration, since they are (unintelligible) transition state, and would you be able to tell us what's their stand on this.

A. The President and the Vice President both have followed these developments very closely, and they have reviewed each of them—this most recent development—and they both agree that under these circumstances, the conditions for a substantive dialogue, which we have had in place since 1975, have been met, and so we should state that we are ready to undertake that dialogue. Now, as far as what will be the efforts of the Administration of President-elect Bush, that is for them to determine, and that remains to be seen.

Q. Than [sic] you Mr.—

Q. Mr. Secretary—

A. I've been dismissed.

Permissions*

Maps following the Table of Contents are reproduced by permission of the Office of the Geographer, Department of State.

Resolution Adopted by the Arab League Sending an Arab Peace Force into Lebanon to Replace Syrian Troops, Cairo, June 9–10, 1976, is reprinted with the permission of the *Journal of Palestine Studies*.

Agreement Signed by Syrian Foreign Minister Abdul Halim Khaddam and PLO Political Department Chairman Farouq Qaddoumi on the Fundamental Points for Ending the Fighting in Lebanon, Damascus, July 29, 1976, is reprinted with the permission of the *Journal of Palestine Studies*.

Prime Minister Begin's Press Conference on Relations between Israel and the United States, the PLO, and Alternatives to the Geneva Conference, July 20, 1977, is reprinted with permission of the Embassy of Israel, Washington, D.C.

Israeli Government Policy Statement Delivered in the Knesset by the Minister of Foreign Affairs, Moshe Dayan, on Relations with the U.S., the Arabs, and the Palestinians, September 1, 1977, is reprinted with the permission of the Embassy of Israel, Washington, D.C.

Address by President Sadat to Israel's Knesset, November 20, 1977, is reprinted with the permission of *Keesing's Contemporary Archives: Record of World Events*.

Response by Prime Minister Begin to President Sadat's Knesset Speech, November 20, 1977, is reprinted with the permission of *Keesing's Contemporary Archives: Record of World Events*.

Security Council Resolution 425 Establishing the U.N. Interim Force in Lebanon and Requesting Israeli Withdrawal from Lebanon, March 19, 1978, is reprinted with the permission of the United Nations.

Report of the Secretary-General on the Implementation of Security Council Resolution 425 (1978), March 19, 1978, is reprinted with the permission of the United Nations.

Resolutions on the Arab Situation Passed by the Sixty-Ninth Session of the Council of the Arab League Following the Israeli Invasion of Lebanon, Cairo, April 1, 1978, are reprinted with the permission of the *Journal of Palestine Studies*.

Security Council Resolution 427 Increasing the U.N. Interim Force in Lebanon from 4,000 to 6,000 Troops and Taking Note of the Partial Israeli

* Permissions are listed to correspond to the sequence of the materials included in this volume.

Withdrawal, May 3, 1978, is reprinted with the permission of the United Nations.

Security Council Resolution 434 Renewing the U.N. Interim Force in Lebanon Mandate, September 18, 1978, is reprinted with the permission of the United Nations.

Security Council Resolution 378 Renewing the U.N. Emergency Force Mandate, October 23, 1975, is reprinted with the permission of the United Nations.

Security Council Resolution 381 Renewing the U.N. Disengagement Observer Force Mandate, November 30, 1975, is reprinted with the permission of the United Nations.

General Assembly Resolution 3525 (XXX) on the Report of the Special Committee to Investigate Israeli Practices Affecting the Human Rights of the Population of the Occupied Territories, December 15, 1975, is reprinted with the permission of the United Nations.

General Assembly Resolution 31/15 on the U.N. Relief and Works Agency for Palestine Refugees in the Near East, November 23, 1976, is reprinted with the permission of the United Nations.

General Assembly Resolution 31/20 on the Question of Palestine, November 24, 1976, is reprinted with the permission of the United Nations.

Security Council Resolution 398 Calling for the Implementation of Security Council Resolution 338 (1973) and Renewing the U.N. Disengagement Observer Force Mandate, November 30, 1976, is reprinted with the permission of the United Nations.

General Assembly Resolution 31/61 on the Situation in the Middle East, December 9, 1976, is reprinted with the permission of the United Nations.

General Assembly Resolution 31/62 on the Peace Conference on the Middle East, December 9, 1976, is reprinted with the permission of the United Nations.

General Assembly Resolution 31/106 on the Report of the Special Committee to Investigate Israeli Practices Affecting the Human Rights of the Population of the Occupied Territories, December 16, 1976, is reprinted with the permission of the United Nations.

General Assembly Resolution 31/110 on the Living Conditions of the Palestinian People, December 16, 1976, is reprinted with the permission of the United Nations.

Resolutions of the Thirteenth Palestine National Council, Cairo, March 21–25, 1977, is reprinted with the permission of the *Journal of Palestine Studies.*

Prime Minister Begin's Speech to the Knesset Presenting the New Government and Outlines of Its Policy, June 21, 1977, is reprinted with the permission of the Embassy of Israel, Washington, D.C.

General Assembly Resolution 32/5 on Recent Illegal Israeli Measures in the Occupied Arab Territories Designed to Change the Legal Status, Geographic Nature and Demographic Composition of Those Territories in

Contravention of the Principles of the Charter of the United Nations, of Israel's International Obligations Under the Fourth Geneva Convention of 1949 and of United Nations Resolutions, and Obstruction of Efforts Aimed at Achieving a Just and Lasting Peace in the Middle East, October 28, 1977, is reprinted with the permission of the United Nations.

General Assembly Resolution 32/20 on the Situation in the Middle East, November 25, 1977, is reprinted with the permission of the United Nations.

General Assembly Resolution 32/40 on the Question of Palestine, December 2, 1977, is reprinted with the permission of the United Nations.

Six-Point Programme Agreed by All Palestinian Factions, Announced by Fateh Central Council Member Salah Khalaf at a Press Conference in Tripoli, December 4, 1977, is reprinted with the permission of the *Journal of Palestine Studies*.

General Assembly Resolution 32/90 on the U.N. Relief and Works Agency for Palestine Refugees in the Near East, December 13, 1977, is reprinted with the permission of the United Nations.

General Assembly Resolution 32/91 on the Report of the Special Committee to Investigate Israeli Practices Affecting the Human Rights of the Population of the Occupied Territories, December 13, 1977, is reprinted with the permission of the United Nations.

State Department Legal Advisor's Letter to the Congress Concerning the Legality of Israeli Settlements in the Occupied Territories, April 21, 1978, is reprinted with the permission of *International Legal Materials*.

General Assembly Resolution 3516 (XXX) on Permanent Sovereignty Over National Resources in the Occupied Arab Territories, December 15, 1975, is reprinted with the permission of the United Nations.

State Department Memorandum of Law on Israel's Right to Develop New Oil Fields in Sinai and the Gulf of Suez, October 1, 1976, is reprinted with the permission of *International Legal Materials*.

General Assembly Resolution 31/186 on Permanent Sovereignty Over National Resources in the Occupied Arab Territories, December 21, 1976, is reprinted with the permission of the United Nations.

Israeli Ministry of Foreign Affairs Memorandum of Law on the Right to Develop New Oil Fields in Sinai and the Gulf of Suez, August 1, 1977, is reprinted with the permission of *International Legal Materials*.

General Assembly Resolution 32/161 on Permanent Sovereignty Over National Resources in the Occupied Arab Territories, December 19, 1977, is reprinted with the permission of the United Nations.

General Assembly Resolution 3474 (XXX) on the Establishment of a Nuclear-Weapon-Free Zone in the Region of the Middle East, December 11, 1975, is reprinted with the permission of the United Nations.

General Assembly Resolution 31/71 on the Establishment of a Nuclear-Weapon-Free Zone in the Region of the Middle East, December 10, 1976, is reprinted with the permission of the United Nations.

The excerpt from General Assembly Resolution S-10/2 Calling for the

Security Council Resolution 444 Renewing the U.N. Interim Force in Lebanon Mandate and Deploring Israel's Lack of Cooperation with the Force, January 19, 1979, is reprinted with the permission of the United Nations.

Security Council Resolution 450 Renewing the U.N. Interim Force in Lebanon Mandate and Calling for Israel to Stop Its Actions in Lebanon, June 14, 1979, is reprinted with the permission of the United Nations.

Security Council Resolution 459 Renewing the U.N. Interim Force in Lebanon Mandate and Approving the General Armistice Agreement, December 19, 1979, is reprinted with the permission of the United Nations.

Security Council Resolution 467 Reaffirming the U.N. Interim Force in Lebanon Mandate and Deploring Israeli Intervention in Lebanon, April 24, 1980, is reprinted with the permission of the United Nations.

Security Council Resolution 474 Renewing the U.N. Interim Force in Lebanon Mandate and Condemning the Continued Violence, June 17, 1980, is reprinted with the permission of the United Nations.

Security Council Resolution 483 Renewing the U.N. Interim Force in Lebanon Mandate and Reactivating the Israel-Lebanon Mixed Armistice Commission, December 17, 1980, is reprinted with the permission of the United Nations.

Security Council Resolution 488 Renewing the U.N. Interim Force in Lebanon Mandate and Reaffirming the Call for Respect of Lebanon's Territorial Integrity, June 19, 1981, is reprinted with the permission of the United Nations.

Security Council Resolution 490 Calling for a Cessation of All Armed Attacks and Reaffirming Its Commitment to Territorial Integrity in Lebanon, July 21, 1981, is reprinted with the permission of the United Nations.

Security Council Resolution 498 Calling for a Cease-Fire in Lebanon, Israeli Withdrawal, and Renewing the U.N. Interim Force in Lebanon Mandate, December 18, 1981, is reprinted with the permission of the United Nations.

Security Council Resolution 501 Reaffirming the U.N. Interim Force in Lebanon and Increasing Its Size to 7,000 Troops, February 25, 1982, is reprinted with the permission of the United Nations.

Security Council Resolution 438 Renewing the U.N. Emergency Force Mandate, October 23, 1978, is reprinted with the permission of the United Nations.

Security Council Resolution 441 Calling for the Implementation of Security Council Resolution 338 (1973) and Renewing the U.N. Disengagement Observer Force Mandate, November 30, 1978, is reprinted with the permission of the United Nations.

General Assembly Resolution 33/28 on the Question of Palestine, December 7, 1978, is reprinted with the permission of the United Nations.

General Assembly Resolution 33/29 on the Situation in the Middle East, December 7, 1978, is reprinted with the permission of the United Nations.

General Assembly Resolution 33/113 on the Report of the Special Committee to Investigate Israeli Practices Affecting the Human Rights of the Population of the Occupied Territories, December 18, 1978, is reprinted with the permission of the United Nations.

General Assembly Resolution 33/147 on Assistance to the Palestinian People, December 20, 1978, is reprinted with the permission of the United Nations.

Security Council Resolution 446 Calling Upon Israel to Cease Changing the Legal Status and the Geographic and Demographic Nature of the Occupied Arab Territories and Establishing a Commission to Examine the Situation, March 22, 1979, is reprinted with the permission of the United Nations.

Resolutions on the Palestine Question Passed at the Conference of the Foreign Ministers of Islamic Countries, Fez, May 8–12, 1979, are reprinted with the permission of the *Journal of Palestine Studies*.

First Report of the Security Council Commission Established Under Resolution 446 (1979) and Annexes III, IV, and V, July 12, 1979, is reprinted with the permission of the United Nations.

Security Council Resolution 452 Deploring Israeli Settlements Policy in the Occupied Arab Territories, July 20, 1979, is reprinted with permission of the United Nations.

The excerpt from the Resolutions on the Situation in the Middle East of the Sixth Conference of Heads of State of Non-Aligned Countries, Havana, September 3–9, 1979, is reprinted with the permission of the *Journal of Palestine Studies*.

Address to the 34th General Assembly of the U.N. by Israeli Foreign Minister Moshe Dayan on the PLO, Lebanon, Jerusalem, Syria, Egypt, the U.N. Role in the Peace Process, and the Soviet Union, September 27, 1979, is reprinted with the permission of the United Nations.

Israeli Supreme Court Judgment with Regard to the Elon Moreh Settlement in the Occupied West Bank, HCJ 390/79, October 22, 1979, is reprinted with the permission of *International Legal Materials*.

Excerpts from the Resolutions of the World Conference on Palestine, Lisbon, November 2–6, 1979, are reprinted with the permission of the *Journal of Palestine Studies*.

General Assembly Resolution 34/29 on the Situation in the Occupied Territories, November 16, 1979, is reprinted with the permission of the United Nations.

General Assembly Resolution 34/65 on the Question of Palestine, November 29, 1979, is reprinted with the permission of the United Nations.

Second Report of the Security Council Commission Established Under Resolution 446 (1979) and Annex, December 4, 1979, is reprinted with the permission of the United Nations.

General Assembly Resolution 34/70 on the Situation in the Middle East, December 6, 1979, is reprinted with the permission of the United Nations.

General Assembly Resolution 34/103 on the Inadmissibility of the Policy of Hegemonism in International Relations, December 14, 1979, is reprinted with the permission of the United Nations.

Israel's Autonomy Model, January 24, 1980, is reprinted with the permission of the Embassy of Israel, Washington, D.C.

Israel's Proposed Model for a Self-Governing Authority (Administrative Council) to Be Elected by the Palestinian Arab Inhabitants of Judea, Samaria, and the Gaza District, January 24, 1980, is reprinted with the permission of the Embassy of Israel, Washington, D.C.

The excerpt from Resolutions on the Palestine Question and Jerusalem by the Islamic Conference of Foreign Ministers Meeting in Its First Extraordinary Session, Islamabad, January 27–29, 1980, is reprinted with the permission of the *Journal of Palestine Studies*.

Hebron, Information Background, February 15, 1980, is reprinted with the permission of the Embassy of Israel, Washington, D.C.

Security Council Resolution 465 Deploring Israeli Policy on Settlements in the Occupied Arab Territories, Jerusalem, and the Holy Places, March 1, 1980, is reprinted with the permission of the United Nations.

The Jewish Quarter of Hebron, Israel Cabinet Decision, March 24, 1980, is reprinted with the permission of the Embassy of Israel, Washington, D.C.

Jewish Settlement in the Land of Israel, April 1980, is reprinted with the permission of the Embassy of Israel, Washington, D.C.

Jewish Settlements in Judea-Samaria: A Deterrent to War, April 1980, is reprinted with the permission of the Embassy of Israel, Washington, D.C.

Security Council Resolution 468 Deploring Israeli Expulsion of Mayors from Hebron and Halhoul, May 8, 1980, is reprinted with the permission of the United Nations.

Israel's Statement Before the Security Council Regarding Resolution 468, May 8, 1980, is reprinted with the permission of the United Nations.

Report by the Secretary-General Under Security Council Resolution 468, May 13, 1980, is reprinted with the permission of the United Nations.

Security Council Resolution 469 Deploring the Israeli Failure to Implement Resolution 468, May 20, 1980, is reprinted with the permission of the United Nations.

Political Programme Approved by the Fourth General Conference of the Palestinian Liberation Movement Fateh, Damascus, May 22–31, 1980, is reprinted with permission of the *Journal of Palestine Studies*.

Security Council Resolution 471 Reaffirming Resolution 465 and Expressing Concern for Israeli Settlements Policy in the Occupied Arab Territories, June 5, 1980, is reprinted with the permission of the United Nations.

Position of the Government of Israel on the Declaration on the Middle East Issued by the Leaders of the European Community at the Venice Summit, June 12–13, 1980, is reprinted with the permission of the Embassy of Israel, Washington, D.C.

Security Council Resolution 476 Deploring Israeli Settlements Policy in the Occupied Territories and Jerusalem, June 30, 1980, is reprinted with the permission of the United Nations.

Letter from the Permanent Representative of Israel to the U.N. Secretary-General Concerning an Israeli-Sponsored Study of the Rights of Palestinians Under International Law, June 27, 1980, is reprinted with the permission of the United Nations.

Israel, the United Nations, and International Law: Memorandum of Law, June 1980, is reprinted with the permission of the United Nations.

The excerpt from the Resolutions Adopted by the Conference of Foreign Ministers of Islamic Countries at an Extraordinary Session to Discuss the Present Situation in Occupied Palestine, Amman, July 11–12, 1980, is reprinted with the permission of the *Journal of Palestine Studies*.

General Assembly Resolution ES-7/2 on the Question of Palestine, July 29, 1980, is reprinted with the permission of the United Nations.

Security Council Resolution 478 Censuring Israeli "Basic Law" on Jerusalem, August 20, 1980, is reprinted with the permission of the United Nations.

Resolutions Adopted by the Emergency Session of the Conference of Foreign Ministers of Islamic Countries, Fez, September 18–20, 1980, is reprinted with the permission of the *Journal of Palestine Studies*.

Text of the Treaty of Friendship between the Soviet Union and the Syrian Arab Republic, Signed in Moscow by Soviet President Brezhnev and Syrian President Hafez Al-Assad, October 8, 1980, is reprinted with the permission of the *Journal of Palestine Studies*.

General Assembly Resolution 35/75 on the Living Conditions of the Palestinian People, December 5, 1980, is reprinted with the permission of the United Nations.

General Assembly Resolution 35/111 on Assistance to the Palestinian People, December 5, 1980, is reprinted with the permission of the United Nations.

General Assembly Resolution 35/122 on the Report of the Special Committee to Investigate Israeli Practices Affecting the Human Rights of the Population of the Occupied Territories, December 11, 1980, is reprinted with the permission of the United Nations.

General Assembly Resolution 35/169 on the Question of Palestine, December 15, 1980, is reprinted with the permission of the United Nations.

General Assembly Resolution 35/207 on the Situation in the Middle East, December 16, 1980, is reprinted with the permission of the United Nations.

Security Council Resolution 484 Expressing Concern for Israeli Expulsion of Mayors from Hebron and Halhoul and Calling for Their Return, December 19, 1980, is reprinted with the permission of the United Nations.

The excerpt from the Final Resolutions of the Third Islamic Summit on Palestine and Jerusalem, Taif, January 25–28, 1981, is reprinted with the permission of the *Journal of Palestine Studies*.

The excerpt from the Resolutions Adopted by the Fourth Congress of the PFLP, April 1981, is reprinted with the permission of the *Journal of Palestine Studies.*

General Assembly Resolution 36/73 on the Living Conditions of the Palestinian People, December 4, 1981, is reprinted with the permission of the United Nations.

General Assembly Resolution 36/120 on the Question of Palestine, December 10, 1981, is reprinted with the permission of the United Nations.

Israel: Law on the Golan Heights, December 14, 1981, is reprinted with the permission of *International Legal Materials.*

Statement Issued by the Syrian Government After the Israeli Decision to Annex the Syrian Golan Heights, December 14, 1981, is reprinted with the permission of the *Journal of Palestine Studies.*

Excerpts from the Statement Issued by the Jordanian Government After the Israeli Decision to Annex the Syrian Golan Heights, December 15, 1981, are reprinted with the permission of the *Journal of Palestine Studies.*

General Assembly Resolution 36/146 on the U.N. Relief and Works Agency for Palestine Refugees in the Near East, December 16, 1981, is reprinted with the permission of the United Nations.

General Asembly Resolution 36/147 on the Report of the Special Committee to Investigate Israeli Practices Affecting the Human Rights of the Population of the Occupied Territories, December 16, 1981, is reprinted with the permission of the United Nations.

Security Council Resolution 497 Deploring Annexation of the Golan Heights, December 17, 1981, is reprinted with the permission of the United Nations.

General Assembly Resolution 36/226 on the Situation in the Middle East, December 17, 1981, is reprinted with the permission of the United Nations.

The excerpt from the Statement Issued by the PLO Central Council at the End of Its Meetings in Damascus, December 29, 1981, is reprinted with the permission of the *Journal of Palestine Studies.*

Excerpts from the Syrian-Soviet Joint Communiqué Issued at the End of Talks between Syrian Foreign Minister Abd Al-Halim Khaddam and Soviet Foreign Minister Gromyko, Moscow, January 16, 1982, are reprinted with the permission of the *Journal of Palestine Studies.*

General Assembly Resolution ES-9/1 on the Situation in the Occupied Arab Territories, February 5, 1982, is reprinted with the permission of the United Nations.

General Assembly Resolution ES-7/4 on the Question of Palestine, April 28, 1982, is reprinted with the permission of the United Nations.

General Assembly Resolution 34/136 on Permanent Sovereignty Over National Resources in the Occupied Arab Territories, December 14, 1979, is reprinted with the permission of the United Nations.

General Assembly Resolution 36/15 on Recent Developments in Connection with Excavations in Eastern Jerusalem, October 28, 1981, is reprinted with the permission of the United Nations.

General Assembly Resolution 36/150 on Israel's Decision to Build a Canal Linking the Mediterranean Sea to the Dead Sea, December 16, 1981, is reprinted with the permission of the United Nations.

General Assembly Resolution 33/64 on the Establishment of a Nuclear-Weapon-Free Zone in the Region of the Middle East, December 14, 1978, is reprinted with the permission of the United Nations.

General Assembly Resolution 33/71 on the Review of the Implementation of the Recommendations and Decisions Adopted by the General Assembly at Its Tenth Special Session: A) Military and Nuclear Collaboration with Israel, December 14, 1978, is reprinted with the permission of the United Nations.

General Assembly Resolution 34/89 on Israeli Nuclear Armament, December 11, 1979, is reprinted with the permission of the United Nations.

Statement by the International Atomic Energy Agency Director-General on the Application of Safeguards to the Tamuz (Osirak) Reactor Facility, June 12, 1981, is reprinted with the permission of *International Legal Materials*.

Iraq's Statement Before the Security Council Concerning Israel's Attack on the Osirak Reactor, June 12, 1981, is reprinted with the permission of the United Nations.

Israel's Statement Before the Security Council Concerning Its Actions Regarding the Osirak Reactor, June 12, 1981, is reprinted with the permission of the United Nations.

Resolution by the International Atomic Energy Agency on the Military Attack on Iraqi Nuclear Research Center and Its Implications for the Agency, June 15, 1981, is reprinted with the permission of the United Nations.

Iraq's Statement on Behalf of the Islamic Group Before the Security Council Concerning Israel's Attack on the Osirak Reactor, June 16, 1981, is reprinted with the permission of the United Nations.

Security Council Resolution 487 Condemning Israel's Air Strike on Iraq's Osirak Reactor, June 19, 1981, is reprinted with the permission of the United Nations.

Israel's Statement Before the Security Council Concerning Its Actions Regarding the Osirak Reactor, June 19, 1981, is reprinted with the permission of the United Nations.

General Assembly Resolution 36/27 on Armed Israeli Aggression Against the Iraqi Nuclear Installations and Its Grave Consequences for the Established International System Concerning the Peaceful Uses of Nuclear Energy, the Non-Proliferation of Nuclear Weapons, and International Peace and Security, November 13, 1981, is reprinted with the permission of the United Nations.

General Assembly Resolution 36/87 on the Establishment of a Nuclear-

Weapon-Free Zone in the Region of the Middle East, December 9, 1981, is reprinted with the permission of the United Nations.

General Assembly Resolution 36/98 on Israeli Nuclear Armament, December 9, 1981, is reprinted with the permission of the United Nations.

General Assembly Resolution 34/145 on Measures to Prevent International Terrorism Which Endangers or Takes Innocent Human Lives or Jeopardizes Fundamental Freedoms and Study of the Underlying Causes of Those Forms of Terrorism and Acts of Violence Which Lie in Misery, Frustration, Grievance and Despair and Which Cause Some People to Sacrifice Human Lives, Including Their Own, in an Attempt to Effect Radical Change, December 17, 1979, is reprinted with the permission of the United Nations.

International Convention Against the Taking of Hostages, December 17, 1979, is reprinted with the permission of the United Nations.

Council of Europe: Recommendation No. R (82) 1 of the Committee of Ministers to Member States Concerning International Co-operation in the Prosecution and Punishment of Acts of Terrorism, January 15, 1982, is reprinted with the permission of *International Legal Materials*.

Statement by Foreign Minister, Yitzhak Shamir, to the Knesset on the Issue of U.S. Arms Sale to Jordan and Saudi Arabia, June 25, 1980, is reprinted with permission of the Embassy of Israel, Washington, D.C.

Communiqué on American-Israeli Strategic Cooperation Issued by the Arab Foreign Ministers After Their Emergency Meeting in New York, October 3, 1981, is reprinted with the permission of the *Journal of Palestine Studies*.

Security Council Resolution 508 Calling for a Cease-Fire in Lebanon, June 5, 1982, is reprinted with the permission of the United Nations.

Security Council Resolution 509 Calling for Israeli Withdrawal from Lebanon, June 6, 1982, is reprinted with the permission of the United Nations.

Security Council Resolution 511 Renewing the U.N. Interim Force in Lebanon Mandate, June 18, 1982, is reprinted with the permission of the United Nations.

Security Council Resolution 512 Stressing the Need for Humanitarian Aid and Refraining from Violence Against Lebanon's Civilians, June 19, 1982, is reprinted with the permission of the United Nations.

Text of Israeli Government Peace Proposal, June 27, 1982, is reprinted with the permission of The New York Times Company, copyright 1986.

General Assembly Resolution ES-7/5 on the Question of Palestine, June 26, 1982, is reprinted with the permission of the United Nations.

Security Council Resolution 513 Calling for Respect of the Rights of All Non-Combatants in Lebanon, July 4, 1982, is reprinted with the permission of the United Nations.

Security Council Resolution 515 Demanding That Israel Lift Its Blockade of Beirut, July 29, 1982, is reprinted with the permission of the United Nations.

Communiqué of Arab Foreign Ministers Conference, Jeddah, July 29, 1982, is reprinted with the permission of the *Journal of Palestine Studies*.

Security Council Resolution 516 Calling for a Cease-Fire in Lebanon and Immediate Israeli Withdrawal, August 1, 1982, is reprinted with the permission of the United Nations.

Security Council Resolution 517 Renewing the Call for a Cease-Fire in Lebanon and Asking the Secretary-General to Report on the Resolution's Implementation, August 4, 1982, is reprinted with the permission of the United Nations.

Security Council Resolution 518 Calling for Israeli Cessation of Military Activities in Lebanon, Particularly in Beirut, August 12, 1982, is reprinted with the permission of the United Nations.

Security Council Resolution 519 Renewing the U.N. Interim Force in Lebanon Mandate, August 17, 1982, is reprinted with the permission of the United Nations.

Text of "Talking Points" Sent to Prime Minister Begin by President Reagan, September 9, 1982, is reprinted with the permission of The New York Times Company, copyright 1982.

Israeli Cabinet Communiqué on President Reagan's Peace Proposal, September 2, 1982, is reprinted with the permission of the *Journal of Palestine Studies*.

Knesset Speech by Foreign Minister Yitzhak Shamir on President Reagan's Proposals, September 8, 1982, is reprinted with the permission of *International Legal Materials*.

Final Declaration of the Twelfth Summit Conference of Arab Heads of State, Fez, September 6–9, 1982, is reprinted with the permission of *International Legal Materials*.

Report of PLO Central Council, November 25, 1982, is reprinted with the permission of the *Journal of Palestine Studies*.

PLO Statement Outlining Its Position on Dialogue with Jordan and Rejecting the Reagan Peace Plan, Damascus, April 12, 1983, is reprinted with the permission of the *Journal of Palestine Studies*.

Security Council Resolution 520 Condemning the Israeli Incursion into Beirut and Calling for Immediate Withdrawal from Lebanon, September 17, 1982, is reprinted with the permission of the United Nations.

Security Council Resolution 521 Condemning the West Beirut Massacre, September 19, 1982, is reprinted with the permission of the United Nations.

Lebanon's Letter Informing the Security Council That It Desires the Reconstitution of the Multinational Force in Lebanon, September 20, 1982, is reprinted with the permission of the United Nations.

General Assembly Resolution ES-7/9 on the Question of Palestine, September 24, 1982, is reprinted with the permission of the United Nations.

Security Council Resolution 523 Renewing the U.N. Interim Force in Lebanon Mandate and Authorizing Interim Humanitarian Acts, October 18, 1982, is reprinted with the permission of the United Nations.

Security Council Resolution 529 Renewing the U.N. Interim Force in Lebanon Mandate, January 18, 1983, is reprinted with the permission of the United Nations.

Excerpts from the Lebanese Government Statement on the Lebanese Agreement with Israel, Beirut, May 16, 1983, are reprinted with the permission of the *Journal of Palestine Studies*.

Agreement between the Government of the State of Israel and the Government of the Republic of Lebanon, May 17, 1983, is reprinted with the permission of *International Legal Materials*.

PFLP-DFLP Joint Communiqué on the Developments on Palestinian and Arab Levels, Damascus, June 6, 1983, is reprinted with the permission of the *Journal of Palestine Studies*.

The excerpt from the Final Statement of the Geneva Conference on Lebanese National Dialogue, Geneva, November 4, 1983, is reprinted with the permission of the *Journal of Palestine Studies*.

Security Council Resolution 542 Requesting a Cease-Fire in Northern Lebanon, November 23, 1983, is reprinted with the permission of the United Nations.

Joint Statement by the Popular and Democratic Fronts for the Liberation of Palestine on Proposed Five-Point Palestinian Initiative for Ending the Tripoli Fighting and Protecting Palestinian National Unity, Damascus(?), November 23, 1983, is reprinted with the permission of the *Journal of Palestine Studies*.

Statement by the Council of Ministers of Lebanon on the Decision to Abrogate the May 17 Agreement, Beirut, March 5, 1984, is reprinted with the permission of the *Journal of Palestine Studies*.

Security Council Resolution 549 Renewing the U.N. Interim Force in Lebanon Mandate, April 19, 1984, is reprinted with the permission of the United Nations.

Security Council Resolution 564 Expressing Concern Over the Continuing Violence in Lebanon and Calling for Respect for U.N. Agencies and the Lebanese Government, May 31, 1985, is reprinted with the permission of the United Nations.

Lebanese Leaders' Statement of National Accord, Damascus, July 8, 1985, is reprinted with the permission of the *Journal of Palestine Studies*.

General Assembly Resolution 40/229 on Assistance for the Reconstruction and Development of Lebanon, December 17, 1985, is reprinted with the permission of the United Nations.

General Assembly Resolution ES-7/6 on the Question of Palestine, August 19, 1982, is reprinted with the permission of the United Nations.

General Assembly Resolutoin ES-7/8 on an International Day of Innocent Children Victims of Aggression, August 19, 1982, is reprinted with the permission of the United Nations.

Security Council Resolution 524 Calling for Implementation of Security Council Resolution 338 (1973) and Renewing the U.N. Disengagement Observer Force Mandate, November 29, 1982, is reprinted with the permission of the United Nations.

General Assembly Resolution 37/86 on the Question of Palestine, December 10 and 20, 1982, is reprinted with the permission of the United Nations.

General Assembly Resolution 37/120 on the U.N. Relief and Works Agency for Palestine Refugees in the Near East, December 16, 1982, is reprinted with the permission of the United Nations.

General Assembly Resolution 37/123 on the Situation in the Middle East, December 16 and 20, 1982, is reprinted with the permission of the United Nations.

General Assembly Resolution 37/134 on Assistance to the Palestinian People, December 17, 1982, is reprinted with the permission of the United Nations.

General Assembly Resolution 37/222 on the Living Conditions of the Palestinian People in the Occupied Palestinian Territories, December 20, 1982, is reprinted with the permission of the United Nations.

Statement by the Conference of Palestinian Resistance Groups Meeting in Tripoli, Libya, January 16, 1983, is reprinted with the permission of the *Journal of Palestine Studies*.

The Palestinian People's Legal Right to Exercise Self-Determination, June 20, 1983, is reprinted with the permission of the United Nations.

The Status of Jerusalem, June 22, 1983: Report to the U.N. International Conference on the Question of Palestine is reprinted with the permission of the United Nations.

Geneva Declaration on Palestine and Programme of Action for the Achievement of Palestinian Rights, September 16, 1983, is reprinted with the permission of the United Nations.

Excerpts from the Fateh Central Committee Statement on the Problems Facing the Palestinian Cause and the PLO, Kuwait, October 16, 1983, are reprinted with the permission of the *Journal of Palestine Studies*.

General Assembly Resolution 38/58 on the Question of Palestine, December 13, 1983, is reprinted with the permission of the United Nations.

General Assembly Resolution 38/79 on the Report of the Special Committee to Investigate Israeli Practices Affecting the Human Rights of the Population of the Occupied Territories, December 15, 1983, is reprinted with the permission of the United Nations.

General Assembly Resolution 38/166 on the Living Conditions of the Palestinian People in the Occupied Palestinian Territories, December 19, 1983, is reprinted with the permission of the United Nations.

Ministry of Defense Statement on Commission Findings Regarding Murder of Commandos (4/12/84), Jerusalem, May 28, 1984, is reprinted with the permission of the *Journal of Palestine Studies*.

Excerpts from the Aden-Algiers Agreement between Fateh Central Committee and the Palestinian Democratic Alliance, Aden, June 27, 1984, are reprinted with the permission of the *Journal of Palestine Studies*.

Excerpts from the Final Communiqué of the Seventeenth Session of the Palestine National Council, Tunis, December 5, 1984, are reprinted with the permission of the *Journal of Palestine Studies*.

General Assembly Resolution 39/49 on the Question of Palestine, December 11, 1984, is reprinted with the permission of the United Nations.

General Assembly Resolution 39/169 on the Living Conditions of the Palestinian People in the Occupied Palestinian Territories, December 17, 1984, is reprinted with the permission of the United Nations.

General Assembly Resolution 39/223 on Economic Development Projects in the Occupied Palestinian Territories, December 18, 1984, is reprinted with the permission of the United Nations.

Text of Jordanian-Palestinian Accord, February 11, 1985, is reprinted with the permission of the *Journal of Palestine Studies*.

Communiqué of the Executive Committee of the PLO on the Plan of Joint Palestinian-Jordanian Action, February 19, 1985, is reprinted with the permission of the *Journal of Palestine Studies*.

Excerpts from the Final Communiqué on the Work of the Emergency Arab Summit Conference, Casablanca, August 9, 1985, are reprinted with the permission of the *Journal of Palestine Studies*.

The Syrian-Jordanian Joint Communiqué, Damascus, November 13, 1985, is reprinted with the permission of the *Journal of Palestine Studies*.

General Assembly Resolution 40/96 on the Question of Palestine, December 12, 1985, is reprinted with the permission of the United Nations.

General Assembly Resolution 40/161 on the Report of the Special Committee to Investigate Israeli Practice Affecting the Human Rights of the People of the Occupied Territories, December 16, 1985, is reprinted with the permission of the United Nations.

General Assembly Resolution 40/165 on the U.N. Relief and Works Agency for Palestine Refugees in the Near East, December 16, 1985, is reprinted with the permission of the United Nations.

General Assembly Resolution 40/168 on the Situation in the Middle East, December 16, 1985, is reprinted with the permission of the United Nations.

General Assembly Resolution 40/170 on Assistance to the Palestinian People, December 17, 1985, is reprinted with the permission of the United Nations.

General Assembly Resolution 40/201 on the Living Conditions of the Palestinian People in the Occupied Palestinian Territories, December 17, 1985, is reprinted with the permission of the United Nations.

Text of Joint Communiqué Issued by Israel and Morocco, July 24, 1986, is reprinted with the permission of The New York Times Company, copyright 1986.

Memorandum to British Prime Minsiter Margaret Thatcher from Palestinian Leaders in the Occupied Territories, May 27, 1986, is reprinted with the permission of the *Journal of Palestine Studies*.

Fateh Revolutionary Council Statement, Tunis, June 19, 1986, is reprinted with the permission of the *Journal of Palestine Studies*.

Jordan's Five-Year Development Plan for the Occupied Territories, Amman, August 1986, is reprinted with the permission of the *Journal of Palestine Studies*.

The PLO Executive Committee Statement, Baghdad, August 10, 1986, is reprinted with the permission of the *Journal of Palestine Studies*.

The Prague Declaration issued by Fateh, the Democratic Front for the Liberation of Palestine, and the Palestinian Communist Party, Prague, September 6, 1986, is reprinted with the permission of the *Journal of Palestine Studies*.

The Alexandria Declaration read by President Husni Mubarak of Egypt and Prime Minister Shimon Peres of Israel, Alexandria, Egypt, September 12, 1986, is reprinted with the permission of the *Journal of Palestine Studies*.

Statement of Israeli Prime Minsiter Shimon Peres on Return from Summit with Egyptian President Husni Mubarak, Alexandria, Egypt, September 12, 1986, is reprinted with the permission of the *Journal of Palestine Studies*.

The Seven Points of the Jordanian Development Conference, Amman, Jordan, November 10, 1986, are reprinted with the permission of the *Journal of Palestine Studies*.

European Community Declaration on the Middle East, Brussels, February 23, 1987, is reprinted with the permission of the *Journal of Palestine Studies*.

Cancellation of the Amman Agreement, Algiers, April 19, 1987, is reprinted with the permission of the *Journal of Palestine Studies*.

Resolution of the Political Committee of the Eighteenth Session of the PNC, Algiers, April 26, 1987, is reprinted with the permission of the *Journal of Palestine Studies*.

Palestinian Memorandum to U.S. Secretary of State George Shultz, Jerusalem, October 1987, is reprinted with the permission of the *Journal of Palestine Studies*.

Memorandum Submitted to French Prime Minister Jacques Chirac by Palestinians from the Occupied Territories, Jerusalem, November 3, 1987, is reprinted with the permission of the *Journal of Palestine Studies*.

Excerpt from the Resolutions of the Arab Summit, Amman, November 11, 1987, is reprinted with the permission of the *Journal of Palestine Studies*.

Report of the Secretary-General of the United Nations to the Security Council regarding the Situation in the Occupied Territories, January 21, 1988, is reprinted with the permission of the United Nations.

General Assembly Resolution 37/122 on Israel's Decision to Build a Canal Linking the Mediterranean Sea to the Dead Sea, December 16, 1982, is reprinted with the permission of the United Nations.

General Assembly Resolution 37/135 on Permanent Sovereignty Over National Resources in the Occupied Palestinian and Other Arab Territories, December 17, 1982, is reprinted with the permission of the United Nations.

Economic Activity and Access to Natural Resources: Legal Restrictions on Access to Land and Water in Israel, June 20, 1983, is reprinted with the permission of the United Nations.

General Assembly Resolution 40/167 on Israel's Decision to Build a Canal Linking the Mediterranean Sea to the Dead Sea, December 16,1985, is reprinted with the permission of the United Nations.

General Assembly Resolution 37/18 on Armed Israeli Aggression Against the Iraqi Nuclear Installations and Its Grave Consequences for the Established International System Concerning the Peaceful Uses of Nuclear Energy, the Non-Proliferation of Nuclear Weapons and International Peace and Security, November 16, 1982, is reprinted with the permission of the United Nations.

General Assembly Resolution 37/75 on the Establishment of a Nuclear-Weapon-Free Zone in the Region of the Middle East, December 9, 1982, is reprinted with the permission of the United Nations.

General Assembly Resolution 37/82 on Israeli Nuclear Armament, December 9, 1982, is reprinted with the permission of the United Nations.

General Assembly Resolution 38/9 on Armed Israeli Aggression Against the Iraqi Nuclear Installations and Its Grave Consequences for the Established International System Concerning the Peaceful Uses of Nuclear Energy, the Non-Proliferation of Nuclear Weapons and International Peace and Security, November 10, 1983, is reprinted with the permission of the United Nations.

General Assembly Resolution 38/69 on Israeli Nuclear Armament, December 15, 1983, is reprinted with the permission of the United Nations.

General Assembly Resolution 39/14 on Armed Israeli Aggression Against the Iraqi Nuclear Installations and Its Grave Consequences for the Established International System Concerning the Peaceful Uses of Nuclear Energy, the Non-Proliferation of Nuclear Weapons and International Peace and Security, November 16, 1984, is reprinted with the permission of the United Nations.

General Assembly Resolution 40/6 on Armed Israeli Aggression Against the Iraqi Nuclear Installations and Its Grave Consequences for the Established International System Concerning the Peaceful Uses of Nuclear Energy, the Non-Proliferation of Nuclear Weapons and International Peace and Security, November 1, 1985, is reprinted with the permission of the United Nations.

General Assembly Resolution 40/93 on Israeli Nuclear Armament, December 12, 1985, is reprinted with the permission of the United Nations.

General Assembly Resolution 38/130 on Measures to Prevent International Terrorism Which Endangers or Takes Innocent Human Lives or Jeopardizes Fundamental Freedoms and Study of the Underlying Causes of Those Forms of Terrorism and Acts of Violence Which Lie in Misery, Frustration, Grievance and Despair and Which Cause Some People to Sacrifice Human Lives, Including Their Own, in an Attempt to Effect Radical

Change, December 19, 1983, is reprinted with the permission of the United Nations.

Security Council Resolution 573 Condemning the Israeli Air Raid on the PLO Headquarters in Tunisia, October 4, 1985, is reprinted with the permission of the United Nations.

Statement by the Egyptian Ministry of Foreign Affairs in Reaction to the Interception by U.S. Warplanes of an *Egypt Air* Plane Carrying the Hijackers of the *Achille Lauro*, Cairo, October 11, 1985, is reprinted with the permission of the *Journal of Palestine Studies*.

Warrant for Arrest and Criminal Complaint of Individuals in the *Achille Lauro* Incident, October 12, 1985, is reprinted with the permission of *International Legal Materials*.

Cairo Declaration on the PLO and Terrorism as Read by PLO Chairman Yasir Arafat, November 7, 1985, is reprinted with the permission of the *Journal of Palestine Studies*.

Communiqué Issued by the Central Council of the Palestine Liberation Organization, Baghdad, November 25, 1985, is reprinted with the permission of the *Journal of Palestine Studies*.

General Assembly Resolution 40/61 on Measures to Prevent International Terrorism Which Endangers or Takes Innocent Human Lives or Jeopardizes Fundamental Freedoms and Study of the Underlying Causes of Those Forms of Terrorism and Acts of Violence Which Lie in Misery, Frustration, Grievance and Despair and Which Cause Some People to Sacrifice Human Lives, Including Their Own, in an Attempt to Effect Radical Change, December 9, 1985, is reprinted with the permission of the United Nations.

Security Council Resolution 579 Condemning Hostage Taking, December 18, 1985, is reprinted with the permission of the United Nations.

The "London Document" on Peace Concluded between King Hussein of Jordan and Israeli Foreign Minister Peres, London, April 1987, is reprinted with the permission of the *Journal of Palestine Studies*.

Excerpts from the Speech Given by Israeli Foreign Minister Shimon Peres to the Forty-second Session of the U.N. General Assembly, New York, September 30, 1987, is reprinted with the permission of the *Journal of Palestine Studies*.

King Hussein's Speech on the West Bank, Amman, July 31, 1988, is reprinted with the permission of the *Journal of Palestine Studies*.

General Assembly Resolution 43/21 on the Uprising (Intifadah) of the Palestinian People, November 3, 1988, is reprinted with the permission of the United Nations.

The Palestinian National Council's "Palestinian Declaration of Independence," November 15, 1988, is reprinted with the permission of the *Journal of Palestine Studies*.

Excerpts from the Speech Given by Yasir Arafat to the Forty-third Session of the U.N. General Assembly, December 13, 1988, is reprinted with the permission of The New York Times Company.

The Arab-Israeli Conflict and International Law:

1975–1988

A Selected Bibliography

Articles

I. UNDERLYING ISSUES

A. *Palestinian Autonomy, Israeli Security, and the Intifadah*

Allon. "Israel: The Case for Defensible Borders." 55 *For. Aff.* 38 (1976).

Bar-On, M. "Israeli Reactions to the Palestinian Uprising." 17 *J. Pal. Stud.* 46 (Summer 1988).

Dunn, M. "Five Smooth Stones: Israel, the Palestinians and the Intifada." 16 *Defense and For. Aff.* 15 (1988).

Feldman. "Peacemaking in the Middle East." 59 *For. Aff.* 756 (1981).

Gabriel, J. "The Economic Side of the Intifadah." 18 *J. Pal. Stud.* 198 (Autumn 1988).

Kanafi, M. "A Digest of Selected Judgements of the Supreme Court of Israel." 22 *Isr. L. Rev.* 219 (1987).

Kapeliouk, A. "New Light on the Israeli-Arab Conflict and the Refugee Problem and Its Origins." 16 *J. Pal. Stud.* 16 (Spring 1987).

Khalidi. "Thinking the Unthinkable: A Sovereign Palestine State." 56 *For. Aff.* 695 (1978).

Kuttab, J. "The Children's Revolt." 17 *J. Pal. Stud.* 26 (Summer 1988).

Lederman. "Dateline West Bank: Interpreting the Intifada." 72 *For. Pol'y* 230 (1988).

Lewis. "Israel: The Peres Era and Its Legacy." 65 *For. Aff.* 582 (1987).

Mandelbaum. "Israel's Security Dilemma." 32 *Orbis* 355 (1988).

Miller. "The Palestinians: Past as Prologue." 87 *Current History* 73 (1988).

Nakhleh. "The West Bank and Gaza: Twenty Years Later." 42 *Mid. East J.* 209 (Spring 1988).

———. "The Palestinians and the Future: Peace Through Realism." 18 *J. Pal. Stud.* 3 (Winter 1989).

Peretz. "Intifadeh: The Palestinian Uprising." 66 *For. Aff.* 964 (1988).

Perlmutter. "A Palestine Entity?" 5 *Int'l Security* 103 (1981).

Rostow. " 'Palestinian Self-Determination': Possible Futures for the Unallocated Territories of the Palestine Mandate." 5 *Yale Stud. in World Pub. Ord.* 147 (1979).

Roy. "The Gaza Strip: A Case of Economic De-Development." 17 *J. Pal. Stud.* 56 (Autumn 1987).

Sahliyeh. "West Bank Politics Since 1967." 10 *Wash. Q.* 137 (1987).

Segal. "A Foreign Policy for the State of Palestine." 18 *J. Pal. Stud.* 16 (Winter 1989).

Shadid and Seltzer. "Political Attitudes of Palestinians in the West Bank and Gaza Strip." 42 *Mid. East J.* 16 (1988).

Shalev. "Unilateral Autonomy in Judea and Samaria: Israel's Options." 43 *Jerusalem Q.* 71 (1987).

Shamir. "Israel's Role in a Changing Middle East." 60 *For. Aff.* 789 (1982).

———. "Israel at 40: Looking Back, Looking Ahead." 66 *For. Aff.* 574 (1988).

Sohn. "The Concept of Autonomy in International Law and the Practice of the United Nations." 15 *Isr. L. Rev.* 180 (1980).

Tillman. "Israel and Palestinian Nationalism." 9 *J. Pal. Stud.* 46 (Autumn 1979).

B. Jerusalem and the Holy Places

Cattan. "The Status of Jerusalem." 10 *J. Pal. Stud.* 3 (Spring 1981).

Crane. "Status of Jerusalem." 21 *Harvard Int'l L. J.* 784 (1980).

Gruhin. "Jerusalem: Legal and Political Dimensions in a Search for Peace." 12 *Case W. Res. J. Int'l L.* 169 (1980).

Neff. "Struggle over Jerusalem." 23 *Am.-Arab Aff.* 15 (1988).

C. Freedom of Navigation through the Strait of Tiran, the Gulf of Aqaba, and the Suez Canal

El Baradei. "The Egyptian-Israeli Peace Treaty and Access to the Gulf of Aqaba: A New Legal Regime." 76 *Am. J. Int'l L.* 532 (1982).

Lapidoth. "The Strait of Tiran, the Gulf of Aqaba, and the 1979 Treaty of Peace between Egypt and Israel." 77 *Am. J. Int'l L.* 84 (1983).

Riyadh. "Israel and Arab Waters." 6 *Arab Researcher* 5 (1986).

II. HOSTILITIES SINCE THE OCTOBER WAR

A. The Entebbe Incident

Knischer. "The Entebbe Operation: A Legal Analysis of Israel's Rescue Action." 12 *J. Int'l L. & Econ.* 57 (1977).

Krift. "Self-Defense and Self-Help: The Israeli Raid on Entebbe." 4 *Brooklyn J. Int'l L.* 43 (1977).

Paust. "Entebbe and Self-Help: The Israeli Response to Terrorism." 2 *Fletcher F.* 86 (1978).

Sheehan. "The Entebbe Raid: The Principle of Self-Help in International Law as Justification for State Use of Armed Force." 1 *Fletcher F.* 135 (1977).

B. The PLO, Israel, and the Conflict in Lebanon

Boyle. "Upholding International Law in the Middle East." 4 *Arab Stud. Q.* 336 (1982).

Cobban. "Lebanon's Chinese Puzzle." 53 *For. Pol'y* 34 (1983–84).

Friedlander. "Retaliation as an Anti-Terrorist Weapon: The Israeli Lebanon Incursion and International Law." 8 *Isr. Y. B. Hum. Rts.* 63 (1978).

Golan. "The Soviet Union and the PLO Since the War in Lebanon." 40 *Mid. East J.* 285 (1986).

Hassan. "The Legal Implications of the United States Involvement in the PLO Evacuation from Beirut." 19 *Tex. Int'l L. J.* 509 (1983).

———. "The PLO's Return to the Lebanese Equation." 293 *Mid. East Int'l* 17 (1987).

Hudson. "The Palestinian Factor in the Lebanese Civil War." 32 *Mid. East J.* 261 (1978).

Ignatius. "How to Rebuild Lebanon." 61 *For. Aff.* 1140 (1983).

Kemp. "Lessons of Lebanon: A Guideline for Future U.S. Policy." 6 *Mid. East Insight* 61 (Summer 1988).

Levenfeld. "Israel's Counter-Fedayeen Tactics in Lebanon: Self-Defense and Reprisal Under Modern International Law." 21 *Columbia J. Transnat'l L.* 1 (1982).

Lieber and Yanir. "Personal Whim or Strategic Imperative: The Israeli Invasion of Lebanon." 8 *Int'l Security* 117 (1983).

Malone. "The Kahan Report, Ariel Sharon and the Sabra-Shatilla Massacres in Lebanon: Responsibility Under International Law for Massacre of Civilian Populations." 373 *Utah L. Rev.* (1985).

Pipes. "Lebanon: The Real Problem." 51 *For. Pol'y* 139 (1983).

Pogany. "International Law and the Beirut Massacre." 16 *Bracton L. J.* 32 (1983).

Schiff. "Dealing with Syria." 55 *For. Pol'y* 92 (1984).

———. "Green Light, Lebanon." 50 *For. Pol'y* 73 (1983).

Seelye. "The Role of Syria in Lebanon." 21 *Am.-Arab Aff.* 87, 103 (1987).

C. The Threat of Nuclear Proliferation and the Israeli Air Strike on Iraq's Osirak Reactor

Barnaby. "The Nuclear Arsenal in the Middle East." 17 *J. Pal. Stud.* 97 (Autumn 1987).

D'Amato. "The Legality of Israel's Destruction of Iraq's Nuclear Reactor." 70 *Mid. East Focus* 12 (1988).

Feldman. "The Bombing of Osirak—Revisited." 7 *Int'l Security* 114 (1982).

Gaffney. "Prisoners of Fear: A Retrospective Look at the Israeli Nuclear Program." 22 *Am.-Arab Aff.* 75 (1987).

Haselkorn. "Arab-Israeli Conflict: Implications of Mass Destruction Weapons." 3 *Global Aff.* 120 (1987).

Ja'far. "The June 1982 War and the Future of the Arab-Israeli Arms Balance." 1 *Arab Aff.* 78 (1987).

Kaplan. "The Attack on Osirak: Delimitation on Self-Defense Under International Law." 4 *N.Y. J. Int'l & Comp. L.* 131 (1982).

Mallison and Mallison. "The Israeli Aerial Attack of June 7, 1981, Upon the Iraqi Nuclear Reactor: Aggression or Self-Defense?" 15 *Vand. J. Transnat'l L.* 417 (1982).

Marom. "Israel's Position on Nonproliferation." 8 *Jerusalem J. Int'l Rel.* 100 (December 1986).

Mintz. "Arms Production in Israel." 42 *Jerusalem Q.* 89 (1987).

Perlmutter. "The Israeli Raid on Iraq: A New Proliferation Landscape." 10 *Strategic Rev.* 34 (1981).

Power. "Preventing Nuclear Conflict in the Middle East: The Free-Zone Strategy." 37 *Mid. East J.* 617 (1983).

Quester. "Nuclear Weapons and Israel." 37 *Mid. East J.* 547 (1983).

Ramati. "Israel and Nuclear Deterrence." 3 *Global Aff.* 175 (1988).

Shoham. "The Israeli Aerial Raid upon the Iraqi Nuclear Reactor and the Right of Self-Defense." 109 *Mil. L. Rev.* 191 (1985).

Snyder. "The Road to Osirak: Baghdad's Quest for the Bomb." 37 *Mid. East J.* 565 (1983).

Steinberg. "Indigenous Arms Industries and Dependence: The Case of Israel." 2 *Def. Analysis* 291 (1986).

Stork. "Arms Industries of the Middle East." 144 *MERIP Mid. East Report* 12 (1986).

———. "Nuclear Shadow over the Middle East." 143 *MERIP Mid. East Report* 4 (1986).

D. Humanitarian Law and the Protection of Civilians and Prisoners of War

Adams. "Israel's Treatment of the Arabs in the Occupied Territories." 6 *J. Pal. Stud.* 19 (Winter 1977).

Butovsky. "Law of Belligerent Occupation: Israeli Practice and Judicial Decisions Affecting the West Bank." 21 *Can. Y. B. Int'l L.* 216 (1983).

Clagett and Johnson. "May Israel as a Belligerent Occupant Lawfully Exploit Previously Unexploited Oil Resources of the Gulf of Suez?" 72 *Am. J. Int'l L.* 558 (1978).

Cohen. "Justice for Occupied Territory? The Israeli High Court of Justice Paradigm." 24 *Columbia J. Transnat'l L.* 471 (1986).

Gerson. "Off-Shore Oil Exploration by a Belligerent Occupant: The Gulf of Suez Dispute." 71 *Am. J. Int'l L.* 725 (1977).

Hertzberg. "Israel and the West Bank." 61 *For. Aff.* 1064 (1983).

"Human Rights and Peace in the Middle East." 13 *Syracuse J. Int'l L. and Commerce* 391 (1987).

Lederman and Tabory. "Criminalization of Racial Incitement in Israel." 24 *Stanford J. Int'l L.* 55 (1987).

Lee. "The Right to Compensation: Refugees and Countries of Asylum." 80 *Am. J. Int'l L.* 532 (1986).

Lustick. "Israel and the West Bank After Elon Moreh: The Mechanics of De Facto Annexation." 35 *Mid. East J.* 557 (1981).

Mallison and Mallison. "Israeli Settlements in Occupied Territory versus International Humanitarian Law." 1 *Arab Persp.* 15 (1980).

———. "The Right of Return." 9 *J. Pal. Stud.* 125 (Spring 1980).

Meron. "West Bank and Gaza: Human Rights and Humanitarian Law in the Period of Transition." 9 *Isr. Y. B. Hum. Rts.* 106 (1979).

Neff. "U.S. Policy and Palestinian Refugees." 18 *J. Pal. Stud.* 96 (Autumn 1988).

Radly. "The Palestinian Refugees: The Right to Return in International Law." 72 *Am. J. Int'l L.* 586 (1978).

U.S. Department of State. "The Occupied Territories." In *Country Reports on Human Rights for 1987* (1988).

III. BOYCOTTS, EMBARGOES, AND ECONOMIC COERCION

A. OPEC, OAPEC, and the Oil Crisis

Bagnasco. "Oil and Money: A Note on the Western Financial Community." 23 *Orbis* 875 (1980).

Haig. "Reflections on Energy and Western Security." 23 *Orbis* 755 (1980).

Levy. "Oil and the Decline of the West." 58 *For. Aff.* 999 (1980).

Moore. "Foreign Policy Dimensions of the Crisis in Oil." 17 *Willamette L. Rev.* 111 (1980).

———. "United States Policy and the Arab Boycott." 71 *Am. Soc. Int'l L. Proc.* 174 (1977).

Shihata. "Arab Oil Policies and the New International Economic Order." 16 *Va. J. Int'l L.* 261 (1976).

B. The Oil Weapon and Responses to It Under International Law

Blaustein and Paust. "The Arab Oil Weapon: A Reply and Reaffirmation of Illegality." 15 *Columbia J. Transnat'l L.* 57 (1976).

Boorman. "Economic Coercion in International Law: The Arab Oil Weapon and the Ensuing Juridical Issues." 9 *J. Int'l L. & Econ.* 205 (1974).

Bowett. "International Law and Economic Coercion." 16 *Va. J. Int'l L.* 245 (1976).

Lillich. "The Status of Economic Coercion Under International Law: The United Nations Norms." 12 *Tex. Int'l L. J.* 17 (1977).

Von Lazar. "Memories of Embargoes Past: Petro-Politics in 1973." 10 *Harvard Int'l Rev.* 19 (1988).

C. The Arab Boycott Under International Law

Blum. "Economic Boycotts in International Law." 12 *Tex. Int'l L. J.* 5 (1977).

Greene. "The Arab Economic Boycott of Israel: The International Law Perspective." 11 *Vand. J. Transnat'l L.* 77 (1977).

Lowenfield. "Sauce for the Gander: The Arab Boycott and United States Political Trade Controls." 12 *Tex. Int'l L. J.* 25 (1977).

Turck. "The Arab Boycott of Israel." 55 *For. Aff.* 472 (1977).

———. "A Comparative Study of Non-United States Responses to the Arab Boycott." 8 *Ga. J. Int'l & Comp. L.* 711 (1978).

IV. THE STATUS OF THE PALESTINE LIBERATION ORGANIZATION UNDER INTERNATIONAL LAW

Friedlander. "The PLO and the Rule of Law: A Reply to Dr. Anis Kassim." 10 *Den. J. Int'l L. & Pol.* 221 (1980).

Kassim. "A Response to Dr. Evyatar Levine." 10 *Den. J. Int'l L. & Pol.* 259 (1981).

———. "A Response to Professor Robert A. Friedlander." 10 *Den. J. Int'l L. & Pol.* 237 (1981).

———. "The Palestine Liberation Organization's Claim to Status: A Juridical Analysis Under International Law." 9 *Den. J. Int'l L. & Pol.* 1 (1980).

Levine. "A Landmark on the Road to Legal Chaos: Recognition of the PLO as a Menace to World Public Order." 10 *Den. J. Int'l L. & Pol.* 243 (1981).

O'Brien. "The PLO in International Law." 2 *Boston U. Int'l L. J.* 349 (1984).

V. THE ROLE OF THE UNITED NATIONS

Blum. "The Seventh Emergency Special Session of the U.N. General Assembly: An Exercise in Procedural Abuse." 80 *Am. J. Int'l L.* 587 (1986).

Finger. "The United Nations and International Terrorism." 10 *Jerusalem J. Int'l Rel.* 12 (March 1988).

Gross. "Voting in the Security Council and the PLO." 70 *Am. J. Int'l L.* 470 (1976).

Halberstam. "Excluding Israel from the General Assembly." 78 *Am. J. Int'l L.* 179 (1984).

Keyes. "The United Nations and Human Rights." 10 *Mid. East Focus* 14 (1988).

Koszinowski. "The Middle East Problem and the United Nations." 36 *Aussenpolitik* 306 (1985).

Perry. "Security Council Resolution 242: The Withdrawal Clause." 31 *Mid. East J.* 413 (1977).

Rivlin. "Changing Perspectives on Internationalism at the United Nations: The Impact of the Ideological Factor on the Arab-Israeli Dispute." 10 *Jerusalem J. Int'l Rel.* 1 (March 1988).

Rosenne. "Israel and International Organizations." 17 *Bracton L. J.* 22 (1984).

Sharif. "The United Nations and Palestinian Rights, 1974–79." 9 *J. Pal. Stud.* 21 (Autumn 1979).

Sommereyns. "United Nations Peace-Keeping Forces in the Middle East." 6 *Brooklyn J. Int'l L.* 1 (1980).

Stone. "Palestine Resolution: Zenith or Nadir of the General Assembly." 8 *N.Y.U. J. Int'l L. & Pol.* 1 (1975).

Urquhart. "United Nations Peacekeeping in the Middle East." 36 *World Today* 88 (1980).

Weinberger. "Peacekeeping Options in Lebanon." 37 *Mid. East J.* 341 (1983).

VI. THE CONTINUING PEACE PROCESS

A. From the Sinai Accords to Camp David

Avineri. "Peacemaking: The Arab-Israeli Conflict." 57 *For. Aff.* 51 (1978).

Bailey. "Changing Attitudes Towards Jordan in the West Bank." 32 *Mid. East J.* 155 (1978).

Ball. "How to Save Israel in Spite of Herself." 55 *For. Aff.* 453 (1977).

Ghorbal. "The Way to Perceive Peace in the Middle East." 2 *Int'l Security* 13 (1978).

Jiryis. "Israeli Rejectionism." 8 *J. Pal. Stud.* 61 (Autumn 1978).

Nes. "Egypt Breaks the Deadlock." 7 *J. Pal. Stud.* 62 (Winter 1978).

Sheehan. "Step by Step in the Middle East." 5 *J. Pal. Stud.* 3 (Spring/Summer 1976).

Shoufani. "The Reaction in Israel to the Sadat Initiative." 7 *J. Pal. Stud.* 3 (Winter 1978).

Whetten. "Changing Perceptions about the Arab-Israeli Conflict and Settlement." 34 *World Today* 252 (1978).

B. The Camp David Accords and the Egyptian-Israeli Peace Treaty

Bassiouni. "An Analysis of Egyptian Peace Policy Toward Israel: From Resolution 242 (1967) to the 1979 Peace Treaty." 12 *Case W. Res. J. Int'l L.* 3 (1980).

Bercovitch. "A Case Study of Mediation as a Method of International Conflict Resolution: The Camp David Experience." 12 *Rev. of Int'l Stud.* 234 (1986).

Eban. "Camp David: The Unfinished Business." 57 *For. Aff.* 343 (1978–79).

Hassan. "The Legal Status of United States Involvement in the Camp David Process." 16 *Vand. J. Transnat'l L.* 75 (1983).

Kamnel. "The Camp David Accords: A Testimony." 283 *Mid. East Int'l* 22 (1986).

Lapidoth. "The Relationship between the Camp David Framework and the Treaty of Peace: Another Dimension." 15 *Isr. L. Rev.* 191 (1980).

Meron. "Settlement of Disputes and the Treaty of Peace." 15 *Isr. L. Rev.* 269 (1980).

Murphy. "To Bring to an End the State of War: The Egyptian-Israeli Peace Treaty." 12 *Vand. J. Transnat'l L.* 897 (1979).

Peres. "A Strategy for Peace in the Middle East." 58 *For. Aff.* 887 (1980).
Sayegh. "The Camp David Agreement and the Palestinian Problem." 8 *J. Pal. Stud.* 3 (Winter 1979).
Spiegel. "Camp David In Retrospect." 1 *Global Aff.* 141 (1986).

C. From Camp David to the Reagan Peace Initiative

Ben-Yishai. "Israel's Move." 42 *For. Pol'y* 43 (1981).
Dawisha. "Comprehensive Peace in the Middle East and the Comprehension of Arab Politics." 37 *Mid. East J.* 50 (1983).
Hassan ibn Talal. "Jordan's Quest for Peace." 60 *For. Aff.* 802 (1982).
Khalidi. "Regiopolitics: Toward a U.S. Policy on the Palestine Problem." 59 *For. Aff.* 1050 (1981).
Quandt. "Camp David and Peacemaking in the Middle East." 101 *Pol. Science Q.* 357 (1986).
Saunders. "An Israeli-Palestinian Peace." 61 *For. Aff.* 100 (1982).

D. The Reagan Peace Initiative, the Shultz Initiative, and Further Thoughts on Settlement

Ajami. "Lebanon and Its Inheritors." 63 *For. Aff.* 778 (1985).
Aruri and Moughrabi. "The Reagan Middle East Initiative." 12 *J. Pal. Stud.* 10 (Winter 1983).
Atherton. "Arabs, Israelis—and Americans: A Reconsideration." 62 *For. Aff.* 1194 (1984).
Carter. "Middle East Peace: New Opportunities." 10 *Wash. Q.* 5 (1987).
Dawisha. "Comprehensive Peace in the Middle East and the Comprehension of Arab Politics." 37 *Mid. East J.* 43 (1983).
Day. "Hussein's Constraints, Jordan's Dilemma." 7 *SAIS Rev.* 81 (1987).
Gemayel. "The Price and the Promise." 63 *For. Aff.* 759 (1985).
Hassan Ibn Talal. "Jordan: The Quest of a Centrist Position." 13 *J. Pal. Stud.* 3 (Winter 1984).
———. "Return to Geneva." 57 *For. Pol'y* 8 (1984–85).
Hudson. "United States Policy in the Middle East: Opportunities and Dangers." 85 *Current History* 50 (1986).
Indyk. "Reagan and the Middle East: Learning the Art of the Possible." 7 *SAIS Rev.* 111 (1987).
Kaufman. "The *Intifadah* and the Peace Camp in Israel: A Critical Introspective." 17 *J. Pal. Stud.* 66 (Summer 1988).
Khalidi. "Toward Peace in the Holy Land." 66 *For. Aff.* 79 (Spring 1988).
Kreczko. "Support Reagan's Initiative." 49 *For. Pol'y* 140 (1982–83).
Lustick. "Israeli Politics and American Foreign Policy." 61 *For. Aff.* 379 (1982–83).
Miller. "Jordan and the Arab-Israeli Conflict: The Hashemite Predicament." 29 *Orbis* 795 (1986).
———. "The Arab-Israeli Conflict: The Shape of Things to Come." 11 *Wash. Q.* 159 (1988).

Neff. "The Remarkable Feat of George Shultz." 320 *Mid. East Int'l* 14 (1988).

Neumann. "Finally: A U.S. Middle East Policy." 6 *Wash. Q.* 199 (1983).

Perlmutter. "Unilateral Withdrawal: Israel's Security Option." 64 *For. Aff.* 141 (1985).

Quandt. "Reagan's Lebanon Policy: Trial and Error." 38 *Mid. East J.* 237 (1984).

――――. "Thinking about Arab-Israeli Peace." 6 *Brookings Rev.* 3 (Winter 1988).

Saunders. "Arabs and Israelis: A Political Strategy." 84 *For. Aff.* 304 (1985).

Shaw. "Strategic Dissensus." 61 *For. Pol'y* 125 (1985–86).

Shlaim. "The Impact of U.S. Policy in the Middle East." 17 *J. Pal. Stud.* 15 (Winter 1988).

E. Continuing Terrorism and Response

Bush. "Prelude to Retaliation: Building a Governmental Consensus on Terrorism." 7 *SAIS Rev.* 1 (1987).

Crenshaw. "Theories of Terrorism: Instrumental and Organizational Approaches." 10 *J. Strat. Stud.* 13 (1987).

Faris. "The American and Arab Perspectives on Terrorism." 9 *Arab Stud. Q.* 149 (1987).

Halliday. "Terrorism in Historical Perspective." 9 *Arab Stud. Q.* 139 (1987).

Laqueur. "Reflections on Terrorism." 65 *For. Aff.* 86 (1986).

Murphy. "Punishing International Terrorists: The Legal Framework for Policy Initiatives." 65 *For. Aff.* 180 (1986).

Shultz, G. "The Challenge to the Democracies." In *Terrorism: How the West Can Win*, ed. B. Netanyahu, 1986.

Weir. "Reflections of a Former Hostage on Causes of Terrorism." 9 *Arab Stud. Q.* 155 (1987).

Wilkinson. "The Concept of Political Terrorism and the International Rule of Law." 1 *Arab Aff.* 26 (1987).

Books

I. GENERAL BACKGROUND

Abu-Lughod, I., ed. *The Transformation of Palestine* (1971).

Ajami, F. *The Arab Predicament* (1981).

Allen, D. and A. Pijpers, eds. *European Foreign Policy-Making and the Arab-Israeli Conflict* (1984).

American Friends Service Committee. *A Compassionate Peace: A Future for the Middle East* (1982).

Amos, J. *Arab-Israeli Military-Political Relations: Arab Perceptions and the Politics of Escalation* (1980).

――――. *Palestinian Resistance: Organization of a Nationalist Movement* (1980).

Arad, R. *The Economics of Peacemaking: Focus on the Egyptian-Israeli Situation* (1983).

Aronson, G. *From Sideshow to Center Stage: U.S. Policy toward Egypt 1946–1956* (1986).

Aronson, Geoffrey. *Creating Facts: Israel, Palestinians, and the West Bank* (1987).

Bailey, C. *Jordan's Palestinian Challenge, 1948–1983* (1984).

Ball, G. *Error and Betrayal in Lebanon: An Analysis of Israel's Invasion of Lebanon and the Implications for U.S.-Israeli Relations* (1984).

Bar-Siman-Tov, Y. *The Israeli-Egyptian War of Attrition, 1969–1978* (1980).

———. *Israel, the Superpowers, and the War in the Middle East* (1987).

Benvenisti, M. *The West Bank Data Project: A Survey of Israel's Policies* (1984).

———. *Demographic, Economic, Legal, Social, and Political Developments in the West Bank* (1986).

Blitzer, W. *Between Washington and Jerusalem: A Reporter's Notebook* (1985).

Bradley, P. *The Camp David Peace Process: A Study of Carter Administration Policies, 1979–1980* (1981).

Braun. A. *The Middle East in Global Strategy* (1987).

Brookings Institution. *Toward Peace in the Middle East: Report of a Study Group* (1975).

———. *Toward Arab-Israeli Peace* (1988).

Bull, V. *The West Bank—Is It Viable?* (1975).

Bulloch, J. *The Making of a War: The Middle East from 1967 to 1973* (1982).

Caplan, N. *Futile Diplomacy*. Vol. 1. *Early Arab-Zionist Negotiation Attempts, 1913–1931* (1983).

———. *Futile Diplomacy*. Vol. 2. *Arab-Zionist Negotiations and the End of the Mandate* (1986).

Carter, J. *The Blood of Abraham: Insights into the Middle East* (1985).

Chomsky, N. *The Fateful Triangle: The United States, Israel and the Palestinians* (1983).

Cobban, H. *The Palestinian Liberation Organization: People, Power, Politics* (1984).

Cohen, S. *Jerusalem: Bridging the Four Walls—Geopolitical Perspective* (1977).

Cordesman, A. *The Arab-Israeli Military Balance and the Art of Operations* (1987).

Curtiss, R. *A Changing Image: American Perceptions of the Arab-Israeli Dispute*, 2d ed. (1985).

Dawisha, A. *The Arab Radicals* (1986).

Day, A. *East Bank/West Bank* (1986).

Dayan, M. *Breakthrough: A Personal Account of the Egypt-Israel Peace Negotiations* (1981).

Ennes, J. *Assault on the "Liberty": The True Story of the Israeli Attack on an American Intelligence Ship* (1979).

Eveland, W. *Ropes of Sand: America's Failure in the Middle East* (1980).

Fahmy, I. *Negotiating for Peace in the Middle East: An Arab View* (1983).

Feintuch, Y. *U.S. Policy on Jerusalem* (1987).

Findley, P. *They Dare to Speak Out: People and Institutions Confront Israel's Lobby* (1985).

Flapan, Simha. *The Birth of Israel: Myths and Realities* (1987).

———, ed. *When Enemies Dare to Talk: An Israeli-Palestinian Debate* (1979).

Freedman, R. *The Middle East After the Israeli Invasion of Lebanon* (1986).

Freeman, R., ed. *World Politics and the Arab-Israeli Conflict* (1979).

———. *Israel in the Begin Era* (1982).

———. *The Middle East Since Camp David* (1984).

Gabriel, R. *Operation Peace for Galilee: The Israel-PLO War in Lebanon* (1984).

Green, S. *Taking Sides: America's Secret Relations with a Militant Israel* (1984).

Grose, P. *A Changing Israel* (1985).

Heikal, M. *The Road to Ramadan* (1975).

Heller, M. *A Palestinian State: The Implications for Israel* (1983).

Herzog, C. *The Arab-Israeli Wars* (1982).

Hirst, D. *The Gun and the Olive Branch: The Roots of Violence in the Middle East* (1983).

Hishal, S. *The PLO Under Arafat: Between Gun and Olive Branch* (1986).

Hof, F. *Galilee Divided: The Israel-Lebanon Frontier, 1916* (1984).

Hudson, M. *Arab Politics: The Search for Legitimacy* (1977).

Institute for Palestine Studies. *The Karp Report: An Israeli Government Inquiry into Settler Violence against Palestinians on the West Bank* (1984).

Jaber, P. *Not by War Alone: Security and Arms Control in the Middle East* (1981).

Jureidini, P. and R. McLaurin. *Beyond Camp David: Emerging Alignments and Leaders in the Middle East* (1981).

Karem, M. *A Nuclear-Weapon-Free Zone in the Middle East: Problems and Prospects* (1987).

Kerr, M. *America's Middle East Policy: Kissinger, Carter and the Future* (1980).

Khalidi, R. *Under Siege: P.L.O. Decisionmaking during the 1982 War* (1985).

Khalidi, R. and C. Mansour, eds. *Palestine and the Gulf* (1982).

Khalidi, W. *From Haven to Conquest: Readings in Zionism and the Palestine Problem until 1948* (1971, 1987).

Khouri, F. *The Arab-Israeli Dilemma* (1985).

Kirisci, K. *The PLO and World Politics: A Study of the Mobilization of Support for the Palestinian Cause* (1987).

Klieman, A. *Israel's Global Reach: Arms Sales as Diplomacy* (1985).

Lakos, A. *International Terrorism: A Bibliography* (1986).

Lesch, A. *Political Perceptions of the Palestinians on the West Bank and Gaza Strip* (1980).

Ma'oz, M. *Palestinian Leadership on the West Bank* (1984).

Marantz, P. and J. Stein, eds. *Peace-Making in the Middle East: Problems and Prospects* (1985).

Mattar, P. *The Mufti of Jerusalem: Al-Hajj Amin al-Husayni and the Palestinian National Movement* (1988).

Migdal, J., ed. *Palestinian Society and Politics* (1980).

Morris, Benny. *The Birth of the Palestinian Refugee Problem, 1947–1949* (1988).

Mgrov, J. *Beyond Security: Private Perceptions among Arabs and Israelis* (1980).

Miller, A. *The PLO and the Politics of Survival* (1983).

Musalam, S. *The Palestine Liberation Organization: Its Function and Structure* (1988).

Muslih, M. *The Origins of Palestinian Nationalism* (1988).

Nakhleh, E. *The West Bank and Gaza: Toward the Making of a Palestinian State* (1979).

————. *A Palestinian Agenda for the West Bank and Gaza* (1980).

Neff, D. *Warriors at Suez: Eisenhower Takes America into the Middle East* (1981).

————. *Warriors for Jerusalem: The Six Days That Changed the Middle East* (1984).

————. *Warriors against Israel* (1988).

O'Brien, L. *American Jewish Organizations and Israel* (1986).

Peck, Juliana. *The Reagan Administration and the Palestine Question* (1984).

Peretz, D. *The West Bank: History, Politics, Society, and Economy* (1986).

Peri, Y. *Between Battles and Ballots: Israeli Military in Politics* (1983).

Pry, P. *Israel's Nuclear Arsenal* (1984).

Quandt, W. et al. *The Politics of Palestinian Nationalism* (1973).

————. *Decade of Decisions: American Policy toward the Arab Israeli Conflict, 1967–1976* (1977).

————. *Camp David: Peacemaking and Politics* (1986).

Rabin, Y. *The Rabin Memoirs* (1979).

Rabinovich, I. *The War for Lebanon, 1970–1983* (1984).

Rabinovich, I. and J. Reinharz, eds. *Israel in the Middle East: Documents and Readings on Society, Politics, and Foreign Relations* (1984).

Reich, B. *Quest for Peace: United States–Israel Relations and the Arab-Israeli Conflict* (1977).

Richardson, J. *The West Bank: A Portrait* (1984).

Roy, S. *The Gaza Strip Survey* (1986).

Rubenberg, C. *The Palestine Liberation Organization: Its Institutional Infrastructure* (1983).

Rubin, B. *The Arab States and the Palestine Conflict* (1981).

Rubinstein, A. *The Zionist Dream Revisited from Herzl to Gush Emunim and Back* (1984).

————, ed. *The Arab-Israeli Conflict: Perspectives* (1984).

El-Sadat, A. *In Search of Identity: An Autobiography* (1977).

Sahliyeh, E. *The PLO after the Lebanon War* (1986).

————. *In Search of Leadership: West Bank Politics Since 1967* (1988).

Said, E. *The Question of Palestine* (1979).

Saunders, H. *The Other Walls: The Politics of the Arab-Israeli Peace Process* (1985).

Sayigh, R. *Palestinians: From Peasants to Revolutionaries* (1979).

Schenker, H., ed. *After Lebanon: The Israeli-Palestinian Connection* (1983).

Schiff, Z. and E. Ya'ari. *Israel's Lebanon War* (1984).

Schnoll, D. *Beyond the Green Line: Israeli Settlements West of Jordan* (1984).

Segev, T. *1949: The First Israelis* (1986).

Sharabi, H., ed. *The Next Arab Decade: Alternative Futures* (1988).

Sheehan, E. *The Arabs, Israelis, and Kissinger: A Secret History of American Diplomacy in the Middle East* (1976).

Shipler, D. *Arab and Jew: Wounded Spirits in a Promised Land* (1986).

Shlaim, Avi. *Collusion Across the Jordan* (1988).

Smith, C. *Palestine and the Arab-Israeli Conflict* (1988).

Spiegel, S. *The Other Arab-Israeli Conflict: Making America's Middle East Policy, from Truman to Reagan* (1985).

Bin-Talal, H. *Palestinian Self-Determination: A Study of the West Bank and Gaza Strip* (1981).

———. *Search for Peace* (1984).

Taylor, A. *The Arab Balance of Power* (1982).

Teveth, S. *Ben Gurion and the Palestinian Arabs: From Peace to War* (1985).

Thorpe, M. *Prescription for Conflict: Israel's West Bank Settlement Policy* (1984).

Tillman, S. *The United States in the Middle East: Interests and Obstacles* (1984).

Touval, S. *The Peace Brokers: Mediators in the Arab-Israeli Conflict, 1948–1979* (1982).

Vance, C. *Hard Choices: Critical Years in America's Foreign Policy* (1983).

Weiler, J. *Israel and the Creation of a Palestinian State: A European Perspective* (1985).

Weinberger, N. *Syrian Intervention in Lebanon* (1986).

Weizman, E. *The Battle for Peace* (1981).

Wells, S. and M. Bruzonsky, eds. *Security in the Middle East: Regional Change and Great Power Strategies* (1987).

Yaniv, Avner. *Dilemmas of Security: Politics, Strategy, and the Israeli Experience in Lebanon* (1987).

II. LEGAL ISSUES

Abu-Wghod, I. *Palestinian Rights: Affirmation and Denial* (1982).

Bailey, S. *The Making of Resolution 242* (1985).

Beling, W., ed. *Middle East Peace Plans* (1986).

Ben-Meir, Y. *National Security Decisionmaking: The Israeli Case* (1987).

Cattan, H. *Palestine and International Law: The Legal Aspects of the Arab-Israeli Conflict* (1976).

Cohen, E. *International Criticism of Israel Security Measures in the Occupied Territories* (1985).

Congressional Research Service. *Documents and Statements on Middle East Peace, 1979-82: Report Prepared for the Subcommittee on Europe and the Middle East of the Committee on Foreign Affairs, U.S. House of Representatives* (1982).

Elazar, D. *The Camp David Framework for Peace: A Shift toward Shared Rule* (1979).

Feinberg, N. *Studies in International Law: With Special Reference to the Arab-Israeli Conflict* (1979).

George, D. *Israeli Occupation: International Law and Political Realities* (1979).

Gerson, A. *Israel, the West Bank, and International Law* (1979).

Grossman, L., ed. *The Palestinian Liberation Organization: A Documentary Handbook* (1977).

Hiltermann, J. *Israel's Deportation Policy in the Occupied West Bank and Gaza* (1986).

Institute for Palestine Studies. *The Egyptian-Israeli Treaty: Text and Selected Documents* (1979).

———. *The Karp Report: An Israeli Government Inquiry into Settler Violence against Palestinians on the West Bank* (1984).

Israeli League for Human and Civil Rights. *Report on the Violations of Human Rights in the Territories during the Uprising* (1988).

Laqueur, W. and B. Rubin, eds. *The Arab-Israeli Reader: A Documentary History of the Middle East Conflict* (1984).

Lukacs, Y., ed. *Documents on the Israeli-Palestinian Conflict, 1967–1983* (1984).

Mallison, W. and S. Mallison. *An International Law Analysis of the Major United Nations Resolutions concerning the Palestine Question* (1979).

———. *The Palestine Problem in International Law and World Order* (1986).

Nuseibeh, H. *Palestine and the United Nations* (1981).

Pogany, I. *The Security Council and the Arab-Israeli Conflict* (1984).

Rabinovich, I. and J. Reinharz, eds. *Israel in the Middle East: Documents and Readings on Society, Politics, and Foreign Relations, 1948–Present* (1986).

Ramahi, S. *International Law and the Palestine Question: An Analysis of Its Legal and Political Dimensions* (1979).

Reich, Bernard and Gershon R. Keival, eds. *Israeli National Security Policy* (1988).

A Select Chronology and Background Documents Relating to the Middle East: Report Prepared for the Committee on Foreign Relations, U.S. Senate (1975).

Shamgar, M., ed. *Military Government in the Territories Administered by Israel: The Legal Aspects* (1982).

Shedadeh, R. *Occupiers' Law: A Study of Israeli Practices in the West Bank and Gaza* (1985).

———. *Occupier's Law: Israel and the West Bank* (1988).

Sherif, R., ed. *The United Nations Resolutions on Palestine and the Arab-Israeli Conflict, 1975–1981* (1982).

Simpson, M., ed. *The United Nations Resolutions on Palestine and the Arab-Israeli Conflict, 1982–1986* (1987).

Siverberg, S. *The Palestinian Arab-Israel Conflict: An International Legal Bibliography* (1982).

Stone, J. *Israel and Palestine* (1981).

Tomeh, G., ed. *United Nations Resolutions on Palestine and the Arab-Israeli Conflict, 1947–1974* (1975).

U.S. Congress, House Committee on Foreign Affairs, Subcommittee on Europe and the Middle East. *U.S. Policy toward the West Bank and Gaza.* Hearing 14 December 1987 (1988).

U.S. Department of State. *The Quest for Peace: Principal United States Public Statements and Related Documents on the Arab-Iraeli Peace Process, 1967–1983* (1984).

Weiler, J. *Israel and the Creation of a Palestinian State: A European Perspective* (1985).